Applying COM+

New Riders

Selected Titles from New Riders Publishing

Scripting:

Tim Hill:	*Windows Script Host* ISBN: 1-57870-139-2
Tim Hill:	*Windows NT Shell Scripting* ISBN: 1-57870-047-7
Dave Roth:	*Win32 Perl Programming: The Standard Extensions* ISBN: 1-57870-067-1
Thomas Eck:	*Windows NT/2000 ADSI Scripting for System Administration* ISBN: 1-57870-219-4
Dave Roth:	*Win32 Perl Scripting: The Administrator's Handbook* ISBN: 1-57870-215-1

Application and System Development:

Duncan Mackenzie and Joel Semeniuk:	*Exchange & Outlook: Constructing Collaborative Solutions* ISBN: 1-57870-252-6
Luke Kenneth Casson Leighton:	*DCE/RPC over SMB: Samba and Windows NT Domain Internals* ISBN: 1-57870-150-3
Gary Nebbett:	*Windows NT/2000 Native API Reference* ISBN: 1-57870-199-6
Eric Harmon:	*Delphi COM Programming* ISBN: 1-57870-221-6
Paul Hinsberg:	*Windows NT Applications: Measuring and Optimizing Performance* ISBN: 1-57870-176-7
Peter G. Viscarola and Anthony Manson:	*Windows NT Device Driver Development* ISBN: 1-57870-058-2

Architecture:

William H. Zack:	*Windows 2000 and Mainframe Integration* ISBN: 1-57870-200-3
Sean Deuby:	*Windows 2000 Server: Planning and Migration* ISBN: 1-57870-023-X
Todd Mathers:	*Windows NT/2000 Thin Client Solutions: Implementing Terminal Services and Citrix MetaFrame* ISBN: 1-57870-239-9
Eugene Schultz:	*Windows NT/2000 Network Security* ISBN: 1-57870-253-4
Edgar Brovic, Doug Hauger, and William C. Wade III:	*Windows 2000 Active Directory* ISBN: 0-7357-0870-3
Gary Olsen:	*Windows 2000 Active Directory Design & Deployment* ISBN: 1-57870-242-9

Applying COM+

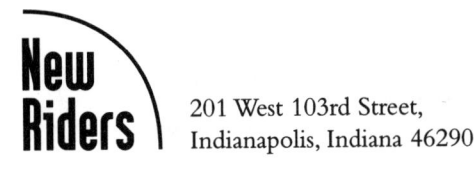

New Riders
201 West 103rd Street,
Indianapolis, Indiana 46290

Gregory Brill

Applying COM+

Gregory Brill

Copyright © 2001 New Riders Publishing

FIRST EDITION: *October, 2000*

All rights reserved. No part of this book may be reproduced or transmitted in any form or by any means, electronic or mechanical, including photocopying, recording, or by any information storage and retrieval system, without written permission from the publisher, except for the inclusion of brief quotations in a review.

International Standard Book Number: 0-7357-0978-5

Library of Congress Catalog Card Number: 00-100520

05 04 03 02 01   7 6 5 4 3 2 1

Interpretation of the printing code: The rightmost double-digit number is the year of the book's printing; the rightmost single-digit number is the number of the book's printing. For example, the printing code 01-1 shows that the first printing of the book occurred in 2001.

Composed in QuarkXPress 4.04 and MCPdigital by New Riders Publishing

Printed in the United States of America

Trademarks

All terms mentioned in this book that are known to be trademarks or service marks have been appropriately capitalized. New Riders Publishing cannot attest to the accuracy of this information. Use of a term in this book should not be regarded as affecting the validity of any trademark or service mark.

Warning and Disclaimer

This book is designed to provide information about Microsoft COM+. Every effort has been made to make this book as complete and as accurate as possible, but no warranty or fitness is implied.

The information is provided on an as-is basis. The authors and New Riders Publishing shall have neither liability nor responsibility to any person or entity with respect to any loss or damages arising from the information contained in this book or from the use of the discs or programs that may accompany it.

Publisher
David Dwyer

Associate Publisher
Al Valvano

Managing Editor
Gina Brown

Product Marketing Manager
Stephanie Layton

Publicity Manager
Susan Petro

Acquisitions Editors
Karen Wachs
Leah Williams

Development Editor
Lisa M. Thibault

Project Editor
Kristy Knoop

Copy Editor
Kelli Brooks

Indexer
Cheryl Landes

Manufacturing
Jim Conway
Chris Moos

Book Designer
Louisa Klucznik

Cover Designer
Brainstorm Design

Proofreader
Sarah Cisco

Composition
Scan Communications Group, Inc.

Contents at a Glance

Introduction   xvii

Part I: COM Basics   1

1   COM+: An Evolution   3

2   COM Fundamentals   41

3   COM Internals   63

Part II: COM+ Components and Services   89

4   Threading and Apartment Models   91

5   Method Invocation and Marshaling   127

6   The COM+ Catalog   157

7   Contexts   193

8   Transactions   225

9   Compensating Resource Managers   255

10   Queued Components   287

11   Events   331

12   Security   359

Part III: Appendixes   397

A   ADO and OLE-DB   399

B   COM+ Synchronization Through Activities   403

v

C Object Pooling 407

D Passing Block Data, SAFEARRAYs 411

E Queue Moniker Parameters 415

F Application Proxies 423

   Index 431

Contents

Introduction xiv
Who Will Benefit From This Book? xiv
Who Is This Book Not For? xiv
Organization of This Book xiv

I COM Basics 1

1 COM+: An Evolution 3
COM+ and the Declarative Model 5
RPC: The Origin of COM Interfaces? 14
IDL: the Beginning or the End? 21
Summary 40

2 COM Fundamentals 41
The Role of IUnknown 41
Where Does COM Live? 53
Summary 62

3 COM Internals 63
Virtual Function Tables (vtables), Abstract Base Classes, and Polymorphism 89
COMCalc C++ Example 75
Summary 87

II COM+ Components and Services 89

4 Threading and Apartment Models 91
Threads and Processes 91
Apartments 97
Marshaling Interfaces 111
Declaring Apartments 117
Summary 126

5 Method Invocation and Marshaling 127
Type Library Marshaling 128
Late Binding 131
Late Binding, Marshaling, and the oleautomation Tag 147
Summary 155
References 156

6 The COM+ Catalog 157
From INI Files to the Registry to the Catalog 157
General COM+ Applications 160
Automating Configuration 171
A Quick Tour: Pre-Installed COM+ Applications 180
CRCs: A Snooper's Best Friend 190
Summary 191

7 Contexts 193
COM and MTS Integration 197
Context: Two Different Definitions 199
COM Context Implementation 207
Understanding and Using the Context Interfaces 218
Summary 223

8 Transactions 225
ROLLBACK and COMMIT 227
Classical Transactions and Traditional Databases 227
A Transaction Scenario 228
The DTC 231
Microsoft's DTC: The Reality 233
COM+ Transactions 239
Transactions, ASP Pages, and IIS 252
Summary 253

9 Compensating Resource Managers 255
The Resource Manager 256
Components of the CRM 258
Aborting Transactions 273
Handling Recovery 274

When In Doubt   275
The Complete Compensator   276
CRMs and Isolation   284
Summary   285

10 Queued Components   287
The Mystery of the Hanging News Feeder   288
Introducing Microsoft Message Queue   289
From MSMQ to COM+ Queued Components   294
Asynchronous COM   327
Summary   330

11 Events   331
Traditional COM Events   332
The COM+ Event Model: Publisher and Subscriber   335
Event Filtering   344
Summary   357

12 Security   359
Declarative Security   359
Programming Security   366
Security Boundaries   369
Lower Level Security   383
Lower Level Security, Roles and Cloaking: Bringing It All Together   384
Summary   395

III Appendixes   397

A ADO and OLE-DB   399
ODBC versus OLE-DB   400
Using ADO in COM+   401
ADO Examples   401

B COM+ Synchronization Through Activities   403
Configuration   405
Activities and Transactions   405

C Object Pooling 407

D Passing Block Data, SAFEARRAYs 411

E Queue Moniker Parameters 415
Parameters That Affect the Destination Queue 416
Parameters That Affect the MSMQ Message 418

F Application Proxies 423
Installing Application Proxies on NT 4 428

Index 431

About the Author

Gregory Brill is founder and president of Infusion Development Corporation, a technology training and consulting firm that specializes in architecting and implementing high-performance trading and market-monitoring systems for Wall Street investment banks. Many of these systems utilize Visual Basic or Visual C++ front-ends acting as hosts for COM components. These components are specifically written to provide high-performance, real-time visual updates, as well as connectivity with MTS-based middle-tier transactional components and/or UNIX/CORBA and mainframe infrastructure.

Gregory holds a M.S. in Computer Science from the Rochester Institute of Technology and a B.A. in English Literature. He has written articles on COM and other Win32 topics for the *C++ User's Journal,* and gives training classes and seminars to companies worldwide. His courses include COM/COM+, Visual Basic, Visual C++, SQL and Relational Database Modeling, Enterprise Java, and CORBA. He can be reached at gmbrill@infusiondev.com or via www.infusiondev.com.

About the Technical Reviewers

These reviewers contributed their considerable hands-on expertise to the entire development process for *Applying COM+.* As the book was being written, these dedicated professionals reviewed all the material for technical content, organization, and flow. Their feedback was critical to ensuring that *Applying COM+* fits our reader's need for the highest quality technical information.

Gene Kellison is a computer specialist working at the Bureau of the Public Debt, part of the U.S. Treasury. He is also a part-time computer consultant. He has 16 years of programming and operating systems experience, from mainframes to minicomputers, to NetWare and Windows NT servers. He is a 1999 graduate of Wheeling Jesuit University, and a two-year graduate of West Virginia University at Parkersburg. Gene lives with his wife and son in Vienna, West Virginia where they enjoy walking, golf, genealogy, and Civil War research.

William McLuskie is a senior consulting partner with Acentron Technologies, Inc. (http://www.acentron.com). He specializes in the development of n-tiered, Web-based applications for national and international clients. Most of his development work is done on the Microsoft Windows platforms using IIS, MTS, ASP, and Visual Studio. Additionally, he has taught object-oriented design, component development, and various programming languages at several universities, as well as in the corporate sector. He holds a B.S. in Computer Science and an M.S. in Computer Information Systems. Bill lives in Charlotte, North Carolina with his wife, Brenda and daughter, Caitlyn. When he is not coding, he is an avid student of Japanese martial arts and currently is the chief instructor at Aikido of Charlotte. He can be contacted at william@mcluskie.com or through http://www.mcluskie.com/william/.

Acknowledgments

First and foremost, I need to acknowledge and thank Sheldon Fernandez, my researcher. With a rapidly growing company to run, I simply could not have researched and tested to the degree a great book requires. Without Sheldon, I fear it would have only been a good book; but thanks to his enthusiasm, intelligence, excellent suggestions, and tremendous hard work, I think it is a great book.

I'd like to thank the people at New Riders, particularly Lisa Thibault and Karen Wachs. True, as my content editor, Lisa did force me to remove much of the poetry and references to quantum physics from early drafts (but I forgive her). Her *other* suggestions definitely yielded a better book. Special thanks to Karen for hooking me up with other New Riders authors when our topics overlapped and for lending a kind ear generally. Of course, I must thank my technical reviewers Gene Kellison and Bill McLuskie for their suggestions; I am hard-pressed to recall a single suggestion of theirs that I did not incorporate. Lastly, I'd like to thank the other folks at New Riders, namely Leah Williams, Kelli Brooks, Kristy Knoop, and Cheryl Landes. I might not have worked directly with all of them, but they were all critical in the creation of this book. Finally, I'd like to thank Alim Somani for his suggestions and, of course, thanks to my colleagues at Infusion Development: Michael P., Brent W., Irene W., Stuart C., Steve A., Fred G., Rex S., Anthony S., and all the rest of the crew that were extremely supportive of this effort.

And, to my wife Deborah: Nowhere near enough room to get into specifics. ☺

Tell Us What You Think

As the reader of this book, you are the most important critic and commentator. We value your opinion and want to know what we're doing right, what we could do better, what areas you'd like to see us publish in, and any other words of wisdom you're willing to pass our way.

As the Associate Publisher for the Networking team at New Riders Publishing, I welcome your comments. You can fax, email, or write me directly to let me know what you did or didn't like about this book—as well as what we can do to make our books stronger.

Please note that I cannot help you with technical problems related to the topic of this book, and that due to the high volume of mail I receive, I might not be able to reply to every message.

When you write, please be sure to include this book's title and author as well as your name and phone or fax number. I will carefully review your comments and share them with the author and editors who worked on the book.

Fax: 317-581-4663
Email: nrfeedback@newriders.com
Mail: Al Valvano
Associate Publisher
New Riders Publishing
201 West 103rd Street
Indianapolis, IN 46290 USA

Introduction

Like most developers, I have a full shelf of technical books. In the lower-right corner, however, I keep three or four books on a ledge of their own, at close reach. I think of these few books as my landmark books—the books that brought me to an entirely new level of understanding and capability. These books all share an uncanny capability: At first reading, they introduce and demystify concepts, and then in later readings, they serve as a detailed technical reference providing critical details I simply can't find anywhere else. From the moment I began writing, my mission was to make *Applying COM+* that kind of book.

If you are a Visual Basic and/or C++ developer and want to understand how COM+ actually works, as opposed to how it is supposed to work or the documentation claims it works—this is the book for you. You can read this book conceptually and understand the capabilities of COM+; but it is, first and foremost, a detailed, declarative book for intermediate to advanced developers who want to fully understand and leverage the capabilities of COM+ in Visual Basic, C++, or both. Traditional COM and related concepts are discussed in the first few chapters; then the book builds on this foundation just as COM+ does—each COM+ service will be explored in detail, with extensive language examples in Visual Basic, C++ and, at times J++. Although many technical books use terms like "Usually" and "For the most part," I put a great deal of effort into making absolute, definitive statements so that explanations and demonstrations are concise and perfectly clear. Such statements require an enormous amount of research and empirical testing to support; but as far as I am concerned, nothing should be left as an exercise for the reader. I have been working extensively with Microsoft technology for 10 years, I have built a successful Wall Street consulting and training firm specializing in COM development, and it is my responsibility to teach you everything I know.

Who Will Benefit From This Book?

Intermediate to advanced C++ and Visual Basic developers will benefit significantly from this book, particularly if they understand COM superficially, but now need a complete understanding of both COM and COM+. Specifically, the book will do the following:

- Provide a thorough grounding in core COM concepts and then demonstrate how these concepts are used to facilitate each COM+ service.
- Explain each COM+ service conceptually and then go into detail using what-if scenarios and extensive code examples.
- Point out "gotchas", where the development reality differs from intuition and documentation, providing workarounds where necessary.
- Fill in many missing details not found in supporting documentation, other books, and articles.
- Fill in many details about supporting technologies not usually discussed in detail—Microsoft's Distributed Transaction Coordinator (DTC), Resource Dispensers, and so on.
- Demonstrate the "how-to" of COM+ with extensive supporting sample code in both VB and C++, and at times, J++.
- Provide extensive source code demonstrating concepts discussed in the book and advanced techniques that, though not specific to COM+, are generally useful.

Development managers might also find the conceptual explanations in this book helpful in understanding the capabilities of COM+. However, the reader should be comfortable programming in Visual Basic, C++, or both.

Who Is This Book Not For?

This book is not intended for junior developers who are just beginning their development careers and are looking for an especially gentle introduction. Similarly, those desiring a purely theoretical, bird's-eye treatment of COM+ might find this book too detailed.

Organization of This Book

Chapter 1, "COM+: An Evolution," provides a high-level discussion of COM+ services and an introduction to COM+'s underlying technology, COM. The concept of interfaces is introduced, and a comparison is drawn between COM interfaces and Remote Procedure Call (RPC) interfaces. Interface Definition Language (IDL) is discussed as it applies to both RPC and COM.

Chapter 2, "COM Fundamentals," bores into the make-up of COM interfaces, exploring the importance of IUnknown and discussing reference counting, querying objects for additional interfaces, and the relationship between COM objects and Dynamic Link Libraries (DLLs). Necessary registry entries, type libraries, and other implementation details are also introduced and discussed.

Chapter 3, "COM Internals," explores COM as it is fully implemented in C++. Interfaces are shown to take the form of abstract base classes, and multiple inheritance is shown to be a convenient mechanism for implementing COM classes in C++. A complete walk-through of a C++ COM component is included.

COM takes advantage of Win32 threading to provide synchronization and protection between components. Chapter 4, "Threading and Apartment Models," begins with a discussion of threading in general and then offers a detailed explanation of the three apartment models: Single-Threaded Apartment, Multi-Threaded Apartment, and the Thread Neutral Apartment.

COM clients can call methods on objects when they have knowledge of the object's interfaces or methods (via a type library). They can also do so, however, even if they do not know anything about the object. These two techniques are referred to as early and late binding, respectively, and they are the subject of Chapter 5, "Method Invocation and Marshaling."

To take advantage of COM+ services, a component must be configured. Configuration data is stored in the COM+ Catalog, a new repository that ships with Windows 2000 and replaces the Registry in many ways. Chapter 6, "The COM+ Catalog," demonstrates how to configure components and their parent COM+ applications using COM+'s Component Services snap-in. The chapter also demonstrates how configuration can be automated via the COM+ administration objects.

Chapter 7, "Contexts," explores how contexts are used to identify an object's runtime capabilities and expectations. As contexts originate with Microsoft Transaction Server (MTS), interactions between MTS objects and their contexts are discussed and demonstrated. The concept of context flow—that is, the flowing of context information from creating object to created—is introduced, and the chapter ends by describing the enhanced roles contexts play in COM+.

COM+ enables multiple objects to participate in distributed database transactions that might span multiple machines and relational databases. Chapter 8, "Transactions," discusses how the Resource Dispenser, objects and their contexts, the Distributed Transaction Coordinator (DTC), and the Dispenser Manager work together to make distributed transactions possible. Object statefulness and voting on a transaction's outcome are also explored in detail.

Writing a fully functional Resource Manager capable of transactions is difficult. Chapter 9, "Compensating Resource Managers," explains how to write a Compensating Resource Manager (CRM) which simplifies this task. The interfaces of a CRM are explored in-depth, and CRM behavior in different transactional scenarios is discussed.

Queued Components is the subject of Chapter 10, "Queued Components." Traditional COM method calls are synchronous, but method calls made on Queued Components may be asynchronous. COM+ Queued Components rely on Microsoft Message Queue (MSMQ) for asynchronous functionality, and MSMQ is discussed in detail. A queued application's interaction with transactional and non-transactional queues are discussed as well as the instantiation of Queued Components via the queue moniker.

Client applications can benefit from being able to receive notification events. Chapter 11, "Events," discusses COM+'s publisher-subscriber metaphor and explains how it is implemented via event classes. It includes additional discussion on synchronous and asynchronous events and techniques of using both.

Chapter 12, "Security," discusses COM+ role-based security and demonstrates how valid NT accounts can be associated with one or many COM+ roles. It then explores how these roles can be associated with components, interfaces, and methods, thereby allowing or disallowing access to these resources for particular users. A lower-level discussion of NT/RPC based security involving impersonation, cloaking, and authentication is also included.

The book concludes with six appendixes: Appendix A, "ADO and OLE-DB," Appendix B, "COM+ Synchronization Through Activities," Appendix C, "Object Pooling," Appendix D, "Passing Block Data, SAFEARRAYs," Appendix E, "Queue Moniker Parameters," and Appendix F, "Application Proxies."

Accompanying source code for *ApplyingCom+* can be found at www.newriders.com/complus.

I
COM Basics

1 COM+: An Evolution
2 COM Fundamentals
3 COM Internals

COM+: An Evolution

INNOVATIONS IN TECHNOLOGY DO NOT ALWAYS take the form of huge leaps and radical paradigm shifts. Often they occur as part of a natural evolution: Two or more related technologies are consolidated into a singular technology that, by virtue of its simplicity, becomes greater than the sum of its parts. So it is with COM+.

COM+ is not so much a new technology as a consolidation of previous Microsoft technologies, mainly transaction processing (MTS) and asynchronous message delivery (MSMQ). These two pre-existing COM-based architectures provide COM+ with a foundation from which many COM+ services originate and others are built. For example, role-based security, object pooling, and synchronization services (all core services of COM+) originated with Microsoft Transaction Server (MTS). Similarly, the architecture of COM+ asynchronous events relies on Microsoft Message Queue (MSMQ).

Although COM+ is built on other technologies, the real benefit of COM+ is that it enables us to focus on features and capabilities as opposed to underlying architecture. And so, we will begin this chapter and our introduction to COM+ by looking at Table 1.1, which shows a list of some of the new features found in COM+.

Table 1.1 **New Features in COM+**

Feature	Description
CORE COM+ SERVICES	
Transaction processing	Related objects that manipulate relational databases (and other Resource Managers) should be able to cooperate with one another under the umbrella of a single transaction. Thus, if one object fails in a chain of related database modifications performed by a chain of related objects, all other objects in the chain will have their changes rolled back.
Queuing	Objects should be able to call the methods of other objects asynchronously. This enables the client object to effectively send a message by calling a method on the object without being required to wait for a response. This message is guaranteed to be delivered.
Event notification	Clients can receive events (messages) from objects synchronously or asynchronously. Client applications, such as stock-tickers and Wall Street trading screens, can benefit greatly from this service.
ANCILLARY COM+ ENHANCEMENTS	
Object pooling	Although an object might be finished with its task and the client who created it might have terminated, COM+ can elect to keep the object alive to service the next request. By using the same object to service the request of different clients, the cost of object creation and initialization can be minimized.
Role-based security	This is a simplified authentication mechanism. Users can be assigned roles, and different roles can have different levels of privilege and access to an object.
Synchronization (Activities)	COM+ components can be configured such that only one logical thread may execute their methods at a time. Although synchronization services have always been an innate part of COM threading, COM+ now externalizes this functionality so that objects may be configured by a developer or system administrator to receive concurrency protection with relatively low performance overhead.

Originally, there were two other core COM+ services that did not make it into the final release of Windows 2000. They were the following:

- **Load balancing**. In times of high system stress when many objects are being used by many clients, COM+ automatically transfers the object creation and method fulfillment to another server that has more available resources. This, of course, is entirely transparent to the client. Microsoft chose not to add this feature to Windows 2000 Server, Advanced Server, and Professional, but relegated it to a future release of a product called AppCenter Server (which would later become Application Center 2000). As this book goes to print, Application Center 2000 is in Beta 2 and expected to be released in the fourth quarter of 2000.
- **In-Memory Database (IMDB)**. IMDB was intended to allow the middle-tier caching of relational database tables. Although it greatly improved data-access times, it was not sufficiently scalable; according to Microsoft, it did not meet the needs of most developers. It was removed from COM+ altogether and is no longer available in Windows 2000.

COM+ and the Declarative Model

New functionality is always welcome, but developers are accustomed to paying a certain price for it. New functionality usually means new APIs to learn and new rules to be aware of. Potentially, it creates unintentional specialists in a development team: "Bob is an expert at working with the security provider APIs"; "Give this project to Anna. She knows how to work with the Distributed Transaction Coordinator"; "Oh, you want to send an asynchronous message. Talk to Mikhail, he's worked with MSMQ a lot." Developers are accustomed to paying a price for new functionality because they are primarily in a functional, process-oriented kind of mind-set. Developers expect new functionality to become available to the process through some form of functional API they will have to master. The API functions might exist in either an operating system or third-party DLL; but at the end of the day, developers will need to know what new functions to call, in what order, in what DLL, and with what arguments.

COM+ changes this environment a bit, however, and challenges the assumption that more functionality equals more work. If the API approach discussed previously can be thought of as functional, the COM+ paradigm can be termed declarative. The following defines these terms in a bit more detail:

- **Traditional functional**. An application's environment is entirely contained in an operating system process (.EXE). This process space has no concept of the developer's programming intent, does not facilitate any form of communication or cooperation between other processes, and does not support or understand objects. Rather, the application is seen as a stream of assembly instructions and is given the absolute minimum of necessary operating system functionality—mainly processor time and an address space (4GB in the case of NT). The application is run entirely in this space, is completely in control of its own lifetime, and calls upon functionality by calling API functions provided by the operating system. Intent is communicated through calling functions. Metaphorically, it is very much like a large, empty, cold-storage warehouse that is entirely the developer's responsibility to fill.

- **COM+ declarative.** COM+ runs objects in special surrogate processes, working with them to create, pool, and facilitate objects. Several programs and events are already in place for which an object can sign up. For example, if an object wants to receive method calls asynchronously, it need only sign up for this service or declare its intent, and COM+ provides it. Interestingly, the declaration is not a function call from within the object as you might expect. In fact, absolutely no code in the object itself states its preference to receive method calls asynchronously. Rather, you set this preference by clicking a check box in an administrative program that is native to Windows 2000.

Because a lot of traditional programming is replaced by declaring your intent with a GUI administration tool, you can think of COM+ as programming by wizard to some extent. Learning to use COM+ effectively has more to do with understanding the paradigm of each of the services it provides than mastering some series of functional steps. Then again, this is nothing new. Even hard-core C and C++ developers well versed in the black art of the Windows SDK could not help but be at least mildly impressed with Visual Basic 3.0. Programming VB 3.0 was fast, relatively simple, and a lot of boilerplate code was instantaneously generated by the Visual Basic form designer. On the down side, there was a lot of low-level functionality missing. The same can be said for COM+—by accepting the simplified abstraction of transactions, queuing, events, and object pooling offered by COM+, you must necessarily relinquish low-level control. However, if you have ever found yourself writing Visual Basic or Java to get something done quickly, this is a sacrifice you have already made and are clearly willing to accept.

The Difference Between COM and COM+

Simply stated, COM+ is an evolved version of COM—not a new technology. COM+ is almost everything that COM is (minus some appendages that are no longer necessary) plus an additional layer of services that ordinary COM objects can declare their intent to use. In short:

COM+ = COM − older, now unnecessary appendages + Event Notification + Object Pooling + Transactions + Queuing + Role Based Security

We will cover a few of these appendages in our review of COM in the next section.

In fact, ordinary COM objects can be COM+ objects and participate in at least some COM+ services with no change in code.

To be precise, COM+ is a fusion of traditional COM, MTS, and MSMQ. Just a couple of years ago, it was not uncommon to find a Microsoft-centric development shop working on a large-scale application incorporating the following:

- **COM**. Objects written in different languages that can create and call methods on one another over a network.
- **MTS**. Enables two or more COM objects to participate in a transaction so that if any object fails to make a change to one or more relational databases (or another type of Resource Manager), all the database work initiated by other objects in the transaction is rolled back.
- **MSMQ**. Enables objects to send asynchronous messages that are guaranteed to arrive at the destination. COM is built on *Remote Procedure Calls* (RPC) and is inherently synchronous. Prior to COM+'s incorporation of MSMQ, it was impossible to call a method on a remote object without waiting for the function to complete and return.

A couple of years ago, I worked on a Wall Street trading application that incorporated all of the preceding technologies. Specifically, it was called a *foreign exchange trading system* (FX system). Basically, foreign exchange traders try to take advantage of any fluctuations in the relative value of different currencies to one another—that is, exchange rates. So, if you were able to buy a British pound (£) for $2 (United States dollars or USD) and the exchange rate changed such that the pound was now worth $2.15 (USD), in converting back you have just made 15 cents! Admittedly, this is not all that compelling an amount at this level; but when you are talking millions of dollars, small percentages add up. At any rate, we used MSMQ to submit trade requests (for example, buy $2,000 (USD) with Yen) and receive events (for example, changes in exchange rates). MTS was used so that different objects involved in changing the database (for example, debiting one account and crediting another) either all succeeded or all failed atomically. COM was used so that our objects could participate in MTS and MSMQ and with one another.

Unfortunately, at the time, MTS, MSMQ, and COM were very separate, distinct entities. They came on different CD-ROMs, had different help files and sample sources, and a different expertise was required to master each technology. Predictably, we had what amounted to an MSMQ team, an MTS team, and a COM team. COM+ unifies these technologies into one cohesive technology. From the developer's perspective, COM+ is basically COM in which the MSMQ and MTS functionality is still provided, but submerged in the operating system.

Fundamental Principles of COM and COM+

To summarize what I've said about COM+ so far, COM+ is COM with new services that are, for the most part, hidden from view and implicitly used by COM objects that declare their intentions to use them. This leaves the traditional COM in the spotlight. Although COM+ does enforce a few conditions and slightly reigns in some freedoms traditionally enjoyed by COM object authors, a good grounding and understanding of COM is the key factor in utilizing COM+ effectively. We will cover features specific to COM+ in depth through most of this book. First, however, we must go over the traditional facets of COM because COM+'s core architecture is, in fact, COM, as it is explained in Chapters 1 through 5. Developers who are already very familiar with COM development can skip ahead to the beginning of Part II, Chapter 4, "Threading and Apartment Models," where we begin our discussion of COM+-specific services.

Of all the courses my company teaches, our COM course is one of the most popular. There is a strange mysticism that surrounds COM and an unwarranted assumption that COM is a complex science, which can only be mastered by a few people. I believe that a host of needlessly complex books and articles exposing and blowing out of proportion very complex but relatively minor facets of COM add to this unfounded fear. Similarly, the evolving nature of COM means that COM carries some of the baggage of its previous incarnation (Object Linking and Embedding, or OLE). This has made it difficult for developers to know which facets in this large-breadth technology are key, which are ancillary, and which are no longer used at all. Learning COM is very much like trying to concentrate on one particular silver-fish in a huge school of them—the fast pitch and sway of the group will consistently confuse your focus. Therefore, let's bring up the whole school, drop it fluttering on the deck, and go through them one by one. Trust me, there really aren't too many fish, and COM isn't too hard to master.

Fundamentally, COM is a distributed object architecture. The basic premise is that you can write objects in any language, and if you (and your language) adhere to a few simple rules, your objects will be able to communicate with client applications that want to use them and with one another across process and network boundaries. All this comes courtesy of COM and Windows NT. Here are the basic rules.

Your object exports its functionality by means of *interfaces*. Interfaces are groups of logically related functions. Your object might have one or many interfaces, which means that your object has one or many groups of related functions. By way of example, imagine that you want to write a calculation object that can add, subtract, multiply, and divide, but also has some financial functions such as `CalculateMortgagePayment`, `GetPrimeRate`, and so on. All of these are essentially mathematical functions, but they actually represent two distinct groups of functions. There are standard mathematical functions (addition, subtraction, and so on), and there are financial functions (`CalculateMortgagePayment`, `GetPrimeRate`, and so on). Your object might be well advised to group these different functions into two distinct groups or interfaces: perhaps `ICalc` and `IFinancial` (the I stands for interface). In linguistic terms, for C++, you might have what is shown in Listing 1.1:

> **Changes from COM to COM+**
>
> Among other things, COM+ demands all components be in-process (that is, reside in DLLs) and have a *type library*. It also heavily discourages the use of the singleton model (multiple clients connected to one object) and discourages the use of threads. These and other differences will be discussed later in this section.

Listing 1.1 A Calculation Object Supporting Two Interfaces in C++

```cpp
class ICalc
{
public:
virtual Add()=0;
virtual Subtract()=0;

};

class IFinancial
{
public:
virtual GetMortgagePayment()=0;
virtual GetPrimeRate()=0;

};

class MyCalcObject: public ICalc, public IFinancial
{
//this class can be cast to either Calc or Financial because it is, in essence
//both classes. The reason will soon be made clear.

Add();
Subtract();
GetMortgagePayment();
GetPrimeRate();

};

C++ pseudo-client

MyCalcObject MyObj;
IFinancial * pFin;
ICalc * pCalc;

pFin=static_cast<IFinancial>(MyObj);
pCalc=static_cast<ICalc>(MyObj);

pCalc->Add();
```

If C++ is the implementation language, COM objects tend to be multiply inherited from different abstract base classes. Interfaces are represented by abstract base classes in C++, and the actual implementation of the methods of the interfaces is the responsibility of the derived class. In the C++ school of thought, because the derived class is both ICalc and IFinancial, the derived class can therefore be cast to either of its base classes (interfaces) depending on which interface the client wants—ICalc or IFinancial. This is probably confusing, and the reasons for this structure might be entirely unclear at this point. A detailed explanation of how this works is found in Chapter 3, "COM Internals."

In Java, this structure is far more clear (for example, see Listing 1.2).

Listing 1.2 Interfaces as a Native Part of Java

```java
// Interface declerations.
//These are analogous to abstract base classes in C++.

interface ICalc {
    public void Add();
    public void Subtract();
}

interface IFinancial {
    public void GetMortgagePayment();
    public void GetPrimeRate();
}

public class MyCalcObject implements ICalc, IFinancial
{
    // Class constructor:
    public MyCalcObject() {}

    // Implementation for ICalc:

    public void Add() {}
    public void Subtract() {}

    // Implmentation for IFinancial:
    public void GetMortgagePayment() {}
    public void GetPrimeRate() {}
}
```

Unlike C++, Java language incorporates the notion of an interface. Viewed in this way, it is clear that the object `MyCalcObject` is the source of two interfaces: `ICalc` and `IFinancial` (see Listings 1.3 and 1.4, and a VB client in 1.5).

Listing 1.3 Java Pseudo-Client

```java
import testcalc.*;   // Imports all coclasses from the COM component

MyCalcObject MyObj;
ICalc pCalc;
IFinancial pFin;

MyObject = new MyCalcObject();
pCalc = MyObj;
pFin = MyObj;
```

Listing 1.4 **Visual Basic Pseudo-Server**

```
VB Class "ICalc"   'Classes are denoted by VB's IDE, the syntax used here
{                  'to denote classes is just for clarification purposes.

Function Add()

End Function

Function Subtract()

End Function
}

VB Class "IFinancial"
{

Public Function GetMortgagePayment()

End Function

Public Function GetPrimeRate()

End Function

}


VB Class "MyCalcObject"
{
implements ICalc
implements IFinancial

Public Function ICalc_add() As Variant
'add implementation
End Function

Public Function ICalc_subtract() As Variant
'add implementation
End Function

Public Function IFinancial_GetMortgagePayment()
'add implementation
End Function

Public Function IFinancial_GetPrimeRate()
'add implementation
End Function


}
```

Listing 1.5 Visual Basic Pseudo-Client

```
Dim FinInterface as IFinancial
Dim CalcInterface as ICalc
Dim MyObj as new MyCalcObject

'all the following will work
Set FinInterface= MyObj
Set CalcInterface=MyObj
Set FinInterface=CalcInterface
Set CalcInterface=FinInterface

CalcInterface.add 1,2
```

Like C++ and unlike Java, Visual Basic does not have the native concept of an interface. The net effect is simulated, however, by the keyword `implements`. When you see this word in Visual Basic, it always means that the class or object in which the `implements` keyword is found also exposes the object that follows the keyword as an interface. In other words, the object that has the `implements` keyword in it is claiming: "I am everything that I am; PLUS, I am also that which I claim to implement, and I guarantee that I will support its methods."

The Theoretical Reason for Interfaces

At this point, you might be puzzled as to what benefit interfaces provide. After all, why not just have an object that supports an array of all its different functions and forget about interfaces altogether? The answer is part theoretical and part practical. From a theoretical perspective, the argument for an object supporting one or many interfaces is obvious—a single object that supports a huge list of ungrouped functions is considered to be a blob by many object-oriented circles; it's just not good style. How would you like it if your local supermarket dumped all of the different items it sells in one big pile? (I'm assuming your supermarket doesn't do this, although mine comes dangerously close.) On the other hand, going to a different store for every category of food—the condiment store, the fruit store, the bread store, the meat store, and so on—would not be easy either. So in life, as in objects, an object (supermarket) best serves the customer when it is in a single geographic place yet offers different interfaces (food aisles grouped by category) of some core product (food).

Java goes so far as to incorporate interfaces into its very language. When you declare an interface in Java like the following, you do not provide any implementation for its methods:

```
interface ICalc {
    public void Add();
    public void Subtract();
}
```

Interface Implementation in C++ and VB

In C++, this role is undertaken by the abstract base class; in VB, it is done by using the `implements` keyword and referencing an interface that exists in a type library and/or another VB ActiveX class in the same project.

The entire purpose of the interface is to act as a kind of contract; when a derived class inherits from the interface, in effect it says, "This interface will be a facet of me. I will honor this contract by fulfilling every method of this interface." Why should a class take on this responsibility? Because if clients and servers agree on what an interface looks like, specifically what functions it has and what arguments those functions take, the client can think solely in terms of functionality of an object with respect to the interfaces it supports. It does not need to be concerned about the actual implementation of the object, its member variables, or any methods it might have that are not part of an interface. The client also doesn't need to worry whether the object's implementation language supports the concepts of objects at all (for example, COBOL or C). Interface-based programming enables you to write entirely generic clients that are only concerned about the functionality of an object and not about its size, member variables, derived class structure, and so on.

In short, clients of objects can think about objects as black boxes that support one or many interfaces. They can look at objects like the one shown in Figure 1.1.

The lollipop-box schematic shown in Figure 1.1 is typical of COM-style schematics. The lollipops represent interfaces, and the box represents the actual COM object whose inner workings are hidden. We have not discussed IUnknown yet, but all COM objects must support the IUnknown interface (a black box with one or many interfaces)—each of which groups one or more related functions.

The server object also benefits from using interfaces because it enables the server to implement this functionality any way it chooses. If we are writing our server in C++, we could implement our object as a derived class multiply inherited from abstract base classes. Alternatively, we could have a solitary class that is not derived from anything and instead contains one or many nested classes. In the former case, the class could cast itself to the interface requested by the client; in the latter case, it could simply pass back a pointer to the appropriate nested class. Either way, the client could care less and can be coded strictly in terms of the interface(s) that it knows the server object will ultimately support. The server, on the other hand, is free to implement the object any way it likes—just as long as it supports interfaces that conform to the client's expectations.

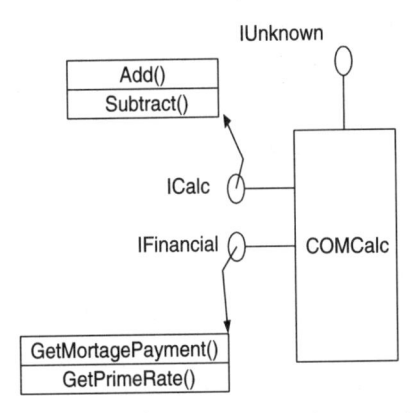

Figure 1.1 A COM object supporting two interfaces—each a grouping of related functions.

The Practical Reason for Interfaces

Theory aside, there are a few practical reasons why interfaces make sense in the context of distributed objects. When we talk about distributing an object, what are we really talking about? In COM, and CORBA for that matter, objects do not travel. When a client application on Machine A requests an object on Machine B, the object does not pack its bags, hop a flight over the network, and move onto Machine A. Rather, the object remains on Machine B, and a channel is opened between the client on Machine A and the object on Machine B. Although Machine A might think it has the object, it really has a proxy to the object. Calls made by Machine A on the object are remoted, or forwarded, to the stub of the object on Machine B.

This channel connecting the proxy and stub takes different forms. COM uses Remote Procedure Calls over TCP/UDP.

No matter what protocol or marshaling architecture (standard or custom) you select, the end result is the same: Some channel of interprocess/internetwork communication is opened between the client and server object, and this is how they talk. In the case of COM, this channel is based entirely on RPC. If we take a brief look at RPC, it might become clear why interfaces play such an important role in COM.

RPC: The Origin of COM Interfaces?

Let us, for the moment, forget entirely about objects and go back a few years and look at an elegant solution to a classic distributed problem: how to call a method on one machine, but have it transparently execute and return values from another machine elsewhere on the network. The solution is RPC. RPC's premise is very simple. I call a function in my C program in an entirely ordinary way. This function, however, executes on another machine and returns its result to me on my machine. Neat trick, but how is it done?

> **Proxies and Stubs**
>
> A *proxy* is an entity that stands in for something else and appears to a client to be an actual instance of that something else. Usually, proxies package and then delegate all client requests made to them over the network to the actual entity on the server. On the server side, the proxy's packaged information is unpackaged by an entity referred to as a *stub*. In the case of RPC, a proxy function appears to the client to be a real, ordinary C function. When called, however, it packages the arguments and sends them to the stub on the server side, which unpacks them and gives them to the actual implementation of the function. Figure 1.2 shows this in greater detail.

> **RPC and Network Protocols**
>
> As mentioned before, COM-based RPC uses TCP/UDP as its base network transport service by default. This can be changed, however; RPC can work on IPX, NetBEUI, TCP/IP, UDP, and a number of others. RPC can also be removed altogether, and developers can define their own protocol using *custom marshaling*. Custom marshaling is an advanced maneuver and should only be done in rare circumstances. Although it is not discussed in detail in this book, for completeness a source code example of custom marshaling can be found in the book's companion source code.

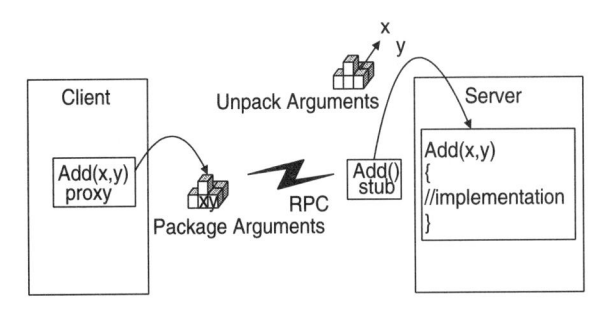

Figure 1.2 An RPC call made to the Add() function on a client.

RPC packages the arguments and sends them across the network to an RPC server. The stub of the RPC server unpacks the arguments and calls the real, server-side implementation of Add(). The first step is to decide what function or functions we want to remote in the first place. Let's use the previous Calculator example and say we want to call the following functions remotely on a server machine separate from the client:

```
int Add(int x, int y)
int Subtract(int x, int y)
```

Let's say that we have a client application (written in C) on Machine A that calls the Add() function. The Add() function actually executes on Machine B, but Machine A does not know that. As far as the programmer developing the client application is concerned, Add() is an ordinary C function just like any other, and the programmer of the client application does not code a call to this function any differently. So what do we need? Consider the following:

- **Client side**. We need a C function Add() for the client that takes two integers and returns one integer. However, the body of this function should not actually perform the arithmetic. Rather, the body of this function should package up the arguments X and Y and somehow send them over the network to the server running on Machine B where the actual work of the function (addition) will occur. Then, Add() should get the result from the server and make it available to the client application, just as if the addition had been done right there on the client. The fact that Add() looks to the client like the real function but is really just delegating the call over a network makes Add() a proxy function.

- **Server side**. We need an application to listen to the network for requests from clients who will call their proxy Add() function. This server should provide the actual implementation for Add() and return the result back across the network to the waiting client.

Interface Definition Language

Theoretically, if RPC knows exactly what my function signatures look like (the number and byte size of the arguments) and whether they are passed by value or reference, RPC can conceivably create a proxy and stub function in C (or any language) for the client and server.

RPC (like COM) has a way of doing this; it is called *Interface Definition Language* (IDL). In the same way a C compiler generates assembly/machine code from a .C source file, the IDL compiler (MIDL.EXE) generates C code from an .IDL file. This generated code defines a proxy and stub .C file that is compiled with the client and server, respectively. Ignoring the generated files for the moment, let's take a look inside the IDL file.

If we define our functions in RPC IDL, we will have something similar to what is shown in Listing 1.6.

Listing 1.6 **A Simple RPC IDL File**
```
[ uuid (C2557720-CA46-1067-B31C-00DD010662DA),
]
interface Calc
{

int Add([in] int x, [in] int y);
int Subtract([in] int x, [in] int y);

}
```

For the moment, let's concentrate solely on the functions. They look like straight C prototypes except for the [in] tags. These tags simply say that the following argument is to be passed by value, so no value is expected to come back and change what the variable holds. RPC needs to know this because it ultimately generates argument-packing and unpacking code based on the argument types and their tags. Therefore, if the server seeks to change the value sent in by the client (indicated in IDL by the tag [in,out] and a variable is a pointer preceded by a *), it needs to generate additional code.

IDL looks a lot like ordinary C with the addition of tags that can remove ambiguities inherent in the C language. There are, as you can imagine, all manner of tags and special handling of strings, arrays, and so on. See the book's source code (www.newriders.com/complus) for some complicated examples of IDL. For now, let's widen our scope a bit and look at the other main part of the IDL (see Listing 1.7).

Listing 1.7 **Interfaces in Traditional RPC IDL**
```
[ uuid (C2557720-CA46-1067-B31C-00DD010662DA),
]
interface Calc
{
```

RPC: The Origin of COM Interfaces? 17

This is interesting. IDL's requirement that we group our functions in an interface and give that interface a numeric identifier (this is called the interface's IID, which is a form of something called a *Globally Unique Identifier* [GUID]) seems to imply that the client needs to specify which specific interface it wants. RPC clients can be presented with many different interfaces from the server; each interface grouping logically related functions. The IDL for a complete `Calculator` object looks like the code shown in Listing 1.8.

Listing 1.8   **Complete IDL Listing with GUIDS.**

```
[ uuid (C2557720-CA46-1067-B31C-00DD010662DA),
]
interface Calc
{

int Add([in] int x, [in] int y);
int Subtract([in] int x, [in] int y);

}
[ uuid (C2557721-CA46-1067-B31C-00DD010662DA),
]
interface Financial
{
double GetMortgagePayment([in] int period, [in] double face_amount, [in] double
↪interest_rate );

double GetPrimeRate();


}
```

The client can look at the server made from this IDL as an object that supports two interfaces, `Calc` and `Financial`. The client can choose which one it wants at any given time or can use both at the same time. Conceptually, a server EXE that exposes one or more interfaces is very much like a classic black box object—it has one or more logical groupings of related functions (interfaces).

Compiling the IDL File

Now that we have an acceptable IDL file that describes the functions we want to remote, what's next? Here are the basic steps for compiling the IDL to generate proxy and stub files. By compiling these C files into the client and server applications, RPC becomes possible:

1. Run MIDL.EXE with this IDL file as a command line argument. Assuming the IDL file was named CALC.IDL, MIDL generates the following files: CALC_C.C, CALC_S.C, and CALC.H.

2. Include CALC_C.C in your client project (that's what the _C stands for, client). This file has the proxy functions for `Add`, `Subtract`, `GetMortgagePayment`, and `GetPrimeRate`. The client programmer calls these functions in the normal way and is unaware that he is actually just forwarding the call to the server.

3. Include CALC_S.C in your server project. This contains the stubs for all the functions defined in your IDL file. Basically, stubs are a jumping off point; they simply serve to receive the marshaled arguments from the client, unpackage them, and immediately want to hand off the unpacked information to your implementation.

4. Write implementations for `Add`, `Subtract`, `GetMortgagePayment`, and `GetPrimeRate`. Sooner or later, someone actually has to write the real code body for these functions, right? So, you do this in the server. If you look at the generated _s.c file, you might notice that the stubs there reference the real versions of the functions that are definitely not in the generated files. It is your responsibility to write them. RPC is just the delivery guy; you have to make the pie.

5. Run the server.

6. Run the client.

What Does COM Have to Do with RPC?

COM has everything to do with RPC. Modern-day COM is built on RPC, and much of its architecture is tied heavily to it. The same compiler (MIDL.EXE) is used to generate traditional C RPC proxy and stub files, or COM C++ proxy files and TLB files (see the next section "From Traditional RPC to COM and COM+"). If you take the concepts discussed so far (an RPC server supports one or many interfaces, each one of which groups one or more logically related functions) and imagine substituting EXE for object, you will begin to understand COM.

> **RPC Details Omitted**
>
> I am leaving a few things out that are not pertinent right now. For example, the client needs to specify the protocol, IP address, and port, and then create a binding to the server. The server, on the other hand, needs to create a pool of threads, register its interface handle(s), and explicitly begin to listen for client connections. Take a look at the example in the book's companion source code (www.newriders.com/ complus). You will find a complete RPC client and server that you can examine to get a sense of the initialization requirements for each.

There are many additions to traditional RPC where COM is involved, and we will soon cover most of them; but the basic idea behind each addition is the same. I have a client on Machine A that wants to instantiate and talk to an object on Machine B. In the same way that RPC solved this problem for C developers in the 1980s, Microsoft RPC has been updated to provide COM support for the object authors of today. In the simplest possible terms, you can think of the traditional multi-interfaced RPC server EXE as having just become an object supporting one or more interfaces. Although the client application has only a few more steps to go through (and more features to take advantage of); an RPC client binding to an RPC server is not all that different from a COM client creating and binding to a COM object.

From Traditional RPC to COM and COM+

RPC was good, but not good enough. It did a great job of interprocess/internetwork communications but was missing several important features. Following are the three features we deal with first:

- Support for languages other than C
- Support for objects, not just flat, ANSI-C style functions
- Capability to automatically find and run server when client requests it

Let's deal with the first item: support for languages other than C. This is a tall order, especially given that MIDL.EXE generates proxy and stub files in C whose purpose in life is to be compiled into the client and server applications. To provide support for other languages, MIDL could, conceivably, generate files for other languages—but for which ones? Also, what about languages, such as Visual Basic, where a significant amount of logic and functionality is built into the development environment itself? What exactly would MIDL generate in this case?

Microsoft devised an answer that turned the problem around. Instead of producing files that supported different languages, other languages would have to learn to support the files MIDL generated. Don't laugh; this is a viable option when you're Microsoft. Thus, the concept of the type library was born. A *type library* (or TLB file) can be thought of as a universal, binary header file. A type library is really a compiled, tokenized form of an IDL file that serves the following two purposes:

- A TLB contains all the function prototypes, interface definitions, and `coclasses` and can be easily parsed and read by any application or development environment via Win32 functions. A `coclass` is a collection of interfaces—a COM object, basically. We will cover `coclasses` in detail throughout the book. Languages such as Visual Basic can read type libraries and determine what methods and properties a COM object supports. This is what fuels IntelliSense in Visual Basic, Visual J++, and Visual C++ (see Figure 1.3). IntelliSense is a productivity enhancer that saves typing and reduces syntactical errors by providing pop-up lists of global functions, objects, constants, and member methods of classes. When you press the period after typing the name of class, a list of that class's methods will automatically appear, allowing you to choose a method. IntelliSense obtains this information by reading type libraries files.

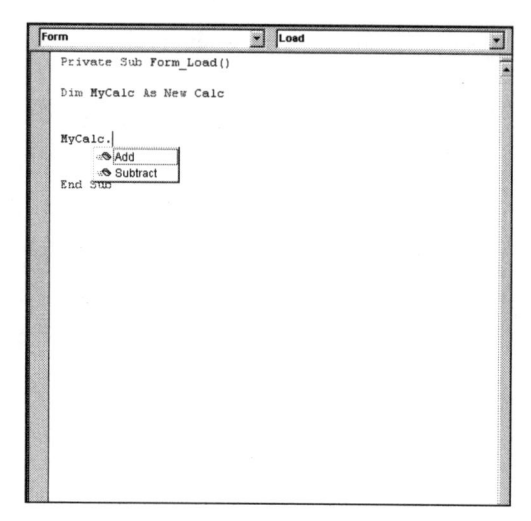

Figure 1.3 IntelliSense is a productivity enhancer that reads the type library and provides context-sensitive lists.

- A TLB is used for marshaling—that is, remoting the function calls. In short, the TLB is used to construct the proxy and stubs necessary for internetwork communications between client applications and objects. Unlike the traditional client/server C files of RPC, however, the TLB does not need to be compiled into the client and server. Rather, the COM subsystem can read the type library at runtime (when the client requests an object defined in the type library) and can set up all the necessary RPC structures at that time. In this way, the networking mechanics do not need to be compiled into the executables; thus, COM does not need to cater to the peculiarities of each particular language. Furthermore, by taking the remoting outside of the executables, you have effectively created a *binary standard* for remoteability. This is a central concept for COM and will come up again when we discuss OLE automation marshaling in Chapter 5, "Method Invocation and Marshaling."

Therefore, the type library both describes the different interfaces defined in an IDL file and provides the necessary networking support to enable the methods to be invoked over process and network boundaries. Can we assume that all COM objects will have a type library? Can we further assume that all COM development first begins with the creation of an IDL file? To answer the first question, if we suppress a few exceptions for the time being, the answer is yes. To function in COM+, COM objects always need type libraries, and every object is described in a type library somewhere. To answer the second question, do we always start with an IDL file? Well, kind of.

> **Rare Type Library Exceptions**
> From a purely technical perspective, a COM object can get away without a type library. In in-process (DLL based) objects accessed from C++ clients, interfaces can be called directly through what are called *vtables* (discussed in Chapter 3) Also, a standard interface called *IDispatch*, which we will cover in the "Inheriting from *IDispatch*" section, can also allow objects to be called without a type library. Practically speaking, however, a type library has become essential.

IDL: the Beginning or the End?

If you understand the true purpose of IDL, you will rightfully assume that writing your IDL is the first step in authoring a COM object. After all, MIDL.EXE, which reads your IDL, looks at the interfaces and their methods and then generates the appropriate proxy/stub code you need to write your client and server. The IDL file is where you universally declare your interfaces and make your contract with the world about what interfaces your object will support. It then follows that writing the IDL file must come first. This is true when you are developing COM components in C++; but when developing in many other languages, such as Visual Basic, Visual J++, Delphi, PowerBuilder, JBuilder, and so on, you might never actually see an IDL file. The IDL file is generated behind the scenes by the development environments.

Implementing COM Objects in Visual C++

To illustrate how to implement COM and COM+ objects, let's take a look at how we would begin to write our `Calculator` object in Visual C++ and then in Visual Basic. Note that this object can operate outside of COM+ as a stand-alone COM object, but it will just as easily operate within COM+ as a COM+ object and be able to participate in COM+ services.

In Visual C++, you have a few options when authoring COM objects. The first option is to write them using the standard Win32 SDK with no help from wizards or class libraries. This is the purest way to do it, but it is also the slowest and most error-prone. Today, most developers use *ATL (Active Template Library)*, which is a template-based class library that exists to speed the development of COM objects. If you use ATL, the Visual C++ Integrated Development Environment (IDE) can aid you in your development. It provides a number of code generation wizards, classes, and so on that can encapsulate and abstract common tasks and leave you little else to do but write functionality. We are going to use ATL for some of our C++ demonstrations; but for now we are going to look at a C++ COM object written using the Win32 SDK.

The first step is to create a Win32 DLL project. COM+ objects always reside in DLLs. Although ordinary COM has a good deal of support for *out-of-process* or *EXE servers*, COM+ demands that your object lives in in-process (DLL) COM components. The reasons for this become apparent shortly; for now, take my word on this, and let's move to the next step.

There is a lot of boilerplate functionality that every COM component needs: four functions the DLL must implement and export, class factories (which are used to actually create COM objects), and additional boilerplate functionality. It is too early yet to delve into all of the details, so I am going to skip a lot for now. Let's assume generic boilerplate code has already been cut and pasted from the last successful COM DLL project and is present.

Include a blank IDL file into the project. In this IDL file, define your interfaces. For our `Calculator` object, we will write something such as that shown in Listing 1.9.

Listing 1.9 COM IDL Describing *ICalc*, *IFinancial*, and the *CalcSDK* Object

```
// comcalc.idl : IDL source for comcalc.dll
//
// This file will be processed by the MIDL tool to
// produce the type library (comcalc.tlb) and marshaling code.

import "oaidl.idl";
import "ocidl.idl";

    [
        object,
        uuid(638094E5-758F-11d1-8366-0000E83B6EF3),
        dual,
        oleautomation,
        helpstring("ICalc Interface"),
        pointer_default(unique)
    ]
    interface ICalc : IUnknown
    {
    [id(1), helpstring("method Add")] HRESULT Add([in] int x, [in] int y,
    ➥[out,retval] int * r );
    [id(2), helpstring("method Divide")] HRESULT Divide([in] int x, [in] int y,
    ➥[out,retval] int * r);
    };

[
    uuid(638094E1-758F-11d1-8366-0000E83B6EF3),
    version(1.0),
    helpstring("calcsdk 1.0 Type Library")
]
library COMCALCLib
{
    importlib("stdole32.tlb");
    importlib("stdole2.tlb");

    [
        uuid(638094E0-758F-11d1-8366-0000E83B6EF3),
        helpstring("Calc Class")
    ]
    coclass CalcSDK
    {
        [default] interface ICalc;
    };

};
```

There is a lot of detail here, but we're going to focus on just one or two things for now. First, let's take a look at the interface declaration for ICalc (see Listing 1.10).

Listing 1.10 **Every Interface Begins with an Attribute Group**

```
[
    object,
    uuid(638094E5-758F-11d1-8366-0000E83B6EF3),
    oleautomation,
    helpstring("ICalc Interface"),
    pointer_default(unique)
]
interface ICalc : IUnknown
{
[id(1), helpstring("method Add")]
HRESULT Add([in] int x, [in] int y, [out,retval] int * r );
[id(2), helpstring("method Subtract")]
HRESULT Subtract([in] int x, [in] int y,
                 [out,retval] int * r);
};
```

This is certainly far more complex than our RPC definition, which looked like that shown in Listing 1.11.

Listing 1.11 **Standard Non-COM RPC Interface Declaration**

```
[ uuid (C2557720-CA46-1067-B31C-00DD010662DA)
]
interface Calc
{

int Add([in] int x, [in] int y);
int Subtract([in] int x, [in] int y);

}
```

However, it doesn't seem that much more complex. The tags you see on top between the [ ]s are often the same or very similar for every interface, and their meaning is not hard to fathom. The following gives a quick run down of some of the more common tags, including some COM+-specific tags:

- `object`. Denotes that this interface belongs to a COM object and is not an ordinary RPC interface. This changes the nature of the code generated by MIDL.
- `uuid`. A 128-bit statistically unique number that uniquely identifies the following interface. Every interface has its own uuid. Technically, this is the interface's "identifier" or IID. Because IIDs are just GUIDs, you sometimes hear people refer to an interface's identifier as its GUID.
- `oleautomation`. The methods of this interface use COM's built-in mechanism for packing and unpacking arguments over the network and remoting function calls.

- `helpstring`. Appears in the user-friendly object browsers provided by many development environments.
- `pointer_default`. Tells RPC how to chase down C-style pointers and arrays (if used).

The following COM+ Specific tags act as configuration hints for COM+. They are not strictly necessary, but they provide information that allows COM+ to automatically configure the components when they are first installed in COM+.

- QUEUEABLE: Indicates that methods of the interface can be called asynchronously via queued components. Queued components are the subject of Chapter 10, "Queued Components." An interface marked with this tag will automatically be configured as "queued" when registered in COM+.
- TRANSACTION_REQUIRED: Indicates that this component requires a transaction and forces this configuration on the component when installed in COM+.
- TRANSACTION_SUPPORTED: Same as above, except transactions are not required but supported.
- TRANSACTION_NOT_SUPPORTED: Same as above, however, transactions are not supported.
- TRANSACTION_REQUIRES_NEW: Same as above, however, a new transaction must be created for such a component when instantiated.

These tags define the interface that follows so that MIDL (and COM+) know exactly how to deal with this particular interface. Let's take a look at the actual declaration of this interface:

```
interface ICalc : IUnknown
```

Notice that this seems to be using a C++/Java syntax for inheritance. `ICalc` seems to be derived from some interface called `IUnknown`. The simple truth is every interface must inherit from `IUnknown`. There are absolutely no exceptions to this rule. We will get into the anatomy of `IUnknown` in Chapter 3, but for now, look at `IUnknown` as a small interface (it only contains three functions) from which every other interface in all of "COM-dom" must inherit. This rule ensures that all interfaces will support the three `IUnknown` functions, and because all interfaces are implemented as C++ abstract base classes, it ensures that the object that derives from them will ultimately be responsible for providing an implementation for these functions.

IDL: the Beginning or the End? 25

The *coclass*

The next interesting section of the COM IDL file contains something we have never seen in our ordinary RPC IDL file—the `coclass` (see Listing 1.12).

Listing 1.12 **IDL with** *coclass*

```
[
    uuid(638094E1-758F-11d1-8366-0000E83B6EF3),
    version(1.0),
    helpstring("calcsdk 1.0 Type Library")
]
library COMCALCLib
{
    importlib("stdole32.tlb");
    importlib("stdole2.tlb");

    [
        uuid(638094E0-758F-11d1-8366-0000E83B6EF3),
        helpstring("Calc Class")
    ]
    coclass CalcSDK
    {
        [default] interface ICalc;
    };

};
```

So far, we have spent most our time talking about interfaces, but we haven't spent much time talking about the objects that will expose and implement these interfaces. This is exactly what a `coclass` represents—the object itself. In COM, a client first asks for an instance of a particular object and then asks for the interface that contains the functionality it wants. Therefore, this IDL says, "I have an object called `CalcSDK`, and that object will support the `ICalc` interface." If there were other interfaces declared in this IDL that made sense for `CalcSDK` to support, they would simply be listed in the `coclass` (see Listing 1.13).

Listing 1.13 **The** *CalcSDK coclass* **Supporting Interfaces**

```
coclass CalcSDK
    {
        [default] interface ICalc;
        interface IFinancial;
        ..other interfaces would be listed here
    };
```

The last unexplained aspect of the IDL file is the library block:

Listing 1.14 **Library Block in the IDL File**

```
[
    uuid(638094E1-758F-11d1-8366-0000E83B6EF3),
    version(1.0),
    helpstring("calcsdk 1.0 Type Library")
]
library COMCALCLib
{
    importlib("stdole32.tlb");
    importlib("stdole2.tlb");

    [
        uuid(638094E0-758F-11d1-8366-0000E83B6EF3),
        helpstring("Calc Class")
    ]
    coclass CalcSDK
    ...
```

This is what is called the type library, or *library block*. All `coclasses` must be defined inside this block. Interfaces, on the other hand, can be declared inside or outside of this block (for the ramifications of each, see the following sidebar "Declaring Interfaces Inside and Outside the Library Block").

You might notice that the type library has a uuid—or as it is more commonly called, a GUID—as does the coclass within the block. This is because COM always refers to entities by their GUIDs (not by string names). The atomic, addressable elements of COM are type libraries, `coclasses`, and interfaces. `coclass` and interface GUIDs are necessary for clients to unambiguously reference the object and interface they want. Type library GUIDs are also important because a client application might want to load, browse, or otherwise manipulate an object's type library.

Implementing the *coclass* in C++

Now that our IDL file is complete, we need to write an actual implementation of the `coclass CalcSDK`. This implementation must actually implement the methods of the interfaces it supports. This raises the following questions:

Declaring Interfaces Inside and Outside the Library Block

Interestingly, if interfaces are declared inside the type library block of an IDL file, MIDL does not generate C and H files when run on this IDL file. If, on the other hand, the interfaces are declared outside of the library block, MIDL does generate C and H files. There is no documentation on this convention, but this is probably because VB-generated type libraries always have their interface declarations inside the library block, whereas C++ COM components tend to declare their interfaces outside of and usually before the type library block. MIDL is, perhaps, assuming that you do not want anything other than a type library when a VB-style IDL file is in use.

- What is the relation or binding between this IDL file and our C++ object?
- How will COM link our C++ class implementation with the type library that will be generated from this IDL file?

In traditional RPC, MIDL generates proxy/stub files that are compiled into the client and server application; the same is true for COM based RPC. If we run MIDL.EXE on the COMCALC.IDL file, MIDL generates (among other things) a file called COMCALC.H. This is all we need to implement our coclass. In C++, our coclass implementation has the form shown in Listing 1.15.

Listing 1.15 **C++ Implementation of the** *CalcSDK coclass*

```
//calcsdkimpl.cpp, the C++ implementation of a COM object

#include "comcalc.h"  //has the necessary C++ abstract base classes
                     //for all interfaces declared in the IDL file.
                     //This is a MIDL generated file.


class CalcSDK: public ICalc //the ICalc abstract base class was
                            //defined in the MIDL generated file
                            //"comalc.h"

{

public:
// IUnknown methods: ignore for now
//NOTE:STDMETHOD is a macro that, among a couple other things, expands to the
// keyword virtual.  Below are the methods of IUnknown
STDMETHODIMP QueryInterface(REFIID riid, void **ppv);
STDMETHODIMP_(ULONG) AddRef(void);
STDMETHODIMP_(ULONG) Release(void);

//
STDMETHOD(Add)(int x, int y, int*r)
{
    *r=x+y;
    return S_OK;
}

STDMETHOD(Subtract)(int x, int y, int*r)
{

    *r=x-y;
    return S_OK;

}
COMCalc() {};

};
```

That's all there is to it—more or less. All of the scary, complex network goo is done by MIDL. You can imagine that the link between our C++ class, and the type library occurs in the MIDL-generated header file `comcalc.h`. This file is where MIDL creates an abstract base class for `ICalc` from which we are inheriting the lines shown in Listing 1.16.

Listing 1.16 **Including** *comcalc*

```
#include "comcalc.h"  //has the necessary C++ abstract base classes
                      //for all interfaces
                      //declared in the IDL file.

class CalcSDK: public ICalc //the ICalc abstract
                            // base class was defined in the
                            // MIDL generated file
                            //after we compiled the IDL file.
{
```

After we implement all the methods of the interface in our implementation class, `CalcSDK` becomes a *bona fide* COM object. The TLB file is created at the same time `comcalc.h` is, and it will be used by COM to pack and unpack (marshal) arguments and remote method calls. The C++ implementation object, MIDL-generated header file, and TLB file combine to create a fully-functional COM object in a DLL.

Visual Basic

Developing a COM component in Visual Basic is far more straightforward. The IDL/Type Library layer is still present, but as we'll see, it is entirely hidden from view and created behind the scenes by the development environment. Let's begin by creating a new ActiveX DLL project as shown in Figure 1.4.

Next, we create a new class module and call it `Calc` (see Figure 1.5).

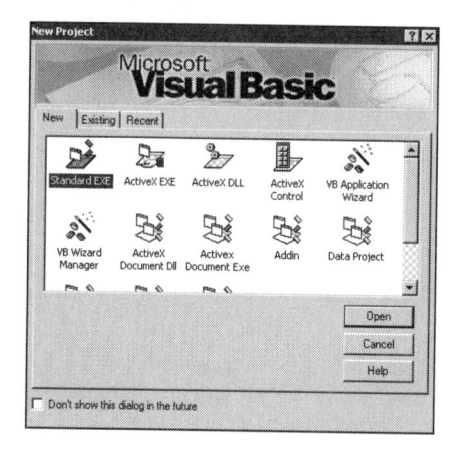

Figure 1.4 Project creation dialogue in Visual Basic.

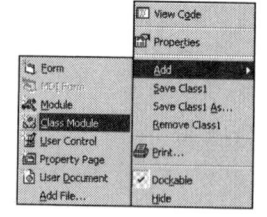

Figure 1.5 New class creation menu for Visual Basic.

Now, we add the `Add` and `Subtract` functions to the class and provide an implementation (see Figure 1.6).

The last step is to compile our application. VB registers our component during the compilation process. There is now a new COM object (`Calc`) with one interface (also called `Calc`, or `_Calc` to be exact) available and ready to use on this machine. We can prove this by creating a new Visual Basic project (a standard EXE this time) and writing a client application for the new object.

After creating a new standard EXE Visual Basic project, select Project, References from the Visual Basic menu. This lists all the type libraries of all COM components currently registered with the system. You will notice that `VBCalc` is now in this list as shown in Figure 1.7.

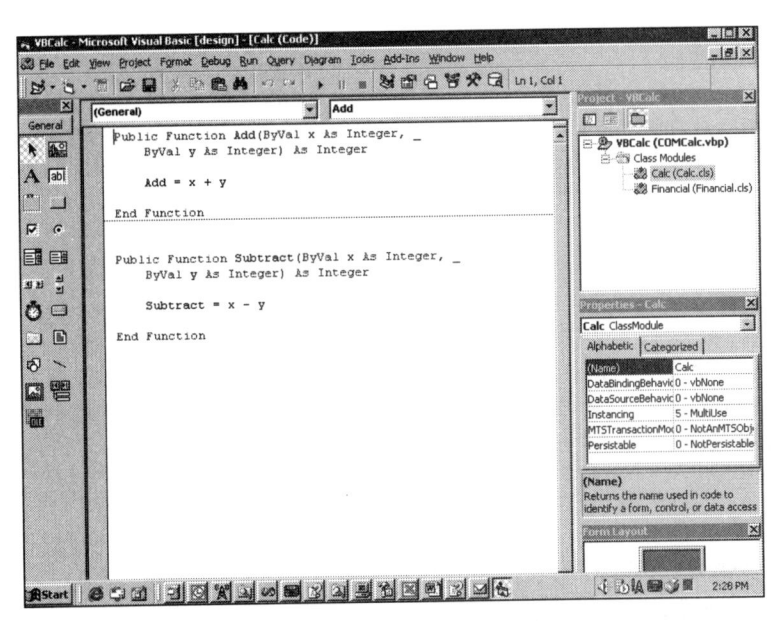

Figure 1.6 Class methods for `Calc`.

Visual Basic Registration

COM components must be registered before they can be used. This means that certain registry entries need to be made so that COM understands how to interact with the object. We will cover registration in Chapter 2, "COM Fundamentals."

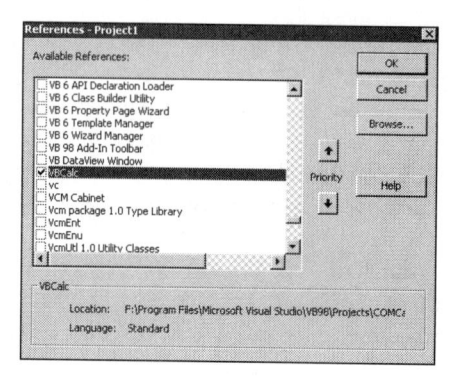

Figure 1.7 The Project References dialogue box:
a listing of registered type libraries.

By selecting VBCalc, you have brought this type library into the current project and extended the development environment to include the Calc object as if it were a native VB object. This is really no different than including a header file containing a class prototype in C++ or importing a package in Java—compilers need information about an object before they can create and use it. By selecting the VBCalc type library, Visual Basic can learn all it needs to know about Calc by simply reading the type library. We can now create a Calc object simply by saying this:

```
Dim MyCalc as New VBCalc.Calc
```

Microsoft introduced a new programmer's aide called *IntelliSense* with Visual Basic 5. IntelliSense can read Calc's (or any object's) type library and offer context-sensitive lists of methods or properties for an object as shown in Figure 1.8.

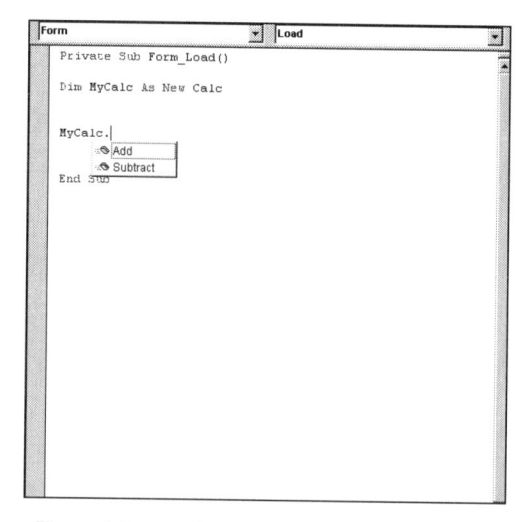

Figure 1.8 IntelliSense reads Calc's type library
and offers some method suggestions.

If this program is completed and run, an instance of the `Calc` object is created, used, and released when the client application exits.

It is important to realize that although we did not interact with an IDL file directly or run MIDL ourselves, a type library was created. The VB IDE created a type library behind the scenes when we compiled the component, and it continues to update this type library as we make changes and additions to the component. So, where is this type library? It is stuffed into the resources of the DLL.

Finding Registered Type Libraries

Every major development environment that advertises the capability to create COM components can probably create type libraries. Some development environments do so explicitly (Visual C++) in such a way that you can interact with the IDL. Others create type libraries implicitly (Visual Basic, Visual J++, Delphi, PowerBuilder, and so on). Whatever your development environment does, however, there will come a time when you need to wean yourself from the abstractions of your IDE and view the type library directly. Visual Basic, for example, encounters some positively ghastly problems and hiccups when developing COM components, particularly when incrementally adding/modifying interfaces and recompiling over time. At some point, you will be dead in your tracks and unable to determine a problem without bypassing VB and looking directly at the type library. How do you do this? The answer can be found in a free program called OLEView.EXE.

OLEView.EXE ships and installs with Visual C++, but it is freely available on the Microsoft Web site at `http://msdn.microsoft.com/downloads/sdks/platform/platform.asp`. (You cannot download the utility by itself. It must be downloaded as part of the PlatformSDK.) Among many other things, this program enables you to browse the type libraries of all components currently registered on your system. There is no substitute for this. When a client application tells you that no such interface exists but you're sure it does, you need to look at the type library to confirm or deny your assumptions. This is easy to do with OLEView.EXE. Just run the program and put yourself in expert mode, as shown in Figure 1.9.

32 Chapter 1 COM+: An Evolution

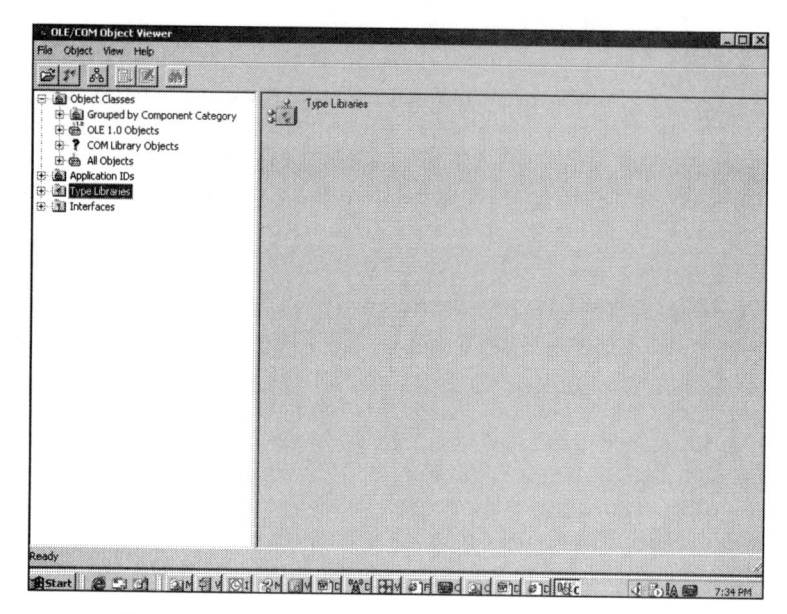

Figure 1.9 The Type Libraries section of OLEView.EXE.

Next, click the Type Libraries portion of the tree and look for the type library you are interested in (See Figure 1.10). Right-click on it.

Now double-click on VBCalc and take a look at the resulting IDL shown in Figure 1.11.

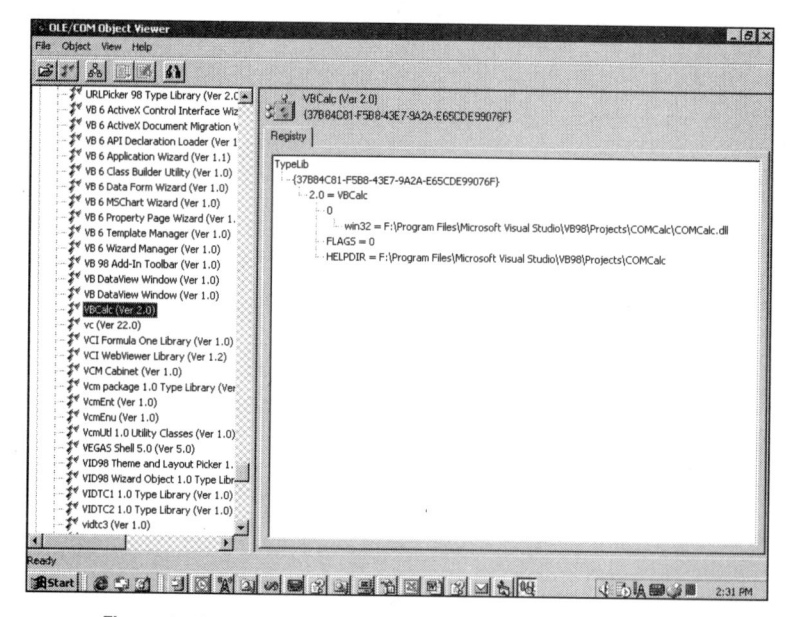

Figure 1.10 Summary information for the VBCalc type library.

IDL: the Beginning or the End? 33

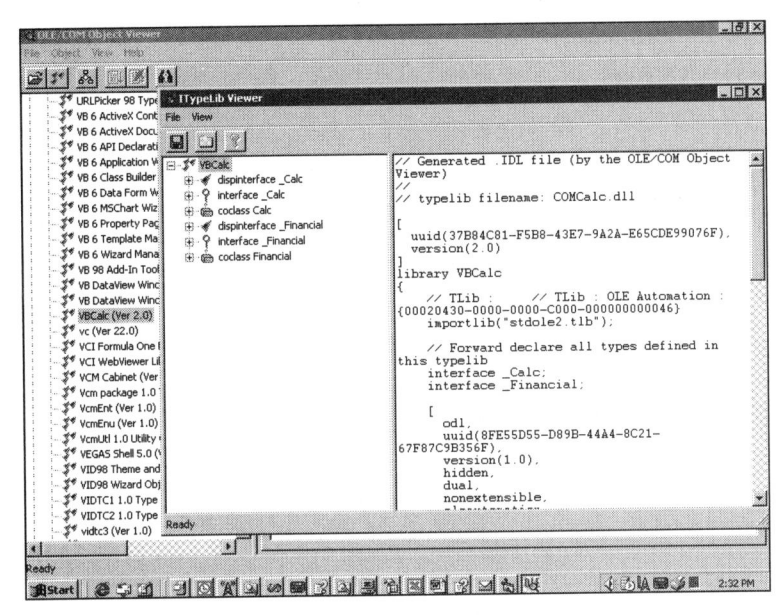

Figure 1.11 Inspecting VBCalc's type library using OLEView.

This is the type library that our VB project generated, which is shown in Listing 1.17.

Listing 1.17 **Reverse-Compiled IDL for *VBCalc***

```
// Generated .IDL file (by the OLE/COM Object Viewer)
//
// typelib filename: VBCalc.dll

[
  uuid(10513762-A601-11D3-8090-00E0811008ED),
  version(2.0)
]
library VBCalc
{
    importlib("STDOLE2.TLB");

    // Forward declare all types defined in this typelib
    interface _Calc;

    [
      odl,
      uuid(1051376B-A601-11D3-8090-00E0811008ED),
      version(1.0),
      hidden,
      dual,
      nonextensible,
```

continues

Listing 1.17 Continued

```
        oleautomation
    ]
    interface _Calc : IDispatch {
        [id(0x60030000)]
        HRESULT Add(
                        [in] short x,
                        [in] short y,
                        [out, retval] short* );
        [id(0x60030001)]
        HRESULT Subtract(
                        [in] short x,
                        [in] short y,
                        [out, retval] short* );
    };

    [
      uuid(10513764-A601-11D3-8090-00E0811008ED),
      version(1.0)
    ]
    coclass Calc {
        [default] interface _Calc;
    };
};
```

The Library Block

Let's break this out by sections. The IDL file begins by declaring a type library block. All interfaces and coclasses can be defined in this block, so you can think of the type library block as containing all the elements that will be in the type library. Library blocks are one of the components of a type library that can be individually referenced, which is why they have a GUID (see Listing 1.18).

Listing 1.18 IDL Declaration Tags for a Type Library Block

```
// Generated .IDL file (by the OLE/COM Object Viewer)
//
// typelib filename: VBCalc.dll

[
  uuid(10513762-A601-11D3-8090-00E0811008ED),
  version(2.0)
]
library VBCalc
{
```

COM uses GUIDs behind the scenes to refer to type libraries—not string names. In VB, for example, when you browse the type libraries on your machine using Project, References, you see the names of the type libraries as shown in Figure 1.12. However, in reality, type libraries are listed in the registry as shown in Figure 1.13.

Therefore, you can see why type libraries are really referenced by GUID and not by name. In fact, it is possible to have two type libraries with identical names but different GUIDs.

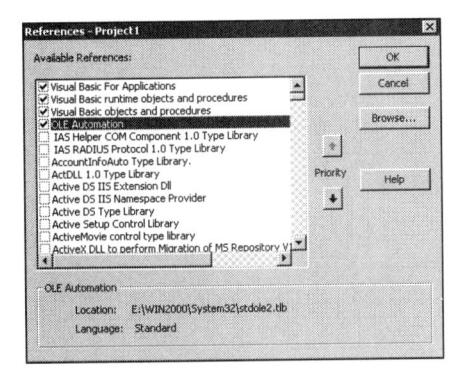

Figure 1.12 Type libraries are listed in VB.

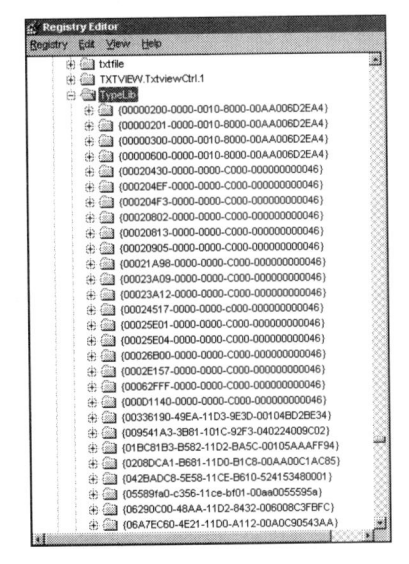

Figure 1.13 Type libraries are listed in the registry by GUID.

Interface Block, Revisited

Moving past the type library definition, we can see our interface definition shown in Listing 1.19.

Listing 1.19 **The VB-generated *Calc* Interface**

```
[
  odl,
  uuid(1051376B-A601-11D3-8090-00E0811008ED),
  version(1.0),
  hidden,
  dual,
  nonextensible,
  oleautomation
]
interface _Calc : IDispatch {
```

We have seen many of these tags before, but there are a few new ones: `odl`, `hidden`, `dual`, `nonextensible`, and `oleautomation`. Many of these tags are informational and not strictly necessary (`hidden`, `dual`, `oleautomation`), and one is a bit of a throwback to earlier days (`odl`). Let's go through them:

- **odl.** This stands for *Object Definition Language.* There was a time early in COM's history when things called ODL (not IDL) files roamed the earth. ODL was the predecessor to IDL and was used before COM and RPC were fully fused to create what Microsoft trumpeted as *DCOM,* or *Distributed COM.* ODL files are not really used anymore except in Microsoft Foundation Class applications, which still coddle the older form of COM. At any rate, the `odl` tag should really be replaced by the `object` tag—the end result would be the same.

- **hidden.** This tag indicates that VB should not display the interface in its object browser or when employing IntelliSense. Note that a hidden interface can still be used, and variables of that type can be declared; it just won't be seen in browsers. In Visual Basic, the same effect can be achieved by preceding an interface name with the _ character. Visual Basic treats these interfaces as hidden.

- **nonextensible.** This tag means the interface is not allowed to support new methods (or stop supporting old ones) at runtime. This might seem strange, but it is possible through something called late binding for objects to support new methods on-the-fly. This tag assures the client that this will not happen.

- **oleautomation.** Simply put, this indicates that all of the arguments of all the methods use Visual Basic data types. COM knows exactly how to pack and unpack these data types to facilitate a remote method call. COM has what it calls an OLE automation marshaler that performs this task. This marshaler exists in a system DLL called oleaut32.dll. Therefore, this tag basically indicates that COM will use oleaut32.dll to marshal data over the network.

- `dual`. This tag indicates that this interface supports early or late binding. We will be discussing this in Chapter 5.

Inheriting from *IDispatch*

The final puzzler of this section is the following line:

```
interface _Calc : IDispatch {
```

In the earlier section "Implementing COM Objects in Visual C++," I said all interfaces must inherit from `IUnknown`, and there are absolutely no exceptions. If this is true, why does `Calc` inherit from something called `IDispatch`? `IDispatch` inherits from `IUnknown`, so `Calc` is sure to inherit those three special methods that I have not yet explained (all in good time, I promise). `IDispatch` is an interface used to support what is called *late binding*, which we will talk about in Chapter 5. For now, just note that by inheriting from `IDispatch`, we are forcing the `coclass` that supports the interface `Calc` to also support the `IDispatch` interface. It will soon become clear why this is useful.

There is some significance to the underscore of the name `Calc`. This is a VBism—Visual Basic treats all interfaces that begin with a '_' as hidden and does not display them in its object browser or IntelliSense. It is clearly VB's intent that the client not see or know about the interface `Calc`, which might seem odd given that COM's whole point is to think of objects solely in terms of the interfaces they support. Unfortunately, this won't be the last time Visual Basic will violate or complicate the COM paradigm: VB sends a lot of mixed messages when it comes to COM. Take a look at the `coclass` declaration shown in Listing 1.20.

Listing 1.20 **The *Calc* coclass**

```
[
    uuid(10513764-A601-11D3-8090-00E0811008ED),
    version(1.0)
]
coclass Calc {
    [default] interface _Calc;
};
```

You might notice that there is an object called `Calc`, and it supports an interface called `_Calc`, which is hidden. Why is this? Because ultimately the VB client does not see the `Calc` object as a black box that supports an interface; instead it lumps the interface and the object together. The VB client looks like Listing 1.21.

Listing 1.21 **Creating the *Calc* Object in VB**

```
Dim MyCalc as new VBCalc.Calc

Msgbox myCalc.add(1,2)
```

If VB were true to COM, however, the code would be (but unfortunately isn't) like that shown in Listing 1.22.

Listing 1.22 **The way VB should do things but doesn't**
```
Dim MyCalc as new VBCalc.Calc
Dim ICalc as _Calc

Set ICalc = Calc      'get the _Calc interface from the Calc object
Msgbox ICalc.add(1,2)
```

To summarize, VB lumps the default interface (this is what the `[default]` tag means) and the `coclass` together so that to the client it appears that the `Calc` object is a simple class that has functions. This isn't COM reality, but it is time you know: VB sometimes lies.

Method Declarations

Finally, let's look at _Calc's method declarations shown in Listing 1.23.

Listing 1.23 **IDL for *Add* and *Subtract* declarations**
```
        [id(0x60030000)]
        HRESULT Add(
                    [in] short x,
                    [in] short y,
                    [out, retval] short* );
        [id(0x60030001)]
        HRESULT Subtract(
                    [in] short x,
                    [in] short y,
                    [out, retval] short* );
```

The `id` tag in front of each method is provided so the methods can be called by number, not just name. This is important for late binding, which is covered in Chapter 5.

Another interesting aspect of these prototypes is that they all return something called an `HRESULT`. An `HRESULT` is a four-byte integer used to indicate the success or failure of the function call. Interface methods cannot return data values as return values—only error codes in the form of `HRESULT`s. This certainly puts a damper on the party and seems to imply that the only way to return values from a method call is by passing variables by reference.

Fortunately, there is the `[out,retval]` tag. This tag indicates that the argument is really the return value of the function. When a development environment, such as VB, sees this tag in the type library, it can generate client-side code that performs some clever rearranging so that the following code is possible:

```
result=Calc.Add(1,2)
```

Technically, `Add()` returns an error code, not a data result. What we are seeing is an illusion created by the client-side development environment. So how can we determine if an error occurred? Exceptions. Exceptions are implemented differently in different languages, but they are basically a mechanism that allows errors to be thrown to some form of catcher/handler. In VB, exceptions take the form shown in Listing 1.24.

Listing 1.24 Exception Handling in VB

```
on error goto eh

result=Calc.Add(1,2)

exit sub
eh:
msgbox "An Error Occurred!"
```

In C++

```
try
{
    ICalc->Add(1,2);
}
catch(_com_error ce)
{
    MessageBox( ce.Description );
}
```

Raw Functions

In Visual C++, you can use exceptions or you can use what are called Raw functions, where the true nature of the method is preserved and can be called in the manner shown in Listing 1.25.

Listing 1.25 Using Raw Functions in C++

```
int result=0;
HRESULT hr=ICalc->raw_Add(1,2,&result);
```

Summary

COM+ is the next evolutionary step from COM: It extends the basic architecture of traditional COM by incorporating additional enterprise-scale services that COM+ objects can take advantage of. However, the more things change, the more things stay the same. COM+ inherits much of the traditional COM architecture including the following:

- The use of interfaces to logically group related methods
- The use of type libraries to describe objects, interfaces, and their methods
- Dependence on RPC for remote method calls from client-to-server object
- A separation of `interface` and `implementation`

In the next chapter, we'll go one level deeper and discuss how COM/COM+ objects are actually implemented.

2

COM Fundamentals

Now that we've covered the basics of COM components, it is time to look at COM in greater detail. Unfortunately, Visual Basic hides a lot of the details, and Visual J++ (VJ++), although exposing more details than VB, still abstracts COM to a large degree. This leaves Visual C++. I have always maintained that COM has its truest representation in C++, and to truly understand COM, you need to understand how it is implemented in this language.

That said, I realize that there are many developers in the world who lead a perfectly satisfying professional life without programming in C++. But, much like learning Latin, your understanding of your present language can be greatly enhanced by a study of its sometimes more verbose and complex predecessor.

The Role of *IUnknown*

Let's focus again on interfaces. A number of times in the last chapter, I said that all interfaces must inherit from `IUnknown`. I said this because `IUnknown` contains three methods that every interface is required to support. The three methods are as follows:

- `QueryInterface()`
- `AddRef()`
- `Release()`

In some languages, particularly VB, you can never call these methods directly; therefore, you can easily forget IUnknown exists. However, every interface you ever use must inherit from IUnknown; because of this, it is guaranteed to support these three methods. This is important, because even if you don't explicitly call these methods, they are called behind the scenes for the following two reasons:

- To control the lifetime of the objects (AddRef(), Release())
- To enable clients to get one or many interfaces from objects (QueryInterface())

This becomes apparent when you take a look at how objects are created. As I said, IUnknown is largely abstracted away in languages like VB, so you need to look at the C++ Win32 way of instantiating an object and getting an interface. In VB, the lines

```
Dim MyCalc as VBCalcLib.Calc
Set MyCalc=new VBCalcLib.Calc
```

are equivalent to the VJ++ lines

```
ICalc MyCalc;
MyCalc = new Calc();
```

which are equivalent to the C++

```
ICalc * pICalc;
const GUID CLSID_Calc =
    {0x638094e0,0x758f,0x11d1,{0x83,0x66,0x00,0x00,0xe8,0x3b,0x6e,0xf3}};
const GUID IID_ICalc =
    {0x638094e5,0x758f,0x11d1,{0x83,0x66,0x00,0x00,0xe8,0x3b,0x6e,0xf3}};

CoCreateInstance(CLSID_Calc, 0,CLSCTX_INPROC_SERVER , IID_ICalc,
↪(void**)&pICalc);
```

Some of the preceding syntax might be unfamiliar to non-C++ developers, but it is not complicated. If you cut it down to its most basic level, you end up with the following:

```
CoCreateInstance(CLSID_COMCalc, NULL, CLSCTX_ALL , IID_ICalc, (void**)&pICalc);
```

Remember, our type library definition of ICalc was:

```
[
    uuid(638094E5-758F-11d1-8366-0000E83B6EF3)
]
interface ICalc : IUnknown
{
```

Our type library definition for the Calc coclass was:

```
[
    uuid(638094E0-758F-11d1-8366-0000E83B6EF3)

]
coclass Calc
```

Here are the C++ lines:

```
const GUID CLSID_Calc =
    {0x638094e0,0x758f,0x11d1,{0x83,0x66,0x00,0x00,0xe8,0x3b,0x6e,0xf3}};
const GUID IID_ICalc =
    {0x638094e5,0x758f,0x11d1,{0x83,0x66,0x00,0x00,0xe8,0x3b,0x6e,0xf3}};
```

This represents how the GUID for the coclass `Calc` and interface `ICalc` are written in C++.

The following code simply says, "COM, please create an instance of the object whose GUID is `CLSID_Calc` and get me the interface of that object whose GUID is `IID_ICalc` and put that interface into the variable `pICalc`:

```
CoCreateInstance(CLSID_COMCalc, _ , _ , IID_ICalc, (void**)&pICalc);
```

The following code then becomes possible:

```
int result=pICalc->Add(1,2);
```

Release( )

When you are finished using the object, how do you tell the object that you're done with it? After all, your application might need `Calc`'s services for only a few milliseconds, but it might run for several hours. You don't want `Calc` hanging around, unused, wasting resources all that time; so there must be some way to let `Calc` know it's time to go. In VB or VJ++, this is easy to do; you can do one of the following two things:

- Do nothing and the language eventually performs some form of garbage collection and cleans up the object for you.
- Get rid of the object by saying the following:

In VB:

```
Set MyCalc= Nothing
```

In J++:

```
MyCalc = null;
```

or

```
com.ms.com.ComLib.release(MyCalc);
```

Implementing *Release( )*

Let's turn our attention to the implementation of `Release`. When it comes to releasing an object, different languages impose different degrees of responsibility on the object developer. In C++, for example, the language has no inherent garbage collection functionality, so the developer must deallocate the object himself. Unlike many 4GL languages, in C++, an equality operator does not natively have an overloaded meaning. So, the following line means that a `0` is placed in the pointer variable `pICalc`:

```
pICalc=NULL;   //BAD!
```

This does not inform the `Calc` object of anything; in fact, you have made an orphan out of the object because you no longer hold a reference to it. How then, can you tell `Calc` that its services are no longer required? Because the `ICalc` interface you hold is inherited from `IUnknown`, it must support a function called `Release()`. This is exactly what `Release()` does—it informs the object that someone has just lost interest in it. Therefore, to ask your object to destroy itself when you are done with it, you simply use the following code:

```
pICalc->Release();
```

The object now destroys itself. If you wonder how `IUnknown` got involved with `ICalc`, just remember that `ICalc` is inherited from `IUnknown`. Look again at the type library in Listing 2.1.

Listing 2.1 **Type Library**

```
[
    object,
    uuid(638094E5-758F-11d1-8366-0000E83B6EF3),
    oleautomation,
    helpstring("ICalc Interface"),
    pointer_default(unique)
]
interface ICalc : IUnknown
{
[id(1), helpstring("method Add")] HRESULT Add([in] int x, [in] int y,
                                                [out,retval] int * r );
[id(2), helpstring("method Subtract")] HRESULT Subtract([in] int x, [in] int y,
                                                [out,retval] int * r );
```

Remember that MIDL.EXE was run on this IDL file, and a header file containing an `ICalc` proxy class was generated. This header file is to be included in the client application so that it is possible to declare `ICalc` pointers. Thus, the following line is possible:

```
ICalc * pICalc;
```

This line is possible because just above it in the source file is the following line, which includes the MIDL-generated header file:

```
#include "calc.h"   //MIDL generated this from the type library
```

If you look in this header file, you will find the code shown in Listing 2.2.

Listing 2.2 *ICalc* **Prototype as Seen in MIDL-Generated File, CALC.H**

```
MIDL_INTERFACE("638094E5-758F-11d1-8366-0000E83B6EF3")
ICalc : public IUnknown
{
public:
    virtual /* [helpstring][id] */ HRESULT STDMETHODCALLTYPE Add(
```

```
            /* [in] */ int x,
            /* [in] */ int y,
            /* [retval][out] */ int __RPC_FAR *r) = 0;

        virtual /* [helpstring][id] */ HRESULT STDMETHODCALLTYPE Divide(
            /* [in] */ int x,
            /* [in] */ int y,
            /* [retval][out] */ int __RPC_FAR *r) = 0;
    };
```

There is no escape from the unknown (or IUnknown). Every interface inherits from IUnknown, so every interface must support AddRef(), Release(), and QueryInterface(). Normally, however, every interface just delegates all of its method calls to the derived object as shown in Figure 2.1.

The point is that every object supports and implements the methods of IUnknown, and the methods of IUnknown can be called from any interface the object supports.

This means that every COM object ever written must know what to do when Release() is called on any of its interfaces. In the C++ case, this responsibility often falls on the developer (unless he is using the Active Template Library [ATL]), and it is typically addressed as shown in Listing 2.3.

Listing 2.3 **A Typical Implementation of *Release( )***

```
SomeObject::Release()
{
    m_ObjectCount--,
    if(m_ObjectCount==0)
        delete this;
}
```

In VB and VJ++, this code is generated automatically, and the developer doesn't have to write it.

AddRef( )

Another method of IUnknown is AddRef(). It is just as critical, but not much more complex. AddRef() is the complementary function to Release(). If Release() is called when you want to notify an object that there is one less outstanding reference to it, AddRef() is called to let an object know there is one more. To be more specific, Release() and AddRef() are called to keep track of the number of *references* held by a client (or clients) to a given object. Basically, whenever you (or COM) give out an interface, AddRef() must be called to let the object know that there is a client somewhere that holds a reference to it.

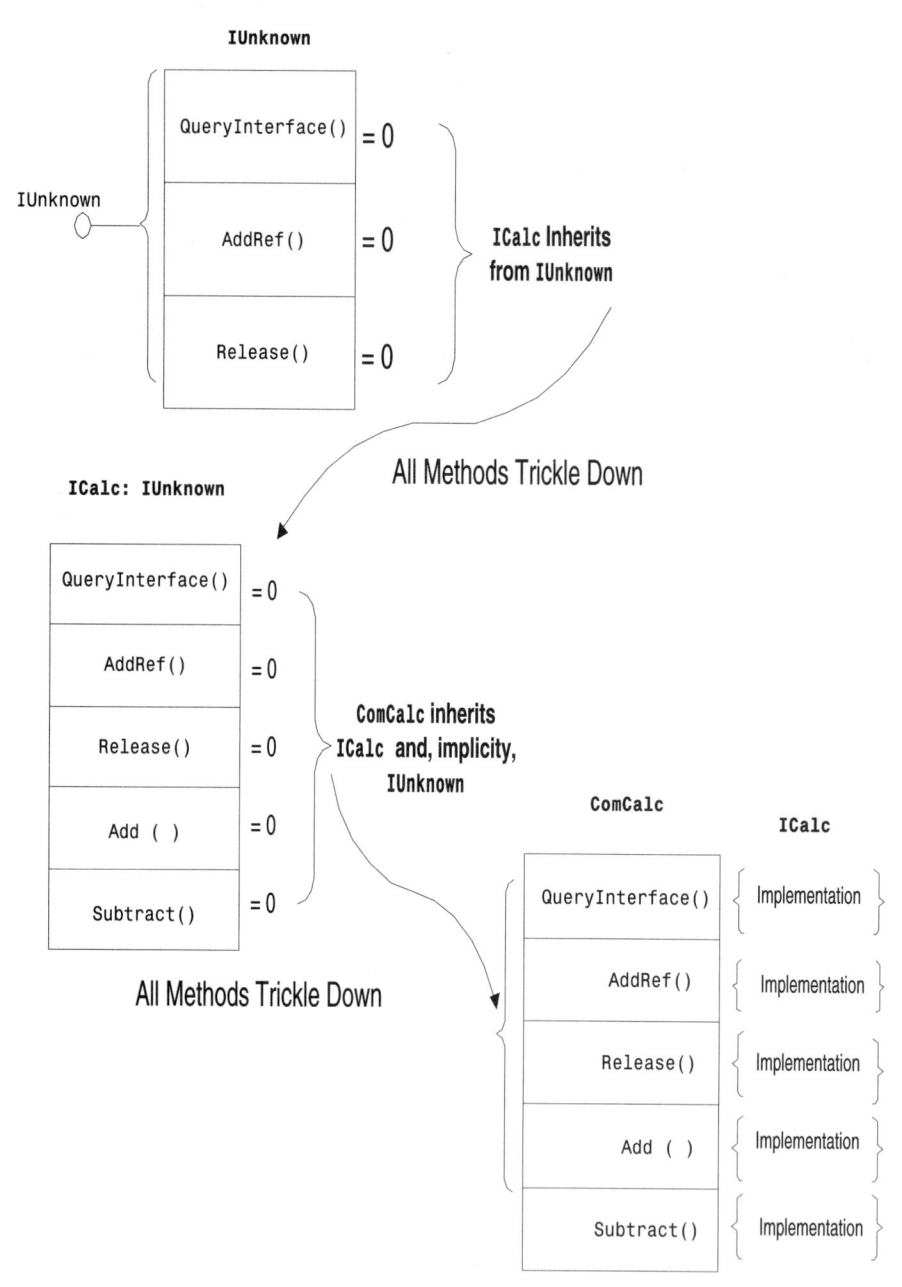

Figure 2.1 A call to a method in an abstract base class trickles down to the implementation in the derived class.

If this is true, you might wonder why we didn't call `AddRef()` in your client code in Figure 2.1. `AddRef()` is actually called; it just happens automatically in `CoCreateInstance()`. For example, if you share your interface in any way, as in the following:

```
ICalc * pICalc1, pICalc2;
CoCreateInstance(CLSID_COMCalc, _ , _ , IID_ICalc, (void**)&pICalc);
pICalc2=pICalc;
```

then you are supposed to call `AddRef()` like this:

```
pICalc->AddRef();
```

You do this to let the underlying `Calc` object know that there is another entity (`pICalc2`) that holds a reference to it, not just one. If this is the case, the following line does *not* cause the object to be released, because every `AddRef()` must be balanced by one complementary `Release()`:

```
pICalc->Release();
```

`Release()` must be called again to balance the number of `AddRef()`s called. In this way, an object can keep a *reference count* so as to track the number of clients the object has. Usually, the reference count is kept in an internal variable of the object and is incremented whenever `AddRef()` is called and decremented whenever `Release()` is called. An object knows it can destroy itself when this internal variable, this reference count, becomes 0.

Guidelines for Reference Counts and Object Lifetime

A client is solely responsible for the lifetime of an object. Always remember that `AddRef()` and `Release()` are member functions implemented by the object itself; they are not COM system functions. They are available to your client only after the object is instantiated and one of its interfaces is delivered to the client. When a client calls `AddRef()` on any interface, the object should take note of it and increment its internal reference count by one. If `Release()` is called, the object should decrement its reference count by one. `AddRef()` never initiates any other kind of action, creation or otherwise. It simply means add one to the reference. Likewise, `Release()` does nothing more than decrement the reference count until the reference count is 0. When this happens, the object should destroy itself because a reference count of 0 indicates that no clients hold any interface pointers to it.

The following are some guidelines for when these functions should be called:

- The client must call `AddRef()` when the client does the following:

    Places the interface pointer in another variable.

    Passes an interface pointer by reference as an `[in,out]` argument to a method.

- `AddRef()` is called implicitly on an object when the following occurs:

    `QueryInterface()` is called and returns the requested interface. Note that when an object is instantiated `QueryInterface()` is implicitly called by the object's class factory during its creation.

- A client should call `Release` when the following occurs:

    It is finished using an interface it `QueryInterfaced` for.

    It is finished using an interface given to it when the client instantiated an object using a COM creation API, such as `CoCreateInstance()`.

    It is finished using an interface passed to it as an output argument from a method.

This is traditional COM. COM+, however, throws a big wrench in all this. Lifetimes are no longer so clear; the reference counting rules should still be followed, but COM+ might elect to keep an object alive even when there are no longer any clients for it and its reference count is zero. I'll explain exactly how this works in Appendix C, "Object Pooling."

QueryInterface( )

`AddRef()` and `Release()` are used by the client application (and COM) to manage the lifetime of an object. It is really only in C++ that you deal with these methods directly, and even then you can avoid calling these functions by using the ATL and what are called *smart pointers*. At this point, don't be concerned about understanding all the possible rules regarding when to call `AddRef()` and `Release()`. They are relatively straightforward, and in many development environments, you don't even see these functions. What is important is that you understand the rules generally. Let's move on to talk about the final method of `IUnknown`, `QueryInterface()`.

`QueryInterface()` is arguably the most important of the three functions of `IUnknown`, and you will understand its use if I introduce two main tenets of COM:

- The only way a client can ever interact with an object is through one of its interfaces.
- The only thing a client can hold is a reference to one of an object's interfaces.

Client applications—be they VB, VJ++, or VC++—can never, ever have a reference or pointer to the object itself; rather, they can only have a reference to one of the interfaces of the object. This makes sense if you begin to look at interfaces for what they really are—channels of communication. An interface is like a radio frequency, and your object is the AM/FM dial that has different programs on different frequencies. When you listen to a talk show during your drive to work, you don't imagine that the host is sitting in the car with you. You realize that this station (or interface) is not the actual show, but a channel into the show, which can be in a far-off city or only two miles away. Either way, you're not concerned where the show is, nor do you care how the show is put together (producer, director, sound engineer, audio equipment, and so on) When you tire of the show, you can always change the station.

This is where `QueryInterface()` comes in. `QueryInterface()` is your tuning dial, allowing you to change the communications *channel*. In the same way you move to another station up or down from whatever frequency you're tuned in to, you can move from any one interface your object supports to any other interface.

`QueryInterface()` is a function available on any interface that allows you to request any other interface that the object supports.

At first glance, our `Calc` object appears to support only one interface, `ICalc`. In actuality, `COMCalc` actually supports both `ICalc` and `IUnknown` because `ICalc` is inherited from `IUnknown`. This brings us to another tenet of COM:

- Every object, without exception, supports the `IUnknown` interface.

This is because every interface of an object must be inherited from `IUnknown`; and because the base object is ultimately responsible for implementing all the methods of all its interfaces, it is also responsible for implementing `AddRef()`, `Release()`, and `QueryInterface()`. By doing this, the object ends up supporting `IUnknown`. Let's prove this. First, recall the following code:

```
ICalc * pICalc;
IUnknown * pIUnk;

CoCreateInstance(CLSID_COMCalc, 0,CLSCTX_INPROC_SERVER , IID_ICalc,
↪(void**)&pICalc);
```

Now, let's use `QueryInterface` on the interface you have (`ICalc`) and ask the object if it supports `IUnknown`:

```
pICalc->QueryInterface(IID_IUnknown, (void**)&pIUnk);
```

You can be sure the object supports `IUnknown` (all objects must); so upon returning from this function, `pIUnk` holds an `IUnknown` reference to object `COMCalc`. You can't really do much with an `IUnknown` reference except control the object's lifetime and query for another interface. As you'll see, there are times when an `IUnknown` reference to an object is a useful thing, but for the most part you don't often ask for it.

Interfaces and Their GUID Identifiers

`IID_IUnknown` is a GUID that is declared in the Windows header files. The GUID for `IUnknown`—and in fact, the GUID for any interface—never changes after it's published. Think of the GUID of an interface as its Social Security Number.

Inheriting from IUnknown

`ICalc` has the `QueryInterface` method because it is inherited from `IUnknown` like all interfaces. Don't get confused—there is not a contradiction between `ICalc` being inherited from `IUnknown` and `COMCalc` supporting both `IUnknown` and `ICalc`. It is *because* `ICalc` inherits from `IUnknown` that `COMCalc` supports `IUnknown`. And it is *because* `ICalc` inherits from `IUnknown` that it has the `QueryInterface()` function that can be used by the client to query the object for another interface it supports.

Using *QueryInterface()*

Let's use `QueryInterface()` in a more common context. If you recall our earlier `Calc` example in Chapter 1, "COM+: An Evolution," we proposed that the object have two interfaces, `ICalc` and `IFinancial`. In this way, the object can partition its functionality into two distinct groups or interfaces, each of which contains methods grouped by functionality. If the client is interested in basic arithmetic functions, it can ask for `ICalc`. If it is interested in financial functions, it can ask for `IFinancial`. If your `COMCalc` supports both interfaces, the IDL file would look like Listing 2.4.

Listing 2.4 **IDL File for *COMCalc***

```
import "oaidl.idl";
import "ocidl.idl";

    [
        object,
        uuid(638094E5-758F-11d1-8366-0000E83B6EF3),
        dual,
        oleautomation,
        helpstring("ICalc Interface"),
        pointer_default(unique)
    ]
    interface ICalc : IUnknown
    {
        [id(1), helpstring("method Add")] HRESULT Add([in] int x, [in] int y,
                                     [out,retval] int * r );
        [id(2), helpstring("method Divide")] HRESULT Divide([in] int x,
                                     [in] int y, [out,retval] int * r);
    };

    [
        object,
        uuid(638094E4-758F-11d1-8366-0000E83B6EF3),
        dual,
        helpstring("IFinancial Interface"),
        pointer_default(unique),

    ]
    interface IFinancial : IUnknown
    {
        [id(1), helpstring("method MortgagePayment")]
        HRESULT MortgagePayment([in] double amount, [in] double percent,
                            [in] int period,
                            [out,retval]float * payment);
```

The Role of IUnknown 51

```
            [id(2), helpstring("method GetPrimeRate")]
            HRESULT GetPrimeRate( [out,retval]double * rate);

    };



[
    uuid(638094E1-758F-11d1-8366-0000E83B6EF3),
    version(1.0),
    helpstring("COMCalc 1.0 Type Library")
]
library COMCALCLib
{
    importlib("stdole32.tlb");
    importlib("stdole2.tlb");

    [
        uuid(638094E0-758F-11d1-8366-0000E83B6EF3),
        helpstring("Calc Class")
    ]
    CoClass COMCalc
    {
        [default] interface ICalc;
        interface IFinancial;

    };

};
```

The C++ client can choose which interface it wants (see Listing 2.5).

Listing 2.5 **Client Code Creating an Instance of *COMCalc* and Using Its *ICalc* and *IFinancial* Interfaces**

```
ICalc * pICalc;
IFinancial * pIFin;

CoCreateInstance(CLSID_COMCalc, 0,CLSCTX_INPROC_SERVER , IID_ICalc,
➥(void**)&pICalc);

int result=pICalc->Add(1,2);
pICalc->QueryInterface(IID_IFinancial, (void**)&pIfin);
float rate=pIFin->GetPrimeRate();
pICalc->Release();
pIFinancial->Release();
```

Where C++ Representations Come From
IID_IFinancial is the C++ name of IFinancial's GUID. It was generated when MIDL was run on the IDL file and the MIDL-generated header file (included in this source file).

52 Chapter 2 COM Fundamentals

A Visual Basic client is much simpler and can be written as shown in Listing 2.6.

Listing 2.6 A VB Client Creating *COMCalc* and Using Its *IFinancial* Interface

```
Dim myCalc as new VBCalc.COMCalc
Dim Financial as IFinancial

Result=myCalc.Add (1,2)
Set  Financial = myCalc
```

In Visual Basic, the `Set` keyword usually translates to a `QueryInterface()` method call. Although you do not see or work directly with the GUIDs as you do in C++, they are present and maintained by the development environment. Specifically, by including your component's type library in your project by choosing Project, References, the component's GUIDs are included and implicitly used. The resulting list of type libraries is shown in Figure 2.2.

VB knows all the GUIDs, objects, and so on that it needs. So, the VB line

```
Set  Financial = myCalc
```

is translated behind the scenes to something like

```
pICalc->QueryInterface({0x638094e4,0x758f,0x11d1,{0x83,0x66,0x00,0x00,0xe8,
    0x3b,0x6e,0xf3}},(void**)&pIFin);
```

When prefaced by the `Set` keyword, VB reads the left side of the =, looks up the GUID for the object (`IFinancial`) in the object's type library, and uses that GUID in a `QueryInterface` call made on the object to the right of the = (which is `myCalc`).

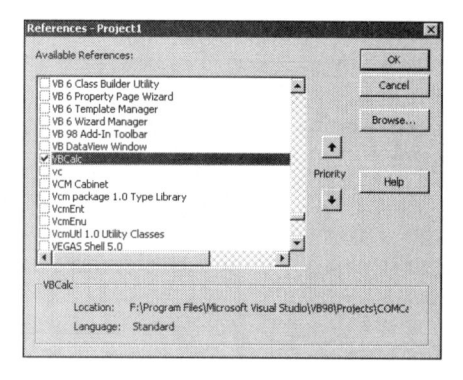

Figure 2.2 Visual Basic lists all the registered type libraries.

Where Does COM Live?

We've talked a lot about COM objects and interfaces and it's important to understand the theory, but we haven't said much about where COM objects reside. I did mention that COM objects can live in DLLs or EXEs; and in the case of COM+, your objects really need to live in the former. But what exactly does it mean for a COM object to be in a Dynamic Link Library (DLL)? How does this DLL get loaded? And how on earth can a client application on one machine get an interface of an object residing in a DLL on another machine? DLLs, after all, are just portable libraries brought into the process space of an application that needs them, so there is really no way for a client application to load and use a DLL across the network. (Well, you could do directory sharing but that is cheating; file sharing is not the same thing as distributed objects.) COM+, however, makes this possible. We'll explore how after we spend a few pages talking about DLLs.

Dynamic Link Libraries (DLLs)

When Windows was originally released, DLLs were really nothing more than groupings of functions that could be loaded into an application when the application wanted them and discarded when the application no longer wanted them. This allowed EXEs to be smaller, because they could outsource a lot of functionality; rather than have a lot of commonly used library routines compiled into the EXE and making the application larger, this functionality could be put in DLLs. DLLs could be loaded and unloaded at will and could even be shared among multiple applications.

Another nice thing about DLLs was that there was a kind of binary standard for them. If your DLLs were compiled properly, you could write the DLL in virtually any language and make your functions available in binary form to any other language. True, your language needed to produce assembly code, and entry points to your functions had to be declared in a certain way so that certain ambiguities were cleared up (who cleans up the call stack, what case will the exported functions be listed in, and so on). That said, however, it quickly became possible to write a DLL in C and call the functions in it from Visual Basic or another language or environment. Now *that* was power.

Today in COM+, DLLs play a more critical and sophisticated role than ever. COM+ DLLs no longer export an arbitrary number of functions (actually, you'll see soon in the sidebar "Functions Exported by COM DLLs" that they only export four utility functions). Their role has changed. The COM class of today's DLLs have far more lofty names for themselves (OCX, ActiveX Component, ActiveX Control) and are even referred to as servers sometimes. This is not to say that there are no longer traditional DLLs that are storehouses for a group of functions; there definitely are. But we're going to concern ourselves with the new role of DLLs—that of COM components.

COM DLLs, sometimes referred to as ActiveX components or servers, are actually repositories for COM objects. When I use the term *COM objects*, I am referring to the actual implementation of a specific coclass in a type library. A DLL can have as many objects in it as the developer wants to put in. That same DLL also has (stuffed into its resources) a .TLB file. A single DLL then can have multiple COM objects and a type library fully describing those objects and interfaces—all inside of one DLL shell. This is shown in Figure 2.3.

COM DLL

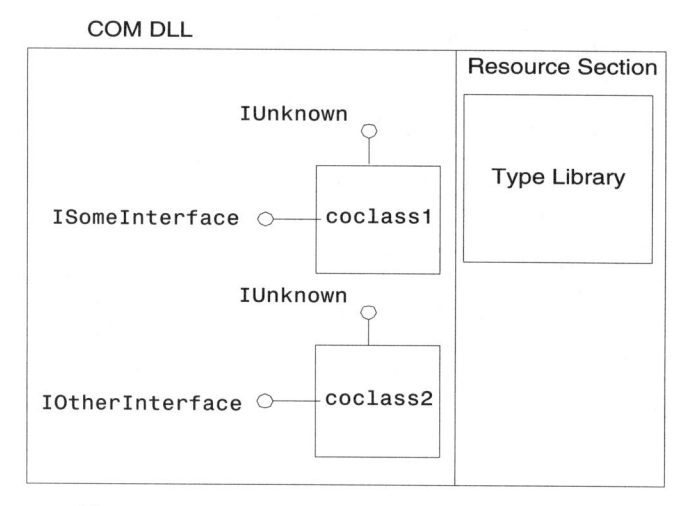

Figure 2.3 A COM DLL that has two coclasses and its type library included in its resource section.

Type Libraries and Resources

So, what does all this have to do with type libraries? Well, another benefit of the resource section of DLLs (and EXEs) is that they are extensible in terms of the kind of data they allow you to store. Think of the resource section as the kitchen junk drawer—it usually has extra twisty-ties, crazy glue, and usually a tape measure, but it can really have just about anything in it. Although there is built-in Win32 support for bitmaps, dialog boxes, icons, and the like, you can put anything you want in the resource section. Some application designers stuff .WAV files or .AVI movie files in the resource section so that they can ship a single DLL or EXE with no dependencies.

What Are Resource Files?

When I teach my COM course, I get to one part of the lesson where I say, "Type libraries are most often stuffed into the resource section of the DLL," and I get a lot of raised eyebrows. At that point, I remember that not all developers have worked with resource files or know what they are. Well, here is the deal with resources: Every dialog box, menu, and most bitmaps, icons, and splash screens used by an application are not compiled into assembly with your program logic. On the contrary, they are stuffed into a reserved section that every DLL and EXE can have called the resources section. You can reverse-compile the resources of most EXEs and DLLs and take a gander at all the dialog boxes, bitmaps, and so on that they use. You can also change any of the resources, and the next time the program is run, you will see that the dialogs, menus, and whatever else you modified have, in fact, changed.

At this point, the students usually get excited and ask if they can change the menus and dialog boxes of Microsoft Word, Excel, and so on. The answer is yes, you can. The Microsoft Compiler (VC++) does not make this easy to do (probably by design), but other compilers include resource editors that make this simple. Personally, I find Watcom's resource editor pretty easy to use when I feel like adding some graffiti to a co-worker's splash screen or changing his menu items to make his day more interesting.

COM takes advantage of this fact, and there is support for stuffing type libraries in the resource section. Remember, this is just a convenience. No one says that type libraries *must* be in the resources of your DLL. Although most COM DLLs do include type libraries in their resources, you can ship two files: your COM DLL and a separate type library. Microsoft Excel does this. Although Excel is a traditional application EXE, it also supports a host of COM objects that you can use to remote control Excel. The type library for Excel is greater than 0.5MB. That's a lot of IDL, and unless you want to make the EXE that much bigger, shipping the type library as a separate file is not a bad idea.

The Registry and Self-Registration

The discussion of type libraries in the previous section begs the following question: If the type library and the component can be two separate things and can even be in separate files, how can COM associate the two? The answer is the component must be officially registered with COM. In the good old days of 16-bit VB 3, the late-cretaceous ancestor of modern ActiveX controls, the VBX roamed the OS. If you wanted to add a new component to the system so that you could use it in VB 3, all you had to do was put a new VBX file in the C:\Windows\System directory, and that was all there was to it. There would be a new control on your tool palette which you could just drag and drop onto your form. I must admit, sometimes I miss the simplicity of this. Modern COM, however, is more exacting. VBXs are gone and replaced by OCXs, which are really just DLLs with COM objects and a type library inside them. The path to the COM DLL, the objects inside of it, and the location of its type library (whether the TLB path is the same as the DLL or is a separate file) must be known to COM before they can be used. COM DLLs, therefore, are *self-registering*. By this, I mean that COM DLLs know exactly what COM needs to know and have the capability to put the appropriate entries in the Registry so that COM knows about them and can use them.

Although COM DLLs know how to put the appropriate entries in the Registry, they are powerless to do so themselves. DLLs are always loaded and acted upon by a host process (EXE), so a COM DLL needs to be loaded by an application and *asked* to register itself. This creates a chicken-or-egg scenario for COM clients: a client needs to know what DLL an object is in if it were to ask the DLL to register itself; but if it knows what DLL the object is in, there is no need for the DLL to register itself. The solution is COM clients do not register COM DLLs—either you do it manually using a utility called regsvr32.exe or some Windows Setup.EXE program performs the registration behind the scenes. In the former case, if I send you a COM DLL called `comcalc.dll` and promise you that there is a calculator object in it, you would register it by going to the command prompt and typing the following:

```
regsvr32.exe comcalc.dll
```

VB and Registration

Note to VB Users: Registration is performed automatically when an ActiveX component is compiled. However, if you ship an ActiveX DLL (VB*ism* for COM DLL) by itself without using VB's Setup Builder, the recipient still needs to register it in this manner.

Regsvr32.exe is a very simple program. It simply loads the DLL, looks for an exported function that all COM DLLs have called `DLLRegister()`, and the DLL does the rest. When `DLLRegisterServer()` is complete, the function returns and regsvr32.exe exits. The approximate code in C for regsvr32.exe is something like that shown in Listing 2.7.

Listing 2.7 **Psuedo-Regsvr32 Utility Writing in C**

```c
main(int argc, char **argv)
{
HMODULE h;
HRESULT (STDAPICALLTYPE *v)(void);

h=LoadLibrary(argv[1]);
(FARPROC&)v = GetProcAddress(h, "DllRegisterServer");

(*v)();

}
```

You get the idea. `DLLRegisterServer()` takes the ball and runs with it. In VB and VJ++, the code for this function is created for you. In C++, you write it yourself unless you are using a class library like ATL and using the accompanying VC++ IDE ATL wizard support. Fundamentally, `DLLRegisterServer()` must do the following two things:

- Put path, GUID, friendly string names, and threading information in the Registry
- Register the type library

The first point is not that complex. COM needs to know where the DLL can be located, what the coclasses (objects) are, and what their GUIDs are. It must also indicate how thread-safe the DLL is—that is, can it handle concurrent access from many different threads at once. If the answer is no, COM automatically makes the component thread-safe by providing protection for it. Threads and thread safety are discussed in depth in Chapter 4, "Threading and Apartment Models." Specifically, the minimum Registry entries a DLL enters are shown in Figure 2.4.

Where Does COM Live?

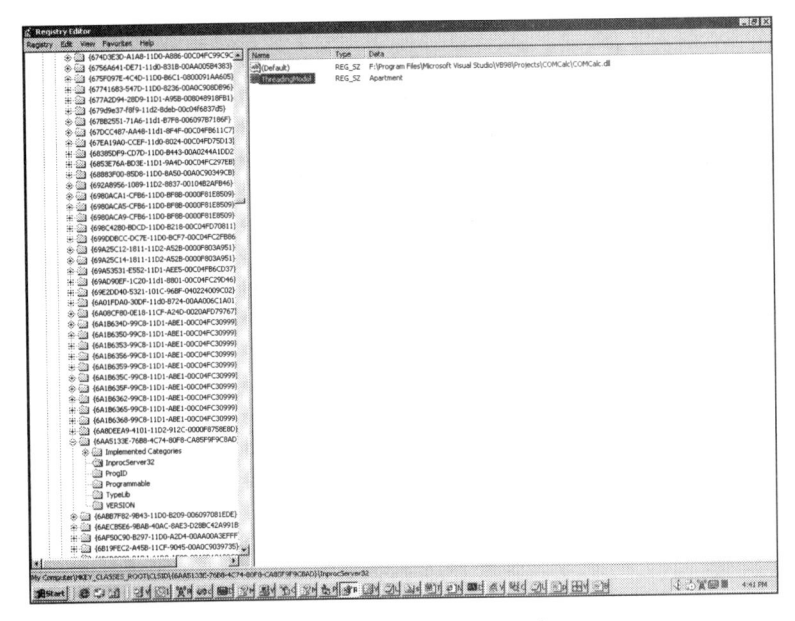

Figure 2.4 Registry settings for a typical component.

Common Registry Entries for COM/COM+ Classes

Following is a list (which is by no means all-inclusive) of common Registry settings. Note that most are optional:

- **Implemented Categories (Optional).** Clients and utilities can look at this entry to determine what a given coclass is capable of and/or what its requirements are. Specifically, there are a number of GUIDs established by Microsoft (check MSDN for details), each one of which indicates a specific capability or requirement. One or many of these GUIDS can be added as subkeys under this key.

- **InprocServer32 (Required).** Contains the path and DLL where the coclass being described can be found. Also has a data entry indicating the coclass's threading affinity (discussed in Chapter 4, "Threading and Apartment Models").

- **Programmable (Optional).** Indicates that the object supports OLE automation. We'll talk more about automation in Chapter 5. This key is no longer necessary.

- **Typelib (Suggested but optional).** Lists the GUID of its type library. This GUID can be looked up under the HKEY_CLASSES_ROOT\TypeLib key, and the actual path to the type library can then be found.

- **Version (Optional).** Can be used to indicate a version of the coclass. This is only important if different versions of the same coclass are co-existing, but all need to be available to the client.

The second point is also simple. Type libraries must be separately registered. As I said, they might very well be located in the same DLL as the objects it describes, but this doesn't matter. When registering, the DLL registers its type library by calling a Win32 function called, appropriately, `RegisterTypeLib()`. This function takes as an argument the path of the type library, and from here, Windows performs some magic. This magic takes the form of placing the type library path and GUID in the Registry in a section called TypeLib, shown in Figure 2.5.

This list is what you see when you select Project, References in VB. This Registry entry, however, is not all that happens. COM reads the type library and also registers additional information about the interfaces contained in the type library. In fact, if you look in HKEY_CLASSES_ROOT\Interface\, you will find your `ICalc` and `IFinancial` interfaces listed by their GUID, as shown in Figure 2.6.

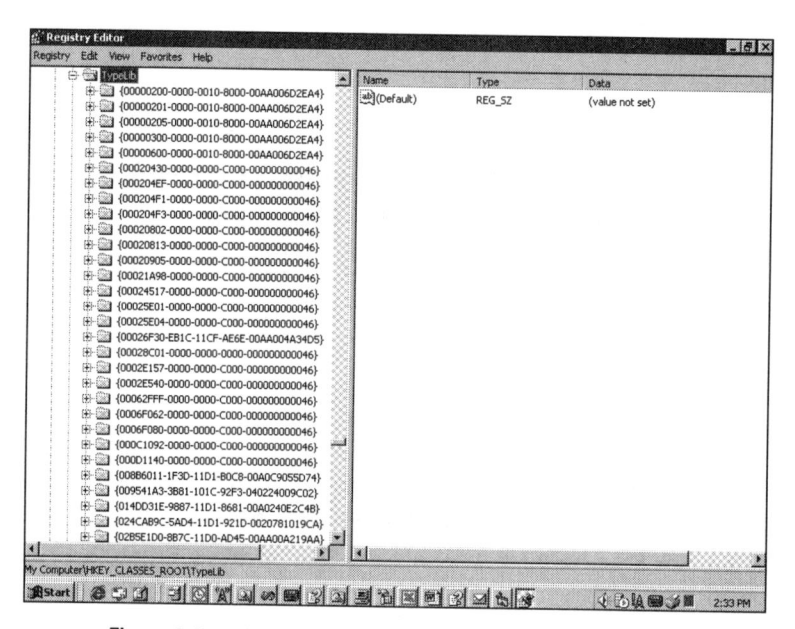

Figure 2.5 The section of the Registry where type libraries are listed (HKEY_CLASSES_ROOT\TypeLib).

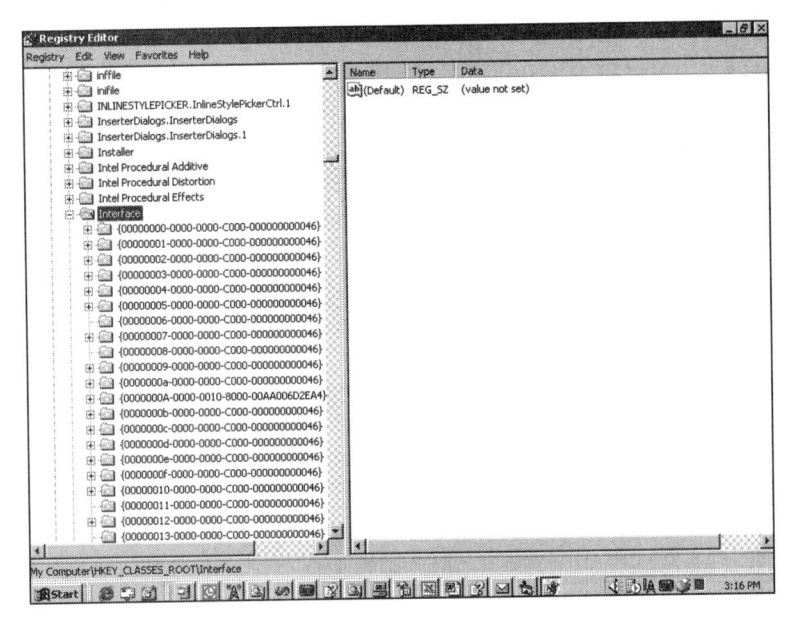

Figure 2.6 Information on interfaces are kept in the
Registry at HKEY_CLASSES_ROOT\Interface.

Functions Exported by COM DLLs

All COM DLLs must export the following four functions:

- **DLLRegisterServer()**. As we discussed, this function makes Registry entries necessary for COM to use your objects and also registers the type library.

- **DLLUnregisterServer()**. If you are sure you will never use a certain COM DLL again, this function can be called (call regsvr32.exe with a /U option) and will undo everything done by DLLRegisterServer(). Prior to Service Pack 4 DLLRegisterServer() would sometimes unregister Windows core oleautomation marshaler (oleaut32.dll) This would prevent OLE automation from working correctly. Thankfully, this was fixed in NT SP 4.

- **DLLCanUnloadNow()**. This is called by COM every few minutes or so to make sure that COM DLLs that are loaded have a reason for being loaded. In the event that a COM DLL is loaded in a process, but that process no longer has any references to interfaces of any object in the DLL, the DLL should be unloaded to conserve resources. DLLCanUnloadNow() tells COM whether it is safe to automatically unload the DLL.

- **DLLGetClassObject()**. COM calls this function to reach into a COM DLL and request that an object be created. Specifically, this function gives the client an interface to the object's class factory. Every object has a class factory, which is itself a COM object that knows how to create objects of a specific type; every object has one class factory. We will touch on class factories a bit more in Chapter 3 "COM Internals", but this function is a critical step in the creation of a COM object; though the process is hidden for the most part, a class factory is always used to create a new instance of a COM object.

A COM+ Variation—Surrogate Processes

We have discussed traditional COM so far, but COM+ adds a few twists and you should take note. Earlier I said that COM+ objects would live in COM DLLs. DLLs always require a process space (an EXE) to house them, so let's call this space a *surrogate*.

A remote client application must go through a surrogate process to talk to a COM object that is in a COM DLL. The architecture looks like that shown in Figure 2.7.

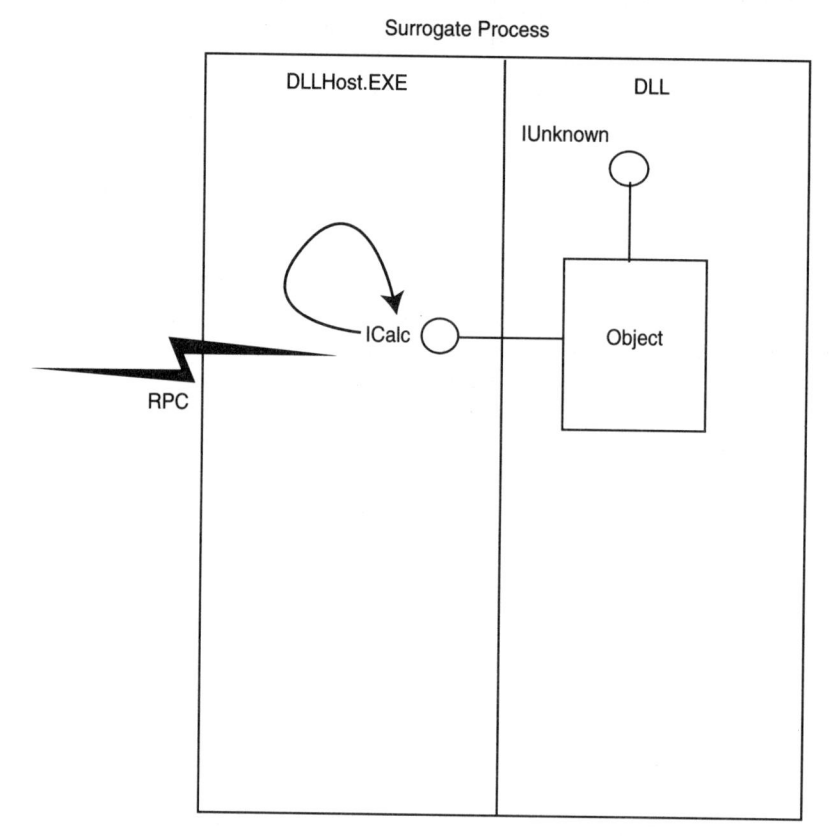

Figure 2.7 A DLL containing COM coclasses is hosted by a surrogate that provides the process space and thread(s).

Because a DLL is a passive bit of code that needs to be acted upon, the surrogate process is responsible for providing the body which a COM DLL needs to make its objects available to the outside world. This body consists of an operating system (OS) process space as well as the threads (we will talk more about threads in Chapter 4) necessary to give the body a brain. As you can imagine, this gives the surrogate an enormous amount of power. After all, the surrogate always stands between the client and the COM DLL; so it could, for example, keep an object alive even if the client calls `Release()` the appropriate number of times and no longer has a reference to it. The surrogate could then present the same object to another client requesting a new instance of the object. In short, the surrogate could provide a form of object pooling.

What else could the surrogate theoretically do? Well, one surrogate could also be the host for a number of different COM objects and allow them to cooperate in different ways; maybe it could track all the database changes of a group of related objects and allow all database modifications to be rolled back if any one of the objects complained.

There have undoubtedly been many developers who have been entranced by the power of surrogates and have undertaken vast development efforts to do what COM+ does—furnish a value-added surrogate that provides additional services to objects. COM+, like MTS before it, uses a surrogate process (DLLHost.exe) for COM DLLs and their objects. By sticking its nose (and its nose comes in the form of something called *interceptors*) between the client and the objects, it can provide an additional range of services for both the client and the captive objects. This book is all about those services and will detail each one *ad nauseum*. If, however, you understand the structure that gives rise to these services, I believe you'll write better objects.

A History of Surrogates

Prior to NT Service Pack 4, developers were required to write their own surrogates if the client EXE and COM DLL were on separate machines. SP4, however, provided a default surrogate. With SP4, it was now possible for a client to instantiate and use a remote COM object in a COM DLL over the network.

Summary

The following summarizes some of the key points discussed:

- COM objects support one or many interfaces.
- Interfaces are groups of logically related functions.
- Interfaces are really RPC channels of communication, as discussed in Chapter 1.
- If a client has any one interface, it can get any other interface the object supports by calling `QueryInterface()` in C++ or the `Set` keyword in Visual Basic (Java's native support for interfaces allows this to be done implicitly).
- An object's interfaces and coclass are described in a type library file.
- A type library file is really a tokenized, binary IDL file and can be generated from an IDL file using MIDL. It can also be created directly through Win32 calls.
- A type library can be reverse-compiled into an IDL by using OLEVIEW.EXE, as we saw in Chapter 1.
- Type libraries are usually stored inside the resources section of the DLL component.
- A single DLL can have one or many coclasses in it, and each coclass can support one or many interfaces.

3

COM Internals

At this point, those of you developing in Visual Basic and VJ++ have enough basic understanding to move forward into COM+ services and begin the in-depth exploration of these topics. Discussion of these services begins in Chapter 6, "The COM+ Catalog." This section is intended for C++ developers and for VB/VJ++ developers who are interested in seeing COM in its truest form, mainly its C++ implementation. Understanding COM at this level will give you some insight into how COM+ evolved into its present form and why it has the strengths and limitations that it does. Arguably, this chapter deals specifically with the internals of COM and not COM+, though I feel that making this distinction is rather like saying that a study of algebra is not relevant to a study of calculus. One builds on the other. This chapter can be skipped, but if you are really interested in how COM, and therefore COM+, ticks, you might give this section a try. Note that everything contained in this chapter is true for writing both COM and COM+ objects.

Virtual Function Tables (vtables), Abstract Base Classes, and Polymorphism

In this section, I'm not going to walk you through the C++ language. However, I am going to illustrate a few key features of the language that can give you a good sense of why COM is designed the way it is.

No matter what language you work in these days, most have the concept of a class. However, C++ offers the developer a great deal of latitude in terms of how a class is constructed and how it behaves. This often draws criticism from anti-C++ factions. This makes C++ too complicated, they argue, and therefore too difficult to learn and maintain. I always argue that increased latitude comes with the cost of increased complexity. At any rate, there are three aspects of C++ that are key to understanding if you want to really know COM:

- Abstract base classes
- Polymorphism
- Vtables

Interfaces as Abstract Base Classes

In the C++ implementation of COM, interfaces are declared as abstract base classes. Basically, an *abstract base class'* entire purpose is to force a certain structure on classes that will derive from them. In C++, ICalc appears as the following:

```
struct ICalc: public IUnknown
{

  virtual HRESULT Add(int x,int y,int *result)=0;
  virtual HRESULT Subtract(int x,int y,int *result)=0;

};

//NOTE: struct in C++ is really a class where all the methods are public.
//don't confuse this with a C structure.
```

The =0 at the end of the method declarations indicates that these functions have no body. They exist only so that any class derived from ICalc must implement them. The virtual keyword indicates that *polymorphism* is in use.

Polymorphism in Practice

I don't want to get into a quasi-religious object-oriented discussion about the merits of polymorphism; rather, I'll just demonstrate what it does. C++ gurus can skip this paragraph, but if you need a refresher, look at Listing 3.1 and tell me what the output will be.

Listing 3.1 Code Demonstrating the Trickle-Down Effect of Virtual Functions

```
class A
{
public:
    virtual void Func1() {cout<<"This is Func 1 in A\n";}
    virtual void Func2() {cout<<"This is Func 2 in A\n";}


};

class B: public A
{
public:
    void Func2() {cout<<"This is an override of Func 2 in B\n";}
    void Func3() {cout<<"This is Func 3 in B\n";}

};

void main()
{
A * pA;
B * pB;

pB=new B;
pA=pB;

pA->Func2();


}
```

If you believe that the output is "This is Func 2 in A", you are mistaken. The output is "This is an override of Func 2 in B." Why? Because of the `virtual` keyword. In a C++ class hierarchy, although a pointer of the base class type can hold an instance of any derived class, the `virtual` keyword ensures that the correct version of the function is called. In other words, although a pointer of type A is used to hold an object instance of B, when pA is used to call `Func2()`, the call trickles down from A to B, and B's `Func2()` is called. If you take away the `virtual` keyword from the `Func2()` declaration in class A, the wrong version of `Func2()` is called; the one from class A is called, even though the pointer is really holding an instance of class B.

The "trickle-down" behavior provided by virtual functions is very useful, particularly when you want to create some kind of collection class that can hold many different types of classes. As long as all these classes share a common ancestor, you can create a collection class that stores pointers to that ancestor (base) class, and it will be more than happy to store pointers to any derived class no matter how far down the line. Using virtual functions, you can iterate through your collection, call some `virtual` method, and be sure that the correct version of the function is invoked.

Writing COM Objects in C++

Another place virtual functions are useful is when you are writing COM objects in C++. As I said earlier, abstract base classes are used to represent interfaces in C++. You write implementation classes that inherit from one or many interfaces. Keeping in mind that all interfaces are abstract base classes that inherit from `IUnknown`, for our `Calc` object, we have what's shown in Listing 3.2.

Listing 3.2 Code Demonstrating the Pseudo-Implementation of a COM Class

```
//NOTE: the following interfaces have had their arguments and return values
//removed to keep things as simple as possible.

//IUnknown is declared in the Windows header files, you would not ordinarily
//declare it in your source files.  This is done just for example.
struct IUnknown
{
    virtual void QueryInterface(void)=0;
    virtual void AddRef(void)=0;
    virtual void Release(void)=0;

};

struct ICalc: public IUnknown
{
    virtual void a(void)=0;
    virtual void b(void)=0;
    virtual void c(void)=0;

};

struct IFinancial: public IUnknown
{
    virtual void d(void)=0;
    virtual void e(void)=0;
    virtual void f(void)=0;

};

//Implementation class
//we are required to actually implement the
```

Virtual Function Tables (vtables), Abstract Base Classes, and Polymorphism

```
//functions here.
//Note that multiple inheritance is most commonly used in COM/C++.
struct COMCalc: ICalc, IFinancial
{
    void QueryInterface(void){cout<<"QueryInterface"<<endl;}
    void AddRef(void){cout<<"AddRef"<<endl;}
    void Release(void){cout<<"Release"<<endl;}
    void a(void){cout<<"a"<<endl;}
    void b(void){cout<<"b"<<endl;}
    void c(void){cout<<"c"<<endl;}
    void d(void){cout<<"d"<<endl;}
    void e(void){cout<<"e"<<endl;}
    void f(void){cout<<"f"<<endl;}

};
```

Notice that `COMCalc` is responsible for actually implementing all the methods declared by all the interfaces. If you do not implement one of these pure `virtual` methods—for example, `a()`—Visual C++ would have this to say:

```
D:\ demo.cpp(68) : error C2259: 'COMCalc' : cannot instantiate abstract class due
➥to following members:
        D:\demo.cpp(44) : see declaration of 'COMCalc'
D:\ demo.cpp(68) : warning C4259: 'void __thiscall ICalc::a(void)' : pure virtual
➥function was not defined
        D:\ demo.cpp(29) : see declaration of 'a'
```

In other words, at no point is the function `a()` ever implemented. Because interfaces are abstract base classes that have pure virtual functions, you cannot implement the functions in the abstract base class definition. Rather, it is the derived class' responsibility to implement all functions on all the interfaces (abstract base classes) that it inherits from. And because every interface inherits from `IUnknown`, the derived object also must implement `IUnknown`'s methods.

Virtual and Pure Virtual Functions

Any method of a class can be virtual, simply put the `virtual` keyword in front of the method prototype. You don't need to modify any implementation code for that method. From then on, any classes derived from the class containing a virtual function are capable of polymorphism.

In Listing 3.2, you might have noticed that function bodies are not provided for `ICalc` and `IFinancial`. All member functions of these interfaces end with an `=0`. This syntax indicates that the methods are *pure virtual*—that is, they have no implementation. The existence of one or more pure virtual functions turns a class into an abstract class.

Look at it this way: An interface is nothing more than, well, an interface. It doesn't do anything other than guarantee what methods the underlying object supports. All methods called on an interface trickle down the object that supports the interface. In C++, the implementing COM object is usually a class that multiply inherits from all the interfaces it intends to support.

You might be wondering why I am spending this much time focusing on C++ implementation. After all, virtual functions, polymorphism, inheritance. . .these are all things that are specific to C++ and don't have much bearing in other languages, so why look at them so deeply? The simple answer is these concepts are central to COM no matter what language you are developing components in. As you'll see, the mechanism by which virtual functions work (vtables) comes into play in Java and VB as well, so if you truly understand the C++ structure, you will truly understand COM.

Internal Structure of a Vtable

Referring to Figure 3.1, let's look at how this class is put together behind the scenes. You wouldn't know it to look at it, but an instance of this class is 8 bytes in size. Specifically, this class is nothing more than two 4-byte pointers to vtables. A *vtable* is an array of pointers to virtual functions. Graphically, the class looks like what is shown in Figure 3.1.

The *ICalc* and *IFinancial* Vtables and Their Relation to *COMCalc*

Each interface is nothing more than an array of function pointers. Notice also that both ICalc and IFinancial begin with the three methods of IUnknown. As you'll see, this is critical to the functioning of COM. All interfaces must begin with these three methods so that they are available to be called by any client who has a reference to any interface.

> **Virtual Inheritance**
>
> C++ *virtual inheritance* can be used in multiple inheritance scenarios to suppress the repetition of an abstract base class that is inherited from more than once. The following line changes the resulting vtable in COMCalc so that the methods of IUnknown do not repeat:
>
> COMCalc: virtual ICalc, virtual IFinancial
>
> However, this is a bad idea. The three methods of IUnknown must be at the top of every interface and so must repeat. Access violations are certain to occur if virtual inheritance is used.

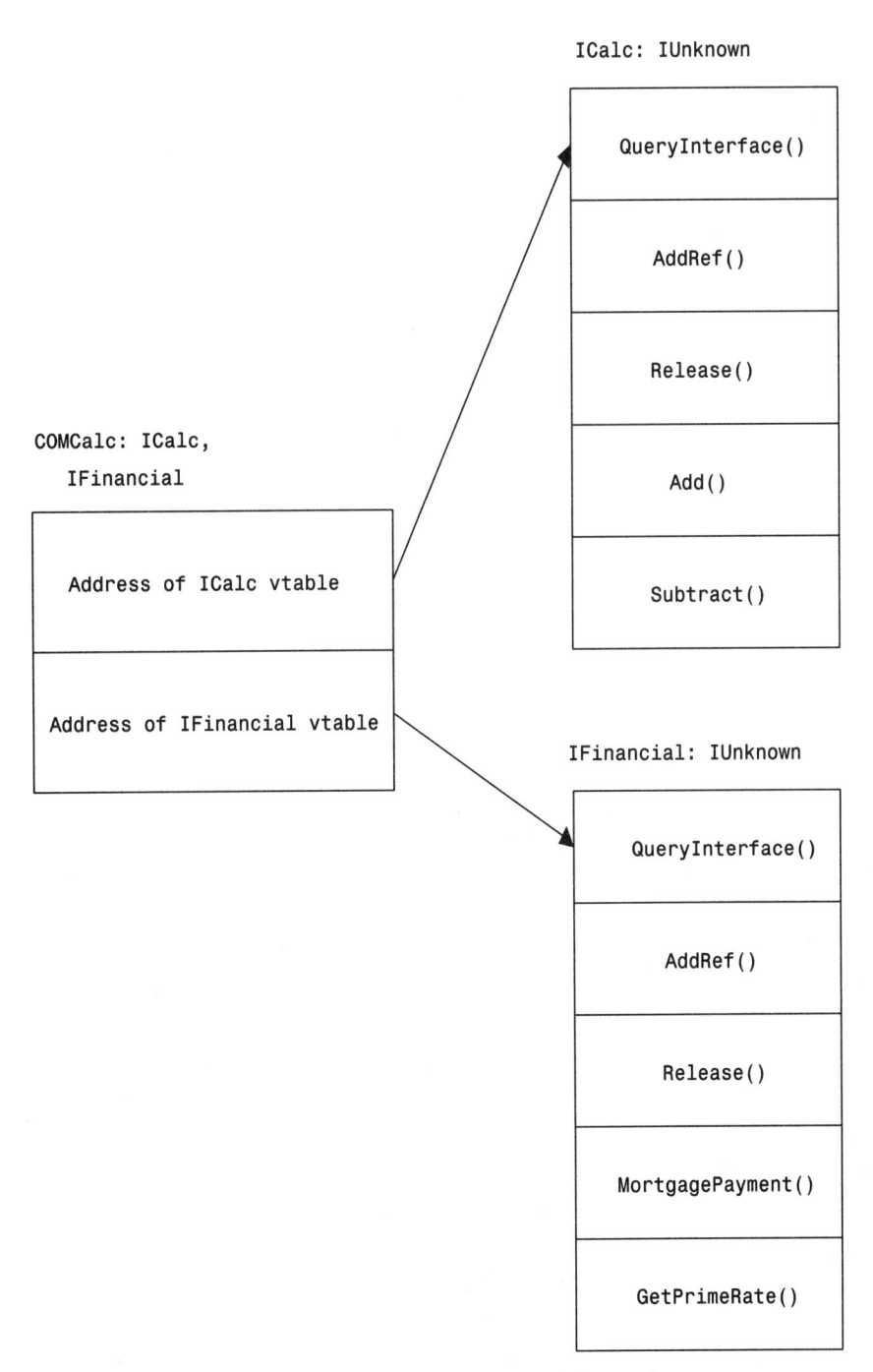

Virtual Function Tables (vtables), Abstract Base Classes, and Polymorphism 69

```
                                          ICalc: IUnknown
                                        ┌─────────────────────┐
                                        │  QueryInterface()   │
                                        ├─────────────────────┤
                                        │     AddRef()        │
                                        ├─────────────────────┤
                                        │    Release()        │
                                        ├─────────────────────┤
   COMCalc: ICalc,                      │      Add()          │
       IFinancial                       ├─────────────────────┤
   ┌─────────────────────────┐          │    Subtract()       │
   │ Address of ICalc vtable │─────────▶└─────────────────────┘
   ├─────────────────────────┤
   │ Address of IFinancial vtable │──┐     IFinancial: IUnknown
   └─────────────────────────┘      │  ┌─────────────────────┐
                                    └─▶│  QueryInterface()   │
                                       ├─────────────────────┤
                                       │     AddRef()        │
                                       ├─────────────────────┤
                                       │    Release()        │
                                       ├─────────────────────┤
                                       │ MortgagePayment()   │
                                       ├─────────────────────┤
                                       │  GetPrimeRate()     │
                                       └─────────────────────┘
```

Figure 3.1 Graphical description of the vtable layout for COMCalc.

If your COM object is implemented in C++ and your client is implemented in C++, an interface is really just a pointer to an abstract base class. Review Listing 3.3:

Listing 3.3 **Client Code Demonstrating Casting to *ICalc* and *IFinancial***

```
ICalc * pICalc;
IFinancial * pIFin;
COMCalc CalcObj;

pICalc=static_cast<ICalc*>&CalcObj;

pICalc->a();
pICalc->AddRef();

pIFin=static_cast<IFinancial*>&CalcObj;
pIFin->d();
```

Note that you cannot create an instance of an ICalc class. ICalc is an abstract base class; it has no implementation. However, an implementation class that derives from ICalc (COMCalc, in this case) and implements its methods can be cast to an ICalc. Of course, any method calls made to COMCalc cast as an ICalc ultimately trickle back down to COMCalc anyway (the methods are all virtual). If a C++ client application has only the abstract class definitions of the interfaces (ICalc and IFinancial) that an object supports (COMCalc), *the client does not need to have any information about the implementation object* (COMCalc). Put simply, if a C++ application could somehow get a pointer to a live instance of COMCalc, it could cast this pointer to either ICalc or IFinancial and be able to call the methods on either. The client would not need to have a prototype for COMCalc because it only loves COMCalc for its interfaces, not its true self.

C++ Clients

What exactly do I mean by C++ client? If I have a pointer to a COMCalc object instance, all my client needs is the prototype class definitions for ICalc and IFinancial; by casting the pointer to either, I can call methods on COMCalc. Why is this a big deal? COMCalc is right there in my source file, so why bother casting at all? You need to remember that interfaces are the only connection between a COM client and a COM object. The only thing a COM client knows about the server is what interfaces it might or might not support. The only thing a COM client can have is a declaration of these interfaces; it may never have a declaration of the underlying COM object.

> **In-Process COM Servers and COM+ Library Applications**
>
> In traditional COM, if a client application requests an object in a COM DLL that resides on the same machine, COM's Service Control Manager (SCM) seeks out this DLL and loads it into the client's process. This is typically the fastest way for clients and objects to talk because the client and server share the same address space. In COM+, the COM DLL is hosted by a surrogate process, and the client application is in a separate process unless the object resides in a *library application*. In this latter case, the COM DLL is brought into the process of the calling client.

Virtual Function Tables (vtables), Abstract Base Classes, and Polymorphism

If a COM client and a COM DLL share the same process, it is possible that the client application could, through a pre-defined COM mechanism, get a pointer to a `COMCalc` object living in the COM DLL. But the actual structure of the object, `COMCalc` in this case, would be unknown to the client who only knows about the interfaces. But then again, this is enough, right? Remember: *If* the client has the pure abstract base class definitions of `ICalc` and `IFinancial` listing nothing but their pure virtual function prototypes, *and* the client is given a pointer of a class instance that inherits from `ICalc` and `IFinancial`, *then* that class can be cast to either `ICalc` or `IFinancial`. Where did the C++ COM client get the abstract base classes for `ICalc` and `IFinancial`? Remember from Chapter 1, "COM+ An Evolution", that comcalc.h is a file generated by MIDL. The client application simply needs to include this file, and it will have class prototypes for `ICalc` and `IFinancial`. Or, if using Visual C++, the `#import` directive can be used to generate a header file from any type library. For more information on `#import`, see the following sidebar, "The `#import` Directive."

The #import Directive

What `#include` is for a header file, `#import` is for a type library: both directives import C++ class/function prototypes, constants, and other constructs into a .CPP file. The difference is that the `#include` brings the contents of a header file which already contains C++ syntax, whereas `#import` reads a type library (type libraries are tokenized Interface Definition Language [IDL] files and do not contain C++ syntax) and converts the contents of the type library into C++ accessible syntax. It does this by creating two hidden header files containing the C++ translated type library ending with the extensions .TLH and .TLI. Thus, a simple client program containing a `#import`, such as

```
//client.cpp
#include "windows.h"
//Note that the DLL below contains a type library
#import "d:\Projects\Calc\Debug\calcsdk.dll"

main()
{
```

will cause the creation of two hidden header files, calcsdk.tlh and calcsdk.tli to be created in the debug directory. These two files contain C++ prototypes for, among other things, interfaces. Thus, if the type library inside calcsdk.dll came from an IDL that included the following:

```
    [
        object,
        uuid(638094E5-758F-11d1-8366-0000E83B6EF3),
        dual,
        helpstring("ICalc Interface"),
        pointer_default(unique)
    ]
    interface ICalc : IUnknown
    {
```

continues

continued

```
            [id(1), helpstring("method Add")] HRESULT Add([in] int x, [in] int y,
                [out,retval] int * r );
            [id(2), helpstring("method Divide")] HRESULT Divide([in] int x, [in] int y,
                [out,retval] int * r);
    };
```

the client application, upon compilation, will include an automatically generated C++ prototype for ICalc. This is because #import implicitly includes the files it creates: calcsdk.tlh and calcsdk.tli. A look at the contents of calcsdk.tlh will reveal a C++ prototype for ICalc:

```
struct __declspec(uuid("638094e5-758f-11d1-8366-0000e83b6ef3"))
ICalc : IUnknown
{
    //
    // Wrapper methods for error-handling
    //

    int Add (
        int x,
        int y );
    int Divide (
        int x,
        int y );

    //
    // Raw methods provided by interface
    //

    virtual HRESULT __stdcall raw_Add (
        int x,
        int y,
        int * r ) = 0;
    virtual HRESULT __stdcall raw_Divide (
        int x,
        int y,
        int * r ) = 0;
};
```

Thus, a client application that uses #import to create C++ prototypes for COM entities containing calcsdk.dll will now be able to declare pointers of type ICalc, because the #import created an appropriate abstract base class based on ICalc's IDL description.

Note that #import recognizes command-line style arguments. Two that I often use are: "named_guids" and "no_namespace." For example:

```
#import "d:\Projects\Calc\Debug\calcsdk.dll"  named_guids no_namespace
```

named_guids puts friendly-named GUID declarations for all interfaces and coclasses in the .tlh file. I would always recommend this option. The no_namespace argument prevents the generated prototypes from existing in a C++ namespace. There are other arguments, but these can be found and easily understood in VC++ documentation.

Assuming that the client gets the prototypes for `ICalc` and `IFinancial` from the MIDL-generated header file, all that remains is for the C++ client to get a pointer to a live instance of `COMCalc`. There is, of course, a mechanism for this. One of the exported functions of all COM DLLs, `GetClassObject()`, is used to get a *class factory* that can be used to create an instance of the object. We will talk about class factories more in the upcoming section "`COMCalc` C++ Example."

Your C++ client could be given a pointer to an instance of `COMCalc` created by COM and given to your client. This pointer has to be of type void, and the client has to cast this pointer to `ICalc` or `IFinancial` pointers before calling any methods on the object. But, after that's done, you have the power to call methods on an object without knowing anything other than the interfaces the object supports. You don't know if `COMCalc` has any member variables, how big it is, if it has any functions in addition to the ones in its interfaces, and so on. You have, in essence, supported another fundamental tenet of COM: Implementation must be separate from interface.

Problems with the Fundamental Tenet of COM

The basic premise of the tenet above is okay, but we have a little problem with implementation. Casting is largely a C++ concept that doesn't even exist in some languages—VB, for example. So, even though having a client cast an object pointer given to it by COM to the appropriate interface works in the C++ case, a Visual Basic client using the same object cannot perform this. VB does not know how to cast. Plus, there is another, huge problem: COM objects can choose not to support an interface that the client requests.

In other words, although `COMCalc` happens to support both `ICalc` and `IFinancial`, how does the client know that? In COM, a client is supposed to ask if an object supports a given interface; it cannot demand that it does. This asking happens through the `IUnknown` function `QueryInterface()` (discussed in Chapter 2, "COM Fundamentals"), which has every right to say upon returning, "No, I don't support that interface. Pick another." In fact, the only interface a client can be sure an object supports is `IUnknown`.

We must, therefore, put the casting responsibility on the object itself. In other words, the client must be able to ask the object to transform itself into `ICalc` or `IFinancial` and return a pointer to the appropriate interface. But this is exactly what `QueryInterface()` is intended to do—produce the vtable of the requested interface and return it to the client. In a C++ object implementation, this is usually done by casting the object's *this* pointer to one of the interfaces the object multiply inherits from (see Listing 3.4).

> **REFIID and QueryInterface**
>
> `REFIID` is simply the GUID of the requested interface. `QueryInterface()` puts the pointer to the appropriate interface (vtable) into the ppv variable and returns it to the client. An `HRESULT` is long and is used to report errors.

Listing 3.4 **A Typical Implementation of** *QueryInterface( )*

```
//If COMCalc is defined:
struct COMCalc: public ICalc, IFinancial
{
    ...
//Then its QueryInterface method would likely be defined:
HRESULT COMCalc::QueryInterface(REFIID riid, void **ppv)
{

    if (riid == IID_ICalc)
        *ppv = static_cast<ICalc*>(this);
    else if (riid == IID_IFinancial)
        *ppv = static_cast<IFinancial*>(this);
    else if (riid == IID_IUnknown)
        *ppv = static_cast<ICalc*>(this);
    else
    {
        *ppv = 0;
        return E_NOINTERFACE;
    }

    AddRef();

    return S_OK;
}
```

You can think of `QueryInterface()` as returning the vtable to the interface you request. If you request an interface that the object does not support, `QueryInterface()` simply returns an error code (`E_NOINTERFACE`) indicating this.

Although it is true that vtables are commonly associated with C++, other languages like Java and Visual Basic can also use vtables. So, although the implementation of `QueryInterface()` looks very different for these languages, the basic principle is the same—the `QueryInterface()` function returns the vtable of the interface the client requests if the object supports that interface. Calls into functions of this interface then trickle down to the implementation object, which implements and executes the function called. At that point, however, you don't care how the object is put together. Think of objects as a black hole and interfaces the event horizon—what lies beyond is unknowable and unreachable.

Putting It All Together (RPC, DLL, Type Libraries, vtables)

In Chapter 1, we talked about Remote Procedure Call (RPC) and type libraries. In Chapter 2 and this chapter, we've discussed vtables, interfaces, DLLs, and `IUnknown`. You have now been exposed, at least superficially, to all these things. The real trick to knowing COM is to understand how these seemingly disjoint technologies coalesce into the COM *gestalt*. Here is a logical way to connect the parts to make the whole:

- RPC and type libraries are closely linked. After all, type libraries often come from IDL files, and traditional RPC uses IDL files too. So, a type library is a binary IDL file that COM's RPC can use as a guide when calling interface methods on objects across network boundaries. Marshaling is perhaps the type library's most critical purpose, but the information in the .TLB file can also be used to provide for programmer-friendly features like Visual Basic's IntelliSense (discussed in Chapter 1).
- Objects support interfaces. On the object side, an interface is nothing more than a vtable. On the client side, this is also true; interfaces are nothing more than a vtable. A vtable is just an array of function pointers. The difference is, on the client side, this array of function pointers point to *proxy functions*—that is, plain-Jane RPC ANSI C-style functions that are remoted to the object where they trip their corresponding entry in the object's vtable. Then, the method call falls into the event horizon of the black hole (object) and mysteriously gets executed. Outside of the interfaces it exposes, the object itself is a black box.
- COM interfaces are often defined in type libraries, but a type library is just a binary IDL file. Just as methods described in an ordinary RPC IDL file allow RPC to remote method calls between clients and server, the same is true for methods of COM interfaces described in a type library.

Now that we've taken a look at type libraries, I want to focus again on the C++ implementation of a COM class. For the remainder of this chapter, we'll step through a complete COM server/client implementation in C++.

COMCalc C++ Example

The following example demonstrates the major facets of a COM client and a COM object, both of which exist in the same .CPP file. Although this example is using the actual COM header files and libraries, we are doing all of your work in a single file so that the COM Service Control Manager is not involved. This gives you an isolated example of how COM clients and servers interact. First, examine Listing 3.5. A detailed description of all significant sections follows after the listing.

Listing 3.5 **Implementation of a COM Class and Associated Client All in One CPP File**

```
#include "windows.h"
#include "iostream.h"
const IID IID_ICalc =
    {0x638094E5,0x758F,0x11d1,{0x83,0x66,0x00,0x00,0xE8,0x3B,0x6E,0xF3}};
const IID IID_IFinancial =
    {0x638094E6,0x758F,0x11d1,{0x83,0x66,0x00,0x00,0xE8,0x3B,0x6E,0xF3}};
const IID CLSID_COMCalc =
    { 0x61305038, 0x396f, 0x11d2, { 0x80, 0x10, 0x0, 0xe0, 0x81, 0x10, 0x8, 0xed } };
```

continues

Chapter 3 COM Internals

Listing 3.5 **Continued**

```
//Abstract base class for the ICalc interface.
//Like all interfaces, it must inherit from IUnknown
//and it does not supply implementation for its methods.

struct ICalc: public IUnknown
{
//=0 means "pure virtual"
 STDMETHOD(Add)(int x,int y,int *r)=0;
 STDMETHOD(Subtract)(int x,int y,int *r)=0;

};


struct IFinancial: public IUnknown
{

    STDMETHOD(Mortgage)(int,int,int,int *r)=0;

};

//The COM class, COMCalc, multiply inherits from
//both ICalc and IFinancial.  It gets IUnknown
//in the bargain since both interfaces inherit
//from IUnknown.
struct COMCalc: public ICalc, IFinancial
{
    STDMETHODIMP QueryInterface(REFIID riid, void **ppv);
    STDMETHODIMP_(ULONG) AddRef(void);
    STDMETHODIMP_(ULONG) Release(void);


    STDMETHOD(Add)(int x,int y, int *r);
    STDMETHOD(Subtract)(int x,int y,int *r);
    STDMETHOD(Mortgage)(int,int,int,int *r);


};

STDMETHODIMP COMCalc::Add(int x,int y, int *r)
{
        cout<<"add\n";
        *r =x + y;
        return S_OK;

}

STDMETHODIMP COMCalc::QueryInterface(REFIID riid, void **ppv)
{
```

```cpp
//Because we are using multiple inheritance,
//the class can cast itself to any of its
//interfaces. It CANNOT cast itself to
//IUnknown. The reason and solution for and
//to this problem is discussed in the code
//walk-through which follows.

    if (riid == IID_ICalc)
        *ppv = static_cast<ICalc*>(this);
    else if (riid == IID_IFinancial)
        *ppv = static_cast<IFinancial*>(this);
    else if (riid == IID_IUnknown)
        *ppv = static_cast<ICalc*>(this);
    else
    {
        *ppv = 0;
        return E_NOINTERFACE;
    }

    AddRef();

    return S_OK;
}

STDMETHODIMP_(ULONG) COMCalc::AddRef(void)
{
//Since this is a pseudo-implementation,
//AddRef() and Release() don't do anything.

    cout<<"COMCALC add ref\n";
    return 0;
}

STDMETHODIMP_(ULONG) COMCalc::Release(void)
{

    cout<<"COMCALC release\n";
    return 0;
}


STDMETHODIMP COMCalc::Subtract(int x,int y,int *r)
{
    cout<<"subtract\n";
    *r= x - y;
    return S_OK;
}
```

continues

Listing 3.5 **Continued**

```
STDMETHODIMP COMCalc::Mortgage(int amount, int percent, int c, int *r)
{
    cout<<"mortage\n";
    cout<<percent<<endl;
    *r= -22; //just a bogus value
    return S_OK;
}

//Class factories are used to create
//instantiate COM objects. We'll discuss
//in the following walk-through.
struct ClassFactory: public IClassFactory
{
    STDMETHODIMP QueryInterface(REFIID riid, void **ppv);
    STDMETHODIMP_(ULONG) AddRef(void){return 1;}
    STDMETHODIMP_(ULONG) Release(void){return 1;}


// *** IClassFactory methods ***
    STDMETHODIMP CreateInstance(IUnknown *pUnkOuter, REFIID riid, void **ppv);
    STDMETHODIMP LockServer(int fLock) {return S_OK;}

};

//Class factories are COM objects, so they must
//support QueryInterface.
STDMETHODIMP ClassFactory::QueryInterface (REFIID riid, void * * ppvObj)
{

    if (riid == IID_IClassFactory)
        *ppvObj = static_cast<IClassFactory*>(this);
    else if (riid == IID_IUnknown)
        *ppvObj = static_cast<IUnknown*>(this);
    else
    {
        *ppvObj = 0;
        return E_NOINTERFACE;
    }


    AddRef();

    return S_OK;

}

//This method is called by COM or the client application directly
//to create a COM object.
STDMETHODIMP ClassFactory::CreateInstance(IUnknown *pUnkOuter, REFIID riid, void
↪**ppvObj)
}
```

```
    COMCalc * pC;
    HRESULT hr;
    pC=new COMCalc;
    hr=pC->QueryInterface(riid, ppvObj);
    return hr;

}

ClassFactory g_CF;

namespace PHONYCOM      //so that my bogus override
                        //doesn't name clash  with the
                        //real CoGetClassObject()
{
STDAPI CoGetClassObject(    REFCLSID rclsid,    //CLSID associated with
                                                //the  class object
                            DWORD dwClsContext,//demand in-proc or out-of proc
                            ⮕or both
                            COSERVERINFO * pServerInfo,  //Pointer to machine on
                                                        ⮕which the
                                                        //object is
                                                        ⮕to be instantiated
                            REFIID riid,    //Reference to the identifier of
                                            ⮕the interface
                            LPVOID * ppv    //Address of output variable that
                                            ⮕receives the // interface pointer
                                            ⮕requested in riid
)
{

    if(rclsid==CLSID_COMCalc)
    {
        g_CF.QueryInterface(riid, ppv);

    }


    return S_OK;

}

}//end namespace

main()
{
int result;
IClassFactory * pCF;
IFinancial *pIf;
ICalc * pIc;
```

continues

Listing 3.5 **Continued**

```
//begin psudocom

CoInitialize(0);   //must call this or CoInitializeEx() for EVERY thread that
                   //uses COM.

PHONYCOM::CoGetClassObject(CLSID_COMCalc, CLSCTX_ALL, NULL,IID_IClassFactory,
                          (void**)&pCF);

pCF->CreateInstance(NULL,IID_IFinancial, (void**)&pIf);
pCF->Release();

pIf->Mortgage(0,0,0,&result);
cout<<"Mortgage is "<<result<<endl;
pIf->QueryInterface(IID_ICalc, (void**)&pIc);

pIf->Release();

pIc->Add(1,2,&result);

pIc->Release();
CoUninitialize();

}
```

Specifying GUIDs in Code

```
const IID IID_ICalc =
↪{0x638094E5,0x758F,0x11d1,{0x83,0x66,0x00,0x00,0xE8,0x3B,0x6E,0xF3}};
const IID IID_IFinancial =
↪{0x638094E6,0x758F,0x11d1,{0x83,0x66,0x00,0x00,0xE8,0x3B,0x6E,0xF3}};
const IID CLSID_COMCalc = { 0x61305038, 0x396f, 0x11d2, { 0x80, 0x10, 0x0, 0xe0,
↪0x81, 0x10, 0x8,
```

In COM, every interface is uniquely identified with what is called a Globally Unique Identifier (GUID). As mentioned in Chapter 1 a GUID is a 128-bit statistically unique number generated by GUIDGEN.EXE.

In COM, the following entities need individual GUIDs:

- Interfaces
- coclasses
- Type libraries

In the preceding declarations, we have run GUIDGEN.EXE and created GUIDs for the coclass `COMCalc` and the interfaces `ICalc` and `IFinancial`. (Remember, in COM, you always ask for an interface or a coclass by GUID, not by name.)

Inheriting from *IUnknown*

```
struct ICalc: public IUnknown
{
    ...
```

Note that every interface must inherit from IUnknown. IUnknown provides the reference counting functions AddRef() and Release(), as well as QueryInterface(), which is the only way to get the interface pointer to another interface that the underlying object may also support.

STDMETHOD, STDMETHODIMP, and Method Implementation

```
STDMETHOD(Add)(int x,int y,int *r)=0;
//      STDMETHOD expands to virtual HRESULT _stdcall.
```

The virtual keyword is critical in this code so that polymorphism is in effect. This allows calls made to the methods of ICalc or IFinancial to trickle down to the base client. In COM, you never implement functions in your interface declarations. Rather, interface declarations should be abstract base classes. The implementation, then, should occur in the class that inherits from your interface. You might notice that implemented functions in the derived class are declared as STDMETHODIMP (the IMP meaning implementation).

All COM methods must return an HRESULT, which is simply a long data type. HRESULT indicates the success or failure of a method call. Because COM methods cannot return application specific data, they must modify variables passed in by reference. As you'll soon see in Chapter 5, "Method Invocation and Marshaling," there are ways to fool the client into believing that the methods return values, even though in reality, they only return HRESULTs.

Multiple Inheritance

```
struct COMCalc: public ICalc, IFinancial
{
    ...
```

Multiple Inheritance (MI) is extremely common in COM. It provides the most efficient and elegant method of writing COM classes. The alternative to MI is *nested classes*. The term is used to describe a class that is declared in another class. A class instance that is held in a member variable of another class can also be thought of as a nested class. Although MI is thought by many to add too much complexity and ambiguity, when used with pure abstract base classes (interfaces), it makes the implementation of QueryInterface(), AddRef(), and Release() very simple.

Implementation of *QueryInterface( )*

```
//note that STDMETHODIMP simply expands to HRESULT __stdcall
STDMETHODIMP QueryInterface(REFIID riid, void **ppv);
...
//You are now in the derived class. This is where you will actually implement
// all the pure virtual functions of your interfaces.
STDMETHODIMP COMCalc::QueryInterface(REFIID riid, void **ppv)
{
    if (riid == IID_ICalc)
        *ppv = static_cast<ICalc*>(this);
    else if (riid == IID_IFinancial)
        *ppv = static_cast<IFinancial*>(this);
    else if (riid == IID_IUnknown)
        *ppv = static_cast<ICalc*>(this);
    else
    {
        *ppv = 0;
        return E_NOINTERFACE;
    }

    AddRef();

    return S_OK;
}
```

This is the actual implementation of the `QueryInterface()` function. Because the `COMCalc` class inherits from `ICalc` and `IFinancial`, it can cast itself to either of these classes or to `IUnknown`, because both `ICalc` and `IFinancial` inherit from it.

Because `ICalc` and `IFinancial` are abstract base classes with pure virtual functions, when `COMCalc` casts itself to either of these types, it is really assigning *ppv to the vtable of either `ICalc` or `IFinancial`. This is all an interface pointer really is, a pointer to a vtable.

One cast that might seem puzzling, however, is this one:

```
else if (riid == IID_IUnknown)
        *ppv = static_cast<ICalc*>(this);
```

You might be wondering, if you want `IUnknown`, why don't you simply cast to `IUnknown`? Because you can't. Because both `ICalc` and `IFinancial` inherit from `IUnknown`, `IUnknown` actually exists in `COMCalc` twice. In other words, the vtable of `IUnknown` repeats and sits on the top of both `ICalc` and `IFinancial`'s vtables. If you try to cast `COMCalc` to `IUnknown`, the compiler is unsure which `IUnknown` to cast it to—remember, there are two. The compiler then issues an error, claiming an ambiguous cast.

The solution is simple and a little odd. Because all interfaces inherit from IUnknown, all interfaces have IUnknown's three methods at the top of their vtables. It is, therefore, permissible to simply cast COMCalc (or any COM class) to any of its interfaces when QI (QI is a shortcut term for QueryInterface) is calling for IUnknown. Although technically, the QI client gets a pointer to a vtable larger than it asked for, it doesn't matter because the client asked for IUnknown, the first three methods of any interface are IUnknown's, and the client never calls deeper than the third method.

Class Factories

```
struct ClassFactory: public IClassFactory
{
    STDMETHODIMP QueryInterface(REFIID riid, void **ppv);
    STDMETHODIMP_(ULONG) AddRef(void){return 1;}
    STDMETHODIMP_(ULONG) Release(void){return 1;}


    // *** IClassFactory methods ***
    STDMETHODIMP CreateInstance(IUnknown *pUnkOuter, REFIID riid, void **ppv);
    STDMETHODIMP LockServer(int fLock) {return S_OK;}

};
```

This is COMCalc's class factory. A class factory is the only way to instantiate a COM object. It must, at the very least, inherit from an interface called IClassFactory. The derived class factory must then implement the CreateInstance and LockServer functions of this interface.

There is a one-to-one relationship between a COM coclass and its class factory. Every COM coclass must have a class factory (which is itself a COM object) that knows how to create objects of that type. The client application must first get the IClassFactory pointer for the specific class factory of a specific coclass, then call CreateInstance to create an instance of that coclass, and return the requested interface pointer to the client application. Functions like CoCreateInstance() undergo this process behind the scenes.

If you want your client to contact the class factory of an object directly, you can do what CoCreateInstance() does and call a Win32 method, CoGetClassObject(). We won't discuss CoGetClassObject() in detail, but if you look it up in Microsoft Developer Network (MSDN), you'll find it is simply a way to get an interface from the class factory of any object.

> **Don't use SWITCH...CASE**
> We use IF. . .ELSE here because SWITCH. . .CASE doesn't work with GUIDs since they are structures.

While it is usually unnecessary to interact with the class factory directly to create an object, it is extremely useful when trying to debug components that will not instantiate. For example, when VB client's return runtime error 429, "ActiveX component can't create object," it is impossible to know what went wrong. All you know is that creation failed, but you don't know where in the chain the failure occurred. If, however, you are able to contact the class factory, but the class factory fails to create the object, then you know that the component is at least partially registered in the OS and was found by COM+, but the problem probably lies in the object's code. If, on the other hand, you fail to contact the class factory, then the component is either not registered, or not registered correctly in the system. I have used this technique many times to resolve creation problems.

Class Factories, *IClassFactory*, and Other Interfaces

```
STDMETHODIMP ClassFactory::QueryInterface (REFIID riid, void * * ppvObj)
{

    if (riid == IID_IClassFactory)
        *ppvObj = static_cast<IClassFactory*>(this);
    else if (riid == IID_IUnknown)
        *ppvObj = static_cast<IUnknown*>(this);
    else
    {
        *ppvObj = 0;
        return E_NOINTERFACE;
    }


    AddRef();

    return S_OK;

}
```

Class factories often inherit from interfaces in addition to `IClassFactory`. Following are some examples:

- `IClassFactory2`. Provides object creation with licensing verification.
- `IOleItemContainer`. Provides moniker support (monikers, an advanced COM concept, are covered in the "Creating a Queued Object using a Moniker" section in Chapter 10, "Queued Components").
- `<your own interface>`. Perhaps you want to provide a special interface that has methods providing special object creation and initialization functionality. Languages like Visual Basic cannot use it, and C++ clients using `CoCreateInstance()`, by default, request `IClassFactory` only. However, a C++ client can ask for this customized creation interface using `CoGetClassObject()`.

IClassFactory's *CreateInstance( )* Method

```
STDMETHODIMP
ClassFactory::CreateInstance(IUnknown *pUnkOuter, REFIID riid, void **ppvObj)
{
    COMCalc * pC;

    pC=new COMCalc;
    pC->QueryInterface(riid, ppvObj);
```

It might be surprising and even counter-intuitive, but creating a new instance of `COMCalc` and then `QueryInterface`ing for the requested interface via the second parameter (`riid`) is pretty much all `CreateInstance()` does. Note that every call to `CreateInstance()` creates a new COM object. Although it is discouraged in COM, your customized class factory could return an interface pointer to a COM object it previously created, instead of creating a new one, thereby turning the object into a singleton. The reasons why singletons are a bad idea will become apparent when we talk more about object lifetimes in Chapter 8, "Transactions."

Global Scope for Class Factories

```
ClassFactory g_CF;
...
```

Unlike other COM objects, class factories are usually declared globally and are, therefore, automatically instantiated and available to the COM sub-system when the DLL containing the COM class is loaded. Also, class factories do not destroy themselves. Interestingly, the `IClassFactory` interface has one method, `LockServer`, that actually forces a DLL (or EXE, although this type of server is not relevant to a COM+ discussion) to stay loaded even if there is no client with any outstanding references to any objects of the COM DLL. This is to prevent the DLL from being unloaded while a client is talking to a class factory.

The Win32 *CoGetClassObject( )* Method

```
    namespace PHONYCOM        //So that my bogus override
                              //doesn't interfere with the
                              //real CoGetClassObject().
{
    STDAPI CoGetClassObject(REFCLSID rclsid,   //CLSID associated with the class
                                               //object.
                            DWORD dwClsContext, //demand in-proc or out-of proc
                                               //or both.
                            COSERVERINFO * pServerInfo,//Pointer to machine on
                                                // which the object is to
                                                //be instantiated (can be NULL).
                            REFIID riid, //Reference to the identifier of the
```

continues

continued

```
                          interface.
                          LPVOID * ppv //Address of output variable that receives
                          the
                                          //interface pointer requested in riid.
)
...
```

The client application calls `CoGetClassObject()` to get an interface pointer (usually `IClassFactory`) from the class factory of a specific coclass. This method is a Win32 system function, but I have overridden and greatly simplified it here for the purpose of demonstration. In the real `CoGetClassObject()`, COM does all the work in terms of finding the appropriate EXE or DLL (called a *COM server*) where the coclass resides, running it, and handling all networking issues in the Out-of-Process case.

To simulate real COM in a single .CPP file, I've written a grossly oversimplified `CoGetClassObject()` function so the client code seems real. I declare it in the PHONYCOM namespace so that it doesn't conflict with the real `CoGetClassObject()`:

```
main()
{
int result;
IClassFactory * pCF;
IFinancial *pIf;
ICalc * pIc;

//begin psudocom

CoInitialize(0);  //must call this or CoInitializeEx() for EVERY thread that
                  //uses COM.

PHONYCOM::CoGetClassObject(CLSID_COMCalc, CLSCTX_ALL, NULL,IID_IClassFactory,
                     (void**)&pCF);
```

The `main()` is pretty much identical to the `main()` you might find in a COM client application. The difference here is you are calling `PHONYCOM::CoGetClassObject`, instead of the real thing, which would do the following:

- Find the appropriate class factory on the client's machine (or another machine altogether)
- Run the COM server
- Return the IClassFactory pointer to the client

You are actually initializing the COM libraries by calling `CoInitialize(0)`, even though you are not taking advantage of their services.

Summary

In this chapter, we looked at the implementation of COM classes and interfaces in C++. Interfaces, you learned, are always pure abstract base classes—that is, classes containing only pure virtual functions. Pure virtual functions, by definition, have no implementation. It is always the responsibility of the derived class to provide the implementation for the methods of all interfaces it inherits from. Any calls made by clients to the methods of an interface ultimately trickle down to the base class' implementation.

MI is the simplest mechanism by which a derived class can support multiple interfaces. MI makes it possible for a COM class to simply cast itself to any of the multiple interfaces that it inherits from. This makes the implementation of `QueryInterface()` trivial.

A class factory is used to create an instance of a specific COM class (each class has its own). A client application can call `CoGetClassObject()` as opposed to `CoCreateInstance()` if it wants to work with a specific class' class factory directly. Otherwise, `CoCreateInstance()` does this behind the scenes.

II

COM+ Components and Services

4 Threading and Apartment Models
5 Method Invocation and Marshaling
6 The COM+ Catalog
7 Contexts
8 Transactions
9 Compensating Resource Managers
10 Queued Components
11 Events
12 Security

4

Threading and Apartment Models

THE TREACHEROUS TOPIC OF COM threading models has been approached many times before, but I feel compelled to revisit this challenge because I have never read an explanation of COM threading models that satisfied me. You can have a very pleasant trip through this book, bypassing this section altogether. I think, however, that a basic understanding of threading, specifically, the COM+ apartment threading models, will help you understand how COM+ performs a lot of its magic.

Threads and Processes

Threads and processes are so simple, yet so misunderstood. To learn about them, let's first concentrate on a concept everyone understands—the process. The process is what your EXE lives in. Any memory your EXE uses, variables it declares, functions it calls, and so on exists inside a process that your operating system creates specifically for it. A process is like a playground surrounded by an invisible fence. Your application code can do what it likes in the playground specifically created for it and does not need to worry about the outside world. However, should your code try to escape the playground and overreach the fence, it will be terminated by the operating system. In fact, when you see a dialog box bearing the great big, red X that tells you the memory cannot be written or read, it usually means that your application tried to go beyond the fence and was terminated by the OS. In NT, the playground boundary is about

4GB, but it really has only 2GB (in Windows NT Enterprise Edition and, more recently, Windows 2000 Advanced Server, this is extended to 3GB) of memory to play with; the other 2GB is reserved by the OS.

A playground is only empty space. The existence of a playground implies that there is someone who will play in it. This someone is your application, and your application appears to the OS as a *primary thread*. At first, *thread* seems like a strange term to use, but it makes sense when you think about it. An application is a series of instructions threaded through time. It is fair, then, to refer to your application as a thread. Of course, your thread is not the only thread the OS is concerned with. There are many processes running, and thus, many threads executing at any given time on NT. Because most machines have only one processor, processor time must be distributed round robin to each thread in each process. To take the playground metaphor further, it is like all the threads in all the playgrounds are playing Red Light, Green Light with the OS who calls "Green Light! Now Red Light!" to each thread in turn. So every thread gets a short period of time to play in its playground, and then it must wait for its turn to come around again.

So far, we are assuming that every process (playground) has only one thread (player) in it. This can happen, but it is quite limiting because the process becomes myopically focused on one task and appears to the user as frozen until the task is complete. An application might want to do more than one thing at one time. Wall Street analytic systems, for example, have some calculations that can take hours to perform. You wouldn't like it very much if, after clicking the Calculate Yield Curve button, the user interface remained unresponsive for several hours. On the contrary, you expect to keep working with the application *while* it performs some task in the background.

Although there are some workaround (`PeekMessage()`, for example) methods of doing this (most of which can be found in Windows 3.1 cooperative multi-tasking), multiple threads are the answer. Let's say there are two kids (threads) doing different things but sharing all the toys (resources) in the same playground (process). When the CPU comes around to your application's playground, it calls Red Light! Green Light! to each of the two threads in your one process, giving each a limited time to play.

This brings up an important distinction—the OS gives time slices to threads, not processes. There simply can be no process without a primary thread, because it is the thread that is actually executing code; the process is just the place where a thread does its work. Thus, it is possible for a process to have more than one thread, that is, it becomes a multi-threaded process. A multi-threaded process has the capability to perform many tasks with what appears to be the same time in single-CPU systems or is actually at the same time in the case of multiple-CPU systems. Our analytic system can now undergo a long calculation in one thread, but keep the user interface responsive to the user with another thread.

Race Conditions and Threading Issues

Many threads that require access to finite resources of a process must adhere to some form of *thread synchronization*—that is, multiple threads must share resources in an orderly fashion, one thread at a time. Basically, if threads are not kept in line, one thread might interrupt another at precisely the wrong time and take control of some resource that the first thread was not finished using. Threads are simply not aware of one another, so it is possible that one thread in a process might be modifying a file, for example, when the CPU suddenly suspends it (in OS terminology, "puts it to sleep" or "blocks" the thread) and activates the second thread. This newly running thread then, unaware of the first thread's modification, proceeds to read the file but gets inconsistent data because the first thread did not complete its write. You now have a *race condition*.

Writing multi-threaded code that protects against race conditions is not the easiest of tasks. The multi-threaded programmer has a host of tools available: mutexes, semaphores, critical sections, events, and others. An in-depth discussion of each primitive is outside the scope of the book, however, a brief introduction is not. The following code demonstrates how a process (which automatically contains one primary thread) can spin off a second, worker thread.

```
#include <process.h>

DWORD WINAPI PrintSomething100Times(char *lpszSomething)
{
        for(int i=0; i<100; i++)
           cout<<lpszSomething<<", i="<<i
              <<" and my thread id is "
              <<GetCurrentThreadId()<<endl;
}

void WorkerThreadFunc(LPVOID v)
{
     PrintSomething100Times("I am the worker thread");

}


main()
{
DWORD dwThreadId;

        CreateThread(0,0,WorkerThreadFunc,0,0,&dwThreadId);

        PrintSomething100Times ("I am the primary thread");


}
```

The output of the program in Listing 4.1 is something like:

Listing 4.1 A Simple Multi-Threaded Program

```
I am the worker thread, i=0 and my thread id is 2088
I am the worker thread, i=1 and my thread id is 2088
I am the worker thread, i=2 and my thread id is 2088
I am the worker thread, i=3 and my thread id is 2088
I am the primary thread, i=0 and my thread id is 806
I am the primary thread, i=1 and my thread id is 806
I am the worker thread, i=4 and my thread id is 2088
I am the worker thread, i=5 and my thread id is 2088
I am the worker thread, i=6 and my thread id is 2088
I am the primary thread, i=2 and my thread id is 806
I am the worker thread, i=7 and my thread id is 2088
I am the primary thread, i=3 and my thread id is 806
I am the primary thread, i=4 and my thread id is 806
I am the worker thread, i=8 and my thread id is 2088
I am the worker thread, i=9 and my thread id is 2088
```

If the intent of `PrintSomething100Times()` is to print something 100 times without interruption, we clearly have a problem. You will notice that the two threads are, in a sense, competing for `PrintSomething100Times()` such that one thread can't finish executing the function before it is usurped by the other thread. Suppose that this constitutes a race condition, and you wanted to make sure that one thread needs to be completely finished with the `PrintSomething100Times()` resource (that is, the thread should complete 100 contiguous prints statements without interruption) before the other thread gains access. You can use a Win32 critical section to get this behavior by protecting the `PrintSomething100Times()` resource. Simply add a critical section object and few method calls such that we have

```
CRITICAL_SECTION pCriticalSection;
DWORD WINAPI PrintSomething100Times(char *lpszSomething)
{
    EnterCriticalSection(&pCriticalSection);

    for(int i=0; i<100; i++)
        cout<<lpszSomething<<", i="<<I
            <<" and my thread id is"
            <<GetCurrentThreadId()<<endl;

    LeaveCriticalSection(&pCriticalSection);
}

main()
{
//other code ommitted for brevity
...
    InitializeCriticalSection(&pCriticalSection);
...
}
```

In Listing 4.1, only one thread may enter `PrintSomething100Times()` at a time because it is protected by a critical section.

Only one thread is allowed in a critical section at a time, so neither thread will be able to call `PrintSomething100Times()` as long as this function is executing in the context of the other thread. Thus the output of the improved application will now consist of one hundred strings printed by one thread followed by one hundred strings printed by the other thread with no intermixing.

There are other synchronization primitives aside from critical sections, but they all operate under the same premise: Prevent concurrent access to some resource from multiple threads that are running at the same time.

Note that while VB does not natively allow multiple threads, VB developers can take advantage of the Win32 API from VB to nonetheless create both threads and synchronization primitives. For example, one can declare an external reference to the Win32 function, `CreateThread()`, as follows:

```
#include <process.h>

DWORD WINAPI PrintSomething100Times(char *lpszSomething)
{
    for(int i=0; i<100; i++)
       cout<<lpszSomething<<", i="<<i
          <<" and my thread id is"
          <<GetCurrentThreadId()<<endl;
}

void WorkerThreadFunc(LPVOID v)
{
    PrintSomething100Times("I am the worker thread");
}


main()
{
    DWORD dwThreadId;

    CreateThread(0,0,WorkerThreadFunc,0,0,&dwThreadId);

    PrintSomething100Times ("I am the primary thread");

}
```

One can then take advantage of VB's AddressOf operator and can spin off a new thread. See Listing 4.2.

Listing 4.2 **Creating a Thread Using the Win32 in VB**

```
Sub NewThreadFunc(Dim NoArg as Long)
        'do something
End Sub

Sub NewThread_Click

Dim ThreadHandle as Long
Dim ThreadId as Long

  ThreadHandle = CreateThread(0, _
                    0, _
                    AddressOf NewThreadFunc, _
                    0, _
                    0, ThreadId)

End Sub
```

Aside from using Win32 function calls, there is no way to directly create threads in VB6 or earlier versions. These versions of VB simply do not support multi-threading, and VB IDE and debugger will not operate correctly if you execute the code shown in Listing 4.2. Some VB developers might disagree and point to the Project Properties dialog box (shown in Figure 4.1) which allows VB programmers to create a pool of threads.

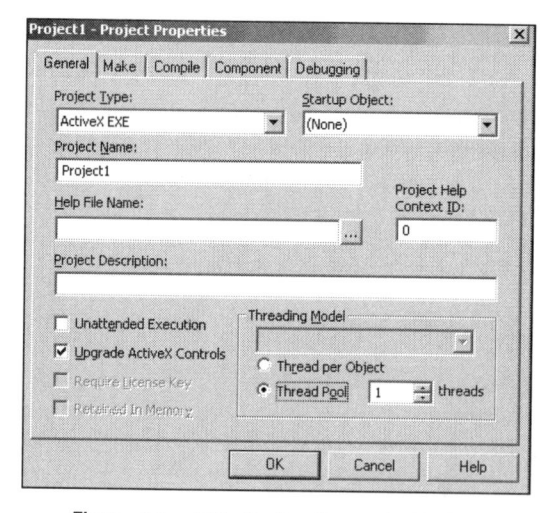

Figure 4.1 VB's Project Properties Dialog

Note that this option is greyed out and unavailable except in the case of out-of-process-(EXE) based servers. Because all COM+ components must be DLLs, this facility has no bearing on COM+. It is intended to provide load balancing for heavily used EXE-based automation servers by alternating new object creations on alternating threads in a pool or by creating a new thread to service each new object. Regardless, COM+ components are not allowed to spin threads and, as I said, they must be DLLs. Thus, this option is not relevant to COM+.

Apartments

Threads are useful and offer the developer a great deal of additional latitude. But with latitude always comes responsibility and complexity. Developers today want to leap right into the enterprise! They don't want to worry about writing thread-safe code when authoring objects that can, potentially, be used by multiple clients and threads at the same time. So, if the objects themselves are not going to be written to handle the rigors of multi-threaded clients, they must have some kind of guardian angel that protects them. They do, and the guardian angel is called, oddly enough, an *apartment*. The apartment provides COM+ with the "magic" ability to prevent race conditions from occurring; even though multiple threads/clients appear to access the same object at the same time.

It takes most developers time to grasp the concepts of COM threading and apartments. When you first hear that COM protects objects from concurrent access from multiple threads by means of an apartment model, you might then go hunting for apartments. If you know what a process is and how threads work, you might try to find some OS entity that corresponds to an apartment. But you won't find one, because apartments don't exist in any literal way. They are simply a concept, a term used to describe groupings of related objects and threads for the purpose of protecting COM objects from concurrent multi-thread access when the objects are not written to handle this. To be complete, I should mention that the role of apartments has evolved to accommodate COM+ contexts, which is discussed in Chapter 7, "Contexts."

For this chapter, however, we will focus on apartments in the context of their original intended purpose—protection. The concept of an apartment makes sense only after we understand why protection is critical for a COM object. So, we will revisit apartments in the section "Enter the Apartment" later in the chapter after exploring some of the synchronization problems inherent in multi-threaded applications and how apartments help to resolve them.

Message Queues as Synchronization Aides

Languages like Visual Basic (up to version 6, at any rate) are single-threaded. Other languages like Java and C++ allow you to create threads. COM+, however, insists that any client, multi-threaded or not, should be able to safely use any server, multi-threaded or not. So, to make good on this promise, COM+ steps in and provides protection in the case of, for example, a multi-threaded C++ client application using a single-threaded VB server object. How does COM+ do this?

At the heart of every Windows' application, and potentially every thread, there is a *message queue*. There is also a *message loop* whose purpose in life is to process messages from this queue. The code that processes a message loop—that is, retrieves the messages from the message queue and makes them available to the application for processing—is often referred to as a *message pump* (see Listing 4.3).

Listing 4.3 **A Simple Message Pump**
```
while(GetMessage(&msg,0,0,0))
{
TranslateMessage(&msg);
DispatchMessage(&msg);
}
```

Every mouse click, mouse movement, minimize, maximize, DDE message. . .basically every event that can happen in the Windows operating system gets stuffed into a queue that this loop perpetually reads from. When an application's UI becomes unresponsive or freezes, it is because this bit of code is hung.

In fact, if you strip away all the abstractions provided by most modern development environments and return the core Win32 API calls, the simplest possible Windows application is very simple. At its most basic, it creates a window, associates a windows procedure with that window to receive all the events (menu selections, windows resizing/movement, repaint, mouse clicks, and so on), runs a message pump to read these events from the queue, and processes them one at a time through the windows procedure (see Listing 4.4).

Listing 4.4 **A Win32 Message Pump and Window Procedure**
```
LRESULT CALLBACK WndProc(HWND hWnd, UINT message, WPARAM wParam, LPARAM lParam)
{
   int wmId, wmEvent;

   switch (message) {

     case WM_COMMAND:
         wmId    = LOWORD(wParam);
         wmEvent = HIWORD(wParam);
         //Parse the menu selections:
         switch (wmId) {

           case IDM_ABOUT:
              DialogBox(hInst, "AboutBox", hWnd, (DLGPROC)About);
              break;

           case IDM_EXIT:
              DestroyWindow (hWnd);
              break;
```

```
                // Here are all the other possible menu options,
                // all of these are currently disabled:
                case IDM_NEW:
                case IDM_OPEN:
                case IDM_SAVE:
                case IDM_SAVEAS:
                case IDM_UNDO:
                case IDM_CUT:
                case IDM_COPY:
                case IDM_PASTE:

                default:
                    return (DefWindowProc(hWnd, message, wParam, lParam));
            }
            break;

        case WM_NCRBUTTONUP: // RightClick on windows non-client area...
<do the appropriate thing>
            break;

        case WM_RBUTTONDOWN: // RightClick in windows client area...
<do the appropriate thing to respond to a right click>
            break;

        case WM_DISPLAYCHANGE: // Only comes through on plug'n'play systems
        {
        break;

        case WM_PAINT:
         <repaint the window>
            break;

        case WM_DESTROY:
            PostQuitMessage(0);
            break;

        default:
            return (DefWindowProc(hWnd, message, wParam, lParam));
    }
    return (0);
}

//Creation of window and a message loop

int APIENTRY WinMain(HINSTANCE hInstance,
                     HINSTANCE hPrevInstance,
                     LPSTR     lpCmdLine,
                     int       nCmdShow)
{
  MSG msg;
  WNDCLASS  wc;
```

continues

Listing 4.4 **Continued**

```
// the main window.
        wc.style         = CS_HREDRAW | CS_VREDRAW;
        wc.lpfnWndProc   = (WNDPROC)WndProc;
        wc.cbClsExtra    = 0;
        wc.cbWndExtra    = 0;
        wc.hInstance     = hInstance;
        wc.hIcon         = LoadIcon (hInstance, szAppName);
        wc.hCursor       = LoadCursor(NULL, IDC_ARROW);
        wc.hbrBackground = (HBRUSH)(COLOR_WINDOW+1);

RegisterClass(&wc);

HWND hWnd;

hWnd = CreateWindow(szAppName, szTitle, WS_OVERLAPPEDWINDOW,
      CW_USEDEFAULT, 0, CW_USEDEFAULT, 0,
      NULL, NULL, hInstance, NULL);


  // Main message loop:
  while (GetMessage(&msg, NULL, 0, 0)) {

        TranslateMessage(&msg);
        DispatchMessage(&msg);

  }

  return (msg.wParam);

}
```

Basically, as the message pump gets each message from the window's message queue, it messages it briefly with `TranslateMessage()` and then calls `DispatchMessage()`, which calls `WndProc()`. `WndProc()` was associated with the window before the window was created and contains a large `switch/case` statement. Every event that can happen to the window must be either handled by the developer in the `switch/case` block or delegated to the default handler via `DefWindowProc()`.

You might be wondering what a window's message queue has to do with protecting COM objects from concurrent access, but think about it. Queue means an orderly, one-at-a-time delivery. The architects of Windows chose to employ queues to tame the huge number of messages that can arrive at any time. Without a queue, a Windows application would become swamped with the sheer volume of messages; but with a queue, it gets orderly, synchronized delivery. And message queues are a built-in service of the operating system that any thread can create and use.

So, can message queues somehow be used to synchronize method calls made by different threads? Yes. And this is exactly what COM does to protect single-threaded objects. It turns all method calls made by clients into messages and stuffs them into the message queue. Prior incarnations of COM actually directed these messages into the message queue of a special, hidden window (COM+ still performs the same trick, but uses a new type of window, the message-only window, discussed later in the section, "Serialization Through Message Queues"). The server-side COM object then read from the queue, one method at a time (see Figure 4.2).

Threads and Objects

Remember that processes (EXEs) are nothing without their primary thread. It is the primary thread that performs tasks; the process is the place where it does the work. If a client application can be said to create a COM object, you are really saying that the primary thread of a client EXE process created a COM object. In a distributed case, a proxy of the object can be brought into the process for the thread to act on, although the object itself is created and remains on the server machine. When the creating thread calls a method on an interface of the proxy, that call gets remoted through the RPC channel to the implementation of the object on the server—so far, so good.

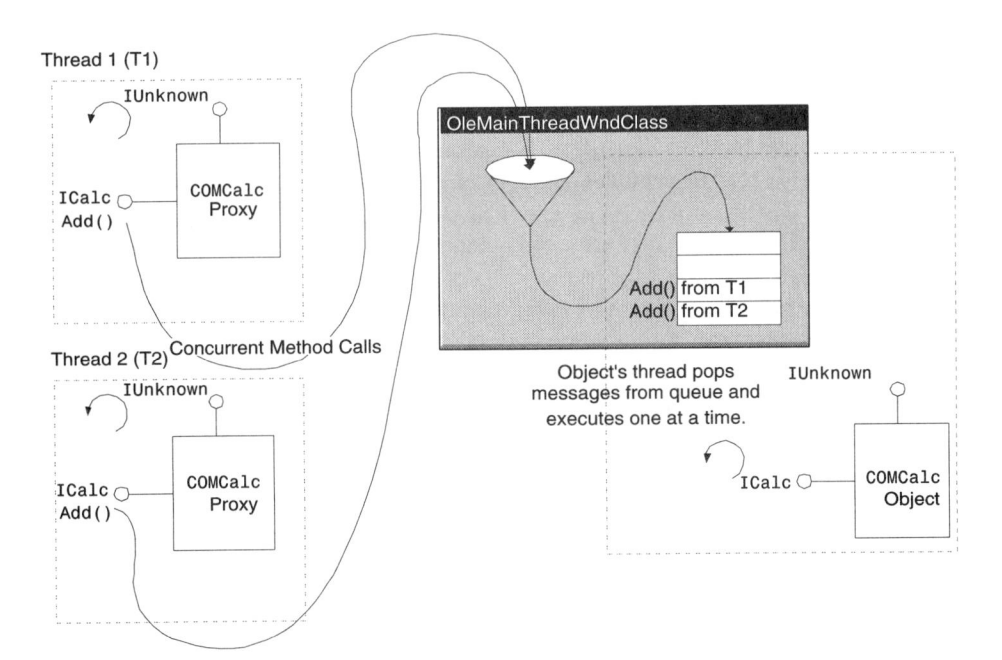

Figure 4.2 A Windows message queue being used to serialize method calls to a single-threaded object.

But what happens if the primary thread is not the only thread in the process? Let's suppose, for example, there are two threads in the process. Thread 1 creates the object and wants to give the object's interface it is holding to thread 2. If your object is not thread-safe, it is in trouble because now there are two threads that can call its methods at any time. For the purpose of example, assume this COM object books seats on planes as part of an airline reservation system. Now, thread 1 can call `ReserveSeat()` one millisecond before Thread 2 calls `ReserveSeat()`. If there is only one seat left on the plane, Thread 1 might reserve the seat but might not finish changing the seat status to Reserved before Thread 2 barrels in and, seeing the erroneous Open status, also reserves the now unavailable seat. COM protects against this by serializing all method calls through a message queue. In other words, COM redirects all concurrent method calls to a single-lane, one at a time queue.

This solves the problem of concurrency, but isn't there an efficiency cost? Yes. A COM object protected in this way does not scale well to meet the demands of a many-threaded client or multiple clients. As you'll see, however, COM+ provides an infrastructure where this scenario tends not to occur, and so the limitations of serialized messages are not that limiting.

Serialization Through Message Queues

You might be wondering what exact form this serialization takes. The answer is surprising. Every thread in the operating system is allowed to have its own queue. In fact, message queues are the only way threads can talk to one another. Threads can share variables and other resources, but if Thread 1 wants to say something to Thread 2, 1 can send a message to 2 if 2 has created and is servicing a message queue (see Figure 4.3).

In "traditional" COM as implemented in NT 4, Windows 95, and 98, recall that a hidden window with a message queue was used to serialize method invocations on a COM object. In fact, on these operating systems you can actually "see" this window using a platform SDK utility called *Spy++*. In COM+, however, this hidden window can no longer be found using Spy++, but that doesn't mean it isn't there. Windows 2000 introduces a special kind of window called a *message-only window*. Basically, it has the primary mechanisms of a traditional window—a valid system handle (`HWND`) and message queue, but lacks any kind of UI component. You might wonder what the point of such a window is. There are times when a mechanism intended for one purpose becomes useful for another. Without getting into too much detail, the use of a message-only window provides the simplest mechanism for COM+ to provide serialized method delivery for COM objects that need it. These windows can be "seen" programmatically by executing the code in the following sidebar "Finding Message-Only Windows."

At any rate, the hidden, message-only window is the protection, and it is erected by COM whenever protection is required. But how does COM know when this protection is required? Returning to the earlier example, how does COM even know that Thread 1 gives the interface of an object it creates to Thread 2? And what does any of this have to do with apartments?

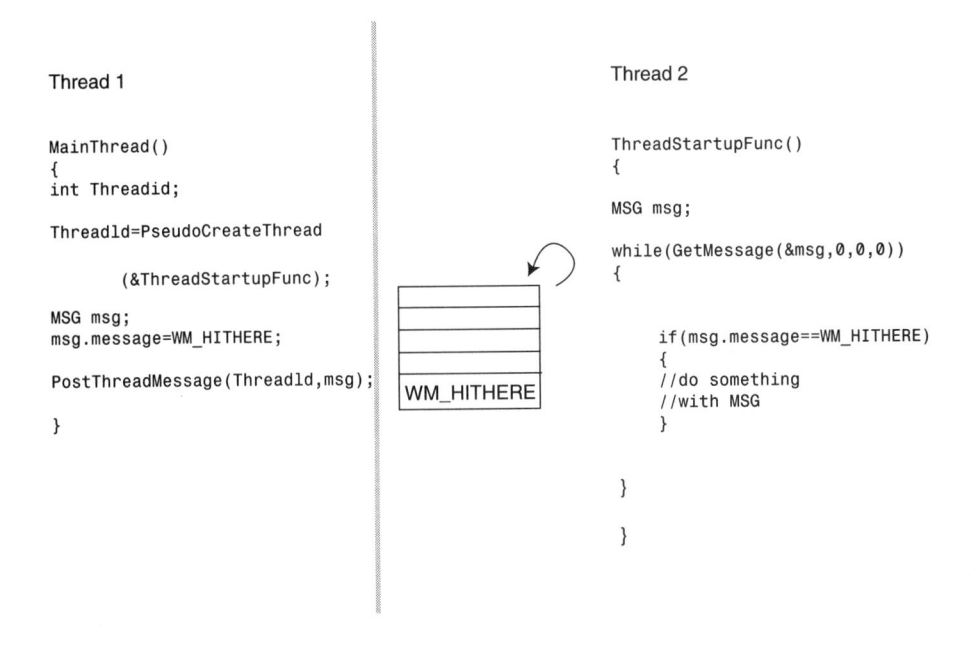

```
Thread 1                                    Thread 2

MainThread()                                ThreadStartupFunc()
{                                           {
int ThreadId;
                                            MSG msg;
ThreadId=PseudoCreateThread
                                            while(GetMessage(&msg,0,0,0))
    (&ThreadStartupFunc);                   {

MSG msg;
msg.message=WM_HITHERE;                         if(msg.message==WM_HITHERE)
                                                {
PostThreadMessage(ThreadId,msg);                //do something
                                                //with MSG
}                                               }

                                            }
                                            }
```

Figure 4.3 Thread 1 creates a second thread and sends a message to it.

Finding Message-Only Windows

Finding message-only windows is not difficult; one needs only to use a few Win32 function calls that are easily accessible from Visual Basic. A VB application demonstrating the process follows.

```
'Declare the Win32 APIs we need:
Public Declare Function FindWindowEx Lib "user32" Alias "FindWindowExA" (ByVal hWnd1 As
↪Long, ByVal hWnd2 As Long, ByVal lpsz1 As String, ByVal lpsz2 As String) As Long
Public Declare Function GetClassName Lib "user32" Alias "GetClassNameA" (ByVal hwnd As
↪Long, ByVal lpClassName As String, ByVal nMaxCount As Long) As Long
Public Declare Function GetWindowText Lib "user32" Alias "GetWindowTextA" (ByVal hwnd As
↪Long, ByVal lpString As String, ByVal cch As Long) As Long
Public Declare Function GetWindowThreadProcessId Lib "user32" (ByVal hwnd As Long,
↪lpdwProcessId As Long) As Long

'Win32 API Constant used with FindWindowEx to indicate we only
'want to search for message-only windows:
Const HWND_MESSAGE = -3

Dim WindowHandle As Long
Dim ClassName As String * 100
Dim WindowText As String * 100
Dim ThreadId As Long
Dim ProcessId As Long
```

continues

continued

```
'Iterate through all the message-only windows on the system.
'When FindWindowEx has enumerated through all of them, it will
'return a window HANDLE of 0.

Do

    WindowHandle = FindWindowEx(HWND_MESSAGE, WindowHandle, vbNullString, vbNullString)
    ClassName = "": WindowText = ""
    GetClassName WindowHandle, ClassName, 100
    GetWindowText WindowHandle, WindowText, 100
    ThreadId = GetWindowThreadProcessId(WindowHandle, ProcessId)

    'Output the information to the debug log:
    Debug.Print WindowHandle, Trim(ClassName), Trim(WindowText), ThreadId, ProcessId

Loop Until WindowHandle = 0
```

Enter The Apartment

You might expect that COM simply creates a message-processing thread whose job is to receive these redirected messages (method calls converted by COM to Windows-style messages) and distribute them, one at a time, serially to the COM object. You would almost be right.

Prior to COM+, COM intercepted the method calls from RPC, turned them into Windows messages, and redirected them to a hidden window of type `OleMainThreadWndClass`. This window was an ordinary, if invisible, window, and you could verify its existence with Spy++. The message queue for that window was used in the fashion just described to serialize the method calls (turned into messages by COM). After the messages were posted to the window's queue, they could be fed one-at-a-time to the server object that could not otherwise handle concurrent access by multiple method calls from multiple threads.

Finding a good real-world analogy for apartments and message queues is difficult, so I have to draw on a little bit of personal history to explain them. When I went to summer camp, all campers were given swim tests and put in one of two categories—Bluefish or Whale. As stronger swimmers, whales were allowed to swim together in the deep end of the swim area with minimal supervision. Bluefish, on the other hand, were considered weaker swimmers. They could only swim in the shallow, heavily supervised end, and if that wasn't enough, each Bluefish had to stay in his own little 4 square-foot area. When it was time for swimming, we all had to line up on the dock and declare our affiliation—Whale or Bluefish. Whales walked to the far end of the dock where they could swim together, mostly unsupervised, and Bluefish were stuck in the shallows in their little 4 × 4 areas. This is a sad, but true story. This is all COM apartments are—Whale and Bluefish affiliations. In COM, the Multi-Threaded Apartment (MTA) is the Whale and the Single-Threaded Apartment (STA) is the

Bluefish. Threads and objects in the MTA are left alone to sink or swim together (they are strong swimmers), but threads and objects in the STA are considered weaker swimmers that need protection.

A thread must declare its apartment affiliation before it can do anything with COM or a COM object. So, the thread goes to the dock and has to declare Whale or Bluefish (MTA or STA). In Visual Basic 6 and earlier (the final features for VB7 have not been finalized at the time of this writing, but Microsoft has announced that VB7 applications will be able to spin threads), where an application can only have one thread, it declares itself implicitly as belonging to the STA (Bluefish). In C++, however, the declaration is explicit and clear cut. Every thread in a COM C++ application must declare its affiliation. It does so with the following statement in Listing 4.5.

Listing 4.5 **Declaring a Thread to be MTA or STA in C++**

```
main()
{
    CoInitializeEx(0, COINIT_MULTITHREADED); //MTA/Whale
  // Or
    CoInitializeEx(0, COINIT_APARTMENTTHREADED); //STA/Bluefish

}
```

Threads always establish their affiliation from the outset. You might wonder why a thread would ever say it is in the STA when the MTA seems like a lot more fun. The answer has to do with the COM object the thread creates. If the object can handle concurrent access by multiple threads and the client is written in C++, absolutely, go MTA all the way and initialize your thread to be `COINIT_MULTITHREADED`. Unfortunately, however, Visual Basic client applications and VB-generated COM objects can only live in an STA. This means that the C++ client thread that instantiates and uses a VB COM object should be STA too.

Conversely, if the client application is written in VB, the server object gains nothing by swimming alone in the MTA because the VB application is putting around in the shallows of the STA. This is not to say that differing apartments can't mix; they absolutely can. But imagine a Whale trying to play catch with a Bluefish. The swimming areas we had at camp were divided by a wood decking, so if a Whale wanted to throw a ball to a Bluefish, the lifeguard probably had to step between the two and pass the ball from one to the other. That's a waste of resources and not much fun.

Single-Threaded Apartments (STA)

When a client thread is created and calls `CoInitializeEx()`, it declares whether it is in an STA or the MTA. If it chooses the STA, a new STA apartment is created for it. A process might have many STAs in it, one for every COM thread (if every thread so chooses). Note that exactly one thread lives in one STA. Using the Bluefish metaphor, every thread is like a swimmer in his own 4 × 4 area. If a thread in an STA creates a COM object and the object declares itself STA friendly (we will talk about how a COM DLL can declare its thread affinity in the section "Declaring Apartments"), that object can be thought of as moving into the STA with the thread.

Because an STA has, at the very most, one thread in it, there is no way that the poor, single-threaded object living in an STA can get walloped by multiple method calls from multiple threads. No matter how you look at it, there is no way for an object to get hurt.

Let's look at the following two scenarios:

- **Scenario 1—STA Client Thread Creating an STA Object on the Same Machine (Library Application).** In COM+, it is possible for a COM object to be brought into the process space of the client who requests it if the client and component are on the same machine. Such an application is called a *library application*. If the client thread is STA and the object is STA, the client thread's STA apartment has just one thread and one object. An object can only be called on by the thread or threads in the apartment in which the object resides. So in this case, you're safe—there is only one thread in the apartment.

- **Scenario 2—STA Client Thread on One Machine and STA Object on Another (Server Application).** In the previous scenario, you imagine that the thread and object live in the same STA. This is still true in this scenario, true in a philosophical if not a literal sense. Even though, technically, the client is in one STA and the server object is in another STA (possibly on a different machine), you can think of the client thread and server object as being in the same *conceptual apartment*. In COM+, most often, you have a client thread in an EXE on one machine that creates and calls methods on an object that resides in a server thread on another machine. In this case, you really have two STAs—one that the client thread and the object's proxy live in and another STA where the server object lives with a single thread provided by the COM+ surrogate EXE. See Figure 4.4 for a simplified representation (serializing hidden windows omitted).

At the end of the day, however, the object is still safe. Take each thread in the two STAs and imagine that they blur into one logical thread that sweeps from the client EXE into the surrogate where it calls into the object. When you look at it this way, there is only one thread that can call into the object.

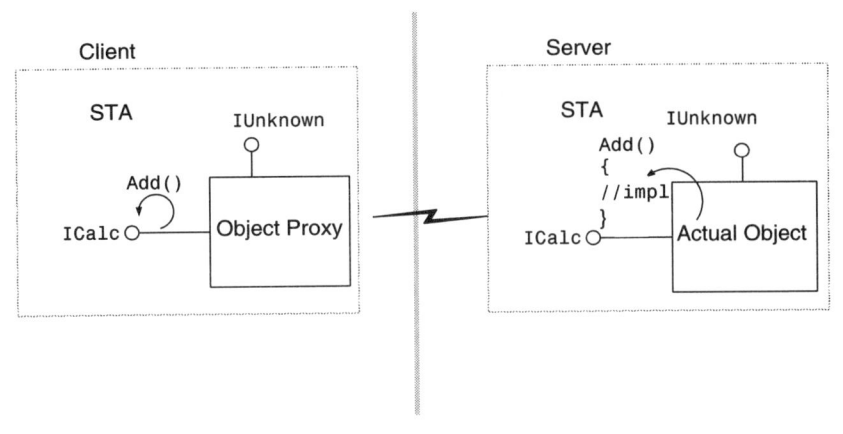

Figure 4.4 Simplified view of a method call being made from one STA to another over the network.

Multi-Threaded Apartments (MTA)

Although every thread that enters an STA always ends up as the sole tenant of its own apartment, an MTA is a big apartment where many different threads can move in together. This means a process can have many STAs but only one MTA. A thread-safe server object can live in an MTA because it is prepared to be hit by any number of threads living in the same apartment. Graphically, you have what is shown in Figure 4.5.

MTA is the easiest scenario to envision if you understand how an RPC server works. In the simplest case, an RPC server is an EXE that is running and listening for remote clients to connect to it and call methods on it. Remember that the client application has proxy functions that remote the call to this waiting, listening server where the function call executes.

The server might have many clients running that can call methods on it at any time, so all code in the server must be thread-safe. The fact is when a client makes an RPC call, this call is carried into the server on an arbitrary thread from the RPC server's *thread pool*. A thread pool is simply a collection of living threads that are waiting for a method call request to come in. When a method call does come in over the wire, one of the threads in the pool is dispatched to handle it. When the call is complete, the thread goes back into the pool. Although the server could create a new thread for every call, the server avoids the expensive overhead of creating a new thread on demand by creating them ahead of time in a pool. Of course, if more method calls come in than there are threads in the pool to handle them, new threads are created (although their lifetimes might not extend far beyond the completion of the call).

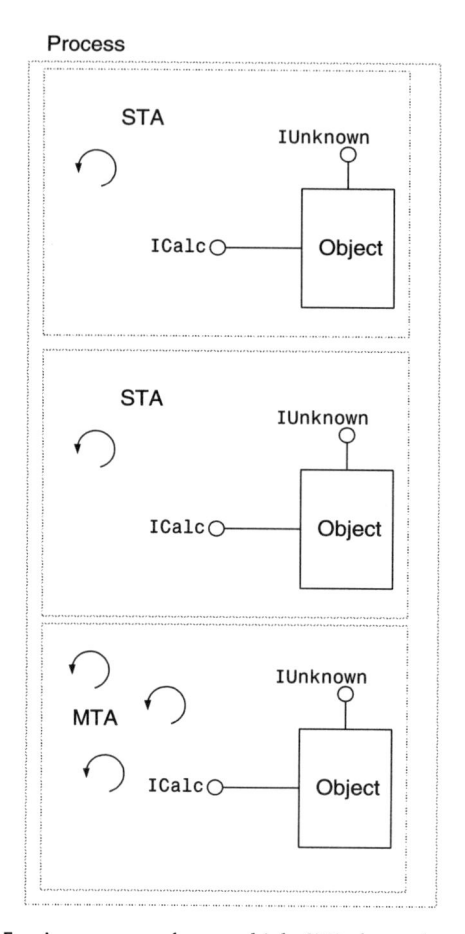

Figure 4.5 A process can have multiple STAs but only one MTA.

MTA is basically the RPC client/server scenario—method calls come into an object living in an MTA on some random thread, at any time and possibly at the same time. Objects that want to live in an MTA must be thread-safe. The simplest possible scenario to envision is one where a multi-threaded C++ client application accesses a thread-safe COM object. In this situation, every thread in the client calls `CoInitializeEx(0, COINIT_MULTITHREADED)`, thus entering the MTA. If the server object declares itself as MTA friendly (again, we will discuss how to do this in the section "Declaring Apartments"), you have a fairly ordinary RPC client/server configuration. COM does not step in and give any form of protection to the object.

Protecting the STA with Message Queues

COM determines what objects need protection by evaluating the following:

- Where each new thread declares it wants to be—STA or MTA
- What each object declares its capabilities to be—STA, MTA, or either
- What thread creates what object

If COM sees that an STA client thread creates an STA-compatible object, there is really no danger of race conditions. If the client and server object share the same process as in the case of a COM+ library application, direct vtable pointers are used, and COM does not insert any kind of protection. In most cases, however, COM still creates the hidden, messaging windows. However, COM does not need to do a thing if you have an MTA client thread that creates an MTA-compatible object. In this MTA-MTA case, the author of the object is responsible for making sure that the object is thread-safe or *re-entrant*. COM only needs to step in when you have mixed models—an STA client thread to MTA object, or vice versa.

Practically speaking, this doesn't happen as much as you might think. There is a heavy performance hit incurred when mixing models, so developers try to keep things the same. Visual Basic can only produce STA clients and server objects, and most commercial COM clients, particularly those having a GUI and/or acting as host for ActiveX controls, such as Internet Explorer, tend to rely on the STA. In my experience, you are likely to find mixed models in the following cases:

- **Scenario 1—Inexperienced C++ Client-Side Developers Writing Code.** Inexperienced C++ client application developers often take the path of least resistance. If they have a UI, STA is easiest; they will already have a message pump running for their window, which picks up COM method messages as well. If they do not have a UI and are not especially comfortable with message queues (or just don't want to be bothered to write extra code), inexperienced C++ developers opt for the simplicity of the MTA. MTAs do not require message processing. This results in faster development of the client, but drastically reduced performance when the MTA client thread instantiates and uses an STA object.
- **Scenario 2—High Performance Out-of-Process (EXE based) COM Singleton Server Used by C++, Visual Basic, and Visual J++ Clients.** The concept of the singleton server—that is, one big EXE server supporting multiple clients—is completely out of vogue these days. COM+ demands that your servers are DLLs and that your objects try not to rely on keeping internal state for extended periods of time. These two factors make this type of mixed model less likely and is found mostly in legacy scenarios.

- **Scenario 3—High-Performance Infrastructure Objects Used by VB Clients.** Free-threaded COM objects are written in C++ with the explicit purpose of servicing multi-threaded clients in some form of high-stress infrastructure capacity. These objects are low-level system objects and are not intended to be used by UI clients. Then, someone comes along and, for whatever reason, decides to write a Visual Basic client for one of these objects.

As you can see, only the C++ developer has the latitude to play with the MTA. Due to the widespread use of STA-only Visual Basic, you are unlikely to find many MTA-only client and servers on the market.

At any rate, it is difficult to explain all possible interactions between clients and servers with different threading models, so I will not get into the depths of it right now. For now, here is what I want you to remember:

- The server threads of STA-inhabiting objects and STA client threads always have running message loops. Remember that all remote method invocations made on STA objects are transformed from RPC calls into windows messages and redirected to a hidden window (`OleThreadWndClassName`). In languages like VB, the message loop is automatically written into your code. Message loops are optional in J++, and although you can run your own in an ugly fashion, a default STA is created by the J++'s VM (Virtual Machine). In C++, however, you must write this loop yourself. The nice things about STAs are that all method calls to an STA object are serialized through a hidden window. The result: Race conditions never occur, so the object does not need to be thread-safe.

- MTA client threads and server threads of MTA-compatible objects do not have message loops. There are no hidden windows or COM tricks. The internals of this process are straightforward RPC, and there is very little COM-inspired complexity. Clients send RPC methods from any thread that calls `CoInitializeEx(0, COINIT_MULTITHREADED)`, and the server receives the method calls from an arbitrary thread in its RPC pool, which carries the call into the server and into the object. MTA objects can get hit by multiple requests at the same time, so they must be written to be thread-safe.

- If you mix models, COM needs to step in and provide protection. This inevitably affects performance, so it is best not to mix your models if you can avoid it.

- If you develop your clients and server objects solely in Visual Basic, you never need to worry. Visual Basic 6 and earlier can only produce STA clients and objects, although VB7 will probably allow for a new type of apartment known as the Thread Neutral Apartment, or TNA (discussed later in this chapter).

Marshaling Interfaces

I begin this section by stating an absolute, immutable mandate of COM. And although only C++ programmers have the option to violate the following rule, it is important for developers of all languages to understand it:

You can never, ever, pass an interface pointer directly from one thread to another.

First of all, why would you want to do this? You might have a situation where Thread 1 creates a COM object and obtains an interface, but wants to give this interface to Thread 2. In this way, Thread 2 could call a method that might take awhile to execute, leaving Thread 1 free to go about its business. Visual Basic users never have this scenario because a VB application has, at most, one thread of execution. Only J++ and C++ developers have the option to share interfaces between threads. J++ developers, however, can rely on the VM to automatically take care of all the messy details of moving an interface between threads. As always, it is the C++ developer who bears the responsibility of total freedom and must be disciplined in his practices and familiar with all the gory details. So J++ and VB readers, if you're interested, read on; if not, skip ahead.

Let's revisit our previous scenario to see if we can spot the problem. Thread 1 creates a COM object, obtains an interface, and then gives that interface to Thread 2. Remember that in C++, an interface is simply a pointer to a vtable, so in this scenario, you pass a pointer from one thread to the other. Let us further assume that the COM object is *apartment-threaded,* meaning it can only exist in an STA because it needs protection from concurrent access. Do you see the difficulty? Both threads have an interface pointer to the object, so both threads can call into the object at the same time. The object simply cannot handle this, so you have a problem. But can't COM take care of this by converting all method calls from both threads into messages via a hidden window and then feeding them to the object one at a time? Yes, it can. But to perform this synchronization magic, COM must first know what thread created what object and what threads have which interfaces. In short, you must inform COM that you are sharing an interface between two threads so that COM can decide what needs to be done to provide protection.

In plain C++, passing an interface pointer from one thread to another does not, in any way, involve COM. You are simply passing a variable (that happens to have an address of a vtable) from one thread to another. As far as C++ is concerned, the variable can have anything in it. At the end of the day, it is just assembly code that is manipulating bytes in an address, and there is no way for COM to know what you're up to. Imagine COM's surprise then when Thread 2 comes out of nowhere and starts firing methods at the poor object.

You must tell COM that you want to share an interface between threads, and predictably, there is an API call you must make—`CoMarshalInterThreadInterfaceInStream()`. The name of this API is not exactly intuitive, but its purpose is straightforward. Just as you would want to send a delicate item across the country in a sturdily boxed, bubble-wrapped package complete with the sender's address, COM wants to send interfaces between threads in a special kind of package. The package in this case is a *stream*, which is nothing more than an array of bytes. `CoMarshalInterThreadInterfaceInStream()`, then, simply packages up the interface into an array of bytes (`Stream`) for transport. You might be interested to know what the stream contains, but for now just think of it as holding all the housekeeping details, particularly the sender's apartment address.

After you have called `CoMarshalInterThreadInterfaceInStream()` from the thread that first obtained the interface, you are left with an `IStream` pointer (see Listing 4.6).

Listing 4.6 **Marshaling an Interface Into a Stream**

```
//Thread 1
IStream *pIStream;

hr = CoMarshalInterThreadInterfaceInStream(
        IID_ICalc,
        pICalc,
        &pIStream);
```

This pointer can be sent between threads. If this `IStream` pointer is given to Thread 2, Thread 2 can then call `CoGetInterfaceAndReleaseStream()` to turn the stream back into the original interface which Thread 2 can now use (see Listing 4.7).

Listing 4.7 **Retrieving a Marshaled Interface From a Stream**

```
//Thread 2
ICalc *pICalc;
hr = CoGetInterfaceAndReleaseStream(
        pIStream,
        IID_ICalc,
        (void **)&pICalc);
```

Actually, Thread 2 might end up with a proxy, a direct pointer, a proxy to a proxy. . . . COM takes care of the housekeeping details and gives Thread 2 whatever illusion is necessary to make it think it has a direct interface to the object while protecting the object from any possibility of concurrent access. By calling `CoGetInterfaceAndReleaseStream()` and `CoMarshalInterThreadInterfaceInStream()`, you are giving COM the opportunity to do the right thing. Determining the right thing to do, so as to provide protection for all scenarios, gets you into a hornet's nest of combinatorial possibilities dependant on threading models, process contexts, and so on. If you follow the rules of marshaling interfaces, you can remain blissfully unaware of the implementation details. A thread's apartment affiliation is one of the housekeeping details stuffed into the stream as it informs COM what protection is necessary.

Listing 4.8 is a code snippet demonstrating how to pass an interface pointer between two STA threads in C++.

Listing 4.8 **Demonstration of Marshaling and Unmarshaling an Interface Pointer Between Two Different Threads**

```
//Source in: book/code/c++/ThreadPassInterface/ThreadPassInterface.cpp


//Stream can be global, available to all threads in the process
IStream* g_pIStream;        // The stream we will be passing


//Thread 1, packaging interface for delivery to another thread
...
    hr = CoMarshalInterThreadInterfaceInStream(
            IID_ICalc,
            pICalc,
            &g_pIStream);
...
//Thread 2, unpackaging the interface
ICalc *pICalc;

    hr = CoGetInterfaceAndReleaseStream (
            g_pIStream,
            IID_ICALC,
            (void**)&pICalc);
```

In J++, this code is unnecessary because marshaling occurs automatically. Specifically, COM classes are represented as *Java Callable Wrappers (JCW)*, which contain additional attributes that inform J++ when and how to marshal interfaces between threads.

Similarly, there is nothing to do in VB because VB client applications and servers can have only one thread. In situations where ActixeX classes (interfaces) are used as method arguments to pass an ActiveX class reference between processes or machines, the marshaling is done automatically.

Global Interface Table (GIT) Marshaling

The marshaling method discussed in the previous section is fine, but has a couple of limitations. One limitation is that after an interface is marshaled (packaged), it can only be unmarshaled (unpackaged) once. (Actually, `CoMarshalInterface()` can be called with the

TABLE_STRONG attribute. But even this can encounter problems if the interface being marshaled is a proxy.) In other words, if I call `CoMarshalInterThreadInterfaceInStream()`, send the stream to another thread, and call `CoGetInterfaceAndReleaseStream()`, the interface is obtained, but the stream is, for lack of a better word, spent.

The one-unmarshal-per-marshal is not that big of a deal, but it can be limiting in certain circumstances. For example, imagine that Thread 1 obtains an interface pointer for some kind of event notification object. This notification object might be useful for all the threads of the client process that want to send notifications. It is nice if Thread 1 can post this useful interface in some globally accessible area, and all other threads simply get this interface when they need it. You might imagine that Thread 1 can simply call `CoMarshalInterThreadInterfaceInStream()` and put the resulting stream pointer in a global variable where any thread can unmarshal it via `CoGetInterfaceAndReleaseStream()`. But this call only succeeds for the first thread and fails for all subsequent attempts by other threads.

I have seen a number of different workarounds for this problem. However, Microsoft introduced something called the *Global Interface Table (GIT)* in NT 4.0 Service Pack 3. The GIT's purpose is to solve this problem and allow a global space where popular interfaces can be placed and then be unmarshaled by different threads in different apartments again and again.

The GIT is a system object that you create and obtain an interface for (see Listing 4.9).

Listing 4.9 **Obtaining an Interface to the GIT**

```
IGlobalInterfaceTable *pIGIT;
// Create an instance of IGlobalInterfaceTable:

HRESULT hr = ::CoCreateInstance(CLSID_StdGlobalInterfaceTable,
                NULL,
                CLSCTX_INPROC_SERVER,
                IID_IGlobalInterfaceTable,
                (void**)&pIGIT);
```

You can then add the interface you want to make available as shown in the following:
```
DWORD m_cookie;
pIGIT->RegisterInterfaceInGlobal(pICalc,
            IID_ICalc,
            &m_cookie);
```
And now, any thread can obtain and use this interface with the following code:
```
pIGIT->GetInterfaceFromGlobal(m_cookie,
    IID_ICalc,
    (void **)&pICalc);
```
A complete example of a multi-threaded client that uses the GIT to pass an interface between threads follows in Listing 4.10.

Listing 4.10 **A Multi-Threaded Client Marshaling an Interface Between Two Threads Using the GIT.**

```c
//full GIT source in book/code/c++/GIT
DWORD g_cookie;

DWORD WINAPI NewThreadFunc(LPVOID );

main()
{
    DWORD dwThreadId;
    HRESULT hr;

    CoInitializeEx(0, COINIT_APARTMENTTHREADED);

    ICalc * pICalc;
    IGlobalInterfaceTable *pIGIT;

    //Below, create a new instance of the CalcSDK object and obtain an ICalc
    →interface.
    hr= CoCreateInstance(CLSID_CalcSDK, 0, CLSCTX_ALL, IID_ICalc,
    →(void**)&pICalc);

    hr = ::CoCreateInstance(CLSID_StdGlobalInterfaceTable,
                NULL,
                CLSCTX_INPROC_SERVER,
                IID_IGlobalInterfaceTable,
                (void**)&pIGIT);

    pIGIT->RegisterInterfaceInGlobal(pICalc,
                                    IID_ICalc,
                                    &g_cookie);

    pIGIT->Release();

    CreateThread(0,0,NewThreadFunc,0,0,&dwThreadId); //spin off a new thread

    CoUninitialize();

}

DWORD WINAPI NewThreadFunc(LPVOID )
{
    ICalc * pICalc;
    IGlobalInterfaceTable *pIGIT;

    hr = ::CoCreateInstance(CLSID_StdGlobalInterfaceTable,
                NULL,
                CLSCTX_INPROC_SERVER,
                IID_IGlobalInterfaceTable,
                (void**)&pIGIT);
```

continues

Listing 4.10 **Continued**

```
            pIGIT->GetInterfaceFromGlobal(g_cookie,
                     IID_ICalc,
                     (void **)&pICalc);

            cout<<pICalc->Add(2,3)<<endl; //call a method of ICalc

            pICalc->Release();
            pIGIT->Release();

}
```

Moving Interfaces Between Processes

If you want to move an interface pointer obtained on one thread to another thread, you must marshal it. This is true if you are moving the interface between two threads in two separate apartments (as shown in the preceding section) and also true if you are moving the interface between two threads in the same apartment as is the case in an MTA.

To a large extent, COM does not distinguish between different threads in one process and threads in different processes. Interface pointers must also be marshaled if they are moved between processes on the same or different machines. Fortunately, you don't need to write the code to do this. Because interfaces are defined in Interface Definition Language (IDL), they can be used as arguments to methods in IDL. It is possible, then, to have a method of an interface that takes another interface pointer as an argument. In fact, this is how a client can create and pass an interface of the one object to another object. The IDL shown in Listing 4.11 allows the holder of the IAlarm interface to pass in an IWakeup interface pointer to the remote implementation object that supports IAlarm.

Listing 4.11 *IWakeUp* and *IAlarm* **IDL Interface Declarations**

```
//tags omitted for brevity
//this interface would be implemented by some object who's implementation resided
➥on the client thread.

      interface IWakeup : IDispatch
      {
          HRESULT WakeupProcedure();
      };


//tags omitted for brevity
//this interface would be implmented by a remote object

      interface IAlarm : IDispatch
      {
          HRESULT SetAlarm([in] IWakeup* Wakeup, [in] long seconds);



      };
```

In this scenario, the `IWakeup` interface belongs to an object that was declared and created in the client thread (a local object) and given to some remote object that supports `IAlarm`—let's call it `AlarmClock`. In this way, `AlarmClock` can call back into the object living in the client thread and ask it to run `WakeupProcedure()`. Basically, you have built an event notification mechanism. The client has an interface pointer to an object residing in a server DLL, but the server object has an interface pointer residing in a client thread.

In this case, you do not need to call `CoMarshalInterthreadInterfaceInSteam()`, even though, technically, you are passing an interface pointer to different threads (albeit, they are different machines). COM does this for you. Because you are invoking an IDL-defined interface and using COM's underlying RPC, COM is directly involved in helping you pass the interface and can call the appropriate marshaling code on your behalf.

In Visual Basic, when you pass an ActiveX class (in reality, ActiveX classes are just interfaces) as an argument to a function or subroutine, the interface is being marshaled. Remember that Visual Basic ultimately uses type libraries and RPC, just like C++ and J++.

Marshaling Interfaces the Hard Way

On a more esoteric note, it is possible to marshal an interface between different processes on different machines without even involving the network. Packing up an interface into a stream is serious business—the stream contains a great deal of bookkeeping information including IP address of the originating object, apartment affiliation, and much more. A stream is an entirely self-contained, self-describing binary package. Nothing is needed by the destination process to rehydrate the stream and obtain a live interface. The stream contains all the information needed to re-establish a connection to the host object. A stream, then, can be passed from one machine to the other via floppy disk, email attachment, or zip disk. As long as the binary structure of the stream is preserved, all the destination process needs to do is read the stream from disk into an in-memory stream, unmarshal via the `CoUnmarshalInterface()` function, and *voila!*—a live, connected interface is obtained.

Floppy disks are not, obviously, an efficient way to move interfaces about. FedEx and UPS are expensive to incorporate in a distributed architecture. Plus, a stream thus packaged and transported had better reach its destination in about 5–6 minutes, at which time COM will invalidate it.

Declaring Apartments

Up until now, I have said that in-process objects can specify what types of apartment they can live in. Now, I will tell you how. In-process objects have a Registry entry called `ThreadingModel`, which can be one of the following four values:

- **Apartment.** Object is not thread-safe and must live in an STA.

- **Free.** Object is thread-safe and insists on living in an MTA. Such an object will be serviced from a dedicated pool of threads. Any calls made to an MTA object from an outside STA will involve a performance-impacting thread switch, as the STA thread must hand off execution to one of the pooled MTA threads (this thread-switch happens in spite of the fact that all threads are in the same process and the object, being thread-safe, wouldn't be in danger.) However, if the client thread making the call happens to originate in the MTA or enters the MTA via a call to CoInitializeEx(0, COINIT_MULTITHREADED), that thread will make the call directly into the object without requiring a thread-switch to a pool thread.

- **Both.** Object doesn't care; it can live in an STA, MTA, or TNA (Thread Neutral Apartment). The value Both comes from the days when the choice was between Apartment and Free. An object so marked must be thread-safe (or have synchronization services configured), but it will enjoy improved performance because it will dwell in the apartment of its creating thread regardless of whether the apartment is STA or MTA. Thus, threads in the host's apartment will be able to execute methods of the object directly without a thread switch. However, thread switches will still occur if an interface to an object marked "both" is passed to another apartment.

- **Neutral.** This is the preferred setting as of Windows 2000. Objects so marked will live in a new apartment known as the TNA. We will discuss this new addition in the upcoming section "The Thread Neutral Apartment (TNA)."

In the Registry, ThreadingModel appears as shown in Figure 4.6.

Sometimes there is some confusion as to why this Registry entry is necessary. Doesn't every thread explicitly state its threading model by calling CoInitialize() with COINIT_APARTMENTTHREADED or COINIT_MULTITHREADED? Yes, but remember that DLLs are passive blocks of code. They require a process to load them and initiate any form of action. So, although the client threads of the process that will load and use the DLL will declare their threading model, how is COM to know whether the COM objects that the threads will create require protection? Simply put, COM reads the Registry. If client thread T1 declares that it is free-threaded (MTA) and it creates an object that is marked in the Registry as Apartment, COM knows that there's a potential problem and performs the appropriate actions.

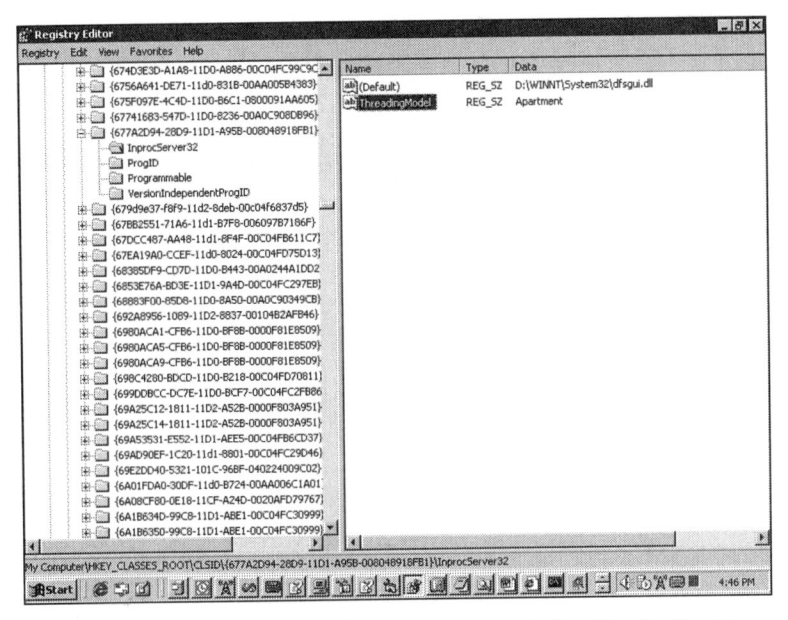

Figure 4.6 Threading model for a component as declared in the Registry.

The Free-Threaded Marshaler (FTM)

Simply put, the free-threaded marshaler lets you violate the rules of COM threading. Normally, when a thread from one apartment in a process invokes the method of an object residing in another apartment a thread switch occurs, the thread that makes the invocation is *not* the thread that executes the method. Even if an object is thread-safe and lives in an MTA, contrary to your intuition perhaps, calls to the MTA-bound object originating from a thread in an STA still result in a thread switch. This is shown in Figure 4.7.

Many developers are puzzled by this. If an object is thread-safe and lives in an MTA that can house any number of threads (and these threads can call directly into the object at any time), why can't an STA thread call directly into the object? The simple fact is that only those threads which have specifically entered the MTA by calling CoInitializeEx(0, COINIT_MULTITHREADED), or were already in the MTA (threads in the MTA's thread pool), are allowed direct access to the object. Threads in STAs are not allowed direct access. This is not to protect the MTA-residing object, which can obviously handle the STA thread, but rather to protect any objects that might be living in the calling STA. Problems can arise if the MTA object calls back into an STA object because the MTA object might do so on any thread. For more information on why the FTM compromises STA objects, see the following sidebar, "Danger of the FTM to STA Objects."

120 Chapter 4 Threading and Apartment Models

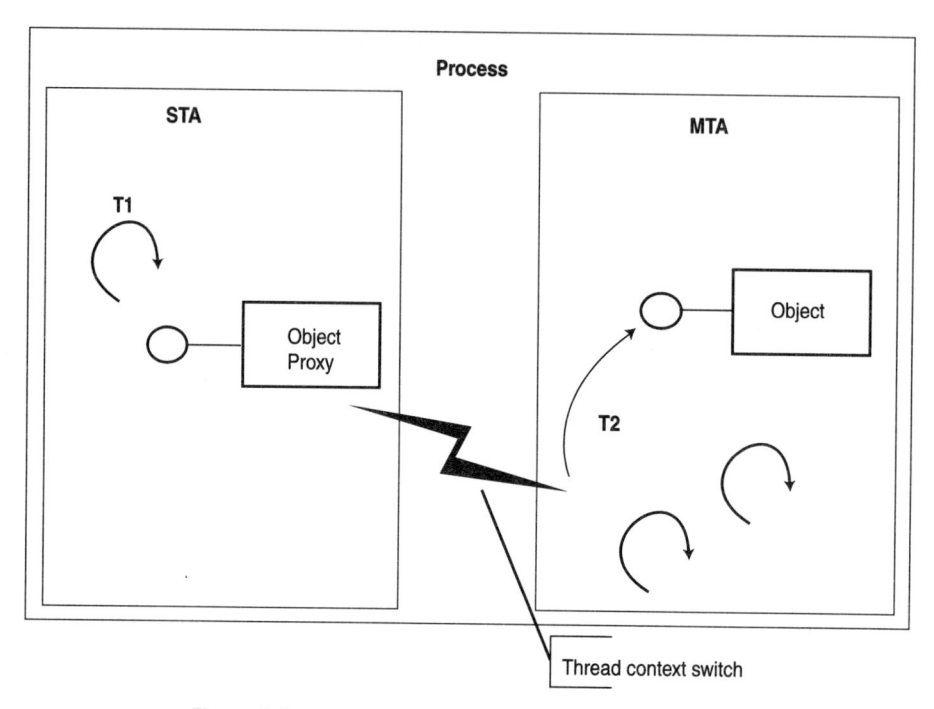

Figure 4.7 Cross-apartment calls result in a thread switch, even if the object is thread-safe and lives in an MTA.

For the time being, suppose that we are certain the MTA object is not going to call back to anything in the STA. Furthermore, suppose you do, in fact, want the STA thread to make a direct invocation on the MTA-residing object without needing a thread switch. In other words, you want the behavior shown in Figure 4.8.

If you want threads in any apartment to directly access and invoke methods on an object in another apartment without a thread switch, the FTM will make this possible.

The FTM performs its magic by allowing the objects that use it to escape the process of marshaling interfaces between threads. Specifically, you continue to marshal your interfaces between threads using the CoMarshal APIs (or let COM+ do it for you when interfaces are passed as object method arguments in IDL), but the presence of the free-threaded marshaler causes the stream to contain an ordinary pointer to the interface. In effect, although you are calling the marshaling APIs as described in the previous section, "Marshaling Interfaces," but with the FTM, you ultimately end up passing an ordinary interface pointer between threads.

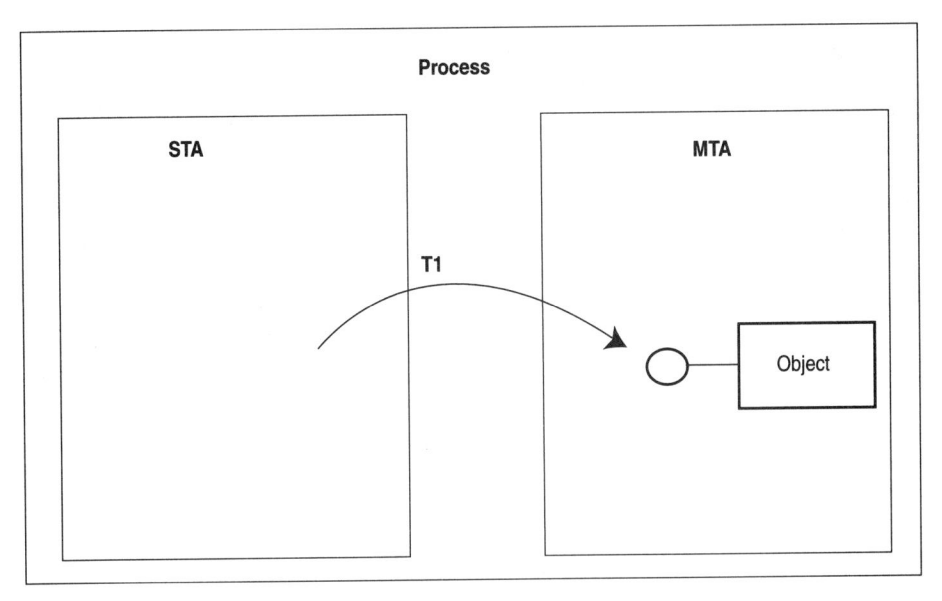

Figure 4.8 Direct invocation on an object in an MTA from a thread in a STA.

Danger of the FTM to STA Objects
Normally, an STA thread monitors a message queue and does not ever block on a method call itself. Rather, this blocking is internally delegated to another hidden thread so that the primary STA thread can keep "pumping" the message loop and can continue to service method calls coming in for other objects in the STA. This is how it is possible for an STA object to call a method and still be able to receive a callback notification from the server object even while that method is still executing. If an object uses the FTM, however, the STA thread calling it *will* become directly involved in the method invocation and will no longer be paying attention to its message loop. The problems here can range from possible deadlock, to concurrent access, to STA objects that are no longer protected by the dynamic duo of the guardian STA thread and its method-serializing message queue. Thus, the FTM should only be used when the interaction between participating components is fully understood and the performance benefit clearly outweighs the dangers and uncertainty its use can bring about.

This might seem like a bad idea with a dangerous downside, but there are circumstances where you need this latitude. For example, if you want to write your own COM+ resource dispenser (discussed in Chapter 8, "Transactions"), you must use the FTM due to issues arising from COM+ contexts (discussed in Chapter 7). Basically, aside from facilitating the development of low-level components like resource dispensers, it has a simpler use—the FTM is an optimization available to authors of thread-safe objects (that do not fire any form of callback event) that are accessed from a client containing one or more STAs. Normally, COM picks up on the differing threading models between the client threads and object and inserts proxy-based protection during the inter-thread marshaling process. For example, if STA thread T1 marshals an interface and hands it to STA thread T2 which unmarshals it, T2 does not get a direct pointer to the object, but gets a proxy instead. This proxy allows COM to set up protection for the object, but this protection isn't always necessary. Because the object is happy in an MTA and can handle concurrent method calls from different threads, it is okay if client STAs do swap a direct interface pointer around.

Direct pointers are faster than proxies, and this can lead to increased performance. So, if the developer imbues his free-threaded object with the power of the free-threaded marshaler, performance can be improved. Always remember though, there is no such thing as a free lunch or a free marshaler. The FTM is never essential (except for certain utility components) and should not be used by objects that intend to take advantage of COM+ services. In other words, if you are writing COM+ components, they should not use the FTM. The FTM can be a performance booster for traditional COM components that operate outside of COM+, but even then only use the FTM when you have worked with and mastered the intricacies of COM threading. You will find in the next section that the Thread Neutral Apartment (TNA) provides the same performance benefits as the FTM, but does so in a COM+-friendly way.

For the most part, the FTM is rarely employed by applications developers, it is more of a low-level tool for systems programmers. For example, if you are writing a Resource Dispenser (RD) like the ODBC driver manager, and are handing out connections (or other resources) to COM+ objects in different contexts (we will talk more about contexts in Chapter 7 and RDs in Chapter 8), you may need to use the FTM to "get around" traditional COM marshaling rules that *need* to be violated in this special case.

In scenarios where you don't need to break the rules, don't; by using the FTM, you disqualify your component from participating in many of the services offered by COM+. Without getting into too much detail before I have a chance to properly introduce contexts in Chapter 7, the FTM makes it impossible for COM+ to properly associate your object with a context. And this, as we'll see, is critical if the object is to take advantage of COM+ services.

To use the FTM, you must *aggregate* it. Basically, aggregation is a way for COM objects to incorporate the functionality of other pre-existing, compiled COM objects. You might think this can be done through simple inheritance, but the idea is to incorporate an object that is already compiled. You cannot inherit from assembly language or Java byte-code, so aggregation provides another way.

At this point, many texts get deep into the intricacies of aggregation. I, however, will relegate the details of such to the book's sample code. A simple way to look at aggregation is as a cross between inheritance and nested classes. It allows you to take two objects and compress them into what appears to the outside world as one. There is an inner object and an outer object. The outer object ultimately presents to the world, as its own, the interfaces of the inner object. The inner object exists in the belly of the outer object and does not necessarily know it is being aggregated (see Figure 4.9).

Obviously, there are all kinds of lifetime and `QueryInterface()` issues that arise, but an aggregatable component is equipped to handle them. Again, consult the book's sample code for more details. For now, just know that aggregation is not intended as a re-use mechanism. It exists for situations just like this, where a COM system object (like the FTM) needs to merge with a standard object (written by you, the developer) to imbue it with some new, system-oriented functionality.

Even though it sounds impressive, aggregating the FTM only requires one function call, one member variable and a modification to an object's QueryInterface( ) method. Listing 4.12 demonstrates how to aggregate the FTM in a simple object.

Chapter 4 Threading and Apartment Models

Listing 4.12 **Aggregating the FTM with a Simple Function Call and Modification to the Class's** *QueryInterface*

```
class COMCalc: public ICalc
{

public:
    LONG        m_cRef;
// IUnknown methods
    STDMETHODIMP QueryInterface(REFIID riid, void **ppv);
    STDMETHODIMP_(ULONG) AddRef(void);
    STDMETHODIMP_(ULONG) Release(void);


    STDMETHOD(Add)(int x, int y, int*r);
    STDMETHOD(Subtract)(int x, int y, int*r);
//FTM Additions below
    IUnknown * pMarshaler; //add a member variable

    COMCalc()
    {
        //Create and aggregate the FTM
        //error checking ommitted for brevity
        CoCreateFreeThreadedMarshaler(static_cast<IUnknown*>(this),
                                      &pMarshaler);

    };
    ~COMCalc()
    {

        pMarshaler->Release();

    }



};

STDMETHODIMP COMCalc::QueryInterface(REFIID riid, void **ppv)
{
    if (riid == IID_ICalc)
    {
        *ppv = static_cast<ICalc*>(this);
    }
    else if(riid==IID_IMarshal)
    {
        pMarshaler->QueryInterface(riid, ppv);

    }
//And so on...
```

The Thread Neutral Apartment (TNA)

There is another facet to COM apartments and threading, new with Windows 2000. So far, we have discussed the STA and MTA. You learned that there is exactly one thread in one STA, but that an MTA can have many threads in it. You also learned that COM sets up protection in the form of hidden windows for objects (apartments) that need it. Lastly, you learned that an apartment, be it STA or MTA, is just a concept, a way of grouping objects and the threads that manipulate them into domains of protection.

If I add a little more detail to the picture, the purpose of the TNA comes to light. There are many possible scenarios that can come about as the result of mixing of models and marshaling interface pointers between threads. Depending on the locality (COM+ library applications that are in-process or COM+ server applications that are in a surrogate), COM's protection schemes can result in threads having direct connections to objects, proxies to objects, or even proxies to proxies. I relegate most of this discussion to Appendix B, "COM+ Synchronization Through Activities." At this point, I only want to address the one, specific scenario that the TNA exists to solve—thread context switching.

In many cases, the thread that calls a method on an interface is not the thread that actually executes the code. At some point, a switch takes place. Consider the example of an STA thread (T1) that creates an STA object, obtains an interface pointer, and then marshals the interface pointer to another STA thread (T2) in the same process. When T2 unmarshals the interface pointer it obtained, T2 does not get a raw pointer; rather, it gets a proxy. Any calls that T2 makes to the proxy are delegated back to T1's STA, and T1 actually makes the call. T2 blocks (or seems to block), waits for the OS to schedule a thread context switch, and gives the green light to T1, which executes the code on behalf of T2. Waiting for a thread context switch is expensive in terms of time and resources.

The TNA exists to allow T2 to make the method call directly. The TNA is sometimes called the *Rental Model*, because T2 enters the TNA momentarily to execute the function. If this is sounding a lot like the FTM, the TNA and FTM are similar in that both allow the calling thread to actually execute the code of an object's method without requiring a thread switch. If this is the behavior you want, TNA is preferable because its services can be obtained declaratively, whereas the FTM requires additional code. Furthermore, and more importantly, an object in a TNA may have a consistent set of attributes (we'll see in Chapter 7 that this is known as a *context*) that is maintained during method calls from different threads. FTM objects, however, always borrow the context of the calling thread; and while this is important for utility objects like resource dispensers, it is deadly for ordinary COM+ objects that want to take advantage of COM+ services. Unlike the MTA and STA, the TNA does not have threads as permanent residents. Conceptually, it is an empty apartment where an object waits with its own sense of identity to be acted on by a thread that can come bursting through the door at any minute.

The Microsoft party line states that the TNA is said to be the preferred threading model for COM+ objects, except in situations where you need a UI, in which case an STA is preferable because you are already running a message pump. Of course, if a TNA allows any thread in at any time, it stands to reason that an object residing in a TNA must be thread-safe. This is true if you are writing an ordinary COM component that will not run in COM+. However, COM+ offers synchronization services that will only allow one thread into a TNA at one time. By externalizing synchronization, COM+ makes it possible for TNA objects to be built in languages that do not support multi-threading. Thus, the TNA offers the best of all worlds to a configured component: direct thread access from a caller in any apartment (like the FTM), a consistent context (unlike the FTM), and external synchronization. All these advantages together finally achieve the much anticipated "rental" model. The rental model is said to be employed when a component is marked as TNA and is configured to use synchronization.

Summary

A Win32 application can have more than one thread, and if it weren't for apartments, developers would be responsible for making their objects and COM DLL's thread-safe.

Apartments are a concept whereby threads and objects are grouped into domains of ownership. By associating threads and objects with a given apartment, if necessary, COM can protect objects by erecting additional proxies and/or serializing method calls made to them through a hidden window.

There are three types of apartments (MTA, STA, and TNA). Client threads and server objects can be of differing types, in which case COM protects thread-unsafe objects (those that require the STA) from concurrent access by multiple client threads.

Protection comes at a cost, however. The hidden serialization windows of the STA impose a great deal of overhead. Higher performance MTA scenarios demand more programming know-how, and there can still be overhead in the form of context switching. The TNA avoids context switching and does not need serialization windows. These advantages have enabled the TNA to become the preferred model for COM+ components.

When a developer wants to pass an interface from one thread to another, he must always do it by marshaling the interface via a call to `CoMarshalInterthreadInterfaceInStream` (or `CoMarshalInterface`). This gives COM the opportunity to set up the appropriate degree of protection for the object if necessary. Note, however, that an interface can be unmarshaled only once. To unmarshal an interface repeatedly, the GIT must be used.

5

Method Invocation and Marshaling

So far, we've talked about the relationship between interfaces, vtables, and RPCs. Interfaces can be looked at as RPC channels of communication, and you saw how the methods of an interface can be defined in IDL and then compiled by MIDL.EXE into proxy/stub code. Although there are a number of additional details, the COM-based interface implementation can be viewed as a more object-oriented version of the traditional RPC implementation—in either case, you define your interfaces and methods in Interface Definition Language (IDL). MIDL.EXE generates the appropriate proxy/stub code necessary to allow method calls made to your object to traverse the network via RPC.

COM RPC borrows from traditional RPC in a few regards, but one of the most important is how data is marshaled over the wire. Remember that method arguments must be packaged by a proxy function into a form that can be transported over the network. If used as method arguments, pointers must be resolved, arrays must be plucked from the caller's memory and packaged for shipment, and an assortment of other mechanisms come into play to allow method calls to span machine and process boundaries. Clearly, IDL provides the information necessary for MIDL.EXE to generate the appropriate proxy/stub code to do this job. In fact, you can use structures, arrays, strings, and even abstract data structures, such as linked lists and binary trees, as method arguments if you define them correctly in IDL. Of course, more esoteric structures like linked lists or the use of most pointer-based arguments disallow Visual Basic clients from using your object; VB allows only a limited range of types. However, your C++ COM clients can happily use these methods.

Once your component is written and its IDL file is compiled into a type library, COM+ offers two ways for a client to call its methods. In COM terminology, these two methods are referred to as *early* and *late binding*, and this chapter describes the implementation of both techniques and details the pros and cons of each.

In this chapter, we look at how COM marshaling works in a little more detail. Then, we discuss two different ways of invoking methods on COM objects: early and late binding.

Type Library Marshaling

As discussed in Chapter 1, "COM+: An Evolution," proxy/stub code does not need to be compiled into your client or server binaries; but in traditional RPC, it must be. In traditional RPC IDL, MIDL.EXE generates C files containing complete proxy and stub functions with the expectation that you will compile them into your existing C client and server projects. COM RPC, or *Object RPC (ORPC)* as it is often called, can still generate complete proxy/stub C files, but they do not need to be compiled in your COM client or server DLL. That is not what they are for. You are probably wondering why MIDL bothers to create them at all, but I am going to delay that discussion for a few paragraphs. For now, imagine that the only MIDL-generated file that really matters is the TLB. The TLB is important because it moves the marshaling responsibility out of the client and server and instead relegates it to COM itself. In other words, the existence of a type library allows COM to perform the marshaling on behalf of the client applications and server objects—relieving them completely of the need to hard-wire or hard-code their marshaling responsibilities in their binaries the way traditional RPC does. Imagine that RPC is the acronym for Real Proxy C files. TLB, then, can be thought of as Totally Liberating Binaries—in other words, type libraries can relieve the binaries from the responsibility of marshaling code.

Because a TLB file seems to be able to assume all marshaling responsibilities for a client and server object, you might imagine that the TLB contains proxy/stub code. It doesn't. Quite the contrary; the TLB file is only a tokenized form of IDL. But, just as traditional RPC IDL is used by MIDL.EXE to generate proxy/stub functions for *compile-time* support of method remoting, type libraries provide for the creation of *run-time* proxy/stub functionality. In other words, COM provides marshaling services when those services are required by a client and server object by using the object's type library as a real-time roadmap. It is like the difference between an interpreted language and a compiled one. Dynamic proxy/stub creation keeps the clients and objects lighter, eliminates any kind of language affinity, and provides a binary, language-independent standard of remotability. The process of using a type library to package and remote (marshal) method calls is sometimes called *type library marshaling*.

If you are using data types that VB cannot understand (C++ pointers, for example), type library marshaling doesn't work. As you see in the section, "Invoke Arguments and Marshaling," type library marshaling uses COM's built-in oleautomation marshaler (OLEAUT32.DLL). But OLEAUT32.DLL can only marshal VB data types (type libraries originated with VB, which is why the two are so closely related). For special C++ types, a type library by itself is no longer enough; you must supply your own marshaler.

Although this sounds complicated, it isn't hard. Take the extra proxy/stub C file that MIDL creates and build a second DLL. This DLL is called a proxy/stub DLL and, because it was created based on your data types defined in IDL, it knows how to marshal your unusual method arguments. This DLL also needs to be registered, just as if it is a COM component, which it is. If you don't like the concept of shipping two DLLs, they can be merged into one. C++ ATL projects give you this option.

It is fair to say that if you have a type library for a specific object registered on a client machine and you are only using VB compatible data types, nothing more is needed for a client application to instantiate and use the remote COM object. However, as useful as type libraries are, there are situations where it is not possible or especially helpful to have a type library present. The following example might be a stretch, but it's one possibility: You work on a locked down NT workstation in a large corporation and are not permitted to modify Registry settings or write to your hard drive (yes, there are such places). However, there is a COM+ object you really want to use in your VB program, but you don't have permissions to install the type library on your machine.

Installation of type libraries is not especially convenient, and certain development environments like Microsoft Internet Information Server cannot access or use a type library when instantiating and calling methods on COM objects. In fact, although IIS' Active Server Pages (ASP) allow you to create and manipulate COM objects to generate HTML, they do not allow the use of a type library to marshal data. Similarly, the scripting engine that executes .VBS (Visual Basic Script or VBScript) files from the command line does not allow the use of type libraries. Why don't these environments facilitate the use of so convenient a mechanism? I suspect it has to do with the complexity of the development environments and the interpretive, non-compilable nature of how they operate. ASP pages, for example, are never compiled; they are interpreted in real-time by IIS. Second, there is no *de facto* development environment for creating ASP pages. Some developers use Visual InterDev, and some use NOTEPAD.EXE. The use of type libraries, however, demands that the development environment read and interpret them. Because there is no development environment for ASP pages, there is no way to associate the VBScript with a particular type library. It might be that future versions of IIS will, in fact, allow the use of type libraries. At present, however, it does not.

We have established that there are certain situations where you do not have a type library but nonetheless want to use a remote COM object. The method you have employed so far to utilize type libraries is called *early binding*, and the method that does not use the type library is called *late binding*. However, as you see later in this chapter where type libraries are used for late binding (see the "Dispinterfaces" section later in this chapter), this is not a hard-and-fast rule. For the moment, however, think of late binding as being required in the absence of a type library. Late binding is easiest to understand in this context.

It is difficult to "show" late binding because on the surface, source code demonstrating early and late binding is almost identical (see Listing 5.1).

Listing 5.1 A VB Client Remotely Controlling Excel Using Early Binding
```
Dim xmlApp as Excel.Application
Set xlApp = New Excel.Application

xlApp.Visible= True
xlApp.Workbooks.Add 'adds a new workbook
```

The code in Listing 5.1 creates a new instance of Excel, makes the new instance visible, and adds a new workbook. This code assumes that Microsoft Excel has been selected in VB's Project references dialog (this dialog is summoned by selecting the Project, References menu item of the VB IDE). This dialog is responsible for including an object's type library into the current VB project. The inclusion of the type library adds component-specific data types (for example, Excel.Application) to the current project so that they can be implemented in the same way as a VB class. The presence and use of a type library *usually* means early binding is being used. Late binding *looks* identical to early binding, but with two small differences (see if you can spot them). Listing 5.2 demonstrates the same functionality as shown in the previous listing, but late binding is being used.

Listing 5.2 A VB Client Remotely Controlling Excel Using Late Binding
```
Dim xlApp as Object 'note the change in data type to Object
Set xlApp = CreateObject("Excel.Application") 'note we are using the CreateObject
➥function

xlApp.Visible= True
xlApp.Workbooks.add 'adds a new workbook
```

Note that the code in Listing 5.2 does not require that type library of Microsoft Excel be included in the project. However, because the type library is not included, we can no longer declare xlApp to be of type Excel.Application (VB is not, without the inclusion of the type library, familiar with the Excel.Application data-type). Instead, we have to declare xlApp as the generic Object data-type. Similarly, we can't implement a new instance of Excel.Application via the New keyword because VB is not natively familiar with this data-type. Thus, we need to use the CreateObject( ) function, passing in the string "Excel.Application." In the next section, "Late Binding," the use of the Object data-type always means late binding is being used. Let's move on to the next session and explore how late binding works and why it is useful.

Late Binding

If you have ever played Marco Polo in some swimming pool in your youth, you understand the basic premise of late binding. Late binding is a cry in the dark. A client shouts the name of the method it wants to call over the network, and the server object responds with a magical number. This number represents a specific method, and when given, the client can invoke the method by using this number.

If you are incensed at the overhead involving two round trips to call one method (the first to get the magic number and the second to invoke the method) and are wondering why this is necessary, you should keep a couple things in mind. First, COM clients do not know with any certainty what functionality an object may support. An early binding `QueryInterface()` can be used to ask an object whether a certain interface is supported. In late binding, however, the actual name of the method is used. In either case, the object has the right to say, "I don't support that functionality."

If COM is based on an object supporting one or many interfaces, the purpose of late binding may not seem apparent at first. There are some COM-savvy developers who love the COM paradigm but feel that because of its reliance on the typeless variant and its overall generality, late binding somehow corrupts the strongly-typed, object-oriented nature of COM. However, there are times in development when, philosophy aside, late binding is the simplest way to solve a problem. You will sometimes come across components actually written by Microsoft that support *only* late binding because of the versatility this mechanism offers. Arguably, late binding simplifies front-end development at the expense of complicating the COM paradigm somewhat, but it is probably not too great a price to pay for the versatility late binding gives you.

> **OLE Automation**
>
> Late-binding used to be known as OLE automation. Soon after, early binding was introduced and sometimes called OLE automation. To add to the confusion, there is also a keyword in IDL files ("oleautomation") which indicates that variables being used in an interface's methods are compatible with OLE automation and implies that only VB-compatible data-types are being used. The word OLE then became *passe*, and it was simply referred to as automation. Before long, the word automation didn't add anything, so people stopped using it to a large degree. COM implies automation. From now on, I will try to minimize my use of the term automation, because of its vague definition. If, however, you encounter the term in an old MSDN article, it can have any of the preceding definitions, depending on the date of the article and the context in which the term is used.

The Architecture of Late Binding

Late binding is all about asking an object what methods it supports instead of what interfaces. Whereas early binding passes a GUID of the interface it is interested in into QueryInterface(), late binding presents the object with a method name in the form of a wide-character string (wide-character meaning 2 bytes per char). If, after interpreting the string, the object supports a method by that name, it returns with a number representing that method. This number is referred to as a *dispatch ID* or DISPID. After the client has this number, it can call the method by invoking the number.

You might think that the mechanism used to provide late binding services might be something non-interface and non-RPC based. This might seem strange, but late binding support is provided whenever an object implements an interface called IDispatch. IDispatch is a standard COM interface that, like IUnknown, is a COM system interface that is already registered in the OS and included in the Windows header files. Specifically, IDispatch has four methods, but we are only going to look at the two most important ones for now (see Listing 5.3).

Listing 5.3 **Partial Prototype for *IDispatch***

```
struct IDispatch: public IUnknown
{
        virtual HRESULT STDMETHODCALLTYPE GetIDsOfNames(
                REFIID riid,
                LPOLESTR *rgszNames,
                UINT cNames,
                LCID lcid,
                DISPID *rgDispId) = 0;

        virtual HRESULT STDMETHODCALLTYPE Invoke(
                DISPID dispIdMember,
                REFIID riid,
                LCID lcid,
                WORD wFlags,
                DISPPARAMS  * pDispParams,
                VARIANT *pVarResult,
                EXCEPINFO *pExcepInfo,
                UINT *puArgErr) = 0;

    //...other functions temporarily ommited for brevity

};
```

GetIDsOfNames is used to get the ID (DISPID) of the method(s) whose name is sent in rgszNames. (You can ask for the DISPID of more than one method at a time.) Invoke is used to call a method by its DISPID. The arguments for this function are stored in pDispParams. Before I get deeper into the specifics of IDispatch's method arguments, let's summarize. A late binding client instantiates a COM object but asks only for `IDispatch`. In C++, this looks like the following:

```
TCHAR progid[255];
IDispatch * idsp;

CLSIDFromProgID(L"comcalc.calc", &pclsid);

HRESULT hr = CoCreateInstance(pclsid , NULL, CLSCTX_ALL,
                              IID_IDispatch, (void **)&idsp);
```

In VB, it looks like this:

```
Dim objSomething as Object
Set objSomething = createobject("Comcalc.Calc");
```

In J++, it looks like the following:

```
Object idsp;


com.ms.com._Guid IID_IDispatch = new _Guid("{00020400-0000-0000-C000-
 000000000046}");
com.ms.com._Guid pclsid;




pclsid = com.ms.win32.Ole32.CLSIDFromProgID("comcalc.calc");
idsp   = com.ms.win32.Ole32.CoCreateInstance
         (pclsid, null,    ComContext.INPROC_SERVER |
          com.ms.win32.win.CLSCTX_LOCAL_SERVER,
          IID_IDispatch);
```

Why does the client bother with `IDispatch` at all and not ask for the interface it really wants? The late binding client presumably has no type library, so it has no clue about any interfaces other than the established Windows ancestral interfaces, such as `IUnknown`, `IDispatch`, and a number of others. These interfaces herald all the way back to the days of Object Linking and Embedding (OLE)—even before there were such things as type libraries. `IDispatch` is really the lowest common denominator—the last possibility for communicating with a COM object when you have no type library, no header files, and nothing other than the name of the function you want to call and the arguments you believe it will take.

> **VB's Object Data Type**
>
> The Object data type in VB always implies late binding. In VB, `Object` is another word for `IDispatch`, and every method call on an object data type is always a late binding call. The intricacies of this call are hidden, however.

Invoke Arguments and Marshaling

It stands to reason that if `IDispatch` is a system interface which ships with Windows and allows clients to invoke methods on remote objects, the system must also have some way to marshal arguments over the wire from the client to the server object. After all, in late binding you don't have a type library to generate run-time proxy/stubs. So, some other marshaling mechanism must already be in place—the oleautomation marshaler. It lives in a DLL called OLEAUT32.DLL. Prior to Windows 2000 (and Service Pack 4 on NT 4) OLEAUT32.DLL could be accidentally unregistered by overzealous unregistration routines. Automation stopped working entirely at that point, and you had to re-register oleaut32.dll to get things working again.

In short, oleaut32 knows how to handle all the networking details of `IDispatch` (late binding) method invocations. It is the `IDispatch` system proxy/stub that replaces the MIDL generated type library you're used to and allows the `IDispatch` interface to invoke method calls over the wire. As far as marshaling the method arguments goes, even though you have no type library, all possible data types are pre-defined by COM. This is possible because oleautomation marshaling is being used, and this form of marshaling only allows the use of a limited number of well-defined data types to be used as method arguments in late binding calls. And does it surprise you that the only data types `IDispatch` allows you to use are those available in Visual Basic? Because `IDispatch` is so closely tied to Visual Basic and its data-types, C++ developers have to deal with slightly more complexities. You see how when we discuss dispinterfaces and dual interfaces a little later in this chapter.

The Variant

In the previous section, I mention that the number of data types that can be used in a late binding call are limited to those data types available to Visual Basic. Visual Basic has a nice array of data types: the unremarkable `long`, `integer`, `double`, `string`, and some interesting ones like `currency`, `date`, and others. COM knows how to marshal all of these over the wire.

There is, however, one small problem: If you look at the structure of `IDispatch`, you might notice that all remote method calls must happen through the `Invoke()` method. How can you write one function that can accept any number of arguments where each can be a different data type? In C, you might look toward *unions*. For non-C programmers, unions are similar to structures with one critical difference—where a structure is as large as the sum of its data members, a union is only as large as its biggest data member. Of course, there's a trade-off for this reduced size—only a single data member of a union can be valid at any given time. Take a look at Listing 5.4 for an example of a C-style union.

Listing 5.4 An Example of a C Union

```
//remember, unlike a structure, a union expects to be only one of these
//type and will only be as big as its biggest type.

union AnyofThese
{
int iVal;
float fVal;
char cVal;
//and every other "Automation Type" that late binding supports
}
```

Conceivably, you can send method arguments into the `Invoke()` function as an array of unions. This allows you to send any number of arguments, each one of which can be of a different type. In other words, although you are sending arguments as an array of homogenous types (`AnyofThese`), each element in the array can represent a different data type by having a different data member with valid data in it.

Unions have most of what we need to represent multi-type method arguments, but they're not quite enough. One of the interesting features of late binding is that it automatically converts your arguments to the type appropriate to your method. In other words, if you call the late-bound method `Add` with two string arguments instead of two integers, the object performs the string-to-integer conversion automatically, if possible.

Because of this, the implementor of `IDispatch` cannot be sure which member of the union has valid data. The solution to this problem is to add a *discriminator* that tells the remote object what member of the union is valid (see Listing 5.5).

Listing 5.5 A Discriminated Union

```
enum types {VT_INTEGER, VT_FLOAT,VT_CHAR};

struct Variant
{
enum types discriminator; //this tells implementor IDispatch what member is
//valid
union AnyofThese
{
int iVal;
float fVal;
char cVal;
...
}
};
```

Now you have a special kind of discriminated union called a *variant*. Variants are used by `IDispatch` to represent method arguments. If you are calling a method via `IDispatch`'s `Invoke()` method, which takes two arguments, you need to give `Invoke` the `DISPID` of the method you want to call and an array of two variants—each with the appropriate discriminator set (see Listing 5.6).

Listing 5.6 **A Pseudo-Late Binding Client Demonstrating How *IDispatch* Uses Variants as Method Arguments**

```
Variant args[2];
Variant retval;
int id;

args[0].discriminator=VT_INT;
args[0].ival=2;

args[1].discriminator=VT_INT;
args[1].ival=3;

IPsudoDispatch->GetIDofFunction("Add", &id);
IPsudoDispatch->RemoteInvoke(id, args, &retval);
cout<<"The sum is "<<retval<<endl;
```

What Can a Variant Hold?

Variants allow you to get around the problem of using heterogeneous data types as arguments by throwing type safety to the wind. Not surprisingly, there is a data type called `Variant` in VB. A VB variant can hold any other type of value. So, the following VB code is perfectly legal:

```
Dim v as Variant:
v=33
v="hi there"
v=CreateObject("comcalc.calc")
v=form1
```

J++ also has the concept of the `Variant`, as in the following:

```
Object v;
v=new Integer(33)
v="hi there"
```

Notice that the `v` can hold object types, as well as data types. Don't confuse Java's `Object` data type with VB's `Object` data type, however. In Java, an `Object` can hold anything (just like a `Variant`), but VB's `Object` can only hold an `IDispatch` pointer.

In C and C++, the variant is implemented as a discriminated union. Its definition can be found in OAIDL.H, and it is very revealing to look at. Basically, its discriminator is a structure that has a union as a data member, as shown in Listing 5.7.

Listing 5.7 **Partial Prototype for a** *VARIANT*
```
struct  tagVARIANT
    {
    union
        {
        struct   __tagVARIANT
            {
            VARTYPE vt;
            WORD wReserved1;
            WORD wReserved2;
            WORD wReserved3;
            union
                {
                LONG lVal;
                BYTE bVal;
                SHORT iVal;
    //      …and every other data-type VB supports
```

You can find every data type that VB (and therefore late binding) supports; and because variants can hold object references as well as flat data values, you can also find `IDispatch` and `IUnknown` data members defined in the following variant structure:

```
…variant code omitted for brevity
            IUnknown __RPC_FAR *__RPC_FAR *ppunkVal;
            IDispatch __RPC_FAR *__RPC_FAR *ppdispVal;
```

Another less apparent capability of the variant is its capability to hold arrays of information. This makes it possible for blocks or blobs of data to be passed to and from a Visual Basic COM object. Internally, arrays in Visual Basic are represented by *safearrays*. Because a variant must be able to hold all VB data types including arrays, it isn't surprising to find safearrays defined in the Variant, as in the following:

```
…
SAFEARRAY __RPC_FAR *parray;
…
```

Safearrays are an entire discussion unto themselves. However, like most things in COM, their explanations are ten times more complicated than their reality.

Invoking a Method on *IDispatch*

In VB, using late binding is as simple as the following:

```
Dim o as Object
Set o=createobject("Comcalc.Calc")

MsgBox o.add (1,2)
```

Chapter 5 Method Invocation and Marshaling

The details are more or less hidden. However, in C++, and to some extent J++, all the intricacies of IDispatch and variants are exposed. And although you might not think this is the most elegant architecture, this is how late binding is done. Here is the real code that performs (or automates) the Add function on a remote object through the IDispatch interface. For C++, refer to Listing 5.8. For J++, refer to Listing 5.9.

Listing 5.8 **C++ and *IDispatch***

```
DISPID dispid;
DISPPARAMS dp={NULL,NULL,0,0};
VARIANTARG vargs[2];
VARIANT arg1,arg2,result;
IDispatch * idsp;

TCHAR progid[255];
CLSID pclsid;

CLSIDFromProgID(L"comcalc.calc", &pclsid);


HRESULT hr = CoCreateInstance(pclsid , NULL, CLSCTX_ALL,
                              IID_IDispatch, (void **)&idsp);

arg1.vt= VT_I2;
arg1.iVal = 1;

arg2.vt= VT_I2;
arg2.iVal = 2;

vargs[0]=arg1;
vargs[1]=arg2;

dp.rgvarg=vargs;
dp.cArgs = 2; //number of args
OLECHAR * name=L"add";

//below: note that is the object did not support this method
//GetIDsOfNames would have returned an error.
idsp->GetIDsOfNames(IID_NULL, &name, 1, GetUserDefaultLCID(), &dispid);

idsp->Invoke(dispid, IID_NULL, GetUserDefaultLCID(), DISPATCH_METHOD,
             &dp, &result,0,0);
//ABOVE:  GetUserDefaultLCID() passed the location identifier to invoke
//so that it can accommodate strings of different spoken languages
//it will be US English for us

cout<<result.iVal<<endl;
idsp->Release();
```

Late Binding 139

Listing 5.9 **J++ and *IDispatch***

```
Object  idsp;
Object  args[];
int     retval[];
int     MethodId;

com.ms.com._Guid IID_IDispatch = new _Guid("{00020400-0000-0000-C000"+
                                            "-000000000046}");
com.ms.com._Guid pclsid;

args=new Object[2];
args[0]="100";
args[1]="200";
retval=new int[1];

pclsid = com.ms.win32.Ole32.CLSIDFromProgID("comcalc.calc");
idsp   = com.ms.win32.Ole32.CoCreateInstance (pclsid, null,
         ComContext.INPROC_SERVER |
         com.ms.win32.win.CLSCTX_LOCAL_SERVER,IID_IDispatch);

MethodId=com.ms.com.Dispatch.getIDOfName(idsp,"Add");

com.ms.com.Dispatch.invoke(idsp,
                           MethodId,
                           Dispatch.Method,
                           args,
                           retval);
```

The C++ code is a bit more complex than the J++ code. However, although some structures in the C++ version of the code seem a bit confusing, they are all pretty simple. Take DISPPARAMS, for example; it is nothing but a structure with four elements, declared as shown in Listing 5.10.

Listing 5.10 **The *DISPPARAMS* Structure**

```
typedef struct  tagDISPPARAMS
    {
    VARIANTARG __RPC_FAR *rgvarg;
    DISPID __RPC_FAR *rgdispidNamedArgs;
    UINT cArgs;
    UINT cNamedArgs;
    }
```

The first element holds a pointer to an array of variants (our method parameters), as emphasized by the following line:

```
dp.rgvarg=vargs;
```

Remember that `vargs` is an array of variants, because this is how you must package your function arguments if you are calling a method using late binding. `rgdispidNamedArgs` is used primarily for compatibility with Visual Basic style function arguments. Visual Basic allows you to have optional function arguments that can be passed as parameters in any order. For example, in VB, the following is possible:

```
VBFunc(arg1:=1, arg5:=5, arg3:=3)
```

If you are taking advantage of this feature, `rgdispidNamedArgs` is important so that you can map the variant argument you are passing to `Invoke()` to the appropriate optional argument on the server-side function. Keep in mind that even if VB considerations offend your C++ or J++ sensibilities, it is important to be aware that VB is a strong driving architectural force in COM.

Late binding and many other COM technologies are entirely based on the VB model. In fact, it's fair to say that a large degree of the complexity you see in COM/DCOM results from the necessity to support Visual Basic. Because many VB programmers (and the development environment itself) do not work with threading, explicit memory allocation, pointers, and networking issues, the COM architecture inherent in the product has to pick up the ball.

If you examine the preceding code and ignore all but the most obvious function parameters, it should be pretty straightforward. You might notice `IDispatch`'s member function `GetIDsOfNames` being called prior to `Invoke()`. As we discussed, `IDispatch` does not let you invoke a method by string name in a single step. The `Invoke()` function takes a `DISPID` as its first argument (`DISPID` is simply defined as a `long`), so you invoke a remote method by number not by name. This is all `GetIDsOfNames` does—it allows you to send an array of method names as strings and get back their specific `DISPID` for use in the `Invoke()` function.

Surprisingly, late binding Visual J++ is much more complicated than you might expect (see Listing 5.11).

Listing 5.11 **Using *IDispatch* Directly from J++**

```
Object  idsp;
Object  args[];
int     retval[];
int     MethodId;

com.ms.com._Guid IID_IDispatch = new _Guid("{00020400-0000-0000-C000-"+
                                            "000000000}");
```

```
com.ms.com._Guid pclsid;

args=new Object[2];
args[0]="100";
args[1]="200";
retval=new int[1];


pclsid = com.ms.win32.Ole32.CLSIDFromProgID("comcalc.calc");
idsp   = com.ms.win32.Ole32.CoCreateInstance (pclsid, null,
            ComContext.INPROC_SERVER |
            com.ms.win32.win.CLSCTX_LOCAL_SERVER,IID_IDispatch);

MethodId=com.ms.com.Dispatch.getIDOfName(idsp,"Add");

com.ms.com.Dispatch.invoke(idsp,
                    MethodId,
                    Dispatch.Method,
                    args,
                    retval);
```

Keep in mind, however, that in most cases the preceding code is only necessary when a Java client has no prior knowledge of the object it is automating. This might seem like an odd statement, given that is what late binding is all about (asking what methods an object supports at run-time). However, you see in the next section that there are situations where a type library can actually help out late binding clients.

Late Binding, Type Libraries, and the Tale of *IDispatch*

It seems that late binding should have absolutely nothing to do with type libraries. Late binding is, after all, a way to remote method calls without a type library, right? It probably surprises you, then, to find out that the first type libraries only provided for late binding.

This is what makes COM complicated. It is not that any one facet of the technology is difficult; it is just that COM has evolved such that an appendage useful for one thing ended up serving another purpose. Such is the nature of evolution. When climates change, creatures change, which is what happened to IDispatch.

In the early days of COM, IDispatch was the only mechanism for remoting objects, and there were no type libraries. COM was the underlying technology for something called OLE. The main thrust of OLE was about integrating desktop applications, such as Word, Excel, PowerPoint, and so on, with one another (as in placing an

Excel spreadsheet inside a Word document) and with programs that any developer could write to, remote control, or automate these same applications. `IDispatch` was the interface that all OLE automatable applications had to support. In this way, it was possible to call `CoCreateInstance( )` to create an instance of Microsoft Word, ask for `IDispatch`, and then ask Word to load and print a file, all from an external client application.

Visual Basic was, and arguably still is, the pre-eminent Windows development environment. Much of VB's popularity has to do with its simplicity. No matter how complicated the back-end development had to become to support VB's front-end simplicity—`IDispatch` wasn't simple enough. But VB users could easily create and manipulate instances of Word, Excel, and so on with the following code:

```
Dim objApp as Object
Set objApp=CreateObject("Excel.Application")
objApp.Visible=True
objApp.Workbooks.Add
objApp.ActiveSheet.Cells(1,1) =123
```

There was no way that the development environment could perform any kind of compile-time checking. Because `IDispatch` resolves method names at run-time via the function `GetIDsofNames()`, the methods for a given object are not known at compile-time. The concept of a type library was introduced so that method calls could be resolved at compile-time and to allow nice, GUI-based object browsers to exist.

Object Definition Language (ODL) Files

Type libraries were originally introduced to give development environments and object browsers a way to see what methods an object would support. `IDispatch` still needed to be used, but its use could be simplified by the presence of a type library. In Microsoft Foundation Classes (MFC), for example, a wizard was introduced that could read a type library for an automatable application (for example, Microsoft Word) and automatically generate a friendly C++ class (derived from `ColeDispatchDriver`) which had methods corresponding to those listed in the type library. The MFC client could simply instantiate an instance of this class, call its methods, and all the ugly details of `IDispatch` were completely hidden from view.

COM+ and Microsoft Office

It is important to note that EXE-based applications that support OLE Automation, such as Word and Excel, can not be COM+ components. This is primarily because they are not in-process servers (DLLs), so they can not be run inside COM+'s DLLHOST.EXE surrogate (more on this in the Chapter 6, "The COM+ Catalog"). This is not to say that they can not be used by COM+ objects or clients, or that they themselves do not contain COM classes (EXE servers definitely do); they just can't participate in COM+ services, such as queueing, transactions, and pooling.

Visual Basic users also benefited from these early (and later) type libraries. With the advent of IntelliSense, method suggestions now pop up whenever the developer presses a period following an object in the editor (you can find a screen-shot in Figure 1.4 of Chapter 1). And if this isn't enough help, the developer can simply press F2, and an object browser appears.

Where did these early type libraries come from? Today, type libraries come from IDL files, or they are created by development environments like VB with Win32 calls behind the scenes. Back then, type libraries came from ODL files. ODL was the COM predecessor to IDL. IDL files are compiled using MIDL.EXE; ODL files are compiled with an older utility called MkTypeLib.EXE. ODL is the ancestor of modern IDL; just as you can see evolutionary echoes from millions of years ago in the forms of alligators and crocodiles, you can still see pure ODL alive today in MFC applications. It is possible to generate COM objects using the wizards in MFC, but they only produce `IDispatch` supporting objects with an ODL-based type library. ATL, on the other hand, favors IDL, and its wizards run MIDL.EXE behind the scenes.

Dispinterfaces

Dispinterfaces are an alternate form of interface declaration. They are not necessary anymore, but they still pop up from time to time. Although ODL files are their normal habitat, it is not unusual to find dispinterfaces in IDL files. Until recently, *advisesinks* for *connectionpoints* (VB's event notification scheme as implemented in COM) had to be described in IDL by dispinterfaces as opposed to regular interfaces. What does a dispinterface look like? See Listing 5.12.

Listing 5.12 **An Example of a Dispinterface**

```
dispinterface DICalc {
        methods:
            [id(0x00000064), helpstring("Add")]
            int Add([in] long Param1,
                    [in] long Param2);

            [id(0x0000006d), helpstring("Subtract")]
            void Subtract([in] long Param1,
                    [in] long Param2);
};

...

coclass DispCalc
{
    dispinterface DICalc;

};
```

As you can see, dispinterfaces are pretty straightforward. In fact, it is fair to say that they are simpler than ordinary IDL interfaces (or *custom interfaces*, as user-created, non-dispinterfaces are commonly called). Dispinterfaces don't inherit from anything; their methods are actually allowed to return real values (unlike ordinary interface methods that must return an HRESULT), and they have the concept of properties, just like classes in Visual Basic.

When you see a dispinterface, think IDispatch. The two are synonymous; a dispinterface's methods may only be accessed through late binding. This may seem odd, but dispinterfaces were introduced early in COM's evolution at a time when OLE automation relied on IDispatch. IDispatch does not require a type library, but a type library was nonetheless desirable to fuel developer tools such as IntelliSense, Object Browsers and MFC's (Microsoft Foundation Class) object wrapper wizards (they generated friendly client-side C++ classes that allowed clients to easily call IDispatch methods on a server). Dispinterfaces were therefore introduced so that type libraries could be created for clients, even though it was not yet possible to use interfaces other than IDispatch for OLE automation.

Thus, the developer of DispCalc must implement IDispatch. A client wishing to call a method of DispCalc would then execute the GetIDsofNames function against this interface, which would return the DISPIDs of all the methods listed by the dispinterface.

Similarly, the client then calls Invoke( ), passing in the DISPID of method it wishes to call, followed by an array of Variants representing arguments to the method. The implementor of IDispatch must therefore implement the Invoke() function. This involves the following:

- Perform some form of switch/case on the DISPID passed into Invoke().
- Unpackage the variant array of arguments.
- If possible, convert arguments to the appropriate data type in the event that the discriminator of a specific variant/argument indicates it is a type different from what the type library promises.

It is tedious, if not especially difficult work, to implement IDispatch. No matter what language you use, you almost never do this by hand. The ATL class IDispatchImpl provides this functionality automatically for the C++ developer, and VB/J++ insists on providing IDispatch support automatically. For the most part, aside from some nuances having to do with the difference between properties and methods, the implementation of a coclass that supports a dispinterface does not look much different from one that provides optional late binding support for a custom interface. Remember, some clients (ASP pages, command-line VBScript) can only use late binding, and it is not unusual for a COM object to support both early and late binding. In other words, the object supports one or many custom interfaces like ICalc and IFinancial, but also supports IDispatch. The implementor of IDispatch then responds positively if the string names of any of the methods of either ICalc or IFinancial come in through

`GetIDsOfNames()`. You might imagine that the IDL for such an object would have an ordinary interface declaration, as shown in Listing 5.13.

Listing 5.13 **An Ordinary IDL Interface Declaration**
```
[
    odl,
    uuid(1051376B-A601-11D3-8090-00E0811008ED),
    version(1.0),
    hidden,
    dual,
    nonextensible,
    oleautomation
]
interface ICalc : IUnknown
{
    [id(1), helpstring("method Add")]
    HRESULT Add([in] int x, [in] int y,
                [out,retval] int * r );
    [id(2), helpstring("method Divide")]
    HRESULT Divide([in] int x, [in] int y,
                   [out,retval] int * r);
};
```

It would also have a dispinterface declaration as shown in Listing 5.12. The coclass, then, might look like the following:

```
coclass CalcSDK
{
    [default] interface ICalc;
    dispinterface DICalc;
};
```

But this is not how it's done. It is, after all, pretty redundant—you are declaring what is essentially the same interface in two different ways. It would be nice if there were some way to consolidate the two interfaces into one declaration that indicates that the interface supports both early binding and late binding. It would be nice if the interface were dual.

Dual Interfaces

Dual interfaces are ordinary custom interfaces that indicate that late binding (`IDispatch`) support will also be implemented by the object. Syntactically, dual interfaces are identical to custom interfaces with one small difference. A custom interface declaration in IDL looks like this:

```
interface ICalc: IUnknown
```

Dual interfaces look like this:

```
interface ICalc: IDispatch
```

In an IDL file, a dual interface inherits from `IDispatch` instead of `IUnknown`. Other than that, there is absolutely no difference in the IDL file. However, the implementation is affected. When MIDL.EXE is run on an IDL file containing a dual interface, MIDL does what it always does and generates an H file containing a C++ prototype that mirrors the interface declaration. This prototype also inherits from `IDispatch` instead of `IUnknown` (see Listing 5.14).

Listing 5.14 **C++ Prototype of *ICalc* Now Inheriting from *IDispatch***

```
//this is in the MIDL generated .h file
MIDL_INTERFACE("638094E5-758F-11d1-8366-0000E83B6EF3")
ICalc : public IDispatch  //as opposed to IUnknown
    {
    public:
```

I said that in C++, the implementation of a coclass is usually a simple class that multiply inherits from each interface it wants to support. Interfaces are always implemented as abstract base classes in C++, and this is exactly what MIDL puts in its generated header file. Remember, MIDL reads the IDL file and creates one C++ interface prototype for each interface it sees declared. It translates each interface into an abstract base class complete with pure virtual prototypes for each method listed in the IDL file. The C++ developer who wants to implement a coclass supporting this interface must inherit from this MIDL-generated C++ prototype. And because the MIDL generated prototype inherits from `IDispatch`, the implementor of the coclass has no choice but to support it.

You're not off the hook in terms of implementing the methods of `IUnknown`, either. Your derived class is required to implement `IUnknown` as well because, like all interfaces in COM, `IDispatch` inherits from `IUnknown`.

Now that there are dual interfaces, there isn't much call for dispinterfaces. It seems that dual interfaces give the best of both worlds. You have the convenience, power, and descriptive IDL of custom interfaces, and you automatically get the late binding support for free—simply by inheriting from `IDispatch` instead of `IUnknown` in the IDL file. But there is a price.

The price is small. The methods of your dual interface can only use those data types that `IDispatch` can accept in its `Invoke()` function. After all, the purpose of a dual interface is to allow the client to access the methods either directly via the vtables of your custom interfaces (early binding) or via `IDispatch` (late binding). However, if the same method can be called either way by a client, the method cannot do anything with early binding that can't also be done with late binding. For instance, you cannot have a dual interface with a method that takes a linked list or a pointer to an array as a parameter. Although this is allowed in an early-bound interface, there is no way to pass these kind of non-VB data types through `IDispatch`'s `Invoke()` function.

`Invoke()` expects method arguments to be passed in as an array of variants. You might, therefore, assume that only variants can be used as the parameters of methods in dual interfaces. Close. Although you can use variants as method parameters, you are limited to those data types that can be represented by a variant. In other words, you can use any data type that a variant can hold. This gives you integers, doubles, longs, strings, and every other VB data type you know and love. Variants can also hold Visual Basic arrays (safearrays).

If you are content with using Visual Basic data types, you should probably make your interfaces dual. Of course in VB, you have no choice; but in C++ and J++, it is up to you.

Late Binding, Marshaling, and the *oleautomation* Tag

Summary and review never hurts. So far, we have discussed the following three scenarios involving late binding:

- No type library late binding
- Type library late binding using dispinterfaces
- Type library late binding using Dual Interfaces

In the first scenario, COM knows how to marshal method calls made through `IDispatch`. Therefore, a COM object that supports `IDispatch` can (to use old terminology), be automated over a network without a type library being present. Just for fun, the VB code in Listing 5.15 instantiates and uses an instance of Microsoft Excel on the remote machine Darjeeling.

Listing 5.15 **VB Late Binding with No Type Library Used**
```
Dim o as object
Set o=createobject("excel.application", "Darjeeling")
o.visible=true
o.workbooks.add
o.cells.range("A1")="hi there"
```

Permissions on Darjeeling must allow this, so an administrator on Darjeeling must run DCOMCNFG.EXE, a utility used to adjust launch and access permissions for DCOM servers. That done, however, the client can do what it wants with someone else's Excel—all from a remote machine without a type library. This is the miracle of `IDispatch` and late binding.

For the second scenario, a type library can exist for an object and contain one or many dispinterfaces that describe what late binding methods the object(s) supports. In this case, compile-time validation can occur because the development environment can check the developer's function invocation against the type library's definition to make sure he is calling the function correctly. Likewise, `DISPID`s can be gleaned from the type library possibly saving a call to `GetIDsofNames()`. In the end, however, `IDispatch` is still used.

A third late binding possibility is that a type library exists but has dual interfaces as opposed to dispinterfaces (there can be a mix of the two, but this is not common). A client can still choose to automate an object using `IDispatch` even though early binding would also have been possible. Indeed, clients like ASP pages have no other mechanism available.

In each and every scenario described here, something called the oleautomation marshaler is used to remote the late-bound method calls. The marshaler lives in oleaut32.dll and is responsible for packing and moving across the wire anything that comes through `IDispatch`. In fact, although it's not necessary, you will often find the `oleautomation` tag present in an interface's attribute block, as shown in Listing 5.16.

Listing 5.16 **Common IDL Tags for an Interface**

```
[
    odl,
    uuid(1051376B-A601-11D3-8090-00E0811008ED),
    version(1.0),
    hidden,
    dual,
    oleautomation
]
```

This tag makes it clear that the oleautomation marshaler will be used. It is not, however, necessary. The oleautomation marshaler can still be used even if this tag is not present.

One interesting, sometimes confusing, aspect of the oleautomation marshaler is that it can also be helpful to customize interfaces (those that inherit from `IUnknown` in IDL) that do not support late binding. How? Very simply, the oleautomation marshaler can be used to marshal arguments for methods of custom interfaces as long as those methods only use oleautomation (VB) data types. If you don't use oleautomation compatible data types (only C++ gives you this latitude), you need to supply your own, proxy/stub DLL. This DLL is used by COM to marshal your arguments instead of the oleautomation marshaler. Again, you only need to have your own proxy/stub DLL if you want to use data types that are not available in Visual Basic. For more information on creating your own proxy/stub DLL (you can only do this with C++), see the book's companion source code www.newriders.com/complus.

J++ and Dual Interfaces

If you use the standard J++ mechanisms to build a COM object (that is, you allow the environment to produce a type library from your Java source), the COM object will be composed entirely of dispinterfaces. And if that isn't enough, your Java source must be peppered with little non-standard directives that inform the compiler of COM-specific details. Granted, the J++ environment can put the appropriate directives in for you, but you can see why Sun is very angry with Microsoft. In J++, non-Java, platform-specific directives are placed in comment blocks—specifically after a /**. In this sneaky way, non-Java/pro-Microsoft features are included in J++ without affecting the Java language.

Consider the block of J++ code used to build a COM DLL shown in Listing 5.17.

Listing 5.17 **A Simple Implementation of a Class Supporting** *ICalc* **and** *IFinancial* **in VJ++**

```
interface ICalc {
    int Add(int a, int b);
    int Subtract(int a, int b);
}

interface IFinancial {
    public void GetMortgagePayment();
    public void GetPrimeRate();
}

/**
 * This class is designed to be packaged with a COM DLL output format.
 * The class has no standard entry points, other than the constructor.
 * Public methods will be exposed as methods on the default COM interface.
 * @com.register ( clsid=7087BCCA-3571-477C-85C5-B192C1A2C94C, typelib=D1676CBE-
 0B58-44E3-BC0F-83F64A021E39 )
 */

public class Calc implements ICalc, IFinancial
{
    public Calc() {};

    // Implementation for ICalc:
    public int Add(int a,int b) {return a+b;};
    public int Subtract(int a, int b){return a-b;};

    // Implementation for IFinancial:
    public void GetMortgagePayment() {};
    public void GetPrimeRate() {};
}
```

150   Chapter 5 Method Invocation and Marshaling

If you look at the type library of the COM object produced by J++, you get the code shown in Listing 5.18.

Listing 5.18 **Type Library Automatically Generated from the Code in Listing 5.17**

```
// Generated .IDL file (by the OLE/COM Object Viewer)
//
// typelib filename: MyCalc.dll

[
  uuid(D1676CBE-0B58-44E3-BC0F-83F64A021E39),
  version(1.0),
  helpstring("MyCalc")
]
library MyCalc
{
    TLib : OLE Automation : {00020430-0000-0000-C000-000000000046}
    importlib("stdole2.tlb");

    // Forward declare all types defined in this typelib
    dispinterface Calc_Dispatch;

    [
      uuid(B5582180-6C48-4F2B-87E4-E6B26F3C92A6)
    ]
    dispinterface Calc_Dispatch {
        properties:
        methods:
            [id(0x00000064), helpstring("Add")]
            long Add([in] long Parameter0,
                     [in] long Parameter1);
            [id(0x00000065)]
            VARIANT wait([in, out] VARIANT* Parameter0,
                         [in, out] VARIANT* Parameter1);
            [id(0x00000066), helpstring("hashCode")]
            long hashCode();
            [id(0x00000067), helpstring("GetPrimeRate")]
            void GetPrimeRate();
            [id(0x00000068), helpstring("toString")]
            BSTR toString();
            [id(0x00000069), helpstring("equals")]
            VARIANT_BOOL equals([in] IDispatch* Parameter0);
            [id(0x0000006a), helpstring("GetMortgagePayment")]
            void GetMortgagePayment();
            [id(0x0000006b), helpstring("notify")]
            void notify();
            [id(0x0000006c), helpstring("getClass")]
            IDispatch* getClass();
            [id(0x0000006d), helpstring("Subtract")]
            long Subtract([in] long Parameter0,
                          [in] long Parameter1);
            [id(0x0000006e), helpstring("notifyAll")]
```

Late Binding, Marshaling, and the oleautomation Tag 151

```
        void notifyAll();
};

[
  uuid(7087BCCA-3571-477C-85C5-B192C1A2C94C),
  helpstring("Calc")
]
coclass Calc {
    [default] dispinterface Calc_Dispatch;
};
};
```

There are a couple of things worth noting about this code:

- Unlike the Java source code, our generated coclass is not composed of two interfaces (`ICalc` and `IFinancial`), but is an amalgamation of the two interfaces called `Calc_Dispatch`. This is because we did not add any COM compiler directives to our Java interfaces.

- J++ added seven new member functions to the `Calc_Dispatch` interface. These additional methods have nothing to do with COM. These exist because J++ generates the COM interface by scanning the Java object's public methods, including those inherited from java.lang.Object. More information about these methods can be found in the Java API documentation. More information about these methods can be found in the JDK (Java Development Kit). For now, refer to Table 5.1.

Table 5.1 **New Member Functions to the *Calc Dispatch* Interface**

Java Method	Meaning
equals	Returns true if the object passed to this method is the same as the current object. Note that this is only meant to compare two Java objects in the same virtual machine, unless the method is overidden
getClass	This returns an instance of java.lang.Class describing the underlying Java class. A COM client could potentially use and manipulate this through IDispatch, though such a case would be very rare.
hashCode	This method returns the *hashcode* of the object. A hashcode is basically a numeric identifier. In Java, all objects have distinct hashcodes (so they can be stored in hashtables). For two objects to be equal (see the `equal` entry), their hashcodes must be the same.

continues

Table 5.1 Continued

Java Method	Meaning
notify	Wakes up a single thread that is Waiting on this object's monitor. A thread waits on an object's monitor by calling one of the wait methods. This is for multithreading within a single virtual machine, and probably should not be used by COM clients.
notifyAll	Wakes up all threads that are waiting on this object's monitor. A thread waits on an object's monitor by calling one of the wait methods. This is for multithreading within a single virtual machine, and probably should not be used by COM clients.
toString	Returns a string that is represented by the object. This is a combination of the Java class name and the object's hashcode. In J++ 6.0, ToString returns coclassname@hex (hashtable). For example, if your object has a hashcode of 131, ToString returns Calc@83 (131 = hex 83)
wait	Places the current Java VM thread on the object's monitor until signaled by notify or notifyAll. Probably should not be used by COM clients.

- Most importantly, the Calc_Dispatch interface is declared to be a dispinterface. This means that early binding (vtable binding) is not possible.

Supporting Dual or Custom Interfaces in J++

There is a way, however, to produce a COM object in J++ with interfaces that are dual (or even a standard vtable interface). It involves forcing the interface on J++ by importing the type library you want your component to have. The procedure is as follows:

1. Create an IDL file that implements your interfaces as dual—for example, MyObject.IDL (see Listing 5.19).

Listing 5.19 **IDL File Describing Dual Interfaces to be Used by J++**

```
[
    uuid(D544BFC0-BC81-11d0-A982-00AA00C0177B),
    helpstring("javaLib Type Library 1.2a"),
    version(1.2)
]
library javaLib
```

```
{
  importlib("stdole32.tlb");

  [
    object,
    dual,
    uuid(D544BFC1-BC81-11d0-A982-00AA00C0177B),
    helpstring("Itest Interface")
  ]
  interface ICalc : IDispatch
  {
      [id(1), helpstring("method TestLong")]
      HRESULT add([in] long parm1, [in] long parm2, [out,retval] long *ret);
      [id(2), helpstring("method TestString")]
      HRESULT TestString([in] long parm1, [in] long parm2,
                        [out,retval] long *ret);

  }

  [
    uuid(D544BFC2-BC81-11d0-A982-00AA00C0177B),
    helpstring("test Object")
  ]
  coclass MyObject
  {
    [default] interface ICalc;
  };
};
```

2. Run MIDL.EXE (this comes with Visual C++ or the Platform SDK) on the IDL to produce a type library (in this case, MyObject.TLB).

3. Assuming that the type library can be found in the D:\MyCalc directory, start Visual J++, click New Project, select the Existing tab, highlight the MyCalc folder, and click Import Project Folder.

4. Note that the MyObject.TLB file appears in the MyCalc Project Folder. Right-click the MyCalc Project Folder and go to MyCalc Project Properties.

5. In the dialog box, select the COM Classes tab, click Use Existing Type Library, and click Select.

6. In the COM Templates dialog box, click Browse. Go to the MyCalc directory and select the MyObject.TLB file.

7. Click Open and then OK. Click OK again.

8. Visual J++ now creates wrappers for all the COM interfaces and coclasses in the type library. J++ provides an implementation for all methods of all wrapper classes in the form shown in Listing 5.20.

Listing 5.20 J++ coclass Wrapper for IDL File Shown in Listing 5.19

```
/** @com.register(clsid=D544BFC2-BC81-11D0-A982-00AA00C0177B,
typelib=D544BFC0-BC81-11D0-A982-00AA00C0177B, version="1.2",
description="test Object")*/

public class MyObject implements IUnknown,com.ms.com.NoAutoScripting,
            myobject.ICalcDefault
{
  public int add(int parm1, int parm2) {
      throw new com.ms.com.ComFailException(0x80004001); // E_NOTIMPL
  }

  public int TestString(int parm1, int parm2) {
      throw new com.ms.com.ComFailException(0x80004001); // E_NOTIMPL
  }
}
```

9. Next, remove the `E_NOTIMPL` lines and provide your own implementation.

10. Indicate to J++ that this project will be packaged as a COM DLL by doing all of the following:

    - Right-click the MyCalc project folder.
    - Select MyCalc Properties.
    - Click the Output Format tab.
    - Select the Enable Packaging check box.
    - Select the COM DLL as the package type.

11. The COM DLL is now built based on the type library you provided. Your interfaces are thus dual and can be accessed through early and late binding.

Examining the Wrapper

Finally, it is worthwhile to examine the wrapper interface that J++ produced for you, as shown in Listing 5.21.

Listing 5.21 J++ Generated Interface Prototype for IDL Declaration of *ICalc*

```
// Dual interface ICalc
/** @com.interface(iid=D544BFC1-BC81-11D0-A982-00AA00C0177B, thread=AUTO,
type=DUAL) */
public interface ICalc extends IUnknown
{
  /** @com.method(vtoffset=4, dispid=1, type=METHOD, name="add", addFlagsVtable=4)
      @com.parameters([in,type=I4] parm1, [in,type=I4] parm2, [type=I4] return) */
  public int add(int parm1, int parm2);
```

```
/** @com.method(vtoffset=5, dispid=2, type=METHOD, name="TestString",
    addFlagsVtable=4)
    @com.parameters([in,type=I4] parm1, [in,type=I4] parm2, [type=I4] return) */
public int TestString(int parm1, int parm2);

public static final com.ms.com._Guid iid = new com.ms.com._Guid((int)0xd544bfc1,
    (short)0xbc81, (short)0x11d0, (byte)0xa9, (byte)0x82, (byte)0x0, (byte)0xaa,
    (byte)0x0, (byte)0xc0, (byte)0x17, (byte)0x7b);
}
```

J++ determines the properties of the ICalc interface (being dual, for example) by utilizing highlighted @com directives. You can, in fact, use these directives directly to produce a dual interface (see http://www.microsoft.com/java/resource/java_com2.htm for examples of various @com directives and how to use them), or simply write the IDL and let J++ do the work for you.

Is there a downside to creating dual interfaces this way? Not really. In fact, creating COM interfaces through IDL is the preferred approach to preserve COM's philosophy of language independence. Automatically generating a type library with J++ exposes language-specific methods, therefore should probably only be used for prototyping or experimentation.

J++ COM clients, however, do have access to these seven methods because of the approach Microsoft has taken with its Java/COM integration. Because a Java wrapper class is created to represent an underlying coclass, this class is a regular Java object and may be treated as one. Note that under this approach, the seven methods are not exposed as COM methods. They are merely Java object methods, and calls to them will not be remoted or marshaled to the server.

Summary

COM provides two mechanisms for clients to invoke method calls on the interfaces of COM objects—early binding and late binding. Early binding implies the existence and inclusion of a type library. It is generally true that a client using a type library to invoke methods on a server object is using early binding. However, there are type libraries that include dispinterfaces that always require late binding.

Late binding requires two complete round trips to invoke a method. The absence of a type library (or a type library containing only dispinterfaces) mandates that only late binding can be used by a client. The first round trip in a late binding call involves sending the method call as a string to the server object and requesting a special number that represents the function, called a DISPID. The second round trip involves invoking the method using the DISPID and sending arguments as arrays of variants. Variants are discriminated unions that can hold any Visual Basic data type.

Early binding is more efficient than late binding. Early binding calls require only one round trip (late binding calls take two), and in the event of a client EXE using a compatibly threaded in-process server, the calls can actually be very fast, direct invocations on the vtable of the object. Additionally, a development environment can perform compile-time type checking using the type libraries present.

Although the benefits of early binding are many and it should be used wherever possible, late binding is essential in certain circumstances. If a type library is not available or a development environment cannot read a type library (as in the case of ASP pages), late binding might be the only option. An interface might support both early and late binding to be of maximum use in all scenarios. Such an interface inherits from `IDispatch` in its IDL declaration and is referred to as dual.

References

Portions of this chapter are excerpted from the following:
Gregory Brill, "Writing COM Clients with Late and Early Binding," *C++ Users Journal*, Volume 16, No. 10(1988): 37-51.
Reprinted by permission of *C++ Users Journal*.

6

The COM+ Catalog

IN THIS CHAPTER, WE LOOK AT COM+'s administrative layer. Many of the COM+ object attributes we manipulate are introduced in this chapter but not described in detail; subsequent chapters provide the specifics.

In this chapter, I demonstrate how to turn on, turn off, and otherwise configure COM+-specific services. For the most part, we are looking at the "how" and "why" of installing COM+ components and applications, but we also demonstrate how to modify settings (configure) for applications, components, interfaces, and methods using both the COM+ Component Services snap-in and the COM+ Administration Objects.

From INI Files to the Registry to the Catalog

In the beginning, there were INI files. Conceptually simple but somewhat limited, an application could store string-based information in its own INI file. In these quiet, simpler times, books on the shelves with titles like *Secrets of Windows Gurus: Undocumented INI Entries!*, and NOTEPAD.EXE gave you real power (after all, INI files were just text files) to determine how an application (or Windows itself) would run.

Back then, the headlines of the industry trades proclaimed, "Forget about INI Files: Store Your Application's Configuration Data in the new Windows Registry!" Many applications, such as 16-bit Windows, took their first tentative steps with this new medium and began to store their settings in the Registry. Although there still were (and are) a good number of INI files in use, it was hoped the Registry might someday replace them altogether.

COM (then called Object Linking and Embedding [OLE]) was one of the driving forces that propelled the Registry into stardom. As Windows moved toward a component-based architecture, a central database containing detailed information about all the registered COM components became a necessity. At a minimum, the Registry needed to keep track of where a component could be found on the hard disk, its GUID, and its friendly string name (`ProgID`). As time went on, other settings were added having to do with threading, implemented functionality, and other details.

As the complexity of components grew, the amount of information held in the Registry grew. Eventually, things grew and evolved to a point where the Registry no longer seemed like the best medium to keep track of it all. For one thing, the Registry was a highly desegregated hierarchy where COM component information intermingled with non-COM-based operating system and application information. In the same manner as NOTEPAD.EXE could be used to edit INI files, the Registry could by modified by anyone who could double-click REGEDIT.EXE or REGEDT32.EXE. Given Windows' increased reliance on components and their blossoming sophistication, maybe this wasn't such a good idea anymore. The Registry was also ill-equipped to address how related COM components might be grouped together so they could share common properties and functionality. In short, COM had grown up, and it was time to have its own room.

Hence Windows 2000 introduces the COM+ Catalog. Much of the information about how a component runs in COM+ and what COM+ services a component takes advantage of is stored here. There are two ways you can modify declarative information about a COM+ component:

- Administratively using the COM+ Administrative UI
- Programmatically using the COM+ Administrative objects

But we are, perhaps, ahead of ourselves. Before a COM component can be manipulated at all in the COM+ Catalog, the developer or administrator must perform the explicit step of importing the component. This importation of a component marks its change from unconfigured to configured. *Configured components* can take advantage of COM+ services; *Unconfigured components* cannot.

Configured Components and COM+ Applications

In-process components that you might have already written in your pre-COM+ days can still function in COM+ without modification. And although these unconfigured components might need some slight modification to take advantage of the full range of COM+ services (for example, voting on the outcome of a transaction), they can be given the opportunity to participate in most of what COM+ offers. They need only be configured by a system administrator or developer. This brings us to the declarative nature of COM+—that is, the capability to administratively dictate how the object will operate.

The administrative settings made available by COM+ encompass everything from declaring that a certain method will be queueable (the caller will not block on the call or expect any form of return value; this is covered in Chapter 10, "Queued Components") to indicating that a certain object requires synchronization. As you see in Chapter 7, "Contexts," these administratively configured attributes combine to create an object's context.

Although it is true that Windows still keeps some component information in the standard Registry, the vast majority of administrative settings lie within the COM+ Catalog. The COM+ Catalog, like all administrative interfaces in Windows 2000, is configured through a Microsoft Management Console (MMC) snap-in.

To take a look at the Component Services snap-in, go to the Start menu, Programs, click Administrative Tools, and then Component Services. This runs the Component Services Console, and much like the Windows Explorer, the entire COM+ administrative hierarchy is displayed as a set of folders. Navigate your way to COM+ Applications as shown in Figure 6.1, and you can see all the COM+ applications installed on your system.

Although the term *application* is already overused, in the COM+ paradigm, an *application* is a group of configured components that are somehow related. If you are familiar with Microsoft Transaction Server (MTS), you can think of the COM+ application as an MTS package. The terminology is different, but the underlying meaning is the same. Similarly, the Component Services snap-in replaces the MTSExplorer (also a snap-in) used in previous versions of Windows.

MMC

Prior to Windows 2000, different system-oriented programs, such as Disk Manager, User Manager for Domains, and so on, had slightly varied and sometimes wildly different User Interfaces (UIs). Similarly, there was no standard for the UIs that configured NT services—every vendor was free to create its own UI, embracing a custom, though perhaps less-intuitive, paradigm.

To provide a uniform look and feel for all services and system tools, Microsoft began pushing MMC as a standard architecture. Basically, MMC.EXE is a COM container that is hard-wired to work with MMC snap-ins. *Snap-ins* are COM components that implement certain MMC interfaces. The author of the service ships a snap-in with his service that, when loaded by MMC, produces a hierarchical list of all properties that can be configured, viewed, or otherwise interacted with. The COM+ Component Services UI is just the MMC.EXE channeling the Component Services snap-in.

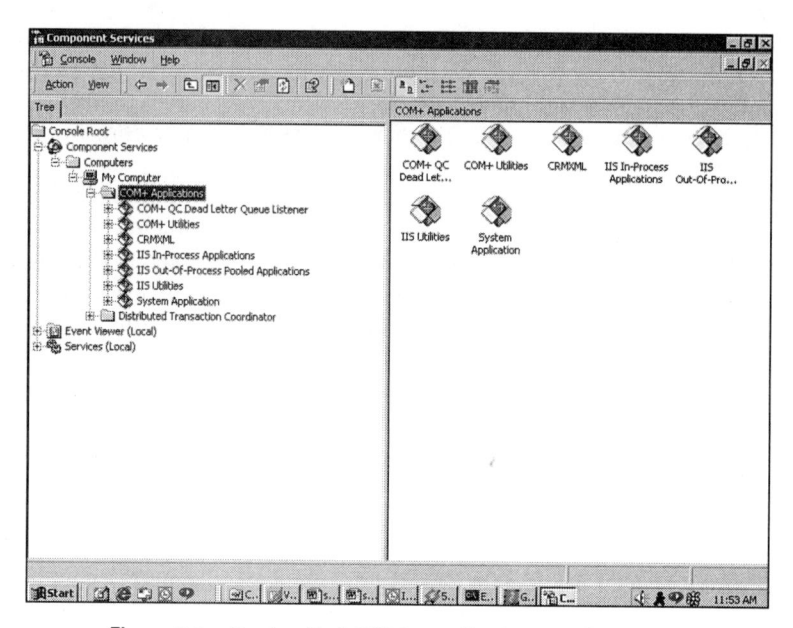

Figure 6.1 Pre-installed COM+ applications on the system.

When you first install Windows 2000, you might notice that there are a number of applications already installed. As you see, many of these pre-installed applications are used internally by COM+ to provide various component services (queuing, transaction capability, and so on). An explanation of these pre-installed applications and their associated components can be found at the end of this chapter. For the time being, let's examine the rules that govern generic applications, components, interfaces, and methods.

General COM+ Applications

In COM+, each and every object you instantiate will run inside a COM+ application. You can think of a COM+ application as a logical grouping of components; but from an OS perspective, a COM+ application is really just a "potential instance" of a process called DLLHOST.EXE. By "potential instance," I mean that a COM+ application has the potential to become a new instance of DLLHOST.EXE, which will house one or more running components. This potential becomes a reality when a client application first requests an instance of a component. COM+ determines the application that the component is associated with, and a new instance of DLLHOST.EXE is run. Thus, when you instantiate an object, the object's application (DLLHOST.EXE) must be run (unless it is already running, in which case the already running instance will be used). The component you instantiate is then loaded into this process. Any number of components may be associated with a COM+ application, and this means that any number of components can be made to run inside the same instance of DLLHOST.EXE.

Because COM+ applications take the physical form of a new DLLHOST.EXE process, the number of components you associate with COM+ applications has a direct effect on performance. If you have many components overall but divide them amongst many different applications, you may end up with a system that is less efficient than it could be; related components should be grouped together in the same application to avoid an excessive number of COM+ applications/DLLHOST.EXEs from running.

There is no absolute rule or guideline to follow when deciding how your components should be grouped. Common sense is often the best guide: don't put every component you write into a single application for the same reason that you don't put every method in one large C++ or Visual Basic class—you end up with an inflexible, monolithic environment. By the same token, avoid creating so many applications in which related components have to talk to one another across process boundaries. Fragmentation results in a system that is inefficient and hard to administrate.

One factor that may dictate how your components are grouped has to do with how the application is *configured*. That is, how the properties of a COM+ application are set. Properties of an application include security settings, asynchronous delivery (queueing), inactivity time-out periods, and other details. A discussion of most these properties is the providence of later chapters of this book (Chapter 10 and Chapter 12). However, to get a sense of how properties may be manipulated for COM+ applications, I show you one set of properties that doesn't require much background. They are the properties that can be found by right-clicking on any COM+ application in Component Services, selecting Properties, and then choosing the Advanced tab. You will see that shown in Figure 6.2

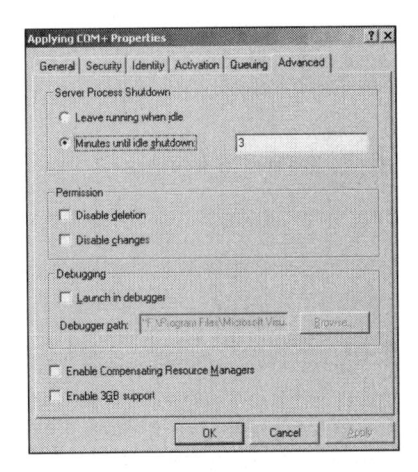

Figure 6.2 Advanced Properties Tab for an Application

These settings affect how the COM+ application behaves. Consider the first two radio buttons: "Leave running when idle," and "Minutes until idle shutdown." These are pretty simple to intuit if you remember that from an OS perspective, a COM+ application is nothing more than a potential instance of DLLHOST.EXE. With that in mind, these settings influence how the new instance of DLLHOST.EXE behaves. Specifically, if you select "Leave running when idle," you are asking that once run, the DLLHOST.EXE for this application should remain running indefinitely even if all clients release their connections to all components, leaving the application empty and idle. By selecting "Minutes until idle shutdown," however, you demand that an application should be terminated after *n* number of minutes of idle time ("idle" being defined as the time the application is not hosting any components for any client applications).

If you anticipate that the components of your application will be used frequently, you may want to "Leave running when idle" to avoid the overhead of starting a new DLLHOST.EXE process. If you are debugging components, however, you will probably want to select "Minutes until idle shutdown" to be something low. When developing a component, it is impossible to recompile while its host application is still running; the component is loaded and in use, so a low minute termination value is a good idea while debugging. Note that any application may be terminated manually at any time by right-clicking the application in Component Services, and selecting the Shut down menu option. Or you can perform the same trick programmatically with the following code:

```
'Must reference comadmin.dll to use COMAdminCatalog

Const APP_TO_SHUTDOWN = "SomeApplication"
Dim Catalog As COMAdminCatalog

Private Sub Command1_Click()

    Set Catalog = New COMAdminCatalog

    On Error GoTo Problem
    Catalog.ShutdownApplication APP_TO_SHUTDOWN

    Exit Sub

Problem:
    MsgBox Hex$(Err.Number) & ": " & Err.Description

End Sub
```

We see that changes to an application's settings affect the components of the application, and this makes sense; they will ultimately be hosted by the application's process, DLLHOST.EXE. So, there is a chain of command involved in COM+ configuration—all components registered under a particular application are affected by the changes you make to that application's properties. Similarly, components themselves have properties you can access (by right-clicking the component and choosing Properties). The Properties dialog box for a component is shown in Figure 6.3.

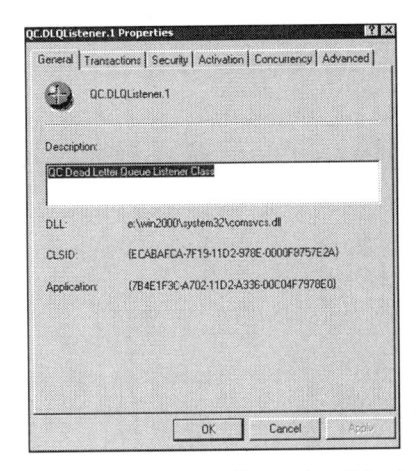

Figure 6.3 Component Properties dialog box.

Where the properties of the application have to do with the system (that is, the DLLHOST.EXE process, timeout intervals and so on), the properties of a component have more to do with the logical functioning of your application. It is here, with these properties, that you specify many operational and application-specific details, for example:

- Will database modifications that your component makes be able to participate in distributed transactions? More on this in Chapter 8, "Transactions."
- Can your object be "pooled" that is, reused between unrelated, successive clients; and if so, under what terms and conditions? This is discussed in Appendix C, "Object Pooling."
- Does your object need to be protected from concurrent access by any outside influence while enlisted in an activity? See Appendix B, "COM+ Synchronization Through Activities," for more details.
- What types of access restrictions do you want to enforce? Security is discussed in Chapter 12, "Security."

Just as the properties of an application affect the functioning of its components, so too do the properties of components affect the interfaces of these components (and, in turn, the methods of those interfaces). For example, if you change the security setting of a component such that certain users are allowed access, you are implicitly allowing these users access to all the interfaces and methods of the component. As we see in Chapter 12, although interfaces and methods have security-related properties just as the component does, there is no COM+ declarative way of refusing access to an interface by any user that the component grants access to.

Installing or Creating a New Application

The most important configuration options are those relating to applications and components. Let's explore them in the context of adding and configuring an entirely new COM+ application and component. We will call the application Trading System, and it will contain one component, Currency.

To create a new COM+ application, click the COM+ Applications folder to highlight it, right-click it, and select New, Application. This brings up the wizard shown in Figure 6.4.

Click the Next button to see the dialog box shown in Figure 6.5.

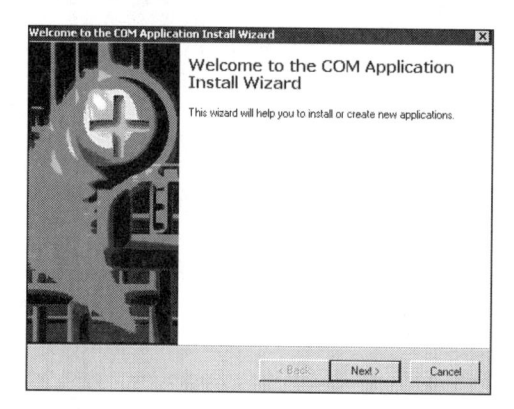

Figure 6.4 Screen 1: COM Application Install Wizard.

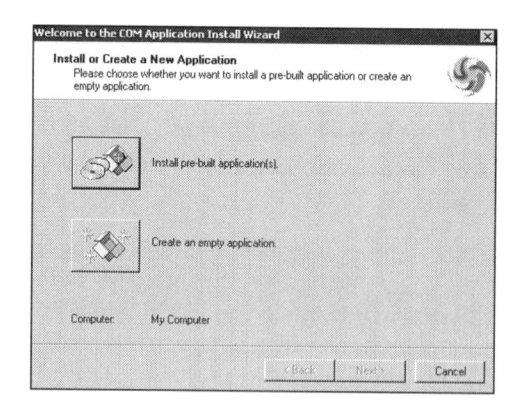

Figure 6.5 Screen 2: COM Application Install Wizard, Install or Create a New Application.

The first button, Install Pre-Built Application(s), is useful if someone gives you a PAK (short for Package) or MSI (Microsoft Installer) file. A PAK comes from the days of MTS and is included for legacy's sake. An MSI file, like a PAK file, is a complete, informational export of all the components and their settings for a specific application. MSI files are created when a COM+ developer chooses to export his application by right-clicking it and choosing the Export menu item. In essence, it is how COM+ applications are distributed.

Of the two choices, select Create an Empty Application. This brings you to the screen shown in Figure 6.6.

Give your application the name Trading System. By accepting the default setting of Server Application, you are saying that all components of this application will run together in one dedicated COM surrogate called DLLHOST.EXE. Although there can be many clients on different machines accessing components of a server application, there will most likely be only one instance of DLLHOST.EXE running that all clients share.

If you select Library Application, however, all components in this application run in the client's address space. Note that the client is intended to be another server application running on the same machine. Library applications often contain utility components that, although not necessarily used on their own, are useful to a running application. In this case, library application components are brought into the application's DLLHOST.EXE. Similarly, client executables running on the same machine as the library application can also bring the application's components in-process. A client executable on a remote machine, however, can not directly use components in a library application because the library application can not cross network boundaries to be brought into the client's process.

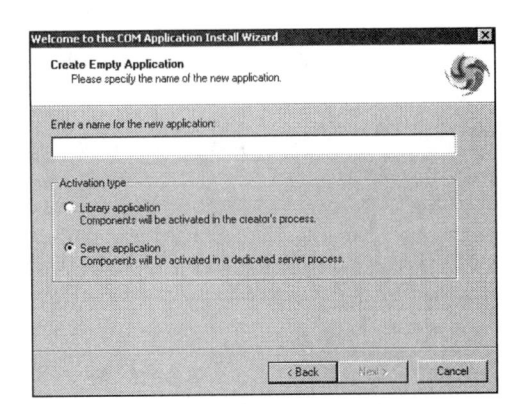

Figure 6.6 Screen 3: COM Application Install Wizard, Creating an Empty Application.

In short, library applications consist of components whose purpose in life is to service the needs of other components and, as such, do not need their own dedicated server process.

Application Identity

Clicking the Next button brings you to a screen like that shown in Figure 6.7. The default in this case is Interactive User. As the description says, the component will run in the NT security context of the user that is currently logged on. COM+ security is explored in detail in Chapter 12; but pushing the finer points of NT security aside for the moment, it is obvious that problems arise when no user is logged on—the server won't run. This setting does have its good points, however, particularly when it comes to debugging. Objects sprung from applications so configured can pop up dialog boxes and other UI elements that can be seen by the currently logged-in user of the server machine. Although server components should never attempt to interact with a user directly via a UI, it can be useful when troubleshooting a component.

On the whole, it is somewhat unbecoming for an enterprise application to be subject to the whims of whoever might be logged in to the server—whatever their privileges happen to be. It is better to create dedicated *software accounts* for your applications—that is, valid NT user accounts configured to provide the specific privileges required by your components. We will examine the details of this option when we revisit security in the "Application Identity" section of Chapter 12.

In this case, do the easy thing—go ahead and accept Interactive User and click Next. This brings you to the final page of the wizard. Just click Finish, and if all goes well, COM+ creates a new application called Trading System. You can now add components to this new application. To demonstrate, let's add a new component called Currency.

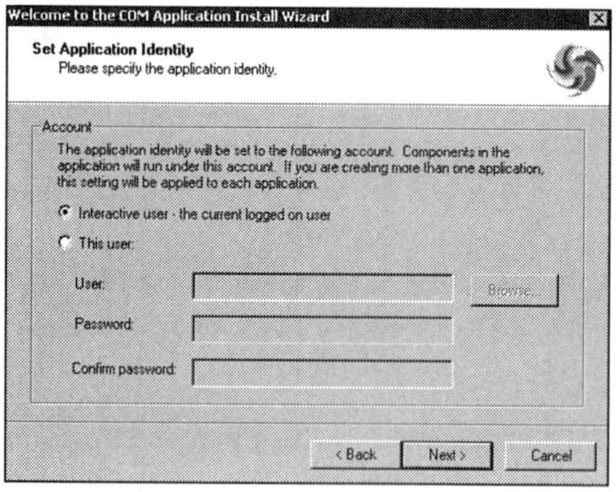

Figure 6.7 Setting the Application Identity

Imagine that the IDL for Currency contains the interfaces shown in Listing 6.1.

Listing 6.1 **The IDL for the Interfaces of the Currency Object**

```
[
        object,
        uuid(3730B8BC-13A3-4F97-8A7E-01F9456793A8),
        dual,
        helpstring("IConvert Interface"),
        pointer_default(unique)
]
interface IConvert : IDispatch
{
        HRESULT CurrencyConvert([in] int SourceCode, [in] int DestCode,
                [in] float InAmount, [out,retval] float* OutAmount);

};

[
        object,
        uuid(4446F2D0-FE18-4902-B91B-95792F4B049D),
        dual,
        helpstring("ITransfer Interface"),
        pointer_default(unique)
]
interface ITransfer : IDispatch
{
        HRESULT TransferMoney([in] int SourceAccount, [in] int DestAccount,
                              [in] float Amount);
};
```

Assume that this IDL has been compiled into a Type Library (.TLB file). Further assume we have created a Visual Basic ActiveX DLL that includes this type library via the Project, References dialog. Now we can create an ActiveX class that implements these interfaces, and not surprisingly, we call this VB ActiveX class Currency. It's code is shown in Listing 6.2.

Listing 6.2 **VB Implementation Code for the Currency Object that Provides Implementation for IConvert and ITransfer.**

```
'The following code is in the ActiveX class, Currency
Implements IConvert
Implements ITransfer


Private Function IConvert_CurrencyConvert(ByVal SourceCode As Long, ByVal DestCode
↪As Long, ByVal InAmount As Single) As Single

'code to perform conversion, not included for brevity
```

continues

Listing 6.2 **Continued**

```
Private Sub ITransfer_TransferMoney(ByVal SourceAccount As Long, ByVal DestAccount
➥As Long, ByVal Amount As Single)

'code to perform transfer, not included for brevity

End Sub
```

Importing versus Installing Components

To add Currency as a component under the Trading System application, right-click the Component folder underneath the Trading System folder and select New, Component, which brings up the Component Install Wizard. The wizard presents you with the options shown in Figure 6.8.

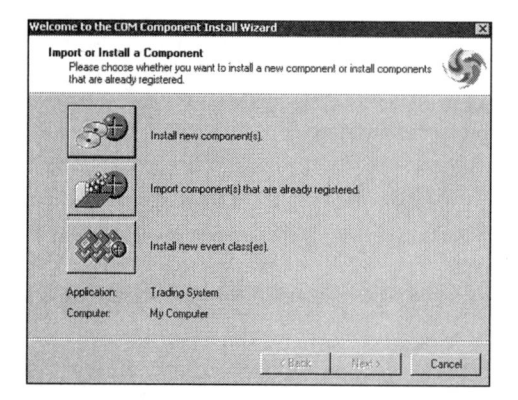

Figure 6.8 Screen 1: COM Component Install Wizard, Importing or Installing Applications.

> **Import versus Install**
>
> There is one other side effect of choosing Import versus Install. If you choose Install, removing the component sometime later from its parent COM+ application results in the component being de-registered entirely. All Registry entries are removed and any applications using this component now find the component unavailable. What's more, COM+ might modify the existing settings (such as its apartment model) when installing the component.
>
> Using Import and then deleting a component from COM+ results in the component becoming unconfigured but still available in a traditional COM capacity—that is, its Registry entries remain, but it can no longer take advantage of COM+ services.
>
> Basically, COM+ regards installed components as belonging entirely to it, but looks at imported components as borrowed and so does not take wide latitudes with their Registry settings.

Install New Component(s) and Import Component(s) That Are Already Registered both allow you to bring a COM DLL into COM+ and make it a configured component. You might imagine that you will use the second option in any case where the component is already registered on the system. However, I suggest that you always use the first option, even if the component is already registered. This is because Install New Component(s) reads the type library of the component and makes information about the interfaces and methods visible in the administrative application. This is important if you want to be able to set security (and other properties) on a particular method or interface. If you use Import Component(s) That Are Already Registered, the interfaces and methods of an object are not listed. True, installing new reregisters the component, but this does not cause any harm.

We discuss the final option, Install New EventClass(es), in Chapter 11, "Events." But just to give you a sense, you can designate a certain interface as being *eventful*. You can then declaratively arrange it so that calls to methods of this interface on the implementing class will result the methods propagation to all (there can be one or many) registered subscribers who support this interface.

For now, choose Install New Component(s). This brings up the Open File dialog box. Choose the COM DLL you want to bring into COM+, which brings up the screen shown in Figure 6.9.

Here, the coclasses in the component are listed. Click the Next button and then Finish. You can now see your component listed as a member of the application.

After the wizard is complete, if you click on the newly installed component and go deeper in the tree, you will see its interfaces and methods, shown in Figure 6.10.

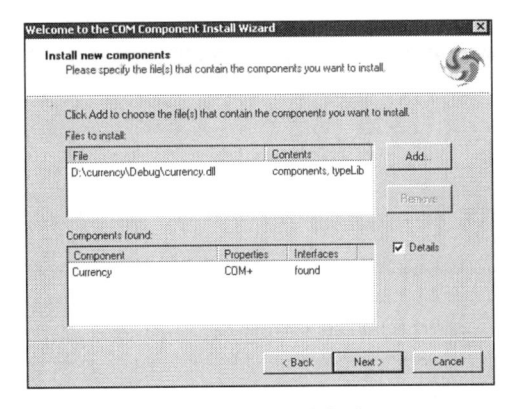

Figure 6.9 Installing a new COM+ component.

> **A Slight Omission: VB's Extra Interface**
> Note that for the sake of simplicity I made one small omission. As Currency is presently written in VB (see Listing 6.2), there should actually be a third interface in front of IConvert and ITransfer named Currency. VB always creates a default interface with the same name as the ActiveX class except it is prepended with an underscore. This interface is not included in Figure 6.10, because I installed a C++ version of Currency for the purpose of this screen capture so as to paint the simplest possible picture.

170 Chapter 6 The COM+ Catalog

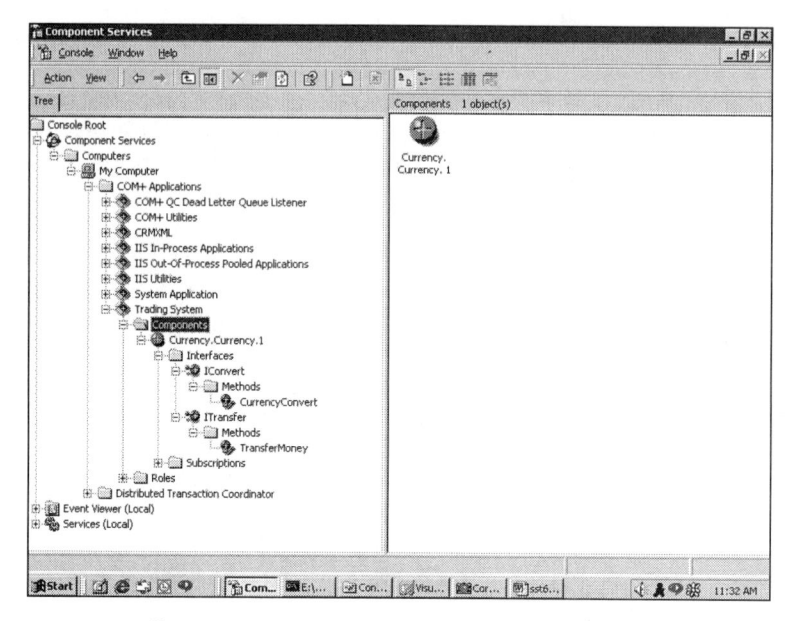

Figure 6.10 Results of installing a new component.

Once again, if you had chosen Import Component(s) That Are Already Registered, interfaces and methods would not be listed (see Figure 6.11).

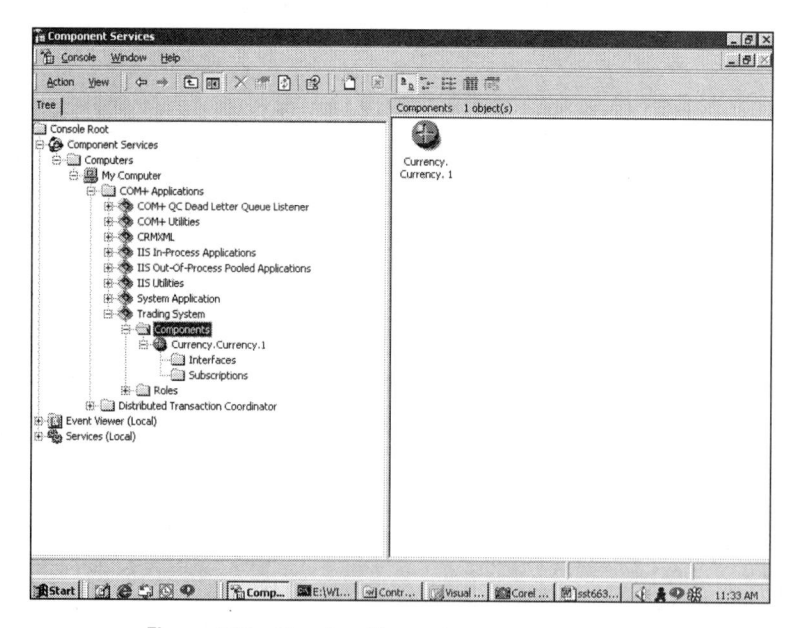

Figure 6.11 Results of importing a new component.

By bringing your component into a COM+ application, it has become a configured component.

Almost every entity that appears in the tree view—Application, coclass, Interface, Method—can be configured. The procedure is always the same: Simply right-click on any one, select Properties, and you can explore all the various settings.

Automating Configuration

The Component Services snap-in is nothing more than an attractive MMC front-end snap-in. The real work of manipulating various settings for configured components and applications is done by interacting with the `Catsrv.CatalogServer.1` component directly (described in the section, "A Quick Tour: Pre-Installed COM+ Applications" at the end of this chapter). However, at the time of this writing, the interfaces of this object are undocumented—a strong indication that they are not to be used by developers, but exist to service other components authored by Microsoft. Fortunately, the "other" components that use CatalogServer are documented and can be used to programmatically change properties of COM+ entities. They are called the COM+ administration objects. These objects implement a series of interfaces that allow an application to modify the declarative settings for COM+ components.

The COM+ Administration Objects Properties

As we have discussed, there are a number of configuration settings that a component can set to take advantage of different COM+ services. It is not my habit to provide laundry lists of properties or methods with brief descriptions (that is why we have MSDN). I do make an exception here, however, just to give you a broad sense of some of the configuration settings and services your object has access to.

Table 6.1 lists the configuration options for a COM+ application and component. (There exist additional security-related settings for interfaces and methods entities, but we will discuss these in Chapter 12.) Many of these options can be found in the property dialog boxes you saw earlier. You access each property programmatically through something called a `ValueProperty`, which is explained momentarily. Note that only brief explanations for properties are provided in Table 6.1, but the underlying concepts will be explored in subsequent chapters.

Table 6.1 **Application Properties**

Value Property	Description
`AccessChecksLevel`	Determines whether access checks are performed at the process level or at the component level. This setting has implications for role-based security.

continues

Table 6.1 **Continued**

Value Property	Description
Activation	Determines whether components within the application will be run in the creator's process (library application) or in a dedicated surrogate (server application).
ApplicationAccessChecksEnabled	Determines whether access checks are performed by components of the application. This setting is related to role-based security.
ApplicationProxy	Determines whether the application is an application proxy. An application proxy can be accessed remotely from other machines, provided the client computer has a subset of the application locally.
ApplicationProxyServerName	The name other machines use when accessing this application remotely. The application must be configured as an ApplicationProxy for this setting to take effect.
Authentication	Determines the level of security COM+ employs when dispatching RPC calls. Because this setting applies only RPC calls, it is available only to server applications. More on this when we discuss security in Chapter 12.
AuthenticationCapability	Determines the impersonation level when RPC calls are dispatched. Again, this applies only to server applications.
Changeable	Determines whether changes to the application's settings are allowed either programmatically or through the MMC.
CommandLine	A command-line string that is passed to the application when it is launched. This is used mostly for debugging purposes.
CreatedBy	A string indicating the creator of the application.
CRMEnabled	Determines if the compensating resource manager is enabled for this application. More on this in Chapter 9, "Compensating Resource Managers."
CRMLogFile	The location of the log for the Compensating Resource Manager. More on this in Chapter 9.

Value Property	Description
Deleteable	Determines whether this application can be removed from the system either programmatically or through the MMC.
Description	A string describing the application.
EventsEnabled	Determines whether events are enabled for the application.
ID	A GUID that represents the application. This can only be written to once—when the application is added to the catalog. If omitted, COM+ generate one for you.
Identity	Applies only to server applications. It allows an application to use the security credentials of an NT account. This property must be set to a valid user account or interactive user, whereby the application assumes the identity of the user who is currently logged in.
ImpersonationLevel	Determines the level of authority this application grants to other applications it uses when they act on its behalf.
IsSystem	Returns whether the application is a system component. This property is read only.
Name	A string that represents the name of the application.
Password	Used in conjunction with the Identity property to allow the application to use the credentials of an NT account.
QueueListenerEnabled	This property only takes effect if the QueuingEnabled property is set to true. This property enables the queue listener so that the application will begin listening for messages when it is run. Queued components will therefore receive asynchronous method calls. Queued Components will be discussed in greater detail in Chapter 10.
QueuingEnabled	Determines whether components within this application can receive method calls asynchronously via MSMQ.

continues

Table 6.1 **Continued**

Value Property	Description
RunForever	Determines if the application stays awake while it is idle. This option is only available to server applications. If this is set to false, the application shuts down after it becomes idle as determined by the ShutdownAfter property.
ShutdownAfter	Determines the interval between when an application becomes idle and when it shuts down. This property is only relevant for server applications. (For development environments, you want to set this value to a low number, so your components don't hang around in memory while you're developing.)
3GigSupportEnabled	Determines whether the application will have 3GB of addressable memory in its process (the default is 2GB).

Similarly, the properties for a component are listed in Table 6.2.

Table 6.2 **Component Properties**

AllowInprocSubscribers	Enables in-process subscribers if the component is an event class.
ApplicationID	Returns the GUID of the application in which this component resides. Changing this property to another application GUID (if it exists) moves the component under that application.
CLSID	The GUID for this component. In plain COM terminology, this is the coclass GUID. This property is read-only.
ComponentAccessChecksEnabled	Determines if role-based access checks are performed on the component.
COMTIIntrinsics	Undocumented, but it is likely that this property specifies whether a component's context inherits COMTI information. COMTI is used to allow COM+ objects to participate in transactions with mainframe systems.
ConstructionEnabled	Determines whether a constructor string (see the ConstructorString property) should be passed to the component when it is instantiated.

ConstructorString	If the `ConstructionEnabled` property is set to true, this string is passed to the component when it is instantiated. This is useful for components that require parameterized construction.
CreationTimeout	If the object supports pooling, this property determines the amount of time the pool has to provide an instance of the component, after which an error is returned. See Appendix C, for more information on object pooling.
Description	A string describing the component DLL—the path and filename where the component resides. This property is read-only.
EventTrackingEnabled	Determines whether events are tracked. This is expanded upon in Chapter 11.
ExceptionClass	If this component is a queued component, specifies the CLSID of an alternative component to be activated when this component repeatedly fails.
FireInParallel	Enables events to be fired in parallel, if the component is an event class. Events are discussed in Chapter 11.
IISIntrinsics	Allows the component's context to inherit Internet Information Server properties, such as session and application objects.
IsEventClass	Returns whether the component is an event class. This property is read-only.
JustInTimeActivation	Determines whether the component supports Just-in-Time (JIT) Activation.
LoadBalancingSupported	Load balancing was removed from Windows 2000 as of Beta 3. Effectively orphaned unless you use Microsoft's new AppCenter Server when it becomes available.
MaxPoolSize	If the component supports object pooling (see `ObjectPoolingEnabled`), determines the maximum number of instances that are kept in the pool.
MinPoolSize	If the component supports object pooling, determines the minimum number of instances that are kept in the pool.
MultiInterfacePublisherFilterCLSID	Sets the CLSID for a publisher filter.

continues

Table 6.2 **Continued**

MustRunInClientContext	If set to true, the component must be activated in the caller's context.
ObjectPoolingEnabled	Determines whether the object supports pooling.
ProgID	Returns the ProgID (friendly identifier) of the component. This property is read-only.
PublisherID	Identifier for the event publisher, if the component is an event class.
Synchronization	Determines if calls to the component are synchronized via Activities. Activities are discussed in Appendix B.
ThreadingModel	Determines the type of thread in which the component will run (STA, MTA or TNA). See Chapter 4, "Threading and Apartment Models," for details.
Transaction	Determines if the component will participate in transactions, and if so, how it will participate in them. This is covered in Chapter 8.
VersionBuild	The major build version of the component.
VersionMajor	The major version of the component.
VersionMinor	The minor version of the component.
VersionSubBuild	The minor build version of the component.

Now that you've seen what properties are available to you, let's take a look at how to configure a component programmatically using the COM+ administrative objects.

Introducing the COM+ Administration Objects

COM+ exposes three components you will use to configure a component. They are the following:

- COMAdminCatalog. Represents the COM+ Catalog database. COMAdminCatalog is the highest level object, and you must go through it to get the collection of COM+ applications. You can also use this object to install components, administer and configure catalogs on other computers, and start and stop services.

- COMAdminCatalogCollection. Used when you have obtained a collection from the COMAdminCatalog object (for example, the Application collection represents all the COM+ applications currently installed on the system). This component allows you to access numerous COMAdminCatalogObjects objects (see the next bullet) in the collection, which you can then manipulate.

- `COMAdminCatalogObject`. Represents an object in a collection. `COMAdminCatalogObjects` can be used to represent an application, component, or any other COM+ entity that can be returned in a `COMAdminCatalogCollection`. Because `COMAdminCatalogObjects` are designed to be generic and to hold any kind of object with any number of properties, they do not have very descriptive (or very many) properties. Aside from a couple of utility methods, these objects have only one property, `Value`.

For the most part, the preceding objects return collections of objects representing either components or applications. You then use one or more of the `ValueProperties` listed in Tables 6.1 and 6.2 to change their settings. Using the `ValueProperty` is a little unusual, because unlike the typical properties you are used to, you must use the `ValueProperty` to get to the underlying real properties of the object that the `COMAdminCatalogObject` is referring to. This is easiest to demonstrate in code. If, for example, you have a `COMAdminCatalogObject` that is representing an application object and you want to make sure that its `3GigSupportEnabled` property is true, you would not say the following:

```
'Don't do this
ApplicationObject.3GigSupportEnabled = True;   'WRONG!!
```

Instead, you would say the following:

```
'do the following
ApplicationObject.Value("3GigSupportEnabled") = True;
```

Note: The string constant `3GigSupportEnabled` is only one possible `ValueProperty`. You can use any of the string constants defined in Table 6.1. Of course, you also need to make certain that the value on the right side of the assignment is the appropriate data type for the property you are setting.

Using the Administrative Objects

Earlier, I made the statement that everything that can be done through the Component Services UI can be done programmatically. To prove this and gain some exposure to the administrative objects, Listing 6.3 demonstrates how to add a new application to COM+ programmatically in Visual Basic.

Listing 6.3 **Adding an Application Programmatically to the Catalog**

```
'This example adds a 'Trading System' application and a Currency component
'residing under it to the COM Catalog.

'Note that this code does NOT check to see if an existing application of
'the SAME name already exists.  The Catalog will not automatically reject
'duplicates, so this is important. See the source code accompanying the
'book for a more complete example.

'Application and Component Information:
Const APPLICATION_NAME = "Trading System"
```

continues

178 Chapter 6 The COM+ Catalog

Listing 6.3 **Continued**

```
Const COMPONENT_PROGID = "Current.Currency"
Const COMPONENT_LOCATION = "\somedir\Currency.DLL"

Dim Catalog  As New COMAdminCatalog 'reference to the Catalog DataBase
Dim Application  As COMAdminCatalogObject   'represents a single application
Dim Component As COMAdminCatalogObject    'represents a single component
Dim colApp  As COMAdminCatalogCollection 'Collection of Applications
Dim colComp As COMAdminCatalogCollection 'Collection of components

'obtain the Application collection from the Catalog
Set colApp = Catalog.GetCollection("Applications")

'Add our Application to the Application Collection:
Set Application = colApp.Add

'The Application variable now points to the newly added application.
'We can let COM+ choose default properties for us, or set some
'ourselves:

Application.Value("Name") = APPLICATION_NAME
Application.Value("Activation") = COMAdminActivationInproc 'Library Activation
Application.Value("ShutdownAfter") = 0 'Shut down immediatley
Application.Value("3GigSupportEnabled") = True 'Enable 3 gig support

'Write changes to the database:
colApp.SaveChanges
```

If you now want to add the Currency component to Trading Systems, you execute the code in Listing 6.4 (this code continues from the prior section).

Listing 6.4 **Adding a Component Programmatically to the Catalog**

```
'Install the Currency component using the catalog object.

'The code below installs a COM component in the Catalog under the
'specified application.  COM+ will read the type library of the DLL
'to determine the necessary registry entries.

'Note that the final two arguments for the line of code below, are for
'the type library and the proxy DLL.  Pass nothing as the third
'argument if the type library is embedded in the DLL (normal) and nothing
'in the fourth argument unless the component needs a special proxy DLL
'(highly unlikely, and impossible if the component is written in VB).

'Note that this code does not check for a pre-existing component of the
'same name.  Attempting to install an already configured component
'results in an internal error (COMADMIN_E_OBJECTERRORS).  See the source
'code accompanying the book for a more complete example.

Catalog.InstallComponent Application.Key, COMPONENT_LOCATION, "", ""
```

```
'Obtain the component from the component collection so we can
'modify its settings:

Set colComp = colApp.GetCollection("Components",
                                    Application.Key)
colComp.Populate

For Each Component In colComp
    if Component.Value("ProgID") = COMPONENT_PROGID Then Exit For
Next

'Did we find our component?
If Component Is Nothing Then
    'component was not found, report the error
    MsgBox "Error: Component was not found."
Else
    'component was found, modify some of its settings:
    Component.Value("JustInTimeActivation") = False 'Just in time activation off
    Component.Value("MustRunInClientContext") = False 'Run outside client's context
    colComp.SaveChanges
End If
```

Some of the code might seem a little indirect, but it is simple enough. After you become familiar with the basic collection-to-object flow, any task involving the administrative objects becomes routine. You can, of course, programmatically configure properties of the newly installed application or components as well. By way of example, the code in Listing 6.5 programmatically shuts down a COM+ application, changes the account identity it runs under (see Chapter 12 for details regarding server identity), and restarts the application. Error checking is omitted for brevity.

Listing 6.5 **Shutting Down a COM+ Application, Changing Its Identity, and Restarting It Programmatically**

```
'This code stops the specified application, configures it
'such that it runs under the specified account, and then
'restarts it.

'This code does not perform error checking.  For example, if
'the account password specified is incorrect a
'COMADMIN_E_USERPASSWDNOTVALID error will be raised. See the
'source code accompanying the book for a more complete example.

Const APPLICATION_NAME = "Trading System"
Const APPLICATION_ACCOUNT = "SomeAccount"
Const ACCOUNT_PASSWORD = "AccountPassword"

Dim Catalog As New COMAdminCatalog
Dim Application As COMAdminCatalogObject
Dim colApp As COMAdminCatalogCollection
```

continues

Listing 6.5 **Continued**

```
'Shut down the application if it is running:
Catalog.ShutdownApplication APPLICATION_NAME

'obtain the Application collection from the Catalog:
Set colApp = Catalog.GetCollection("Applications")

'Search for the specified application:
colApp.Populate
For Each Application In colApp
    If Application.Value("Name") = APPLICATION_NAME Then Exit For
Next

'Did we find our Application?
If Application Is Nothing Then
    MsgBox "The application is not in the Catalog. "
    End
End If

'Change the identity application runs under:
Application.Value("Identity") = APPLICATION_ACCOUNT
Application.Value("Password") = ACCOUNT_PASSWORD
colApp.SaveChanges

'Restart the application
Catalog.StartApplication APPLICATION_NAME
```

A Quick Tour: Pre-Installed COM+ Applications

When you first run Component Services on Windows 2000, you find a number of pre-installed COM+ applications. These applications contain one or many components, some of which seem mysteriously named and do not appear to be documented. Although these components may be thought of as "plumbing," understanding the purpose of these components can be helpful in constructing a "big picture" understanding of how COM+ provides its services.

If your present interest in applied COM+ drastically outweighs your interest in its plumbing, the remainder of this chapter may be skipped (perhaps you might return to it later), and you can begin reading about COM+ contexts in Chapter 7.

COM+ QC Dead Letter Queue Listener

This application group consists of one COM+ system component, `QC.DLQListener`. As you'll see in Chapter 10, when queued components are in use, it is understood that the client who sends an asynchronous message does not run at the same time as the server who ultimately receives it. Therefore, there are circumstances when a message might never be received. `DLQListener` is involved in the tracking of such dead messages—that is, those that fail to arrive at a destination. `DLQListener` is an internal system object, and it does not support any interfaces that would make it useful to your clients.

COM+ Utilities

COM+ utilities consists of system components that are involved in queuing, events, and transactions. Specifically, this application group contains the following:

- QC.ListenerHelper.1. Used on the server side to create and feed messages to a queueable server object. It works hand-in-hand with a coclass called QC.Player, but we talk more about these in Chapter 10. You do not explicitly create objects of this type.

- QC.Recorder.1. Used on the client side to record method calls of a client object to a queueable object. These calls are later replayed for a newly instantiated server object with the help of the ListenerHelper. You do not explicitly create objects of this type.

- RemoteHelper.RemoteHelper. Completely undocumented at the time of this writing. Some sleuthing, however, indicates that it is most likely used by the system to facilitate the COM+ security; see the book's companion source code for more information (www.newriders.com/complus). You do not explicitly create objects of this type.

- TxCTx.TransactionContext. An object of this type is created by a client EXE when it instantiates transactional objects and wants to vote on the outcome of a transaction. As you see in Chapter 8, an EXE itself does not, on its own, have the capability to vote with objects it creates to determine the outcome of a transaction they all share. Chapter 8 demonstrates how objects of this type can be created and used in your applications.

   TxCTx.TransactionContextEx: A more comprehensive version of the previous object. Basically, it supports a more C++-friendly interface—nothing to write home about.

IIS In-Process Applications and IIS Out-Of-Process Pooled Applications

COM+ is frequently described as a merging of COM and MTS. Actually, Microsoft's Web server product Internet Information Server (IIS) and MTS entered into a symbiosis much earlier in IIS 4.0. You could not install IIS 4.0 without getting MTS in the bargain.

With IIS 3.0, Microsoft introduced Active Server Pages (ASP). These were HTML pages laced with VBScript so that when the client browser requested a page, IIS ran the ASP page. This meant that all the VBScript on the page was run, and through the use of an IIS-provided COM object called response, the VBScript dynamically injected HTML into its host page. See Listing 6.6 for a simple example.

Listing 6.6   **A Simple ASP Example**

```
<html>
<body>
<p> This is simple ASP Page</p>

<%
'NOTE: the '<%' tag denotes script that will be processed
'by IIS.  Response.write can be used to produce
'ordinary html that will be injected in to the resulting
'HTML page that is handed back to the client browser

   response.write("<b> The date is " & _
           CStr(Date) & "</b>"
%>

</body>
</html>
```

IIS merged with MTS in version 4.0. The merger made sense—the only way the VBScript in an ASP page could reach out to the outside world was through COM objects. And MTS was, basically, a value-added COM surrogate that could provide for better performance and allow different objects to cooperate in distributed transactions.

IIS also had its own suite of components that could benefit from running inside MTS. One component specifically was, and still is, called the *Web Applications Manager* (WAM). The purpose of WAM was to protect IIS's process (INETINFO.EXE) from in-process entities (called ISAPI DLLs) that could, if they failed, bring the entire Web server down.

The WAM itself is a COM component, and as such, it ran in MTS. Now, it runs in COM+, and you find two different incarnations of it in the following two COM+ applications:

- `IISWAM.OutofProcessPool`. This WAM manages DLLs that are pooled together in a process outside of IIS's processes.

- `IISWAM.W3SVC`. This is the WAM that wraps DLLs that are brought into the IIS process. This component is owned and operated by IIS.

Incidentally, if you look at the application settings for `W3SVC`, you might notice that the application is configured to be a library application. This means that all components in that application (mainly `IISWAM.W3SVC`) run in the process space of its caller. `OutofProcessPool`, however, is configured as a server application, which means it always runs in a process separate from the caller.

To see that this is true, right-click on Out-Of-Process Pooled Applications and select Properties. Then click the Activation tab (see Figure 6.12).

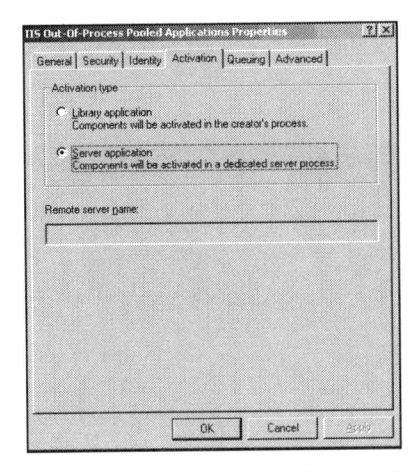

Figure 6.12 IIS Out-Of-Process Applications Properties.

If you look at the application properties for IIS In-Process Applications, you might notice that the radio button reads Library Application. These settings make sense if you remember that, as described previously, W3SVC handles IIS in-process scenarios (IIS being the client), and OutofProcessPool handles the out-of-process ones.

IIS Utilities

With the introduction of IIS 4.0, different ASP pages that modified data could now share in the same transaction. Simply put, different ASP pages that used Active X Data Objects (ADO) (or some other ODBC-supporting data access technology) to modify one or many databases could cooperate in a single distributed transaction. Practically, this meant that if any ASP page reported an error, data modifications would be rolled back for all ASP pages. To do this, an ASP page creates one of four IIS objects depending on how it wants to participate in a transaction. It is early yet to discuss this in detail; we cover the specifics in Chapter 8. For completeness, the objects are as follows:

- ASP.ObjectContextTxNotSupported
- ASP.ObjectContextTxRequired
- ASP.ObjectContextTxRequiresNew
- ASP.ObjectContextTxSupported

You do not create these objects explicitly. They are created implicitly when you put a @Transaction= tag in the beginning of your ASP page. You learn more about this in Chapter 8.

System Application

The following components are used by COM+ to facilitate certain services and the management of the COM+ Catalog:

- `Catsrv.CatalogServer.1`. This is the component that makes changes to the COM+ Catalog. Any higher-level administrative tool—for example, the COM+ Component Services snap-in or the COM+ Administrative Objects—ultimately must go through this component to make changes to the catalog.
- `COMSVCS.TrackerServer`. This component is completely undocumented at the time of this writing; however, some investigating into its Registry settings reveals a self-description of COM+ Instance Tracking Component. What's more, lack of documentation aside, an object of this type can be instantiated and used to iterate through running instances of applications, and a variety of performance-oriented statistical data can be obtained. See the following sidebar, "Using *TrackerServer*," for a code example of this component in use.

Using TrackerServer

The following code demonstrates how the `IGetAppData` interface of `TrackerServer` can be used to iterate through and obtain information about running COM+ applications.

```
// Demonstration of IGetAppData, contained in the TrackerServer coclass.
// Note that these interfaces are undocumented by Microsoft and
// subject to change.

#include <windows.h>
#include <iostream.h>
#include <Rpcdce.h>

// We have to #import comsvcs.dll because comcvcs.h does not
// contain the interface declerations for IGetAppData.

// To look at the methods of these functions, you have
// to use a utility like OLEView to examine the type library
// embedded inside comsvcs.dll:

#import "comsvcs.dll" no_namespace named_guids


int main() {

HRESULT         hr;
IGetAppData*    pGetAppData;
ULONG           nApps;
ULONG           nCLSIDs;

// The following structs are defined in the embedded type
// library, and are used with IGetAppData's methods:

appData*        pAppData;
CLSIDDATA*      nCLSDATA;
```

```cpp
// Initialize the COM Library:
CoInitialize(NULL);

// Get an interface pointer for IGetAppData:
hr = CoCreateInstance(
        CLSID_TrackerServer,
        NULL,
        CLSCTX_ALL,
        IID_IGetAppData,
        (void**)&pGetAppData);


if (hr!=S_OK)
{

    // There was a problem getting IGetAppData:
    cout << "Problem obtaining IGetAppData processing"
            "component." << endl;
    return 1;
}

// If you look at the IDL generated by the type library, you
// will see that IGetAppData has 4 methods.  There is no
// documentation, so the purpose of these methods must be determined
// empirically.  Looking at the data structures these methods
// return is a good place to start. The interface decleration
// has been extraced from the type-library and is provided below:

/*

interface IGetAppData : IUnknown {

    HRESULT _stdcall SetPushRate([in] unsigned long dwPushRate);

    // Enumerates all the currently running
    // COM+ applications on the system:

    HRESULT _stdcall GetApps(
                    [out] unsigned long* nApps,
                    [out] appData** aAppData);

    // Returns Information on all the components
    // of a COM+ application. Some of this information
    // can be be found using the COM Admin objects (whether
    // a component is queued or not), others, can only be
    // obtained through this interface (# of live references
    // to the object, calls completed etc):

    HRESULT _stdcall GetAppData(
                    [in] unsigned long idApp,
                    [out] unsigned long* nCLSIDs,
                    [out] CLSIDDATA** aAppData);
```

continues

186   Chapter 6   The COM+ Catalog

```
continued Same as GetAppData, except it doesn't return ALL
    // the components in a COM+ application, just the
    // one specified by the GUID given:

    HRESULT _stdcall GetCLSIDData(
                    [in] unsigned long idApp,
                    [in] GUID clsid,
                    [out] CLSIDDATA** ppAppData);

        HRESULT _stdcall Shutdown();

};
*/


// Get all the running COM+ applications:
pGetAppData->GetApps(&nApps,
                    &pAppData);

cout << "Number of COM+ Applications currently running: "
    << nApps << endl << endl;

// Iterate through each running application, print some information,
// and also get information about running components:

for (int k=0; k < nApps; k++)
{
    cout << "Application #: " << k+1 << endl << endl;
    cout << "    Process ID: " << pAppData[k].m_dwAppProcessId << endl;
    cout << "    AppGUID: ";

    // Print out the Application GUID:
    for (int n=0; n<39;n++)
        cout << (char)pAppData[k].m_szAppGuid[n];
        cout << endl;

    cout << "    Total times Called: "
            <<pAppData[k].m_AppStatistics.m_cTotalCalls
            << endl;
    cout << "    Total Classes:       "
            <<pAppData[k].m_AppStatistics.m_cTotalClasses
            << endl;
    cout << "    Total Instances:    "
            <<pAppData[k].m_AppStatistics.m_cTotalInstances << endl;

    cout << "    Calls per second:   "
            << pAppData[k].m_AppStatistics.m_cCallsPerSecond << endl << endl;
    // Get information on running components within the application:
    pGetAppData->GetAppData(pAppData[k].m_idApp,
                    &nCLSIDs,
                    &nCLSDATA);
```

```
        cout << "Number of Components in the Application running: "
            << nCLSIDs << endl << endl;

        // Print out information on each of the running components:
        for (unsigned int i=0; i < nCLSIDs; i++)
        {

            // We use the bstr class to make printing of
            // the progID simpler:

            _bstr_t sComponentName;
            OLECHAR *pProgID;
            ProgIDFromCLSID(nCLSDATA[i].m_clsid,&pProgID);
            sComponentName= pProgID;

            cout << "Component #" << i << ": " << sComponentName
                << ": CallsCompleted: " << nCLSDATA[i].m_cCallsCompleted
                << ", CallsFailed: " << nCLSDATA[i].m_cCallsFailed << endl;

            ::CoTaskMemFree(pProgID);

        }
        cout << endl << endl;
}

}
```

The output is similar to what is seen below:

Number of COM+ Applications currently running: 2

Application #: 1

    Process ID: 2400
    AppGUID: {02D4B3F1-FD88-11D1-960D-00805FC79235}
    Total times Called: 0
    Total Classes: 1
    Total Instances: 5
    Calls per second: 0

Number of Components in the Application running: 1
Component #0: COMSVCS.TrackerServer: CallsCompleted: 6, CallsFailed: 0

Application #: 2

    Process ID: 2448
    AppGUID: {E0A989B7-277F-4461-8067-17782524607F}
    Total times Called: 0
    Total Classes: 0
    Total Instances: 0
    Calls per second: 0

Number of Components in the Application running: 0

188 Chapter 6 The COM+ Catalog

- `EventPublisher.EventPublisher.1.` This is the COM+ Event Notification Server and is used in conjunction with the COM+ Event Service to broadcast events to interested subscribers.

- `Mts.Mtsgrp.1.` As its name implies, this heralds the days of MTS. It was used to enumerate through running MTS packages. In COM+ terminology, packages are now known as applications. An object of this type enumerates through running applications. Information can be gathered about each application, although not as much as can be gleaned from an instance of `TrackerServer` (described in a previous bullet). See the following sidebar, "Using *Mtsgrp*," for an example of how this component may be used.

Using Mtsgrp

The following code demonstrates how the `Mtsgrp` may be used to obtain information about currently running applications (specifically, this application will list all applications currently running):

```
#include "iostream.h"
#include "comdef.h"
#include "comsvcs.h"

int main(int argc, char* argv[])
{

IMtsGrp *pIMtsGrp;
IMtsEvents *pIMtsEvents;
IUnknown *pIUnknown;

LONG nApps;
HRESULT hr;
CLSID CLSID_MtsGrp;
_bstr_t bstrMtsGrpProgID("Mts.MtsGrp.1");

// Initalize the COM Library:
CoInitialize(0);

// Obtain the MtsGrp CLSID:

CLSIDFromProgID( bstrMtsGrpProgID, &CLSID_MtsGrp);

// Obtain an IMtsGrp interface pointer. Error
// checking has been omitted for brevity. Consult
// the book's source code for a complete example.
```

```cpp
CoCreateInstance(CLSID_MtsGrp,
                 0,
                 CLSCTX_ALL,
                 IID_IMtsGrp,
                 (void**)&pIMtsGrp);

// Determine the number of applications running,
// and cycle through them, printing out their names:

pIMtsGrp->get_Count(&nApps);
cout << "Number of applications running is: " << nApps <<endl;

for(int i=0; i < nApps; i++)
{

    pIMtsGrp->Item(i,&pIUnknown);

    hr=pIUnknown->QueryInterface(IID_IMtsEvents,
                                 (void**)&pIMtsEvents);

    if(hr!=S_OK)
    {
        cout<< "Did not support IMtsEvents."<<endl;
    }
    else
    {
        // Determine the Application name:
        BSTR bstrAppName;
        pIMtsEvents->get_PackageName( &bstrAppName);
        _bstr_t bstrHelper(bstrAppName, FALSE);

        cout<< "Application: " << i+1 << " is named "
            << bstrHelper << endl;
        pIMtsEvents->Release();
    }
    pIUnknown->Release();
}

pIMtsGrp->Release();
CoUninitialize();

return 0;
}
```

Visual Studio APE Package

Application Performance Explorer (APE) was written originally for MTS. It is written entirely in Visual Basic and ships with Visual Studio 6.0. It may or may not be installed on your machine, depending on the options you chose during the setup routine. It is a template application that simulates a real application by moving money around to different accounts in one or many databases. Its behavior can be changed by UI tools to play what-if scenarios and test the impact of different architectures. It is not a core part of COM+ and need never be used; it is an external application, useful perhaps, but in no way necessary or required. You can find out more about the APE in MSDN.

CRCs: A Snooper's Best Friend

An unimportant, though perhaps revealing, question remains—where exactly does COM+ keep its catalog information? Although it is not documented anywhere (and it relies on some roundabout techniques to prove it), the evidence suggests that COM+ keeps its catalog information in the \%winroot%\Registration directory.

There are two ways to prove this, but first let's briefly go over what exactly a Cyclical Redundancy Check (CRC) is—it will inevitably benefit you at some point in your development career. CRC is a common technique for detecting data transmission errors. It examines a file and based on a certain algorithm, provides you with a 16- or 32-bit signature of that file. If you send a file to a friend over email, he can perform a CRC check on the file to determine if he received it correctly. If the CRC he computes matches yours, he can say with reasonable certainty that his file is the same as yours. (Two different files can have the same CRC, but this is a remote possibility—especially for 32-bit CRCs.) In fact, several compression utilities do this implicitly to ensure that what was compressed is what is uncompressed.

Now, back to our investigation of the COM+ Catalog. If you look in the \%winroot%\Registration directory, you should see something like the following:

```
R000000000155.clb        24,100
R000000000156.clb        24,100
{02D4B3F1-FD88-11D1-960D-00805FC79235}.crmlog    1,048,576
```

To prove that this is where COM+ Catalog information is stored, perform a CRC on these files (several CRC/CRC32 utilities can be downloaded from various freeware and shareware sites). If you perform the check several times in succession, you should note that the CRC values stay constant (the file contents are not changing). Now use the snap-in and do something (such as, add a component, change a property). Return to this directory and perform the CRC check again. You should observe that the CRCs of some files are different (their contents have changed). From this little exercise, can you conclude that this is where COM+ Catalog information is stored? You be the judge.

Try one more thing. If you have a copy of Visual Basic, run the following code (add the COM+ administrative components as reference):

```
Dim catalog As New COMAdminCatalog 'reference to the Catalog Database

catalog.BackupREGDB "test.dat"
```

According to the MSDN, the `BackupRegDB` method, "Backs up the COM+ class registration database (RegDB) to a specified file." If you now run a CRC on `test.dat` and compare it to one of the clb files in the \systemroot\Registration directory, you should observe their CRCs are the same (they are the same file!). Once again, draw your own conclusions as to what this might mean.

Employing a more sophisticated tracking mechanism (such as using some type of file monitoring utility) explicitly shows that COM+ does in fact keep its catalog information here.

Summary

Ordinary COM components that pre-date COM+ can be used by COM+ objects and ordinary executables. To take advantage of COM+ services, however, a component must be configured. This involves either installing or importing the component using the COM Application Install Wizard; installing is the preferred option.

A configured object must exist in a COM+ application that you create. Both applications and components have various properties that can be set using the Component Services snap-in. Alternatively, the COM+ administration objects can be used by your applications to accomplish the same result programmatically.

Property settings for applications, components, interfaces, and methods are hierarchical in nature—configuration changes made to an application affect components in that application, changes to components affect interfaces, and so on.

7

Contexts

IN THE SUMMER OF 1996, MY MSDN supplement came to my office as it always did—via UPS in a little brown box. I opened the box, and there was a little red CD-ROM labeled Microsoft Transaction Server (MTS) 1.0.

I, along with my peers, had heard about MTS (code named Viper). We knew it would somehow, magically, enable COM objects to share in transactions, but we weren't sure what that meant. The basic idea was that a number of related objects could manipulate a database, but if any one of the objects encountered a problem it could shout "Abort!" Then the database modifications for all the objects would be undone. But how could this be?

By design, COM objects do not know anything about the objects that created them and do not transfer any information to the objects they create (aside from Remote Procedure Call [RPC]-based security information), except for what is explicitly communicated through interface methods. MTS promised that developers could write objects without any *a priori* knowledge of other objects, and only very minor changes were needed to allow any number of objects to share in a single transaction.

In this chapter, I show you exactly how objects can share—not only in transactions, but in other regards as well. It all has to do with a mechanism that originated in MTS: the context. The first stop on the road to understanding contexts is to return to the days of MTS and take a look at the role of a new interface that this value-added surrogate introduced: `IObjectContext`.

Introducing *IObjectContext*

In the days of MTS, Object A could create Object B who could create C and so on. All could manipulate one or more databases, but if any of the objects reported a problem, all changes would be rolled back for all objects in each database.

This brings us to the first significant modification to traditional COM programming—MTS required that objects participating in transactions should vote on the success or failure of their database operations.

They did this in two parts. The first part involved an object requesting and getting an interface to a special object called the *context object* from MTS. Every object would have access to its own context object, and when obtained, each object participating in a transaction would call special voting methods on it to state whether the object's database modification (insert, delete or update) was successful. In VC++, they would do this by requesting a special interface called `IObjectContext` via a method called `CoGetObjectContext()`. In VB, the developer would call the method `GetObjectContext` which would return a `ContextObject` object.

As we discussed in Chapter 1 "Com +: An Evolution," VB tends to treat interfaces as if they were objects. The `ObjectContext` object is really the `IObjectContext` interface, and this interface was only available to objects running in MTS. It has eight methods, and I'll describe the purpose of each one. Note that the first three methods I list are informational in that they retrieve information from an object's context and make it available to the object. The next four methods have to do with voting on the outcomes of transactions, and the final method has to do with something called *context flow*. Context flow enables information to pass from the creating object to the created.

The informational methods are as follows:

- `IsCallerInRole`: This method is used to facilitate COM+ security and is discussed in detail in Chapter 12, "Security." An object calls this method to test whether the identity of the current caller (by identity, I mean the NT account of the client making the call) is in a particular role (passed in as a string, for example "Managers").

- `IsInTransaction`: Returns a simple Boolean indicating whether the object is currently involved in a transaction or not. As we learn in Chapter 8, "Transactions," a component may be set such that it can participate in a transaction should its parent be participating in one; however, it can also operate without inheriting a transaction from its parent. In situations where an object absolutely must participate in a transaction (even if a system administrator declares it otherwise by manipulating the component's settings in Component Services) the object author can use this method to determine whether a transaction is present. If a transaction isn't present, the object author can prevent the object from performing a modification. The following code snippet demonstrates how this is done:

```
If Not GetObjectContext.IsInTransaction Then
        ' I'm not in a transaction - raise an error
End If
```

- `IsSecurityEnabled`: As we will see in Chapter 12, COM+ security may be turned off depending on how the component's properties are set. This method returns a Boolean indicating whether security is on or off. Because it is too easy for a systems administrator (or, perhaps a malicious intruder) to turn security off for a component via Component Services, I have seen this method used by security-minded developers who want to make sure that their component will never operate unless security is turned on.

```
if Not GetObjectContext.IsSecurityEnabled Then
    'Role based security is NOT being used,
    'so raise a permission denied error.
    Err.Raise 70
End If
```

The Distributed Transaction Voting methods are as follows:

- `SetAbort()`: As we see in Chapter 8, an object calls this method when it wishes to set flags in its context to indicate that it failed while performing database modification or is otherwise unhappy with the transaction it is involved in. These context flags (called the Happy and Done bit as we see in the next chapter) tell COM+ whether to commit or abort the transaction. If this method is called, the Happy bit will be set to 0 and the transaction will be aborted.

- `SetComplete()`: Same as `SetAbort()`, except this method will set the context flags to indicate that the object successfully completed database modification.

The Lifetime methods are as follows:

- `DisableCommit`: An object in a transaction should call this method if it performs a database modification and is unhappy with the result, but wishes to remain alive in hopes that a subsequent method call will make the object Happy. This method and its sister method, `EnableCommit()`, are used to temporarily keep COM+'s rather zealous object deactivation policies at bay. We discuss these two methods in depth in Chapter 8 when we discuss object statefulness, Just-In-Time Activation (JITA), and object lifetime. For now, it is enough to know that `DisableCommit()` sets flags in the object's context so that the object will remain alive between method calls. However, if ultimately forced to deactivate, it will cause the distributed transaction it is involved in to abort.

- `EnableCommit`: This method works identically to `DisableCommit` (it keeps the calling object alive between method calls); however, when an object that calls this method is forced to deactivate, its vote will be interpreted as a "yes." In other words, the distributed transaction has the possibility of succeeding and being committed provided other objects participating in the transaction also vote positively.

The Context Flow method is as follows:

- `CreateInstance( )`: This method is used to create a new instance of an object. It works in a fashion identical to `CreateObject()` and can, in fact, be used wherever `CreateObject()` is used in a configured object. The difference is,

`CreateInstance()` passes on context information from the caller to the created object, whereas `CreateObject()` does not.

As discussed in the previous bullet points, an object participating in a transaction can call `SetAbort()` or `SetComplete()` to indicate the success or failure of its modifications. We will explore this process in-depth in Chapter 8. For now, the most interesting function is `CreateInstance()`. An object can use this method to create another object, but unlike the standard COM creation mechanisms (`CoCreateInstance` or VB and Java's `New`), this method allows the context to flow from the creator to the created. In other words, information kept in the context of the creator (such as the transaction it is involved in) can be passed, or flow, to the created object so that it too can participate in the transaction.

The `CreateInstance()` method of `IObjectContext` is no longer necessary in COM+, but in the MTS days it was critical. Unlike in traditional COM, if you want a transaction to flow from MTS Object A to an MTS object it creates—for example, B—you cannot use VB's `New` or `CreateObject()` methods, nor can you use VC++'s `CoCreateInstance()`. Instead, A must get its `ObjectContext` and must use its `CreateInstance()` method to create B.

Note that the following code is specific to MTS programming prior to the introduction of COM+. COM+ does not require the use of `IObjectContext->CreateInstance` to allow context to flow.

For VB, instead of using the following code:

```
Dim myB as B
set myB=CreateObject("SomeObject.B")
```

you can use this:

```
set myB=GetObjectContext.CreateInstance("SomeObject.B")
```

For VC++ (Microft's Visual C++), instead of using the following:

```
IB * pB;
CoCreateInstance(CLSID_B,0,CLSCTX_ALL,IID_IB, (void**)&pB);
```

you can use this:

```
IObjectContext * pIObjectContext;

CoGetObjectContext(IID_IObjectContext, (void**)&pIObjectContext);
pIObjectContext->CreateInstance(CLSID_B,IID_IB, (void**)&pB);
```

So, if an Object A creates another Object B using the `IObjectContext->CreateInstance()`, MTS has the opportunity to get involved. In fact, in these early, pre-COM+ days, you could consider the `IObjectContext` interface as an interface that MTS supported and made available to your objects. Certainly then, by calling the `CreateInstance()` of this MTS interface, A is really asking MTS itself to create the instance of B on its behalf. Therefore, if A is participating in a transaction, and A asks MTS to create B, MTS can bring B into the transaction as well. Again, the transaction can be said to flow from A to B, courtesy of MTS. This is shown in Figure 7.1.

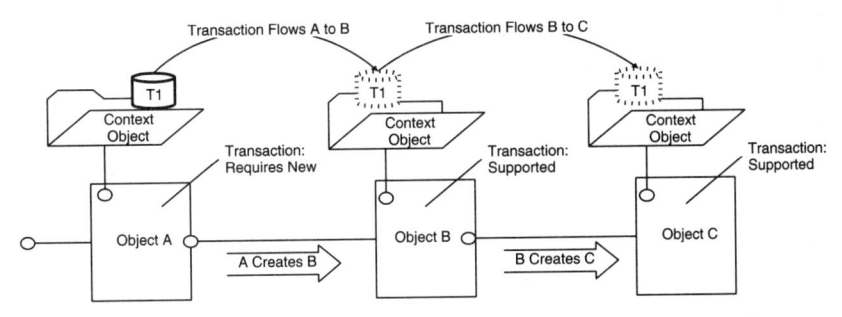

Figure 7.1 Transactions can flow from creator to created via contexts.

Prior to COM+, context was only available to MTS objects. If non-MTS objects asked for a context, COM refused them. Furthermore, if an Object A running in MTS created B without going through the context, the transaction failed to flow from A to B, and the objects did not share in the transaction.

COM and MTS Integration

Originally, COM and MTS were two separate things:

- MTS was only a value-added surrogate for COM objects.
- COM was a base level of service, and MTS provided the value-added benefit of allowing objects to cooperate by providing contexts that could allow attributes (transactions) to flow from creator to the created.

As a surrogate, however, MTS was never truly part of COM. To function in MTS and be able to work with contexts, an object needed to be associated with MTS. Because the COM creation mechanisms were well-defined and unalterable, a slight-of-hand had to be employed; a non-MTS COM object would list its Dynamic Link Library (DLL) name in the Registry like that shown in Figure 7.2.

Non-graphically, the registry entries are:

```
Registry Key:HKEY_CLASSES_ROOT\CLSID\{ 638094E0-758F-11d1-8366-0000E83B6EF3}\
➥InprocServer32\
Value for Above Key:
C:\components\comcalc.dll
```

If this same object was brought into MTS, MTS changed the key's value to something like the following:

```
C:\WINNT\System32\mtx.exe /p:{ 638094E0-758F-11d1-8366-0000E83B6EF3 }
```

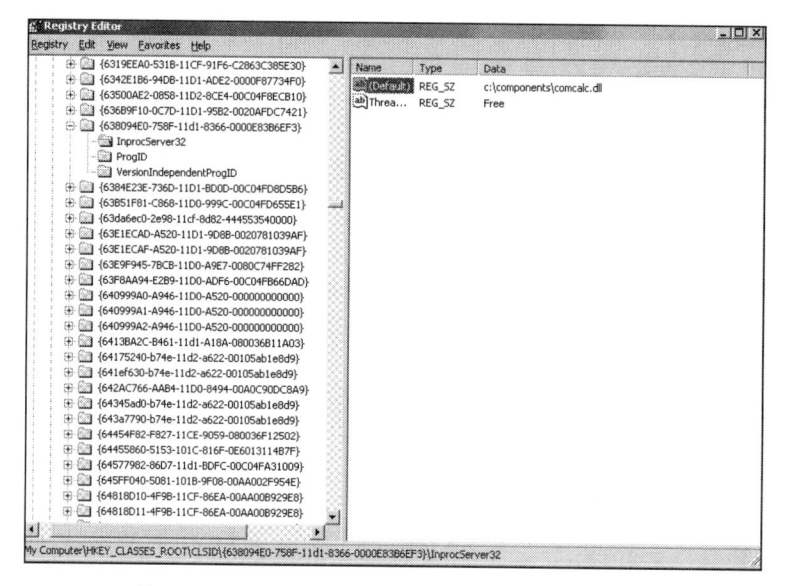

Figure 7.2 A typical registry entry for a COM DLL.

Clearly, the authors of MTS were not much more privileged in what they were trying to do than COM surrogate developers outside of Microsoft; they clearly weren't allowed to make any changes to COM's internal mechanisms. The mechanics of COM are separate and immutable to MTS—COM knows nothing about MTS; it simply creates objects according to COM's rules. By surreptitiously modifying the Registry settings to include the MTS surrogate (MTX.EXE), MTS fools COM into creating another instance of the MTX.EXE server (or further utilizing an already running instance of MTX.EXE), which knows what real object to create based on a command-line argument. MTS's approach to COM is very much like a virus's approach to a cell—both entities hijack existing mechanisms of their host and redirect them to other purposes without knowledge of the host.

COM and MTS Merge

As of Windows 2000, MTS is no more. But its spirit lives on in COM+. The two development teams were merged at Microsoft, the wall came crumbling down, and an era of cooperation between two formally separate kingdoms ensued. It was no longer necessary to use `IObjectContext`'s `CreateInstance()` method to create objects; any ordinary COM creation mechanism would do.

In-process components that you might have already written in your pre-COM+ days can still function in COM+ without modification. And although these *unconfigured components* might need some slight modification to take advantage of the full range of COM+ services (for example, voting on the outcome of a transaction), they can still participate in most of what COM+ offers after they are configured by a system administrator or developer.

It is important to note that unconfigured components (that is, those COM DLLs that have not been brought into COM+), do not have their own contexts. Instead, they are brought into the context of their creator (threading model compatibility permitting). If their creator is a standard EXE (which always lacks a context), an unconfigured object (that is, an instantiated coclass from an unconfigured COM DLL) does not have one either. If, however, a configured object instantiates an unconfigured object, the latter dwells in the context of the former. Basically, unconfigured components are empty vessels without a context of their own.

Context: Two Different Definitions

Before we explore the mechanics of contexts in greater depth, it is important that we first define context. I fear that the term *context* is destined for the same ambiguous use as the terms *objects*, *servers*, *applications*, and *components*. So, I want to make my stand early—there is the concept of context, and then there is the implementation of context. We discuss implementation in the upcoming section "COM Context Implementation." For now, let's explore the concept of context.

Context: The Concept

In everyday language, the word "context" is used to describe the environment within which something occurs. Celebrities often complain that newspaper columnists print their quotes "out of context," implying that columnists change the meaning of their words by not taking into account the context in which they were said. It is fair then to say that context gives meaning to an action, COM+ would certainly agree.

If an object calls `GetObjectContext.SetAbort`, it means absolutely nothing unless the object is in the context of a transaction. To be "in" the context of a transaction means the object is associated or somehow "tied" to an actual, system-level distributed transaction (COM+ creates this transaction on the object's behalf as discussed in Chapter 8). The association between the object and the real transaction (call this transaction T1) is kept in the object's context object. In other words, the context of the object holds a reference to the transaction T1. Thus, a call to `SetAbort` means that the transaction T1 should be aborted.

Transactions and information about transactions are kept in an object's context. This information is in no way hidden from the object; on the contrary, an object can always query its context object to find out about its current environment. In the book's sample code (www.newriders.com/complus) you find a component called `ContextDemo`. Although `ContextDemo` is written in VC++ (it needs to manipulate Globally Unique Identifiers [GUIDs]), it can be used by both VB and VC++ components to find information about their current context. A listing of `ContextDemo`'s primary function, `ContextInformation()`, is shown in Listing 7.1.

200 Chapter 7 Contexts

Listing 7.1 *ContextDemo* Uses the *IObjectContext*, *IobjectContextInfo*, and *ITransaction* Interfaces to Find Information About the Host Object's Current Context

```
// Note: these two example are snippets of the ContextDemo
// component of the book's accompanying sample code

HRESULT CContextDiag::ContextInformation() {

// Demonstration of an object that determines information about
// its context using IObjectContext and IObjectContextInfo.

IObjectContext *pObjectContext;
IObjectContextInfo *pObjectContextInfo;

bool bIsInTransaction, bIsSecurityOn, bIsSyncronizationOn;
GUID contextGUID, transactionGUID, activityGUID;
char achSecurityString[3],achContextInfo[1024];
unsigned char *pContextGUIDString, *pTransactionGUIDString, *pActivityGUIDString;

HRESULT hr;
RPC_STATUS rpcstat;

// Obtain an IObjectContext interface pointer:

hr = GetObjectContext (&pObjectContext);
if (hr !=S_OK)
{
    // Could not get IObjectContext:
    sprintf(achContextInfo,"ContextInformation: Could not get IObjectContext");
    MessageBox(NULL,achContextInfo,"Context Information",MB_OK);
    return hr;
}

// Obtain an IObjectContextInfo interface pointer:

hr=pObjectContext->QueryInterface(IID_IObjectContextInfo,
                 (void**)&pObjectContextInfo);
if (hr !=S_OK)
{
    // Could not get IObjectContextInfo:
    sprintf(achContextInfo,"ContextInformation: Could not get
    ➥IObjectContextInfo");
    MessageBox(NULL,achContextInfo,"Context Information",MB_OK);
    return hr;
}

///////////////////////////////////////////////
// Obtain information about the object's context:
///////////////////////////////////////////////

// Obtain the Context GUID:
pObjectContextInfo->GetContextId(&contextGUID);
rpcstat = UuidToString(&contextGUID, &pContextGUIDString);
```

```
if (rpcstat !=RPC_S_OK)
{
    return E_FAIL;
}

// Obtain the Transaction GUID
bIsInTransaction = pObjectContext->IsInTransaction();

if (bIsInTransaction)
{
    pObjectContextInfo->GetTransactionId(&transactionGUID);
    rpcstat = UuidToString(&transactionGUID, &pTransactionGUIDString);
    if (rpcstat !=RPC_S_OK) return E_FAIL;
}
else
{
    pTransactionGUIDString = new unsigned char[4];
    sprintf((char*)pTransactionGUIDString,"N/A");
}

// Obtain the Activity GUID:
pObjectContextInfo->GetActivityId(&activityGUID);

// If GetActivity returns GUID_NULL, then the object does have
// synchronization protection on:
if (activityGUID==GUID_NULL)
{
    bIsSyncronizationOn=false;
    pActivityGUIDString = new unsigned char[4];
    sprintf((char*)pActivityGUIDString,"N/A");
}
else
{
    bIsSyncronizationOn=true;
    rpcstat = UuidToString(&activityGUID, &pActivityGUIDString);
    if (rpcstat !=RPC_S_OK) return E_FAIL;
}

// Determine if the object is using role based security:
bIsSecurityOn = pObjectContext->IsSecurityEnabled();
if (bIsSecurityOn)
    sprintf((char*)achSecurityString,"YES");
else
    sprintf((char*)achSecurityString,"NO");


// Display a message box with all the information we
// have garnered above.
sprintf(achContextInfo,"Context Information\n\nContextID: %s\nActivityID:"
        "%s\nTransactionID: %s\nRole based security on:%s",
        pContextGUIDString,pActivityGUIDString,
        pTransactionGUIDString,achSecurityString);
```

continues

Listing 7.1 **Continued**

```
MessageBox(NULL,achContextInfo,"Context Information",MB_OK);

//string deallocation code with delete [] and
//RpcStringFree() ommitted for brevity

return S_OK;

}
//The following function obtains more transactional information
//about an object. some code ommitted for brevity, see the book's
//companion source (www.newriders.com/complus) for the complete
//example.
HRESULT CContextDiag::TransactionInformation() {

// Demonstrates additional transaction information that can be
// obtained from an object's context. This is obtained through
// the ITransaction interface, which is obtained using
// IObjectContextInfo::GetTransactionInfo.

IObjectContext *pObjectContext;
IObjectContextInfo *pObjectContextInfo;
ITransaction *pTransaction;

bool bIsInTransaction;
char achTransactionInfo[1000];

HRESULT hr;
XACTTRANSINFO xTransInfo;

// Use the _bstr_t class to make our message
// parsing and displaying a little easier:
_bstr_t sTransInfo="";

// Obtain IObjectContext and IObjectContextInfo interface pointers:

hr = GetObjectContext (&pObjectContext);
if (hr !=S_OK)
{
    // Could not get IObjectContext:
    sprintf(achTransactionInfo,
        "TransactionInformaion: Could not get IObjectContext");
    MessageBox(NULL,achTransactionInfo,"Transaction Information",MB_OK);
    return hr;
}

hr=pObjectContext->QueryInterface(IID_IObjectContextInfo,
                            (void**)&pObjectContextInfo);
if (hr !=S_OK)
{
    // Could not get IObjectContextInfo:
```

```
        sprintf(achTransactionInfo,
                " TransactionInformaion: Could not get IObjectContextInfo");
        MessageBox(NULL,achTransactionInfo,"Transaction Information",MB_OK);
        return hr;
}

bIsInTransaction = pObjectContext->IsInTransaction();

if (!bIsInTransaction)
{
    // If the componenent is not participating in a transaction,
    // abort the method:

    sprintf(achTransactionInfo,"Error: this component is not"
            " partcipating in a transaction.");
    MessageBox(NULL,achTransactionInfo,"Transaction Information",MB_OK);
    return S_OK;

}

// We can get an ITransaction pointer from IContextInfo::GetTransaction.
// This interface pointer will give us additional information about the
// transaction the object is partcipating in:

pObjectContextInfo->GetTransaction(((IUnknown**)&pTransaction);

// GetTransactionInfo populates a XACTTRAMSINFO structure
// with additional information:

pTransaction->GetTransactionInfo(&xTransInfo);

// The XACTsTransInfo structure is given below. Most
// of the information is really only important
// when you are working with transactions on a very
// low level (working with the DTC etc):

/*

typedef struct XACTTRANSINFO {
    XACTUOW   uow;                          // The UNIT OF WORK associated with the trans
    ISOLEVEL  isoLevel;                     // Isolation information
    ULONG     isoFlags;                     // Always zero
    DWORD     grfTCSupported;               // Transaction Capabilties
    DWORD     grfRMSupported;               // Always zero
    DWORD     grfTCSupportedRetaining;      // Always zero
    DWORD     grfRMSupportedRetaining;      // Always zero
} XACTTRANSINFO;

*/

// The UNIT OF WORK field is just a byte array of length 16.
// This is really used for internal purposes, but we show it
```

continues

Listing 7.1 **Continued**

```
// here just for demonstration:

sTransInfo = "Transaction Information: \n\n";
sTransInfo += "Unit of Work: ";

for (int k=0; k<=15; k++) {
    char cUow[1];
    sprintf(cUow,"%x",xTransInfo.uow.rgb[k]);
    sTransInfo+= cUow;
}


// The isoLevel field indicates information about the
// transaction's isolation level.  Again, this type of information
// is generally of importance only to components interacting with
// transactions on a system-level (RMs):

sTransInfo +="\n\nIsolation Levels of the transaction: \n";


if (xTransInfo.isoLevel == ISOLATIONLEVEL_UNSPECIFIED)
    sTransInfo += "    ISOLATIONLEVEL_UNSPECIFIED\n";
else {
    if (xTransInfo.isoLevel & ISOLATIONLEVEL_CHAOS)
        sTransInfo +="    ISOLATIONLEVEL_CHAOS\n";

    if (xTransInfo.isoLevel & ISOLATIONLEVEL_READUNCOMMITTED)
        sTransInfo +="    ISOLATIONLEVEL_READUNCOMMITTED\n";

    if (xTransInfo.isoLevel & ISOLATIONLEVEL_BROWSE)
        sTransInfo +="    ISOLATIONLEVEL_BROWSE\n";

    if (xTransInfo.isoLevel & ISOLATIONLEVEL_CURSORSTABILITY)
        sTransInfo +="    ISOLATIONLEVEL_CURSORSTABILITY\n";

    if (xTransInfo.isoLevel & ISOLATIONLEVEL_READCOMMITTED)
        sTransInfo +="    ISOLATIONLEVEL_READCOMMITTED\n";

    if (xTransInfo.isoLevel & ISOLATIONLEVEL_REPEATABLEREAD)
        sTransInfo +="    ISOLATIONLEVEL_REPEATABLEREAD\n";

    if (xTransInfo.isoLevel & ISOLATIONLEVEL_SERIALIZABLE)
        sTransInfo +="    ISOLATIONLEVEL_SERIALIZABLE\n";

    if (xTransInfo.isoLevel & ISOLATIONLEVEL_ISOLATED)
        sTransInfo +="    ISOLATIONLEVEL_ISOLATED\n";
}

// The grfTCSupported field indicates that capabilities
// of the transaction associated with the component.
```

Context: Two Different Definitions 205

```
sTransInfo +="\nTransaction Capabilities: \n";
sTransInfo +="    Synchronous Committs allowed: ";

if ((xTransInfo.grfTCSupported & XACTTC_SYNC) || (xTransInfo.grfTCSupported &
➥XACTTC_SYNC_PHASEONE))
    sTransInfo += "YES\n";
else
    sTransInfo += "NO\n";

sTransInfo += "    Asynchronous Committs allowed: ";
if ( (xTransInfo.grfTCSupported & XACTTC_ASYNC) || (xTransInfo.grfTCSupported
    & XACTTC_ASYNC_PHASEONE))
    sTransInfo += "YES\n";
else
    sTransInfo += "NO\n";

// Display all the transaction information we have obtained:
MessageBox(NULL,sTransInfo,"Transaction Information",MB_OK);

return S_OK;
//Interface release code
}
```

When `ContextDemo` is unconfigured (that is, running as an ordinary COM component outside of COM+), it will automatically share the context of the COM+ object that calls it. This is the behavior of all unconfigured COM components and the behavior we want, so don't install this component into COM+ or it will cease to operate properly. So, in its unconfigured state, when a host object calls `ContextDemo`'s `ContextInfo()` method, `ContextDemo` will actually be investigating its host's context. It will query for information regarding the host's context, activity, transaction, and security configuration and display this information in one or two message boxes. See Figures 7.3 and 7.4 for examples of `ContextDemo`'s output.

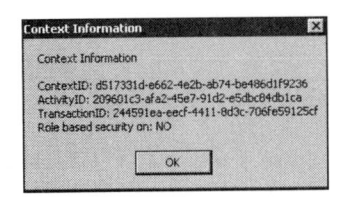

Figure 7.3 `ContextDemo` obtaining its Context Information.

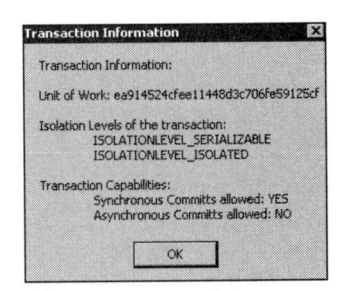

Figure 7.4 `ContextDemo` obtaining Transactional Information.

`ContextDemo` can be helpful in solidifying your understanding of contexts; try writing your own objects, configuring them in different ways, and calling upon `ContextDemo` to report on their differences. You might also try adding to `ContextDemo`, for example, to report on the current thread ID as well. This can help you understand the effect the threading model affiliations Apartment, Free, Both, and Neutral have. You will find that the behavior of calling and executing threads change (hopefully, as you expect) when the threading model of the component is changed. To determine the current thread ID, simply use the code:

```
DWORD dwThreadID=GetCurrentThreadId();
```

Let's return now to contexts and note that even though an object can reach outside of itself and interact with its context, it is not required to. In fact, some objects (and some object authors) are happiest when blissfully unaware of their context; it is perfectly acceptable to write an ordinary COM component that does not use `IObjectContext` (or any other context-oriented interface) in any way. However, even though an object might not interact with its context explicitly, a context is still critical; as with transactions, there are other COM+ services that must put information in an object's context in order for the object to participate in that service. COM+ synchronization is a good example of this. An object that is configured as requiring synchronization services (discussed in more detail in Appendix B, "COM+ Synchronization Through Activities") will end up participating in something called an "activity." Information about this activity is stored in the object's context. Although the object may not "know" that it is in an activity or be explicitly written to take advantage of the fact, activity information in its context is always available and readable to COM+. Thus, when this object interacts with another object, COM+ will know by reading the context that it needs to protect this object from concurrent access.

A context is rather like a transparent bucket attached to each object—one that can hold information about transactions, activities, and any other information that links an object with one or more COM+ services. These buckets follow the object around throughout its life. They are transparent so that COM+ can see inside, and just as one bucket may be tipped so that its contents may flow to another bucket, so too can COM+ contexts flow. Specifically, when Object A creates another object (Object B), the bucket of the first object is tipped such that its contents (the transaction it is involved in, the activity is involved in, etc.) can flow from creator to created. Thus, if Object A participates in a transaction, Object B inherits that transaction and participates in it as well. And so, if either object calls `GetObjectContext.SetAbort()`, data modifications for both objects are aborted.

In the last paragraph, the interaction between Object A and Object B is based on a simplifying assumption: that Object A and Object B are completely compatible and both are interested in transactions. Suppose this is not the case. Imagine that Object A participates in a transaction, but Object B performs no database modifications and wants nothing to do with transactions. In this case, the transactional attributes should not flow because the contexts of the objects are incompatible, as far as transactions are concerned. But why are these objects incompatible, and how did they get that way?

When you configure your components (set its transactional properties, request synchronization services, and so on), you give your object a context—that is, you describe a world that your component expects to live in. It is COM+'s responsibility to ensure that it sees the world as you have defined it. At present, there are a fixed number of context-influencing attributes, although in the future, developers might be able to create their own.

Let's move on now, and discuss contexts and context flow in a little more detail.

COM Context Implementation

Contexts are created when an object is instantiated; that is, when `CoCreateInstance()` or Visual Basic's `New` is invoked and a new instance of a component is brought into being.

If the object creator is a configured component, then it will have a context, and COM+ will seek to make its contextual information flow from creator to created. But exactly what information is it that flows? And suppose information existing in the context of the creator is not relevant to the created object? Addressing the first question will give us insight into the second, how incompatibilities in context are handled.

As I discuss in the previous paragraph, the attributes you set in Component Services will effect what information exist in an object's context. It should not surprise you then, to find that information regarding the following can be found in an object's context:

- Transaction Information: If an object is participating in a transaction (more on this in Chapter 8) then transactional information including a transaction identifier will exist in the object's context. Should this object create another object, this context information passes (flows) from creator to created (provided, of course, that the created object's class is configured to support transactions). Transaction information is available at all times to the object, it need only request the `IObjectContext` and `IObjectContextInfo` as demonstrated in Listing 7.1.

- Activity Information: COM+ synchronization services rely entirely on activities to protect objects. An activity is simply a way of grouping a series of objects together, such that they are all protected from outside interruption while a single logical thread of method invocations weaves its way through. Activities are deeply intertwined with transactions to the extent that if an object is involved in a transaction, it *must* be in an activity. Therefore, transaction and activity information often flow together from the context of the creating object to the created. We will discuss activities (and their association with transactions) in greater detail in Chapter 8 and in Appendix B. Activity information may be retrieved by an object by using the `IObjectContext` and `IObjectContextInfo` interfaces as demonstrated in Listing 7.1.

- Security Information: Information about the current caller, as well as successive callers can be found in an object's context. Obtaining security information from an object's context is demonstrated in Listing 7.1.

- Apartment Information: Although an apartment may have any number of contexts associated with it, a context can only be associated with a single apartment. Although it is not documented, it is highly likely that this association is maintained in an object's context. An object may not obtain information about its apartment directly through Microsoft supplied interfaces, however, if you are not faint of heart, the code in Listing 7.2 will do the trick:

Listing 7.2 **A Component Which Obtains Its Apartment "GUID"**

```
HRESULT CContextDiag::ApartmentInformation() {

    // This method obtains the Apartment "GUID" of the component.
    // This cannot be obtained using COM+'s context interfaces, but rather
    // it must be ascertained using a little ingenuity.

    // Recall from chapter 4 that to pass an interface pointer
    // from one thread to another, you must convert the interface
    // to a stream using CoMarshalInterThreadInterfaceInStream.

    // With this stream, and an understanding of how COM functions
    // on a network packet level, we can obtain the object's OXID
    // (its Object Export Identifier) which is unique to every
    // apartment in the system.  The OXID can thus serve as
    // the apartment GUID of a component — since it is unique
    // for every apartment.

    // For more information on how COM works at a network level,
    // consult Guy and Henry Eddon's excellent article,
    // "Understanding the DCOM Wire Protocol by Analyzing Network
    // Data Packets" in the May 98 issue of the Microsoft's systems
    // journal, or consult the DCOM draft from Microsoft.

    IStream *pStream;
    BYTE    cStreamArray[1024];
    ULONG   nBytesRead=0;
    HRESULT hr;

    // Use the _bstr_t class to make message
    // parsing and displaying a little easier:
    _bstr_t sApartmentInfo="";

    // Convert the current interface to a stream:
    hr=CoMarshalInterThreadInterfaceInStream(
        IID_IContextDiag,
        (IUnknown*)(IContextDiag*)this,
        &pStream);

    if (hr!=S_OK)
    {
        // We couldn't convert the interface pointer to a stream:
        sApartmentInfo="ApartmentInformation: Problem converting"
                    " pointer to stream";
```

```
        MessageBox(NULL,sApartmentInfo,"Apartment Information",MB_OK);
        return S_OK;
    }


    // Deposit the contents of the stream into a byte array
    // so we can analyze it:
    hr=pStream->Read(cStreamArray,1024,&nBytesRead);

    if (hr!=S_OK)
    {
        sApartmentInfo="ApartmentInformation: Problem reading stream.";
        MessageBox(NULL,sApartmentInfo,"Apartment Information",MB_OK);
        return S_OK;
    }

    // The contents of the converted stream are now in the stream array.
    // The data is formatted according to the Standard Marshall Object
    // Reference as specified by the DCOM draft.  The first
    // 4 bytes of the stream should spell out MEOW:

    if (cStreamArray[0]!='M' ||  cStreamArray[1]!='E' ||
        cStreamArray[2]!='O' ||  cStreamArray[3]!='W')
    {
        // The stream's contents are not as we expect, so abort:
        sApartmentInfo="ApartmentInformation: Unexpected Stream Contents.";
        MessageBox(NULL,sApartmentInfo,"Apartment Information",MB_OK);
        return S_OK;
    }

    // The object's OXID is contained in array positions 32 to 39 as
    // defined by the DCOM draft:
    sApartmentInfo = "APARTMENT GUID (OXID) = ";

    for (int k=32; k<=39; k++)
    {
        char cHexbyte[1];
        sprintf(cHexbyte,"%x",cStreamArray[k]);
        sApartmentInfo += cHexbyte;
        if (k!=39) sApartmentInfo += "-";
    }

    // Display apartment information:
    MessageBox(NULL,sApartmentInfo,"Apartment Information",MB_OK);

    return S_OK;
}
```

- Because unconfigured components are also contained in apartments, this method will work on either configured or unconfigured components. The output of this method is given in Figure 7.5.

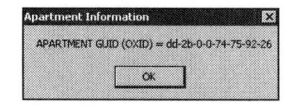

Figure 7.5 An unconfigured object share its creator's context.

- Other COM+ Objects: I don't want to raise your hopes—only Microsoft can perform this magic. If you are Microsoft, it is actually possible to have the object context contain (and act as a dispenser for) interfaces to other COM+ objects. In this way, an object can get an interface to another object through its context. Object's accessed from ASP pages can actually obtain interfaces to IIS objects such as Response, Request, and Session. This is discussed in greater depth in the section, "Context and ASP Pages."

When a configured object (Object A) seeks to create another object (Object B), COM+ first goes to the COM+ catalog and examines the attributes of component B. In other words, it looks to see how you configured this component and determines to what extent B's configuration is compatible with A's. In the simplest, most ideal case, Object B is configured exactly the same way as Object A; all contextual information can flow from A to B. I say flow from the context of A to context B, because although the contexts of A and B may be 100% compatible, they will not share a context; rather each object will have its own. To prove this we need only look at the context GUIDs of both A and B when they are instantiated. A and B are going to be VB objects, so we do have a slight problem in that IObjectContextInfo's GetContextId() method returns a GUID and VB6 cannot handle a GUID. So, we create a VC++ wrapper component called VBGUID that will obtain its host's context GUID, convert it into a VB string (which is represented as the C++ data-type BSTR), and return it to the host object. The code for the key function of this wrapper is shown in Listing 7.3.

Listing 7.3 **A C++ Component Which Returns the Context GUID of an Object as a String**

```
HRESULT VBGUID::ContextGuid(BSTR *CntxGuid ) {

//This method returns a STRING of the current context GUID. Since
//Visual Basic has no native support for GUIDs, this component can serve
//as a way for a Visual Basic component to obtain its contextGUID.

//This component must NOT BE CONFIGURED!  Doing so would give the
//object its own context, and thus the Context GUID this method
//will return will be its own — not its caller.  By keeping
//the component unconfigured, one ensures that it shares the context
//of its creator, and thus the reported Context GUID is in fact
//that of the caller.

//This component should only be called from configured components,
//since it attempts to examine the context of its creator.
```

```
IObjectContext *pObjectContext;
IObjectContextInfo *pObjectContextInfo;

GUID contextGuid;
unsigned char *pContextGuidString;
WCHAR wContextGuidString[40];

HRESULT hr;
RPC_STATUS rpcstat;

// Obtain IObjectContext and IObjectContextInfo interfaces:

hr = GetObjectContext (&pObjectContext);
if (hr !=S_OK)
{
    // Could not get IObjectContext:
    MessageBox(NULL,"Could not get IObjectContext",
               "Context Information",MB_OK);
    return hr;
}

hr=pObjectContext->QueryInterface(IID_IObjectContextInfo,
                            (void**)&pObjectContextInfo);
if (hr !=S_OK)
{
    // Could not get IObjectContextInfo:
    MessageBox(NULL,"Could not get IObjectContextInfo",
                  "Context Information",MB_OK);
    return hr;
}

// Obtain the Context Guid:
pObjectContextInfo->GetContextId(&contextGuid);
rpcstat = UuidToString(&contextGuid, &pContextGuidString);
if (rpcstat !=RPC_S_OK)
{
    return E_FAIL;
}


// The Context GUID is currently in a character array.
// Convert to UNICODE and then to a BSTR:

if (MultiByteToWideChar(
    CP_ACP,
    0,
    (char*)pContextGuidString,
    -1,
    wContextGuidString,
    sizeof(wContextGuidString)/sizeof(wContextGuidString[0]))==0)
{
```

continues

212 Chapter 7 Contexts

Listing 7.3 **Continued**

```
    // Could not convert to UNICODE.
    return E_FAIL;

}

// Convert the UNICODE string to a BSTR:
*CntxGuid=SysAllocString(wContextGuidString);

return S_OK;

}
```

Now that we have a wrapper component that will perform the context GUID-to-string conversion, we can use VB objects to prove that contexts differ. Let's begin with Object B shown in Listing 7.4.

Listing 7.4 **A VB Component Which Obtains Its GUID Using the Component Above, and Exposes a Method That Returns It**

```
'ObjectB

Dim retrieveGuid As VBGUID

Private Sub Class_Initialize()
    Set retrieveGuid = New VBGUID
End Sub

Function GetContextGuid() As String
    GetContextGuid = retrieveGuid.ContextGuid
End Function
```

Object B does little more than create a new instance of VBGUID and defines a method that will return its own context GUID as a string. Object A, shown in Listing 7.5, will perform three actions: it will create a new instance of VBGUID, it will use this object to determine its own context identifier, and then it will determine the context identifier of Object B. The code for Object A is shown in Listing 7.5.

Listing 7.5 **A VB Component Creates ObjectB, Obtains Its Context GUID, Obtains Its Own Context GUID, and Compares Them**

```
Dim retrieveGuid As VBGUID
Dim ObjectB As ContextB

Sub ContextDemo()

    Dim sCompare As String
    Dim sContextA As String
    Dim sContextB As String
```

```
    'Obtain the Context Guids of both objects:
    sContextA = retrieveGuid.ContextGuid
    sContextB = ObjectB.GetContextGuid

    sCompare = "Comparison of Object Contexts: " & vbNewLine & vbNewLine
    sCompare = sCompare & "Context GUID of Object A: " & sContextA_
            & vbNewLine
    sCompare = sCompare & "Context GUID of Object B: " & sContextB_
            & vbNewLine
    MsgBox sCompare

End Sub

Private Sub Class_Initialize()
    Set retrieveGuid = New VBGUID
    Set ObjectB = New ContextB
End Sub
```

If both Object A and Object B are configured components, when Object A is instantiated you will find that Object A's and Object B's contexts differ as shown in Figure 7.6.

On the other hand, if we don't configure Object B, it will share the context of its creator (Object A); and both contexts have the same context indentifiers as shown in Figure 7.7.

Prerelease COM+ documentation and articles mention that if contexts between two objects are fully compatible, it will be possible for the two objects to actually share the same context. You will, however, be hard-pressed to find any scenario where this is the case; empirically, you will find that each configured object has its own context no matter how similar they are, and contexts never seem to be shared. Don't expect the "Must Be Activated in the Callers Context Check Box" on the component's Activation tab to help; this checkbox exists to prevent an object from being created unless it can run in its creator's context. In almost all cases, sharing a context isn't possible. Selecting this checkbox will have the effect of preventing your object from ever being created.

It may very well be that a less-common scenario exists where contexts may be shared, or future incarnations of COM+ will allow it. At present, however, it seems as though the designers of COM+ found it simpler (or perhaps more expedient) to give every object its own context. In the interim, if you need an object to share the context of its creator, make sure that its component is unconfigured. Unconfigured components share their caller's context by default.

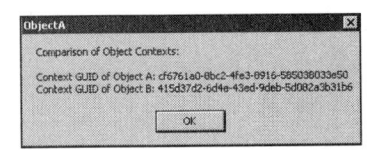

Figure 7.6 Objects configured similarly have different contexts.

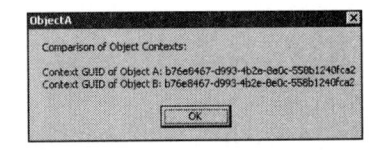

Figure 7.7 An unconfigured object shares its creator's context.

Returning now to the concept of context flow, we know that COM+ examines the context of the creator and context of the created. What properties are compatible will flow; it would seem, those properties that aren't compatible will not flow. But it is not quite so Boolean as that. Shades of grey exist between contexts where some form of mediation is employed between contexts so that objects with different contexts (and, therefore, different needs) can work together. The mediation that makes this possible is, in COM+ terminology, known as *interception*.

Interception

The premise of interception is simple: If two objects have incompatible contexts, COM+ should step in between the two and act as a translator between the objects. To use a grossly simplified analogy, if Object A's context is French and Object B's context is German, then an interceptor should step between the two objects and translate French to German one way and German to French the other. Giving examples in more detailed terms is not as clear cut, largely because the implementation of interception is not documented at the time of this writing. Rather, most discussion of interception is conceptual. In the Microsoft Press book, "Understanding COM+," David Platt (one of my favorite technical authors) speaks of the concept of interception and mentions that between the client side proxy, RPC channel, and the server stub there exists chains of "policy objects." The number and functions of these policy objects depend on how the component is configured. Basically, these objects are responsible for performing the actual grunt work of mediation. The example Platt gives involves a server-side object that requires synchronization services. In this event, a server-side policy object will "intercept" the method invocation and try to acquire a lock to the server's process before allowing the method invocation through.

In the September 1999 Microsoft Systems Journal section, "House of COM," Don Box says "An interceptor acts as a proxy to the 'real' object." As such, interceptors implement the same interfaces as the real object. Box does not mention policy objects even once, but he does go on to show how an interceptor is created beneath `CoCreateInstance()` and is used to set up the context for the created object. This leads us to see interceptors as a proxy to our configured object. This interceptor/proxy will transparently and automatically propagate attributes from creator to created and mediate communications between two different contexts, regardless of the differences.

While interesting, knowledge of the inner workings of interceptors is not critical or especially important when writing components. The implementation is not published and is certain to change. However, the fundamental tenant of COM+ says essentially, "Don't worry...be happy"; COM+ will take care of the details—concentrate instead on what you want your application to do.

Contexts, Apartments and the Free Threaded Marshaler

If I can borrow another line from the "House of COM," a context is the "innermost scope of an object." All configured objects exist in a context, but what does a context exist in? The answer is: an apartment. Before I go into greater detail, I should pause for a moment and alert the reader that this section discusses more esoteric, lower-level aspects of contexts that, while interesting, are by no means a prerequisite in using contexts effectively. This section may, therefore, be safely skipped without harm.

An apartment, remember, is a declarative affiliation between threads and objects. Threads declare what type of apartment they wish to be in, whereas objects are bound to the apartment of the thread that created them (note that by "creating thread" I don't mean the thread of the client executable that called `CoCreateInstance()` or `New`; rather, I mean the thread in DLLHOST.EXE on which a new instance of the object was created). Now, let's bring contexts into the picture. Recall that a thread in one apartment is not allowed to share a raw interface pointer with a thread in another apartment, and instead must call `CoMarshalInterthreadInterfaceInStream()` or use the global interface table (GIT) to package the interface into a portable form.

When the portable, or marshaled, form of an interface is unmarshaled by another thread, COM+ will automatically tie the resulting proxy to the unmarshaling thread's apartment and context. For the purpose of example, let's assume that we have a client thread executing on behalf of a configured component and, therefore, has a context. When this thread unmarshals a marshaled interface, the resulting interface proxy will be automatically tied in to the thread's context and calls made by this thread on this interface will be cross context. Both the thread's context and the object's context will be taken into account and ordinary interception can take place. If the object investigates its context, it will see exactly what it (and you) would expect: Its own context, not that of the client. Suppose, however, that you want the object to execute in the context of the client thread that calls into it? In other words, you want the object to give up any claim to its own context and instead always operate in the context of the object that calls it. In COM+ terminology, you want your object to be context-neutral.

We know that unconfigured objects share the context of their creator (though the server and creator's apartment model needs to be compatible), which is part of what we want. But there is a problem. If the creator marshals its interface pointer into a stream—(or uses the GIT) and this packaged interface is unmarshaled by a thread executing on behalf of another configured object—the unconfigured object will still execute in the context of its creator and not in the context of the calling thread's object. However, we want our object to share the context of its caller, regardless of whether the caller is the creator. This is shown in Figure 7.8.

216 Chapter 7 Contexts

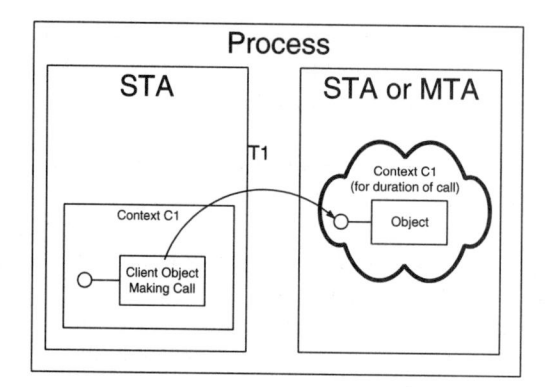

Figure 7.8 An object that always executes in the context of its caller.

If you want your object to "borrow" the context of the calling object it must be unconfigured, and it must aggregate the free-threaded marshaler (FTM). This may not sound so simple, but it actually is pretty simple to do, though it can only be done in C++.

Recall from Chapter 4, "Threading and Apartment Models," that when an interface is unmarshaled, the thread that performed the unmarshaling receives an apartment-relative (that is, bound to a certain apartment) interface proxy. This proxy will tie itself into the thread's context; so, it can now be said to be context-relative as well. The FTM, however, interferes with this proxy creation and, in a sense, violates the rules of COM+ by forcing "raw" object pointers to be returned to the unmarshaling thread. This has a couple of effects. The first effect is that COM+ can no longer perform Single Threaded Apartment (STA) synchronization effectively because COM+ can no longer tell from which apartment the method call originates. Furthermore, because a thread receives a raw interface pointer to an object aggregating the FTM, that particular thread is now the one that actually executes the method in the object. Thus, the object better be thread-safe because it is opening itself up to access by any and all threads in the process. The second effect is that any method invocation made on the interface executes in the context of the calling thread and *not* in the context of the receiving object. This means that an object that uses FTM finds that calls to `GetObjectContext()` return an interface to the context of its *caller,* and not to its own context.

By and large the only components that benefit from executing in caller context are utility components. A class of component known as resource dispensers (the Open Database Connectivity [ODBC] driver manager is a Resource Dispenser [RD]), for example, hand out resources—often transactional connections to a relational database or other form of Resource Manager (RM). RDs may, therefore, make use of the FTM because they often need to "see" into the context of the caller. By looking into the caller's context, an RD can determine such things as the transaction the caller is currently involved in.

One final aspect of contexts and apartments has to do with the thread neutral apartment (TNA). Recall that, unlike the STA and MTA, the TNA does not contain any threads. While the STA has one thread that is usually monitoring a message queue and the MTA has a pool of threads "hanging out" waiting to be dispatched, a TNA contains only objects and the contexts of those objects. An object residing in a TNA shares a similarity with an object that aggregates the FTM. The thread that calls a method on the object is the thread which actually executes that method and the usual thread switch does not occur. However, in the case of the FTM, the object always executes in the context of the calling thread; an object that uses the FTM is saying that it does not want a context of its own. An object residing in a TNA, however, *does* want its own context and its methods will, in fact, always execute in that context no matter what thread enters the TNA. This is shown in Figure 7.9.

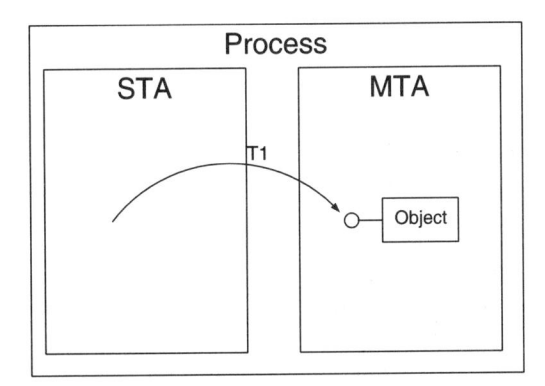

Figure 7.9 A TNA allows the calling thread direct access but preserves the object's context.

If you are developing components in VB6, TNA- and FTM-specific functionality is not available. All VB components execute in an STA, and it is not possible for them to aggregate the free-threaded marshaler. Of course, it certainly doesn't hurt to know a little about how these entities operate. So now that we have at least a cursory understanding of contexts at a lower level, we should take a look at how to leverage them for the benefit of our applications. Specifically, we will take a look at the context-oriented interfaces, mainly `IObjectContextInfo`, `IContextState`, `ISecurityCallContext`, and `IGetContextProperties`.

Understanding and Using the Context Interfaces

We discussed the methods of `IObjectContext` in the section, "Introducing *IObjectContext*." There are four other interfaces that are especially useful in interacting with the context object.

IObjectContextInfo

Frustratingly, `IObjectContextInfo` is not usable from VB6; its methods return GUIDs, which VB rejects with a message box proclaiming that the interface uses non-automation datatypes. It may be, however, that the designers of `IObjectContextInfo` did not feel that its methods were of much use to VB components. Granted, `IsInTransaction()` might be useful, but that method is already available in the VB-friendly `IObjectContext`. That leaves `GetTransaction()`, `GetTransactionId()`, `GetActivityId()`, and `GetContextId()` for us to consider.

Aside from `GetTransaction()`, which returns an `ITransaction` interface pointer (we'll talk more about this in the next chapter), these methods are informational. Arguably, they are only useful to components that perform tasks that VB components can't. Take object pooling for example. If your object can be aggregated and is thread-safe (neither of which is possible in VB—at least not yet), it can be temporarily deactivated (but kept alive) as opposed to destroyed when its client releases it. In other words, it is "pooled." At a later point in time, when another client requests that a new instance of the same type of object be created, creation and initialization overhead is eliminated as the deactivated object is simply reactivated and bound to the client. The methods of `IObjectContextInfo` are important for such an object because when it is reactivated, it might find itself in a strange new context. The object may need to determine exactly what transaction and activity now finds itself in and compare this state with its previous state. In the case of transactions, for example, a reactivated object will need to reenlist its database connection if the transaction ID it gets from `GetTransactionId()` upon activation differs from the transaction ID it had when it was deactivated. For performance reasons, we would prefer not to reenlist a connection if the transaction ID had not changed. `IObjectContextInfo` gives our object the information it needs to make the right decision. See Listing 7.6 for an example of a pooled, transactional object that investigates its current transaction upon being reactivated.

Listing 7.6 **A Transactional, Pooled Object Determining Its Current Transaction Upon Being Activated**

```
HRESULT PooledAndTransactional::Activate() {

IObjectContext *pObjectContext;
IObjectContextInfo *pObjectContextInfo;
```

Understanding and Using the Context Interfaces 219

```
bool bIsInTransaction;
HRESULT hr;
GUID transactionGuid;


// Obtain IObjectContext and IObjectContextInfo interface pointers:
hr = GetObjectContext (&pObjectContext);
if (hr !=S_OK)
{
    // Could not get IObjectContext:
    return hr;
}

hr=pObjectContext->QueryInterface(IID_IObjectContextInfo,
                  (void**)&pObjectContextInfo);
if (hr !=S_OK)
{
    // Could not get IObjectContextInfo:
    return hr;
}

bIsInTransaction = pObjectContext->IsInTransaction();
if (!bIsInTransaction)
{
    // The componenent is not participating in a transaction,
    // so we don't have to enlist anything:

    m_TransactionID = GUID_NULL;
    return S_OK;

}

pObjectContextInfo->GetTransactionId(&transactionGuid);

if (transactionGuid != m_TransactionID)
{

    // We are in a new transaction, enlist with the DTC:
    m_TransactionID = transactionGuid;

    // See chapter 8 for the implementation of EnlistDTC():
    EnlistDTC();
}

return S_OK;


}
```

ISecurityCallContext

`ISecurityCallContext` is used by an object to find out security-related information about its current caller. The methods of `ISecurityCallContext` will be familiar to you already, because you have seen them before as members of `IObjectContext`—specifically as the following:

- `IsCallerInRole`
- `IsSecurityEnabled`
- `IsUserInRole`

I imagine you would agree that given the security-orientation of these methods, it makes the most sense to put them in a separate interface instead of lumping them together with voting and state functionality in `IObjectContext`. And `ISecurityCallContext` offers additional functionality as well. Specifically, this interface also acts as a VB-style collection. VB users can loop through different security properties via FOR..EACH. See Listing 7.7 for an example.

Listing 7.7 Enumerating Through the Items In *SecurityCallContext*

```
Option Explicit

Dim iItemNum As Long
Dim sItems As String
Dim vntItem As Variant

Sub securityinfo()

sItems = "Items in the SecurityCallContext collection: " & vbNewLine & vbNewLine

'Loop through all the items in the SecurityCallContext collection.
'In VB you obtain this using GetSecurityCallContext(). In C++ you
'would use CoGetCallContext() and ask for ISecurityCallContext

For Each vntItem In GetSecurityCallContext()
    iItemNum = iItemNum + 1
    sItems = sItems & iItemNum & ".) " & vntItem & vbNewLine
Next

'Display the results:
MsgBox sItems
```

Executing the code in Listing 7.7 produces the following output shown in Figure 7.10.

In Chapter 12, I show you how to actually use these properties to determine the chain of callers and other security information. For now, however, while we're on the subject of properties, let's move on to the final interface we will be discussing in this chapter—the strange and intriguing `IGetContextProperties`.

Figure 7.10 The items in the `SecurityCallContext` object.

IGetContextProperties

`IGetContextProperties` is an interesting method with very generic, non-specific method names like `Count()`, `EnumNames()`, and `GetProperty()`. This interface is purposefully vague because it is used to retrieve arbitrary interfaces from the context object. I say arbitrary, because a context object may actually act as a dispenser for other objects.

As I mentioned earlier in this chapter, the context object is extensible, at least by Microsoft. Just how to make it extensible is not documented for the benefit of non-Microsoft developers, but Microsoft's Internet Information Server (IIS) can and does extend the context object. `IGetContextProperties` can be used by COM+ objects running in ASP pages to obtain interface pointers to IIS intrinsic objects. Specifically, IIS makes five of its internal objects globally accessible by placing their interfaces in the context of objects that are created by Active Server Pages (ASP).

If you are not familiar with ASPs, here's a little history. In version 3.0, IIS introduced the concept of ASPs to provide the same functionality as CGI-bin scripts—that is, they allow HTML pages to be dynamically generated when requested by the client. In the ASP model, there exists an ordinary HTML file with pockets of VBScript (or JavaScript) interspersed throughout the page and denoted by the special tags `<%` and `%>`.

When a client requests an ASP from IIS, IIS runs the ASP. All the script in the page is run, and the code ultimately resolves to HTML. This process is sometimes referred to as *server-side scripting*.

Aside from the basic functionality offered by VBScript, the only way an ASP page can reach out and call upon external functionality is by creating and using COM objects. For example, if an ASP page wants to modify a database, it must call on a COM object to do the work. If the ASP page wants to retrieve data, it must also go through a COM object (perhaps RDO or ADO) to retrieve the records. After these records have been obtained, the ASP page converts the data into HTML and IIS ferries an ordinary (though dynamically created) HTML page to the client.

The relationship between IIS ASP and COM objects is interesting. If an ASP page instantiates a configured COM+ object, that object will have a context. If the ASP instantiates an unconfigured object, it will not. Because it stands to reason that most components that you use with ASPs will be configured, let's assume that all objects created and used by ASPs will have access to their context object.

222 Chapter 7 Contexts

ASP-created objects can, therefore QueryInterface (*QI*) for IGetContextProperties. With this interface, it is possible to enumerate through and access other objects and/or interfaces that might have been placed in the object's context. For example, if an ASP-created object requests this interface, the object can use it to snoop through other objects/interfaces that might have been placed in its context. In doing so, an ASP-created object finds that IIS has added the following IIS intrinsic objects to its context:

- Request (IRequest)
- Response (IResponse)
- Server (IServer)
- Application (IApplicationObject)
- Session (ISessionObject)

Here is an example of how a configured object can get this list in VC++ using IObjectContextProperties. It is long and somewhat clunky and, as we see, requires many lines to obtain the same result as VB can with a single line. Listing 7.8 demonstrates how a configured C++ component run from an ASP page may obtain an IResponse interface to IIS's intrinsic Response object.

Listing 7.8 **A VC++ Object Component Retrieving an *IResponse* Interface from Its Context**

```
// obtaining of context and error checking omitted for brevity,
// see the book's accompanying source code for a complete example.

_bstr_t bstrPropName=L"Response";
VARIANT varProp;
VariantInit(&varProp);

// Obtain the IGetContextProperties interface from the
// IObjectContext interface:

pObjectContext->QueryInterface(
    IID_IGetContextProperties,
    (void**)&pGetContextProps);

// Now ask IGetContextProperties for the Response object.
// This method is somewhat awkward, in that it returns
// a VARIANT of the requested interface, which is really
// an IDispatch pointer of the Response object.

pGetContextProps->GetProperty(bstrPropName,&varProp);

// Obtain the IDispatch pointer the variant contains,
// and then QI this interface for the Response object.
// Again, error checking has been omitted:
pIDispatch = V_DISPATCH(&varProp);
```

```
pIDispatch->QueryInterface(IID_IResponse,(void**)&pIISResponse);

// Write something to the ASP page using the
// response object we have obtained:

pIISResponse->Write(CComVariant(
    OLESTR("Hello from an object being used by an ASP page!")));

return S_OK;
```

The following VB example is simpler but more abstracted:

```
GetObjectContext.Item("Response").Write "Hello from an object being used by
➥an ASP page!"
```

The preceding code, if placed in a configured VB object used by an ASP, results in the sentence "Hello from an object being used by an ASP page!" in the HTML page that IIS gives to the client browser. The object is using its context object to gain access to IIS's `Response` object. Note that although the `IGetContextProperties` is not directly available to VB, it is most likely used behind the scenes.

Summary

In this chapter, we talk about contexts. Contexts are unique to each object and can be thought of as the universe that the object lives in. It encompasses all the attributes that you use to configure your component. You manipulate these attributes by using the Component Services snap-in or the COM administrative objects, as discussed in the previous chapter.

Information can flow from one object's context to the next in a creation chain. This allows different objects to cooperate in COM+ services, such as transaction management, because COM+ can look into the context of the creating object, set attributes of the created object; and if it determines that the two objects are compatible, COM+ can allow information to flow from the creator's context to the context of the created.

The concept of context originated with MTS. Any MTS object could, at any time, get in touch with its context object by asking MTS for an `IObjectContext` interface. When obtained, an MTS object could create other objects via `IObjectContext`'s `CreateInstance( )` method. By using this method instead of the standard COM creation functions, transactional information could flow from the context of the creating object to the context of the created object. In this way, multiple objects could share in a transaction.

Microsoft's IIS also takes advantage of contexts. As of IIS 4.0, IIS and MTS work closely together, so that the context of MTS objects can carry IIS-specific entities as well. The integration is so tight that an MTS object created from an ASP can obtain interfaces to a number of IIS-useful objects simply by querying its context object.

8

Transactions

AUNIVERSE THAT IS CLEARLY GUIDED by the relationship between cause and effect is often referred to as *Newtonian*. Your enterprise-scale application seems to live in a predictable, Newtonian universe, but every time it wants to make a permanent record of its state, it enters a period of uncertainty. In physics, this period of uncertainty is described by the laws of quantum mechanics; in development, it is the law of transactions.

Most large applications and IT infrastructures keep their state in relational database management systems (RDBMSs). Microsoft SQL Server, Sybase, Oracle, Informix, and Ingres are all examples of RDBMSs. All these systems are transactional, meaning that sequences of data modifications succeed or fail together as an atomic group allowing no chance for inconsistent, partially updated data to exist in the system. RDBMS architects employ a transactional model because they realize that there is a certain chance that one or many related modifications could fail; and should that happen, the entire series of modifications must be undone.

Grouping one or many data modifications into an atomic unit of work is the hallmark of what is called a *transaction*. What goes on inside a transaction as all the possibilities are explored (and the dice of chance is rolled) is not viewable to the outside world. If all goes well, the transaction ultimately collapses into a codified, singular result as the data modifications are committed to permanent record. If things do not go well, all intermediate changes are undone and the transaction evaporates into nothingness—that is, rollback affecting no permanent record.

> **COM+ Performance: Top Rated According to TPC-C Benchmarks**
>
> While developers should always strive to write efficient components, it is good to know that COM+ itself is a top performer. At the time of this writing, COM+ claims the number one spot on the Transaction Processing Council's (www.tpc.org) TPC-C benchmark. According to this benchmark, when run on an IBM Netfinity 8500R c/s with DB2 7.1 and Advanced Server, COM+ is able to originate 440,879.95 tpmC (transactions per minute). The TPC-C is a scenario-based test that simulates a high-traffic order entry system. 440,879.95 tpmC means that COM+ was able to process 440,879.95 new order requests while the system was simultaneously processing other requests. To quote TPC's own FAQ, "Throughput, in TPC terms, is a measure of maximum sustained system performance. In TPC-C, throughput is defined as how many New-Order transactions per minute a system generates while the system is executing four other transactions types (Payment, Order-Status, Delivery, Stock-Level). All five TPC-C transactions have a certain user response time requirement, with the New-Order transaction response time set at 5 seconds. Therefore, for a 710 tpmC number, a system is generating 710 New-Order transactions per minute while fulfilling the rest of the TPC-C transaction mix workload."
>
> Although the top performance slot seemingly relies on an all-IBM platform, COM+ claims the top six positions when ranked according to price and performance. That is, according to the TPC, when you look at the total cost of the system, your best performance for the price comes in the form of a Dell, Compaq, or Hewlett Packard running an all Microsoft backbone: SQL Server 7 or 2000, Windows 2000 or (NT 4 Enterprise Edition), and COM+ (or Microsoft Transaction Server [MTS]).
>
> Certainly, one should keep in mind that all benchmarks have arguable points. The components used in this test are certainly highly optimized, and the cost of development is not taken into account. Similarly, system reliability is not considered. Nonetheless, this metric correlates well to the industry perception; for years UNIX/Oracle systems running the BEA Tuxedo transaction processing monitor have dominated. However, COM+ has made a resoundingly strong entrance, beating out its closest performance rivals by a factor of three. If you are using COM+, feel good about it; you are not giving up anything for ease of use and development. And if you are not using COM+ and shopping around for the appropriate transaction processing system, know that Microsoft is a real player in this arena.
>
> To find out more about the TPC-C benchmark, be sure to go to www.tpc.org.

ROLLBACK and COMMIT

If your life supported transactions as a relational database does, you could immediately remove yourself from any embarrassing, unexpected, or dangerous situation arising from your actions. In fact, all you would need to do is shout the word "ROLLBACK" at any time, in any situation you didn't plan (or want) to be in, and you would immediately be whisked back in time to a safe point before the unpleasant situation arose.

Of course, the question arises: What would this safe point in time be? Well, if you know you are just about to embark on a series of actions that might not turn out in a way you'd like, you first shout the words "BEGIN TRANSACTION." This establishes your *rollback point*—that is, the point in time to which you want to return in the event your actions don't produce the result you want or expect.

In the previous example, we discussed BEGIN TRANSACTION and ROLLBACK, but you're missing one other key component—COMMIT. BEGIN TRANSACTION is used to specify a safe place in time where everything is okay or, in database terminology, consistent. As discussed earlier, after BEGIN TRANSACTION, a ROLLBACK can always be called and it undoes all actions occurring after the BEGIN TRANSACTION, bringing you back to your safe or consistent point.

However, suppose things go well for you in your transaction-enabled life, and all your actions produce the desired results. But, way back in your history, there is a dangling BEGIN TRANSACTION—for which there was no COMMIT.

Assuming that this is an unappealing prospect, the time soon comes when you should really commit to the actions you've executed, close out that BEGIN TRANSACTION, and make everything permanent. You do this simply by uttering the word "COMMIT." That command closes out the transaction and makes all your actions permanent; you can never roll them back.

Classical Transactions and Traditional Databases

Sadly, you acknowledge that you cannot have transactions in real life. Your database systems, however, are more fortunate. And although they might not be especially concerned with rolling back to prevent from being embarrassed or making a bad life decision, they are deeply concerned with ACID. ACID is an acronym representing the following four guiding principles of transactions:

- Atomicity
- Consistency
- Isolation
- Durability

Atomicity

Transactions need to be atomic. There was a time in classical physics when atoms were thought to be the absolute smallest constituents of matter, and the term *atomic* meant all or nothing. To a database, this means that if a sequence of data modification statements are made within the context of a transaction (that is, they occur between a BEGIN TRANSACTION and a COMMIT TRANSACTION statement), they either all succeed or none of them succeed. If four of the five modification statements succeed but the fifth one doesn't, the four that did succeed are rolled back and the database is returned to the consistent state it was in at the time BEGIN TRANSACTION was declared.

Consistency

No matter what happens in a transaction, data in the database should remain accessible, any partial changes should be rolled back, and any internal data structures the database might use to keep track of the data (memory-cached indexes, for example) must be correct.

Isolation

Today, we know that the atom is no longer truly atomic—there are smaller elements of matter. Quantum mechanics gave scientists insight into how things work at a sub-atomic level and postulates a theory that might be true for both transactions and sub-atomic physics—an observer must necessarily affect the outcome of what he observes. Therefore, it might sometimes be best in physics and transactions just not to look.

This is what isolation means—Transaction A might not see or influence the data as it is being manipulated by another transaction, Transaction B. Transaction A might see the data before Transaction B operates on it, or after Transaction B commits, or rolls back, but cannot see or influence anything in between. If you are a fan of quantum mechanics, think of a transaction as unwatched particles expanded into their wave probabilities, exploring every possible trajectory at once.

Durability

After changes are committed, the changes must be durable. If the power is switched off, the changes must still be there when the power is turned on. In other words, when a change is committed, the transaction is over and the modifications are permanent.

A Transaction Scenario

Now that you're familiar with the concept of what transactions are, let's get into some examples. In a relational database system, all modifications occur as a result of an INSERT, DELETE, or UPDATE statement. If you are not familiar with relational databases, you can still follow these examples—just keep your eye on the INSERT.

Imagine you have an accounting database where different ledgers or accounts are represented by different database tables. The golden rule of accounting is that everything should balance; so for every debit, there must be a corresponding credit, and vice versa. For example, if you want to pay a $100 bill to XYZ Corp, you debit Cash for 100 and credit Accounts Payable for 100. Imagine that these two T ledgers (so called because they often resemble a capital T when drawn in paper ledger books) are represented by database tables. The SQL that the accounting software sends to the database to make these changes to these tables might resemble the following:

```
Insert into cash
(
explanation,
debit
)
VALUES
(
'payment to XYZ corp. for widget',
100
)

Insert into accounts_payable
(
explanation,
credit
)
VALUES
(
'payment to XYZ corp. for widget',
100
)
```

The preceding SQL works fine most the time, but in computer science it is always the boundary, fringe conditions that take the most work to accommodate. What if the system crashes just after executing the first statement, debit from cash, but before applying the cash to Accounts Payable? When the system comes up again, your books will be out of balance. Money has been taken from cash, but not applied to any other account. You lost money, got nothing for it, and this glitch will likely be buried by thousands of subsequent entries applied after the system comes up again, making it very difficult to track down. How can you prevent this from happening?

The *BEGIN TRANSACTION* and *COMMIT TRANSACTION* Commands

If you make both of these statements an atomic unit of work by wrapping them in a transaction (atomicity), you are assured that data will always be consistent (consistency) because all transactions will be isolated from one another until their unified success or failure (isolation) and that their ultimate modifications will be a permanent, durable part of the database (durability). In other words, rewrite slightly to add the BEGIN TRANSACTION and COMMIT TRANSACTION statements to produce the following:

```
BEGIN TRANSACTION

Insert into cash
(
explanation,
debit
)
VALUES
(
'payment to XYZ corp. for widget',
100
)

Insert into accounts_payable
(
explanation,
credit
)
VALUES
(
'payment to XYZ corp. for widget',
100
)

COMMIT TRANSACTION
```

Distributed Transactions

Relational databases typically implement transactions (and other features, such as replication) by keeping *log files*. Log files record all data modifications made to the database. In the simplest implementation, when a DBMS encounters BEGIN TRANSACTION, it writes all data modifications from that point on to the log. In this way, if it encounters a ROLLBACK command, it systematically works backward through the log and undoes any changes that have been made up until the BEGIN TRANSACTION is reached. If a system crash occurs, the DBMS notices upon restart that the transaction did not complete and likewise undoes all changes. If, on the other hand, the database encounters a COMMIT statement, the changes are made permanent, the log may be purged (or *truncated)*, and the transaction is closed out.

This is a simplified case. Logging strategies differ widely among database systems—some keep a perpetual log for replication and transactional purposes, others truncate their log files after a transaction is complete. Whatever they do, however, is implementation (and setting) dependent and need not concern you. It is the transaction that is important.

So, transactions are relatively straightforward when you have one database. Any user can, at any time, group a series of data-modification statements between a `BEGIN TRANSACTION` and `COMMIT` and rest assured that all SQL statements will either all succeed or all fail atomically. Suppose, however, that a developer wants to have a transaction that spans multiple database systems, perhaps from different database vendors? Suddenly things become more complex.

A transaction is normally specific to a particular database connection. (The system interprets a broken connection or dead client as a reason to `ROLLBACK`.) The developer needs a different database connection for each database he wants the transaction to span, but how can he juggle the transaction between these databases over different, isolated connections? Internally, databases from different vendors use entirely different, incompatible mechanisms for handling transactions.

Clearly some form of third-party referee or transaction monitor (TM) is needed to coordinate transactions across multiple databases, and all databases must support some form of industry-standard protocol to communicate with this TM. We discuss the database-to-TM protocols in more detail in the Chapter 9, "Compensating Resource Managers." For now, let's take a look at Microsoft's transaction manager, the Distributed Transaction Coordinator (DTC).

The DTC

If you have ever bought any form of real estate in the United States, you know exactly how the DTC operates. To protect two or more parties (usually a buyer and a seller) who want to enter into a real-estate or other business transaction, a protocol has evolved to ensure that all parties participating in the transactions successfully discharge their contractual responsibilities. If all parties do, the transaction completes; if one or more do not, the transaction is aborted.

Escrow and the Two-Phase Commit

This protocol centers around something called *escrow*. I am simplifying somewhat, but *escrow* can be thought of as a neutral third party acting as a temporary holder of assets and a kind of transaction referee. The way it works is—if you agree to buy my house, we have effectively agreed to enter into a transaction together. For you to buy my house, you need to give me money, and I need to give you the title. Sounds simple, but a lot can happen in between.

If you give me the money first, but I don't give you the title after depositing your check, the transaction is not complete. However, there isn't much chance that I'm going to return the money, and you will have a very difficult time finding me, I can assure you. So, I am a fugitive of the law, and you are out a lot of money with no house to show for it. There is no way to roll back. On the other hand, if I give you the title to my house first, you might move in, change the locks, and never give me my check. I have no legal recourse because, officially, you own the house. Again, we have an aborted transaction leaving one of the transaction's participants out of balance.

The escrow system was developed so that a neutral third party can mediate the transaction and prevent these kinds of problems. In the escrow way of doing things, the buyer and seller agree on a third-party agent, an *escrow agent*, who has the following responsibilities:

- Holds all assets in an *escrow account*, including house title and cash. Neither the buyer nor seller has access to this account.
- Makes certain that both parties do what they promise before releasing any assets and closing out the transaction.
- Returns assets to original owners if either party fails to perform his contractual duties, thus aborting the transaction.
- Acts as the guardian of the transaction.

If we use an escrow agent, let's call him David T. Cohen (DTC for short), our transaction is not much more complex but is safer for both parties. You and I agree to engage DTC or, in database terminology, you and I *enlist* in the transaction with DTC.

Each of us is hoping for a permanent change of our fortunes—you want the title, and I want the money—but we need to let the DTC manage this process. Normally, in real estate, the buyer and seller do not have any direct contact with one another; it is all done through an escrow attorney.

The Two-Phased Commit Protocol

At this point, the following two phases must occur before DTC is happy and allows the house to change title from me to you:

- **Phase One (Prepare).** DTC asks each of us to prepare to discharge our specific financial responsibilities. This preparation is unique to each of us. You should probably get a certified check from your bank for the purchase price of the house, and I need to dig up the deed for my home. If your bank says you don't have the funds, or if I can't find my deed in the attic or my kitchen junk drawer, we need to tell DTC. The DTC then tells the other party that the transaction is over. If we both can complete our preparations, we tell the DTC that we are both prepared.

> **The DTC Does Not Know Details**
> In real life, your money and my deed are placed in an attorney's escrow account after the Prepare phase, but a database DTC does not have any knowledge of or interaction with actual resources and data being modified.

We have completed the Prepare phase, but the change of title or acceptance of money has not occurred yet. No official change of record takes place for either of us. However, because we have each indicated that we are prepared, we are obligated to go through with this transaction if and when the DTC asks us to sometime in the immediate future.

- **Phase Two (Commit).** After we have both indicated that we are successfully prepared, the DTC notifies both of us that the sale will go through. We need to sign the final contracts and make whatever changes necessary to make the deal permanent. At this point, you can put the deed in your safe, and I can put the money in the bank. There is no going back at this point. Our states are permanently changed.

During the Prepare and Commit phases, in broker's lingo, the house is said to be under contract. This means no one else can bid on it or deliver another offer to the seller. What's more, specific information about the transaction is not made available to parties outside of the transaction until it is concluded. This provides the same effect isolation does according to ACID.

System Failure and Reconciliation

The DTC is a busy guy, and he only waits around for a set period of time when listening for a response from the buyer or a seller. During the Prepare phase, if the buyer or seller does not contact the DTC for some set period of time, the DTC calls off the whole transaction, and he notifies all parties that the deal is off.

If both parties indicate that they are prepared, the DTC then asks both parties to commit. If he doesn't hear from someone for some set period of time thereafter (maybe the seller slipped in the shower), the DTC becomes uncertain about the entire transaction. There is still the possibility of a reconciliation, however, after the seller regains consciousness and checks in with the DTC.

If both parties successfully complete the Prepare and Commit phases, the DTC's job is done.

Microsoft's DTC: The Reality

If you understand the preceding analogy, you understand the basic function of the real DTC, Microsoft's Distributed Transaction Coordinator. The DTC acts as a managing third party that a client application can call on to enlist two or more databases in one distributed transaction. The DTC that the client contacts becomes the *controlling DTC* and initiates contact with DTCs on each machine where a participating database is located. Together, they work under the management of the controlling DTC to make sure that all participating databases succeed in their data modifications, or none of the modifications are allowed to take place. In this way, the DTC facilitates a distributed transaction that can span many databases.

The DTC does so by employing the same two-phased commit discussed in the preceding section. Phase one involves asking the participants, each in turn, to prepare to make their proposed modifications. The second phase involves actually asking them to commit these changes. Any discontinuity or failure occurring with any participant in either of these two phases results in the DTC demanding that each participant roll back. In this way the entire conceptual transaction can be rolled back. We revisit the two-phase commit in greater detail in Chapter 9.

My escrow analogy is okay for explaining the concept of the DTC, but it is imperfect in one regard. An escrow attorney actually has knowledge of the details of the transaction. He knows that a house is being sold, and he even holds onto the deed and payment temporarily. A real DTC, however, knows nothing about what the participants are trying to accomplish. It relies entirely on the participating databases to inform it of their success or failure (or failure to report at all, which is seen as failure) and simply uses this knowledge as it walks them through the two-phase commit, telling the participants what they should do.

Microsoft's DTC first shipped with SQL Server 6.5 in April 1996. Specifically, it runs as an NT service, and it is always listening for some database client to call out and request its service. And call out they do. Let me show you how.

Using Raw DTC to Coordinate Transactions Across Multiple Databases

Like all COM+ services, the mystery surrounding transactions quickly dissipates if you understand the underlying internal processes. In this spirit, then, I propose the following scenario: Process A wants to make a data modification on Database 1 (DB1) and Database 2 (DB2). These two database modifications are, however, related, and must succeed or fail together. A distributed transaction is needed to span the two databases.

It is the responsibility of the client application to request the assistance of the DTC and enlist all the database connections it holds in the distributed transaction. The exact mechanism differs depending on what database API the client is using. Generally, there are three steps:

1. Contact a DTC on a specific machine (or default to the local) and ask for a new ITransaction interface.
2. Enlist each database connection in the transaction with this interface.
3. Commit the distributed transaction by calling ITransaction->Commit().

Steps 1 and 3 seldom vary, but step 2 differs, again, depending on what client-side database access technology you are using. If Open Database Connectivity (ODBC) is being used, Listing 8.1 demonstrates how to use the DTC to create a distributed transaction.

Listing 8.1 **Using the DTC to Create a Distributed Transaction**

```cpp
//This is a C++ client application that has two database connections
//on two different database servers on different machines.

//It demonstrates how to use the DTC to create a distributed transaction
//that spans both databases.

//Also note that there will actually be two DTCs involved. The DTC
//we are contacting here will be the controlling DTC and it will
//automatically coordinate with the DTC on the second machine
//behind the scenes.

ITransactionDispenser   *pTransactionDispenser;
ITransaction            *pTransaction;
HRESULT hr;

//below: perform ODBC style login
//and put valid connection handles
//into gCon1 and gCon2
MyDBLogon(&gCon1, "server1", "sa", "sasparilla");
MyDBLogon(&gCon2, "server2", "sa", "humtulumpus");

//Step 1
hr = DtcGetTransactionManager(
                    NULL, //get the DTC on the local machine
                    NULL,
                    IID_ITransactionDispenser,
                    0,
                    0,
                    NULL,
                    (void **)&pTransactionDispenser
                    );

hr = pTransactionDispenser->BeginTransaction(
                    NULL,
                    ISOLATIONLEVEL_ISOLATED,
                    ISOFLAG_RETAIN_DONTCARE,
                    NULL,
                    &pTransaction
                    );

//Step 2 in ODBC:
SQLSetConnectOption (gCon1->hdbc,
                    SQL_COPT_SS_ENLIST_IN_DTC,
                    (UDWORD)pTransaction);

SQLSetConnectOption (gCon2->hdbc,
                    SQL_COPT_SS_ENLIST_IN_DTC,
                    (UDWORD)pTransaction);
```

continues

Listing 8.1 **Continued**

```
//execute on database 1
MyExecuteStatement(&gCon1,"delete from current_customer where custid=22");
//execute on database 2
MyExecuteStatement(&gCon2,"delete from legacy_customer where custid=22");


// Step 3: Commit the distributed transaction
hr = pTransaction->Commit(0,0,0);

pTransaction->Release();
pTransactionDispenser->Release();

//deallocate ODBC handles
```

The following are the basic steps outlined in the code:

1. Call `DtcGetTransactionManager()` to get a transaction dispenser. (Note: This function does not return a true COM interface, however, just a vtable. This is why you don't see any calls to `CoInitialize()` and the like—it looks like a COM, but COM is not involved.)
2. Call `ITransactionDispenser->BeginTransaction` to obtain an `ITransaction` pointer.
3. Enlist your separate database connections with the `ITransaction` pointer.
4. Execute your SQL statements.
5. Call `ITransaction's->Commit()` to commit the transaction.

This general flow is always the same for client applications using the DTC directly. Obviously, the client applications need to be able to use COM, but their interaction with the DTC is pretty straightforward—request a couple of transaction-oriented interfaces and call their methods. Only the enlisting of the transaction differs significantly, depending on what database technology your client uses.

Differences in Transaction Enlistment

If your client is using ODBC, its database connections are enlisted in transactions via the `SQLSetConnectOption()` function:

```
SQLSetConnectOption (gCon2->hdbc,
                     SQL_COPT_SS_ENLIST_IN_DTC,
                     (UDWORD)pTransaction);
```

If your client application is not using ODBC, the enlistment process is different. For example, if you are only using Microsoft SQL Server databases and choose to use SQL Server's native database library, dblib, you enlist your transactions this way:

```
dbenlisttrans (dbp, pTransaction);
```

There are, of course, differences between dblib and ODBC in terms of how database connections are made and SQL statements are executed. There is one important thing to note while we are on the subject of dblib—unlike ODBC, dblib does not support the automatic transaction enlistment that gives rise to COM+ transactions. dblib cannot participate in implicit COM+ transactions because it does not support the interfaces necessary to coordinate with the COM+ Dispenser Manager.

We talk more about the Dispenser Manager in the upcoming section, "Resource Dispensers: A First Look." For now, you need only understand that although COM+ objects can use dblib to connect with SQL Server, they do not get automatic, context-based transaction support. It is best to stick with ODBC.

Transaction Enlistment by Pooled Objects

Transaction enlistment is automatic except in the case of pooled objects that participate in transactions. Object Pooling is discussed in Appendix C, "Object Pooling," but the premise is simple and can be described here. When an object is released by the client, if that component is configured to be pooled, COM+ will not destroy it. Instead COM+ keeps it alive but deactivated in some form of object pool. Then, when an object of this type is requested at a later time by another client, COM+ will reactivate a pooled object instead of creating a new instance. The client will get an interface to this pre-existing object and be none the wiser. Obviously, pooling improves performance.

Unfortunately, pooling does complicate transaction enlistment. Resource Dispensers (RDs) automatically enlist connections on behalf of the objects at the time the objects first receive the connections. Pooled objects, however, hold on to the same database connection no matter how many different parent objects they may ultimately serve because obtaining a database connection is an expensive process. Because different parent objects may be participating in different transactions, it is necessary for a pooled object upon reactivation to determine what transaction its new parent is participating in. Because context will flow from the parent to the pooled object, the pooled object need only investigate its own context to find the transaction identifier it has inherited from its new parent. If the object determines that the transaction has changed (that is, it has a new parent in a different transaction) it must obtain an ITransaction pointer from its context and manually enlist its database connection with this new transaction. In the "IObjectContextInfo" section of Chapter 7, "Contexts," I include a code example that demonstrates how a transactional, pooled object determines if its transaction had changed. In the Chapter 7 example, if the object finds that its transaction changed, it calls the `EnlistDTC()` method. We are now ready to see what is inside this method. Listing 8.2 shows the contents of `EnlistDTC()`.

Listing 8.2 A Pooled Object Reenlisting a Database Connection with a New Transaction

```
// This method enlists the current transaction with the DTC.  COM+
// usually does this implicitly when an object is created, but in the
// case of a pooled object that changes transactions without ever being
// destroyed, re-enlistment must occur.  This involves:
//
// 1. Obtaining an ITransaction pointer from IObjectContextInfo::GetTransaction
// 2. Using the ITransaction pointer to enlist in the transaction with the DTC.
//
// This code was adapted from the account.vc example, included in the Platform
➥SDK.

HRESULT PooledObject::EnlistDTC() {

// Error checking omitted for brevity:

HRESULT hr;
IObjectContext * pIObjectContext;
IObjectContextInfo *pIObjTx;

// Obtain IObjectContext and IObjectContextInfo interfaces:

hr = CoGetObjectContext(IID_IObjectContext, (void**)&pIObjectContext);

if (hr!=S_OK) {
   return hr;
}

hr = pIObjectContext->QueryInterface(IID_IObjectContextInfo, (void **)&pIObjTx);


if (SUCCEEDED(hr))
{
    // Retrieve the ITransaction pointer from IObjectContextInfo
    ITransaction *pITx;
    RETCODE rc;

    hr = pIObjTx->GetTransaction ((IUnknown **)&pTx);

    if (SUCCEEDED(hr)) {

        // Enlist with the DTC.  This is a demonstration of
        // enlistment using ODBC — it will differ depending
        // on the Resource Manager the component is using.
        // In this case, we are using
        // an OLE-DB provider on top of ODBC.

        rc = SQLSetConnectOption(m_hdbc, SQL_ATTR_ENLIST_IN_DTC, (UDWORD)pTx);

        if ((rc) != SQL_SUCCESS && (rc) != SQL_SUCCESS_WITH_INFO) {
```

```
            hr = E_FAIL;
        }

        pITx -> Release();
    }

    pIObjTx -> Release();
}

pIObjectContext->Release();
return hr;

}
```

VB6 objects cannot, as yet, be pooled. So, although they cannot benefit from the increased performance of pooling, they do not need to be concerned with manually enlisting their connections in transactions.

Summary of Distributed Transactions and the DTC

If you have never worked with distributed transactions before, you might be surprised at the relative simplicity of the preceding code. All the real difficulty involved in coordinating distributed transactions is handled by the DTC and the database systems themselves. For an in-depth look at the DTC, consult the book's sample code (www.newriders.com/complus) on Resource Managers. Among other things, this code demonstrates how DTCs on different machines communicate with one another.

Regardless of how the DTC performs its magic on the lowest level, at the highest level all the developer needs to do is inform the DTC of his intentions using a couple of simple interfaces (`ITransaction`, `ITransactionDispenser`). Then, with only a couple of additional Win32 API calls (`DtcGetTransactionManager`, `SQLSetConnectOption`, or `dbenlisttrans`), the functionality comes for free.

Keep in mind that all the distributed transaction functionality described here has been around since SQL Server 6.5 shipped, and you can see that COM+ does not add much. COM+ simply leverages the capabilities of the DTC and the transactional capabilities of most relational databases. COM+ does provide, however, a simplified, more abstracted method of using this capability without requiring the object developer to be familiar with the DTC. COM+ objects that participate in transactions do not need to call any Win32 API functions, nor do they ever need to request and manipulate any DTC-specific interfaces in the manner demonstrated in Listing 8.1.

COM+ Transactions

Science fiction writer Arthur C. Clarke once wrote, "Any sufficiently advanced technology is indistinguishable from magic." Of course, advanced is a relative concept. If you don't understand the role of the DTC and are not aware of how the data modifications of COM+ objects are automatically enlisted in transactions by COM+, it all seems like magic. If you do understand these processes, however, the magic and mystery dissolve, and COM+ becomes entirely fathomable. Toward this end, it is now time to take a look at a simple COM+ transaction and discuss what goes on under it.

COM+ Transaction Declarative Settings

Let's assume that you have two configured COM+ objects, A and B, both of which are going to modify data on two different databases. A creates B. First, how does COM+ know that these two objects are transactional? Second, how does COM+ know that the two objects are related and will be working together under the umbrella of one distributed transaction?

The answer to the second question is COM+ does not know that these objects will be working together. And the answer to the first question explains why COM+ doesn't need to know—both objects are configured in the COM+ catalog as one of the following, shown in Figure 8.1:

- **Disabled** (Developers only). Seldom used except in rare situations where the developer wants to work with the DTC directly.

- **Not Supported** (Don't participate at all). If A has a transaction and creates B, B wants nothing to do with it. What B does with a database (if anything) has nothing to do with A. B lives in a world (context) where there is no such thing as a transaction, and it doesn't want to deal with one in any way. In a sense, the transaction stops dead at B's doorstep. B does not propagate the transaction downstream to any objects it might create.

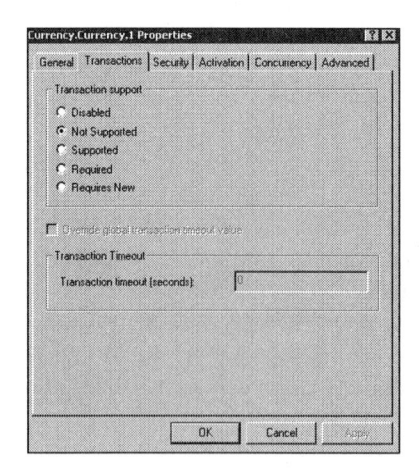

Figure 8.1 Transaction properties for a component.

- **Supported** (Participate but don't originate). B should know about transactions and can participate in them if it is created by an object that has a transaction in its context. So, if A has a transaction, and it creates B in the context of that transaction, then B's data modifications should succeed or fail in concert with A's. What's more, B propagates the transaction to any objects it creates if the context of those downstream objects doesn't forbid it. B can call its object context's `IsInTransaction()` method to determine if it is participating in a transaction or not.

- **Required** (Use existing transaction if available; create a new one if not). If A's context has a transaction, B inherits it, participates in the transaction, and passes it on to objects it creates. If A does not have a transaction, B creates a new transaction and, in the process, becomes the root of that new transaction. The term *Required* might lead you to believe that an object so marked demands that a transaction be present in the context of its creator, A, and that COM+ will not allow B to be created if B's creator lacks a transaction. This last assumption is not true, however. An object marked *Required* is saying that it needs a transaction one way or another, and if its creator doesn't supply one, B creates a new one and passes it downstream to objects it creates.

- **Requires New** (Demand a new transaction). B needs its own transaction. In B's context, only its own transaction is important; it is only interested if objects that it creates succeed or fail in their data modifications. It does not care what transaction came before it, because an object so configured will always create a new transaction of its own. This setting is often used when you want to nest one transaction in another. For example, if you want to keep some permanent record, perhaps a transactional event log of each attempt at data modification by the outer transaction, Requires New is a good setting for the inner objects that have the job of logging the attempt. This way, the inner logging objects and the outer data modification objects can commit or abort independently. Remember, if both the data modification objects and the logging objects share the same transaction, a `SetAbort()` in any object ultimately causes the data modifications for all the objects to be rolled back. The result is no data modification, but also no log of the attempt.

By setting the configuration options for objects A and B, COM+ knows how the objects are to behave in all transactional scenarios. Again, you are confronted with COM+'s declarative model. A functional mindset writes A and B so that they work with *a priori* knowledge of one another and programmatically enlist their transactions with the DTC. This is in sharp contrast to the COM+ declarative mindset that dictates that you state how the objects will behave in any situation.

We trust that COM+ can handle any discontinuity between objects whose configured attributes conflict by using interceptors or by disallowing the cooperation altogether.

In this case, assume A is configured as Requires New and B is configured as Supported. These settings allow the transaction to flow from A to B. The stage for the distributed transaction is now set. The actual source code for A and B is in Listing 8.3 and 8.4.

Listing 8.3 **Component A Source, Crediting an Account Database**

```
Sub CreditAccount()

'A reference to the component that will Debit Accounts:
Dim DebitComponent As ComponentB

'An ADO Connection object to perform database manipulation:
Dim adoConn As New ADODB.Connection

'If we encounter any problems abort the transaction:
On Error GoTo Problem

'Obtain an instance of ComponentB, and tell it to perform its
'operation (debit the account):
Set DebitComponent = New ComponentB
DebitComponent.DebitAccounts

'Assuming the operation above proceeded smoothly, credit the
'appropriate account:

'Establish a connection with SQL Server:
adoConn.Open "Driver={SQL Server};Server=Tetley;Database=CreditAccount"

'Add 10% to the account balances in the CreditAccount Database:
adoConn.Execute "UPDATE CreditAccountTable SET AccountBalance =" & _
                (AccountBalance * 1.1)", Connection, _
                adOpenDynamic, adLockOptimistic
adoConn.Close

'Let COM+ know everything went smoothly by calling SetComplete:
GetObjectContext.SetComplete
Exit Sub

Problem:
'There was a problem, so tell COM+ to abort the transaction
'by calling SetAbort:
GetObjectContext.SetAbort

End Sub
```

Listing 8.4 **Component B Source, Debiting an Account Database**

```
Sub DebitAccounts()

'ADO Data objects we will be using:
Dim adoConn As New ADODB.Connection

'If we encounter any problems, we will abort the transaction:
On Error GoTo Problem

'Establish a connection with SQL Server:
adoConn.Open "Driver={SQL Server};Server=Tetley;Database=DebitAccount"

'Subtract 10% to the account balances in the DebitAccount Database:
adoConn.Execute "UPDATE DebitAccountTable SET AccountBalance =" & _
                "(AccountBalance / 1.1)", _
                Connection, adOpenDynamic, adLockOptimistic

adoConn.Close

'Let COM+ know everything went smoothly:
GetObjectContext.SetComplete
Exit Sub

Problem:

'There was a problem, so tell COM+ to abort the transaction
'by calling SetAbort:
GetObjectContext.SetAbort

End Sub
```

As you can see, we are using ActiveX Data Objects (ADO) for database manipulation. ADO is the preferred database access technology for a number of reasons outlined in Appendix A, "ADO and OLE-DB," but RDO or the direct ODBC API also can be used.

Notice that neither A nor B do anything other than send an update statement to the database for which they have a connection. They do not explicitly engage the DTC, and they don't share any interfaces or other data. Both A and B do call `SetComplete()` (or `SetAbort()` if they encounter an error), but other than that, A simply creates B in an ordinary COM fashion.

Where to Find the Source Code

Visual C++ and Visual Basic source code can be found on this book's Web site: www.newriders.com/complus.

If A completes its data modifications and calls `SetComplete()` but B calls `SetAbort()` (or has an access violation, hangs indefinitely, or so on), all the changes for A are ultimately rolled back. The reverse is also true—if B succeeds but A fails, the data modifications for A and B are undone as the distributed transaction is aborted.

It is very important to realize, however, that `SetAbort()` and `SetComplete()` do not initiate any kind of immediate `ROLLBACK` or `COMMIT` action at the time they are called. It is tempting to think of `SetAbort()` as triggering an immediate RDBMS `ROLLBACK` statement and `SetComplete()` as firing a `COMMIT` statement, but as you see in the upcoming section, "COM+ Transaction Behavior: Voting," this is not the literal truth. That said, conceptually at least, this line of reasoning is not far off—a `SetAbort()` call probably does result in a `ROLLBACK` (and `SetCommit()` results in a `COMMIT`) statement to be issued down the line, but it doesn't happen at the moment `SetAbort()` or `SetComplete()` are called. In the section "COM+ Transaction Behavior: Voting," the reasons for this delayed committing are made clear.

Returning now to the code in Listing 8.3, clearly A and B are sharing in a distributed transaction mediated by the DTC, but how is COM+ making this happen? This question can be answered in multiple parts. This first part has to do with *Resource Dispenser* (RD).

RDs: A First Look

The concept of a RD is simple—a Dynamic Link Library (DLL) that creates and hands out resources such as database connections, threads, or live connections to any resource. RDs are, in themselves, architecturally interesting. In the book's Resource Manager (RM) source code, you find an example of how they operate and interact with other components of COM+.

As I've said, an RD is a DLL that hands out resources. Database connections are resources, and in fact, the ODBC driver manager is a COM+-compatible RD. This means that no matter what database access technology A and B use (ADO, RDO, ODBC API) to get an ODBC connection, they ultimately come into contact with the ODBC driver manager/RD. However, to support COM+ transactions, an RD must do more than simply hand out database connections to requesting objects. Specifically, the RD must be able to look at the context of the object to determine if that object is in a transaction. If the object is in a COM+ transaction, the RD must enlist the connection it gives to the object with the DTC.

The ODBC driver manager is an RD, but RDs cannot investigate the context of objects requesting resources from them on their own. There is another COM+ entity called the *Dispenser Manager (DispMan)* that has precisely this job. When an RD is first called upon by a client, the RD registers itself with DispMan (all RDs must if they want to propagate transactions). After DispMan and the RD have established a relationship (they hold interfaces to one another), they work together—the RD tells DispMan that a client object has requested a connection, and DispMan investigates the context of the requesting object on behalf of the RD and tells the RD whether to enlist the connection in a distributed transaction with the DTC.

The relationship between DispMan, the ODBC driver manager, and other RDs is interesting, complex, and worthy of detailed discussion. In fact, the Resource Manager example included with the book's source code is dedicated to exploring the roles and interrelationships of RDs, RMs, and DispMan. For now, realize that DispMan and the driver manager work together to determine whether there is a transaction in the object's context and, if so, enlists the database connection with the DTC. This is how COM+ transactions occur.

COM+ Transaction Behavior: Voting

Now that you understand the basic mechanisms underlying COM+ transactions, you can learn the behavior of objects that participate in them.

I have said that objects can vote on the outcome of a transaction by calling `SetAbort()` or `SetComplete()` on the `IObjectContext` interface (introduced in Chapter 7) they obtain from COM+. The question then arises, when are the results of this vote tallied?

Contrary to intuition, a distributed transaction is not necessarily rolled back the moment an object calls `SetAbort()`. In this way, `SetAbort()` is not like `ROLLBACK TRANSACTION` which has an immediate effect on a relational database. For an object, `SetAbort()` initiates no action whatsoever—all it does is flip the object's commit bit (this bit is in the object's context) to 0. This bit only becomes significant when COM+ systematically checks the status of all participating objects. This occurs when the root object (the object that originated the transaction) has completed its work and is deactivated.

COM+ attempts to commit a transaction when the root object that originated the transaction deactivates. The root object might deactivate when the object has called `SetAbort()` or `SetComplete()` (or even `SetDeactivateOnReturn(TRUE)`) and has returned from a method call to its client. As you see in the next section and all subsequent sections of this chapter, calling these methods flips one or both status bits in the object's context. Although these status bits can let COM+ know that the root object is allowed to be deactivated, they don't directly cause the object to deactivate. Another entity known as *JITA (Just-In-Time Activation)* does this.

> **Deactivate**
>
> The phrase *completed work* is somewhat vague, and the term *deactivate* can further furrow the brow. It is important to realize that, in COM+, objects are not necessarily deleted when the client releases all references or completes a method call to them. If the object supports pooling, it is disassociated with the client and put in a pool to be used again by other clients. If the object does not support pooling, it is destroyed. The term *deactivation* covers both cases. Because VB objects do not support pooling, they are destroyed when deactivated.

In the preceding case, COM+ attempts to commit a transaction when the root object has completed its work and is deactivated. Somewhere up the creation chain, however, there must be some client EXE that created the root object. This brings about a third scenario where COM+ can try to commit a transaction: The client EXE itself calls `SetAbort()` or `SetComplete()`.

Base Clients, Voting, and the *TransactionContext* Object

It might seem impossible for a *base client* (another term for a client executable) to vote on a transaction given that `SetAbort()` and `SetComplete()` are methods of the context object. Remember, a client executable does not run in COM+, so it does not have a context. Without a context, any request the client executable makes to obtain an `IObjectContext` or an `IContextState` interface fails. You might, therefore, imagine that it is impossible for a client executable to call `SetAbort()` and `SetComplete()` directly. You would be right, except that COM+ provides a special object that a client executable can create and then use to vote on a transaction. The following code, shown in both VC++ and VB, creates a transaction object that a client executable (lacking a context of its own) can use to vote on the transaction it kicked off by creating first (root) transactional object:

In VC++:

```
ITransactionContextEx *m_pTransactionContext
CoCreateInstance(CLSID_TransactionContextEx, NULL, CLSCTX_INPROC,
            IID_ITransactionContextEx,
        (void**)&m_pTransactionContext);
```

In VB:

```
Dim myTranContext As New TransactionContextEx
```

The only hitch is the client EXE must use `ITransactionContextEx->CreateInstance()` to create the first object. This might seem very similar to MTS coding where it was necessary for object A to create objects using `IObjectContext->CreateInstance()` so that the context would flow from A to B. The situation you have with `ITransactionContextEx` is exactly the reverse—COM+ is providing a way for the context to flow from Object A back to the client executable that created it. Technically, the client still does not have a true context, but it does have one of the key advantages of one—the capability to vote on the outcome of a transaction.

The Methods of *IObjectContext*

Now that we have laid the groundwork for understanding COM+ transactions, let's take a look at each method of `IObjectContext`. Note that I am not listing these methods in vtable order; rather, they are grouped by category.

COM+ Transactions

CreateInstance: A Legacy Method

The `CreateInstance` method is included for backward compatibility but need never be used again. In the old days of MTS years prior to COM+, it was important for one transactional object to create another using this method call so that MTS had an opportunity to pass transactional information from the creating object to created object. In other words, this was how context flowed in MTS. Prior to COM+, however, COM had no sense of context, so creating an object with the `CoCreateInstance` method in C++, or `New` or `CreateObject` methods in VB and J++, resulted in an object that did not know about and could not share in its parent's transaction.

Basic Voting and Associated Methods

As we've discussed, transactions are democratic, and every object gets to vote. An object wears its vote much like a politically active person might return from the voting booth wearing a pin on his lapel saying, "I voted for Candidate X."

An object's lapel pin has the form of two bits stored in its context. These two bits are often referred to as the *Happy* and *Done* bits (*HD*). When an object calls `SetAbort()`, `SetComplete()`, `DisableCommit()`, or `EnableCommit()`, all these functions are doing is flipping these bits into one of four configurations, which follow:

- I am happy and finished with all my work: HD 11.
- I am unhappy with what I've done, but am finished: HD 01.
- I am happy so far, but am not done; things could still go wrong: HD 10.
- I am unhappy so far, but am not done; things might improve : HD 00.

Let's take a look at how each of the four voting methods map to these configurations:

- `SetComplete()`: HD 11

    An object calls this method to indicate that it has performed all of its database modifications, and they have been successful. This method flips a bit in the object's context (sometimes called the *Happy bit*) and COM+ interprets that as a yes vote. Remember, `SetComplete()` does not necessarily initiate any kind of action; you are not calling `Commit` on your database. It simply flips a bit or a vote that will be tallied later.

- `SetAbort()`: HD 01

    This method is called when an object encounters an error during its data modifications or, for whatever reason, becomes unhappy and wants to abort the transaction (see Listing 8.5). Calling this method registers a vote; it does not initiate an immediate action. Specifically, the Happy bit is flipped to a state of sadness. Note that `SetAbort()` must be called explicitly by the object to indicate a negative vote; it does not happen automatically in the event of a database error. Thus, it is common to encounter code that checks the success or failure of a database modification method and calls `SetAbort()` or `SetComplete()` accordingly.

Listing 8.5 **How to Properly Abort a Transaction**

```
Sub DataModify()

'If we encounter any problems, abort the Transaction:
On Error GoTo Problem

<DO SOMETHING WITH DATABASE>

'if an error occurs in VB, control jumps
'to the error block defined in the "On Error" statement.

'if we get to this portion of the code, then
'everything proceeded smoothly.  We indicate this
'to COM+ by calling SetComplete().

'Note that this DOES NOT mean that the transaction will
'commit.  COM+ must tally ALL components particpating in
'the transaction and get their approval before it
'commits.

GetObjectContext.SetComplete
Exit Sub

Problem:

'Let COM+ know there was a problem by calling SetAbort.

GetObjectContext.SetAbort

End Sub
```

JITA, Object Statefulness, and Stateful Voting Methods

The next two voting methods, `EnableCommit()` and `DisableCommit()`, are more complex than `SetAbort()` and `SetComplete()`. To understand them fully, we first need to talk about object state.

With the introduction of MTS, the term *stateless objects* was whispered in the corridors of many an IT shop. Esoteric Socratic discussions of statelessness ensued, and confusion gripped the MTS landscape.

This confusion arose because some said that, to scale well, objects needed some form of pooling and/or automatic deallocation. The traditional client/server mechanism where many clients have dedicated connections to one singleton server did not scale well. Of course, many developers disagreed. At the time of MTS's introduction, COM allowed (and still does allow) *out-of-process* or EXE servers. An out-of-process server gave the developer fine-grain control of threading, memory allocation, object instantiation, and other tools allowing the seasoned developer to write a very scalable COM component if his ability allowed.

The problem with writing a scalable singleton server was that everyone would end up reinventing the wheel. Inevitably, different developers in different places would end up creating schemes for pooling connections, pooling object instances, and so on. This kind of infrastructure was, however, of common use to all object developers, so Microsoft decided to write it for them.

Singleton servers simply did not fit in the MTS model where objects were expected to flit in and out of existence like quantum particles. MTS wanted lifetime control, which meant developers had to give up some control. Specifically, developers had to accommodate the fact that a client application might create an instance of an object, but the client might actually call methods into a different object each time it made a method invocation. After all, you wouldn't want to keep an object alive consuming precious resources for a client that made a method call once a day, right?

But this was a shot across the bow for many developers. If they could not count on the client controlling the lifetime of an object, and could not even assume a dedicated connection, it meant they could not keep state information in member variables or anywhere else in their object. There was, however, something called the *shared property manager*, which is a kind of global storage area where stateless objects can keep information for their own use or the shared use of other objects. But, responding much like the French mob at King Louis XVI's gates to Marie Antoinette's, "let them eat cake"—riots ensued.

Left out, however, was the fact that an MTS object could keep state. In fact, by default, objects were stateful. The state could only be kept for a limited duration and you would ask for it explicitly only when you needed it. If you treated state as a privilege to be invoked only when needed, as opposed to an absolute entitlement, you opened the way for greater scalability.

This scalability was brought about by something called *JITA*. JITA (sometimes referred to as JIT) is the consummate downsizer. It tries to deactivate your object whenever possible (usually after a method call returns), and if your object doesn't explicitly state its desire not to be deactivated (either by COM catalog configuration or method call), you cannot be sure when it will be knocked out of commission.

In traditional COM, there was the implicit assumption that when a client application instantiated an object, they were bound to one another via a dedicated connection. Until the client called the final `Release()` on the object's interface, that particular object instance serviced that particular client. With JITA employed, however, this is no longer true. Your client might call into a different object instance with every method call even though it is holding on to the same proxy. COM+ is keeping the RPC channel alive, but is switching the object instance on the stub side, unbeknownst to the client.

With JITA, it seems impossible to write a transactional object that can keep state. JITA always wants to deactivate your object wherever possible. So the only option it seems is to declaratively disable JITA support for an object in the COM+ catalog. However, all transactional objects must use JITA. Fortunately, getting JITA off your object's back is simple even for transactional objects—just call `DisableCommit()` or `EnableCommit()`.

- `DisableCommit()`: HD 00

    This method flips the Done bit in the object's context. When JITA comes calling and sees this bit flipped, it knows that the object isn't done yet. Although the object might not be doing anything at that moment, it is expecting other method calls from its client. Although JITA likes to deactivate the object as soon as the first method call completes, it leaves it alone and goes off and bothers some other object.

However, if the root object deactivates or the transaction timeout interval of 60 seconds elapse, JITA comes back with a vengeance. COM+ looks at the combination of the two bits and says, in effect, "I see that you are not done, but it is too late now. You will be deactivated, and I will abort the transaction given that you are obviously not happy."

- `EnableCommit()`: HD 10

   The object that calls this method is saying that it is expecting other method calls from its client, is keeping state, and that JITA should leave it alone for the time being. JITA, however, comes back when the root object deactivates or 60 seconds elapse. COM+ then interprets these settings and says, "You aren't done, but I guess whatever else you where planning to do wasn't so important that the transaction should be doomed by your not finishing it. It is time to be deactivated, but because you are happy with everything, I will commit the transaction if everyone else is happy too."

Note that when transactional objects are first activated, it is as if they implicitly call this method. "Happy yes, Done no" is their default disposition. So, if you do not call `SetAbort()` or `SetComplete()` before returning from a method call, JITA assumes your object is stateful and does not deactivate it after a method call to it completes.

Basic Informational Methods

The `IObjectContext` methods that follow in this section are used by objects to gather information about their present context. We begin with a method that allows an object to find out about the security context of the caller:

- `IsCallerInRole`. COM+ has a role-based security system (fully described in Chapter 12, "Security") that works with and simplifies NT's more sophisticated authentication paradigm. As its name implies, this method allows the developer to determine if the current user of the object is a member of a particular role group; for example, is he a manager?

   Although security can be set on the interface of the method declaratively, this gives the developer finer-grained control. Declarative security allows you to permit or deny access to a method or interface, but `IsCallerInRole` might be used when you want to provide access to a method for everyone, but want to change what the method does depending on the role of the user.

- `IsInTransaction`. It is as simple as its name implies. Although transaction participation is a declarative attribute, you might want to call this method to make absolutely sure that a given object will or will not function within a transaction in the event the declarative attributes in the COM+ catalog are improperly set. This is probably overkill, but you can imagine writing an object that manipulates incredibly sensitive data, and you want to make certain that it never runs outside a transaction.

- `IsSecurityEnabled`. It is possible to set security for a COM+ application so that role-based security is not used. This method returns `FALSE` in this instance. As with `IsInTransaction`, this method can be used to enforce security requirements for an object independent of what the COM+ catalog says. Of course, you cannot force role-based security to be reinstated at the moment of a method call, but you can prevent your object from operating without security.

Finer Granularity Control with *IContextState*

A transactional object can get all it needs from the `IObjectContext` interface. However, `IObjectContext` is kind of a blunt instrument when it comes to setting an object's Consistency Happy and Done bits. You might have noticed `IObjectContext` offers no way to change the consistency or Done bit independently. Each method in this interface sets both bits at the same time.

Another drawback to `IObjectContext` is that all four of its voting and duration methods assume that you are in a transaction; they all manipulate the consistency bit, as well as the Done bit. Suppose, however, that your object is not in a transaction but wants to flip its Done bit to indicate to JITA that it is ready to be deactivated or wants to stick around. It is true that your non-transactional object still can do this by calling `EnableCommit()`, `DisableCommit()`, `SetAbort()`, or `SetComplete()`, but these methods result in the manipulation of the consistency bit (which is not looked at in a non-transactional context) and results in misleading source code. `IContextState`, however, is a refinement of `IObjectContext` that lets you set the consistency and Done bit separately. It is also logically simpler and can make for clearer code because it only contains methods that have to do with voting on a transaction or deciding whether to allow deactivation. This is in sharp contrast to `IObjectContext` with its hodgepodge of creation, voting, and informational methods.

Now that I've made the case for `IObjectContext`, let's look at its methods:

- `SetDeactivateOnReturn`. Sets the Done bit to 1 or 0 depending on the Boolean that is passed in. It ultimately has the same effect as `IObjectContext-> EnableCommit()`, but does not affect the consistency bit.
- `GetDeactivateOnReturn`. Returns the value of the Done bit as a Boolean.
- `SetMyTransactionVote`. Sets the consistency bit to true or false by taking in a type library defined enumeration (see code listing immediately following), and has the same effect as `SetAbort()` or `SetComplete()`, but does not modify the Done bit.

```
typedef enum {
    TxCommit = 0,
    TxAbort = 1
} tagTransactionVote;
```

- `GetMyTransactionVote`. Returns either `TxCommit` or `TxAbort` depending on the value of the consistency bit.

Transactions, ASP Pages, and IIS

In the previous chapter, I speak a little about Internet Information Server (IIS) as Active Server Pages (ASP). For interest's sake, I'm going to revisit this topic because ASP pages have some unique transactional requirements. Read this section only if you are interested in how IIS operates; if you aren't, skip ahead to the next chapter.

Just a few sections ago, I mention that a client EXE needs to create a new instance of `TransactionContext` object if it wants to vote on the outcome of a transaction. This is because, unlike the objects it creates, an EXE does not have a context and has no access to `SetAbort()` or `SetComplete()`. When the EXE creates its first transaction object, it is left out of the loop in terms of voting—the root object it creates might father a whole line of descendents, and the transaction might flow to each one. The client is, however, cut off from the transaction after the root object takes over. Fortunately, the client EXE can borrow a context by creating a `TransactionContext` object and can use it to both create descendent objects and vote with them.

ASP pages have a similar kind of problem and solution. Much like client executables, ASP pages cannot, on their own, enlist in or vote on a transaction. Although COM objects that the ASP pages create can participate in transactions, suppose you have a series of related ASP pages that do nothing more than modify databases via ADO. How can they use transactions?

The answer is as simple as placing one of the following tags at the beginning of an ASP page:

```
<%@ Transaction=Required%>
```

After doing this, the script can, at any point, call `ObjectContext.SetAbort` or `ObjectContext.SetComplete` to vote on the outcome of the transaction.

A transaction can span multiple ASP pages providing that a parent ASP page transfers control to another page by using the `Server.Execute` or `Server.Transfer` commands:

ASP/VBScript

```
Server.Execute ("SomeOther.asp") //Server.Transfer would also work
```

This is eerily similar to the MTS-style of object creation and transaction propagation:

```
GetObjectContext.CreateInstance("SomeObject.Object")
```

The principles are quite similar. When an ASP page is run, IIS creates a `Page` COM object that represents that page. The `Transaction=` tag at the beginning can make the `Page` object transactional. And just like in MTS, the transaction can flow to descendent `Page` objects (other ASP pages) if their `Transaction=` tags are compatible. Interestingly, the following four components you can find in the IIS Utilities Application are used for this purpose:

- `ASP.ObjectContextTxNotSupported.1`
- `ASP.ObjectContextTxRequired.1`
- `ASP.ObjectContextTxRequiresNew.1`
- `ASP.ObjectContextTxSupported.1`

Summary

A transaction is an atomic unit of work that can either be committed permanently or completely undone by a relational database. A distributed transaction is a conceptual transaction that can span more than one database. For distributed transactions to work, an RD, such as the ODBC driver manager, needs to enlist the connections to different databases used by different clients with the DTC. The DTC, by virtue of a two-phased commit protocol, ensures that all participating databases succeed in each of these two phases, Prepare and Commit.

COM+ objects can participate in the same transaction because their contexts allow transaction information to flow from the creator to the created if their transactional settings are compatible. When an object participating in a transaction requests a database connection, the COM+ DispMan checks the context of the requesting object and informs the RD whether it should enlist that connection in the transaction.

If the data modifications made by multiple objects are related, those objects should share in the same COM+ transaction. When participating in the same transaction, any single object can notify COM+ of the success or failure of its data modifications by voting, thereby influencing the success of the overall transaction. An object can vote by requesting an `IObjectContext` from its context object and calling `SetCommit()`, `SetAbort()`, `EnableCommit()`, or `DisableCommit()` on this interface. These methods do not immediately cause any action; rather, they flip bits in an object's context called the Happy and Done bits. When the root object of a transaction has completed its work and is deactivated, COM+ inspects these bits in the context of all objects participating in a transaction. By checking the status bits, COM+ can make sure that all objects voted positively. If one or more objects voted negatively, COM+ commands all DTCs involved to roll back their changes.

9

Compensating Resource Managers

FRUSTRATED WITH THE INADEQUACIES OF the prevailing hierarchical storage schemes of the day, in 1970 an IBM researcher named Edgar Codd published a general specification for a relational database (Codd, Edgar. 1970. A Relational Model of Data for Large Shared Data Banks. *Communications of the ACM,* Vol. 13, No. 6, June, 377-387.). Codd did not say much about how his relational calculus might be implemented in a server, but he fired the starting gun for a new era in data storage technology.

Companies like Oracle, Ingres, and of course IBM rushed to provide actual, salable implementations of Codd's work. After a period of contention about the query language (Oracle and others favored SQL—Ingres held out for something called QUEL), relational database technology became, more or less, industry standard.

Relational database systems have grown significantly in terms of their capabilities. Far from simply being efficient, convenient repositories for data, they have also become safe, robust places to put data. Although each Database Management System (DBMS) handles transactions and disaster recovery differently, they all promise a high degree of fault-tolerance.

> **Enabling A CRM**
>
> For components of a COM+ application to use a CRM, the "Enable Compensating Resource Managers" check box needs to be clicked on the Advanced tab of the application's (that is, the one hosting the CRM) properties.
>
> For additional configuration settings, including transactional and JIT settings for the worker and compensator, the MSDN offers a concise list so there is no need to duplicate it here. Simply query MSDN for the string, "Installing CRM Components."

For all that relational databases offer, however, there are simply times when you need to manipulate data that just doesn't fit well into a relational model. And although it is a relatively straightforward process to write code to query from and modify data in some proprietary form, it is exponentially more complex to make the process fail-safe.

Fortunately, COM+ provides a framework for writing server-side components that can modify data at the behest of a transactional client (and be governed by the Distributed Transaction Coordinator [DTC]), just as Microsoft SQL Server does. This framework is called the *Compensating Resource Manager (CRM)* and is the subject of this chapter.

The Resource Manager

Reinventing the code necessary to handle power-outages, user-requested rollbacks, interrupted modifications, and so on for non-relational data is not something most developers have the time and resources to do. Fortunately, COM+ provides an architecture that helps—that of the CRM.

Before we talk about the CRM, we need to introduce some new terminology. Microsoft's technology can sometimes be confusing because they often attach new names to existing technologies. For example, the terms *OCX*, *ActiveX*, *OLE*, and *COM* can all be used to describe the exact same technology.

Usually, Microsoft reinvents a technology when it is refitted to play a part in some new, larger initiative. For example, the term *OCX* was once used to describe a graphical COM control that could be put on a VB form. When Microsoft took on Java on the Web-front, however, it adapted the concept of the OCX so that it could exist on an Internet Explorer 3 Web page. At this point, the humble OCX became an ActiveX control even though it didn't fundamentally change. The term *ActiveX* became a more general term that described Microsoft's overall Web strategy in a more generic fashion. According to the party line, the ActiveX control was a particular implementation and utilization of ActiveX technology.

Just as Microsoft's sudden emphasis on the World Wide Web warped established terminology and made strange bedfellows of previously unrelated or loosely related technologies, now COM+'s emphasis on the Enterprise is doing the same thing. In the new Enterprise philosophy, the term database (or worse, relational database) is thought to be too limiting. These words evoke images of SQL and relational tables, but not all corporate data repositories are based on relational databases. And so, Microsoft has adopted a term already used in the industry that can refer to any type of application that manages data and can participate in COM+ transactions—*Resource Manager (RM)*.

Strictly speaking, an RM must support COM+ transactions, but this is really to say that it can talk to the DTC and knows how to handle a two-phased commit. Specifically, an RM must support one or both of the following two-phased commit protocols:

- **X/Open XA.** X/Open (www.opengroup.com) is an international standards body that defined the XA standard. XA is not an acronym, rather it is the name of a protocol. Specifically, it is a two-phased commit protocol originating in the UNIX world. Most popular transaction monitors (TMs) systems—BEA Tuxedo and Encina, to name a couple—interoperate with a variety of relational databases such as Oracle, DB2, and Sybase (all are examples of RMs) to make distributed transactions possible. UNIX-style TMs perform the same functionality as Microsoft's DTC, and XA is the protocol that the TMs use to govern one or many XA-compliant RMs during a distributed transaction.
- **OLE Transactions.** This protocol is a two-phased commit protocol just like XA. OLE Transactions is based on methods callable from COM interfaces; XA, on the other hand, is API-based. In the end, however, both protocols accomplish the same result. OLE Transactions can be said to be DTC's native two-phase protocol. For the DTC (and therefore COM+ transactions) to work with an RM, the RM must support OLE Transactions or must supply an OLE Transaction-to-XA conversion mechanism. As discussed in "XA and the DTC," sidebar, this conversion mechanism is usually located in the ODBC driver or OLE-DB provider supplied by the vendor.

Most major relational databases support one or both of these protocols. If they support OLE Transactions, they can automatically participate in COM+ transactions. If they only support XA, they can only participate in COM+ transactions if the ODBC driver (or some other form of resource dispenser the vendor makes available) works with the DTC to translate the OLE Transaction calls to XA-compliant ones. If the RM supports both, it gets the best of all worlds.

So, RMs are commonly relational databases, but do not need to be. Microsoft Message Queue (MSMQ) is an example of an RM that is not a relational database. As you will see, COM+ messaging relies on MSMQ. It gives you the ability to send asynchronous transactional messages. We'll discuss this more in Chapter 10, "Queued Components."

XA and the DTC

XA is not natively handled by the DTC. The DTC uses the OLE Transactions protocol (described in the next section, "Components of the CRM"). It is important to realize that although the DTC has facilities (a series of conversion interfaces) to convert an OLE-based transaction to an XA-based one, this is not an automatic process. The DTC cannot, on its own, interoperate with an XA-based RM like an older version of Oracle. However, if the ODBC driver (or other connection resource dispenser) supplied by the RM's vendor is specifically designed to work with the DTC to perform this conversion behind the scenes, it may seem as though the DTC does automatically govern transactions on XA-only RMs. Don't be fooled—the DTC is biased toward OLE Transactions. To work with XA-only RMs, the vendor has to supply a translator—usually buried in its ODBC driver or OLE-DB Provider.

By supporting either XA or OLE Transactions, an RM is indicating it knows how to temporarily buffer changes to its data source, whatever that may be, and roll them back or commit them whenever asked by the DTC. This implies that the RM needs to keep some kind of log that records all changes. If the RM crashes, it can reopen the log when it is run again and either complete or undo whatever changes are necessary to ensure the integrity of its data.

Furthermore, the RM must serialize all database changes while in the midst of a transaction. It would be very difficult to roll back changes indicated in the log, if other processes were continually allowed to change data underneath it. Most relational databases lock the table(s) or row(s) when a transaction is in progress and block all data modifications for all connections other than those enlisted in the transaction. The locks are released only after the transaction is complete.

In short, writing a proper RM is difficult. The CRM is a kind of template and protocol that, if followed, takes a lot of the complexity out of writing an RM.

Components of the CRM

You have data that is non-relational in nature and have decided to write your own CRM to manage this data on behalf of transactional COM+ objects. Although writing a true RM poses quite a challenge, writing a CRM is not difficult.

A CRM consists of two separate COM coclasses that you must implement. The first coclass is the `Worker`. The second coclass is the `Compensator`.

Worker

The `Worker` coclass supports whatever methods you choose to give it. In our example (Listing 9.1), we have a `Worker` class with methods like `AddAccount()`, `ChangeAccount()`, and so on. In the transactional examples we've discussed so far, COM+ objects are manipulating relational databases (which are RMs) via ADO methods like `Execute()`. Philosophically, an object that calls `ChangeAccount()` on our `Worker` object is doing the exact same thing as an object executing an update statement via some method of ADO; it is requesting that a data change be made by an underlying RM in the context of a transaction.

Listing 9.1 **Constants Common to Both *Worker* and *Compensator***

```
'Constants shared by both the compensator and worker components:

'Error Code indicating that the compensator is in recovery mode:
Public Const XACT_E_RECOVERYINPROGRESS = &H8004D082

'Constants used when writing the log file:
Public Const ADD_ACCOUNT_COMMAND = 1
Public Const REMOVE_ACCOUNT_COMMAND = 2
Public Const CHANGE_ACCOUNT_COMMAND = 3
```

The Worker knows about the structure of the underlying data and knows how and where to make changes. However, and this is the interesting part, although the Worker coclass might make changes to the underlying data, these changes require the participation of the Compensator to make these changes permanent or to undo them altogether should any COM+ object participating in the transaction call SetAbort().

The relationship between the Worker and Compensator is very much like the relationship between an office worker and his office manager. It is often, though not necessarily, the case that a worker (Worker) does most of the legwork, but ultimately it is the manager (Compensator) who applies a rubber stamp to make the change permanent and official. On the other hand, the manager might say, "This work is no good!" or "One of the higher-ups have canceled the project, so what you've done is no longer valid" and see to it that all the work is undone. Of course, different offices have different balances of responsibility between workers and their managers. In some companies, the clerk might merely propose a thing, and the manager actually does most the legwork to make it happen. There is no absolute rule about who does what, except that both the Worker and Compensator must work together.

It is important to realize that, just as with our office example, a Worker and Compensator are not necessarily working at the same time. It might be the case that the Worker works the evening shift and leaves some kind of information log about what he has done with an office clerk. When the manager (Compensator) comes in the next morning, the Clerk gives the manager the log and says, "This what the Worker proposed doing, can you approve this and make it permanent?"

The *CRMClerk*

Note that we have introduced another player in our drama—the Clerk. The Clerk keeps log information on behalf of the Worker and shares it with the Compensator when the Compensator is available. In this metaphor, there are three roles or characters—that of Worker, Compensator, and Clerk. I have chosen these characters because they have direct parallels when writing a real CRM.

The Worker object must support interfaces and methods that transactional COM+ objects can call to make modifications to your data. In a very real sense, the Worker is your RM, so these methods can be whatever you want them to be and can do whatever you deem appropriate. Whatever these methods do, however, it is critical that the Worker record any actions resulting from each method call to some kind of log before the Worker makes any kind of physical change. Remember, just as with our office example, there is a clerk who records a log of what the Worker intends to do and passes it from Worker to Compensator. It is ultimately the Compensator who either approves the changes and makes them permanent or undoes them. If the Worker fails to record his actions before doing them and then decides to quit (or crash), the Compensator has no idea how to undo the Worker's changes. This is why it is important that the Worker log his actions with the Clerk before making any physical changes. In the CRM, this clerk is called, appropriately, the CRMClerk. The CRMClerk is a COM object defined in the comsvcs.dll type library that all `Worker`s must ask for and use. It creates a log on behalf of the `Worker`; after the `Worker` obtains an instance of the `CRMClerk`, it can call the `Clerk`'s methods to make additions to this log. Getting the `Clerk` is as simple as using the following code:

```
Dim Clerk as CRMClerk
Set Clerk = New CRMClerk
```

The `Clerk` allows the `Worker` to write to a log file (created and maintained by `Clerk`) by supporting the `ICrmLogControl` interface. The `Worker` need only `QueryInterface` (QI) for it, as demonstrated:

```
Dim CrmLogControl As ICrmLogControl
Set CrmLogControl = Clerk
```

Note that in VB, the `ICrmLogControl` interface is the `CRMClerk`'s default interface. You can either call `ICrmLogControl`'s methods through a variable of type `ICrmLogControl` or directly on the `Clerk` object itself.

After the `Worker` has the `ICrmLogControl` interface, it can write to the `Clerk`'s log file. The `Worker` can either write an array of variants or a binary large object (BLOB). Let's demonstrate using variants (see Listing 9.2).

Listing 9.2 **Writing an Array of Variants to the Log File**

```
Dim vntLogFileEntries(2) As Variant
vntLogFileEntries(0) = "LEDGERID:66:MAKEBALANCE:4500"
vntLogFileEntries(1) = "LEDGERID:176:MAKEBALANCE:5500"
vntLogFileEntries(2) = "WRITEEVENT: Debit and Credit for $500 complete"

On Error GoTo ErrorHandler
'Write to the log file, and ensure it is durable:
CrmLogControl.WriteLogRecordVariants LogFileEntries
```

It really is as simple as it seems. The `Worker` writes arrays of variants via the `CRMClerk` to the log file the `CRMClerk` will maintain (a complete CRM Worker is provided in Listing 9.3). It is completely up to the developer to decide how much and what kind of data should be logged. Ultimately, the log file is presented to the `Compensator` in one of the following two ways:

- If all COM+ objects participating in the transaction vote that the transaction is good, the `Compensator` is told to commit the changes and is given the log.
- If one or more objects vote for the transaction to fail, however, the `Compensator` is asked to roll back the changes and once again, is given the log to do so.

Whatever logging protocol you create and use, it must be understood by both the `Worker` and `Compensator`. What's more, the log should contain all the information that the `Compensator` could possibly need to either commit or roll back the changes.

Let's take a moment and summarize what we have so far. We know that the Worker writes data changes to a log file, and we know that that log file will be given to the Compensator and asked by COM+ to either commit or roll back the changes. This question, however, arises: Who does the physical work of modifying the data, the Worker or the Compensator? Writing to a log file is one thing, and it is clear that the Worker writes to the log file via the CRMClerk, and the Compensator is given the log when the COM+ transaction as a whole commits or aborts. When it comes to actual, physical changes, the developer determines how much actual work the Worker and Compensator each perform. It is really governed by what kind of data the CRM is supposed to modify and how many steps are necessary to modify it.

The first example most developers see of a CRM is one that creates and modifies flat files. In this CRM, the Worker creates the file in a temporary directory after writing the file's path in the log. The Compensator then receives the log and from it, figures out where the temporary file is. If the Compensator is called in the context of a commit, it copies the file to the permanent directory. If it is called because a participating object named SetAbort(), it deletes the file from the temporary directory. Without getting too complex but adding a little spice, Listing 9.3 displays the code for a CRM Worker that performs modifications to an XML file using Microsoft's XML Document Object Model (DOM). If the listing seems daunting, just read the source comments along the way and you'll find that there is nothing at all complicated about a CRM Worker.

Listing 9.3 **A Complete CRM Worker Component that Modifies Account Balance in an XML File**

```
'XMLWorker: Worker component for the XML CRM.
'
'This component exposes the interface that a client sees and interacts with.
'It is responsible for associating itself with a compensator component that
'understands the log it writes, and can commit/abort the operations that it
'performs

Option Explicit

'The worker component needs an instance of the CRM clerk, to associate itself
'with a compensator and to write its operations to the log:
Dim Clerk As CRMClerk
Dim CrmLogControl As ICrmLogControl

'The progID of the compensator this worker component is associated with:
Const COMPENSATOR_ProgID = "XMLCRMVB.XMLCompensatorVB"
Const COMPENSATOR_DESCRIPTION = "XML VB Compensator component"

'Indicates if the compensator has been registered:
Dim bIsCompensatorRegistered As Boolean

'A Variant array that is used to write to the log:
Dim vntLogFileEntries(3) As Variant
```

continues

Listing 9.3 **Continued**

```
'This Worker component uses Microsoft's XML Document
'Object Model (DOM) components to perform XML manipulation:
Dim xmlDoc As New DOMDocument
Dim xmlNodes As IXMLDOMNodeList
Dim xmlNode As IXMLDOMNode
Dim xmlBalanceNode As IXMLDOMNode
Dim xmlAccountNode As IXMLDOMNode
Dim xmlAccountBalanceNode As IXMLDOMNode
Dim xmlAccountNumberNode As IXMLDOMNode
Dim xmlRootNode As IXMLDOMNode


Private Sub Class_Initialize()
    bIsCompensatorRegistered = 0
End Sub


'This routine is called by the Initialize method.  It
'obtains an instance of the Clerk for writing to the log.
Private Sub ObtainCRMClerk()

    On Error GoTo ErrorHandler
    Set Clerk = New CRMClerk
    Set CrmLogControl = Clerk
    Exit Sub

ErrorHandler:
    MsgBox "ObtainCRMClerk ErrorHandler " + Err.Description

End Sub

'This procedure associates this worker component with
'the compensator:
Private Sub RegisterCompensator()

    'If we have already registered the compensator then
    'exit the subroutine:
    If bIsCompensatorRegistered = True Then
        Exit Sub
    End If

    'Register the componensator with the DTC.
    'There is the possibility that the Compensator is in the
    'the process of recovering from a previous shutdown, hence
    'the error checking loop:
    On Error Resume Next
    Do
        CrmLogControl.RegisterCompensator COMPENSATOR_ProgID, _
        COMPENSATOR_DESCRIPTION, CRMREGFLAG_ALLPHASES
        DoEvents
```

```vb
        Loop Until Err.Number <> XACT_E_RECOVERYINPROGRESS

        'Was there an error registering the compensator?
        If Err.Number <> 0 Then GoTo ErrorHandler

        'Indicate that the compensator has been registered, so
        'subsequent calls to register the compensator abort:
        bIsCompensatorRegistered = True
        Exit Sub

ErrorHandler:
        MsgBox "XMLVBWorker: RegisterCompensator" & Err.Description & " - " &
    ➥Hex$(Err.Number)

End Sub


'The following methods are exposed by the worker component to
'client applications.  They perform the desired XML operations
'on the specified file, and write to the system log
'indicating what operations were performed. Note that each of these
'methods calls Initialize(), which registers the XML compensator
'if it has not already been registered:

Sub AddAccount(AccountNumber As Long, Balance As Double, Filename As String)

        Dim dAccountBalance As Double
        Dim iNode As Integer

        On Error GoTo ErrorHandler
        Initialize

        'Check to see if the account already exists.  We do this BEFORE
        'writing to the log, because if it does exist we don't want
        'add an already existing account. Any easy way to check for existence
        'is to run the GetBalance function against the account. If there IS
        'a balance, then the account already exists so we have a problem:

        If GetBalance(AccountNumber, Filename, dAccountBalance) Then
            MsgBox "Account already exists"
            GetObjectContext.SetAbort
            Exit Sub
        End If

        'Before we perform ANY operations on the XML file,
        'we have to write to the log to indicate what we are doing.

        'Our entry in the log will contain:

        '   1.) The operation (Adding an Account)
        '   2.) The AccountNumber we are adding
```

continues

Listing 9.3 **Continued**

```
'     3.) The Balance it will start with
'     4.) The XML filename we are writing to:

vntLogFileEntries(0) = ADD_ACCOUNT_COMMAND
vntLogFileEntries(1) = AccountNumber
vntLogFileEntries(2) = Balance
vntLogFileEntries(3) = Filename

'Write to the log file, and ensure it is durable:
CrmLogControl.WriteLogRecordVariants vntLogFileEntries
CrmLogControl.ForceLog

'Log file was written, so now try to add the account to the
'XML file.  This uses Microsoft's XML Parser:
xmlDoc.Load Filename
Set xmlNodes = xmlDoc.childNodes.Item(0).childNodes

'Check to make sure we are not adding an account that
'already exists. We already did this, but make sure
'since we don't have an exclusive lock on the file:
For iNode = 0 To xmlNodes.length - 1
    Set xmlNode = xmlNodes.Item(iNode).childNodes.Item(0)
    If xmlNode.Text = AccountNumber Then
        GetObjectContext.SetAbort
        Exit Sub
    End If
Next

'The account does not exist, so we can add it without any problems:
Set xmlRootNode = xmlDoc.documentElement
Set xmlAccountNode = xmlDoc.createElement("ACCOUNT")
Set xmlAccountNumberNode = xmlDoc.createElement("ACCOUNTNUMBER")
Set xmlAccountBalanceNode = xmlDoc.createElement("BALANCE")

xmlAccountBalanceNode.Text = Balance
xmlAccountNumberNode.Text = AccountNumber

xmlAccountNode.appendChild xmlAccountNumberNode
xmlAccountNode.appendChild xmlAccountBalanceNode

xmlRootNode.appendChild xmlAccountNode
xmlDoc.save Filename
GetObjectContext.SetComplete
Exit Sub
```

```
ErrorHandler:
    MsgBox "An error occured in ADD " & Err.Description

End Sub


Sub RemoveAccount(AccountNumber As Long, Filename As String)

    Dim dBalanceBefore As Double
    Dim iNode As Integer
    On Error GoTo RemoveAccountProblem

    Initialize

    'Since we are changing the account balance we need to obtain
    'the CURRENT balance and write to the log file (in case the
    'transaction is rolled back)
    If Not GetBalance(AccountNumber, Filename, dBalanceBefore) Then
        'There was a problem getting the current balance
        'from the XML file, so abort the operation:
        MsgBox "Couldn't get balance!"
        GetObjectContext.SetAbort
        Exit Sub
    End If

    vntLogFileEntries(0) = REMOVE_ACCOUNT_COMMAND
    vntLogFileEntries(1) = AccountNumber
    vntLogFileEntries(2) = dBalanceBefore
    vntLogFileEntries(3) = Filename

    'Write to the log file, and ensure it is durable:
    CrmLogControl.WriteLogRecordVariants vntLogFileEntries
    CrmLogControl.ForceLog

    xmlDoc.Load Filename
    Set xmlNodes = xmlDoc.childNodes.Item(0).childNodes

    'Check to make sure we are not adding an account that
    'already exists:
    For iNode = 0 To xmlNodes.length - 1
        Set xmlNode = xmlNodes.Item(iNode).childNodes.Item(0)
        If xmlNode.Text = AccountNumber Then
            Exit For
        End If
    Next

    'Is the account we wish to remove there?
    If xmlNode.Text <> AccountNumber Then
        GetObjectContext.SetAbort
        Exit Sub
    End If
```

continues

Listing 9.3 **Continued**

```
    'Remove it from the file:
    xmlDoc.childNodes.Item(0).removeChild xmlNodes.Item(iNode)
    xmlDoc.save Filename
    GetObjectContext.SetComplete
    Exit Sub

RemoveAccountProblem:
    MsgBox "Account was NOT removed!"

End Sub


Sub CreditAccount(AccountNumber As Long, Amount As Double, Filename As String)
    ChangeAccount AccountNumber, Amount, 1, Filename
End Sub

Sub DebitAccount(AccountNumber As Long, Amount As Double, Filename As String)
    ChangeAccount AccountNumber, Amount, 0, Filename
End Sub

Private Sub ChangeAccount(AccountNumber As Long, Amount As Double, creditOrDebit
➥As Boolean, Filename As String)

    Dim dBalanceBefore As Double
    On Error GoTo ChangeAccountProblem
    Dim iNode As Integer
    Initialize

    'Since we are changing the account balance we need to obtain
    'the CURRENT balance and write to the log file (in case this
    'transaction is rolled back)
    If Not GetBalance(AccountNumber, Filename, dBalanceBefore) Then
        'There was a problem getting the current balance
        'from the XML file, so abort the operation:
        GetObjectContext.SetAbort
        Exit Sub
    End If

    vntLogFileEntries(0) = CHANGE_ACCOUNT_COMMAND
    vntLogFileEntries(1) = AccountNumber
    vntLogFileEntries(2) = dBalanceBefore
    vntLogFileEntries(3) = Filename

    'Write to the log file, and ensure it is durable:
    CrmLogControl.WriteLogRecordVariants vntLogFileEntries
    CrmLogControl.ForceLog

    On Error GoTo ChangeAccountProblem
```

```
    xmlDoc.Load Filename
    Set xmlNodes = xmlDoc.childNodes.Item(0).childNodes

    'Check to make sure we are not adding an account that
    'already exists:
    For iNode = 0 To xmlNodes.length - 1
        Set xmlNode = xmlNodes.Item(iNode).childNodes.Item(0)
        If xmlNode.Text = AccountNumber Then
            Exit For
        End If
    Next

    'Is the account we wish to remove there?
    If xmlNode.Text <> AccountNumber Then
        GetObjectContext.SetAbort
        Exit Sub
    End If

    Set xmlBalanceNode = xmlNodes.Item(iNode).childNodes.Item(1)

    'Debit or Credit the Account:
    If creditOrDebit Then
        xmlBalanceNode.Text = xmlBalanceNode.Text + Amount
    Else
        xmlBalanceNode.Text = xmlBalanceNode.Text - Amount
    End If

    xmlDoc.save Filename
    GetObjectContext.SetComplete
    Exit Sub

ChangeAccountProblem:
    GetObjectContext.SetAbort

End Sub

'The GetBalance function places the Balance of the desired account in the Balance
'variable. This function exists because in both the RemoveAccount and
➥ChangeAccount
'routines we need the balance of the Account before any changes are made,
'so we can write it to the log file.
Private Function GetBalance(AccountNumber As Long, Filename, ByRef Balance As
➥Double) As Boolean

    Dim iNode As Integer

    On Error GoTo GetBalanceProblem
    xmlDoc.Load Filename
    Set xmlNodes = xmlDoc.childNodes.Item(0).childNodes

    'Find the Account Number we want:
```

continues

Listing 9.3 **Continued**

```
    For iNode = 0 To xmlNodes.length - 1
        Set xmlNode = xmlNodes.Item(iNode).childNodes.Item(0)
        If xmlNode.Text = AccountNumber Then
            Exit For
        End If
    Next

    'Is the account we wish to remove there?
    If xmlNode.Text <> AccountNumber Then
        GetBalance = False
        Exit Function
    End If

    'Determine the Balance:
    Set xmlBalanceNode = xmlNodes.Item(iNode).childNodes.Item(1)
    Balance = xmlBalanceNode.Text
    GetBalance = True
    Exit Function

GetBalanceProblem:
    GetBalance = False

End Function


'Initialize obtains the interface to access the log
'and registers the compensator component:
Private Sub Initialize()

    'Have we obtained a ICrmLogControl interface yet?
    'If not obtain it from the CRMClerk:
    If CrmLogControl Is Nothing Then
        ObtainCRMClerk
    End If

    'Register the compensator with the DTC:
    Call RegisterCompensator

End Sub
```

Compensator

The Compensator's job is to either commit the changes initiated by the Worker or roll them back. COM+ notifies the Compensator of which action to perform, commit or roll back, and presents the Compensator with each and every entry in the log, one at a time. Interestingly, if the Compensator is asked to commit, it is given each log entry in the same order as it was written by the Worker. If, on the other hand, the Compensator is asked to roll back, it is given each log entry in reverse order. We look at this process in the next couple paragraphs.

COM+ objects call on the `Worker`, but COM+ itself calls on the services of the `Compensator`. A given `Compensator` is associated with a particular `Worker` by virtue of the `Worker` executing the following code early in its life:

```
Clerk.RegisterCompensator "MyCompensator.Comp", "[put your description here]",
➥CRMREGFLAG_ALLPHASES
```

The last argument is a flag that indicates which phases the `Compensator` wants to be involved in. It can choose to be called during the Commit phase and not in the Prepare phase, if there is nothing it needs to do in the latter and thus wants to improve performance. For now, we're going to assume that our `Compensator` wants to be involved in all phases as this is the norm. For completeness, however, a description of each registration flag can be found in the subsequent section, "Phase I: Prepare."

Note that although a `Worker` explicitly associates itself with a particular class of `Compensator`, they are not necessarily running at the same time. And under no circumstances does the `Worker` call methods on the `Compensator`, or vice versa. Their only form of communication, by design, is the log. Upon instantiating the `Compensator`, COM+ gives it an `ICrmLogControl` interface; however, the `Compensator` cannot use this interface to read the log, only to write to it. To read the changes made by the `Worker`, a `Compensator` must implement one of the following two interfaces:

- `ICrmCompensator`
- `ICrmCompensatorVariants`

COM+ automatically QIs the `Compensator` for one of the above interfaces and uses its methods to "feed" the Worker's changes to the `Compensator`. The particular interface your `Compensator` should implement depends on the type of data it works with. Specifically, if the `Compensator` is dealing with binary data, it implements the `ICrmCompensator`; if it is dealing with data that can confidently be represented by variants, it uses `ICrmCompensatorVariants`. In either case, COM+ calls methods on these interfaces to inform the `Compensator` what the specific changes are (that is, what the `Worker` wrote to the log) and whether it should commit them or roll them back.

For simplicity, let's assume that variants are sufficient to represent our data modifications in the log. In this case, our `Compensator` only needs to implement the `ICrmCompensatorVariants` interface.

The complete source code for our XML `Compensator` can be found under the section, "The Complete *Compensator*," found toward the end of this chapter. I am not going to show its source code here because the `Compensator` has a more complicated job than the `Worker`, and we need to lay a little more groundwork before its implementation will make perfect sense. Remember that COM+ transactions occur in two distinct phases—a Prepare phase and a Commit phase. If all objects participating in a transaction vote positively, your CRM is asked to commit. For now, let's assume this is the case—all the objects have voted positively and COM+ wants to commit the transaction. After instantiating the `Compensator`, COM+ QIs for its `ICrmCompensatorVariants` interface. It then calls the methods of this interface to walk your CRM through the Prepare and Commit phases. I'll talk about the former case first.

Phase I: Prepare

This phase involves three method calls, described in section "Step 1: General Prepare." Before I discuss them fully, note that it is only possible for a CRM to abort a transaction during this phase. One of the methods of the `CRMClerk`'s default interface, `ICrmLogControl`, is `ForceTransactionToAbort()`. Because the `Compensator` is given this interface on instantiation (COM+ calls its `SetLogControlVariants` method), you might think that the `Compensator` can call this method to abort the transaction; it doesn't work. This method is for the `Worker`, and as you see, the only way a `Compensator` can abort a transaction during the Prepare phase is by returning `FALSE` when COM+ calls its final preparation method.

The Prepare phase is crucially important, because after a `Compensator` indicates it has successfully completed this phase, the CRM can no longer abort the transaction. COM+ expects the `Compensator` to be able to commit the changes, no matter what else might happen.

Although the Prepare phase is important, it is allowable for a `Compensator` to opt out of this phase altogether. This is not to say that the Prepare phase doesn't happen; it is an inherent part of Object Linking and Embedding (OLE) Transactions and always occurs when COM+ attempts to commit a transaction. The `Compensator` does, however, have the option not to be notified of this phase or to participate in it. It does this by specifying one or a combination of five enumerated values in the third argument to `ICrmLogControl`'s `RegisterCompensator()` method, as follows:

```
'remember, the Worker calls this method early in its life
'to associate itself with a specific class of Compensator

Clerk.RegisterCompensator "MyCompensator.Comp", "[put your description here]",
WhatToParticipateIn
```

`WhatToParticipateIn` can be one of the following:

- `CRMREGFLAG_ALLPHASES`
- `CRMREGFLAG_PREPAREPHASE`
- `CRMREGFLAG_COMMITPHASE`
- `CRMREGFLAG_ABORTPHASE`
- `CRMREGFLAG_FAILIFINDOUBTSREMAIN`

These flags are made to be bit-wise OR'd, meaning they can be combined where their effects are additive. `CRMREGFLAG_ALLPHASES` is just a combination of all the flags except for `CRMREGFLAG_FAILIFINDOUBTSREMAIN`. We will talk about this last flag in the subsequent section "When In Doubt," but the other flags are pretty straightforward. The word PHASE does not refer to the two phases of OLE Transactions; they refer to the various phases of interaction between the CRM and COM+.

There are no absolute rules as to what CRM phases your `Compensator` should participate in; only the developer can make this judgment (the `Compensator` example in Listing 9.4 participates in all of them). They are included to provide the `Compensator` developer with a means of improving performance by eliminating unnecessary method calls. And, in case you might be thinking it—no, you cannot register different `Compensators` to handle different phases for the same `Worker`.

Keep in mind that by not participating in a phase (particularly the Prepare phase), your `Compensator` is implicitly indicating its approval and is saying, in effect, "I wouldn't do anything if you did call me during this phase, and I would have given you the okay anyway. So, don't bother me, and proceed as if I said everything was fine."

Assuming that the `Worker` asked the `Compensator` to be involved in all phases (`CRMREGFLAG_ALLPHASES`), COM+ undertakes the following steps and calls the following methods during the Prepare phase of a commit.

Step 1: General Prepare

```
BeginPrepareVariants()
```

The first step in the two-phase commit involves COM+ calling the CRM's `BeginPrepareVariants()` method. It takes no arguments, and COM+ makes no assumptions about what the `Compensator` will do when this method is called. It is really just a notification. COM+ wants the `Compensator` to do whatever it needs to do to prepare to commit a transaction. Some `Compensators` might not do anything; others might allocate a new block of memory, disk space, and so on.

Step 2: Prepare to Make Changes for Each Log Entry

```
PrepareRecordVariants( [in] VARIANT * pLogRecord,
                       [out, retval] VARIANT_BOOL * pbForget
);
```

This method is called once for every log entry made in the `CRMClerk` by the `Worker` object. COM+ hands each entry to the `Compensator`, one at a time. The `Compensator` knows when it has received every entry, because COM+ calls the `EndPrepareVariants()` (discussed in the next section) function to indicate when this is the case.

The first argument contains the current log entry; so if this is the fifth time COM+ has made this call, this argument contains the fifth log entry made by the `Worker`. Note that one entry can contain one or many variant values. Basically, I am using the term entry to describe one call made by the `Worker` to `WriteLogRecordVariants()`.

The second argument, `pbForget`, gives the `Compensator` the opportunity to remove an item from the log. A `Compensator` might want to remove items from the log that are purely informational and relate only to the Prepare phase but not the Commit phase. In other words, the `Worker` might want to send the `Compensator` information about something it needs to prepare for. This information might not, however, be pertinent after the preparation is complete and the CRM is in the Commit phase, so the `Compensator` has an opportunity to remove it while still in the Prepare phase. There are no absolute rules; this is only one possibility. Don't feel pressured to use this (or any argument) just because it is there.

It is important to realize that, like `BeginPrepareVariants()`, the `EndPrepareVariants()` method is informational. What the `Compensator` does or doesn't do when this method is called is up to it. COM+ just wants to be sure that the `Compensator` knows what it is in for and makes preparations for the upcoming commit—whatever those preparations might be. The nature of such preparations, is dependent on the details of the CRM implementation.

Step 3: Finalize Changes

```
EndPrepareVariants( [out, retval] VARIANT_BOOL * pbOkToPrepare);
```

When COM+ calls this method, it is notifying the CRM that it has received all the log entries and the Prepare phase is about to complete. The CRM can return `TRUE` or `FALSE` indicating whether it has successfully completed the Prepare phase. If you return `FALSE` (or don't return anything until the timeout period), COM+ asks all other RMs also participating in the transaction (if any) to roll back. It also calls the `Abort` methods on your CRM (to be discussed soon) and gives the `Compensator` the opportunity to undo any changes that the `Worker` might have made.

Do not tell COM+ that it is okay to prepare unless you really mean it. By returning `TRUE`, you are promising COM+ that you are confident that you can commit the transaction in the future. COM+ reserves the right to reinstantiate and pester your `Compensator` repeatedly until it reports a successful commit.

Phase II: Commit

The Commit phase is very similar to the Prepare, except this is where the CRM is expected to make the `Worker`'s changes permanent. It is important to understand that after your `Compensator` has completed its Prepare phase and moves to the Commit phase, COM+ expects the `Compensator` to be able to commit and might keep rerunning your `Compensator` until it reports to COM+ that the commit ultimately succeeded. You must also realize that COM+ might use a different instance of your `Compensator` in the Prepare phase than what it uses in the Commit phase, so don't keep any kind of state in member variables, globals, and so on that you need to span the two phases.

You might experience a sense of *déjà vu* when you look at these methods because some have the identical form of their counterpart functions in the Prepare phase.

Step 1: Prepare to Commit

```
BeginCommitVariants([in] VARIANT_BOOL * bRecovery, );
```

COM+ calls this method to notify the CRM that it should prepare to commit what the `Worker` has done.

The second argument has a value of `TRUE` if something catastrophic happens after the `Compensator` completes its Prepare phase successfully and tries unsuccessfully to commit on a prior occasion. After the CRM completes its Prepare phase without indicating an error, it is on the hook to commit the transaction. Although your

Compensator might take special, additional steps to handle the case of a recovery, you are still obligated to commit. If your Compensator crashes again in this or another method call during a recovery, COM+ reruns your Compensator yet again and again indicates that it is committing in the context of a recovery. For an in depth look at recovery, forcing transactions to abort, and other boundary conditions consult the book's source code on RM.

Step 2: Make Changes for Each Log Entry

```
CommitRecordsVariants( [in] VARIANT * pLogRecord,
[out, retval] VARIANT_BOOL * pbForget
);
```

This method has the same form and purpose as its counterpart PrepareRecordVariants() in the Prepare phase. COM+ calls this method once for every log record made by the Worker. The Compensator is to make these changes permanent, and it has the option of removing or forgetting a record if it is certain that it is complete or deems it no longer necessary.

Step 3: Commit Changes

```
EndCommitVariants()
```

This method notifies the Compensator that it has received all log entries. As the Compensator does not return an error code or crash, the commitment is complete as far as COM+ is concerned, and the log is discarded.

Aborting Transactions

Sadly, we acknowledge that not every transaction can commit. Even if all COM+ objects vote Yes on the transaction and COM+ attempts to commit it via the DTC, any participating RM or CRM can fail. The RM or Compensator for the CRM can specifically indicate failure in the Prepare phase by returning FALSE when EndPrepareVariants() is called or by crashing. Similarly, any COM+ object that is manipulating an RM or CRM can call SetAbort() in the context of a transaction. In either case, COM+ asks all RMs and CRMs to roll back their changes.

In the event of a rollback request by the Distributed Transition Coordinator (DTC), COM+ calls the following methods of the CRM's ICrmCompensatorVariants (or ICrmCompensator if using binary data) interface. However, these methods are only called if the transaction aborts in the following manners:

- A COM+ object calls SetAbort().
- During the Prepare phase, the CRM crashes or returns FALSE when COM+ calls its EndPrepareVariants() method.
- Another RM reports failure or fails to check in during its Prepare phase.

- Your CRM crashes after its Prepare phase but before it receives a commit command from the DTC. This is called an in-doubt state, and we talk about it in the section "When In Doubt."

Also note that the CRM abort methods are not called if the CRM crashes during the Commit phase. Remember: if the CRM successfully completes its Prepare phase, aborting the transaction is no longer an option. We talk about how to handle this case after we take a look at the abortive functions of `ICrmCompensatorVariants`.

Step 1: Prepare to Abort

```
BeginAbortVariants [in] VARIANT_BOOL * recovery)
```

This method notifies the `Compensator` that it should prepare to abort all changes made by the `Worker`.

The recovery argument is `TRUE` if the `Compensator` crashes during or after its Prepare phase but before it receives a commit command from the DTC. If it previously aborted gracefully via `ForceTransactionToAbort()`, or the transaction was voted down by a COM+ object, this argument is `FALSE`.

Step 2: Undo Each Log Entry

```
AbortRecordVariants ([in] VARIENT * pLogRecord,
                    [out, retval] VARIANT_BOOL * pbForget)
```

This method is called once for every record in the log. Note that the entries are in reverse order. The `Compensator` can then undo changes made by the `Worker`, from the latest to the earliest, and can, of course, remove the record from the log by returning `TRUE`.

Step 3: Finalizing Abortion

```
EndAbortVariants()
```

`EndAbortVariants()` notifies the `Compensator` that it has received all log records and the abort is complete.

Handling Recovery

We have discussed that the successful completion of the Prepare phase is a commitment, and the `Compensator` is obligated to commit the transaction. But what happens if a CRM never can commit its transaction? Suppose some resource it depends on becomes forever unavailable moments after the Prepare phase, forever dooming its attempts to commit. COM+ runs your CRM, asks it to commit every time a `Worker` calls `RegisterCompensator()`, and identifies your particular class of `Compensator`.

There is no simple answer. Ideally, you design your `Compensator` such that after it has completed the Prepare phase, it is certain to be able to complete the commit. However, your `Compensator` might rely on some technology or OS service that proves flaky. To protect against the possibility of never being able to commit, you can check the recovery argument of `BeginCommitVariants()`. If it is `TRUE`, you know that the CRM crashed during a previous attempt to commit. You can keep track of how many times the commit has failed by adding additional entries to the log. Remember that the `ICrmLogControl` interface is given to the `Compensator` after it is instantiated (COM+ calls its `SetLogControlVariants` method), and so, like the `Worker`, it has the capability of adding entries. These entries can be interpreted by the `Compensator` on a subsequent commit attempt; after a number of attempts, your CRM might throw up its hands and report a completed commit to get COM+ off its back. It might then send an email to the system administrator or write to some system event log, "Critical Failure: I tried and I tried, but was never able to commit. Data modifications that certain objects thought happened never did. Human intervention is required."

There is one final important point I want to make about recovery—that of *idempotence*. You won't find the term *idempotence* in the dictionary, but you will hear it bantered about in mathematical and development circles. An action is said to be idempotent if it can occur any number of times, but the frequency does not affect the result. For example, if you hit the elevator Up button in the lobby, get impatient, and keep hitting it, your action is idempotent—no matter how many times you hit the button, the elevator does not move any faster and the ultimate outcome is the same.

In the event of crash recovery, it is possible that your `Compensator` is asked to commit changes more than once, so make sure that entries to the log are written in such a way as to be idempotent. For example, if the log indicates that an account should be debited once by $50, there is the possibility that the `Compensator` will end up debiting the account repeatedly if asked to commit multiple times during the recovery process. It is better if the log entries indicate the account's last balance, as well as the amount it should be debited by. In this way, the `Compensator` can check the account balance, and if it sees the balance is already reduced by $50, choose not to debit the amount again. Alternatively, it might be better design for the `Worker` to specify what the new balance of the account should be, including the $50 debit. Setting the absolute balance is idempotent because no matter how many times you do it, the effect is same.

When In Doubt

In the process of a two-phase commit, there is a period of time between the Prepare phase and the Commit phase where an RM or CRM can be said to be in doubt about the ultimate success of the distributed transaction. This occurs when a transaction is spanning more than one RM on more than one machine—thus, more than one DTC is involved. If you have a transaction spanning two machines, A and B, each machine has its own DTC that controls the RM on that machine. The primary or controlling DTC communicates with the DTCs on other machines, propagates prepare and commit notifications to the other DTCs, and coordinates the responses to these commands. During a distributed transaction, RMs become interdependent as their DTCs must gather consensus and coordinate with one another to make sure each RM completes its Prepare phase.

Thus, an RM might get a prepare notification from its DTC, complete it, but wait for some time while other participating RMs are completing their Prepare phases. The prepared RM has said it is ready to commit, but the possibility still exists that another RM might fail its Prepare phase or crash. If this happens, the prepared RM does not get a commit command from the DTC; rather, it is asked to roll back. On the other hand, if all the other RMs do complete their Prepare phase, the controlling DTC issues a commit notification, and the prepared RM enters its Commit phase. The period of time for an RM, after the preparation is complete but before a `commit` command is received from the DTC, is called the *in-doubt state* because the RM, though ready, is not sure (or is in doubt) about whether the transaction will ultimately succeed.

Doubt should be fleeting and probably last no more than a fraction of a second. However, if an RM crashes during the in-doubt state, the DTC records that the whole distributed transaction becomes in doubt. When the failed RM is next run, it contacts the DTC, asks about the status of the transaction, and both parties try to reconcile the transaction. If the other RMs complete their Prepare phase and the controlling DTC issues a commit command, the recovering RM is on the hook to commit its transaction. If, after reawakening, the failed RM discovers that another RM has not completed its Prepare phase, it rolls back all changes made during the Prepare phase.

The Complete *Compensator*

Now that we've stepped through the phases of `Compensator` committal and abortion, the complete listing of our XML `Compensator` should make sense. Listing 9.4 details the implementation of the XML sample `Compensator`. The listing is somewhat long, but not especially complex; the source file comments will provide a running commentary.

Listing 9.4 **CRM *Compensator* Component that Commits or Aborts Changes to an XML File Made by the *Worker***

```
'XMLCompensator: Compensator component for the XML CRM.
'
'This component is called when a transaction involving the XMLWorkerVB component
'aborts or commits.  Either one of two interfaces MUST be implemented by all
'compensator components:

'ICrmCompensator          — for unstructured storage in the log
'                           (C++ components)
'ICrmCompensatorVariants  — for structured storage in the log
'                           (VB/Java):
```

```
Option Explicit

'The worker component this compensator is associated with writes
'variants to the log, so this component implements the ICrmCompensatorVariants
'interface:
Implements ICrmCompensatorVariants

'The DTC gives the ICrmLogControl interface to the compensator
'in the SetLogControlVariants method so the compensator can access
'the log:
Dim CrmLogControl As ICrmLogControl

'Like the worker, this compensator uses Microsoft's XML Document
'Object Model (DOM) components to perform XML manipulation:
Dim xmlDoc As New DOMDocument
Dim xmlNodes As IXMLDOMNodeList
Dim xmlNode As IXMLDOMNode
Dim xmlAccountNode As IXMLDOMNode
Dim xmlAccountBalanceNode As IXMLDOMNode
Dim xmlAccountNumberNode As IXMLDOMNode
Dim xmlRootNode As IXMLDOMNode

'Variables to read from the log file:
Dim vntCommand, vntAccountNumber, vntBalanceBefore, vntFilename


'AbortRecordVariants is called after BeginAbortVariants.
'This method delivers log records that were written by the
'worker.  The compensator must "undo" the changes indicated
'by such records.
Private Function ICrmCompensatorVariants_AbortRecordVariants(pLogRecord As
➥Variant) As Boolean

    Dim iNode As Integer

    'Obtain information from the logfile that indicates what was done:
    vntCommand = pLogRecord(0)
    vntAccountNumber = pLogRecord(1)
    vntBalanceBefore = pLogRecord(2)
    vntFilename = pLogRecord(3)


    On Error GoTo AbortRecordVariantProblem
```

continues

Listing 9.4 **Continued**

```
'Determine what operation was performed and "undo" it:
If vntCommand = ADD_ACCOUNT_COMMAND Then

    'The log indicates that an account was ADDED, and so we must remove it:
    xmlDoc.Load vntFilename
    Set xmlNodes = xmlDoc.childNodes.Item(0).childNodes

    For iNode = 0 To xmlNodes.length - 1
    Set xmlNode = xmlNodes.Item(iNode).childNodes.Item(0)
    If xmlNode.Text = vntAccountNumber Then
            Exit For
        End If
    Next

    'Is the account we wish to remove there?
    If xmlNode.Text <> vntAccountNumber Then
        'The account is already gone, so we are ok.
        Exit Function
    End If

    'Remove the account from the XML file:
    xmlDoc.childNodes.Item(0).removeChild xmlNodes.Item(iNode)
    xmlDoc.save vntFilename

ElseIf Command = REMOVE_ACCOUNT_COMMAND Then

    'An account was removed. To undo this action we must
    'add the account with its previous balance. A true
    'rollback scenario would add the account in its proper
    'place in the XML file.  For our purposes, we just
    'add the account to the end of the XML file.

    xmlDoc.Load vntFilename
    Set xmlNodes = xmlDoc.childNodes.Item(0).childNodes

    'Check to make sure we are not adding an account that
    'already exists.
    For iNode = 0 To xmlNodes.length - 1
        Set xmlNode = xmlNodes.Item(iNode).childNodes.Item(0)
        If xmlNode.Text = vntAccountNumber Then
            ICrmCompensatorVariants_AbortRecordVariants = True
            Exit Function
        End If
    Next

    Set xmlRootNode = xmlDoc.documentElement
    Set xmlAccountNode = xmlDoc.createElement("ACCOUNT")
    Set xmlAccountNumberNode = xmlDoc.createElement("ACCOUNTNUMBER")
    Set xmlAccountBalanceNode = xmlDoc.createElement("BALANCE")
```

```
            xmlAccountBalanceNode.Text = vntBalanceBefore
            xmlAccountNumberNode.Text = vntAccountNumber

            xmlAccountNode.appendChild xmlAccountNumberNode
            xmlAccountNode.appendChild xmlAccountBalanceNode
            xmlRootNode.appendChild xmlAccountNode
            xmlDoc.save vntFilename

        ElseIf vntCommand = CHANGE_ACCOUNT_COMMAND Then

            'The account was debited/credited.  To undo this we
            'just have to restore the previous balance:
            xmlDoc.Load vntFilename
            Set xmlNodes = xmlDoc.childNodes.Item(0).childNodes

            For iNode = 0 To xmlNodes.length - 1
                Set xmlNode = xmlNodes.Item(iNode).childNodes.Item(0)
                If xmlNode.Text = vntAccountNumber Then
                    Exit For
                End If
            Next

            If xmlNode.Text <> vntAccountNumber Then
                ICrmCompensatorVariants_AbortRecordVariants = True
            End If

            Set xmlNode = xmlNodes.Item(iNode).childNodes.Item(1)
            xmlNode.Text = vntBalanceBefore
            xmlDoc.save vntFilename

        End If

        ICrmCompensatorVariants_AbortRecordVariants = True
        Exit Function


AbortRecordVariantProblem:
    MsgBox "XMLWorker, AbortRecordVariant error: " & Err.Description

End Function

'BeginAbortVariants is called to let the compensator know that it
'must abort the current transaction. A call to this method is followed
'by a call to AbortRecordVariants, where the compensator recieves
'log records of the operations it must undo.  In this phase
'the compensator will do any preparatory work it has to, to undo these
'changes (this compensator does not have any such preparatory work)
```

continues

Listing 9.4 Continued

```
Private Sub ICrmCompensatorVariants_BeginAbortVariants(ByVal bRecovery As Boolean)

End Sub

'BeginCommitVariants is called to let the compensator know that the
'second phase of the two phase commit has been reached.  A call to this
'method is followed by a call to CommitRecordVariants, where the compensator
'receives log records of the operations is must commit.  In this phase
'the compensator will do any preparatory work it has to, to commit these changes
'(this compensator does not have any such preparatory work)
Private Sub ICrmCompensatorVariants_BeginCommitVariants(ByVal bRecovery As
➥Boolean)

End Sub

'BeginPrepareVariants is called to let the compensator know that the
'first phase of the two phase commit has been reached.  A call to this
'method is followed by a call to PrepareRecordVariants, where the compensator
'receives log records of the operations is must prepare.  In this phase
'the compensator will do any preparatory work it has to, to prepare these changes
'(again, this compensator does not have any such preparatory work)
Private Sub ICrmCompensatorVariants_BeginPrepareVariants()

End Sub

'CommitRecordVariants is called after BeginCommitVariants.
'This method delivers log records that were written by the
'worker.  The compensator must do whatever it has to do
'to make the changes specified in the log records permanent.
'In this example, since the XML operations have already
'been performed by the worker, the compensator doesn't
'have to do anything to make them permanent (the only work
'the compensator has to do is during the abort phase — see
'AbortRecordVariants).
Private Function ICrmCompensatorVariants_CommitRecordVariants(pLogRecord As
➥Variant) As Boolean

    ICrmCompensatorVariants_CommitRecordVariants = False

End Function

'EndAbortVariants is called at the end of the abort phase, after
'AbortRecordVariants.This is the last method called during the
'abort phase.  This is where the compensator
'would do any cleanup operations associated with its entire abort phase.
```

```vb
Private Sub ICrmCompensatorVariants_EndAbortVariants()

End Sub

'EndAbortVariants is called at the end of the commit phase, after
'ComitRecordVariants. This is the last method called during the
'commit phase.  This is where the compensator would do any cleanup
'operations associated with its entire commit phase.
Private Sub ICrmCompensatorVariants_EndCommitVariants()

End Sub

'EndPrepareVariants is called at the end of the prepare phase, after
'PrepareRecordVariants. This is the last method called during the
'prepare phase.  This is where the compensator would do any cleanup
'operations associated with its entire prepare phase. In addition,
'this compensator returns a boolean in this method: if the prepare
' phase proceeded smoothly, the compensator indicates it is ready for
'the commit phase by returning true. If there was a problem during the
'prepare phase, the compensator returns false, at which point the
'transaction is aborted.

Private Function ICrmCompensatorVariants_EndPrepareVariants() As Boolean

    ICrmCompensatorVariants_EndPrepareVariants = True

End Function

'PrepareRecordVariants is called after BeginPrepareVariants.
'This method delivers log records that were written by the
'worker.  The compensator must do whatever it has to do
'to prepare the records for the commit phase of the transaction.

Private Function ICrmCompensatorVariants_PrepareRecordVariants(pLogRecord As
↪Variant) As Boolean

End Function

'SetLogControlVariants is called by the DTC to give the compensator
'an instance of ILogControl so it can access the log:
Private Sub ICrmCompensatorVariants_SetLogControlVariants(ByVal pLogControl As
COMSVCSLib.ICrmLogControl)

    Set CrmLogControl = pLogControl

End Sub
```

282 Chapter 9 Compensating Resource Managers

Listing 9.5: **XML Wrapper Component (This Allows Clients to Explicitly Abort or Commit the Transactions of The Worker Component):**

```vb
'XMLCRMWrapper.

'This component "wraps" the four methods of the XML CRM Component
'(AddAccount, RemoveAccount CreditAccount, DebitAccount). In addition
'to wrapping these methods, it exposes two methods called
'Abort and Commit, which Abort and Commit the transaction by calling
'SetAbort and SetComplete.

'Wrapper components give a client the ability
'to explicitly abort or commit a transaction. Alternatively, a client
'could use the TransactionContext object to accomplish the same thing.

Option Explicit

'The following error code results when one tries to execute a method call
'on a COM+ component that has a transaction and has already aborted or
'in the process of aborting that transaction.  See ErrorHandler for details
Const CONTEXT_E_ABORTING = &H8004E003

Dim pObjectContext As ObjectContext
Dim pObjectState As IContextState
Dim XMLWorker As XMLWorkerVB


Private Sub Class_Initialize()
    'Get an instance of the Object's context, so we can call
    'SetAbort and SetComplete
    Set pObjectContext = GetObjectContext()
    Set pObjectState = pObjectContext

    'Also get an instance of the XMLWorker component we are wrapping:
    Set XMLWorker = New XMLWorkerVB
End Sub

'Wrapper functions:

Public Sub AddAccount(AccountNumber As Long, Balance As Double, filename As
↪String)
    On Error GoTo addproblem
    XMLWorker.AddAccount AccountNumber, Balance, filename
    Exit Sub
addproblem:
    Call ErrorHandler

End Sub

Public Sub RemoveAccount(AccountNumber As Long, filename As String)
    On Error GoTo removeproblem
```

```
        XMLWorker.RemoveAccount AccountNumber, filename
        Exit Sub
removeproblem:
        Call ErrorHandler

End Sub

Public Sub CreditAccount(AccountNumber As Long, Amount As Double, filename As
➥String)
        On Error GoTo creditproblem
        XMLWorker.CreditAccount AccountNumber, Amount, filename
        Exit Sub
creditproblem:
        Call ErrorHandler

End Sub

Public Sub DebitAccount(AccountNumber As Long, Amount As Double, filename As
➥String)
        On Error GoTo debitproblem
        XMLWorker.DebitAccount AccountNumber, Amount, filename
        Exit Sub
debitproblem:
        Call ErrorHandler

End Sub

'The following two methods are exposed so a client application can
'explicitly abort or commit the transaction.
Public Sub Abort()
        pObjectContext.SetAbort
End Sub

Public Sub Commit()
        pObjectContext.SetComplete
End Sub

'Our errorhandler is executed when a call to the XMLWorker component has failed.
'A common error with wrapper components is to try to execute a method against
'an underlying component has already aborted the transaction:

Private Sub ErrorHandler()

   If Err.Number = CONTEXT_E_ABORTING Then
        MsgBox "Could not perform the operation. The transaction has been
            ➥aborted."
        pObjectContext.SetAbort
   Else
        MsgBox Err.Number & " : " & Err.Description
   End If

End Sub
```

CRMs and Isolation

One critical property of a transaction, isolation, is not automatically provided by the CRM. Isolation implies that what happens inside a transaction is hidden and protected. Normally, an RM places some form of lock on the resources involved. Most relational databases, for example, provide *row level locking* so that rows whose data is involved in a transaction are protected from modification by clients outside the transaction. The CRM architecture, however, does not provide any facility to aid the developer in terms of enforcing isolation. This is not to say that synchronization support is not provided—it is. All COM+ transactions are synchronous and have only one logical thread (transactions always run a COM+ *Activity*, discussed in Appendix B, "COM+ Synchronization Through Activities"). But don't confuse synchronization and concurrency with isolation; they are altogether different.

Although you can be certain that only one method call will execute on the Worker of your CRM at any one time, you cannot be certain where that method will come from. For example, it is possible that two transactions executing concurrently involve the same CRM. Unlike a true RM whose interfaces have method arguments to keep track of transaction IDs, the CRM architecture does not include any direct facility to keep track of what objects are calling into it or what transactions they are involved in. Thus, Object A from Transaction T1 might ask an instance of your CRM to make a modification to some region of data in one method call, and Object B from Transaction T2 might ask for a change to the same region in another. Although different instances of your CRM might be used, the same underlying data source is being modified in both cases. The CRM, therefore, needs to employ some method of protecting specific regions of the data source involved in a transaction and blocking would-be data modification requests from clients outside of that transaction.

You can choose whatever method you want to enforce isolation. File locking, or some other form of OS lock, often works well. Just keep in mind that a CRM is not a singleton, and you cannot count on the same instance of a CRM servicing different clients in different transactions. So, if you are a C++ developer and want to employ mutexes, semaphores, critical sections, and so on, make sure they are named so that they are at system-wide scope and can synchronize access across multiple processes.

The CRMREGFLAG_FAILIFINDOUBTSREMAIN Flag

It is possible that some form of crash, network outage, and so on can result in a CRM that, after recovering, is unsure about the success or failure of a transaction it participated in. If you want to prevent your CRM from being involved in any new transactions while a pre-existing transaction is still in doubt, you need only code the following:

```
Clerk.RegisterCompensator "MyCompensator.Comp", "[put your description here]", 
➥CRMREGFLAG_ALLPHASES OR CRMREGFLAG_FAILIFINDOUBTSREMAIN
```

Summary

If a relational database system is capable of handling transactions, and it supports the OLE Transaction two-phase commit protocol, it is considered by COM+ to be an RM. If an RDBMS only supports the XA protocol, but its ODBC driver (or some other form of Resource Dispenser) can convert an XA to an OLE Transaction, this database also qualifies as an RM.

An RM does not necessarily need to be a relational database system, however. The CRM is an example of an RM that can make changes to any structure of data within the context of a COM+ transaction. The CRM is a template and protocol that a developer can use to simplify the complex task of writing an RM.

The author of the CRM must implement two coclasses: the Worker and the Compensator. The Worker is instantiated and used by any client executable or object to make changes to some resource kept by a given CRM. When COM+ attempts to commit a transaction involving a CRM, it instantiates an instance of the Compensator and interacts with it during the Prepare and Commit phases of a transaction. Typically, the Worker is responsible for making initial changes of state to underlying data, and the Compensator is responsible for bringing this change to its final state and making such changes permanent. Both the Worker and Compensator can write to a log maintained on their behalf by COM+, but only the Compensator is presented with the actual entries of this log. The log, kept by the CRMClerk object, is the only form of communication between the Worker and Compensator, and COM+ gives an interface (ICrmLogControl) to both objects upon their instantiation.

A Worker can explicitly abort the transaction by calling the ForceTransactionToAbort() method of the CRMClerk, but the Compensator may not call this method. The Compensator might indicate failure by returning FALSE during the final steps of the Prepare phase, or it can simply crash. If, however, the Compensator successfully completes its Prepare phase, it is obligated to commit its changes if asked.

COM+ does not provide isolation for CRMs. There can be any number of CRM instances running at a given time, so CRM authors should take care to protect data relevant in a particular transaction from corruption by another CRM instance in a different transaction. Additionally, the CRM author must make sure that actions made by the Compensator are idempotent—that is, they can safely be implemented more than once without negative consequence.

10

Queued Components

WHEN MOST PEOPLE THINK OF Wall Street traders, they imagine a frenetic trading floor, countless arms outstretched, waving tickets under a green-dotted, scrolling marquee. But not all trading is like that. Take bond trading, for example. Bonds and bond trading are commonly referred to as Fixed Income (FI) trading on Wall Street. The FI trading environment is more reserved than you might expect. In many firms, FI traders sit quite closely to each other at long desks laden with electronic news feeds, telecommunications consoles, and something called a *Hoot and Holler* (used for hollering announcements throughout the office).

These days, proprietary monitors and news feeds are giving way to Windows desktops, and there is growing acceptance of Windows-based, message-oriented information systems. But at one investment bank I worked with, a major problem occurred regarding an inherent limitation of COM when it applies to messages. With this problem I introduce the concept of *asynchronous messaging* with Microsoft Message Queue (MSMQ), and ultimately, our discussion works its way up the evolutionary timeline to COM+ Queued Components.

In this chapter, we take a look at how to call methods asynchronously using Queued Components. As you'll see, Queued Components rely on MSMQ, and this chapter also includes as a detailed discussion of this their inter-relationship.

The Mystery of the Hanging News Feeder

As you can imagine, the prompt receipt and processing of a high volume of messages is critical for a trading system. Price corrections, small and large, need to be packaged, processed, and presented to the trader immediately through some sort of user interface.

One firm I consulted for developed a proprietary, centralized system to deliver messages to a number of clients. The system was based on traditional COM (not COM+; this was a couple years ago) and used a mechanism called *connection points*. Connection points are discussed in greater detail in Chapter 11, "Events," but in the simplest terms, connection points give rise to a scenario where a server COM object holds an interface to its client. This enables the server to call methods on the client's interface (a client can be or create a COM object for the purpose of receiving notification) or, to use other terminology, trigger events on the client.

My client's notification server was found to hang indefinitely on occasion and required someone to kill the process. The client asked me to troubleshoot the system, but I had a pretty good guess as to what was going on without looking at the code. I asked if any kind of modal dialog box was popping up in the event routine of their client application. A modal dialog box, I further explained, is one that suspends any further code execution until it is dismissed. I received a blank look, which was in itself revealing.

Basically, any COM method call is *synchronous*. This is because COM is based on traditional Distributed Computing Environment (DCE), an industry standard style Remote Procedure Calls (RPC) where a client application blocks until the server-side implementation of a function completes. In more specific terms, an RPC client thread always blocks—that is, freezes—while it is waiting for the server-side RPC thread to run the function implementation and return. If the server takes an arbitrarily long time to complete the function, the client waits just as long. If you turn the tables, you find that the same holds true for connection point clients. If the client-side event hangs somewhere in its implementation code after being called by the server, the server thread that called the event hangs as well. If the server is single threaded, the server is now blocked on the method call to the client, giving the impression that it is hung.

This, in fact, is exactly what was happening with my client's news feed server. The author of the VB client application had implemented a certain event such that it popped up a modal dialog box in response to certain messages. If, however, the trader did not dismiss the form, the server blocked on the call and ceased to deliver any further messages to this or any other client. So, by replacing the modal dialog box with a modeless one, the immediate problem was resolved.

Clearly, an architecture that can be held hostage by one rogue (or badly-written) client is not going to cut it in the enterprise. If, however, your remote method calls are synchronous, there is no convenient way of avoiding the hanging client problem. But what if your method calls could somehow be *asynchronous*? In other words, what if the client did not need to block on a method call, but could return the moment after it called it? Microsoft offers two COM-based mechanisms toward this end:

- Queued Components (QC)
- Asynchronous COM

QC by far the easier of the two to use, is a COM+ core service, and does not suffer significant limitations of Asynchronous COM (mainly, COM+-configured components cannot use it!). This chapter, therefore, focuses on QC, but I discuss Asynchronous COM at the end.

For an asynchronous architecture to work, you need to forego the use of return values and output parameters in methods you want to call asynchronously. After all, if the client returns from a method call before the method executes, there is certainly no way output parameters can contain valid values.

Assuming you are willing to give up any output or return parameters, there remains the problem of delivery. Often, the return value of a function is used to indicate its success or failure, but if a client returns immediately after invoking a remote method and cannot rely on any kind of return values, it cannot be certain that the server even received the client's invocation. It is awkward to force the developer to write his own acknowledgement scheme, but it is just as awkward for the system to notify the client of a failed method call—how and when should it do so? Many different schemes have arisen to address failed asynchronous calls. Some schemes demand that the server-side implementation of the method be idempotent such that the system can call it multiple times without harm if needed. (We discuss idempotence in Chapter 9, "Compensating Resource Managers," in the section "Handling Recovery.") Other schemes simply ignore the problem altogether and say, "Call at your own risk—no guarantees of delivery."

Providing asynchronous method invocation services that also guarantee delivery is a tricky business, and Microsoft has taken up the challenge in small steps over the years, which has culminated in COM+ Queued Components. The first step, on which others are built, was introduced in November 1997 (as part of the NT 4 Option Pack), and it was called *Microsoft Message Queue (MSMQ)*.

Introducing Microsoft Message Queue

Simply put, MSMQ is a service that allows applications to send messages to one another asynchronously and can guarantee the successful delivery (or notification of the failure to deliver) of a given message. A *message* can be anything the developer wants it to be—arrays of bytes, strings, numbers, and so on—but it is important to realize that an asynchronous message is not the same thing as an asynchronous method call. MSMQ has no provision or charter to package the arguments of a method call and ferry it asynchronously from client and server. Rather, MSMQ is a relatively simple C API and a collection of COM objects (presumably based on the C API) that developers can use to send information, again in the form of a message, from point A to point B asynchronously with a guarantee of delivery.

MSMQ as Middleware

MSMQ is itself an NT service that runs on Windows 2000. It is also a proper Resource Manager (RM) that allows messages to be sent in the context of a transaction. In fact, many developers classify MSMQ as *middleware* because it is not truly an innate service of the operating system, nor is it an application in its own right. It is a middle-tier message delivery mechanism that developers can leverage to send information from one application to another. Granted, developers can use TCP/IP sockets, named pipes, RPC, and a number of other established Inter-Process Communication (IPC) mechanisms, but MSMQ has the following advantages:

- Guaranteed message delivery (if requested).
- Asynchronous message delivery. The sender and recipient do not need to be running at the same time.
- Message logging services. A *journal* of all messages sent can be recorded and stored for later review.
- Security. Access permission can be set on queues (we talk about queues in the next section) and the message bodies themselves can automatically be encrypted.

I could add a number of additional bullets, but MSMQ is probably simplest to understand if you take a look at the code for the simplest possible MSMQ sender and receiver.

MSMQ Sender Implementation

MSMQ ships with a small collection of COM objects that wrap the underlying C API in a more friendly, language-independent abstraction. An example of a VB client that uses these objects follows in Listing 10.1.

Listing 10.1 **A Simple VB Client that Sends a Message to a Queue**

```
Dim qInfo As New MSMQQueueInfo
Dim msgSend As New MSMQMessage
Dim qDest As MSMQQueue

msgSend.Body = "Hello World"

qInfo.PathName = " darjeeling \private$\MSMQTest"
qInfo.Label = "Test Queue"
qInfo.Create
```

```
Set qDest = qInfo.Open(MQ_SEND_ACCESS, MQ_DENY_NONE)

msgSend.Label = "Test Message"
msgSend.Send qDest

qDest.Close
```

Creating and Opening a Queue

You might notice that *queues* seem to play a large part in MSMQ code. Intuitively, you might imagine that all messages must travel through a queue to reach their destination; it is more precise to realize that the queue is the destination. Much like a database table, a queue is a persistent repository for messages that can be read from any MSMQ recipient in an FIFO (First-In-First-Out) fashion. You will see such a recipient in the section "MSMQ Receiver Implementation," but let's continue our queue discussion for the moment.

There can be as many queues as you care to create, and they can be created by a sender, receiver, or any application. In Listing 10.1, it is the sender who creates a queue called MSMQTest. The following lines describe the location of, and then create, a queue:

```
Dim qInfo As New MSMQQueueInfo
qInfo.PathName = "darjeeling\private$\MSMQTest"
qInfo.Create
```

It is important to realize that a queue is not a connection nor is it an asynchronous path between two points. Queues do not have a sense of direction relative to the clients and servers that use them in the same way (for example, as TCP/IP sockets do). One end of the queue can be used by any client anywhere to *push* messages into the queue, and the other end can be read by any server anywhere to *pop* messages off the queue and interpret them in some way. A message queue is simply a persistent entity that acts as a repository and FIFO-style distribution center for messages. It is probably best to think of MSMQ as the RM it is. The MSMQ RM transactionally handles its own proprietary data store and provides methods allowing for the storing and retrieving of your messages to that store.

Now, back to queues. After a queue is created, it exists completely independently of the entity that created it and can (security permitting) be used by any client and server pair at any time for any purpose. If you want to see message queues that have been created and are currently in existence, you can open the Computer Management Microsoft Management Console (MMC) snap-in and look under the Message Queuing tree-view item, as shown in Figure 10.1.

292   Chapter 10   Queued Components

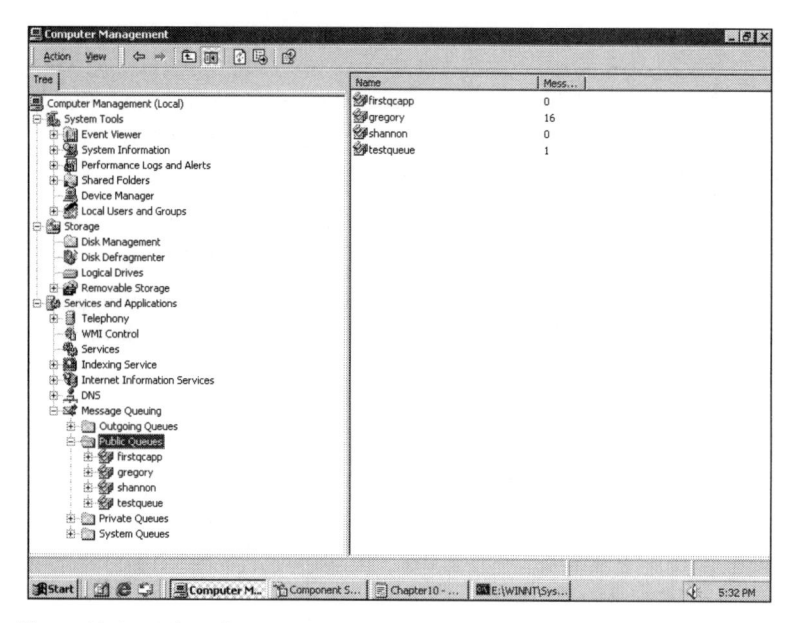

Figure 10.1   A list of message queues currently in existence, including the queue for a COM+ example application we will be using in this chapter, `FirstQCApp`.

Sending the Message

After a queue has been created, it can be opened for reading or writing. A sender of a message typically opens a queue for writing (though technically, it can open and read from the same queue if it wants) with the following line:

```
Set qDest = qInfo.Open(MQ_SEND_ACCESS, MQ_DENY_NONE)
```

The arguments used in the preceding method call are typical, and we'll hold off on a more detailed discussion of these arguments; interested readers should consult Appendix E, "Queue Moniker Parameters." For now, note that the `Open` method of an `MSMQQueueInfo` object returns an `MSMQQueue` object. The `MSMQQueue` object represents a connection to a queue and is used to send and retrieve messages from the queue.

Not surprisingly, the message itself is represented by an object, one of type `MSMQMessage`. The following code demonstrates how to set the simplest of an `MSMQMessage` object's properties and then send the message:

```
msgSend.Body = "Hello World"
msgSend.Label = "Test Message"
msgSend.Send qDest
```

In this example, you are setting the `Body` property equal to the string `"Hello World"`. The `Body` property is really a variant, and so it can hold any type of Visual Basic data type or array. The question arises as to whether you can set the `Body` of a message to an instance of an object and send that object through a queue. The short answer is yes, provided the object supports the `IPersistStream` interface. We discuss this in more detail in the subsequent section "Persistence: Passing Objects Through Messages."

You might notice that the `MSMQMessage` object has a `Send()` method that takes the current queue connection (represented by the `MSMQQueue` object returned from an `MSMQQueueInfo`'s `Open` method) as an argument. Thus the following line of code sends the message represented by the `myMessage` object to the `myQueue` queue:

```
myMessage.Send myQueue
```

When this method returns, the message is sent. All the sender needs to do is close its connection to the queue. You do this by using the following code:

```
myQueue.Close
```

Remember, the preceding line does not destroy the queue. When created, a message queue stands on its own and can outlive its creating object or process. Queues must be explicitly deleted as shown in the next section.

MSMQ Receiver Implementation

The MSMQ receiving application is, as you might expect, the mirror image of the sending application (see Listing 10.2).

Listing 10.2 **A Simple VB Client that Receives a Message from the Queue**
```
Dim qInfo As New MSMQQueueInfo
Dim msgRec As MSMQMessage
Dim qSource As MSMQQueue

qInfo.PathName = "darjeeling\private$\MSMQTest"

Set qSource = qInfo.Open(MQ_RECEIVE_ACCESS, MQ_DENY_NONE)
Set msgRec = qSource.Receive

MsgBox msgRec.Body
qSource.Close
```

Receiving a Message

All the basic objects, `MSMQQueueInfo`, `MSMQQueueMessage`, and `MSMQQueue`, are used in a similar fashion to the sender—the location of a queue is specified, a queue is opened, and a message is popped from the queue with the following line:

```
Set msgRec = qSource.Receive
```

By default, the `Receive` method is a blocking call. This means that if there are no messages in the queue, the calling thread freezes when making this method call. You can, however, specify a timeout period using one of `Receive`'s optional arguments, or you can ask MSMQ to notify you when a message comes in. In the C API, you can enable this feature by giving a callback function to MSMQ; in VB, you can implement the `MSMQEvent` interface in a form or class and pass it as an argument to the `EnableNotification()` method of the `MSMQQueue` object. See the companion source (www.newrider.com/complus) for greater detail.

Closing and Deleting a Queue

When a receiving application no longer wants to process messages, like the sender, it can simply call the following:

`qSource.Close`

Of course, the preceding line does not delete the queue, it only closes the receiver's connection to it. If you want to delete the queue, do so with the following line:

`qInfo.Delete`

This assumes, of course, that the caller's `myQueueInfo` is describing an existing queue and that the caller has the permissions to delete it. The ability to delete a queue, as well as privileges to send, receive, and peek (that is, look but don't remove) messages can be set on a per-queue basis.

From MSMQ to COM+ Queued Components

In this chapter, I flip quite a bit between MSMQ and QC, interpolating the two technologies until they ultimately converge. So, let's take a first look at COM+ QC.

Asynchronous Methods Calls with Queued Components

If a developer wants the methods of a specific interface to be asynchronous, it is simple to do with QC. Go to the Component Services snap-in, select the Properties and then the Queuing tab for an interface as shown in Figure 10.2. Then, click the Queued check box.

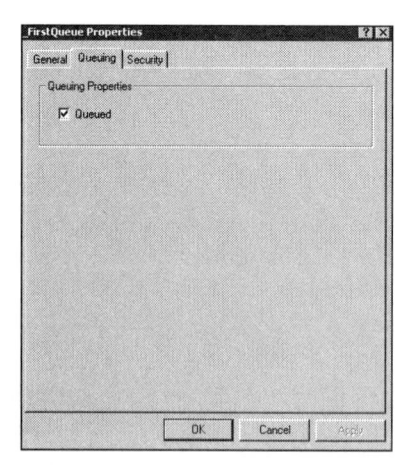

Figure 10.2 The QC dialog box.

Or, using the COM+ administrative objects, the code shown in Listing 10.3 does just as well.

Listing 10.3 **Marking an Application and Interface Queueable Using the COM+ *Admin* Objects**

```
'Error check omitted for brevity.  Consult the book's
'accompanying source code for fully-complete example

Dim Catalog As New COMAdminCatalog
Dim Application As COMAdminCatalogObject
Dim Component As COMAdminCatalogObject
Dim Interface As COMAdminCatalogObject

Dim colApp As COMAdminCatalogCollection   'Collection of Applications
Dim colComp As COMAdminCatalogCollection  'Collection of components
Dim colInt As COMAdminCatalogCollection   'Collection of components

'The interface we will attempt to make QUEUEABLE and
'the component and application it resides in:
Const APPLICATION_NAME = "Trading System"
Const COMPONENT_PROGID = "Current.Currency"
Const INTERFACE_NAME = "_Currency"

'obtain the Application collection from the Catalog:
Set colApp = Catalog.GetCollection("Applications")

'Search for the our application
colApp.Populate
For Each Application In colApp
    If Application.Value("Name") = APPLICATION_NAME Then Exit For
Next

'Did we find our Application?
If Application Is Nothing Then
    MsgBox "Did not find the Trading System Application!"
    End
End If

'Turn on queueing support for this application:
Application.Value("QueuingEnabled") = True
Application.Value("QueueListenerEnabled") = True
colApp.SaveChanges

'obtain a component collection of all the components in our application:
Set colComp = colApp.GetCollection("Components", _
                                    Application.Key)

'Search for our component:
colComp.Populate
```

continues

Chapter 10 Queued Components

Listing 10.3 **Continued**

```
'For Each Component In colComp
If Component.Value("ProgID")=COMPONENT_PROGID Then Exit For
Next

'Did we find our component:
If Component Is Nothing Then
    MsgBox "Did not find the Currency Component!"
    End
End If

'obtain an interface collection of all the interfaces in the component
Set colInt = colComp.GetCollection( _
                    "InterfacesForComponent", Component.Key)

'Search for the interface we wish to make queueable
colInt.Populate
For Each Interface In colInt
    If Interface.Name = INTERFACE_NAME Then Exit For
Next

'Did we find our interface?
If Interface Is Nothing Then
    MsgBox "Did not find the desired Interface"
    End
End If

'Is queueing even supported on this interface?
If Interface.Value("QueuingSupported") = True Then
    'Queueing is supported on this interface, so turn it on:
    Interface.Value("QueuingEnabled") = True
End If

'Save changes to the Catalog.
colInt.SaveChanges
```

Or, if in the IDL declaration of your interface, you included the QUEQUEABLE tag thus (see Listing 10.4):

Listing 10.4 **Adding the *QUEQUEABLE* Tag in the Interface's IDL Declaration**

```
//Be sure to include "mtxattr.h" so that the QUEUEABLE tag will be recognized
[
    object,
    uuid(1E14A3F0-FEC5-4114-A3A6-796EA40D51A4),
    pointer_default(unique),
    QUEUEABLE
]
interface ITest : IDispatch
{
```

You might imagine that method calls made to an interface become asynchronous the moment you mark it as Queued. Not so. The object supporting this interface behaves identically, synchronously, as before. By marking an interface queueable, you are declaring its *candidacy* to receive asynchronous calls, but you'll soon see in the section "Creating a Queued Object Using a Moniker" that an object implementing a queued interface needs to be instantiated in a particular way, via a *moniker*, before it will exhibit queued behavior.

Assuming the object implementing the queued interface is instantiated appropriately, instead of synchronous RPC, MSMQ is used as the underlying transport. As you've seen, MSMQ does not demand or even expect that the client and server run at the same time, so you effectively de-couple the client using this interface from the object implementing it. A method call made to a queueable interface is turned into an MSMQ message that is delivered to the recipient object at some later time after being turned back into a method call.

So, MSMQ is an asynchronous messaging middleware accessed through an API (or a group of COM objects shipping with MSMQ that are layered on top of that API). Knowing that COM+ is leveraging MSMQ to provide asynchronous method calls, you can intuit the following:

- COM+ is providing some form of abstraction on top of MSMQ and hiding the details of MSMQ's involvement to clients and objects utilizing QCs.
- The existence of QCs implies the existence of MSMQ queues created and maintained by COM+.
- If MSMQ is a separate service, it must be installed on a machine for QCs to work. The possibility exists that it might not be installed, and therefore QCs might not work with a new Windows 2000 installation.
- QCs are ultimately subject to the strength and limitations of MSMQ.
- Methods of interfaces marked as queueable cannot have return or output parameters because the method call must be turned into an MSMQ message and sent asynchronously through a queue.
- Certain native MSMQ features are inaccessible and/or incompatible with the QC's paradigm.
- A certain degree of cooperation between pure MSMQ and QCs is possible.

The following sections explore each of these points.

Restrictions on Queued Interfaces

An interface can only be marked queued if its methods contain no output parameters and it uses only OLE automation compatible types—that is, VB-compatible types the OLE automation marshaler knows how to handle.

The Queued Components Abstraction: Introducing the Player, Listener, and Recorder

By now, you are probably tired of me telling you that QC relies on MSMQ. The question then becomes the following: How does COM+ leverage MSMQ to the degree that you can simply click a check box, and when done, your method calls are suddenly asynchronous without you ever creating a queue or calling the MSMQ APIs in any way?

To provide for MSMQ's hidden involvement, COM+ introduces a new paradigm involving the following three objects:

- The `Recorder`
- The `Listener`
- The `Player`

Before any of these objects come into play, however, a queueable object must first be instantiated via something called a *queue moniker*, as shown in the next section.

Creating a Queued Object Using a Moniker

Let's assume that you want to instantiate and obtain an interface (one designated as queued) from an object called `FirstQueue`. To create this object and obtain this interface, you need to go through the queue object via a moniker. This is demonstrated in Visual Basic in Listing 10.5.

Listing 10.5 **Examples of Creating Queued Objects Via Monikers**

```
//VB

Dim QC as IFirstQueue
Set QC = GetObject("queue:/new:FirstQC.FirstQueue")

//C++

IFirstQueue* pFirstQueue;
CoGetObject (L"queue:/new:FirstQC.FirstQueue", NULL, IID_IFirstQueue, (void**)
➥&pFirstQueue);
```

In the event you are not entirely comfortable with monikers, I will offer a brief explanation. A moniker string can allow you to create a COM object and pass it arguments in the process. The ordinary COM creation mechanisms (mainly `CoCreateInstance`, `New`) do not provide a way to actually send construction arguments to an object. Although monikers are certainly useful in helping you bypass this restriction, they don't seem especially impressive until you take into account that the arguments they let you send can be other COM objects. And if this still isn't compelling, the COM objects specified in a moniker string can coordinate with one another and, in effect, cooperate to produce the object ultimately returned by a call to VB's `GetObject` (`CoGetObject` in C++). By way of example, examine the following moniker string:

`queue:/new:FirstQC.FirstQueue`

This moniker string has two COM classes in it, `queue` and `new`. If you look in the Registry, you will find both are COM classes with the ProgIDs of `queue` and `new`.

Both `queue` and `new` are ordinary COM objects, but they are also written to support certain interfaces (`IMoniker` being one) that make them monikers. An object wants to be a moniker if it wants to have its creation influenced by other monikers specified in a moniker string. The implementation details of a moniker are complex to describe, but from the client's perspective, it is pretty simple. When the preceding string is given to VB's `GetObject()` method, COM+ processes the string from left to right. It creates the queue object and feeds it the rest of the string. The queue object processes as much of the string as it can, but then gives the remainder back to COM, usually after detecting and chopping off some kind of character delimiter, a / in this case. COM then repeats this process with the remainder of the string by creating the new object and giving the portion of the string remaining to that object. This can be thought of as the *parsing process*, but another process, the binding process, remains.

As moniker objects are created left to right, a common context (called a `BindContext`) groups them together and relates them to one another. A moniker object is given an interface (`IMoniker`) to the moniker at its left (queue in this case); thus, the new moniker knows that a queue moniker is at the left of it and can interact with it in any fashion. This negotiation between monikers from right to left is often called *binding*. The binding process is like a snowball rolling down a hill, right to left, getting bigger as more creation information is amassed, ultimately resulting in a single object being created. By way of example, the moniker string `queue:/new:FirstQC.FirstQueue` can be described in the following conversation:

COM: Create the object whose ProgID is queue and hand it the string `/new:FirstQC.FirstQueue`.

queue: I am expecting some arguments that only I understand, but I don't see any supplied. All I see is a delimiter, /, which tells me that I am at the end of any string information intended for me. Therefore, I am going to chop off the / delimiter (COM defines a number of such delimiters; the / is only one) and hand the rest of the string back to COM.

COM: Create the object whose ProgID is new and hand it the string `FirstQC.FirstQueue`.

new: I see arguments. I understand. I will create a new instance of the object whose ProgId is `FirstQC.FirstQueue` because this is my purpose in life, to create new objects. But wait, I see through the binding context that I share with other monikers that there is a queue object to my left. I am written to work with this type of object, so rather than create a new instance of `FirstQueue`, I will retrieve its GUID and pass that to the queue object.

queue: The new moniker on my right has given me a GUID. I will create an instance of the object specified by this GUID and return its default queueable interface to the caller of `GetObject()`.

The queue object mentioned in the moniker string ultimately produces an `IFirstQueue` interface. VB places a reference to this interface in the QC variable (as shown in Listing 10.5), and the client can call methods on it in a normal fashion. It is always true of moniker strings that no matter how complex, they always result in one single interface to one particular object.

Although creating objects via monikers might seem like an unnecessary step (after all, why not just create a queue object directly?), remember that monikers allow for arguments to be passed to objects. Although the moniker string `queue:/new:FirstQC.FirstQueue` is relatively simple, it is more common to pass additional information to the queue object in strings like the following:

queue: **Priority=6,ComputerName=Darjeeling**/new:FirstQC.FirstQueue

If you cannot pass arguments in the moniker string, the author of the queue object is forced to write the queue object such that it has properties corresponding to every possible argument. You end up with code like the following:

```
'We wouldn't want to do this:
Dim q as new Queue
q.Priority=6
q.ComputerName="Darjeeling"
'And every other possible property
```

Keep in mind that, although you are creating a queue object in the moniker, the queue object is ultimately returning `IFirstQueue`, an interface normally implemented by the `FirstQueue` object. Ultimately then, the queue object is merely a way station, a staging area for the creation of another object. As you see in the next section "The Recorder," the queue moniker does not return an actual RPC interface pointer to an instantiated `FirstQueue` object, it returns an MSMQ-based entity called a *Recorder*.

Before we move on to the next section, note that some other variations of the queue moniker are detailed and explained in Appendix E.

The Recorder

The Recorder is a COM+ system object that pretends to be a given, queueable object. When you create a queueable object via the queue moniker shown in the previous section, you get back an interface to a Recorder, not an interface to the object itself (which COM+ does not even bother to instantiate). The Recorder is a kind of proxy that stands in for the requested object and implements the interfaces of this object (those marked as Queued), such that the client is unaware of the deception. To be fair, the Recorder cannot deceive the client completely; attempts by a client to QueryInterface (QI) for a non-queueable interface that the real object would ordinarily support is met with an error code. A Recorder is an imperfect proxy then, supporting only an object's queueable interfaces.

Proxies are certainly nothing new. Remember, a client application on Machine A can only have an interface proxy to an object on Machine B—that is, the client side of an RPC channel—not a pointer to the object itself. In this traditional case, there is a synchronous RPC connection between the two. The client can rely on the fact that when it calls a method on the interface proxy it holds, the call is immediately, synchronously delivered to a living object.

This is not the case with the Recorder. Think of the Recorder as exactly that, a recorder. The same way a tape recorder translates your spoken word to magnetic imprints and stores them on a tape to be played back to another party at some later time, the COM+ Recorder records method calls, translates them into messages, and stores them in a queue. When you record your voice on a tape recorder, you don't need to be around when the tape is played for someone else, and you certainly don't need to be around while someone is listening (processing) what you said on tape. To be fair, the person listening can play the tape recording whenever he is ready and prepared to, and the tape itself can outlive both you and the listener. If you think of the tape as an MSMQ queue and the listener and recorder as the COM+ Player and Recorder, you begin to get the idea.

The Player

The Player performs actions opposite the Recorder. It reads messages from a queue, turns them back into method calls, and invokes these method calls (plays them) on the queueable object. The Player can only play messages if the COM+ application in which the queueable object resides is running and listening for messages.

The next section demonstrates how to make a COM+ application listen, but basically an application listens to its queues through an instance of the `ListenerHelper` COM class. When a message arrives, the `ListenerHelper` object instantiates an instance of the Player and gives it the message(s) received. The Player, in turn, instantiates an instance of the recipient object, translates the message back into method invocations, and invokes them on the recipient object, security settings permitting.

As with the client's interaction with the Recorder, the recipient queueable object is unaware that the method invocations it is receiving on its interfaces are coming from the Player. They have the security context, privileges, and so on as though they are arriving via direct RPC invocation.

> **Creation Conditions for the Recorder**
>
> Note that a client comes into contact with the Recorder if and only if it instantiates a queueable object via the queue moniker. If it creates the COM object and/or QIs for the queued interface in the normal COM fashion (`CoCreateInstance` in C++, or VB's New keyword), it gets an ordinary, synchronous RPC connection to a real instance of the object.

Writing Queueable Objects

Queueable objects are ordinary COM objects. Aside from the fact that the methods of their interfaces cannot have output parameters and their method arguments can only take OLE automation compatible data types, they are not written any differently. Such objects can be used in the ordinary COM fashion, and it is only when they are instantiated via the queue moniker that their special nature becomes apparent. Keep in mind also that their queueableness can be taken away at any time by simply removing the check from the Queued check box for its interface(s), as illustrated in Figure 10.2. An attempt to instantiate a non-queueable object via this moniker results in an error.

Writing a queueable object is straightforward; any ActiveX Dynamic Link Library (DLL) will do (again provided that its interface methods do not have output parameters and it uses only OLE automation compatible types). In VB, after a new ActiveX DLL project has been created, adding even one subroutine, as in the following, is all you need:

```
'In VB ActiveX class FirstQC

Sub DisplayNumber(ByVal Number As Integer)
    MsgBox Number
End Sub
```

But in VB, beware! The following method renders the class unqueueable:

```
'Can't be queued
Sub DisplayNumber(Number As Integer)
    MsgBox Number
End Sub
```

The reason is that, in VB, all arguments are passed by reference (implicitly `ByRef`) unless otherwise stated by using the `ByVal` keyword. In VB, `ByRef` translates to an `[in,out]` parameter in the underlying type library, which is not allowed for a queueable interface.

Assuming our object is named `FirstQC`, after you compile this object (VB registers it during the compilation process), you then need to import it into COM+ through mechanisms described in Chapter 6, "The COM+ Catalog." At this point, you designate the `_FirstQC` interface as queued. (Note that VB prepends its default interfaces with a _.) One additional step is required. Even though `FirstQC` is now, technically, a queueable object, the COM+ application that `FirstQC` lives in must also have the appropriate settings. These settings will be discussed next.

Queueable Settings for the Application

One of the property pages that appear when you right-click on an application using Component Services is the Queuing page, show in Figure 10.3.

If you find that these boxes are grayed out, you might check to make sure that the application is a Server Application and not a Library Application. QC-based applications must always be Server Applications.

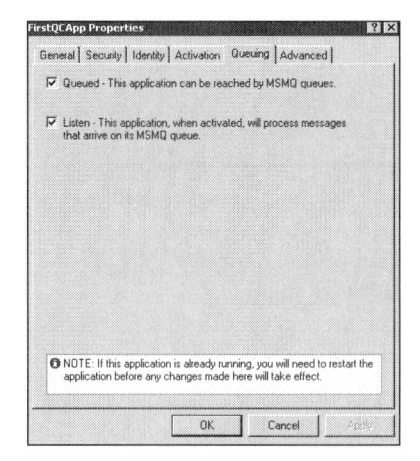

Figure 10.3 The Queuing tab for an application.

If you click the Queued check box, by default, COM+ creates seven queues. You can see them using the Computer Management snap-in, shown in Figure 10.4.

The first queue has the same name as the application, and it is followed by five similarly named queues numbered 0 to 4. There is one last queue, known as the *dead queue*. Basically, a message works its way through all these queues as COM+ repeatedly attempts to deliver the message to the receiver in the context of a transaction.

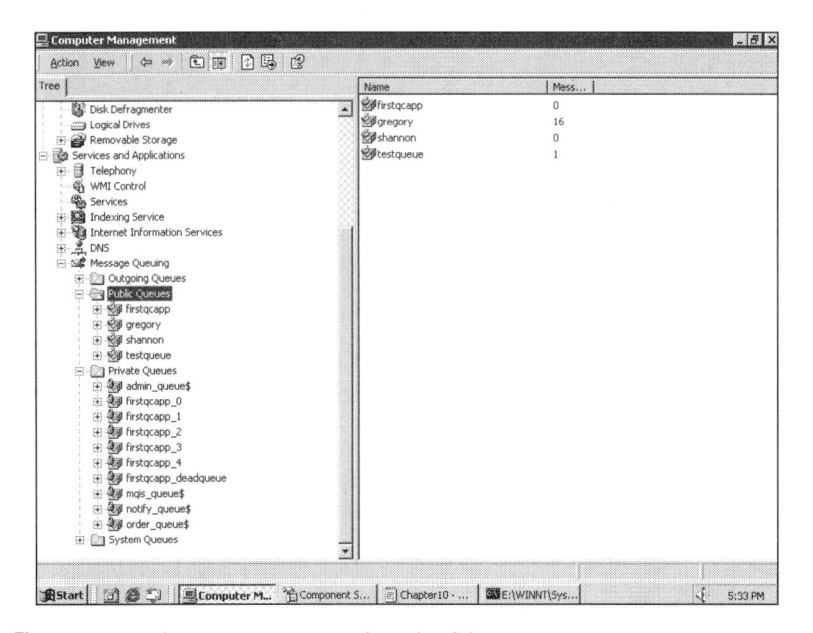

Figure 10.4 The Message Queuing branch of the Computer Management snap-in.

The fact that the message delivery is attempted as part of a transaction should not surprise you, given that MSMQ is a *bona fide* RM. To MSMQ, delivering a message to or from a queue is akin to a more traditional RM, such as a database receiving a SQL update. As far as MSMQ is concerned, the queue is the data store, and the main purpose of its transaction is to ensure that the message successfully gets placed in the queue or removed from it completely. It is also possible to use solitary non-transactional queues with QC, but we will delay the discussion of these until the section "Transactional and Non-Transactional Queues."

After the Queued check box is clicked and the queues are created, `FirstQC` can be instantiated via a queue moniker and can begin receiving messages. Keep in mind, however, that it is the Recorder standing in as a proxy for the object that is getting the method calls from the client, turning them into messages, and storing them in the queue for later retrieval.

This brings us to the other check box shown in Figure 10.3. The second check box, Listen, seems simple enough, especially with the helpful sentence imprinted on the dialog box. This check box causes the `ListenerHelper` to monitor the queues for the application. If the `ListenerHelper` detects a message, it hands it to the `ListenerHelper` object, which gives it to the Player, which creates a new instance of `FirstQC` and replays the method invocations made by the client.

One final, critical point to make is that `FirstQC`'s parent application must be running for `FirstQC` to receive any messages. To make certain that your application is running, simply right-click on it in the Component Services and select Start. Note that clients can still send messages via the Recorder even if the application is not running—they just aren't picked up and played to a new instance of the `FirstQC` until the application is next run. It might seem odd that the application needs to be explicitly run by the user or otherwise started using the COM+ administrative objects. After all, COM+ applications are normally run automatically when a client calls on one of its components. It is the asynchronous, monitoring nature of QC and MSMQ that make explicit startups a necessity.

QC Internals

Now that we've discussed the Player, Recorder, and Listener, let's explore implementation of a QC and track method calls/messages as they move through a COM+ application's queues.

Disabling Security

Security settings paired with your specific NT domain topology and other administrative issues add another, more complicated layer to this process, which we'll explore in Chapter 12, "Security." For the examples in this chapter, let's explore the simplest possible QC scenario first, where security and other network considerations are removed. To cut out the security layer altogether, go to the Properties page for the `FirstQCApp` application and click on the Security property tab. Adjust the settings such that Authentication Level for Calls is set to None, as shown in Figure 10.5.

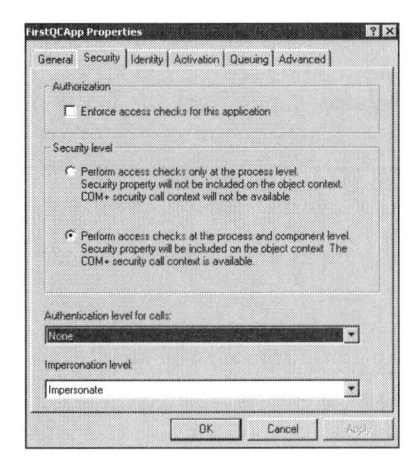

Figure 10.5 The Security settings tab for FirstQCApp.

Viewing Method Calls as Messages

You know that the Recorder translates method calls into MSMQ messages and puts them in an application's queue. If you are wondering exactly when the method calls are put into the queue by the Recorder, always remember that MSMQ is an RM. Therefore, by the rules outlined in Chapter 8, "Transactions," the message is placed in the queue when the transaction is committed—that is, when the root object is deactivated with its Happy bit set to TRUE. Given that your base client executable does not have a context and, therefore, does not have a transaction, COM+ automatically creates a new transaction when the Recorder is instantiated. If you check the transactional settings for the COM+ Recorder, you'll notice that it is set to Required. As you learned in Chapter 8, this setting means that the object inherits a transaction if its creator had one, or COM+ creates a new transaction for the object if it did not. Thus, all QC method calls are transactional, and the method calls are committed to the queue as messages when the Recorder object, the root object in this case, is deactivated and Happy.

> **Authentication Problems with Windows 2000 Workgroup Mode**
>
> Although I don't want to get into Windows 2000 administration too much at the moment, I want to save a few hours of frustration for you if I can. If you are experimenting with Windows 2000, perhaps you just have Windows 2000 Professional on your desktop but are not logged in by a *bona fide* Windows 2000 Server (or Advanced Server) domain controller, you must disable security entirely. This is because you are in *workgroup mode*, and in this mode, the Windows 2000 Active Directory services are not available to provide user authentication. Calls to create or otherwise use your queued components will fail.
>
> Authentication will be discussed in greater detail in Chapter 12 where you will also find that role-based security can still operate, even if authentication is turned off.

Chapter 10 Queued Components

Let's take a look at how method calls turn into messages. Imagine the following code exists in a simple VB client:

```
Dim QC As FirstQC.FirstQueue

Sub Form_Load()
Set QC = GetObject("queue:/new:FirstQC.FirstQueue")
End Sub

Sub Command1_Click
QC.DisplayNumber 4
End Sub
```

Further, imagine that you perform the following steps:

1. Run this client.
2. Click the button once.
3. Close the application.
4. Run the application again.
5. Click the button 10 times.
6. Close the application.

Keeping in mind that because `FirstQCApp` is not running (you haven't explicitly started it), you can go to this application's queues and take a look at the messages. Using the Computer Management Console, you can navigate to `FirstQCApp`'s queues, as shown in Figure 10.6.

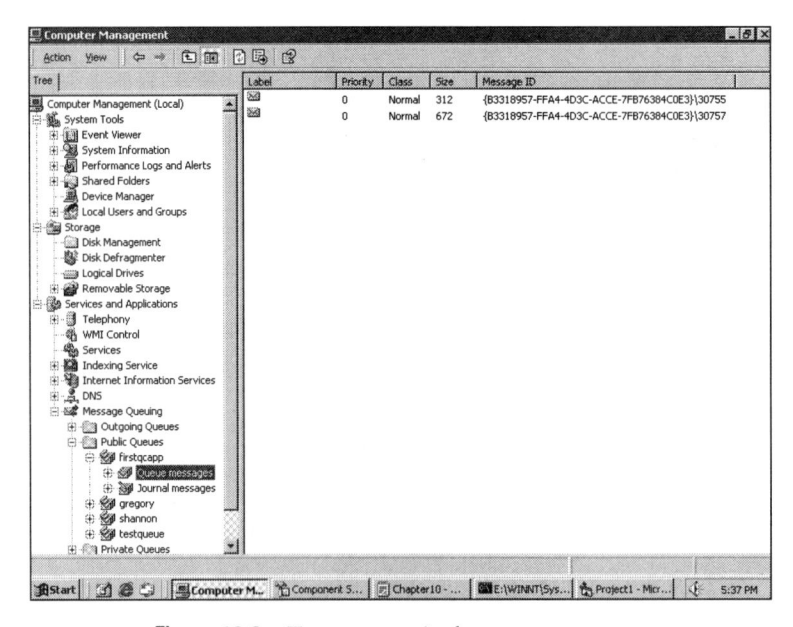

Figure 10.6 Two messages in the `FirstQCApp` queue.

You might have expected 11 messages because you made 11 method calls. But, if you think about it, you'll find it makes perfect sense. As an RM, MSMQ attempts to commit a transaction when the root object completes its work. In our example, our base client made one method call and was closed, thus deactivating the `Recorder` object (the root object of the transaction) and forcing the transaction to commit. The result of this operation was one message.

Next we reran the application, made 10 method calls, and again forced the transaction to complete. It seems logical and efficient then that the 10 method calls should be bundled into a singular message.

There is one large caveat, however. If any single method call of the 10 in the message causes the recipient to crash or call `SetAbort`, the message is retried (according to the rules laid out in the upcoming sidebar "Timeout Periods and Retry Attempts for Failed QC Messages"). This message, however, contains 10 method invocations, and they are all played to the recipient again, not just the one that failed. This implies that your method calls should be idempotent, or at the very least, any data modifications performed by queued methods should be under the umbrella of the recipient's transaction, which given that the modifications are undone in the event of an aborted transaction, amounts to the same thing, more or less. These messages can, of course, be viewed. Double-click on the first one (or solitary method call), and you will see something like Figure 10.7.

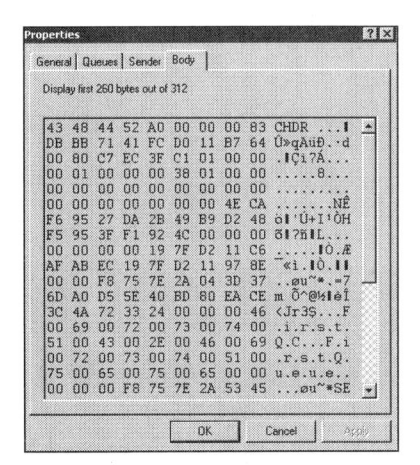

Figure 10.7 The contents of the message resulting from a method call to `FirstQC`.

308 Chapter 10 Queued Components

You don't need to understand the contents of the message, only that this is the binary representation of your queued method call. In the section, "Manually Reading the Message," I demonstrate how to take the contents of this message and put it into a queue directly via an ordinary, non-COM+ MSMQ client. For the moment, however, let's continue our exploration.

Playing the Messages

Because `FirstQCApp` is not running, method calls made by clients requesting queueable objects from this application simply pile up in the queues. So, by the simple action of right-clicking the application in the Component Services Console and selecting the Start menu item, you are ultimately greeted by 11 message boxes, some of which are minimized, as shown in Figure 10.8.

If you dismiss the 11 message boxes and look into `FirstQCApp`'s queues, you find them empty. The messages have been detected by the Listener; and the Player was created, which then instantiated a `FirstQC` object and played the messages as method calls for the object. Messages are removed from the queue after they are successfully played for the recipient.

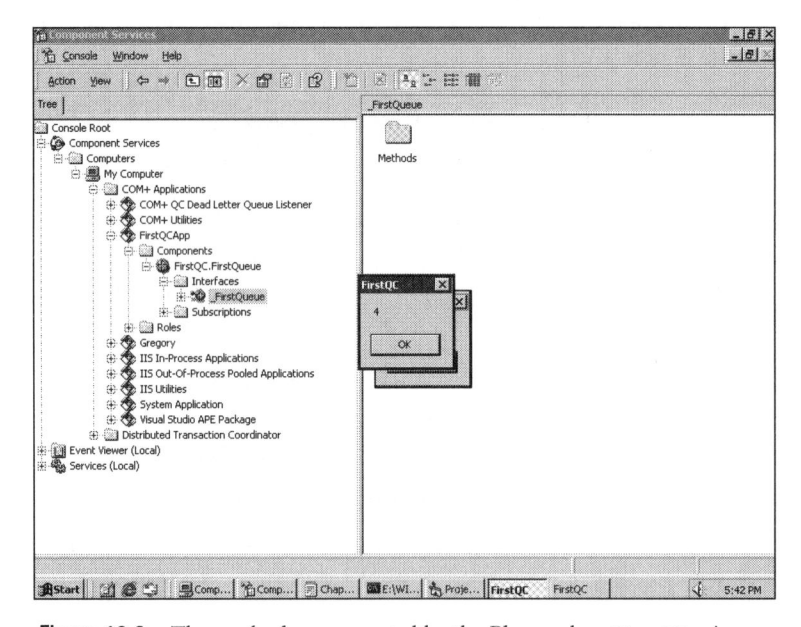

Figure 10.8 The methods are executed by the Player when `FirstQCApp` is run.

Transactional and Non-Transactional Queues

By default, when you click the Queued check box for a COM+ application, you get seven transactional queues. As COM+ tries repeatedly to deliver a transactional message to an object that keeps crashing, keeps calling SetAbort(), or is involved with some other RM that keeps failing, it moves through the numbered queues—lowest to highest. Ultimately, if the message cannot be delivered, it ends up in the dead message queue (or played to your exception class as discussed in the section, "Exception Classes") where a system administrator should probably take a look at the message. Note that each of the seven queues are transactional, but the movement of a message from one queue to a queue of a higher number as it fails to be delivered is not part of what it means to be a transactional queue. The upward movement through six queues and ultimately to a dead message queue is a convention of COM+—not of transactions or MSMQ. For more information on the way COM+ attempts to deliver messages, see the following sidebar, "Timeout Periods and Retry Attempts for Failed QC Messages."

It is possible to have a single queue that is transactional. You can even choose to create one such queue before creating your application, but COM+ quickly creates the other six queues as soon as you mark the application as Queued. Alternatively, you can create a single non-transaction queue, and if you later create an application of the same name, COM+ does not create six other queues. However, there's no good reason to do this unless you don't want COM+ to redeliver the message if the receiver calls SetAbort() or some other failure occurs.

Timeout Periods and Retry Attempts for Failed QC Messages

The protocol for retrying delivery and moving a message upward through the queues toward the dead message queue can be empirically discovered. Assuming that you have a client that crashes or calls SetAbort() continuously, you will find the message moves as follows:

- BLOWUP_0 queue. COM+ waits 60 seconds before re-attempting delivery three times.
- BLOWUP_1 queue. COM+ waits 120 seconds before re-attempting delivery three times.
- BLOWUP_2 queue. COM+ waits 240 seconds before re-attempting delivery three times.
- BLOWUP_3 queue. COM+ waits 480 seconds before re-attempting delivery three times.
- BLOWUP_4 queue. COM+ waits 960 seconds before re-attempting delivery three times.
- BLOWUP_dead queue. The message should now be examined by a system administrator unless an exception class is set up to be notified. Exception classes are discussed in the subsequent section by that name.

Note that the retry times are individual—not cumulative. In other words, after 60 seconds of waiting on the first failure, COM+ waits 60 seconds after the second failure, and so on. At present, these times are not changeable by the system administrator.

In the context of COM+, QC transactional queues guarantee that a message will be delivered. However, although you might read in Microsoft publications that it is delivered only once, this is not necessarily true—remember that one message might translate to several method calls played for the client. As discussed in the previous section, if any of these method calls cause a crash or `SetAbort()` to occur in the recipient, the entire message is replayed and the nine good methods are executed again along with the failed tenth. It is important, then, to make sure that the method calls are idempotent and/or data modifications they make will be aborted and undone if the recipient's transaction should fail.

Transactional queues have some very desirable attributes, so the following question arises: Why would you not want to use a transactional queue? Perhaps performance might be far more important than reliability in some scenario, and you want to avoid the overhead of MSMQ transaction enlistment by using non-transactional queues. Alternatively, you might want to bypass the transactional `Recorder` and `ListenerHelper` (both are marked `transaction=Required`) and access the queues directly with non-transactional clients or objects.

Non-transactional queues do not, obviously, require transactions, nor do they support them. These queues do not guarantee delivery, and messages could, conceivably, be lost altogether.

The Different Queue Types: Private and Public

There are certain points where development efforts and NT system administration converge, and you cannot understand one fully without understanding the other. Private and public queues sit at such a point.

Basically, a *private queue* is one that an MSMQ application must explicitly know about. Senders and recipients must know the exact location and name of this queue. If you are familiar with IPCs mechanisms, queues have a very similar naming convention as named pipes. Although private queues are often created on the local machine and used when the sender and recipient are also on the local machine, the sender, receiver, and queue can all be on different machines. Private queues do not suffer any limitations except that they do not advertise their existence in any way.

Public queues, on the other hand, advertise their existence through the Active Directory. Active Directory was introduced with Windows 2000. You can think of it as a hierarchical database that is automatically replicated on all domain controllers (DCs) that are part of the same *forest*. A forest is a group of logically related domains that agree on a particular *schema*—that is, they share a common hierarchical view consisting of specific system and user-definable objects whose meaning and organization are relevant to them. Unfortunately, to give Active Directory its proper due and to explain schemas, forests, and so on in the appropriate depth would take a book of its own. For that reason, we are going to look at Active Directory from a high level.

The Active Directory database contains user account information for authentication purposes, as well as information about printers, fax machines, and, among other things, public queues. The existence of public queues are broadcast by Windows 2000 using Active Directory, and this makes them easy to find. A client might need only the name of the public queue and does not need to know where the queue was. This is not the case with a private queue.

Before we leave the topic of the Active Directory, know that it can also hold and replicate any form of hierarchical information that you care to enter into it programmatically via Active Directory Service Interfaces (ADSI). I will not get deep in a discussion about Active Directory because that would take us into the field of NT administration and is outside the scope of this book. For completeness, however, the companion code for this book includes a simple VB client that uses ADSI to find out information about public queues. Additional information on Active Directory can be found in New Riders's *Windows 2000 Active Directory*, by Edgar Brovick, Doug Hauger, and William C. Wade III. For additional information on ADSI scripting, see New Riders' *Windows NT/2000 ADSI Scripting for System Administration*, by Thomas Eck.

Other than their self-aggrandizing, showy nature, public queues are identical in functionality to private queues, and either type can be transactional or non-transactional. COM+ applications marked as Queued create their first, primary queue as public, and the six other queues are private because they are an implementation detail of QCs and are not meant to be accessed directly by MSMQ clients.

Interoperability Between MSMQ and QC

You know that QC is based on MSMQ. It stands to reason, then, that it must be possible for an MSMQ application to interact with a QC and *vice versa*. Although this is certainly the case, it is probably best to stick with one or the other. After all, QC uses a proprietary binary format when it translates method calls to messages, so although an MSMQ recipient can receive the message, in all likelihood, it cannot do anything meaningful with it.

To prove that MSMQ and QC are truly interoperable and to further explore the details of this symbiosis, I am going to demonstrate how to write an MSMQ client that masquerades as a QC client. Specifically, I'm going to simulate a method call to a QC object by writing a message directly to the queue using an ordinary MSMQ client, bypassing the Recorder altogether.

You know that the Recorder translates method calls made by a client on a queueable object (created by the client through the queue moniker) into messages and puts them in the object's application's queue. It is also true that the destination COM+ application might not be running/listening at that time the method call is made, and even if it is, the calling client and receiving object are uncoupled—the Receiver monitors the queue and does not know or care about how a message got into its queue, only that a message is in it.

Manually Reading the Message

The algorithm used by the Recorder to translate method calls to messages is not documented. Assume that the following code is executed by a QC client:

```
Dim QC As FirstQC.FirstQueue
Set QC = GetObject("queue:/new:FirstQC.FirstQueue")
QC.DisplayNumber 4
```

You can see the resulting message in `FirstQCApp`'s queue by navigating to `FirstQCApp`'s primary queue, viewing its messages section, and double-clicking the resulting message. You see a message similar to that shown in Figure 10.7.

We are going to simulate the preceding client-side code using an ordinary, non-transactional MSMQ client. For simplicity, I am assuming you are in Workgroup mode (that is, not using Active Directory). Follow these steps:

1. Because COM+ uses transactional queues by default and your MSMQ client is going to be an ordinary non-transactional EXE, you need to create a new, non-transactional private queue. This is easy to do, however. Simply choose Computer Management MMC, Services & Applications, Message Queuing, and right-click Private Queues. Then select New. The dialog box shown in Figure 10.9 appears.

2. Give the queue the name `SecondQCApp` and don't check the Transactional check box. This creates a private queue on the system called `SecondQCApp`.

3. Now create a COM+ application called `SecondQCApp` and make it queue-enabled (also, don't forget to turn authentication off). Instead of creating seven new queues as before, COM+ uses the existing non-transactional queue you just created for the queued components on this system.

4. Delete the `FirstQC` component from `FirstQCApp` and install it into `SecondQCApp`. Then, mark its interface as queued. The stage is now set—you have created a new application, `SecondQCApp`, that is using the new non-transactional queue you explicitly created for it. By installing `FirstQC` in `SecondQCApp`, queued calls you now make to `FirstQC` will reach `FirstQC` through the new, non-transaction queue.

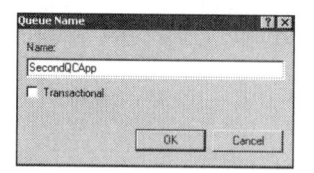

Figure 10.9 The New Queue dialog box.

5. Using the application described in the "Viewing Method Calls as Messages" section, try the following:

   Click the command button once.

   Close the application.

Now examine the contents of the queue as shown in Figure 10.10.

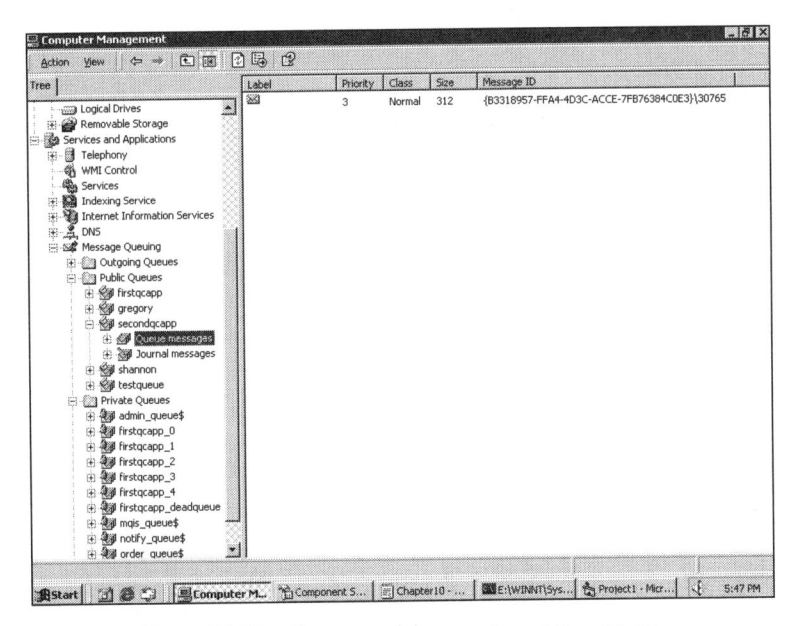

Figure 10.10 Contents of the new `SecondQCApp` queue.

Predictably, there is one message in the queue that corresponds to the method call you just made. But this queue can be read from or written to by MSMQ-aware applications, so it is legal to read and remove a QC-generated message using a pure MSMQ application. The code in Listing 10.6 demonstrates how this message can be read by an ordinary MSMQ application.

Listing 10.6 **Reading a Message and Dumping Its Contents into a Binary File**

```
Dim qInfo As New MSMQQueueInfo
Dim qSource As MSMQQueue
Dim msgRec As MSMQMessage
Dim vntBody As Variant

'Specify the queue we will be reading from, in this case
'the non-transactional queue we created before. Note that
'if this queue was transactional, an attempt to open it
'would fail since a client application has no transaction
'associated with it.

'Note that this code assumes you are in Workgroup mode
'in other words authentication via Active Directory is not being used

qInfo.PathName = ".\private$\MSMQTest"

'Open the queue and try to retrieve the message
Set qSource = qInfo.Open(MQ_RECEIVE_ACCESS, MQ_DENY_NONE)
Set msgRec = qSource.Receive(ReceiveTimeout:=1000)

If msgRec Is Nothing Then
    MsgBox "Nothing in Queue"
Else

    'dump the message body contents to a binary file:
    vntBody = msgRec.body
    Open "body.dat" For Binary As #1
    Put #1, , vntBody
    Close #1

    'dump the message extension contents to a binary file:
    vntBody = msgRec.Extension
    Open "extension.dat" For Binary As #1
    Put #1, , vntBody
    Close #1

End If

qSource.Close
```

The code in Listing 10.6 reads the message from the queue (thus removing it) and dumps the message body and extension into two binary files. The message extension is a new property in MSMQ 2.0 (the version that comes with Windows 2000) and is used to specify additional application-defined information that is associated with the message.

These two binary files completely describe the message that results in the method call you want. To illustrate this, you can construct a program that uses the binary files to package a message and put it back in the queue. Listing 10.7 demonstrates this process.

Listing 10.7 **Manually Placing a Message into a Queue**

```
Dim qInfo As New MSMQQueueInfo
Dim qDest As MSMQQueue
Dim msgSend As New MSMQMessage
Dim vntBody As Variant

qInfo.PathName = ".\private$\MSMQTest"
Set qDest = qInfo.Open(MQ_SEND_ACCESS, MQ_DENY_NONE)

'Construct the message by reading the binary files:

Open "body.dat" For Binary As #1
Get #1, , vntBody
Close #1
msgSend.body = vntBody

Open "extension.DAT" For Binary As #1
Get #1, , vntBody
Close #1
msgSend.Extension = vntBody

'Send the same message 5 times:
For k = 1 To 5
    msgSend.Send qDest
Next

qDest.Close
```

If the code in Listing 10.7 is run, an examination of SecondQCApp's queue reveals five new messages. If you were expecting one large message, remember that you do not have a transactional queue, and this is not a transactional client, so each Send corresponds to exactly one message. That said, it should come as no surprise that when SecondQCApp is started, five message boxes appear as the FirstQC object is instantiated and played its messages.

Although it is possible to examine the contents of body.dat and try to understand the binary layout of QC messages, such an effort would probably bear little fruit. The layout can always change, and if authentication were on, the contents would be encrypted.

Persistence: Passing Objects Through Messages

A message's body property can store pretty much anything—any kind of variable and even binary data can be sent from sender to the recipient object. If you are wondering whether objects themselves can be passed through messages, the answer is sort of.

The terminology *passing an object* is a bit of a euphemism—that is, a friendly, simplified way of describing a more complicated, ugly reality. Objects are not passed in COM+; they do not travel. Rather, references to objects are passed in the form of marshaled interfaces. You can certainly use an interface pointer as an argument to a method and hand out access to some Object A to other objects throughout the network for callback purposes. In this scenario, however, the fundamental Object A remains rooted on the machine in the process in which it was created. This paradigm, that of singleton server handing out references to multiple clients, simply doesn't fit in the QC framework.

Even if you could pass an interface to a living object as a message, there is no way to tell when the receiving application will be running. Therefore, you cannot tell when the recipient object in that application will be playing the message as a method call, and as such, you cannot be sure when it will be given this interface pointer as a method argument. By this time, the original client object referenced by the interface might have been destroyed, and the receiver might unmarshal an orphaned interface to a dead object. And even if the object somehow remained alive, data contained in a marshaled interface pointer is only valid for about five to six minutes.

Ideally, if you are going to send objects from sender to receiver using QC, you need to move the entire object from sender to recipient. And by supporting an interface called `IPersistStream`, an object can elect to take such a trip. An object that supports `IPersistStream` is indicating that it knows how to save its state into a binary stream of bytes and, upon request, gives this stream to any requesting client. Such an object is said to be *persistable,* and persistable objects also know how to reconstruct themselves if some other client instantiates a new instance then and hands them back this stream.

Listing 10.8 demonstrates a C++ implementation of `IPersistStream`. This listing shows a portion of the code for a COM class called `NumberClass`. `NumberClass` simply keeps an array of 1,000 integers, and by inheriting from and implementing `IPersistStream`, it can save and restore its state when asked.

Listing 10.8 **A Portion of C++ COM Component Demonstrating** *IPersistStream*

```
// This is only a partial listing of the persistent component. Consult
// the book's accompanying source code for a complete example.

/************************************************************************
IPersistStream implementation

The implementation of the IPersisStream interface.  COM+ asks the component
for this interface if this component is passed as a parameter to a method
of a queued componenet.

IPersistStream inherits from IPersist, and thus must support the one
method of IPersist (GetClassID). In addition IPersistStream contains
four other methods, all of which are explained below:

*************************************************************************/


// GetClassID is required by IPersist (and hence IPersistStream).
// For persistant objects, COM requires that we provide the component's
// CLSID, so that it can associate the component with the persistent data
// it will be writing/reading.
```

```
HRESULT NumberClass::GetClassID(CLSID *pClassID) {
    *pClassID = CLSID_NumberClass;
    return S_OK;
}


// Before COM asks an object to write its state to a stream,
// it calls the IsDirty method.  This method informs
// COM if the object's state has changed since the last save.
// If it is hasn't, then COM can forgo the write.
//
// In our case, inform COM to always perform the write:

HRESULT NumberClass::IsDirty(void) {
     return S_OK;
}

// The Load method is called when COM wants the object
// to restore its state from a stream.  If this component
// were passed as a parameter to a method of a queued component,
// this method would get called when the QC.Player unpacks
// the MSMQ message and instantiates the queued component.

HRESULT NumberClass::Load(IStream *pIStream) {

    ULONG lBytesRead;

    // Read the collection of numbers from the stream.  From the
    // Save method (below), we know that all 10000 array elements
    // were written to the stream regardless of how many of them
    // contain valid information (that information is kept
    // in the p_Numbers variable).

    for (int i=0; i < 10000; i++) {

        pIStream->Read((void*)&p_NumberCollection[i],
                    sizeof(p_NumberCollection[i]),&lBytesRead);

        if (lBytesRead != sizeof(p_NumberCollection[i])) {
            // For some reason, we didn't read proper number of
            // bytes from the stream:
            return E_FAIL;
        }

    }

    pIStream->Read((void*)&p_Numbers,sizeof(p_Numbers),&lBytesRead);
    if (lBytesRead != sizeof(p_Numbers)) return E_FAIL;

    pIStream->Read((void*)&p_Sum,sizeof(p_Sum),&lBytesRead);
    if (lBytesRead!= sizeof(p_Sum)) return E_FAIL;
```

continues

318 Chapter 10 Queued Components

Listing 10.8 **Continued**
```
        return S_OK;
}


// The Save method is called when COM wants an object to
// save its state to the stream. If this component were
// passed as a method to a queued component, this method
// would be called when COM+ packages method calls made
// against the component into an MSMQ message — (most likely)
// when the application closes.

HRESULT NumberClass::Save(IStream *pIStream, BOOL fClearDirty) {

    ULONG           lBytesRead;
    HRESULT         hr;


    // This objects state consists of:
    //
    // 1.) The 10000 element array
    // 2.) The p_Numbers variable indicating how many #'s are in the collection
    // 3.) The p_Sum variable which keeps a running Sum of the numbers.

    for (int i=0; i < 10000; i++) {

        pIStream->Write((void*)&p_NumberCollection[i],
                        sizeof(p_NumberCollection[i]),&lBytesRead);

        if (lBytesRead != sizeof(p_NumberCollection[i])) {
            // For some reason we couldn't write the # of bytes
            // we wanted to the stream:
            return STG_E_CANTSAVE ;
        }

    }

    pIStream->Write((void*)&p_Numbers,sizeof(p_Numbers),&lBytesRead);
    if (lBytesRead != sizeof(p_Numbers)) return STG_E_CANTSAVE;

    pIStream->Write((void*)&p_Sum,sizeof(p_Sum),&lBytesRead);
    if (lBytesRead != sizeof(p_Sum)) return STG_E_CANTSAVE;

    return S_OK;

}


// GetSizeMax is called by COM to determine the maximum amount
// of bytes the object will need to save its state.  This method
```

```
// is commonly called before the Save method so COM can reserve
// space in the stream before an objects stores its state to the stream.

HRESULT NumberClass::GetSizeMax(ULARGE_INTEGER *pcbSize) {

    // The amount of space to save this object's state is determined
    // by the private member variables of our class.  These include:

    // Array of 10000 elements + p_Numbers + p_Sum.

    pcbSize->QuadPart = (DWORD)(sizeof(p_NumberCollection[0])
                        *10000+sizeof(p_Numbers)+sizeof(p_Sum));
    return S_OK;

}
```

Visual Basic's support for persistable components is far easier to use, if less versatile. First, your must set the VB class's `Persistable` property to 1 as shown in Figure 10.11. After this is done, the VB programmer is responsible for implementing two new methods as shown in Listing 10.9.

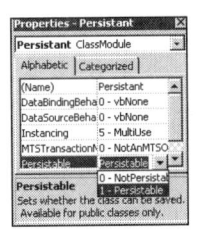

Figure 10.11 Making an object persistable in Visual Basic 6.

Listing 10.9 A Persistable Component Written in Visual Basic 6

```
'An example of a persistable component written in Visual Basic.
'This is a new feature provided by Visual Basic 6.

'This component implements a simple object that provides
'statistical information for a collection of numbers.
'The state of the object is thus the collection of numbers, stored
'in the private class array. The visual basic example does not have
'the 10000 collection limit of its C++ counterpart.

Option Explicit

'Private member variables:
Private m_vntNumberCollection As Variant
```

continues

Listing 10.9 **Continued**

```
Private m_vntNumbers As Variant
Private m_dSum As Double

'Class constructor. Initialize private class variables:
Private Sub Class_Initialize()
    m_vntNumbers = 0
    m_dSum = 0
    ReDim m_vntNumberCollection(0)
End Sub

'AddNumber allows the user to add a number to the collection.
'Redimension the array to accomodate for this newly added number
Sub AddNumber(ByVal Number As Double)
    m_vntNumbers = m_vntNumbers + 1
    ReDim m_vntNumberCollection(m_vntNumbers)
    m_vntNumberCollection(m_vntNumbers) = Number
    m_dSum = m_dSum + Number
End Sub

'Average returns the average of all the numbers in the collection.
'Since we keep a running total of the sum of the numbers this is easy:
Function Average() As Double
    Average = m_dSum / m_vntNumbers
End Function

'Sum returns the Sum of all the numbers in the collection:
Function Sum() As Double
    Sum = m_dSum
End Function

''''''''''''''''''''''''''''''''''''''''''''''''''''''
'Persistable objects in Visual Basic must implement the
'following two procedures:

'The ReadProperties procedure in Visual Basic is like
'the IPersistStream::Load method in C++. It allows
'an object to restore its state from disk.

Private Sub Class_ReadProperties(PropBag As PropertyBag)
    Dim iNumber As Integer

    'The property bag where we write the object's state to
    '(much like the stream in C++):
    m_vntNumbers = PropBag.ReadProperty("Numbers")
    m_dSum = PropBag.ReadProperty("Sum")

    'Dimension the array to the amount of numbers
    'that were previously saved:
```

```
    ReDim m_vntNumberCollection(m_vntNumbers)

    'Read in each element of the array:
    For iNumber = 0 To m_vntNumbers - 1
        m_vntNumberCollection(iNumber) = PropBag.ReadProperty("Number" & _
                                                                iNumber)
    Next

End Sub

'The WriteProperties procedure in Visual Basic is like
'the IPersistStream::Save method in C++. It allows
'an object to store its state from disk.

Private Sub Class_WriteProperties(PropBag As PropertyBag)
    Dim iNumber As Integer

    PropBag.WriteProperty "Numbers", m_vntNumbers
    PropBag.WriteProperty "Sum", m_dSum

    'The property bag CANNOT write arrays, so we must iterate
    'through it ourselves:
    For iNumber = 0 To m_vntNumbers - 1
        PropBag.WriteProperty "Number" & iNumber, m_vntNumberCollection(iNumber)
    Next

End Sub
```

Notification and Callbacks

By default, you can never be sure that a method call made to a queueable object will ultimately be processed by that object. Although it is true that you can be sure that the message will be placed in a queue and queued for processing (provided the object's application is using transactional queues), you cannot be certain that the object's application will ever be run or that, if running, it is listening for new messages.

Certain mission-critical applications generate messages like BUY or SELL that need some form of acknowledgement. The acknowledgement might also need to contain additional information like what an item was sold or purchased for. Fortunately, QC provides for such a mechanism in the form of *callbacks*.

As convenient as it might seem, you cannot simply instantiate an object locally on the sending machine and pass an interface via a method call argument to a QC object. As we've discussed, by the time the recipient even gets the method call, the callback object probably has perished along with the sender. Persistent objects don't help you either—the recipient is getting a completely new instantiation of the object that would run locally. The QC framework does, however, provide a callback solution. It is allowable for a queueable object to exist on the sender's machine and, after being instantiated via a queue moniker, can be passed as an argument to the recipient object. In other words, you can pass a Recorder as an argument to another Recorder.

There is a kind of duality involved in dealing with recorders in that you sometimes treat them as living callback objects and other times as references to objects that will be instantiated some time in the future. The latter treatment is closer to the truth, but the former is more easily understood. It might even be fair to say that you shouldn't care about the fact that you get a Recorder and not a real interface to a queued object. Due to the declarative nature of COM+, it is certainly true that your code should never make the assumption to write your server's objects as if they really are getting true interface pointers and not Recorders. It is COM+'s job to make sure everything works.

Writing an interface with a method that can take a callback object as an argument is simple. For the purpose of example, imagine that you have two queueable objects, `CallBackObject` and `ServerCallback`. The former object belongs to the client and provides the client with callback notifications from `ServerCallback`. An interface of `CallBackObject` (a Recorder) is passed as an argument to a method of `ServerCallback` so that `ServerCallback` can use it to send acknowledgements back to the client. The VB code in Listing 10.10 demonstrates how to implement `ServerCallback`.

Listing 10.10 **Implementation of *ServerCallback* ActiveX Class**

```
'Remember the ByVal keyword is important!
Sub ServerMethod(ByVal CallBackObject As CallBack.CallBackObj, ByVal Message)
    On Error GoTo problem
    MsgBox "Server received the following message: " & Message
    CallBackObject.CallBackMethod Message

    Exit Sub
problem:
    MsgBox Err.Description & " - " & Hex$(Err.Number)

End Sub
```

Assume the subroutine in Listing 10.10 is located in a VB class called `ServerCallback` in an ActiveX DLL project. Remember that in VB, a class is really an interface. So according to VB's conventions, there is a coclass called `ServerCallback` that supports an interface called `CallBackObject`. The following is the generated IDL:

```
interface _ServerCallback : IDispatch {
    [id(0x60030000)]
    HRESULT ServerMethod(
                [in] _CallBackObj* CallBackObject,
                [in] BSTR SomeString);
};
```

If a client application executes the code in Listing 10.11, the client is, in effect, creating two Recorder objects—one representing the `ServerCallback` object and another representing `CallBackObject` on the client machine.

Listing 10.11 Client-Side Code Demonstrating Callbacks Using *CallBackObj*

```
Dim callBck As callback.CallBackObj
Dim srvr As server.ServerCallback

'Use the queue moniker to get a recorder to the local client component:
Set callBck = GetObject("queue:/new:Callback.CallBackObj")

'Use the queue moniker to get a recorder which points the remote machine:
Set srvr = GetObject("queue:CompuerName=Sajid,QueueName=Gregory" & _
                     "/new:Server.ServerCallBack")


'Call a method
srvr.ServerMethod callBck, "This is a message for the server!"
```

Because `CallBackObject` has one method, `ServerMethod()`, that can take a `CallBackObject` interface as an argument, the client can send its local `CallBackObject` to the server, which can use it to send notifications back to the client.

You might imagine that passing a Recorder is like passing a persistable object, but it isn't. When you pass a Recorder, you are really passing little more than a moniker string that tells the recipient what object in what location to create. For example, if you examine the method/message recorded to the queue for the `ServerMethod` method call, you will find something like the following:

```
computername=MSMQHEAD,queuename=Gregory,formatname=PUBLIC=92df4d1c-a62a-48c0-ae43-
➥690e9d46a5cc,authlevel=1Æ¯«ì_Ò —Zøu—*V_∫π¯AyI‰*'( ¯÷t(Callback.CallBackObj)
```

Additional information might be automatically added to the moniker string by COM+, such as the sender's queue's GUID if public queues are used. You are not, however, passing an object interface or Recorder, just a string and a little extra contextual information. The recipient uses this string and automatically instantiates a new Recorder back to the sender.

In that case, the following client code, although seemingly correct, does not work unless `CallBackObj` is persistable:

```
Set c = new CallBack.CallBackObj 'Won't work, did not create with a queue moniker
➥s.ServerMethod c, "This is a message for the server!"
```

Of course, if it is persistable, a new instance of `CallBackObj` is instantiated on the recipient machine. But this is not what you want because this new object has no ties back to the client, thus invalidating its use as a callback mechanism. So, although they look syntactically similar, passing a Recorder and passing an object interface are very different things.

One final point worth mentioning is that the client might want callbacks to be sent, not to itself, but to another machine altogether. The client can create a Recorder via a `queue` moniker that points to a callback object on another machine and pass that to some recipient. There is no rule that says the callback object must be on the same machine as the original sender. The asynchronous nature of QC grants an enormous amount of flexibility in terms of acknowledgements because you are not passing interfaces, you are passing locations, addresses in the form of a string.

Exception Classes

Callbacks and acknowledgements are one thing, but failure is another. If you want to be explicitly notified when a queued method call fails to be delivered, you need only declare an *exception class*. The Properties dialog box of any COM+ component has a tab labeled Advanced. It looks like the one shown in Figure 10.12.

Type the ProgID (or ClassID) of an object that you want COM+ to call in the event of a failed message delivery. Most commonly, you set this property on both the sending and receiving applications on different machines. This is because COM+ triggers the exception class on the sending machine if it cannot reach the destination machine at all (perhaps the network is down); it triggers the exception on the destination machine if it can reach the destination, but ultimately it cannot play the message for the recipient.

In the event of a failed delivery, COM+ instantiates your exception class and then QIs for an interface called `IPlayBackControl`. If your object implements this interface, COM+ calls one of its two methods, which follow:

- `FinalClientRetry`. COM+ calls this method on the exception object on the sending client if the message cannot be delivered to the server at all. This most likely occurs if the server is down or otherwise unreachable. Although this method has no arguments, upon receiving this call, a client knows to check its dead queue.

- `FinalServerRetry`. COM+ calls this method on your exception object on the receiving server after repeated attempts to play the message fail. This method is called when the failed message enters the dead message queue for the application.

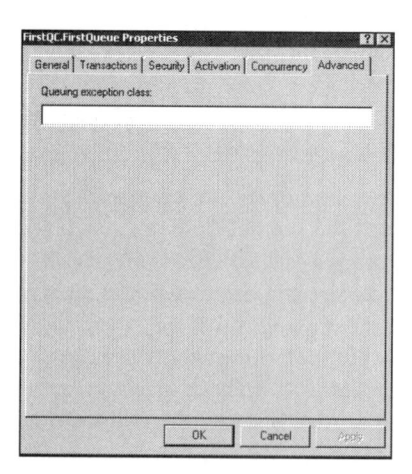

Figure 10.12 The Advanced tab.

If you don't feel like peeking into a queue and analyzing the failed message, you can request that COM+ play the failed method call to your exception class. All your exception class needs to do is simply implement the queued interface containing the failed method call in question. In other words, you can write your exception class such that it is, in a sense, the recipient object's evil twin; if the method call fails to be played to the recipient object, then your exception class will receive the method call instead, just as if it were the originally targeted object. Of course, by receiving method calls originally slated for the recipient object, your implementation of these method calls would probably do little more than announce "This function was attempted but failed!"

For example, imagine some interface, `IExample`, is declared queued in some recipient object, and it has one method called `Test()`. If a client calls `IExample->Test()`, and the message resulting from that call fails to successfully play for the recipient, COM+ instantiates the event class you established for that object, and after QIing for `IPlaybackControl`, it then QIs for `IExample`. Predictably, the Player for your exception class invokes the `Test()` method on this interface of your exception class. So, when authoring such an event class and implementing `IExample`, you can write code to take whatever actions you deem appropriate given that you know exactly which method(s) failed to be delivered to the recipient.

An event class might support the `IPlaybackControl`, the queueable interface of the recipient, or both.

Callbacks and Events

At this point, you might be envisioning schemes that allow the client executable to receive acknowledgements while it is running. Maybe you're thinking about writing a trade-entry front end that allows the user to submit a trade via QC and soon after get back an acknowledgement that perhaps populates some control on the currently running form. For this type of application, however, COM+ *events* are better suited. As you see in the next chapter, COM+ events can use either synchronous Distributed COM (DCOM) or MSMQ as an asynchronous transport but provide a generic, extensible architecture for real-time acknowledgements.

Some Subtle Requirements for QC: Parallel Application Configurations Required for Sender and Receiver

Originating with terminals and mainframes, the idea of thin clients is once again in vogue (that is, after a brief interlude with client/server in the early 1990s). Its maxim: Configure the server to handle the work, not the client.

In QC, you would expect the recipient machine receiving a queued method call to have a configured COM+ application, complete with queues, in which the destination component had been imported. You would further expect the interfaces of that component to be marked as Queued. It is surprising then to learn that the client must also have a fully configured COM+ application, complete with queues, in which the destination component is likewise locally installed and configured.

This kind of forced symmetry seems analogous to installing a brick oven in your home and donning an apron to order out for pizza. According to the rules of traditional COM, a client machine need only have the type library for the server object registered locally (and even then, only if the client wants to use early binding instead of late binding). Requiring an entire configured application complete with queues, however, seems a bit much. In addition, if the recipient application's queues are transactional, your client-side queues need to be transactional as well. And if you imagine that the sender's local queues are somehow used to temporarily stage a message before sending it to the recipient queues, you will be disappointed—the local queues on the sender's machine are not used.

At the time of this book's writing, Microsoft documentation doesn't specifically mention this client-side symmetry as a requirement. However, empirical research indicates this symmetry is necessary; it seems likely that COM+ uses the locally configured application, queue, and component settings to determine exactly how a message should be sent to a recipient. If, for example, the recipient application's queues are transactional, the sender must know this so that it adds transaction information as part of the message when sending it. The existence of similarly configured local queues can give the sender this information, even if they are not otherwise used. If your client COM+ application is configured to use non-transactional queues but the recipient application uses transactional queues, your QC method call will appear to work. However, if you check the event log, you will find that the QC.Recorder logs an error message like that shown in Listing 10.12.

Listing 10.12 **Error Message Reported by the Recorder When the Locally Configured Queue of the Client Application is Not Transactional but the Recipient Queue is Transactional**

```
An unexpected error was returned by the MSMQ API function indicated. The following
➥error message was retrieved from MSMQ.
MQSendMessage : Transaction usage is invalid.
Server Application ID: {E3D43E4D-D73C-4AC1-8318-36DF1BEFDF69}
Server Application Name: shannon
Error Code = 0xc00e0050 :
COM+ Services Internals Information:
File: .\channelmanager.cpp, Line: 388
```

Forgetting about queues for the moment, a locally configured COM+ application also makes it possible to specify exception classes on the sender, as well as the receiver. This requires a configured, sender-side COM+ application.

Asynchronous COM

Sometimes two (or more) different technologies originate to solve the same problem, but they take different evolutionary paths. Eventually, one might dominate and force the other into obscurity and, perhaps, kill it altogether. This is perhaps the case with QC and another technology *Asynchronous COM*. However, regardless of what the future brings or whichever technology wins out, QC and Asynchronous COM are both around—documented and clamoring for use at present. So a discussion of Asynchronous COM is helpful if only so you recognize it when you see it described or in use, and you are able to distinguish it from QC.

QC is a native COM+ service. QCs can leverage MSMQ transparently to make asynchronous method calls and can utilize other COM+ services such as transactions and role-based security. Asynchronous COM, though far more complicated to implement, can do almost none of these things except provide for asynchronous method calls. Asynchronous COM components cannot even be configured COM+ components, so they can't use any COM+ services.

Asynchronous COM Implementation

If you think of QC as an inherent COM+ service and Asynchronous COM as an RPC enhancement, you are not far from the truth. Simply put, Asynchronous COM begins at the IDL level. To demonstrate, imagine you have the IDL shown in Listing 10.13, but with the additional attribute shown in bold.

Listing 10.13 **Simple IDL Declaration of an Interface with an** *async_uuid* **Attribute**

```
[
object,
uuid(8183C0C6-8AB3-4445-9D31-D2F7A575F7FB),
helpstring("ITester Interface"),
async_uuid(340C09D1-E06B-41f3-85BD-70FF4D205807),
pointer_default(unique)
]
interface ITester : IUnknown
{
[helpstring("method Info")] HRESULT TestMethod([in] int x, [out] int * y);

};
```

The async_uuid attribute causes an additional interface prototype to be created when MIDL.EXE is run on this IDL file. If you examine the resulting header file, you find that shown in Listing 10.14.

Listing 10.14 **MIDL-Generated Prototype for *AsyncITester***

```
MIDL_INTERFACE("340C09D1-E06B-41f3-85BD-70FF4D205807")
AsyncITester : public IUnknown
    {
public:
virtual /* [helpstring] */ HRESULT STDMETHODCALLTYPE Begin_TestMethod(
/* [in] */ int x) = 0;
virtual /* [helpstring] */ HRESULT STDMETHODCALLTYPE Finish_TestMethod( /* [out]
↪*/   int
 __RPC_FAR *y) = 0;
    };
```

MIDL has created an entirely new interface, one not specified in the IDL file. This new interface has the same name as the original, ITester, but is prepended with the tag Async: result AsynchITester. An Asynchronous COM client must use this interface if it wants to make method calls asynchronously, but as you see in a few paragraphs, the client does not QI for it.

You might also notice that the single method, TestMethod(), which contained both an in and an out parameter has been split into two methods, Begin_TestMethod() and Finish_TestMethod().

The Begin method contains all the in parameters. The Asynchronous COM client calls this method, and it returns immediately, *asynchronously,* allowing the client to continue with other work. Some time later, however, the client needs to call the Finish method (which contains all the out parameters) unless it wants to cancel the call altogether. Obviously, the client needs to know when the server is finished, so the server supports an interface called ISynchronize which the client can use to determine when the server is finished.

Clearly, Asynchronous COM imposes a more complex protocol that the developer of the client and server object must adhere to. The server author, in particular, has to support the ISynchronize interface, and it normally does so by aggregating one of the COM system synchronization objects, CLSID_StdEvent or CLSID_ManualResetEvent. Don't look for these objects in the Registry, and you won't find them especially well-described in Microsoft documentation (at least at the time of this writing); they exist entirely in the COM sub-system. The platform SDK demonstrates the use of these objects in the context of implementing an Asynchronous COM server object, so you might want to check out the Async examples that come with the SDK if you are interested in greater detail.

You might imagine, then, that all the client needs to do is create an instance of the object, QI for AsynchITester and ISynchronize, and then call the Begin method to execute the async function call. After the async call is made, the client should use the methods of ISynchronize to determine when the server is finished and then call Finish when ISynchronize says it is okay to retrieve any out parameters.

Well, there is one additional step. The server object must also support an interface called `ICallFactory` that is used to create the `call` object. It is through the `call` object that the client must get its `AsynchITester` interface. Examine Listing 10.15.

Listing 10.15 **Client-Side Code Using Asynchronous COM**

```
ISynchronize * pSync;
ICallFactory * pCallF;
AsyncITester * pAsynchTest;
ITester * pTester;
int result;

//Not shown: COM Inititalization

CoCreateInstance(CLSID_Test, NULL, IID_ITester, (void **)&pTester);
pTester->QueryInterface(IID_ICallFactory, (PVOID*)&pCallF);
pCallF->CreateCall(IID_AsyncITest, NULL, IID_AsyncITester, (LPUNKNOWN*)
➥&pAsyncTest);
pAsyncTest->Begin_ TestMethod(1);
pAsyncTest->QueryInterface(IID_ISynchronize, reinterpret_cast<void**>(&pSync));

while ((hr = pSync->Wait(0, 1000)) == RPC_S_CALLPENDING)
    {
        //do anything you like while the server is still processing
    }

hr = pAsyncTest->Finish_TestMethod(&result);

//Not Shown: Release all interfaces
```

Asynchronous COM Drawbacks

The complexity outlined in the previous section makes it difficult to use Asynchronous COM with clients not written in C++. When compared with the simplicity of marking an interface as Queued and creating an object through a moniker, Asynchronous COM doesn't have a lot going for it. Add to this the following:

- Asynchronous COM does not work with interfaces that inherit from `IDispatch`. Therefore, Asynchronous COM cannot be used with late binding or implemented by an object supporting only dual interfaces. This precludes its use from scripting environments, such as ASP.
- Asynchronous COM does not work with configured components—that is, components that are part of a COM+ application. Thus, Asynchronous COM servers cannot take part in transactions, role-based security, or any other COM+ service. This incompatibility between Asynchronous COM and COM+ was announced at the Microsoft Professional Developers Conference (PDC 1999), and at the time of this writing, no plans have been announced to make Asynchronous COM COM+-compatible.

When you take into account the preceding points, it is hard to make a compelling argument for the use of Asynchronous COM. Given the existence of QC, it is puzzling to contemplate why Asynchronous COM was introduced at all. My feeling is that the Asynchronous COM paradigm fits into the DCOM camp. DCOM was an evolutionary step that allowed COM to cross network boundaries via RPC, but the considerations that weigh on DCOM developers (mainly, writing their own out-of-process servers and devising their own services) no longer concern a COM+ developer. So, where Asynchronous COM is attractive to the DCOM developer, it might be considered redundant and needlessly complex by the COM+ developer.

You can go further and claim that Asynchronous COM stands in direct contradiction to the COM+ declarative model. Components should not explicitly be written to support specific services; rather, a system administrator should be able to declare his intent to use them. But I've been hard enough on Asynchronous COM. I will not go into greater detail on Asynchronous COM because it is outside of COM+. Keep in mind that it is there, and now that you know its capabilities and limitations, you can be the judge regarding if and when it should be used.

Summary

Traditional COM uses synchronous RPC to connect client applications and running objects. This mechanism demands that both the client and server object are running at the same time; it has no provision for recovering from failed method calls, and a poorly coded server can cause the calling client to hang.

QC removes the limitations inherent in RPC by using MSMQ as a transport for method calls. By marking an interface as Queued, a client that obtains this interface via a queue moniker gets a special proxy for the recipient object called a Recorder. From the client's perspective, the Recorder appears to be the actual object, yet all method calls return immediately. COM+ translates the method calls into MSMQ messages and places them in the message queues of the recipient object's application. When the recipient application is next run (and if it is configured to listen), COM+ creates an object called the Player, handing it the messages. The Player then instantiates the recipient object (if it is not already running), translates the messages back into method calls, and invokes them on the object, security permitting.

11

Events

IF MOST OF YOUR PROFESSIONAL EXPERIENCE involves the development of applications for Microsoft Windows, the concept of event-driven programming is obvious and intuitive. However, developers who have not written applications for Windows, X-Windows, MacOS, or another GUI-based operating system might find the concept difficult to get a handle on. I've seen some very sophisticated and senior developers with years of experience in UNIX or mainframe development get very frustrated trying to write a simple Visual Basic application. They scour the code looking for a `main()` function or some definitive place where the program can be said to begin execution. They often get moody when you explain that in an event-driven paradigm, you cannot necessarily specify such a place, nor can you be sure what event will fire when.

In the traditional functional paradigm (C or COBOL on a mainframe or a nongraphical UNIX system), your program dictates; but in an event-driven paradigm, your program is dictated to. In Windows, this means that you write code to handle specific events generated by the operating system. These events often start life as a Windows system message. A system message is generated when the OS detects that some event has happened that is important to a particular application—for example, the user clicks a button. After a Windows message is posted to your application's message queue, a development environment like VB retrieves the message from the queue and translates the message into an event. In VB, this event takes the form of a subroutine, and a VB developer only needs to fill in this subroutine with code specifying what the application should do if this event is fired. This is often referred to as *implementing* the event.

There are a great many system messages, but a VB developer only needs to provide implementation code for events he is interested in. VB provides a listing of events, many of which map directly to Windows messages. Some events, however, are generated by VB itself or by COM objects and do not start out as Windows messages. Either way, the application developer should not be concerned about the underlying mechanics of the event itself.

Traditional COM Events

When COM first came on the Windows scene in its first incarnation (Object Linking and Embedding [OLE]), many developers got their feet wet by writing OLE automation controllers. These were applications that used OLE automation to remote control other applications—for example, a VB program might automate Microsoft Excel to offload complex calculations. As important as it was to control an *OLE automation server*, it was almost equally critical for the server to be able to notify the client of events that occurred to it. To give servers the capability to trigger events on the client, Microsoft introduced *connection points*. Connection points were COM's primary event mechanism and were originally used when an automation server (such as Excel) wanted to report a change (such as a modification to a cell) to its controlling VB client application. For example, the VB code in Listing 11.1 demonstrates how a VB client can be notified when the user makes a change to a cell in an Excel spreadsheet.

Listing 11.1   **A VB Client That Connects to a Currently Running Instance of Excel and Receives Event Notification When Any Cells Change**

```
Dim WithEvents xlWorksheet As Worksheet

Private Sub Form_Load()

    'Below: obtains the active worksheet of the currently running
    'instance of Excel.  Use CreateObject if you wish to instantiate
    'a new instance.
    Set xlWorksheet = GetObject(, "excel.application").ActiveSheet

End Sub

Private Sub xlWorksheet_Change(ByVal Target As Excel.Range)

    MsgBox "New value for cell is " & Target

End Sub
```

Note that the declaration in the first line includes the `WithEvents` directive. In VB, this keyword indicates that the server will fire events on the client, which really means that the server implements connection points. VB does a very good job at keeping the somewhat complex realities of connection points hidden from the developers. VC++ clients, however, must deal with the connection point interfaces (`IConnectionPointContainer` and `IConnectionPoint`) directly unless they are using a class library (such as Active Template Library [ATL]) which abstracts these details from them.

The basic premise of connection points, however, is simple: A client instantiates a server object and obtains interfaces to that object in the normal COM fashion. The client then instantiates an internal COM object within itself, often called an *event sink*, and gives an interface of this sink to the server object. What had been client-server becomes peer-to-peer. Because both the client and event server must run simultaneously and are tightly bound together, connection points qualify as a tightly coupled event (TCE) system. Each entity, the server and the client, holds interfaces (that they agree on in advance) to one another and can call methods on one another—the client to issue commands to the server and the server to issue event notifications to the client. Figure 11.1 demonstrates this graphically.

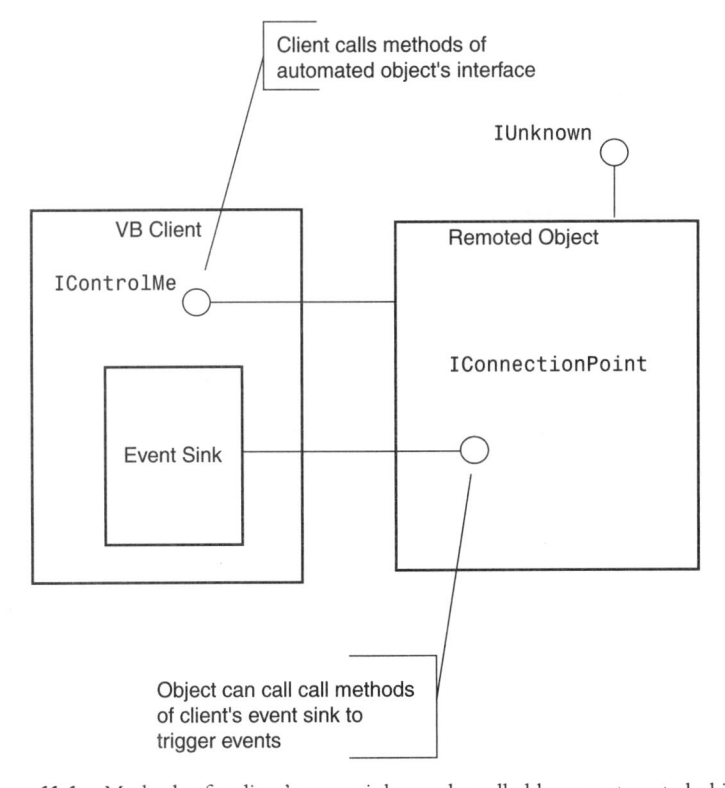

Figure 11.1 Methods of a client's event sink may be called by an automated object.

The connection point mechanism itself is a relatively simple protocol that enables this exchange to take place in a generic fashion. Going over it at a very high level, a server object that wants to publish events according to the connection point protocol first needs to support the `IConnectionPointContainer` interface. This interface, when obtained by the client, enables the client to iterate through all the available connection points offered by the server object.

From the server side, think of a connection point as a point of registration for a client's event sink. A particular event sink fits into a particular connection point on the server. For example, a client's event sink might have three methods that, when called by a server, tell the client about the changes to stock or bond prices. There is only one connection point offered by the server that is the appropriate match for this sink. The client finds it by iterating through all the connection points via the `IConnectionPointContainer` obtaining the `IConnectionPoint` interface representing each connection point. The client knows when it has found the right connection point for its particular sink by using a method of `IConnectionPoint` to determine the Globally Unique Identifier (GUID) of a particular connection point. When the client finds the `IConnectionPoint` interface it is looking for, the client calls the `Advise()` method of that `IConnectionPoint` interface, passing in the `IUnknown` pointer to its own advise sink. At this point, the connection point server has and does hold onto the client's advise sink and can send the client notifications via synchronous method calls from then on.

The Doubtful Future of Connection Points

Connection points are falling out of favor. For one thing, they are very expensive to use in terms of system resources—simply finding the right connection point and then registering a client's advise sink with a connection point server can take many network round trips. Connection point functionality is also somewhat redundant. It has always been possible for a client to simply send an interface pointer to itself as an argument to one of the server's interface methods. Although this requires special coding for the server, in reality, it is probably simpler to do this than to undertake the trouble of implementing proper connection points.

The synchronous nature of connection point method calls drives another nail into the connection point coffin. Connection points rely on synchronous Remote Procedure Call (RPC), as do all COM interfaces. Thus, a hanging or frozen client hangs the server thread that attempts to trigger an event on it. This is because when firing an event, a connection point server iterates through all registered client-side interfaces in a serial fashion on one thread. If the 99th client out of 100 pops up a modal "hello world!" message box in its event implementation, the server will hang, never reaching the 100th client until someone has the good graces to click the OK button.

Given all the bad press that connection points get, why learn about them at all? After all, there is an alternative event paradigm, COM+ events, which I introduce shortly. Connection points will likely stick around (particularly as the event mechanism for OLE automation servers like Microsoft Excel, Word, and so on), and you need to be able to differentiate between connection points and COM+ events. Certain languages like VB have hard-wired allegiance to connection points and demand that a COM object support them for language-specific features to work. For example, the VB declaration `Dim With Events` is used when a VB program wants not only to create a COM object, but to receive events from it as well. If, however, you return to the fundamental *declarative* paradigm of COM+, you don't want to write extra code to receive event functionality. You would prefer that a component can simply be declared administratively to receive events. And this is precisely what COM+ provides.

The COM+ Event Model: Publisher and Subscriber

The publisher/subscriber paradigm is commonly used by architects of large systems, but it is simple to understand. There is an entity that *publishes* events, and there are other entities that, by *subscribing* to these events, are alerted by the publisher when the events occur. In this model, the publisher keeps track of all *subscriptions*—that is, all requests made by clients who want to be notified of specific events. When the publisher broadcasts an event, it iterates through its subscriptions and fires the event only on subscribers to that event.

In the COM+ event model, any application can be a publisher, and any COM object can be declaratively named a subscriber. You need only declare it to be so. This generality paired with the fact that the subscriber need not be written with the publisher in mind (or be running at the same time) qualifies COM+ events as a loosely coupled event (LCE) system. In this way, COM events are similar to Queued Components (QCs), but with the following two important differences:

- Events adhere to a one-to-many publisher/subscriber metaphor, whereas QCs assume one-to-one relationship between the sender and recipient.
- There must be a definitive, singular source of events—a kind of broadcasting radio tower that fires events for any number of subscribers.

The Event Class

Think of an event class as a radio tower and all the subscribers as tuned into (subscribed to) the radio frequency (station) broadcast by the tower. You don't assume that the music that subscribers are listening to is generated by the tower; it is only broadcast from there. The content of the broadcast can come from any number of studios, and these studios can be located anywhere.

An event class is similar to the radio tower in that it does not generate events, but acts as a central point of departure for events generated elsewhere. An application that wants to fire an event for multiple subscribers only needs to instantiate the event class, and the events radiate outward from there. Like a radio tower, the event class doesn't have any logic of its own, and although the event class must be a fully functional COM+ Dynamic Link Library (DLL), it is never instantiated and its code never executes. To COM+, an event class is nothing more than a type library containing interface declarations, and it is the interface declarations of an event class that are of prime importance.

Creating an Event Class

As mentioned in the previous section, an event class is an ordinary COM+ DLL with a type library. As with QCs, the interface methods declared in the event class's type library must not contain [out] parameters. As you will see, this is because it is possible to fire events asynchronously (via QCs) or synchronously (via DCOM). As we discuss in Chapter 10, "Queued Components," methods of QCs cannot have any return values because the client thread does not block on the call to a queued object and, therefore, might not even be running by the time the method returns.

When writing an event class, it is not important to implement the interfaces by providing functionality for their methods. Other than implementing DLLRegisterServer and DLLUnregisterServer, the event class can otherwise remain a kind of skeleton object; when client applications that want to send an event instantiate an instance of your event class, the event class object itself is not actually run. Rather, it is the subscribers to the event class that are instantiated and receive the event(s)! We discuss the subscription process in detail in the section "Subscriptions," but I first want to discuss how to create an event class.

The first step in writing an event class is, as with any COM component, deciding on your interfaces. The critical thing to realize about the interfaces of an event class is that it is not the event class that implements them but the subscribers. A *subscriber* is just a fancy word for an object with an event sink. A client with an event sink becomes a server in the sense that it can receive callbacks. So when a client (subscriber) registers its event interface with some form of server (publisher), the server can start sending the subscriber events in the form of COM method calls. In the traditional connection point model, the connection point server's type library contains the interface declaration that the client needs to create and adhere to, so as to construct an event sink that is compatible with the server.

The COM+ event model shares a couple of common elements with connection points. As with a connection point server, the event class offers a complete declaration of the event interface(s) that the subscriber needs to support. The author of a Subscribing Object A needs to implement only the interface(s) specified by the event class and declare that A's interface implementation should therefore be intertwined with the event class's. (This is done via a subscription.) Thus, when the event class is instantiated by some application that wants to send out events, calls to the event class's interface are redirected to Object A's implementation (due to the subscription) and all other subscribing objects that, by subscription, state that they implement this interface.

Writing and Installing an Event Class

Now that you know a little bit about the structure of COM+ events, I explore them in greater detail by walking you through an implementation of an event class. The first step is to declare your interfaces. Keeping in mind that event class interfaces can only use OLE automation types (they must be Microsoft Message Queue [MSMQ]-compatible) and their code implementation isn't used, VB might seem like the easiest way to write an event class. However, I strongly recommend using VC++, even if you are a VB developer and not necessarily familiar with the C++ language. The Visual Studio IDE for C++ has a number of wizards that, without requiring C++ coding, can help you put together an event class. You can, of course, write an event class in VB, however, VB is sometimes in an odd kind of limbo when it comes to COM. On one hand, it relies entirely on COM and the concept of interfaces, and yet it is designed to provide the illusion that interfaces don't really exist, instead representing interfaces as VB classes. Furthermore, VB "name mangles" interfaces of its ActiveX DLLs by prepending their names with an underscore. Certainly this is not that big a deal; however, if you want control over exactly how your event class interfaces look, it is simpler to create an ATL-based C++ project for your event class (you can use the ATL COM AppWizard to do this). Then, using the Visual Studio wizards and basic features of the IDE, it is possible to automatically add interfaces to the Interface Definition Language (IDL) and provide empty C++ implementations for these interfaces. Fundamentally, you are using the ATL C++ project as a shell. You do all the important work in the IDL file.

Assuming you have a skeleton ATL DLL project (see the books source code, www.newriders.com/complus, if you are not sure how to create one), you can now declare your event interfaces in the project's associated IDL file. In this example, assume that your event class is going to be used to send stock and bond information to interested subscribers. An appropriate interface declaration is shown in Listing 11.2.

Listing 11.2 **An Event Interface Declaration in IDL**

```
[
   object,
   uuid(5E0137B5-BBDB-4689-9A8D-6D9C09525C35),
   dual,
   helpstring("ITradeTicker Interface"),
   pointer_default(unique)
]
interface ITradeTicker : IDispatch
{

[id(1), helpstring("method BondPriceChanged")]
HRESULT BondPriceChanged([in] BSTR cusip, [in] double price);
[id(2), helpstring("method StockPriceChanged")]
HRESULT StockPriceChanged([in] BSTR Symbol, [in] double price);
};
```

After the component containing the IDL in Listing 11.2 is compiled, you are ready to configure it as an event class. In Chapter 6, "The COM+ Catalog," we discuss how to add a new component to an existing application. The process is more or less the same with an event class but with one difference. Right-click on the Components folder (for an application in the COM+ Component Services snap-in) and select New, Component. The dialog box shown in Figure 11.2 appears.

Select the Install New Event Class(es) option. Doing so brings up a File Open dialog box that requests you select a type library or DLL. Although selecting a type library is an option presented by this dialog box, it should be ignored. An event class needs to exist in a fully fleshed out, functional COM DLL so that other attributes can be configured. If you select the DLL you just compiled, the rest of the installing process is identical to that of an ordinary COM+ component. After you click the Finish button on the installation wizard, your event class is registered.

Subscriptions

If an event class is akin to a radio tower broadcasting events at a certain frequency, subscribers are the radios tuned to that frequency. *Tuning in* implies that a subscriber implements an interface of the event class. Remember, in classical connection points, the connection point server's type library lists but does not implement the interfaces that it expects a client to support if that client is to receive events. After reading the server's type library, the client implements that interface and hands it back to the server to receive callbacks (events). Though similar, the COM+ event paradigm is somewhat less complicated.

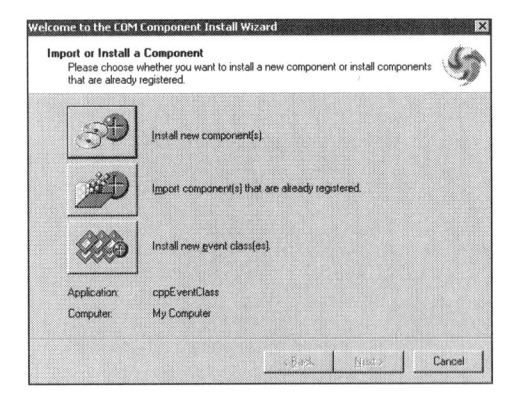

Figure 11.2 Install a component dialog box.

A subscriber needs to do two things to receive events: First, it must implement one (or more) of the interfaces of the event class; Second, it must subscribe to the event class. In this subscription, the subscriber must explicitly specify which method calls of this interface it wants to receive. In other words, if some application instantiates the event class and calls methods on the event class's interface that a subscriber supports and subscribes to, the subscription must specify which of these methods should be fired on the subscribing object.

An example will make this clearer. Imagine that a COM class exists that implements `ITradeTicker` (shown in Listing 11.2). We'll call this object `Ticker`. `Ticker` is an ordinary, configured COM+ class existing in a COM+ application called `SubscriberApp`. Its code can be as simple as that shown in Listing 11.3.

Listing 11.3 **VB Source Code for the Subscribing Component,** *Ticker*

```
'NOTE: the type library for the event class of Listing 11.1
'must be included in this VB project

Implements ITradeTicker

Private Sub ITradeTicker_BondPriceChanged(ByVal cusip As String, _
                                          ByVal price As Double)

    'Do something with information

End Sub


Private Sub ITradeTicker_StockPriceChanged(ByVal Symbol As String, _
                                           ByVal price As Double)

    'Do something with information

End Sub
```

For `Ticker` to make the transition from ordinary COM+ object to subscriber requires that a new subscription be created for the `Ticker` class. In the COM+ Component Services snap-in, you might have noticed that under every registered component is a folder called Subscriptions. `Ticker` is no exception, and by right-clicking on the Subscriptions folder, shown in Figure 11.3, you are presented with the dialog box shown in Figure 11.4.

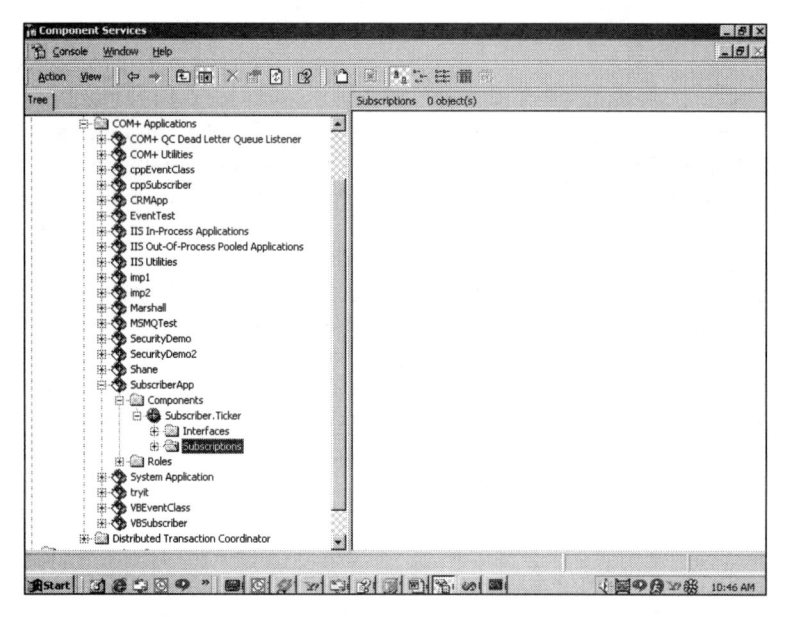

Figure 11.3 The Subscriptions folder. A component may subscribe to a particular event class by adding a subscription here.

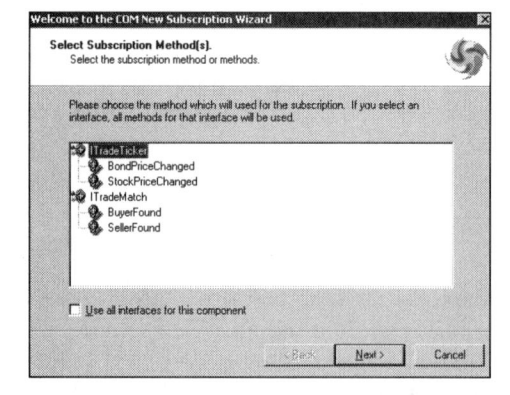

Figure 11.4 Select Subscription Method(s). A component may choose which method and/or interface(s) of the event class it would like to subscribe to.

The Select Subscription Method(s) dialog box lists all the interfaces supported by the subscribing COM+ class. It is not at all surprising to see ITradeTicker here because you know that the Ticker subscriber implements this interface. But note that this dialog box says nothing about the event class from which the ITradeTicker declaration originated. You are only looking at interfaces implemented by the Ticker class, and this dialog box is asking you a theoretical question: Assuming that there exists an event class that also supports the interface(s) listed, which methods do you want to be invoked on your subscribing object if the same method on the same interface is invoked on the event class?

By selecting the `ITradeTicker` interface, you are saying that you want this object to receive all method calls made on this interface if this interface is implemented by an event class, and if some application instantiates the event class and calls the methods of `ITradeTicker`. If you then click the Next button, the dialog box shown in Figure 11.5 pops up.

It might take a moment or two for the list control to fill in. COM+ actively searches through all registered event classes, looking for one or more that support the interface(s) of your subscriber. Remember, you selected the subscriber's interface(s) in the previous dialog box, so you are now looking for the event classes (or, more specifically, the event class interfaces) that can act as broadcasters for your subscriber. If the list view does not fill in, COM+ is telling you that no event class supporting the interface you selected exists. Therefore, you cannot proceed because you are trying to create a subscription to an event class that does not exist. In this scenario, you can, however, select the Use All Event Classes That Implement the Specified Interface check box. This indicates that you want to subscribe to any event classes registered now or in the future that will support this interface.

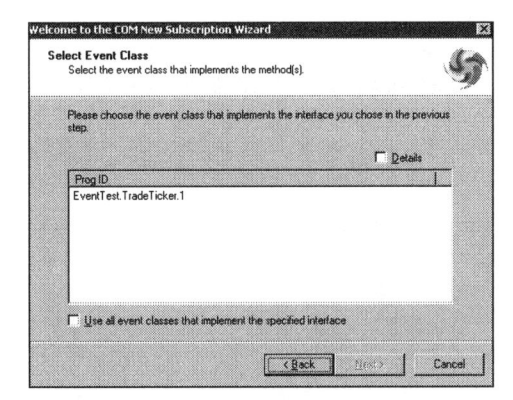

Figure 11.5 Select Event Class dialog box. All event classes containing interfaces compatible with the subscriptions will be listed.

> **Event Class and Subscription Publisher IDs**
>
> Although it is not documented at the time of this writing, you notice that the Advanced tab of an event class has a field called "Publisher ID." You may also notice that when creating a new subscription, if you check the "Use all event classes that implement the specified interface" checkbox, the subscription will also give you the opportunity to fill in a Publisher ID field.
>
> Basically, a subscription may specify the Publisher ID (its ProgID) of a particular event class (if the event class was given one), and thereby be notified whenever that event class is instantiated and called by some client. The Publisher ID is simply another, more generic way to bind subscribers to event classes.

In the case where the event class containing the declaration of `ITradeTicker` is registered, you can see its ProgID in the list control as shown in Figure 11.5. At this point, you only need to click the Next button. This brings you the final screen of the wizard where you only need to enter the name of your subscription. That's it. Your subscriber and event class are now bound together. It is much like the old standby of vaudevillian comedy—the doctor hits one knee of the patient with a reflex hammer, but the other leg kicks. It is much the same with COM+ events, in that you can hit the event class with a hammer, but it is the subscriber(s) that kicks.

Propagating Events Across a Network: The Machine-Specific Nature of Subscriptions

One final note about subscriptions: They are machine-specific. You can only make subscriptions on a per-machine basis—that is, you cannot say, "Tell me when this event fires on any machine on the network." However, it is possible for events to propagate across multiple machines by creating the appropriate chain of subscriptions, although the process is not intuitive.

If you examine a subscriptions properties using Component Services, specifically its Options tab, you will see that shown in Figure 11.6.

Note the Server name text box. If you enter the name of another server in this box, this subscription will no longer invoke its subscribing component on the present machine; it will instead invoke the subscribing component on the machine you enter in this field. Thus, if the subscription is attached to a component called Subscriber1 on the present machine but the Server name box specifies another server called "Darjeeling," this subscription remotely instantiates the Subscriber1 component on Darjeeling—not on the present machine. Thus, you have effectively delegated the event to Darjeeling (assuming, of course, that Subscriber1 is installed and configured on Darjeeling, as well as the present machine).

Delegation is fine, but you may want *both* the subscribers on the present machine and Darjeeling to receive events. You can always create two subscriptions—one alerting Subscriber1 on the present machine, and another alerting Subscriber1 on Darjeeling. This can, however, become somewhat messy, especially if your intent is to simply propagate all events of an event class on multiple machines for the benefit of any and all subscribers on the network.

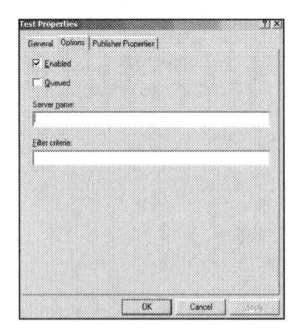

Figure 11.6 The Options tab for a subscription

If you want to effectively propagate an event class across multiple machines, a good topology to employ is that of a centralized event server. Configure the event class on this central server, and create subscriptions under that particular event class. This may seem somewhat recursive and odd; an event class certainly can't be a subscriber to itself. However, if you set the Server name property of each of these subscriptions to the names of different machines on your network (each with a local copy of our event class) you get a propagation effect. Calls made to the event class on the central machine are repeated and forwarded to the local event class on all other machines referenced in the central server's subscriptions. The result is that all subscribers to a particular event class on all machines will be notified when a method call is made to the event class on the central server.

One final note about propagating event class subscriptions. When adding subscriptions to an actual event class (as discussed in the previous paragraph), the dialog shown in Figure 11.5 does not include the event class you are adding subscriptions to; an event class can't be a subscriber to itself. However, by clicking the "Use all event classes that implement the specified interface" checkbox, you are permitted to create the subscription. Once the subscription is created, you can change its Server name attribute by selecting its properties and clicking on the Options tab.

Firing Synchronous and Asynchronous Events

To send events to subscribers, a client simply instantiates an instance of the event class, obtains one or many of its interfaces, and calls methods on them. The COM+ event mechanism makes sure that these invocations propagate to all subscribers. The application that instantiates the event class does not need to worry about any of the details.

Earlier in this chapter, I mention that connection points suffer because all connection point events are synchronous. Thus, if a client's implementation of an event hangs the client's thread, the server's thread calling the event also hangs, waiting for the client to return. COM+ events can free you from this limitation, but only if you explicitly ask for the event to be queued. By default, COM+ uses traditional, synchronous DCOM to fire events just like connection points. If an application instantiates an event class in this mode, COM+ is really instantiating each subscriber and firing events on them synchronously. Thus, if any subscriber pops up a modal message box, the client application will hang and the remaining subscribers will not receive the event.

Fortunately, there is a Fire in Parallel check box that can be found on the Advanced Property tab for the component. This causes COM+ to use multiple threads when firing events on subscribers; so if one subscriber hangs, other threads are available to trigger the events on the remaining subscribers. Surprisingly, even in the multi-threaded case, the client application still hangs. Firing events via COM+'s QCs service is, perhaps, the safest way to fire events. You see in the next section that there are a couple of ways to leverage QC.

Queued Event Classes versus Queued Subscribers

The simplest way to escape the hanging client problem is to mark your event class interfaces as Queued. A client should then instantiate the event class as it would any queued component via a queue moniker, as discussed in the previous chapter. The client gets a COM+ recorder, returns from its method invocations immediately, and is otherwise off the hook—COM+ makes sure the event(s) fired by the client reach all subscribers when the application containing the event class is next run.

A second way to leverage QC in COM+ events is to mark one or more subscriber interfaces as Queued but to leave the event class configured as Unqueued. In this scenario, the client instantiates the event class in a normal COM+ fashion without a queue moniker and can call the methods of the event class. COM+ delivers the events some time later to queued subscribers according to the rules outlined for QCs in the previous chapter.

There can also be subscribers that are not queued which receive their events via synchronous RPC. There is nothing wrong with mixing synchronous and asynchronous subscribers; COM+ permits a number of interesting arrangements. For example, the following scenario is possible:

1. The client application uses the queue moniker to instantiate an event class. Method calls made against it are packaged as messages to the event class's COM+ application.

2. At some point later, the event class's application awakens (is run) and receives the method calls made in step 1. As a result, COM+ fires the event to all subscribers' components (some of which might be QCs). Those components that are not queued receive the events immediately via synchronous DCOM. Components that are queued do not receive messages until their parent application is run. In the interim, all messages are posted to their parent application's queue.

3. When a queued subscriber's COM+ application is started, it is played the event posted by COM+ in step 2.

Event Filtering

It is simple to associate a subscriber with an event class, and you can, in the process, even perform some rudimentary filtering. For example, you can specify that only certain methods of an event class's interface should result in an event being fired on a specific subscriber. For example, in Listing 11.2, even though ITradeTicker supports two methods, you can specify that only the BondPriceChanged() method should cause an event to be fired in some subscriber and not StockPriceChanged(). This is ideal if the subscriber is only interested in bonds. This type of filtering is still somewhat of a broad stroke; however, the problem is that there are many different categories of bonds—Governments (GOVs), Municipal (MUNIs), Corporate—and it is likely that the subscriber is interested only in one or more categories, not all. Therefore, receiving an event call for every bond price change for every category is a waste of bandwidth.

It is, of course, always possible to break your event interface down into more methods with finer granularity. Instead of `BondPriceChanged()`, you could write `GovPriceChanged()`, `MUNIPriceChanged()`, or `CorpPriceChanged()`, but this would make your interface much larger and more complex, and inherently limits it (new categories of bonds can be brought to market, but interfaces are not allowed to change once published). It is much better to keep `BondPriceChanged()` as it is but add an argument that can identify the category, as in the following:

```
//In IDL
HRESULT BondPriceChanged([in] BSTR BondType, [in] BSTR cusip, [in] double price);
```

With the preceding addition, a subscriber can certainly perform a switch/case or if/else structure to filter out categories it isn't interested in. You are still, however, wasting bandwidth in delivering the message to a subscriber that might not ultimately be interested in it. It is also a waste to bloat every subscriber with code that ignores unwanted messages after it receives them.

COM+'s declarative paradigm provides you with a relatively simple way of dealing with this. If you right-click and ask for the properties of any subscription in the Component Services snap-in, you will notice a Filter Criteria text box on the Options tab. You can see it in Figure 11.7.

You can enter a Boolean statement into this text box that provides automatic filtering based on method arguments. For example, if you only want the subscriber to be notified if the first argument of `BondPriceChanged()` is `"MUNI"`, you simply add the following string where `BondType` is the actual name of a `BondPriceChanged()`'s first parameter:

```
BondType = "MUNI"
```

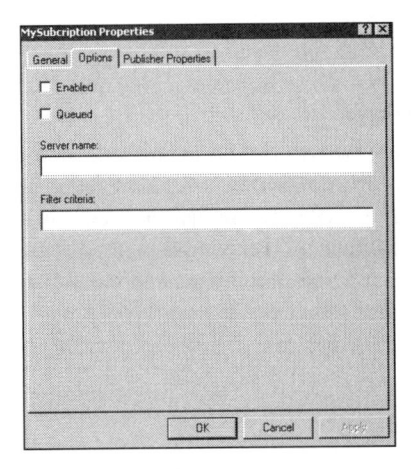

Figure 11.7 The Options tab of a subscription. Additional attributes of a specific subscription can be set.

Although the `Filter` criteria option is somewhat helpful, it is very limited. By establishing that the argument `BondType` must equal `"MUNI"`, you are saying that all methods of all interfaces of the event class that have an argument called `BondType` must equal the string `"MUNI"`. This limitation is devastating if you use the same argument name in more than one method. What's worse is that any event methods that don't have `BondType` as an argument do not pass this criteria, and the subscriber never sees the event. To be precise, the event is delivered to the subscriber, but the subscriber simply rejects it when it arrives. Thus, subscriber filtering cannot help you conserve bandwidth by eliminating unnecessary event traffic. We need a more sophisticated filtering mechanism, and thankfully *publisher filters* fit the bill.

Publisher Filters

Although the `Filter` criteria option discussed in the previous section is useful, it is somewhat limiting. If you want complete and total power over what events reach what subscribers, you will want to write a publisher filter. A *publisher filter* is simply a COM+ class, just like the event class. A publisher filter is associated with an event class such that all events go first to the publisher filter instead of directly to the subscribers. The publisher filter is given a list of all subscribers by COM+ and can be privy to all method calls and arguments intended for these subscribers. Thus, the publisher filter is in a position to evaluate all events and choose which, if any, subscribers should receive those events.

To become a *bona fide* publisher filter, the would-be filter must implement one of the following two interfaces:

- `IPublisherFilter`. Implement this interface if the associated event class has only one event interface. This interface can still be used if the event class has more than one interface, but as you'll soon see, this can lead to ambiguities as to what interface is being triggered.

- `IMultiInterfacePublisherFilter`. Implement this interface if the associated event class has more than one interface. This interface can also be used instead of `IPublisherFilter`, even if the event class has only one interface. In fact, `IMultiInterfacePublisherFilter` would be the preferred interface to use in every situation except for the unfortunate fact that VB filters cannot implement it because it uses a non-standard VB data type, specifically a GUID.

Both interfaces described here support the two methods. (Normally, COM+ QIs for one of these interfaces and calls each of these two methods on them.) A brief description of these two methods follows:

- `Initialize`. This method is called by COM+ (or can be called by you directly, as we discuss in the section, "Explicit Association of Publisher Filters by Clients") when the publisher filter is instantiated. Through this method, COM+ makes a list of all subscribers available to the publisher filter.

In the case of `IPublisherFilter`, COM+ passes you an `IDispatch` pointer as an argument to this method. Your filter then QIs for an interface called `IEventControl` and from that obtains an `IEventObjectCollection`. This last interface allows your filter to iterate through all the subscribers of the event class it is associated with.

If you are using `IMultiPublisherFilter`, COM+ gives you an `IMultiInterfaceEventControl` interface, which serves the same purpose as `IEventControl` and can also be used to obtain an `IEventObjectCollection` interface.

- `PrepareToFire`. This method is called by COM+ on your publisher filter whenever any method of the event class has been called. The filter receives an `IFireControl` interface from COM+ via this method. When in possession of the `IFireControl` interface, it is entirely up the publisher filter as to when (and if) the event should be fired on one or many of the subscribers.

In addition to implementing the interfaces and methods just discussed, a publisher filter can also elect to implement the event interface itself, much as the subscriber does. So, if the event class implements `ITradeTicker`, the publisher filter can also implement `ITradeTicker`. COM+ QIs for it to see if this is the case, and if it is, COM+ calls the methods of the filter's `ITradeTicker` implementation whenever a client calls methods of that interface of the event class. In this way, the publisher filter can examine the actual arguments of the event and decide which subscribers should be notified. It does so via the subscriber's `IFireControl` interface.

To summarize, when a method call is made to an event class, COM+ instantiates the filter, calls `Initialize()` and `PrepareToFire()`; and if the filter implements the event interface, COM+ calls the actual event class method on the publisher filter. We discuss the `Initialize()` and `PrepareToFire()` methods and how their parameters function in greater detail in a couple of sections. For now, just make sure you understand the basics—a publisher filter must implement either `IPublisherFilter` or `IMultiInterfacePublisherFilter`, preferably the latter. Each of these interfaces has two methods: `Initialize()` and `PrepareToFire()`. The arguments differ slightly for these two interfaces, but their overall function is the same. `Initialize()` gives the filter a list of subscribers that it can store. `PrepareToFire()` tells the filter that an event method has been called on the event class and gives the filter the opportunity to fire this event on any of (or none of) the filter's stored list of subscribers.

Associating Publisher Filters with Event Classes

Surprising as it might seem, there is no way to associate a publisher filter with an event class using the Component Services snap-in. It must be done either through the COM+ administration objects or explicitly by the client of the event class. We discuss the former method first.

COM+ Administration Objects

Using the COM+ administration objects, you can associate the event class with a publisher filter supporting `IPublisherFilter` or `IMultiInterfacePublisherFilter` by setting the `MultiInterfacePublisherFilterCLSID` properties of the component. The code in Listing 11.4 demonstrates this.

Listing 11.4 **Setting the Publisher Filter for an Event Class**

```
Const EVENT_CLASS_PROGID = "VBEvent.VBEventClass"
Const EVENT_CLASS_APP = "VBEventClass"

'The CLSID of our Publisher filter.  We could obtain this
'programmatically  but since the CLSID of a component is
'constant, we can hardcode it:

Const FILTER_CLSID = "{C02560AA-95B6-419D-AD0E-8E4F7FFF6493}"

'obtain the Application collection from the Catalog
Set colApp = Catalog.GetCollection("Applications")

'Search for the trading system application
colApp.Populate
For Each Application In colApp
    If Application.Value("Name") = EVENT_CLASS_APP Then Exit For
Next

'Did we find the event class application?
If Application Is Nothing Then
    MsgBox "Did not find the event class application!"
    Exit Sub
End If

'obtain the ComponentCollection of the event class' application
Set colComp = colApp.GetCollection("Components", _
                                    Application.Key)

'Search for our component:
colComp.Populate
For Each Component In colComp
    If Component.Value("ProgID") = EVENT_CLASS_PROGID Then Exit For
Next

'Did we find the component
If Component Is Nothing Then
    MsgBox "Did not find the event class!"
    Exit Sub
End If

Component.Value("MultiInterfacePublisherFilterCLSID") = FILTER_CLSID
colComp.SaveChanges
colApp.SaveChanges
```

The only hitch with this method of associating the filter with the event class is that the filter in question must support `IMultiInterfacePublisherFilter`. This is because COM+ only QIs for `IMultiInterfacePublisherFilter` and does not ask for `IPublisherFilter` if `IMultiInterfacePublisherFilter` is not implemented by the filter. This behavior is surprising and is not documented at the time of the writing. A look inside the eventsys.h header file that contains these interface declarations, exposes a comment that is revealing:

```
/* interface IPublisherFilter */
/* [unique][helpstring][uuid][object] */

// ****************************************************************************
// This is a Deprecated interface - Use IMultiInterfacePublisherFilter instead.
// ****************************************************************************
```

`IPublisherFilter` is slated for depreciation. *Adieu.* This is all well and good, but if you remember that VB filters can only support `IPublisherFilter`, you realize that VB publisher filters cannot be associated with event classes through the COM+ administration objects—COM+ only checks for `IMultiInterfacePublisherFilter` when the association happens through the administration objects. C++ filters supporting `IMultiPublisherFilter` have no such problem, however. The other way to associate a publisher filter with an event class is to have the client do so explicitly. This is discussed in the next section.

Explicit Association of Publisher Filters by Clients

At times, a client executable instantiating an event class might want specific control of what publisher filter is used. For example, imagine a client that doesn't know what types of messages are appropriate for subscribers until after it is already running. Such a client might have a drop-down list box on its UI that specifies which category of bond prices to send out—MUNI, GOVCORPS, and so on. Let's consider each item in the drop-down as a filter the user can select from. When the user selects a specific bond type, the client can initialize the particular publisher filter appropriate for that selection.

Granted, the preceding example is somewhat contrived—the client could include code that checks the drop-down and only fires events on the event class as appropriate. But you can lighten your client considerably and put this responsibility on one or many different filters that the client can choose from. Listing 11.5 demonstrates how a client can associate a publisher filter with an event class at run-time. Note that the filter in this example is written in C++, so `IMultiPublisherInterface` is used.

Listing 11.5 **A Client Associating a Publisher Filter with an Event Class**

```
Dim EventControl As IMultiInterfaceEventControl
Dim PublishFilter As IMultiInterfacePublisherFilter
Dim PubFilter As New myFilter

Set eventClass=new TradeTicker
```

continues

Listing 11.5 **Continued**

```
'Next obtain the IMultiInterfaceEventControl interface from the eventClass itself:
Set EventControl = eventClass

'Register the publisher filter:
EventControl.SetMultiInterfacePublisherFilter PubFilter


'When we register the publisher filter this way, we must
'explicitly call the Initialize() method ourselves.  If we
'had registered the publisher filter using the COM Admin objects,
'COM+ would have called this for us since it instantiates the
'publisher filter.
PubFilter.Initialize EventControl
```

Although associating publisher filters with event classes at run-time is useful, there are a few limitations, which follow:

- The client must explicitly call the `Initialize` method of the filter, passing it the `IMultiInterfaceEventControl`. The client can obtain the `IMultiInterfaceEventControl` by QIing the event class, and COM+ will provide one.

- This method does not work if the event class is configured as Queued. This is because some methods of `IMultiInterfaceEventControl` have `[out]` parameters, something not permitted by QCs.

- If a certain filter that a compiled client relies on is removed from COM+, the client might cease to function.

Dynamic association only stays in place for the lifetime of the client instance that makes the association or at least until the client releases the event class. At the time of this writing, there is no other way for a VB filter to be associated with an event class except via this dynamic method. However, keep in mind that, with a VB filter, these lines

```
Dim EventControl As IMultiInterfaceEventControl
'intervening code omitted for brevity
EventControl.SetMultiInterfacePublisherFilter PubFilter
```

would become

```
Dim EventControl As IEventControl
'intervening code omitted for brevity
EventControl.SetPublisherFilter PubFilter
```

Implementing Publisher Filters

So far, we've discussed how publisher filters operate conceptually. We have also introduced the interfaces `IEventControl`, `IFireControl`, `IMultiPublisherFilter`, and `IPublisherFilter`. In this section, I demonstrate how to write a publisher filter implementing and leveraging these and other interfaces.

As discussed in the previous section, "Publisher Filters," `IMultiPublisherFilter` has two methods: `Initialize()` and `PrepareToFire()`. For this section, we assume that the publisher filter has been associated with the event class statically, using COM+ administration objects.

Initialize

When a client instantiates the event class, COM+ instantiates your filter, QIs for `IMultiPublisherFilter`, and calls its `Initialize()` method. (Remember, the client only calls `Initialize()` if the association is made dynamically by the client, as opposed to using the administration objects.) The prototype of `Initialize()` is as follows:

```
HRESULT Initialize(
    IMultiInterfaceEventControl *pIEC
);
```

It is clear that COM+ is giving your filter a `IMultiInterfaceEventControl` interface. There are a number of methods of this interface that can be used to get and set properties associated with the event class, but one method is by far the most important—`GetSubscriptions()`. The filter can call this method to retrieve a list of all subscribers but, contrary to intuition, the filter cannot call this method right away. If you look at the prototype for `GetSubscriptions`, you will see why:

```
HRESULT GetSubscriptions(
    REFIID Iid,
    BSTR MethodName,                //Event method
    BSTR OptionalCriteria,
    int *pOptionalErrorIndex,
    IEventObjectCollection **ppCollection   //Subscription collection
);
```

To get a collection of subscribers, you need to tell `GetSubscriptions()` what subscribers you are interested in—this is not done for you automatically. At the very least, you need to pass in the IID of the event interface and the method name as a string. At the time the filter's `Initialize()` method is called, however, you don't have any of this information—the client has not yet called any method on the event class. Thus, when the publisher is given an `IMultiInterfaceEventControl` interface, it should save it for later use.

PrepareToFire

The next thing that happens to your publisher filter is a `PrepareToFire()` invocation. This occurs when the client invokes a method on the event class. Because your filter is associated with the event class, COM+ lets you know about the invocation by calling out the `PrepareToFire()` method. The prototype of this method is as follows:

```
HRESULT PrepareToFire(
    REFIID iid,                       //IID of interface being fired
    BSTR bstrMethodName,              //Name of event method
    IFiringControl *pFiringControl    //Firing control
);
```

352 Chapter 11 Events

From these arguments, your publisher filter can determine the method name (as a string) that was called on the event class by the client and the GUID of the interface to whom this method belongs. This is just enough information to call GetSubscribers() (discussed in the previous section), so you can find out which subscribers are interested in receiving this particular event. It's a good thing you saved the IMultiInterfaceEventControl given to you when your Initialize() method was called. You can use it to determine these interested subscribers.

By way of example, let's suppose that a client instantiates the TradeTicker event class, QIs for ITradeTicker, and then calls the BondPriceChanged() method on that interface. Predictably, the filter's PrepareToFire method is called. The recipient filter finds that the first argument passed into its PrepareToFire() method is 5E0137B5-BBDB-4689-9A8D-6D9C09525C35 (the GUID of ITradeTicker), and the second argument is "BondPriceChanged". The third argument gives the filter an IFiringControl interface. A filter uses the IFiringControl interface to actually fire the event on a subscriber(s). All that remains, then, is to get a list of subscribers or, more specifically, get a list of all subscribers of the particular method name (and/or interface) you received as the first and second arguments to your PrepareToFire implementation. If you now bring out the IMultiInterfaceEventControl interface you saved from COM+'s earlier call to Initialize(), you can use it to iterate through a list of these subscribers. Thus, you have that shown in Listing 11.6.

Listing 11.6 **Determining Subscribers to a Particular Interface/Event and Firing the Event**

```
HRESULT Filter::PrepareToFire(
        REFIID iid,
        BSTR methodName,
        IFiringControl *firingControl) {

long lSubscriberCount;
long lAmount;
int  iError;
HRESULT hr;

// The following variables are private member variables
// for the filter class, listed here for reference. Consult
// the publisher filter example of the book's accompanying
// source code for details.

/*
    IEventControl*          m_pControl;
    IEventObjectCollection* m_pCollection;
    IEnumEventObject*       m_pEnum;
    IEventSubscription*     m_pSubscribe;
    IUnknown*               m_pObject;

*/
```

```cpp
// Fire the event to all subscribers.  This requires that we have an
// enumeration of the subscribers of course, and we obtained that
// in the Initialize() method.

// Note that this publisher filter could implement the methods of the
// event class, and COM+ will call them after calling this function.
// See the VBFilter for an example of such an implementation.

// Call the GetSubscriptions method on IEventControl to obtain a
// IEventObjectCollections pointer.  The first parameter of this
// method (the methodName) parameter, allows us to specify which
// methods we are looking for subscriptions on.  A value of NULL
// for this parameter indicates that we want the subscriptions
// on all methods of the event class.

// The second variable, allows us to specify a Query string to
// further eliminate subscribers.  A value of "ALL" indicates that
// we want all subscribers.


hr = m_pControl->GetSubscriptions(NULL,L"ALL",&iError,&m_pCollection);

m_pCollection->get_Count(&lSubscriberCount);

// Reset the event enumeration since it might have been
// previously used:

m_pEnum->Reset();

for (int k=0; k < lSubscriberCount; k++) {

    // The Next method of IEnumEventObject gives us an IUnknown
    // pointer to the next object:
    hr=m_pEnum->Next(1,&m_pObject,(ULONG*)&lAmount);

    if (hr!=S_OK) {
        MsgBox("C++ IPublisher Filter: Problem Obtaining Event Object.");
        return hr;
    }

    // Query the IUnknown pointer of the subscriber, for a
    // IEventSubscription pointer which contains the information we are
    // interested in:

    hr=m_pObject->QueryInterface(IID_IEventSubscription, (void**)&m_pSubscribe);
    m_pObject->Release();

    if (hr!=S_OK) {
        MsgBox("C++ Publisher Filter: Problem Obtaining"
                IEventSubscription pointer.");
        return hr;
```

continues

Listing 11.6 **Continued**

```
    }

    // Fire the event to the subscriber:
    firingControl->FireSubscription(m_pSubscribe);
    m_pSubscribe->Release();
  }

  return S_OK;
};
```

The preceding code might seem a little complex, but this is largely due to the use of enumerations. Enumerations exist for the benefit of VB. VB sees them as collections that can conveniently be iterated via VB's FOR...EACH construct. In C++, they are somewhat messy. Enumerators aside, following are the basic steps to retrieve subscribers:

1. Call the `GetSubscribers()` method of the `IMultiInterfaceEventControl` interface. You received this interface when COM+ called your filter's `Initialize()` method. Pass in the GUID of the interface and method name, the subscribers to which you are want. You get an `IEventObjectCollection` as output of the `GetSubscribers()` method.

2. Call `IEventObjectCollection`'s `get_NewEnum` method. This returns an `IEnumEventObject` interface.

3. Iterate through all subscribers via the `IEnumEventObject` interface. Use its `Next()` method to get the `IUnknown` pointer for each subscriber in turn and QI each `IUnknown` interface for `IEventSubscription`.

4. Call `IFiringControl`'s `FireSubscription` method passing the `IEventSubscription` interface for each subscriber you want to fire the event on.

Publisher Strategies

In the previous section, I demonstrate how to iterate through the subscribers of a specific event and fire events on them from a publisher filter. If this is all you want to do, there isn't much point in writing a publisher filter—simply declaring a subscription provides this functionality. Ideally, you are writing a publisher filter so that you can make intelligent choices about which subscriber should receive specific events. You know from the previous section that a publisher filter automatically receives the GUID of the event interface and the string name of the method—both as arguments to its `PrepareToFire()` method. COM+ calls `PrepareToFire` every time a client calls a method on an interface of the filter's associated event class.

Unfortunately, a GUID and a method name doesn't tell you much. You know the method name, but you don't know what the arguments to the event method are. Similarly, you don't know anything about the subscribers themselves. Clearly, you need to find out more about each if your filter is to make intelligent choices about what subscribers should receive which event.

Publisher Properties

In Listing 11.5, I demonstrate how to loop through subscribers of an event in the simplest possible fashion. This code demonstrates how to get an `IEventSubscription` interface for each subscriber and how this interface can be used as an argument to `IFiringControl`'s `FireSubscription` method. But the `IEventSubscription` interface can also be used to obtain information about a specific subscriber. This information can be used by the publisher filter to determine whether a given subscriber is a candidate for a particular message.

If you right-click on any subscription in Component Services and select Properties, you notice that one of the tabs of the properties dialog box is Publisher Properties. This dialog box is shown in Figure 11.8.

Publisher properties can be used to add arbitrary property names and values. I say *arbitrary* because they can be anything you like. For example, imagine you want to specify that a particular subscriber only wants to receive bond-related events when the bond is GOV or MUNI type. Furthermore, assume the subscriber should only receive the event if there are less than 10,000 MUNIs left and 5,000 GOVs. You might set this criteria as shown in Figure 11.9 for this subscriber's COM+ subscription.

Note that COM+ does not process these properties in any way. It simply makes them available to your publisher filter. Querying publisher properties from a publisher filter is simple to do. After you have obtained an `IEventSubscription` interface, you only need to call its `GetPublisherProperty()` method, as in the following:

```
VARIANT val;
pEventSubscription->GetPublisherProperty(L"MUNI", &val);
```

After the desired property(s) is obtained, you can use these publisher properties to determine whether the subscriber associated with them should receive the event.

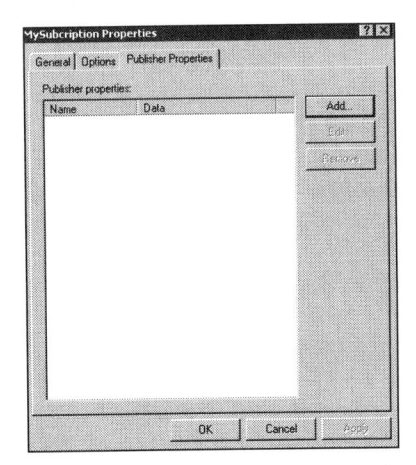

Figure 11.8 The Publisher Properties tab. Property names and values can be added here and retrieved later by the publisher filter.

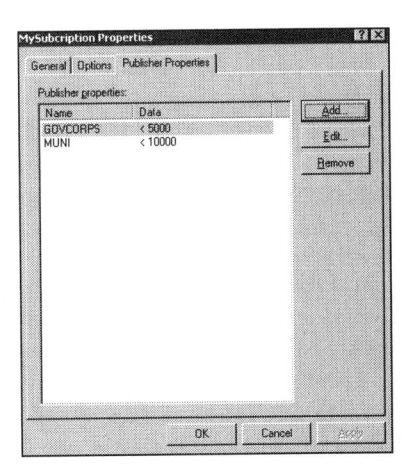

Figure 11.9 Publisher properties for a subscription.

Evaluating Method Arguments

Publisher properties are helpful in that they give you information about a given subscriber. Your filter can pair this information with its knowledge of what method has just been called on an event class. (COM+ informs your filter of the event class method invoked by calling the filter's `PrepareToFire` method, passing it the method name as a string.) There is still something missing, however—method arguments.

When a method of an event class is called, a publisher filter can, thanks to `PrepareToFire()`, determine the method name, the GUID of the event interface, and the publisher properties of a specific subscription. However, the filter can also examine the method arguments passed into the event class. To do this, the filter only needs to implement the event interface in question. For example, imagine you have an event class that implements the `ITradeTicker` interface. If any method of this interface is called on the event class, the associated publisher receives a `PrepareToFire()` method invocation on its `IMultiPublisherInterface` interface. If the filter also implements `ITradeTicker`, COM+ makes the exact method invocation on the filter's `ITradeTicker` as that made on the event class's `ITradeTicker`. Thus, the filter knows the specific parameters of the method call.

Assuming a filter supports `ITradeTicker`, as well as `IMultiPublisherInterface`, the interaction between the filter, COM+, and the broadcasting client is as follows:

1. A client executable wanting to broadcast events instantiates an event class.
2. COM+ instantiates the publisher filter associated with that event class and calls the `Initialize()` method of the filter's `IMultiPublisherInterface`. The `IMultiInterfaceEventControl` interface is passed in as an argument.
3. The client calls the `BondPriceChanged()` method of the event class's `ITradeTicker` interface.
4. COM+ calls the `PrepareToFire()` method on the publisher filter, passing in the name of the method called, the event interface GUID, and an `IFireControl` interface.
5. COM+ QIs the publisher for `ITradeTicker`. If the filter supports it, COM+ calls the `BondPriceChanged()` method of the filter's `ITradeTicker` implementation, passing it the same arguments as were passed to the event class by the client.

If your filter is investigating method arguments to determine which subscribers should receive an event, such a filter should not fire events on subscribers in its `PrepareToFire()` method. This is because, as shown in the previous chronology, the filter doesn't receive the method arguments of the event until after the filter's `PrepareToFire()` invocation is called. Therefore, there is a period of time between when the filter knows what event method has been called (step 4) and what the arguments to the method are (step 5). The filter programmer must delay gratification somewhat. Rather than making the determination of what subscriber should be fired and firing it in the filter's `PrepareToFire()` implementation, the filter should delay firing the event until the actual event method is called on it by COM+ (step 5). In this way, the filter has the opportunity to review the actual parameters to the event method called on the event class.

If you want to store information from `PrepareToFire()` to your filter's implementation of the event method, you can use any form of global data structure you like or, optionally, take advantage of subscriber properties. Subscriber properties are only superficially documented at the time of this writing, but empirically you might find that they work in an identical fashion to publisher properties discussed in the previous section "Publisher Properties." The difference is the subscriber property bag (a *bag* is a term commonly used to denote a group of properties) is empty at first where the publisher property bag can have arbitrary properties put into it by a developer or system administrator via Component Services (see Figure 11.9). A publisher filter can add and retrieve arbitrary properties to the subscriber properties property bag at any time.

Just as with publisher properties, subscriber properties can be accessed through methods of `IEventSubscription`—mainly `GetSubscriberProperties()` and `PutSubscriberProperties()`. Again, it is important to note that COM+ does not process these properties in any way—it just keeps them for you as a convenience. Furthermore, subscriber properties, unlike publisher properties, do not persist between method calls on the event class. In other words, all subscriber properties are purged every time a method on the event class is called, so they are useful mainly to carry information from `PrepareToFire()` (step 4) to method invocation on the filter (step 5).

Summary

The COM+ event mechanism is based on a publisher/subscriber architecture. For any one broadcaster of events, there can be many subscribers. Subscribers are ordinary COM+ objects that implement one or more interfaces of the event class. The event class is a configured COM+ object that serves as the source of events. Any invocation made on the event class by any client is broadcast by COM+ to all subscribers with a declarative association with the event class. This broadcasting can be done through QC or synchronous DCOM. This association between an event class and a subscriber is made by creating a subscription in the COM+ Catalog. A subscription specifies which interface and/or methods should be fired on the subscriber if they are fired on a particular event class.

A publisher filter is a COM+ class that allows you to intercept all events before they are fired on the subscribers. The publisher filter can then determine information about the subscribers and decide whether a specific event is appropriate for a particular subscriber instance. Specifically, a filter can determine the method name, arguments, and interface invoked on the event class and can find out which subscribers have subscribed to this particular event with this information. The filter can then find out more about the subscriber by investigating the publisher properties of its subscription. These are arbitrary values that a system administrator or developer can associate with a subscription via Component Services.

The association between a publisher filter and an event class can be made using the COM+ administration objects. The association can also be made dynamically by a client application. In either case, it is necessary for a publisher filter to support one of two interfaces—`IMultiPublisherInterface` or `IPublisherInterface` (the former being preferred). COM+ calls the `Initialize()` and `PrepareToFire()` methods on a filter implementing these interfaces, providing the filter with all the information and functionality it needs to fire events manually on the subscribers it chooses.

12

Security

My firm works predominantly with Wall Street investment banks, so security is never far from our minds. Billions of dollars move through our trading systems, often at the simple strike of the Enter key. It is critical to make sure that only *that* trader for *that* desk has the authority to trade *that* particular security for *that* amount. That is a lot of conditions. Although most of these institutions have not migrated to Windows 2000 and COM+ at the time of this writing, when they do, they will benefit greatly from COM+'s role-based security architecture. It will give them the ability to group users into domains of privilege (roles) and declaratively apply them to components, interfaces, and even methods.

Declarative Security

COM+ security is declarative in the sense that users can be associated with one or more *roles*. A role groups one or more users together such that if permission is granted to a role, any user in that role has permission. For example, many of the trading desks I've worked with have two distinct roles for their users—traders and operations. *Traders* have the authority to execute trades, but operations people do not. *Operations* people have authority to change the details of a trade after it is submitted (in case pricing errors were made), which traders cannot do. If we were using COM+ security, we would give the

Operations role permissions to call methods on interfaces that modify trading data after it is submitted, but deny this access to the traders. We would, however, give the Traders role the permission to call methods on interfaces that facilitate trade entry, but deny access to trade-entry interfaces for operations people.

Entering Users in a Role

In Component Services, you notice that every application has a Roles folder. By default, it is empty. You can create new roles by right-clicking the Roles folder and selecting New, Role. A dialog box bearing a simple text box pops up asking you for the name of the new role. If you summon this dialog box twice, once for Operations and again for Traders, under the Roles folder, you will see what is shown in Figure 12.1.

You now have two roles, Operations and Traders, but they are empty. You need to place authenticated NT users in these roles. By double-clicking on either the Operations or Traders folders, you see a Users folder. Right-click on this folder, select New, and User, and the dialog box shown in Figure 12.2 pops up.

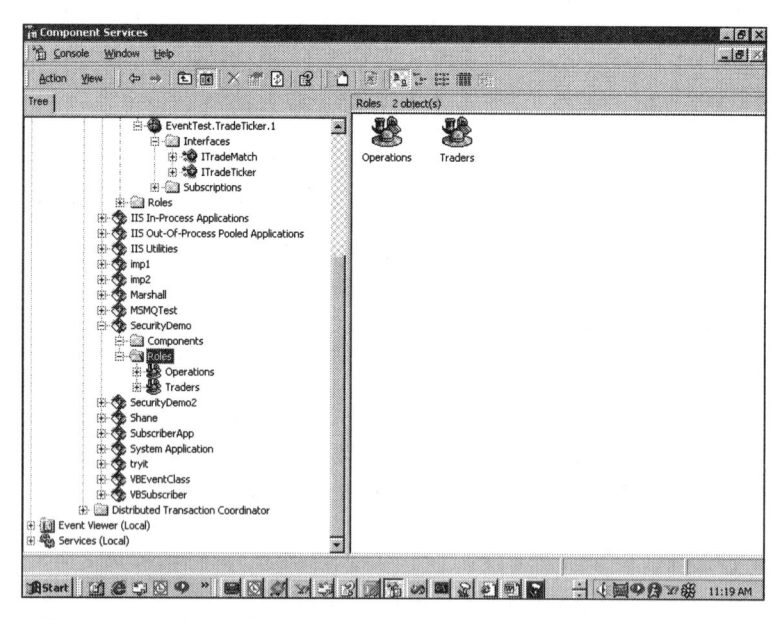

Figure 12.1 New roles can be created or deleted for an application with this dialog box.

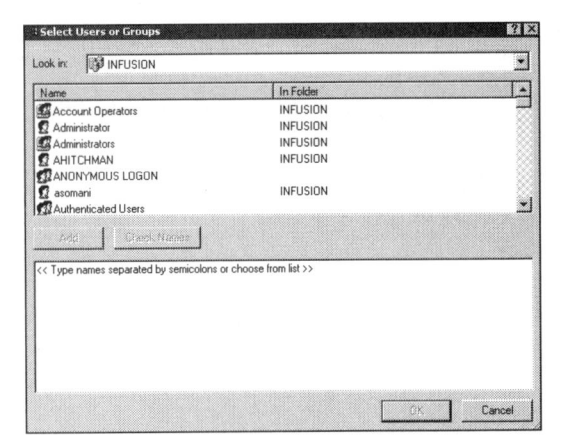

Figure 12.2 List of all NT user accounts, which may be assigned to roles.

Simply double-click on all the registered users you want to be placed in a particular role and click OK. Component Services now lists those users as members of the role.

Granting Permissions to a Role

Roles can be associated with components themselves and to the interfaces and methods of any configured component. To demonstrate how this works, assume that you have a component described by the IDL in Listing 12.1.

Listing 12.1 **Partial IDL for the *TradeEntry* Component**

```
//Note: Definition tags are not shown for the purpose of brevity

    interface ITradeEntry : IDispatch
    {
        HRESULT EnterTrade(BSTR cusip, int qty, double price);
        HRESULT ModifyTrade(BSTR cusip, int qty, double price);
    };

    coclass TradeEntry
    {
        [default] interface ITradeEntry;
    };
```

The TradeEntry component shown in Listing 12.1 appears in Component Services as shown in Figure 12.3.

362 Chapter 12 Security

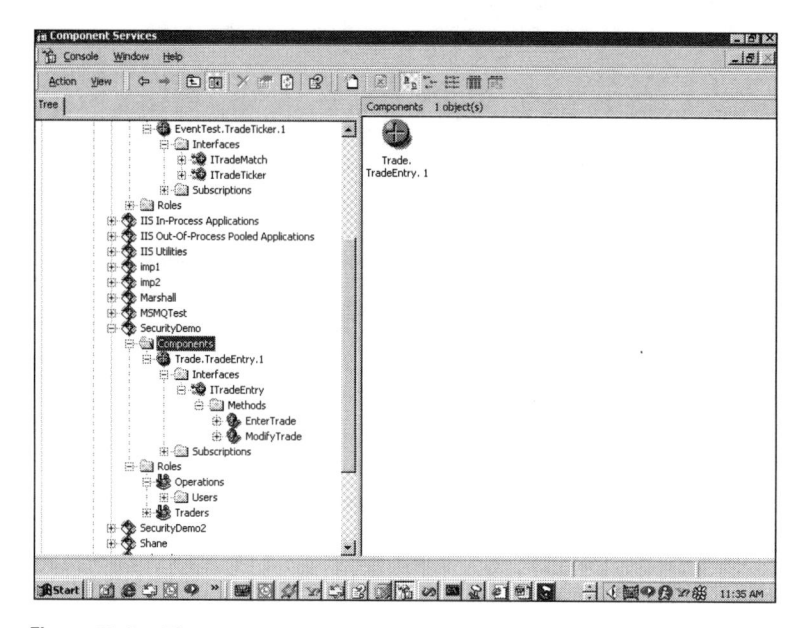

Figure 12.3 The `TradeEntry` component as it appears in Component Services.

The `TradeEntry` component, the `ITradeEntry` interface, and the `EnterTrade` and `ModifyTrade` methods can all have roles assigned to them. For example, I said that the Traders role should be able to enter trades. Thus, you can simply right-click on the `EnterTrade` method, then select Properties, and then select the Security tab of the resulting dialog box. Next, click the Traders role as shown in Figure 12.4.

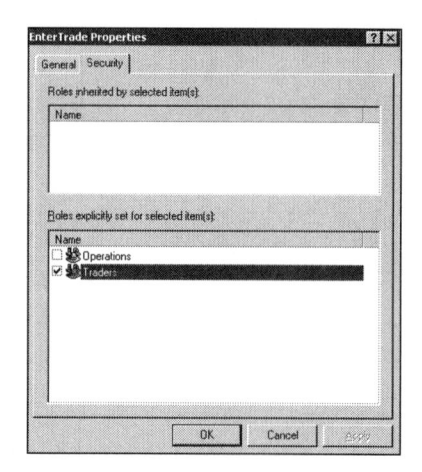

Figure 12.4 Giving traders permission to call the `EnterTrade` method.

By selecting the Traders role and not selecting the Operations role, you are saying that any user in the Traders role has permission to execute this method, but Operations people do not.

Role-based permissions can be set on the `ITradeEntry` interface in the exact same manner as you set role permissions on the `EnterTrade` method. Permissions are inheritable, so if you give the Traders role access to the `ITradeEntry` interface, traders can invoke both the `EnterTrade` and `ModifyTrade` no matter what the security settings are for these two methods.

The same holds true for components. If Traders are given access to the `TradeEntry` component, Traders must necessarily be able to access all interfaces of the component and call all methods on all interfaces of the component. Thus, the following statements are always true regarding COM+ security:

- If you give a role permission on a component, you are giving that role permission to access all interfaces and methods of that component.
- If you give a role permissions on an interface, you are giving that role permission to invoke all methods of that interface.

It can be helpful to think of COM+ security as optimistic and always looking for a yes. You never deny access to a role declaratively, you only grant access. Thus, even though a "parent" component and interface might not explicitly grant access to a certain role, if the role is assigned access to the "child" method, the call succeeds.

Configuring and Programming Security

To enable a COM+ application to take advantage of role-based security, it must first be turned on. When you bring up the properties for an application in Component Services and select the Security tab, you will see what is shown in Figure 12.5.

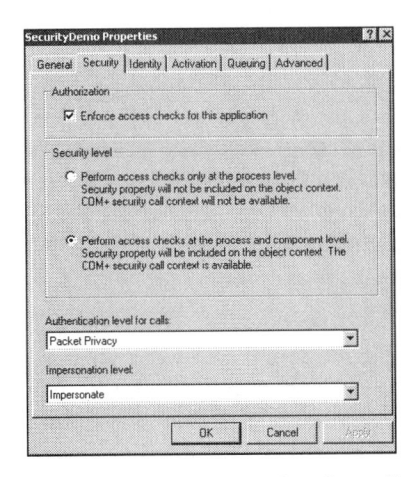

Figure 12.5 The Security dialog box for applications.

Note that the dialog box of Figure 12.5 is specific to server applications in that it contains options only appropriate for these types of applications. There is a similar but slightly different dialog box for COM+ library applications. We are going to discuss security in server applications for most of this chapter, but a discussion of the special security considerations involved in library applications can be found in the sidebar, "Library Application Considerations."

Let's take a look at Figure 12.5. I cover the bottom section of the dialog box (specifically, the bottom two drop-down list boxes) in the section "Authentication." For now, let's begin at the top.

To enable declarative security for a COM+ application, the Enforce Access Checks for This Application must be checked. If it isn't checked, no access checks are performed, and the methods of all components in the application are accessible to any and all callers. (However, a component might still be able to investigate the caller's role programmatically and reject it. More on that in the next section, "Programming Security.")

Following the Enforce Access Checks for This Application check box, in the Security Level section of the dialog box are the following two radio buttons:

- **Perform Access Checks Only at the Process Level**. Selecting this option turns off component-level role-based security. COM+ objects in an application so configured will not have any security information in their context, and you will not be able to associate roles with interfaces, methods, or components of the application (security dialog boxes will be grayed out). There is still security, but it is very broad–stroke: COM+ simply reads all the roles associated with the application (those listed under the Roles folder) and adds all users in every role to the process's Access Control List (ACL). Thus, COM+ will only check to make sure that a caller is in one of the roles associated with the application as a whole and denies the caller if he is not. Other than that, however, no other access checks are performed, and no security context is available to components. Thus, programmatic security will not operate for components of parent applications configured in this way.

- **Perform Access Checks at the Process and Component Level**. This option turns role-based security on. Security contexts will be available to components, and you can declaratively give roles access to components, interfaces, and methods. Validation still occurs at the process level in that the caller needs to be in some role associated with the application, but finer-grain control is permitted. Roles can be granted permission to certain components, interfaces, and methods in the application, but not others. Normally, you will select this option.

It might seem surprising, but both these options are still relevant even if Enforce Access Checks for This Application is not checked. The operative word on this check box is Enforce, and by not selecting this option, you are asking COM+ to stand down and let everyone through. Security information might, however, still be available. For example, if you do not enforce access checks for the application, but you do select the second radio button, Perform Access Checks at the Process and Component Level, components can still programmatically determine what role their caller is in and accept or reject the call. If Enforce Access Checks for This Application is off, acceptance or rejection needs to be implemented manually by the developer because COM+ does not automatically enforce security in this mode.

If you do not select the Enforce Access Checks for This Application option and select the first radio button, Perform Access Checks Only at the Process Level, you are effectively saying that you want no security enforced, and you want to prevent all components of the application from receiving any security information. Thus, programmatic security no longer works. This no enforce, process only pair is the setting to choose if you want to emphatically state that an application and all its components are absolutely public and available to anyone.

Library Application Considerations

As we've discussed, a COM+ library application does not have a process of its own, but lives in the process of another COM+ application (or in the process space of an ordinary client application executable, but that is a rare circumstance and we will not discuss it here). Thus, its security considerations are different from that of a COM+ server application. The first difference you will notice is a library application's Security dialog box (Figure 12.6) has slightly different settings available than does the server application's Security dialog box shown earlier in Figure 12.5.

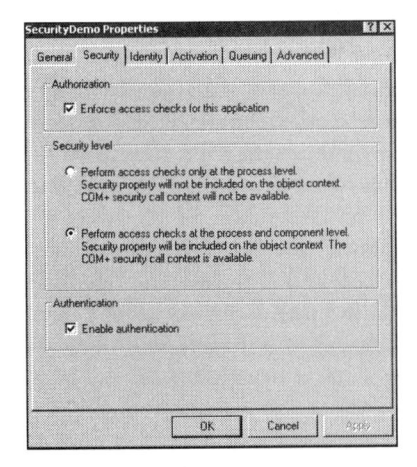

Figure 12.6 The Security tab for a COM+ library application.

continues

continued

Notice that the dialog box shown in Figure 12.6 does not include the Impersonation and Authentication drop-down boxes. This is because a library application always lives in the process of its client application (by client application, I am referring to the COM+ application that contains the component that called on the library application), and it is the client that determines the impersonation and authentication settings. Library applications do, however, have an Enable Authentication check box. If this is checked, the library application is saying that, in addition to its own declarative security, it wants to be accessed according to the security requirements of its host application/process. Specifically, an interface to a library component with Enable Authentication checked cannot be passed as an argument to any component that does not have access to that library's host application. Put another way, the application that will be receiving an interface to a component in the library application must have an identity that exists in some role of the library's host.

At first glance, you might imagine that not checking this check box allows clients to invoke methods of a library component without going through the security of the parent application. This is true in a sense, but for a library application to be run in the first place, a running COM+ server application must first request a component in the library application on behalf of a client. For this to happen, the client must go through the host application and invoke some method that results in the creation of the library application. It follows then that the client must already have access to the host application for it to gain access to the library application. This setting, therefore, is not designed to allow the creating client uncontested access to the library component (it already has it), but to impose additional access restrictions to components that will receive an interface from a component in the library application as an argument.

Programming Security

Declarative security is useful for granting access to a component, interface, or method. It is simple (using Component Services) to declare that the Traders role can call the `EnterTrade()` method but the Operations role cannot. COM+ automatically enforces these permissions for you, and the developer does not need to implement any security-related code in his component. However, if you require finer-grain security control—for example, allowing the `EnterTrade()` method to be invoked by Traders but only if the trade amount is less than one million dollars—declarative security cannot help you. To make access decisions based on method arguments or other fine point considerations, you need to use the security context of your object.

ISecurityCallContext

The primary interface used by components that implement programmatic security is `ISecurityCallContext`. In VB, you can obtain this interface with the following:

```
Dim SecCallCtx as SecurityCallContext
Set SecCallCtx = GetSecurityCallContext()
```

And in C++

```
ISecurityCallContext *pSecCtx;
HRESULT hr;
hr=CoGetCallContext(IID_ISecurityCallContext,(void**)&pSecCtx);
```

The methods of `ISecurityCallContext` are listed in Table 12.1 (source: MSDN) with some additional explanation:

Table 12.1 **Interface Methods**

Interface Method	Description
IsCallerInRole	*Determines whether the direct caller is in the specified role.* The role name is passed as a string in the first parameter of this method.
IsSecurityEnabled	*Determines whether security is enabled for the object.* If Enforce Access Checks for This Application is not selected for the COM+ application, this method returns false.
IsUserInRole	*Determines whether the specified user is in the specified role.* Pass in the string name of the NT account as the first argument, the role (also as a string) as the second argument.

Note that these methods are also available via the IObjectContext interface. However, as IObjectContext is largely a legacy Microsoft Transaction Server (MTS) interface, ISecurityCallContext should be used instead.

Now that your component can obtain its security context, you can provide finer-grain access control. Listing 12.2 demonstrates how to allow or disallow a caller from invoking a method depending on the callers role and the arguments to the method.

Listing 12.2 **The Use of Programmatic Security Combined with Method Arguments to Determine Access**

```
Sub EnterTrade(cusip As String, qty As Integer, price As Double)

Dim SecCallCtx As SecurityCallContext
Set SecCallCtx = GetSecurityCallContext()

If SecCallCtx.IsCallerInRole("Traders") And price < 1000000 Then
    'do the trade
ElseIf SecCallCtx.IsCallerInRole("HeadTraders") And price < 5000000 Then
    'HeadTraders role is allowed a higher limit
Else
    'this raises permissions denied as COM+ does,
    'but you can raise whatever error condition you like.
    Err.Raise 70
End If

End Sub
```

Application Identity

If you have a client executable calling into a single COM+ application, security is pretty straightforward. COM+ determines the calling client's identity, sees what roles that identity is associated with, and determines if the caller's associated role(s) has the appropriate privileges. Things get more complex when a call to a component in one application results in a call to a component in another application.

A COM+ application does not automatically assume the identity of its callers. On the contrary, the application's process (DLLHOST.EXE) always runs as one specific user. Selecting the Identity properties tab for an application results in the dialog box shown in Figure 12.7.

The Identity tab lets you specify who the application will be when it runs—that is, what privileges it will assume. By selecting Interactive User, you are saying that the application will run with the privileges of the currently logged-in user—that is, the user currently logged into the machine on which the COM+ application will be run. There is often some confusion about this setting. Many developers believe that an application so configured assumes the identity of the client application that is calling or interacting with the application. That process is termed *impersonation,* and that is not what is happening. By selecting Interactive User, the COM+ application has only those privileges that the currently logged-in user has.

If no user is logged in, the application will not run and calls to its components fail. Even if someone is logged in, it is simply a bad idea to write a piece of enterprise architecture that relies on the serendipitous fact that the appropriate user will happen to be logged into the server. Thus, this setting should probably not be used except when writing and debugging components. One convenient feature of this setting is that components in an application configured as Interactive User can pop up dialog or message boxes. Note that you should never do this in production, but for debugging it is helpful. A message box only appears because the application is running in the context of the logged-in user, and by being logged into that machine at that moment, the user is sitting in front of a living Windows desktop that can present him with message boxes. If you do not select the interactive user option, message boxes still pop up, but do so in the depths of a non-graphical NT virtual desktop, unseen by anyone, possibly hanging your application by waiting forever for someone to click OK.

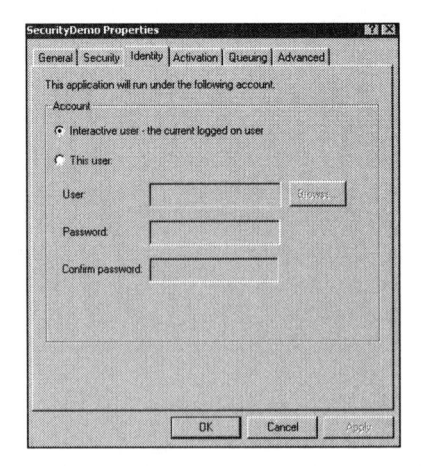

Figure 12.7 The Identity dialog box determines what account the application will run under.

The This User radio button allows you to specify the account you want the application to run under. Never use a real person's account for this. People leave to join other companies, get promoted, demoted, and so on. The last thing you need is to have your application suddenly fail because a system administrator in another building changed the password for an account you were using. It is much better to create dedicated *software accounts*—that is, accounts created by the system administrator specifically intended to service COM+ applications. By setting the application to run as a specific software account, the components of that application have the privileges of that account.

Security Boundaries

Every COM+ application can be thought of living in its own security boundary. Roles, after all, are specific to a particular application. Furthermore, you know that every application runs under one specific account—the one specified in the application's Identity tab. When a component in one application calls a component in another application, security boundaries are said to be crossed.

For the purposes of example, imagine you have an Application A that contains one component, Component A. Further imagine an Application B that contains one component, Component B. If I, user gbrill, run a client executable that invokes a method on Component A, the declarative security for Application A comes into effect. COM+ makes sure the calling account, gbrill, exists in a role that has access to the method I am trying to invoke. If the method I invoke in Component A calls the methods of another component in the same application, no additional security checks are performed. (If you are familiar with relational databases, you might notice a similarity between this and stored procedures security; if you give a database user permission to execute a stored procedure, the procedure can access tables that the user might not have permissions to access directly.)

If, however, Component A calls Component B, which resides in another COM+ application (Application B), a second authentication takes place. Unfortunately, roles do not cross the security boundaries of applications, only the ID of the caller does. If user gbrill invokes a method on Component A in Application A, which then invokes a method on Component B in Application B, you might expect that application B's caller is gbrill; it isn't. Application B's caller is the account that Application A is set to run under in its Identity tab (see Figure 12.7). If the identity of Application A is set to Administrator, the call to component B only succeeds if the Administrator is in the proper role(s) for that component. Although gbrill might be the original caller, that does not come into play for declarative security when security boundaries are spanned. Component B can, however, determine programmatically that gbrill was the original caller by requesting a call list. Examine the code in Listing 12.3.

370 Chapter 12 Security

Listing 12.3 **Retrieving the Chain of Callers**

```
Sub WhoCalledMe()

    Dim SecCallCtx As SecurityCallContext
    Dim Caller As SecurityIdentity
    Dim Callers As SecurityCallers
    Dim iCaller As Integer

    Set SecCallCtx = GetSecurityCallContext()
    Set Callers = SecCallCtx.Item("Callers")

    Debug.Print "Number of Callers in Chain: " & Callers.Count & _
                vbNewLine

    'Note: For…Each will not work with this interface

    For iCaller = 0 To Callers.Count - 1
        Set Caller = Callers.Item(iCaller)
        Debug.Print "Caller " & Caller.Item("AccountName") & vbNewLine
    Next

End Sub
```

Listing 12.3 introduces two new VB objects—`SecurityIdentity` (VB's wrapper for `ISecurityIdentity`) and `SecurityCallers` (wrapper for `ISecurityCallersColl`). For more information about their use, see the following sidebar, "Determining the Call Chain with `ISecurityCallersColl` and `ISecurityCallersColl`."

> **Determining the Call Chain with ISecurityIdentityColl and ISecurityCallersColl**
>
> The `ISecurityCallContext` interface can be used to determine if a caller or user is in a specific role and if security is presently enabled. It is also a VB style collection and, as such, supports a method, `Item()`, that returns a single Variant. This returned Variant holds either a numerical value or an IUnknown pointer that can be QI'd for an `ISecurityIdentityColl` (gives information about a specific caller) interface or an `ISecurityCallersColl` interface (a collection of `ISecurityCallersColl` interfaces). The string value passed into the `Item()` method of `ISecurityCallContext` determines what the returned Variant will have in it. For example, examine the last line of the following VB code snippet from Listing 12.3:
>
> ```
> Dim securityinfo As SecurityCallContext
> Dim callers As SecurityCallers
>
> Set securityinfo = GetSecurityCallContext()
> Set callers = securityinfo.Item("Callers")
> ```
>
> By passing in the string "Callers", you are asking the `SecurityCallContext` object to return a collection of callers. Other string values could have been used, however that would have returned a single `ISecurityCallersColl` interface or numerical value. The table of property values is shown in Table 12.2 (source: MSDN) with some additional explanation.

Security Boundaries

Table 12.2 The Properties of *ISecurityCallContext*

Property	Description
NumCallers	The number of callers in the chain of calls.
MinAuthenticationLevel	The least secure authentication level of all callers in the chain.
Callers	Information about the chain of callers to the current object. In Visual Basic, this returns a SecurityCallers collection object. In C++, it returns a ISecurityCallersColl interface. The SecurityCallers is a collection of SecurityIdentity objects (ISecurityIdentityColl interfaces in C++), which represent the identity of a caller. (More on this in the section following this table).
DirectCaller	Returns a SecurityIdentityColl object of the caller that called the object directly. This is the ISecurityIdentity interface in C++.
OriginalCaller	Returns a SecurityIdentityColl object of the caller who originated the chain of calls to the object. This is the ISecurityIdentity interface in C++.

When a collection of "Callers" is requested from *ISecurityCallContext*, a collection of *SecurityIdentityColl* interfaces is returned. Like *ISecurityCallersColl*, the *ISecurityIdentityColl* is another collection of properties. It also has an *Item()* method that returns a Variant and takes a string value to determine what the returned Variant will hold. Its property table is shown in Table 12.3 (source: MSDN) with some additional explanation.

Table 12.3 The Properties of *ISecurityCallersCall*

Property	Description
SID	The security identifier of the caller. A V_ARRAY. This can be used in low-level, Win32 security APIs.
AccountName	The account name that the caller is using. Returns a string.
AuthenticationService	The authentication service used by the caller, such as NTLMSSP, Kerberos, or SSL. Returns the integer representing the authentication service in use.
ImpersonationLevel	The impersonation level, which indicates how much authority the caller has been given to act on a client's behalf. Returns an integer representing the impersonation level.
AuthenticationLevel	The authentication level used by the caller, which indicates the amount of protection given during the call. Returns an integer representing the authentication level.

continues

continued

The *ISecurityIdentityColl* and *ISecurityCallersColl* interfaces are not, in my opinion, well designed. Although they are relatively straightforward to use in VB, their typeless, Variant-oriented design makes them unwieldy in C++. Furthermore, only *IUnknown* and *IDispatch* interfaces can be returned in a Variant, so the object requesting a collection of callers, for example, gets a collection of *IUnknown* pointers stored in Variants. Thus, the object must extract each interface from the Variant and then explicitly QI for *ISecurityIdentityColl*. This might not seem like much, but needless round trips in a heavily used object add up quickly to degrade performance.

Reviewing this scenario, you have a user, gbrill, who runs a client that invokes a method on Component A in Application A. Application A has its identity declaratively set to run as Administrator. Thus, if Component A then invokes a method on Component B residing in Application B, the caller (from Application B's perspective) is Administrator, not gbrill. If the code in Listing 12.3 is run in Component B, the resulting output would confirm this:

```
Number of Callers in Chain: 2
Caller INFUSION\gbrill
Caller INFUSION\Administrator
```

Although Application B can determine the original caller, gbrill, declarative security is enforced based on the last or current caller (Application A), which is running as Administrator. You might imagine that there must be some way to allow the original caller to persist in cross-application calls, and there is—impersonation and delegation. We discuss the former first.

Impersonation

You know that, by default, a component runs with the security credentials of its host COM+ application and not with the credentials of its caller. The easiest way to prove this is to use a simple NTFS file. Permissions on an NTFS file—that is, a file on an NTFS hard drive partition—can be set to allow certain users to read, write, execute, and so on. Imagine that you have such a file, but access is restricted to user gbrill. Further imagine that you have a COM+ application whose identity is set to softwareaccount1. If I, gbrill, execute a client executable that invokes a method on some component in this application, any attempts by that component to modify the file will fail. Why? Because only gbrill has access to the file, and although the original caller might be gbrill, the component is running with the privileges of its application. In this case, the application's identity is softwareaccount1; thus, the file modification does not succeed even though the original caller, gbrill, has the appropriate access.

There is, however, a way for the component to impersonate the caller. Specifically, a component only needs to call the Win32 method, `CoImpersonateClient()`. This method encapsulates the following:

```
CoGetCallContext(IID_IServerSecurity, (void**)&pServerSec);
    pServerSec->ImpersonateClient();
```

The `CoGetCallContext()` Win32 function can be used to retrieve either `ISecurityCallContext` (covered in the previous section) or the other interface you see here—`IServerSecurity`. `IServerSecurity` has four methods, one of which is `ImpersonateClient()` (shown in the preceding code). If your file modification component calls this `ImpersonateClient()`, the component assumes the credentials of the caller. Thus, the file modification component does have the credentials of gbrill and, therefore, does have the appropriate permissions to manipulate the file. When the component no longer wants to assume the caller's identity, it can call the `IServerSecurity` method, `RevertToSelf()` (or the `CoRevertToSelf` API).

Let's see an example of `CoImpersonateClient()` at work. Imagine you have NTFS file scenario described earlier: User gbrill runs a client application that instantiates a file modification component in a COM+ application. Because this application's identity is set to `softwareaccount1`, the component is unable to open a file owned by gbrill—even though gbrill is the originating caller. The file-modification component shown in Listing 12.4 first tries to do exactly this but will be rebuffed with an `ACCESS DENIED` error. The component then calls `CoImpersonateClient()` to borrow the credentials of the original caller, gbrill, and succeeds in opening the file. Examine Listing 12.4 for the file-modification component's source.

VB and CoImpersonateClient

The only security method COM+ Services type library makes available to VB is `GetSecurityCallContext()`. This global method always returns a `SecurityCallContext` object (`ISecurityCallContext`, in reality). `IServerSecurity` cannot be obtained or used in VB because one of its methods, `QueryBlanket()`, uses non-automation data types. However, you can make an external Win32 function call to `CoImpersonateClient()` and achieve the same result. To call `CoImpersonateClient()` from VB, you need only add the following Win32 declaration to your project:

```
Public Declare Function CoImpersonateClient Lib "ole32.dll" () As Long
```

Listing 12.4 A Component that Borrows the Credentials of Its Caller in Order to Modify a File Owned by the Caller

```
'This example demonstrates a VB component that utilizes
'CoImpersoanteClient. The component tries to open file
'as specified by the protectedfilename parameter, under:

'1.) The identity of the component itself.

'2.) The identity of its caller. Note that the caller does
'not have to be a configured component - it doesn't have
'to have a context.  This is because all CoImpersonateClient
'is doing, is copying the ACL into the thread of the
'component so it runs with its caller's credentials.

'Win32 COM Security functions.  We CANNOT use the underlying interface
'(IServerSecurity) of these APIs in VB, because it uses
'non-ole datatypes

Public Declare Function CoImpersonateClient Lib "ole32.dll" () As Long
Public Declare Function CoRevertToSelf Lib "ole32.dll" () As Long
'Above declarations should be in a VB module

Sub Impersonate(protectedfilename As String, logfile As String)

    Open logfile For Output As #1
    Print #1, "Trying to open file under component identity: "

    If FileOpen(protectedfilename) Then
        Print #1, "Opened: " & protectedfilename
    Else
        Print #1, "Could not open: " & protectedfilename
    End If

    'Impersonate the client:
    Print #1, "Impersonating client"
    CoImpersonateClient
    Print #1, "Trying to open file under inhertied identity: "

    If FileOpen(protectedfilename) Then
        Print #1, "Opened: " & protectedfilename
    Else
```

```
        Print #1, "Could not open: " & protectedfilename
    End If
    Close #1

    'Revert to self:
    CoRevertToSelf

End Sub
```

Assuming the filename specified by `ProtectedFilename` (say c:\protect.txt) is restricted by NTFS such that only the user gbrill can open it, the following log file results as detailed in Listing 12.5:

Listing 12.5   **Output of the VB Component**

```
Trying to open file under component identity:
Could not open: c:\protect.txt
Impersonating client
Trying to open file under inherited identity:
Opened: c:\protect.txt
```

Thus, the log file confirms that the component has successfully borrowed the credentials of the original caller.

Impersonation allows the recipient of a method call to borrow the credentials of the caller, but contrary to intuition, does not assume the caller's identity. An impersonating server is like a thief with your credit card—the thief might be able to purchase things as you, but if anyone checks his real ID, that person can see that the thief is not you. The intent of impersonation is to allow the server to borrow the credentials of its caller so as to manipulate resources it does not ordinarily have security privileges to access. Even here, it is limited—impersonation only works for one network hop.

For example, if a client executable on one machine uses Component A on another Machine, A can impersonate the client. Similarly, if Component A calls another Component, B, in a different application but on the same Machine, B also can impersonate the client. If, however, the impersonating Component A calls a Component C on another Machine, C cannot impersonate the client. This is shown in Figure 12.8.

This behavior is by design. At one time, it was thought dangerous to allow an impersonating server to have all the privileges of the client it was impersonating. Concerns arose about malicious servers that would use this capability and, unbeknownst to the client, manipulate resources elsewhere on the network without limitation. Thus, the privileges of impersonating servers were curtailed somewhat. An impersonating server can have all the privileges of its caller but only on the machine on which the server is running. This is shown in Figure 12.9.

The one network hop limitation for impersonation caused particular havoc with DCOM servers using connection points (connection points are covered in Chapter 11, "Events," in the section "The Doubtful Future of Connection Points"). An impersonating DCOM server running on a machine separate from the client would find itself unable to call back on the client's event sink because as far as NT is concerned, that is a second network hop and is forbidden. An impersonating server is even forbidden to manipulate a file on the network.

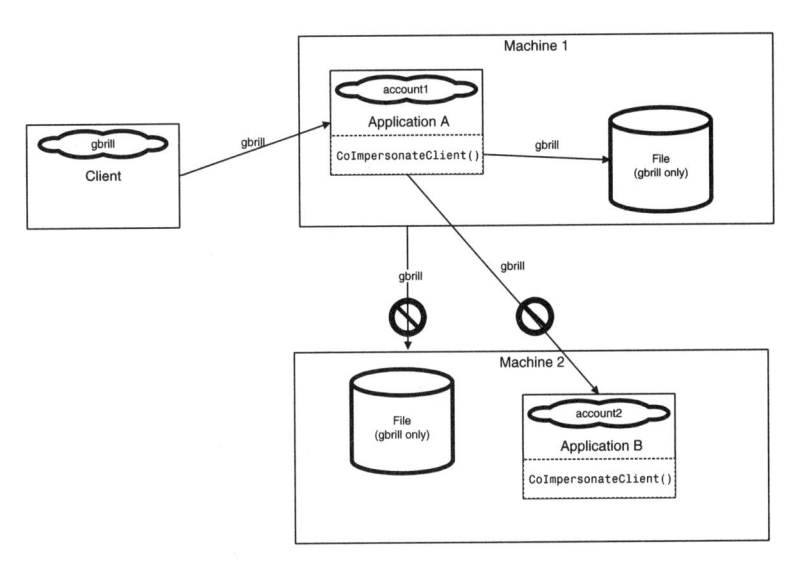

Figure 12.9 Impersonating a server's borrowed credentials only works on the machine on which they are running.

Delegation

To overcome this limitation, Windows 2000 introduced the concept of *delegation*. (Although you might find references to delegation in some of the security dialog boxes of NT 4.0, it was never supported before Windows 2000). Where an impersonating server can borrow the credentials of the caller (but only on the machine where it is running), a delegating server has unrestrictive use of borrowed credentials. Specifically, a delegating server can reach out beyond the machine on which it is running. It can connect to databases, manipulate files on the network, and perform other actions forbidden to impersonating servers. And through the use of a feature called Windows 2000 *cloaking* that is on by default (I discuss cloaking in the next section), delegating COM+ applications can allow the original caller to propagate across any number of application/network hops. Delegation with cloaking is depicted in Figure 12.10.

If delegation and cloaking are enabled and every component involved in a chain of calls invokes `CoImpersonateClient()` before calling another component, the original caller (the user who ran the client application) can propagate to each component. In this scenario, if gbrill calls Component A, which calls B, which calls C, which calls D, D runs with the credentials of gbrill. The combination of delegation, cloaking, and calls to `CoImpersonateClient()` enable the propagation of the original user.

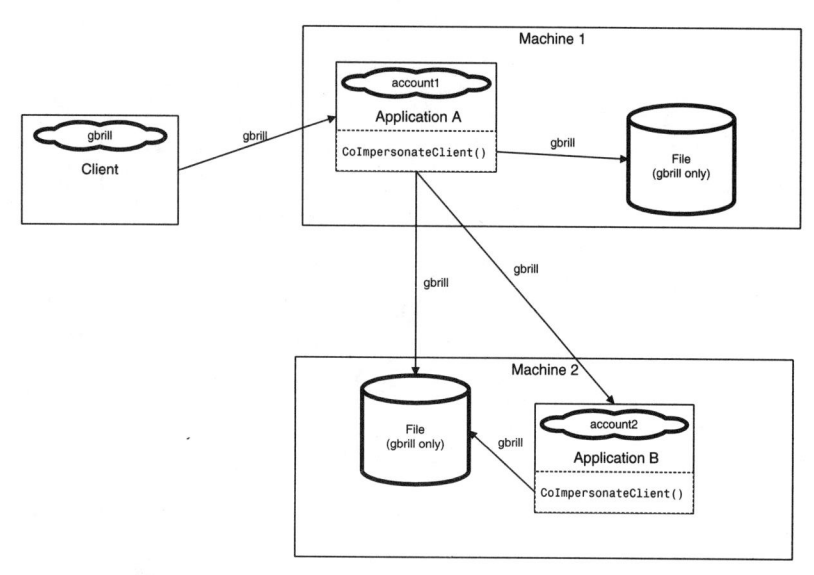

Figure 12.10 Delegation allows impersonated credentials to span any number of network hops.

Cloaking

Impersonation allows a server to use the security credentials of a client for one network hop. Delegation is a form of impersonation that does the same thing, but for an unlimited number of hops. In either case, the server is simply borrowing the credentials of its caller. Normally, if an impersonating or delegating server Application A creates another server Application B, Application B will see Application A in terms of its real identity, not the one it is borrowing from the caller (see Figure 12.11).

Figure 12.11 depicts a delegating server that creates another server, Application B, that calls `CoImpersonateClient()`. Note, however, that Application B ends up impersonating the real identity of Application A, account1, as opposed to the original caller, gbrill. This is precisely what you do not want to happen. Application B cannot obtain the original caller's credentials in any way and ends up impersonating its creating application's identity, account1, which cannot help Application B open gbrill's file.

The solution to this problem comes in the form of *cloaking*. Cloaking can be defined as the capability of an impersonating or delegating server to pass on the capability to impersonate its present caller. With cloaking, Application B can impersonate gbrill even though its immediate caller, Application A, is really running under account1. But because Application A is impersonating gbrill and cloaking is enabled, Application B will see Application A as gbrill and not account1. (A cloaking example, Listing 12.7, can be found toward the end of this chapter).

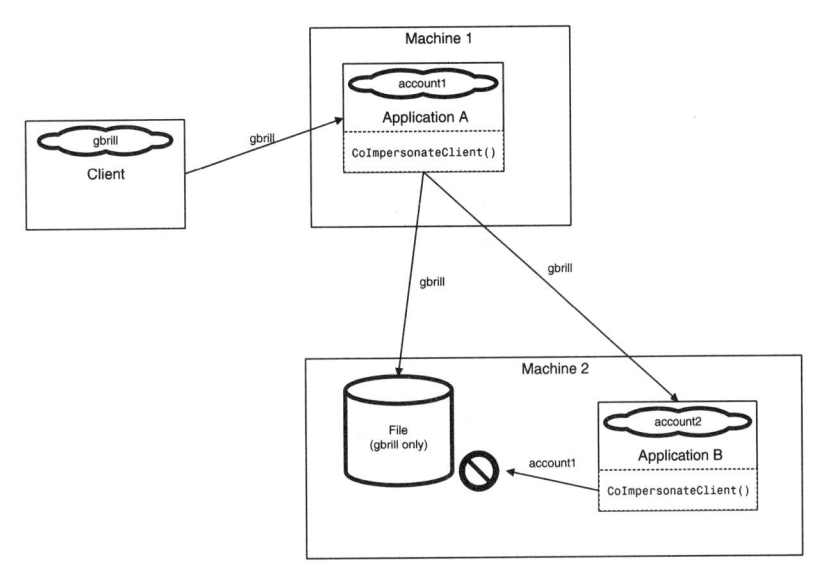

Figure 12.11 Delegation without cloaking prevents the propagation of the original caller.

Cloaking is on by default. This means that impersonating servers automatically pass on impersonation privileges to servers on one machine, and delegating servers can do this across network boundaries on many machines. By and large, this is the behavior you want, although this is a different paradigm than older DCOM servers might have been written to expect. If you like, you can turn cloaking on or off. In fact, all declarative security settings can be explicitly set by and for any thread or process. The section "Lower Level Security" discusses how security can be explicitly set via COM security API calls. For additional details about cloaking, see the following sidebar, "Static and Dynamic Cloaking."

Static and Dynamic Cloaking

There are two types of cloaking—static and dynamic. If there are a number of delegating or impersonating servers along a call chain, the last server in the chain borrows the credentials of the original caller. This is the behavior you expect and want. However, if a client changes its identity or passes its interface to some other client running under a different identity, dynamic cloaking forces all servers in the call chain to re-identify the caller with each new method call and assume the identity of the new caller. By default, dynamic cloaking is enabled.

Static cloaking, on the other hand, does not permit dynamic reidentification and impersonation. Even if the caller changes its identity the downstream servers retain their original impersonation. Thus, though more efficient, static cloaking is not as accommodating.

Authentication

There remains one other security setting we have not discussed—authentication. Like the impersonation level, authentication can be set on per machine or per application level. Its levels are shown in Figure 12.12.

These settings determine to what extent NT should go to protect the integrity of data sent on the network from client to server. These settings range from the least safe but most efficient, to the most safe but least efficient. Note that every setting implicitly includes all settings above it. For example, if Call is selected, Connect is performed as well. Also note that the authentication does not affect role-based security. Role-based security still operates even if the authentication level is set to None.

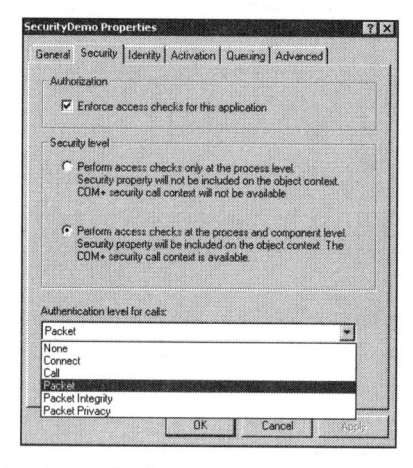

Figure 12.12 Authentication levels can be selected in the middle drop-down box determining what level of network security is to be used for the RPC connection.

> **Impersonation and Delegation and Queued Components**
>
> Impersonation and delegation does not work with queued components. Although a message does retain security information about its sender, such that role-based security will operate, it does not contain the access token or impersonation token of the caller. Impersonation and delegation require this information to reconstruct the caller's security privileges; thus, any attempt to call `CoImpersonateClient()` on a queued component results in an error. When I test this empirically, I get `RPC_E_CALL_COMPLETE`. If you are a C++ programmer, this error is described in winerror.h as "call context cannot be accessed after call completed."

Authentication is designed to protect against replayed method calls, network sniffers, packet hacking, and other security attacks that occur at the network level. The settings are as follows:

- **None.** No authentication is used. Note that impersonation does not operate if this setting is used.
- **Connect.** Authentication is performed when the client first connects to the server. Thereafter, authentication is not performed. A slight and negligible performance hit is incurred during the initial connection.
- **Call.** Authentication is performed on every method call. A performance hit is incurred on every method call, but this is negligible because the authentication occurs very quickly.
- **Packet.** Authentication is performed on every packet of every method call. For connectionless protocols (such as TCP/UDP), the Call and Connect settings are treated as the Packet setting. This also has a negligible effect on performance.
- **Packet Integrity.** In addition to authentication of every packet of every method call, packet integrity is ensured. COM+ does this by computing a checksum of the packet when the call is made and then re-computing the checksum and comparing for equality at the server end. This has a negative effect on performance, because a checksum must be computed twice on every method call—at both the client and server.
- **Packet Privacy.** Packet Privacy is the highest level of authentication that COM+ provides. In addition to performing the operations in the Packet Integrity option (checking for packet integrity by computing a checksum), each packet is encrypted. This setting incurs a relatively large performance hit.

Situations can arise where a server or client might require different authentication levels. In these scenarios, the highest security setting is used. For example, if a client seeks Packet but a server demands Packet Integrity, Packet Integrity is used.

Configuring Impersonation, Delegation, and Authentication

Impersonation and delegation are powerful but somewhat dangerous capabilities for a component to have. If a component delegates as you, it is you as far as NT is concerned. It can open your Outlook account and send nasty emails to everyone in your contact list, all of which have your full name in the FROM field. Thus, clients can explicitly disallow components from delegating or impersonating them. There are two ways to do this. The first is programmatically with a call to a Win32/COM method `CoInitializeSecurity()`. This method is somewhat complex and can only be done from C++. It is somewhat contrary to the declarative nature of COM+. Unfortunately, you might end up calling this API anyway because the alternative method while very simple, is, perhaps, too all-encompassing: you can specify what impersonation settings *all* client applications allow on a machine-wide basis. To specify access rights for all components on a machine, select the properties for the My Computer folder at the root of Component Services' tree and then click on the Default Properties tab; you see that shown in Figure 12.13.

Sadly, someone at Microsoft forgot to set the Sort property of the drop-down to false. Thus, these settings are sorted alphabetically instead of by privilege level, so the order in which they appear in the dialog box is not meaningful. I, however, will order them according to their restrictiveness, with the most restrictive first:

- **Anonymous.** This is the least permissive setting. Anonymous means that the client does not want the server to know who it is. The server cannot impersonate the client and does not receive any security credentials. Note that this setting prevents role-based security from operating because COM+ cannot determine the identity of the caller.

- **Identify.** The client allows the server to determine the client's identity—that is, the server knows what account the client is using. The server cannot, however, impersonate or otherwise assume any of the credentials of the caller.

- **Impersonate.** The client allows the server to impersonate it by assuming its credentials. The server has all the privileges of the account under which the client is run, but only on the computer on which the server is running.

- **Delegate.** This is the most permissive setting. The client allows its server to impersonate it completely, and the server can manipulate resources beyond the computer on which it is running.

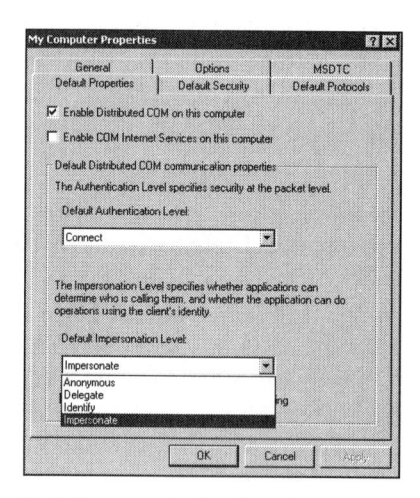

Figure 12.13 Default properties for all applications on My Computer.

These same settings can be set on the Security tab, shown earlier in Figure 12.5, for every COM+ application. This setting indicates the level of privilege the application grants to other applications it might call—that is, to what extent the recipient application can impersonate the calling application. In other words, an application that is set to Delegate is saying, "If a component of mine should ever call another application, that application can impersonate me with my credentials on its machine and/or anywhere on the network." If the application never calls outside of itself to another application, this setting is not referenced.

Lower Level Security

COM+ declarative security eliminates the need for components and processes to explicitly call Win32/COM security APIs. Declarative security is, however, just a higher level abstraction. Security APIs are called by COM+ implicitly on your application's behalf. A detailed description of these functions and their methods would bring us into the internals of security descriptors, Access Control Entries (ACEs), ACLs, and many other facets of NT security used to allow or exclude access to resources. That kind of discussion demands a book of its own. However, for completeness and so that you can understand security-related COM articles you might come across, I'm going to introduce a couple of security functions that every COM+ developer should have a nodding acquaintance with.

The *CoInitializeSecurity* Function

This method determines process-wide security settings. Old style, out-of-process (EXE) DCOM servers often call this function explicitly to determine who has access to them, their authentication level, and so on. If this function is not called for an out-of-process server, COM calls it when an interface is first marshaled to or from the server using values from the Registry. In NT 4.0., the utility DCOMCNFG.EXE was typically used to assign access rights to the DCOM server such that COM could determine the arguments for this implicit call to `CoInitializeSecurity()`.

With COM+, you no longer write out-of-process servers, and more often than not, your clients are Visual Basic. Thus, leave it to COM+ to interpret your security-related declarations and make this call for you. Although a C++ client executable can call this function, it is typically unnecessary—machine-wide default settings are automatically used. Furthermore, the client can always change the security settings of the proxy it holds to a component by calling `CoSetProxyBlanket()`, which is discussed next.

The *CoSetProxyBlanket( )* Function

Typically, when a client holds an interface, it does not have a pointer to the actual object. The client is really holding a *proxy*, and in reality, the proxies a client holds are aggregated inside an object called the *proxy manager*. It is possible, then, for the client to interact with the proxy manager itself. Specifically, when a client QIs an interface proxy for `IClientSecurity`, the real object does not support it, but the QI, according to the rules of aggregation, is passed on the outer object. The proxy manager remains quiet and invisible most of the time, but it picks up on this request and gives the requesting client an `IClientSecurity` interface. A client can use this interface to dynamically change the security settings for a particular interface proxy. The `CoSetProxyBlanket()` method simply encapsulates the process of obtaining the `IClientSecurity` interface and calls its `SetBlanket()` method.

For the most part, you do not want to dynamically change security settings for a proxy. There are, however, a couple rare circumstances where this might be necessary. If you want to turn off cloaking because you have very real security concerns, this is the preferable way to do it.

A client can call this method's counterpart, `CoQueryProxyBlanket()`, to determine what the present security settings are for a proxy.

Lower Level Security, Roles and Cloaking: Bringing It All Together

We've certainly covered a lot of ground in this chapter, so it is appropriate to end with an example that brings all these concepts together in a meaningful way. Let's return to the example we've used so far (that of the file belonging to gbrill) and add some additional dimensions to it.

Assume we have two components, `Impersonate1` and `Impersonate2`, both of which reside in different COM+ applications. The application that `Impersonate1` resides in runs under the account `account1`, and the application that `Impersonate2` resides in runs under the account `account2`.

The component `Impersonate1` is written to create an instance of `Impersonate2` and call a method on `Impersonate2` that will attempt to open gbrill's file. Assuming that both `Impersonate1`'s and `Impersonate2`'s applications have Roles that contain the account gbrill, what do you think happens when a client EXE run by user gbrill kicks off the process by calling `Impersonate1`?

Well, the first thing that happens is that the client gets a `Permission Denied` error. If you are not sure why, you might want to take a second look the section, "Security Boundaries" in this chapter. Remember, `Impersonate1` runs in an application operating under the identity of `account1`. Thus, when `Impersonate1` calls `Impersonate2`, it is doing so from the account `account1`—not from the original caller, gbrill. Therefore, the call is rejected by `Impersonate2`'s application, which has a role for gbrill but not for `account1`.

While we can always add `account1` to a Role of `Impersonate2`'s application, the ideal solution is to have `Impersonate1` call `CoImpersonateClient()` *before* it creates and calls `Impersonate2`. If it does this, `Impersonate2`'s application will see the caller as gbrill and let it through *provided* cloaking is enabled (don't worry, it is enabled by default).

Lower Level Security, Roles and Cloaking: Bringing It All Together 385

Because cloaking is on, Impersonate2 should call CoImpersonateClient() just as Impersonate1 did. Now Impersonate2 inherits gbrill's credentials from Impersonate1, which in turn impersonated them from the original caller. If Impersonate2's call to CoImpersonateClient() succeeds, it is now able to open gbrill's file.

The source example of Listing 12.6 details the relevant functions of Impersonate1 and Impersonate2. Note that Impersonate1 has the ability to turn on and off cloaking via a call to CoSetProxyBlanket() and Listing 12.6 demonstrates what the effect will be.

Listing 12.6 *Impersonate1::CallImpersonate,* **Which Impersonates Its Caller and Instantiates** *Impersonate2*

```
HRESULT Impersonate1::CallImpersonate2(
        BSTR Protectedfile,
        BSTR Logfile,
        int Cloaking) {

// CallImpersonate2 Impersonates its caller. It then
// creates an instance of Impersonate2, which in turn
// attempts to impersonate its caller.  The identity
// Impersonate2 obtains depends on whether or not
// CLOAKING is turned on, as determined by the cloaking
// variable of this method, where:

// cloaking = 0        turns CLOAKING OFF
// cloaking = 1        sets  STATIC CLOAKING
// cloaking = other  sets  DYNAMIC CLOAKING


IImpersonate2 *pImpersonate2;

DWORD AuthnSvc, AuthzSvc, AuthnLevel;
DWORD ImpLevel, Capabilities, Cloaking_Type;
HRESULT hr;
OLECHAR* ServerPrincName;
RPC_AUTH_IDENTITY_HANDLE pAuthInfo;


// Impersonate our caller:
hr=CoImpersonateClient();

if (hr!=S_OK) {
    // CoImpersonateClient failed.
    return hr;
}

// Initialize the COM Library and create an instance
// of Impersonate2:
CoInitialize(NULL);
```

continues

Listing 12.6 **Continued**

```
hr = CoCreateInstance(
        CLSID_Impersonate2,
        NULL,
        CLSCTX_ALL,
        IID_IImpersonate2,
        (void**)&pImpersonate2);


if (hr!=S_OK) {
    // Couldn't get an instance of Impersonate2.
    return hr;
}


// Depending on the cloaking variable, set the
// type of cloaking to be used:

if (Cloaking == 0)
    Cloaking_Type = EOAC_NONE; // No cloaking
else if (Cloaking == 1)
    Cloaking_Type = EOAC_STATIC_CLOAKING; // Static cloaking
else
    Cloaking_Type = EOAC_DYNAMIC_CLOAKING;// Dynamic cloaking


// Before we set the type of Cloaking used,
// Query the Impersonate2 proxy we have
// obtained, to ascertain information we will
// use when we set the proxy:

hr=CoQueryProxyBlanket(
    pImpersonate2,
    &AuthnSvc,
    &AuthzSvc,
    &ServerPrincName,
    &AuthnLevel,
    &ImpLevel,
    &pAuthInfo,
    &Capabilities);
```

```
if (hr!=S_OK) {
    // Problem Querying proxy:
    return hr;
}


// Now set the proxy according to the information
// obtained when we Queried the proxy AND
// the type of Cloaking we desire:

hr=CoSetProxyBlanket(
    pImpersonate2,
    AuthnSvc,
    AuthzSvc,
    ServerPrincName,
    AuthnLevel,
    ImpLevel,
    pAuthInfo,
    Cloaking_Type);          // Set cloaking Type

if (hr!=S_OK) {
    // problem setting proxy:
    return hr;
}


// Call impersonate2:
hr=pImpersonate2->ImpersonateClient(
    Protectedfile,
    Logfile);

pImpersonate2->Release();

return S_OK;

}
```

Chapter 12 Security

The source code for `Impersonate2` follows in Listing 12.7.

Listing 12.7 *Impersonate2*, **Which Impersonates Its Caller and Attempts to Open a File**

```
// ImpersonateClient first tries to open the protected file using its own
// credentials.  It then impersonates its caller, and does two
// things with its newly inherited identity:

// It prints out the security credentials it has inherited (this
// magic is performed by GetTokenUser) and then it tries to
// open the protected file using these credentials.


HRESULT Impersonate2::ImpersonateClient(
          BSTR protectedfile,
          BSTR logfile) {


    HRESULT hr;
    HANDLE fHandle;
    const int BUFFER=200;
    char achInfo[BUFFER];
    char achCallersName[BUFFER];
    char achProtectedFile[BUFFER];
    char achLogFile[BUFFER];
    int size=BUFFER;

    // Convert the incoming BSTR to char *'s required
    // by the C APIs we will be using:

    if (WideCharToMultiByte(CP_ACP, 0,
                     logfile,
                     WC_SEPCHARS, // -1
                     achLogFile,
                     size,
                     NULL, NULL) == 0)
    {
        // Could not convert:
        return E_FAIL;
    }

    if (WideCharToMultiByte(CP_ACP, 0,
                     protectedfile,
                     WC_SEPCHARS, // -1
                     achProtectedFile,
                     size,
                     NULL, NULL) == 0)
    {
        // Could not convert:
        return E_FAIL;
    }
```

```
// Open the log file:
fHandle = CreateFile(achLogFile,
                GENERIC_WRITE,
                FILE_SHARE_WRITE,
                NULL,
                CREATE_ALWAYS,
                FILE_ATTRIBUTE_NORMAL,
                NULL);


if (fHandle==INVALID_HANDLE_VALUE)
{
    // Couldn't open the logfile:
    return E_FAIL;
}


// Try to open to protected file with this
// component's identity:

if (GetTokenUser(achCallersName)) {
    sprintf(achInfo,"Impersonate2: Account credentials BEFORE Impersonation:
    ↪%s\n",achCallersName);
    WriteToFile(fHandle, achInfo, strlen(achInfo));
}
else {
    sprintf(achInfo,"Impersonate2: could not get access token\n");
    WriteToFile(fHandle, achInfo, strlen(achInfo));
    CloseHandle(fHandle);
    return E_FAIL;
}

sprintf(achInfo,"Impersonate2: Trying to open %s\n",achProtectedFile);
WriteToFile(fHandle, achInfo, strlen(achInfo));

if (TryToOpenFile(achProtectedFile)) {
    sprintf(achInfo,"Impersonate2: Successfully opened %s\n",
            achProtectedFile);
    WriteToFile(fHandle, achInfo, strlen(achInfo));
}
else {
    sprintf(achInfo,"Impersonate2: Could not open %s\n",
            achProtectedFile);
    WriteToFile(fHandle, achInfo, strlen(achInfo));
}

// Impersonate the caller:
hr=CoImpersonateClient();
```

continues

Listing 12.7 **Continued**

```
if (hr!=S_OK) {
    sprintf(achInfo,"\nImpersonate2: CoImpersoanteClient failed.: %x\n",hr);
    WriteToFile(fHandle, achInfo, strlen(achInfo));
    CloseHandle(fHandle);
    return hr;
}
else {
    sprintf(achInfo,"\n\nImpersonate2: Successfully"
            Impersonated Caller.\n\n");
    WriteToFile(fHandle, achInfo, strlen(achInfo));
}

// Determine the account this component is running under after
// it impersonates its caller.  Note that if the this component's
// caller is itself a component that has impersonated its caller,
// the identity assumed here will depend on whether CLOAKING
// is ON or OFF.


if (GetTokenUser(achCallersName)) {
    sprintf(achInfo,"Impersonate2: Account credentials AFTER"
            " impersonation: %s\n",achCallersName);
    WriteToFile(fHandle, achInfo, strlen(achInfo));
}
else {
    sprintf(achInfo,"Impersonate2: could not get access token\n");
    WriteToFile(fHandle, achInfo, strlen(achInfo));
    CloseHandle(fHandle);
    return E_FAIL;
}

// Try to open the protected file with the new credentials:

sprintf(achInfo,"Impersonate2: Trying to open %s\n",achProtectedFile);
WriteToFile(fHandle, achInfo, strlen(achInfo));

if (TryToOpenFile(achProtectedFile)) {
    sprintf(achInfo,"Impersonate2: Successfully opened %s\n",
            achProtectedFile);
    WriteToFile(fHandle, achInfo, strlen(achInfo));
}
else {
    sprintf(achInfo,"Impersonate2: Could not open %s\n",
            achProtectedFile);
    WriteToFile(fHandle, achInfo, strlen(achInfo));
}


CloseHandle(fHandle);
return S_OK;
```

```
}


// GetTokenUser determines the security credentials the component is using
// when it attempts open resources etc.  This is not as simple as a call
// to the API GetUserName:

// From the MSDN:

/* "Impersonation is really the ability of a thread to execute in a security
   context different from that of the process owning the thread. The server
   thread uses an access token representing the client's credentials, and
   with this it can access resources that the client can access. */

// Thus to determine the security credentials the component has inherited
// we must:
//
//   1.) Obtain the new Access Token of the current thread
//   2.) Obtain the security identifier (SID) within the Access Token
//   3.) Resolve the SID to an account name.



int GetTokenUser(char *User) {

HANDLE hToken;
const int BUFFER=200;
char achAccountName[BUFFER];
char achDomainName[BUFFER];
DWORD DomainBuffer=BUFFER;
DWORD AccountBuffer=BUFFER;

SID_NAME_USE sidUse;
TOKEN_USER tokenInfo;
DWORD BufferSize;

// Obtain the Access token of the current thread. If the component
// has not attempted to Impersonate its client, the thread may
// not have an access token:

if (!OpenThreadToken(GetCurrentThread(),
                   TOKEN_QUERY,
                   FALSE,
                   &hToken))
{

    // Problem getting Thread Access Token.
    // This could be because there is no Thread
    // token available, which means that the
    // thread is not impersonating anyone.  In this
    // case, get the process Access Token (so we can
```

continues

392 Chapter 12 Security

Listing 12.7 **Continued**

```
    // determine the identity the component itself is
    // running under)

    if (GetLastError()==ERROR_NO_TOKEN)
    {

        if (!OpenProcessToken(GetCurrentProcess(),
                     TOKEN_QUERY,
                     &hToken))
        {

            // There was a problem getting the
            // process token.  This is a problem,
            // so abort the procedure:
            return 0;
        }

    }
    else
    {

        // The Thread token existed, but we couldn't
        // get it for some reason, so abort the
        // procedure:
            return 0;
    }

}

// Now obtain information on the Token's
// user account.  This gives us a structure
// with the user account's SID:

if (!GetTokenInformation(hToken,
          TokenUser,
          &tokenInfo,
          (DWORD)BUFFER,
          (PDWORD)&BufferSize))
{

    // Problem getting user account information:
    return 0;
}


// Resolve the SID obtained above, into
// an NT account name.  This gives us
```

```
// both the Domain and Account of the user:
if (!LookupAccountSid(NULL,
        tokenInfo.User.Sid,
        achAccountName,
        &AccountBuffer,
        achDomainName,
        &DomainBuffer,
        &sidUse))
{
        return 0;
}


// We have the Domain and Account Name the thread's
// token is running under, give this information
// to the user.  We use the _bstr_t class to make
// our string manipulation a little easier:
_bstr_t FullName=achDomainName;
FullName+="\\";
FullName+=achAccountName;
strcpy(User,FullName);

return 1;

}



// TryToOpenFile...tries to open the specified file.
// It Returns 1 if it exists, and 0 otherwise:

int TryToOpenFile(char * Filename) {


HANDLE Hand;
Hand= CreateFile(Filename,
            GENERIC_READ,
            FILE_SHARE_READ,
            NULL,
            OPEN_EXISTING,
            FILE_ATTRIBUTE_NORMAL,
            NULL);


if (Hand==INVALID_HANDLE_VALUE)
{
    return 0;
}
```

continues

Listing 12.7 **Continued**

```
else
{
    CloseHandle(Hand);
    return 1;
}

}

void WriteToFile(HANDLE hFile, char* Contents, int size) {

DWORD nWritten;

int result = WriteFile(hFile,
                Contents,
                size,
                &nWritten,
                NULL);

}
```

Now that you have examined the source code in Listings 12.6 and 12.7, let's turn our attention to the output.

Assume that the user gbrill is logged in and that there exists a file c:\protect.txt, such that it is only accessible to gbrill (through NTFS protection). Imagine we run the following VB code under the gbrill account:

```
Dim impImp1 As Impersonate1
Set impImp1 = New Impersonate1
impImp1.CallImpersonate2 "c:\protect.txt", "c:\log.txt", 0  'Cloaking OFF
```

Assuming that role-based security is turned off for the applications of `Impersonate1` and `Impersonate2`, we need to turn Security off (or add account1 to a Role); because if cloaking is disabled then `Impersonate2`'s application does not see the caller as gbrill, rather it sees the caller as account1 and rejects the call. An examination of the log file created by `Impersonate2` further proves the point

```
Impersonate2: Account credentials BEFORE Impersonation: INFUSION\account2
Impersonate2: Trying to open c:\protect.txt
Impersonate2: Could not open c:\protect.txt

Impersonate2: Successfully Impersonated Caller.
Impersonate2: Account credentials AFTER impersonation: INFUSION\account1
Impersonate2: Trying to open c:\protect.txt
Impersonate2: Could not open c:\protect.txt
```

Because cloaking is OFF, `Impersonate2` gets `Impersonate1`'s security credentials (account1) as opposed to the credentials of the original caller. Thus the attempt to open the file fails because the file belongs to gbrill and not account1. It is true that

`Impersonate1` called `CoImpersonateClient()` before creating `Impersonate2`, and this would allow `Impersonate1` to open gbrill's file if it wishes. However, with cloaking disabled, a downstream server sees its caller for who it really is, as opposed to who it is impersonating.

If we modify the VB client to enable cloaking

```
Dim impImp1 As Impersonate1
Set impImp1 = New Impersonate1
impImp1.CallImpersonate2 "c:\protect.txt", "c:\log.txt", 2  'Cloaking ON
```

the following log file results:

```
Impersonate2: Account credentials BEFORE Impersonation: INFUSION\account2
Impersonate2: Trying to open c:\protect.txt
Impersonate2: Could not open c:\protect.txt

Impersonate2: Successfully Impersonated Caller.
Impersonate2: Account credentials AFTER impersonation: INFUSION\gbrill
Impersonate2: Trying to open c:\protect.txt
Impersonate2: Successfully opened c:\protect.txt
```

Because cloaking is enabled `Impersonate2` is able to obtain gbrill's credentials, and the attempt to open the file succeeds.

Summary

COM+ security is declarative in nature and can enforce access checks without requiring components to call security-related functions. A COM+ application can define one or many roles into which one or many individual NT accounts can be placed. An administrator declaratively grants roles access to components, interfaces, and/or methods using Component Services. If an application and/or the components of the application are configured to enforce access checks, COM+ prevents callers from accessing any components, methods, or interfaces that do not grant access to a role that the caller is associated with.

Programmatic security can augment declarative security by allowing the component programmer to manually determine whether the caller is in a specific role. Furthermore, method arguments can be factored in to decide whether a caller should be accepted or rejected. Programmatic security can also be used to determine the chain of callers, the authentication level in use, and many other security details. `ISecurityCallContext` is the main security interface and provides methods to determine if a caller or user is in a specific role and if security is presently enabled. It is also a VB-style collection and, as such, can be used to obtain the `ISecurityIdentityColl` and `ISecurityCallersColl` interfaces, which can be used to obtain more detailed information about the caller(s).

A COM+ application is assigned a specific NT account to run under. It can either be the interactive user (the user presently logged into the system) or assigned specific NT account. Although interactive user is useful when debugging a component, specific accounts should be used most of the time. If an application wants to borrow the security credentials of its caller so as to manipulate resources as the caller, it can do so on the machine in which it is running by using impersonation. A client specifies whether to allow a server to do this based on how its impersonation level is set, but for the most part, clients allow impersonation. Delegation is a type of impersonation that can allow the server to manipulate resources as the caller, even if those resources are located on another machine. A component that wants to impersonate (or delegate) its caller can call the `CoImpersonateClient()` function.

A new feature of Windows 2000, cloaking, is enabled by default and allows the original caller to propagate across a series of impersonating or delegating servers, such that the last component in a call chain can still borrow the security credentials of the original caller.

III

Appendixes

- **A** ADO and OLE-DB
- **B** COM+ Synchronization Through Activities
- **C** Object Pooling
- **D** Passing Block Data, SAFEARRAYs
- **E** Queue Moniker Parameters
- **F** Application Proxies

A

ADO and OLE-DB

Querying with the search string "database query" in MSDN brings back an inordinate number of references to technologies like DAO, RDO, ODBC, DB-LIB, and others. Except in rare, specific circumstances, you probably should not use any of these legacy data access technologies for new development. This is not to say they don't work; in many cases, they work fine, even in COM+. The reason you shouldn't base new development on them is because Microsoft has changed its data access strategy to become non-RDBMS centric. Where all the aforementioned technologies assume that you are accessing a relational database (Oracle, SQL Server, and Informix, for example), Microsoft's new data access technology, ADO, does not.

In the new nomenclature, ActiveX Data Objects (ADO) is an OLE-DB *consumer*. The term OLE-DB describes Microsoft's new, generic data access strategy. The term consumer is clear enough; it consumes data—that is, a data access client. I cannot, however, imagine a worse name than OLE-DB. OLE is a term falling out of use in favor of COM, and DB stands in direct contrast to what OLE-DB is all about—generic access to any kind of data source whether it is a relational database or not. Bad naming aside, OLE-DB is about providing access to any type of data—hierarchical, relational, flat, it doesn't matter. As long as someone writes an *OLE-DB provider* for the data source, any client can connect with it and retrieve information via ADO.

An OLE-DB provider is nothing more than a COM class that implements the minimum set of interfaces required by the OLE-DB specification. The actual manipulation of data, processing of a query string, and massaging return data into a tabular format is the responsibility of the OLE-DB provider author. OLE-DB is not a technology; it is an interface specification that, if followed, allows your data source to be accessed by OLE-DB based Microsoft technologies. Many database vendors now supply OLE-DB providers for their databases (relational and non-relational) in addition to (or even instead of) ODBC drivers.

ODBC versus OLE-DB

There is often some confusion between Open Database Connectivity (ODBC) and OLE-DB, which is understandable. There is some overlap between the two (Microsoft provides an OLE-DB provider for ODBC, but we'll talk about that in a bit), and they were both created to solve similar problems. ODBC is a standardized relational database API created by Microsoft. As the primary desktop OS, Microsoft was able to coerce every relational database manufacturer to adhere to the ODBC specification and ship an ODBC driver (a DLL exporting this API) with their product. By providing a standard interface (granted, a Microsoft standard), it became possible to write generic query tools and client applications that could be written to the ODBC specification instead of some proprietary API from the database manufacturer. Thus, an ODBC client application could talk to any relational database. As an additional benefit, one database can always be swapped for another without requiring any changes to client code.

There are two problems with ODBC, however. The first is that ODBC is a C API and so is not COM accessible. The second problem is that ODBC is designed solely as an interface to relational databases—its APIs are designed specifically to ferry SQL to an RDBMS and retrieve tabular rowsets. Many of the ODBC method names even contain the word SQL. Although this is certainly no problem if you are only interested in accessing relational databases, it is awkward if you want to access non-relational databases that don't understand SQL. Microsoft wanted to remove this inherent limitation, and as part of something it called Universal Data Access (UDA) it wanted a more generic, interface-based mechanism of accessing any type of data from any type of data source. It should be possible to query an Excel spreadsheet in the same way you can query a database table. It should further be possible to join an Excel spreadsheet with a relational database table (Microsoft SQL Server 7 can do this). Thus, OLE-DB became the preferred back-end interface.

ODBC has not vanished, however. There still exists a large number of ODBC drivers that provide access to many back-end systems, the manufacturers of which might not have written OLE-DB providers yet. Because Microsoft has, for the most part, adopted ADO/OLE-DB approaches in lieu of ODBC-based ones (case in point, the new OLE-DB grid, combo-box, and so on included with VB 6), it would be nice if ADO could have access to ODBC data sources for which there is not an OLE-DB provider. Microsoft provides such a wrapper in the form of a generic OLE-DB provider for ODBC. This means that you can, through this component, use ADO to access any data source for which there is an ODBC driver.

Using ADO in COM+

As we discuss in Chapter 8, "Transactions," the ODBC driver manager is a COM+ Resource Dispenser. This means that when a transactional COM+ object requests an ODBC connection via any data access technology (RDO, ODBC, ADO), the ODBC driver manager enlists the connection with the Distributed Transaction Coordinator (DTC). This is how COM+ transactions operate. If ADO requests an ODBC connection through the OLE-DB provider for ODBC, the connection is enlisted by the ODBC driver manager. If ADO requests a connection directly from an OLE-DB provider (one supplied by the database manufacturer), the provider itself can enlist the connection with the DTC because the ODBC driver manager is not involved.

ADO Examples

Now that you know a little about why ADO should be used, here are a couple ADO examples to start you off. A detailed overview of ADO is a book in itself, but to soften the impact of learning COM+ and ADO at the same time, the examples shown in Listings A.1 through A.3 might be of use.

Listing A.1 **ADO Code to Retrieve a** *Recordset*

```
Dim Query As String
Dim Connection As String
Dim DataSet As New ADODB.Recordset

Query = "SELECT traderName, traderID FROM Traders"
Connection = "DSN=TraderDemo;UID=gbrill;PWD=password;"

DataSet.Open Query, Connection

'Code to iterate through recordset and manipulate individual rows

DataSet.Close
Set DataSet = Nothing
```

Listing A.2 ADO Calling a Stored Procedure, No *Resultset,* But with Output Parameter

```
Dim Connect As New ADODB.Connection
Connect.ConnectionString = "DSN=TraderDemo;UID=gbrill;PWD=password;"
Connection.Open

Set Command = New ADODB.Command
Set Command.ActiveConnection = Connection
Command.CommandText = "sp_GetTraderInfo"
Command.CommandType = adCmdStoredProc
Command.Parameters.Refresh

Command.Execute()

Debug.print "Paramater 1 = " & Command.Parameters(0).Value
Debug.print "Parameter2  = " & Command.Parameters(1).Value
```

Listing A.3 ADO Calling a Stored Procedure with Resultset and Output Parameters

```
Dim Connect As New ADODB.Connection
Dim DataSet As New ADODB.Recordset

Connect.ConnectionString = "DSN=TraderDemo;UID=gbrill;PWD=password;"
Connection.Open

Set Command = New ADODB.Command
Set Command.ActiveConnection = Connection
Command.CommandText = "sp_GetTraderInfo"
Command.CommandType = adCmdStoredProc
Command.Parameters.Refresh

Set DataSet = Command.Execute()

' Code to iterate through recordset and manipulate individual rows

DataSet.Close

Debug.print "Paramater 1 = " & Command.Parameters(0).Value
Debug.print "Parameter2  = " & Command.Parameters(1).Value
```

B

COM+ Synchronization Through Activities

WRITING A THREAD-SAFE COMPONENT—that is, one that can safely be called by multiple threads at any time—has always been a challenge. Such development demands knowledge of semaphores, mutexes, critical sections, and other forms of OS thread locking primitives. These must be set like sentinels at the gates of every resource in a process that requires serialized access.

COM offers protection for objects that might be called concurrently by multiple threads, but cannot or do not employ any form of mutual exclusion primitive (mutex, semaphores, and so on). This protection comes in the form of the Single-Threaded Apartment (STA), which, as discussed in Chapter 4, "Threading and Apartment Models," serializes all method calls made by any thread through a protective message queue. COM then serially pops the messages from the queue one at a time and invokes them on the object.

STA serialization guarantees that only one method is invoked on the object at a time. Thus, if three threads call method `Foo()` on an object in an STA at the same time, the method calls are serialized in an FIFO fashion. There is no danger of the first method invocation, M1, being interrupted by another thread's method invocation, M2, before M1 has completed and returns. The thread protection, then, is at the method level. That is certainly useful, but it cannot guard against more subtle forms of race conditions.

Imagine the scenario where object A creates B which creates C which creates D in the context of a transaction. Object A might call a method on B which, in turn, calls a method on C. If A, B, and C are apartment model (they are protected by their STAs), there is no danger of their individual method calls being interrupted—A's method call to B is guaranteed to complete as is object B's call to object C and C's to D. However, there is the possibility that some other alien thread could butt in between A's call to B and B's call to C and make another method invocation that could interrupt the chain of related method calls. By interrupt, I mean to say that the foreign thread could make a serialized method call that is perfectly legitimate as far as the STA is concerned, but might result in the recipient object being in a state inappropriate for what A, B, and C are trying to accomplish together. Perhaps an example is helpful to visualize this. Examine the pseudo VB code in Listing B.1.

Listing B.1 **Simple VB Objects**

```
'The Client
A.DoSomethingOnBFromA
 'Object A:
Sub DoSomethingOnBFromA()
 'Do something, then:
B.DoSomethingOnCFromB
end sub
 'Object B:
Sub DoSomethingOnCFromB()
 'Do something, then:
    C.DoSomethingOnDFromC
end sub
```

You can see from Listing B.1 that a call to object A's `DoSomethingOnBFromA` method initiates a chain of related method invocations involving four objects (A through D). Now, here's the problem: From the moment A's `DoSomethingOnBFromA` method is called, objects A, B, C, and D become conceptually dependent on one another; they are grouped in a common action. It is as if there is an electric impulse moving along a nerve, jumping synapses from A to B to C to D with a singular purpose. After the current flows from A to B, you want to be certain that D is still there and in the appropriate state to cooperate with the rest of the objects. However, when A first calls B, it is still possible for some alien thread to make a method call on object D before D is reached. All upstream objects are counting on D's contribution, but the danger exists that a foreign thread could manipulate D at the last moment. Thus, D might be put in a state now inappropriate for the method invocation it is about to receive and, therefore, the group action it is about to participate in. Fortunately, there is a way to protect against this scenario—COM+ activities.

I find it helpful to visualize a COM+ activity as a large, transparent dome covering a group of related objects. Any time a method call is made by an outside thread to any one object in the activity, the dome snaps opaque and no outside method invocations—that is, methods invoked by a thread not participating in the activity—are not allowed in to any object under the dome. When the method call completes, the dome turns transparent, and external method calls are again allowed in. This dome can spread to encompass objects on different machines in different processes and, as always, turn opaque the moment any one outside thread calls a method on any object, in any process on any machine within the dome until the call returns. Interestingly, even in the unlikely event that one object independently, spontaneously calls a method on another object within the activity not at the behest of an outside thread, the dome snaps opaque until the call completes.

If you are comfortable with the concept of the STA, it can be helpful to think of an activity as one big STA, serializing access to all objects within itself.

Configuration

Configuration of activities work in a fashion identical to COM+ transactions. The Concurrency tab of the properties for a configured component displays the same options as the Transactions tab. Specifically, it displays the following options:

- **Disabled**. Object does not require synchronization.
- **Not Supported**. Object cannot participate in an activity.
- **Supported**. Inherits an activity if its creator's context holds an activity. Otherwise, no new activity is created.
- **Required**. Inherits an activity if its creator's context holds an activity. If not, a new activity is created, and this object becomes the root.
- **Requires New**. A new activity is always created.

Note that, just as with transactions, an activity can span multiple processes and machines.

Activities and Transactions

All transactions must occur in an activity to make sure that isolation (the I in ACID, introduced in Chapter 8 "Transactions") is properly enforced. The same is true for Just-In-Time Activation (JITA), introduced and discussed in Chapter 8. If JITA is enabled for an object, that object must participate in an activity. Remember that JITA objects tend to be deactivated and pooled (or destroyed altogether in the case of VB6 objects) whenever a method call returns. Thus, JITA objects require activities to protect against a case where a method call made by one thread T1 is interrupted by a method call made by thread T2. If T2 completes its method call while T1 is blocked, JITA deactivates/destroys the object, thus pulling the rug out from T1. Activities prevent this from happening.

Transactions require both JITA support and activities, and Component Services automatically configure your component to use activities if transactions or JITA (or both) settings are enabled.

Object Pooling

CREATING AND DESTROYING OBJECTS IS expensive. Allocations, initialization, and deallocations all take a good deal of processor time that would be much better spent servicing functional requests from clients. COM+ seeks to reduce this overhead by implementing *object pooling*. If an object supports pooling (we talk about the requirements shortly), it has the option not to be destroyed when it is deactivated. Deactivation, as we discussed in Chapter 8, "Transactions," occurs when Just-In-Time Activation (JITA) is enabled for that object and one of the following occur:

- An object's Done bit is set to true, and a method invocation made on it returns.
- The client terminates or otherwise releases the object instance.

Deactivation does not mean termination for poolable objects as it does for non-poolable objects. Quite the contrary; pooled objects are sent to a kind of purgatory (the pool) where they remain alive and functional, albeit in a deactivated state. When COM+ receives a creation request for an object instance matching that in the pool, COM+ activates the pooled object and returns an interface to the client. The client might believe it created a new instance of the object, and even though this isn't the case, the client has no cause for complaint; a reactivated object does not retain any state from its previous caller and functions in a manner identical to a newly instantiated object.

Unfortunately, not every development environment can create poolable objects. VB 6 objects cannot be pooled. This is because to be pooled, an object must have the following characteristics:

- **Be aggregatable.** COM+'s pooling mechanism involves the use of an outer wrapping object that aggregates the pooled object within itself. Objects that do not support aggregation, therefore, cannot be created in the manner required by the COM+ pooling architecture.
- **Support the MTA or TNA threading model.** STA objects cannot be pooled due to the severe performance limitations of requiring all method calls to be serialized through one thread.

VB 6 is capable of neither. For the time being then, you must use C++ (preferably with Active Template Library [ATL]) to write poolable objects. That said, if you write a free or neutral threaded object in C++ that supports aggregation, it is automatically poolable. Although not strictly necessary, it is a good idea to implement the `IObjectControl` interface. The methods of `IObjectControl` are straightforward, as follows:

- `Activate`. COM+ calls this method to notify your object it has been activated and is currently engaged.
- `CanBePooled`. Your object returns true if it wants to give COM+ the permission to put it in the pool when it is deactivated; otherwise, it returns false. If your object returns false, it is destroyed when deactivated and causes a transaction (if it is in one) to be aborted.
- `Deactivate`. COM+ calls this method to let the object know it has been deactivated and is no longer servicing a client.

You are not strictly required to implement `IObjectControl` except in the case where you are writing a transactional pooled object. In this scenario, it is important for the object to know when it is being activated so that it can do the following:

- Get an interface to its new context by calling `CoGetObjectContext()`.
- Determine the transaction ID and/or interface of the transaction it is now participating in.
- Manually enlist its connection in this transaction.

> **CanBePooled: How Can It Return a Boolean?**
>
> This method actually returns a Boolean, as opposed to passing one by reference. Thus, in stark contrast to the protocol governing every established interface method in all of COM, the `Deactivate` and `CanBePooled` methods of `IObjectControl` do not return HRESULTs.

The first two points are self-explanatory. The final point, manually enlisting in the transaction, sounds complicated but isn't. You might remember from Chapter 8 (in the section "Resource Dispensers, A First Look") that when an object gets a connection to a Resource Manager (RM) via a Resource Dispenser (RD), such as the Open Database Connectivity (ODBC) driver manager, the Dispenser Manager (DispMan) investigates the context of the object. If a transaction is present in the object's context, DispMan then tells the RD to enlist the connection in a distributed transaction. COM+ performs this enlistment automatically for non-pooled objects but cannot do this for a pooled object; the same instance of a pooled object might participate in any number of transactions but likely uses the same database connection in every case. Thus, a poolable object must assume responsibility for enlisting the same database connection in the different transactions it finds itself participating in.

Normally, a pooled object does the following in its `Activate()` method:

- Gets its `IObjectContextInfo` interface.
- Calls `IObjectContextInfo`'s `GetTransaction()` method to get an interface to the transaction it is in.
- Calls `SQLSetConnectOption()` passing in the database connection handle and transaction interface. (Assuming it is using ODBC, this step differs depending on the RD used.)

The COM+ Platform SDK contains a good example of how the preceding actions might be implemented in the Account.Vc sample application. Assuming you have installed the Platform SDK (and you should), you can find this and other pooling examples in the following:

```
<install drive>:\Platform
SDK\Samples\COM\Services\Object_Pooling
```

Chapter 8 also includes an explanation of this process with a code example. See Listing 8.2.

D

Passing Block Data, SAFEARRAYs

CERTAIN MICROSOFT TECHNOLOGIES ARE EXTREMELY useful, relatively easy to use, and almost impossible to find coherent documentation or examples for. A *SAFEARRAY* is just such a creature. Simply put, VB arrays are represented internally as something called a SAFEARRAY. SAFEARRAYs can be multi-dimensional, have esoteric locking considerations, and have some of the most confusing, obscure, and unhelpful documentation I've come across. In spite of this, they are very useful; they can allow you to pass arbitrary-length blocks of data over the network using type library marshaling.

Type library marshaling is the default, pre-installed marshaler that enables COM to send basic types as arguments to your interface methods—integers, doubles, strings, and so on. But what about sending large blocks of data with a single method call? If you want to send an array of, let's say, 100 integers, things get tricky. You can either make 100 method calls passing one integer each time, or you can resort to *standard marshaling*. Standard marshaling allows you to pass any C++ data type and most arrays and structures. The downside is that you must use C++ and ship a proxy/stub DLL (unless you merge the proxy/stub DLL into the COM DLL, which is also an option). Even if you go to this trouble of implementing a proxy/stub DLL, VB can only use interfaces that use OLE automation types. The existence of a proxy/stub DLL usually indicates that non-automation types are being marshaled via standard marshaling; thus, a VB client or server would not be able to interact with your component. This means that, for the most part, you cannot send blocks or arrays of data to VB using standard marshaling.

This brings us to SAFEARRAYs. Arrays in VB can be sent using type library marshaling, because VB arrays are considered OLE automation types. As I've said, the underlying representation of a VB array is a SAFEARRAY, and what is simple in VB becomes somewhat complex in C++. However, code examples should make things clear. In the companion code for this book (www.newriders.com/complus), I've included a directory called safearrays that includes a series of examples demonstrating how to pass arrays from C++ to VB and vice versa. SAFEARRAYs don't have anything to do with C++ *per se*, but they are a useful tool to have in COM+ development.

It is difficult to give SAFEARRAYs adequate coverage without a dedicated chapter, so I'm going to leave it to the source code accompanying this book to explore a number of detailed SAFEARRAY scenarios and permutations. However, just to give you a preview, let's take a look at how an array of VB strings can be sent to and interpreted by a C++ component using SAFEARRAYs.

Imagine that you have the following VB client:

```
'Throw a few strings together into an array
Dim astrColour(0 To 3) As String
astrColour(0) = "Purple"
astrColour(1) = "Yellow"
astrColour(2) = "Green"
astrColour(3) = "Red"

Dim UseSafearray As New SERVERLib.UseSafearray
Call UseSafearray.DisplayStrings(astrColour)
```

To receive a VB array (a SAFEARRAY, remember), the IDL for the C++ component UseSafearray needs to be the following:

```
//snippet of IDL
interface IUseSafearray : IDispatch
    {
        [id(1), helpstring("method DisplayStrings")] HRESULT DisplayStrings
        ➥([in] SAFEARRAY(BSTR) *psa);
```

Note that VB strings are BSTRs in C++. A BSTR is simply an array of two-byte shorts, two bytes for every character. The first four bytes of a BSTR constitute a long that indicates the length of the string. Don't worry, there are a number of BSTR wrapper classes that make them much easier to work with.

The following code retrieves and displays the strings of this array in C++:

```
STDMETHODIMP CUseSafearray::DisplayStrings(SAFEARRAY** ppsa)
{

    LONG nLBound = 0;
    //    Get lower bound of first dimension
    hr = ::SafeArrayGetLBound(*ppsa, 1, &nLBound);
    ATLASSERT(SUCCEEDED(hr));
```

```
    //    Get upper bound of first dimension
    LONG nUBound = 0;
    hr = ::SafeArrayGetUBound(*ppsa, 1, &nUBound);

    BSTR* pbstrElement = NULL;

CComBSTR bstrComposite = _
T("We received and unpacked the strings: ");

hr = ::SafeArrayAccessData(*ppsa, (void**)&pbstrElement);

for(LONG nI = nLBound; nI <= nUBound; nI++)
    {
            bstrComposite += pbstrElement[nI];
    }

::MessageBox(NULL, (TCHAR*)bstrComposite, _T("[SERVER] 
   CUseSafearray::DisplayStrings()"), MB_OK);
    //    Done with guts of the array - sew it back up
    hr = ::SafeArrayUnaccessData(*ppsa);

}
```

E

Queue Moniker Parameters

We learn in Chapter 10, "Queued Components," that Queued Components rely on MSMQ for asynchronocity. The queue moniker is used to instantiate queued components and can also be used to set MSMQ-specific properties affecting how messages are delivered to these components. This gives the COM+ client author some additional control over how and where MSMQ ultimately delivers its method calls. For example, consider the following moniker string:

    Set b = GetObject("queue:MaxTimeToReachQueue=10/new:Some.Component")

The `MaxTimeToReachQueue` parameter shown here allows you to specify the maximum time a message has to reach its destination queue before an error is triggered. If you are using MSMQ directly, you will find that one of the properties of an `MSMQMessage` object is `MaxTimeToReachQueue`. Most of the string parameters that queue monikers are designed to understand have direct property equivalents at the MSMQ level.

COM+ exposes only a subset of all the message attributes available directly through MSMQ, because many of these attributes are populated by COM+ itself. (The `Extension` attribute, for example, is populated by COM+ and thus is not exposed as a moniker parameter.)

Some important parameters that can be specified using the queue moniker are given in the following sections. These can be grouped into two sets: one set that affects the queue the message is sent to and another that affects the message itself.

Parameters That Affect the Destination Queue

In MSMQ, there are two ways to specify the location of a queue. One way is to use the `FormatName` property, which allows you to specify the queue location in a number of different formats. The second way is the `PathName` property. I will discuss the former first.

FormatName

`FormatName` can take on the following variations:

- FormatName=PUBLIC=QueueGUID
- FormatName=PRIVATE=MachineGUID\QueueNumber
- FormatName=DIRECT=Protocol:MachineAddress\QueueName
- FormatName=DIRECT=OS:MachineName\QueueName

Let's consider each option in turn.

1. FormatName=PUBLIC=QueueGUID

   You can only use the PUBLIC specifier when operating on an Active Directory network. This option requires that you know the GUID of the queue you want to communicate to, as in the following:

   Example: FormatName=PUBLIC=984A8A7E-6054-42e3-A4C4-F94F3D2DF55A

   If you know the computer name and queue name, this GUID value can be obtained by using the MSMQ API function `MQPathNameToFormatName`. This API takes a given `PathName` (MachineX\QueueY) and provides you with the PUBLIC GUID of that queue. If you have the path name, however, you can use the `PathName` attribute listed in the next section, "*PathName*." This option is really for the rare cases where you only have the queue GUID.

2. FormatName=PRIVATE=MachineGUID\QueueNumber

   Use the PRIVATE specifier to access private queues on the network. Private queues are not registered in Active Directory and require that you specify the machine GUID and the queue number of the destination queue, as in the following:

   Example: FormatName=PRIVATE=AE4D13C4-CE13-4fea-8B8C-0C75FBE47BE8\0000000ff

   The machine GUID can be obtained using the MSMQ: `MQGetMachineProperties` API.

3. FormatName=DIRECT=Protocol:MachineAddress\QueueName

4. FormatName=DIRECT=OS:MachineName\QueueName

   The DIRECT specifier is useful when working with networks that don't have Active Directory or to access queues outside an Active Directory network. Also note that in a Workgroup setup (a network without Active Directory), the only way to access a remote queue is to use the DIRECT specifier.

The `DIRECT` specifier has two parts: the address specifying the location of the destination machine and the name of the queue on that machine. You can specify one of the supported protocols and address (TCP/SPX) or use the computer's underlying protocol and specify the machine name using the OS specifier. The following are all valid examples:

```
Examples:
FormatName=DIRECT=OS:Sajid\SajidsQueue
FormatName=DIRECT=TCP:202.10.6.12\SajidsQueue
FormatName=DIRECT=SPX:00000322:00b3335f1551\SajidsQueue
```

For private queues, note that the queue name is preceded by the `Private$` specifier:

```
FormatName=DIRECT=OS:Sajid\Private$\SomePrivateQueue
```

PathName

The `PathName` parameter is used very much like the last two variants (of the `FormatName` parameter. It allows you to specify the full path name of the destination queue. Use this parameter by specifying both the computer and queue name, as in the following:

```
PathName=Sajid\SajidsQueue
PathName=Sajid\Private$\SomePrivateQueue
```

You can also specify that the local machine should be used by using the `.` specifier, as in the following:

```
PathName=.\SajidsQueue
PathName=.\Private$\SomePrivateQueue
```

This attribute has a maximum string length of `MQ_MAX_Q_NAME_LEN` characters, which at the time of this writing is 124 UNICODE characters.

ComputerName and QueueName

There are two additional moniker parameters that COM+ allows you to specify to determine the location of the destination queue. Recall that the `PathName` parameter consists of two parts: the `computername` and the `queuename`. COM+ allows you to specify these individually using the appropriately named `ComputerName` and `QueueName` parameters.

Thus, the following two initialization strings are the same:

```
Set b = GetObject("queue:PathName=Sajid\SajidsQueue/new:Some.Component")
Set b = GetObject("queue:ComputerName=Sajid,QueueName=SajidsQueue/
↪new:Some.Component")
```

COM+ is amalgamating the `QueueName` and `ComputerName` parameters in the second string, to produce the `PathName` in the first string.

If you use the `QueueName` parameter by itself, COM+ assumes the `ComputerName` to be the local computer. Thus, the following two moniker strings are also the same:

```
Set b = GetObject("queue:PathName=.\SajidsQueue/new:Some.Component")
Set b = GetObject("queue:QueueName=SajidsQueue/new:Some.Component")
```

The only complication that arises is when you use the `ComputerName` parameter without using the `QueueName` parameter. Consider the following string:

```
Set b = GetObject("queue:ComputerName=AnotherComputer/new:Some.Component")
```

In this case, how does COM+ determine what queue it will send messages to on `AnotherComputer`? COM+ makes an educated guess based on the local configuration. Remember that the destination queue is determined by the name of the COM+ application in which the component resides. Because no `QueueName` has been specified on the remote machine, COM+ uses the local application to determine the queue it should send to. (This is why a queued component must be installed locally, even if it will only be run on remote machines.)

Thus, if the COM+ applications housing the queued component are named differently on the local and remote machines (and hence their respective queues are different), COM+ sends the message to the wrong queue on the remote machine—if it exists in the first place. However, queued components exhibit some interesting behavior if this happens; when a COM+ application receives a message not meant for it, it re-routes the message to the proper COM+ application housing the intended component. In addition, unauthenticated messages get authenticated during the process.

Parameters That Affect the MSMQ Message

The parameters described in the following sections affect the underlying MSMQ message sent on behalf of the queued component.

AppSpecific

`AppSpecific` (long) allows you to specify application-specific information to be used by the receiver of the message. This doesn't make sense in the context of Queued Components, because the receiver of the message is most likely the QC.Player, which discards this information anyway. Below is an example of using the `AppSpecific` parameter:

```
Set b = GetObject("queue:AppSpecific=2000/new:Some.Component")
```

AuthLevel

`AuthLevel` (long) determines whether MSMQ should authenticate the messages it sends out. The default value for this attribute is derived from the local application housing the component in question. This attribute gives you explicit control over authentication and is useful in situations where the destination queue resides on a remote computer. It can either be turned ON (MQMSG_AUTH_LEVEL_ALWAYS) or OFF (MQMSG_AUTH_LEVEL_NONE). The following line of code tells MSMQ to authenticate all the messages it sends out:

```
Set b = GetObject("queue:AuthLevel=MQMSG_AUTH_LEVEL_ALWAYS/new:Some.Component")
```

Delivery

Delivery (long) determines if the message being sent is written to disk prior to the delivery attempt. You specify that the message should be written to disk by setting this value to MQMSG_DELIVERY_RECOVERABLE. If speed is of the essence and you are willing to sacrifice the durability this option provides, you can turn it off by setting this value equal to MQMSG_DELIVERY_EXPRESS. Bear in mind that if the destination queue is transactional, COM+ automatically sets this option to MQMSG_DELIVERY_RECOVERABLE, such that the message can be sent repeatedly if required. The line of code below tells MSMQ NOT to write messages to disk before it sends them out:

```
Set b = GetObject("queue:Delivery=MQMSG_DELIVERY_EXPRESS/new:Some.Component")
```

EncryptAlgorithm

EncryptAlgorithm (long) allows you to specify the algorithm MSMQ uses to encrypt outgoing messages. The following are two options that are available:

- CALG_RC2. Microsoft's RC2 block encryption algorithm (default).
- CALG_RC4. Microsoft's RC4 stream encryption algorithm (stronger).

The code below tells MSMQ to encrypt messages using the RC4 encryption scheme:

```
Set b = GetObject("queue:EncryptAlgorithm=CALG_RC4/new:Some.Component")
```

Consult the MSDN documentation on the Crypto API for information regarding these encryption techniques. The portions of your message that are encrypted using the specified technique can be specified using the PrivLevel attribute.

HashAlgorithm

HashAlgorithm (long) determines the hash algorithm MSMQ will use to authenticate the message. MSMQ uses such algorithms to compute a hash value based on the body of the message being sent. It attaches this value to the message itself. When the recipient receives it, it computes a hash value using the same algorithm and compares it to the attached value. If they match, the message is said to be authentic—that is, the contents of the body haven't changed during transmission of the message.

You can specify any of the following algorithms: CALG_MD2, CALG_MD4, CALG_MD5, CALG_SHA, CALG_SHA1, CALG_MAC, CALG_SSL3_SHAMD5, CALG_HMAC, or CALG_TLS1PRF.

```
Set b = GetObject("queue:HashAlgorithm=CALG_MD5/new:Some.Component")
```

Consult the Crypto API documentation for specific information on each.

Journal

`Journal` (long) determines what happens when a message is retrieved from the queue it has been sent to. Options for this attribute are the following:

- `MQMSG_JOURNAL_NONE`. Messages are discarded after they are retrieved from the queue.
- `MQMSG_DEADLETTER`. Messages are moved to the deadletter queue (sometimes referred to as the Dead Message Queue) after they are retrieved.
- `MQMSG_JOURNAL`. Messages are moved to the journal queue after they are retrieved. This is the default setting.

    Set b = GetObject("queue:Journal=MQMSG_JOURNAL_NONE/new:Some.Component")

Label

`Label` (string) allows you to specify a string describing the message. If you specify this attribute, all messages that COM+ sends for this queued component will contain the label you specify. Keep in mind that the `label` attribute has no effect on the operation of queued components themselves and is really only used for information purposes as shown in Figure E.1.

    Set b = GetObject("queue:Label=Your-Label-Here/new:Some.Component")

This attribute has a maximum string length of `MQ_MAX_MSG_LABEL_LEN` characters, which at the time of this writing is 250 UNICODE characters.

MaxTimeToReachQueue

`MaxTimeToReachQueue` (long) determines the maximum amount of time the message has to reach its destination queue, before it is moved to the location specified by the `Journal` attribute. This attribute can take on the following values:

- `INFINITE`. Messages remains in the queue infinitely (default).
- `LONG_LIVED`. This value can be adjusted by an MSMQ administrator. The default value is 90 days.

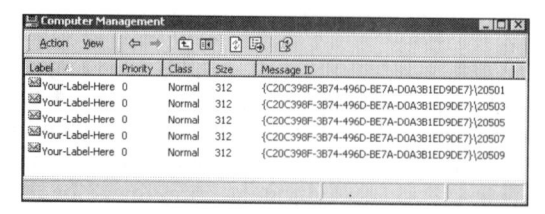

Figure E.1 How the `Label` attribute describes messages in COM+.

Alternatively, you can specify the number of seconds a message will wait in the queue before it is removed to its alternate location. Used in conjunction with the `Journal` `MQMSG_DEADLETTER` setting, this option can be used to trigger an Exception class if the message is not sent within a given amount of time.

    Set b = GetObject("queue:MaxTimeToReachQueue=15/new:Some.Component")

MaxTimeToReceive

`MaxTimeToReceive` (long) is similar to the `MaxTimeToReachQueue` attribute—the difference being that it specifies the amount of time the message has to be removed from its destination queue, before it is moved to the location specified by the `Journal` attribute. Like the `MaxTimeToReachQueue` property, this attribute can take on three values: `INFITE`, `LONG_LIVED`, or an integer equal to the number of seconds to wait.

    Set b = GetObject("queue:MaxTimeToRecieve=LONG_LIVED/new:Some.Component")

Priority

`Priority` (long) determines the priority of the message being sent. MSMQ uses this value to give preference to higher priority messages during the routing process and also to determine where the message is placed in the queue itself. This attribute can take on one of the following values: `MQ_MIN_PRIORITY` (0), `MQ_MAX_PRIORITY` (7), `MQ_DEFAULT_PRIORITY` (3), or a number between 0 and 7.

    Set b = GetObject("queue:Priority=MQ_MIN_PRIORITY/new:Some.Component")

Note that when the destination queue is transactional, MSMQ ignores this attribute and uses a priority of 0.

PrivLevel

`PrivLevel` (long) determines the level to which outgoing messages are encrypted. This attribute can take on the following values:

- `MQMSG_PRIV_LEVEL_NONE`. The message is not encrypted at all (default).
- `MQMSG_PRIV_LEVEL_BODY`. The message body is encrypted using a 40-bit encryption technique.
- `MQMSG_PRIV_LEVEL_BODY_BASE`. The message body is encrypted using a 40-bit encryption technique (same as the preceding option).
- `MQMSG_PRIV_LEVEL_BODY_ENHANCED`. The message body is encrypted using a 128-bit encryption technique. This is the most secure of all the options.

    Set b = GetObject("queue:PrivLevel=MQMSG_PRIV_LEVEL_BODY/new:Some.Component")

When any of the last three options are specified, the encryption technique to be used is determined by the `EncryptAlgorithm` attribute.

Trace

Trace (long) determines whether MSMQ generates report messages when and if it routes this message to a remote machine. Following are the values available for this option:

- MQMSG_TRACE_NONE. MSMQ does not produce any report messages when this message is routed (default).
- MQMSG_SEND_ROUTE_TO_REPORT_QUEUE. MSMQ produces report messages as this message is routed. Report messages are sent to the report queue that is specified by the Queue Manager.

    Set b = GetObject("queue:Trace=MQMSG_SEND_ROUTE_TO_REPORT_QUEUE/ new:Some.Component")

Again, this option only works in the context of an Active Directory setup.

F

Application Proxies

BY DEFINITION, A COM+ APPLICATION expects to have clients on other machines. The following question then arises: What do you distribute to your clients? In traditional COM, you have several options when distributing components to remote users:

- **Distribute nothing**. Client applications can only communicate with your components using late binding.
- **Distribute type library**. Client applications can communicate with your components using early and late binding.
- **Distribute type library and proxy/stub DLL**. If you are using non-automation types as arguments to your interface methods, you need to ship a proxy DLL to your client.

To instantiate your component remotely, assuming NT 4.0 and VB 6.0, the client must do either of the following:

- Use the DCOMCNFG.EXE utility and specify that your component should always be run on a specific remote machine even if requested locally. In this way, any local creation requests made via `CoCreateInstance()` or VB's `CreateObject` or `New` results in the component being instantiated on the remote machine.

Appendix F Application Proxies

- Instead of `CoCreateInstance()`, use `CoCreateInstanceEx()` to specify a remote machine name when creating a component. In VB, two arguments must be passed to `CreateObject()`, the first being the ProgID of the component and the second being the machine name.

COM+ automates the distribution and installation process. Specifically, it can export applications for automatic installation on other machines. During the export process, COM+ packages all facets of the application (contained components, the component and application settings) into one, easily distributable file. This file can then be imported into another machine just as easily as it was exported.

There are two options when exporting a COM+ application. One option is to completely export the application for installation on another server machine. You do this when you are finished developing the application and its components and are ready to deploy it on the production server. The other option is of interest to client machines, and it allows you to export the COM+ application as an application proxy. Application proxies can be installed on a client machine such that all the components on that machine point to components on the server machine. When the component is run on any machine where the application proxy was imported, it executes on the machine where the proxy was exported.

Consider a simple COM component written in Visual Basic called AppProxy. On machine A, you create an application named ProxyApp and install your component under it (see Figure F.1).

Now, let's export this application by right-clicking the application and selecting Export (see Figure F.2).

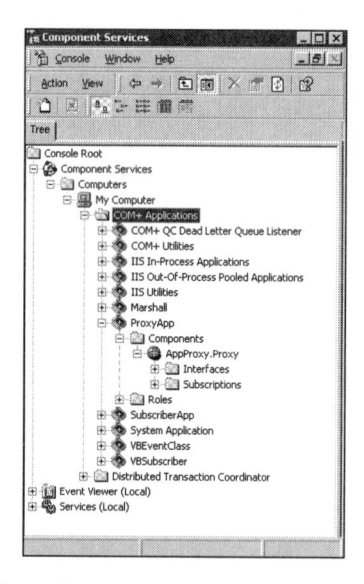

Figure F.1 The ProxyApp application.

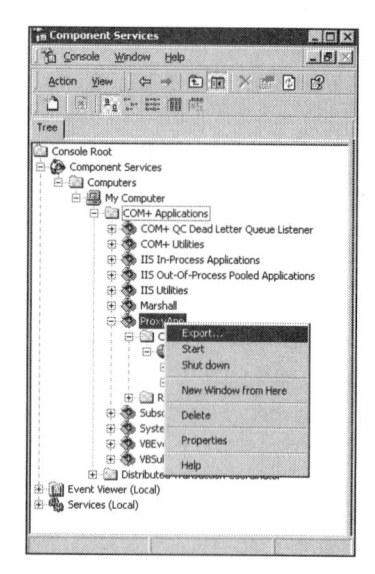

Figure F.2 Exporting the application.

Doing this brings up the COM Application Export Wizard, shown in Figure F.3. Give the exported application a filename (this is the file you will use to reconstruct the application on machine B) and select the Application Proxy option. If you do not select the Application Proxy option, when the application is reconstructed on other machines, all the components are locally installed and run on that machine.

Click Next; if all goes well, COM+ exports the application for you (see Figure F.4).

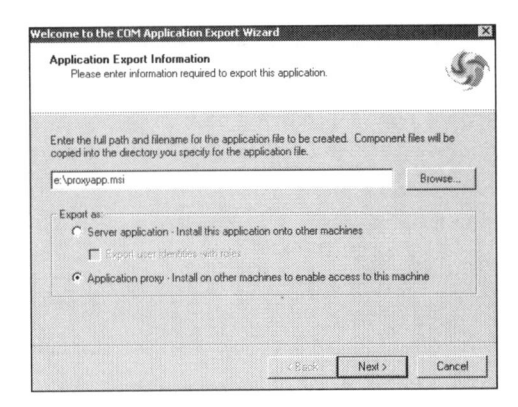

Figure F.3 Exporting to a filename.

Figure F.4 A successful application export.

426 Appendix F Application Proxies

Take the MSI file that COM+ produces and copy it to machine B. Install the application on the machine as an application proxy by starting the COM Application Installation Wizard and selecting Install pre-built application(s) (see Figure F.5).

Selecting the first option allows you to select the filename of the application you want to install. Here, select the proxyapp.MSI file that you created on machine A. Doing so brings up the screen shown in Figure F.6.

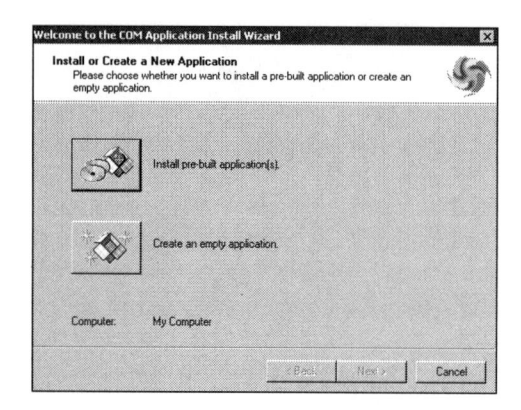

Figure F.5 Installing a pre-built application.

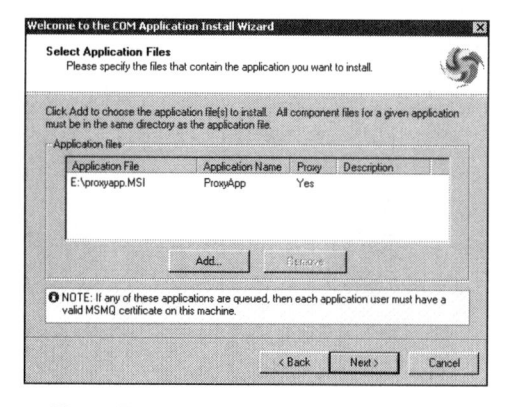

Figure F.6 Installing the application proxy.

Note that COM+ has detected this is as a proxy application. Clicking Next allows you to choose where you want the application installed locally (see Figure F.7).

Accept the default and click Next. If all goes well, COM+ installs the application proxy on your machine, as shown in Figure F.8.

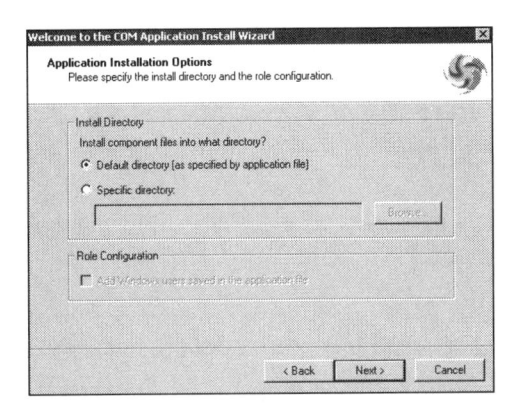

Figure F.7 Selecting the destination.

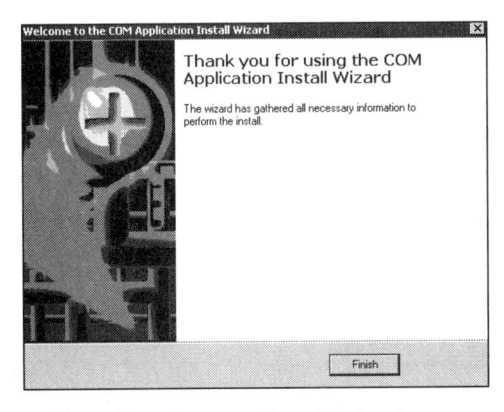

Figure F.8 A successful application import.

During the installation process, COM+ installs the information it needs to access the application remotely. This includes the following information:

- Application identity information (AppIDs, CLSIDs, and ProgIDs).
- The name of the remote machine.
- Marshaling information for all components (type libraries and proxy/stubs).
- MSMQ queue names and identifiers (if the Queued Components service is enabled for the application).
- Application, component, and method attributes.

COM+ actually stores a copy of DLL(s) (and any associated proxy/stub DLLS) on the local computer in the following directory:\Program Files\COMPlus Applications\{Application-GUID}\.

Installing Application Proxies on NT 4

Behind the scenes, components executed on the local machine are instantiated and execute on the remote machine and communicate through DCOM. As such, the only requirement for the local machine is that it be DCOM capable (and have the Windows Installer to process the exported MSI file).

Thus, although a configured component can only execute on a Windows 2000 machine, it can be exported and called by any operating system supporting DCOM. Because this scenario is likely to be commonplace during Windows 2000 migration efforts where NT 4 clients are likely, I will demonstrate it here.

To install application proxies (MSI files) on non-Windows 2000 platforms, you must have the Windows Installer (instmsi.exe), a free utility and SDK available from Microsoft (http://msdn.microsoft.com/downloads/sdks/platform/wininst.asp) installed on the destination machine. As an example, we will install the previously exported application (proxyapp.msi) on an NT 4 machine. Follow these steps:

1. On the Windows NT machine, go to the Control Panel and run Add/Remove Programs, which brings up the dialog box shown in Figure F.9.
2. Click Install and select the proxyapp.MSI file (see Figure F.10).
3. Click Finish.

At this point, the Window Installer takes over and installs the application and its associated components on the NT 4 machine, such that they point to the Windows 2000 machine. Because the components execute on the Windows 2000 machine, they can participate in all COM+ services, even though the calling machine is not COM+ capable.

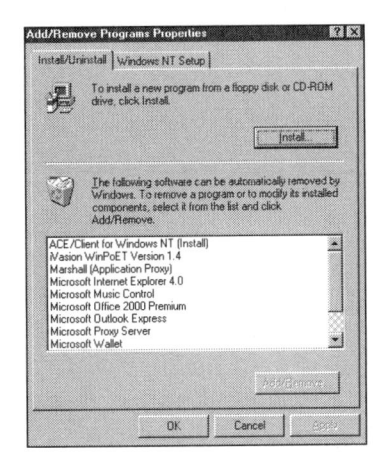

Figure F.9 Add/Remove Programs on NT 4.

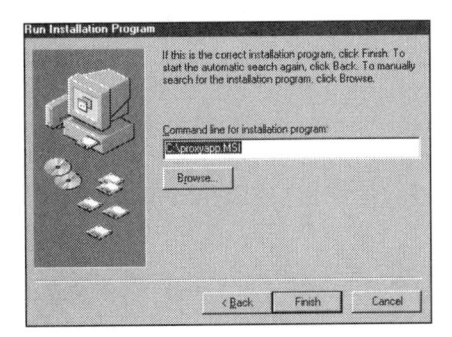

Figure F.10 Selecting the filename on NT 4.

Note that there is one significant restriction with the application proxy technique involving the use of Queued Components. Recall that Queued Components are instantiated using the queue moniker, a feature exclusive to Windows 2000. It is not possible, therefore, to instantiate and use Queued Components directly from non-Windows 2000 machines. During the installation process, the Windows Installer does the following:

- Stores a local copy of DLL(s) and associated proxy/stub DLL(s) in \Program Files\COMPlus Applications\{Application-GUID}\.
- Makes the appropriate Registry entries, such that the component could be accessed on the remote machine using DCOM.

You now can use the component as you do any other standard component. The difference is that it executes on the remote machine.

Index

Symbols

#import directive, 71-72
3GigSupportEnabled property, 174, 177

A

aborting transactions, 248, 273-274
AbortRecordVariants() method, 274
abstract base classes, 63-75, 81-85
access
    programmatic security and method arguments, 367
    Universal Data (UDA), 400
AccessChecksLevel property, 171
account database, 242-243
accounts, software, 369
ACID, 227-228
Activate method, 408-409
activation
    Just-In-Time (JITA), 248, 405
    pooled objects, 218
Activation property, 172
Active Directory, 311
Active Server Pages (ASPs), 181, 183
    contexts, 221
    transactions, 252-253
    type libraries, 129
Active Template Library (ATL), 21
ActiveX control, 256, 302
ActiveX Data Objects (ADOs), 243, 399-401
activities, synchronization, 403-405
activity information, objects, 207
Add() function, 15, 38
adding
    applications
        catalogs, 177-178
        COM+, 164-166
    COMCalc instances, clients, 51-52
    components
        COM, Visual Basic (VB), 28
        catalogs, 178
    distributed transactions, Distributed Transaction Coordinator (DTC), 235-236
    event classes, 336-338
    instances, ICalc class, 70
    objects
        Calc, Visual Basic (VB), 37
        Calculator, 21-28
        COM, C++, 66-68
        intrinsic IIS, contexts, 222-223
        queued, monikers, 298-302
    publisher filters, 350-354
    QUEQUEABLE tags, IDL declarations, 296
    queues, 291-292
    threads, AddressOf operator, 96
AddRef() function, 45-48
AddressOf operator, creating threads, 96
administration objects
    adding applications and components, 177-178
    components, 176-177
    marking applications and interfaces queueable, 295-296
    properties, 171-176
administrative layer. *See* catalogs

ADO (ActiveX Data Objects), 243, 399-401
Advise() method, 334
advisesinks, 143
aggregation
   FTM objects, 124
   support, IObjectControl interface, 408
aides, synchronization, 97-101
AllowInprocSubscribers property, 174
Anonymous setting, 382
apartment GUIDs, components obtaining, 208
Apartment value, 117
apartment-threaded objects, 111
apartments, 97-102, 106, 117, 122, 125, 215
   Multi-Threaded (MTA), 104-108
   Single-Threaded (STA), 104-105, 109-110
      pooled objects, 408
      serialization, 403-405
   Thread Neutral (TNA), 125-126, 217
APE (Application Performance Explorer), 190
Application Performance Explorer (APE), 190
application proxies, 423-428
ApplicationAccessChecksEnabled property, 172
ApplicationID property, 174
ApplicationProxy property, 172
ApplicationProxyServerName property, 172
applications
   COM+
      configuring components, 160-184
      pre-installed, 180-190
      shutting down, changing identities, and restarting, 179-180
   distributing, 423-428

Excel
   changing cells in spreadsheets, notifying VB clients, 332
   as COM+ component, 142
   controlling remotely, 130-131
   exporting, 424-425
   identity, 367-369
   IntelliSense, 19
   library, 70, 106, 365-366
   marking queueable, Admin objects, 295-296
   multi-threaded, 94
   OLEView.EXE, 31-34
   queuable settings, 302-304
   Regsvr32.exe, 56
   Spy++, 102
   TrackerServer, 184
   Visual Studio, 190, 337
AppSpecific parameter, 418
architecture, late binding, 132-133
arguments
   invoke, marshaling, 134
   methods
      determining access, 367
      evaluating, publisher filter properties, 356-357
      variants as, 136
   named_guids, 72
   no_namespace, 72
   pbForget, 271
arrays
   SAFEARRAYs, passing block data, 137, 411-412
   vargs, 140
ASP. *See* Active Server Pages
associated methods, 247-250
associating publisher filters with event classes, 347-350
assuming identify of callers. *See* impersonating callers
async uuid attribute, IDL declarations of interfaces, 327
Asynchronous COM, 327-330
asynchronous events, firing, 343

C++ programming language   433

asynchronous method calls, 288-289, 294-297
AsyncITester interface, 328-329
ATL (Active Template Library), 21
atomicity, transactions, 228
attribute groups, interfaces, 23
attributes
  async uuid, IDL declarations of interfaces with, 327
  Extension, 415
  See also parameters
authentication, 305, 380-383
Authentication drop-down box, 366
Authentication property, 172
AuthLevel parameter, 418
automating configurations, components and applications, 171-179
automation, OLE. *See* late binding

B

bags, 357
balancing, load, 5
base clients, voting, 246
BEGIN TRANSACTION command, 227-231
BeginAbortVariants() method, 274
BeginCommitVariants() method, 272-275
BeginPrepareVariants() method, 271-272
benchmarks, Transaction Processing Council (TPC-C), 226
binary files, dumping message contents into, 314
binding, 299
  early, 128-130
  late, 128-155
bits, Happy and Done (HD), 247

block data, passing, 411-412
blocks
  interface, 36
  type. *See* type libraries
BLOWUP queue messages, 309
Booleans, returning, 408
borrowing credentials of callers to modify files created by, 374
Both value, 118
boundaries, security, 369-383
Box, Don, 214
Brovick, Edgar, 311
BSTR, 412
buttons
  Leave running when idle, 162
  Minutes until idle shutdown, 162
  radio
    Interactive User, 368
    Perform Access Checks, 364-365
    This User, 369
ByVal keyword, 302

C

C programming language, generating files, 26
C++ programming language
  clients, 70-73
  components, returning context GUIDs as strings, 210-212
  implementations
    CalcSDK coclass, 27
    coclasses, 26-28
    COM classes, 75-80
  interfaces
    IDispatch, 138
    IUnknown, 41-51
    support, calculation objects, 9
  raw functions, 39
  Variant data type, 136
  virtual function tables (vtables), abstract base classes, and polymorphism, 63-75, 81-85
  writing COM objects, 66-68

434 Calc coclass

Calc coclass, 37
Calc interface, Visual Basic (VB), 36
Calc objects
   creating, Visual Basic (VB), 37
   method declarations, 38-39
   releasing, 43-48
   support, IUnknown interface, 49
CALC.H header file, 44-45
Calccoclass, 42-43
CalcSDK coclass, implementation in C++, 27
CalcSDK object, Interface Definition Language (IDL) description, 22
calcsdk.tlh header file, 71-72
calcsdk.tli header file, 71-72
calculation objects, support in C++ interfaces, 9
Calculator objects, creating, 21-28
CALG RC2 value, 419
CALG RC4 value, 419
Call setting, 381
CallBackObj class, 323
callbacks, 321-325
caller chains, 370
callers, 367-394
Callers property, 371
calling stored procedures, ActiveX Data Objects, 402
calls
   cross-apartment, 119
   FTM to STA objects, 121
   function, aggregating FTM objects, 124
   method
      asynchronous, 288-297
      indempotent, 307
      synchronous, 288
      viewing as messages, 305-307
   Remote Procedure (RPC), 7, 14, 19, 288

CanBePooled method, 408
candidacy, 297
casting, ICalc and IFinancial objects, 70
catalogs
   COM+ applications, configuring components, 160-184
   Cycle Redundancy Checks (CRCs), 190-191
   origin of, 157-160
Catsrv.CatalogServer.1 component, 184
cells, changing in Excel spreadsheets, 332
chains, caller, 370
Changeable property, 172
changing
   cells in Excel spreadsheets, notifying Visual Basic (VB) clients, 332
   files
      callers, 374
      XML, account balances, 261-268
   identities, COM+ applications, 179-180
   menus and dialog boxes, 54
channels, 48-49
check boxes
   Enable Authentication, 366
   Enforce Access Checks for This Application, 364-365
   Fire in Parallel, 343
   Listen, 304
   Queued, 303-304
   Use All Event Classes That Implement This Interface, 341
Clarke, Arthur C., 239
class factories, 83-85
classes
   abstract base, 63-75, 81-85
   CallBackObj, 323
   COM
      implementations of, 66, 75-80
      Registry entries, 57
   event, 335-338, 347-350

COM objects

exception, 324-325
ICalc, creating instances, 70
implementation supporting ICalc
  and IFinancial interfaces, 149-150
ListenerHelper, 301, 304
nested, 81
new, 299-300
NumberClass, 316
queue, 299-300
ServerCallBack, implementing, 322
See also coclasses

Clerk coclass. *See*
  CRMClerk coclass

client executables. *See* **base clients**

client-server connections, 333

client-side symmetry, 326

clients
  base, voting, 246
  C++, 70-73
  casting, ICalc and IFinancial, 70
  connection points, 334
  creating COMCalc instances, 51-52
  explicit association of publisher
    filters, 349-350
  hung, troubleshooting, 343
  implementations of COM classes,
    75-80
  interface usage, 13
  Java, 10
  multi-threaded
    passing interfaces between threads,
    115-116
  object lifetimes, 47-48
  VB
    notifying of cell changes in Excel
    spreadsheets, 332
  VB, message received from queue by,
    293
  VB, message sent to queue by, 290
  Visual Basic (VB), 12

cloaking, xi, 377-395

closing queues, 293-294

CLSID property, 174

coclasses, 19
  Calc, 37, 42-43
  CalcSDK, implementation in
    C++, 27
  Clerk, 259-260
  Compensator, 259-284
  CRMClerk, 259-260
  implementing, C++, 26, 28
  Interface Definition Language (IDL)
    files, 25-26
  Worker, 258-260, 269-275
  wrappers, Interface Definition
    Language (IDL) file, 154
  See also classes

CoCreateInstance method, 247

CoCreateInstance() function, 84

Codd, Edgar, 255

code, specifying Globally Unique
  Identifiers (GUIDs) in, 80

code listings. *See* **source code**
  listings

CoGetClassObject() function,
  83-84

CoGetClassObject() method, 85-86

CoGetObjectContext()
  method, 194

CoImpersonateClient() method,
  373, 377

CoInitializeSecurity() method,
  381-383

COM Application Install Wizard,
  164-166

COM classes
  implementations of, 66, 75-80
  Registry entries, 57

COM Component Install Wizard,
  168-171

COM component, creating in
  Visual Basic, 28

COM objects
  implementing, Visual C++, 21-28
  location of, 53-61
  writing in C++, 66-68

COM+ administration objects, associating event classes with publisher filters, 348-349

COM+ applications
configuring components, 160-184
pre-installed, 180-190
shutting down, changing identities, and restarting, 179-180

COM+ Queued Components, 294-325

COM+ transactions, 239-252

COMAdminCatalog objects, 176

COMAdminCatalogCollection objects, 176-177

COMAdminCatalogObject objects, 177

CoMarshalInterThreadInterfaceInStream() function, 112-117

CoMarshalInterthreadInterfaceInStream() method, 215

COMCalc object
clients creating instances of, 51-52
example of, 75-81, 83, 85
Interface Definition Language (IDL) file, 50
relationship with ICalc and IFinancial vtables, 68, 70

comcalc.h file, 28

CommandLine property, 172

commands
BEGIN TRANSACTION, 227-231
COMMIT, 227, 231, 244
COMMIT TRANSACTION, 229-230
ROLLBACK, 227-231, 244
Server.Execute and Server.Transfer, 252

COMMIT command, 227, 231, 244

Commit phase, 233-234, 272-275

COMMIT TRANSACTION command, 229-230

CommitRecordsVariants() method, 273

Compensating Resource Managers (CRMs), 255-256
aborting transactions, 273-274
components, 258-259, 269-276, 282-284
handling recovery, 274-275
isolation, 284
two-phase commit protocol, 275-276

Compensator coclass, 259-260, 269-276, 282-284

compilers, changing menus and dialog boxes in Visual C++, 54

compiling Interface Definition Language (IDL) files, 17-18

Component A source code, 242

Component B source code, 243

components
borrowing credentials of callers to modify files owned by, 374
C++, returning context GUIDs as strings, 210-212
Catsrv.CatalogServer.1, 184
COM, creating in Visual Basic (VB), 28
COM+, Microsoft Office as, 142
Compensating Resource Manager (CRM), 258-259, 269-284
COMSSVCS.TrackerServer, 184
configured, 158-160, 329
configuring
  Asynchronous COM, 329
  COM+ applications, 160-184
  as event classes, 338
debugging, class factories, 84
DLQListener, 180
EventPublisher.EventPublisher.1, 188
Mts.Mtsgrp.1, 188
obtaining apartment GUIDs, 208
obtaining GUIDs, 212
persistable, 319-320

QC.DLQListener, 180
QC.ListenerHelper.1, 181
QC.Recorder.1, 181
Queued (QC), 287
   Asynchronous COM, 327-330
   COM+ Queued Components, 294-325
   firing events, 343-344
   hanging news feeders, 288-289
   impersonation and delegation, 380
   installing application proxies, 429
   Microsoft Message Queue (MSMQ), 289-294
   vs. COM events, 335
   registration, 55-56, 59
   RemoteHelper.RemoteHelper, 181
   subscribing, Visual Basic (VB) source code, 339
   TradeEntry, partial Interface Definition Language (IDL), 361
   transaction properties, 240-241
   TxCTx.TransactionContext, 181
   TxCTx.TransactionContextEx, 181
   unconfigured, 158, 198
   Visual Basic (VB), output, 375
   VC++ object, retrieving IResponse interfaces from contexts, 222
   Web Applications Manager (WAM), 182-183
   worker, modifying account balances in XML files, 261-268

ComputerName parameter, 417-418

COMSSVCS.TrackerServer component, 184

COMTIIntrinsics property, 174

Concurrency tab, options, 405

conditions, race, 93-97

configurations
   activities, 405
   Sender and Receiver objects, 325

configured components, 158-160, 329

configuring
   components
      Asynchronous COM, 329
      COM+ applications, 160-184
      as event classes, 338
   impersonation, delegation, and authentication, 381-383
   security, 363-366

Connect setting, 381

connection points, 143, 288, 332-336

connections, databases, 239

consistency, transactions, 228

ConstructionEnabled property, 174

context flow, 194

Context Flow methods, 195-196

context interfaces, 218-223

context objects, 194

ContextDemo, 200-206

ContextInformation() method, 200-204

ContextObject object, 194

contexts, 193, 223
   defined, 199, 201, 203, 205
   extensibility and Internet Information Server (IIS), 221-222
   implementing, Component Object Model (COM), 207-217
   integrating Component Object Model (COM) and Microsoft Transaction Server (MTS), 197-199
   IObjectContext interface, 194-197
   retrieving IResponse interfaces from, VC++ object components, 222

controlling
   Excel remotely, binding, 130-131
   Distributed Transaction Coordinator (DTC), 233

controls, ActiveX, 256

coordinating transactions across multiple databases, 234-236

CoQueryProxyBlanket() method, 384
CoSetProxyBlanket() method, 383-384
counts, reference, 47-48
CPP files, implementing COM classes, 75-80
crashes, handling recovery from, 275
CRC (Cycle Redundancy Checks), 190-191
CreatedBy property, 172
CreateInstance method, 247
CreateInstance() function, 246
CreateInstance() method, 85, 195-196
CreateObject method, 247
CreateThread() function, declaring external references, 95
creating
 COM components in Visual Basic (VB), 28
 COM+ applications, 164-166
 COMCalc instances, clients, 51-52
 distributed transactions, Distributed Transaction Coordinator (DTC), 235-236
 event classes, 336-338
 instances, ICalc class, 70
 objects
  Calc, Visual Basic (VB), 37
  Calculator, 21-28
  COM, C++, 66-68
  queued, monikers, 298-302
 publisher filters, 350-354
 queues, 291-292
 threads, AddressOf operator, 96
CreationTimeout property, 175
credentials, borrowing from callers to modify files owned by, 374
crediting account databases, 242
CRM. *See* Compensating Resource Managers

CRMClerk coclass, 259-260
CRMEnabled property, 172
CRMLogFile property, 172
CRMREGFLAG FAILIFINDOUBTSREMAIN flag, 284
cross-apartment calls, 119
crossed security boundaries, 369
Currency interface, 169
Currency object
 IDLs for interfaces of, 167
 Implementation for IConvert and ITransfer, 167-168
custom interfaces, 143-154
custom marshaling, 14
Cycle Redundancy Checks (CRCs), 190-191

D

data, block, 411-412
data types, 136-137
databases
 account, 242-243
 ACID, 227-228
 Active Directory, 311
 connections, pooled objects re-enlisting with new transactions, 239
 coordinating transactions across, 234-236
dblib, 236-239
Deactivate method, 408
deactivating objects, 245, 407
dead queues, 303
debiting account databases, 243
debugging components, class factories, 84
declaration tags
 type libraries, 34

declarations
  Interface Definition Language (IDL)
    interfaces, 145
      adding QUEQUEABLE tags, 296
      interfaces, 145, 327, 337
    interfaces, 23
    methods, 38-39

declarative model, 5-14

declarative security, xi, 359-366

declarative settings, COM+ transactions, 240-244

declaring
  apartments, 117-125
  external references, CreateThread() function, 95
  interfaces, 337
    inside and outside library blocks, 26
    IWakeUp and IAlarm, 116

Default Properties tab, settings, 382

Delegate setting, 382

delegation, 377, 379
  configuring, 381-383
  event class subscription propagation, 342
  Queued Components, 380

DELETE statement, 228

Deleteable property, 173

deleting
  log entries, 274
  queues, 294

Delivery parameter, 419

Description property, 173-175

destination queues, parameters affecting, 416-418

dialog boxes
  changing, 54
  Security, 364-366
  Select Subscription Method(s), 340

DIRECT specifier, 416-417

DirectCaller property, 371

directives, #import, 71-72

directories, Roles, 360

DisableCommit method, 195

DisableCommit() function, 248-250

Disabled option, 405

Disabled property, 240

disabling
  role-based security, 364
  security, 304-305

discriminated unions, 134-137

discriminators, 135-136

dispatch ID (DISPID), 132-133

Dispenser Manager (DispMan), 244-245

Dispensers, Resources (RDs), 244-245, 401

DISPID (dispatch ID), 132-133

dispinterfaces, 143-148

displaying
  method calls as messages, 305-307
  SAFEARRAYs, 412

DispMan (Dispenser Manager), 244-245

DISPPARAMS structure, 139

Distributed Transaction Coordinator (DTC), 231-239
  Resource Manager (RM), 275-276
  X/Open XA protocol, 257

Distributed Transaction Voting methods, 195

distributed transactions, 230-231, 239
  creating, Distributed Transaction Coordinator (DTC), 235-236
  success of, 275, 284

distributing applications, 423-428

DLL. See **dynamic link libraries**

DLLCanUnloadNow() function, 59

DLLGetClassObject() function, 59

DLLHOST.EXE, potential instances, 160-162

DLLRegisterServer interface, 336
DLLRegisterServer() function, 56-59
DLLUnregisterServer interface, 336
DLLUnregisterServer() function, 59
drop-down boxes, Authentication and Impersonation, 366
DTC. *See* **Distributed Transaction Coordinator**
dual interfaces, 145-154
dual tag, 37
dumping message contents into binary files, 314
durability, transactions, 228
dynamic cloaking, 379
dynamic link libraries (DLLs), 53-61
    listing of names in Registry, non-MTS COM objects, 197
    proxy/stub, 129, 148

E

early binding, 128-130
Eck, Thomas, 311
editing
    cells in Excel spreadsheets, notifying Visual Basic (VB) clients, 332
    files
        callers, 374
        XML, account balances, 261-268
    identities, COM+ applications, 179-180
    menus and dialog boxes, 54
editors, resource, 54
Enable Authentication check box, 366
EnableCommit method, 195
EnableCommit() function, 248-250
enabling
    declarative security, 364
    role-based security, 364
    security, 363-366

EncryptAlgorithm parameter, 419
EndAbortVariants() method, 274
EndCommitVariants() method, 273
EndPrepareVariants() method, 272
Enforce Access Checks for This Application check box, 364-365
enlisting transactions, 236-239
entering users in roles, 360-361
entries
    Implemented Categories, 57
    InprocServer32, 57
    log, removing, 274
    Programmable, 57
    Registry, COM classes, 57
    ThreadingModel, 117-118
    Typelib, 57
    Version, 57
    See also settings
enumerating SecurityCallContext interface, 220
erasing
    log entries, 274
    queues, 294
error messages, similarly configured local queues, 326
escrows, 231-232
evaluating method arguments, publisher filter properties, 356-357
event classes, 335-338, 347-350
event interface declarations, 337
event notifications, 4
event sinks, 333-334
EventPublisher.EventPublisher.1 component, 188
events, 325, 332, 358
    filtering, 344-357
    firing asynchronous and synchronous, 343
    publishers and subscribers, 335-344
    tightly coupled (TCE), 333
    traditional COM, 332-335

EventsEnabled property, 173
EventTrackingEnabled property, 175
Excel
  changing cells in spreadsheets, notifying VB clients, 332
  as COM+ component, 142
  remotely controlling, early binding, 130
  remotely controlling, late binding, 130-131
exception classes, 324-325
exception handling, Visual Basic (VB), 39
ExceptionClass property, 175
executables, client. *See* base clients
exiting queues, 294
explicit association, publisher filters by clients, 349-350
exporting applications, 424-425
extensibility, contexts and Internet Information Server (IIS), 221-222
Extension attribute, 415
external references, declaring with CreateThread() function, 95

F

factories, class, 83-85
failed queued component (QC) messages, timeout periods and retry attempts, 309
failures, exception classes, 324-325
files
  binary, dumping message contents into, 314
  C, generating, 26
  CALC.H, 44-45
  callers, modifying, 374
  comcalc.h, 28
  CPP, implementations of COM classes, 75-80

H, generating, 26
header
  calcsdk.tlh and calcsdk.tli , 71-72
  comcalc.h, 28
INI, 157-160
Interface Definition Language (IDL),
  16, 143
  COMCalc object, 50
  compiling, 17-18
  dual interfaces, 152
  J++ coclass wrapper, 154
log, 230-231, 260
Microsoft Installer (MSI), 165
NTFS, permissions, 372
Object Definition Language (ODL), 142
opening, 388-394
Package (PAK), 165
Regsvr32.exe, 56
resource, 54
type libraries (TLB), 8, 19-20, 44, 74-75
  coclasses, 26
  code for, 150-151
  declaration tags, 34
  late binding, 141-147
  listing, registered COM components, 29
  marshaling, 128-131, 411-412
  registered, finding, 31-32, 34, 37-39
  registration, 55-59
  resources, 54-55
XML, changing account balances, 261-268
Filter Criteria text box, 345
filtering events, 344-357
filters, publisher, 346-357
FinalClientRetry method, 324
FinalServerRetry method, 324
finding
  message-only windows, 103
  registered type libraries, 31-39
Fire in Parallel check box, 343
FireInParallel property, 175

firing events, 343, 352-354
flags, CRMREGFLAG FAILIFINDOUBTSREMAIN, 284
flow, transactions, 194-197
folders, Roles, 360
foreign exchange trading (FX) systems, 7
FormatName parameter, 416-417
Free value, 118
Free-Threaded Marshalers (FTMs), 119-124, 215-217
function calls, aggregating FTM objects, 124
functions
 abstract base classes, implementing, 67
 Add(), 15, 38
 AddRef(), 45-48
 CoCreateInstance(), 84
 CoGetClassObject(), 83-84
 CoMarshalInterThreadInterfaceInStream(), 112-117
 CreateInstance(), 246
 CreateThread(), declaring external references, 95
 DisableCommit(), 248-250
 DLLCanUnloadNow(), 59
 DLLGetClassObject(), 59
 DLLRegisterServer(), 56-59
 DLLUnregisterServer(), 59
 EnableCommit(), 248-250
 GetClassObject(), 73
 Invoke(), 134-147
 LockServer(), 85
 main(), 86
 member, ICalc interface, 151-152
 proxy, 75
 QueryInterface(), 47-51, 73-74, 82-83
 Raw, 39
 RegisterTypeLib(), 58
 Release(), 43-48, 249
 SetAbort(), 243-252, 261
 SetComplete(), 243-252
 SQLSetConnectOption(), 236
 Subtract(), declarations, 38
 ToString, 152
 virtual, trickle down effect of, 65
 See also methods
FX (foreign exchange trading) systems, 7

G

generating C and H files, 26
GetClassObject() function, 73
GetDeactivateOnReturn method, 251
GetMyTransactionVote method, 252
GetObject() method, 299-300
GetObjectContext() method, 194
GetPublisherProperty() method, 355
GetSubscriptions() method, 351
GIT. See Global Interface Tables
Global Interface Tables (GITs), 215
 marshaling, 113-115
 passing interfaces between threads, multi-threaded clients, 115-116
global scope, class factories, 85
Globally Unique Identifiers (GUIDs)
 apartments, 208
 components obtaining, 208, 212
 contexts, C++ components returning as strings, 210-212
 IID IFinancial, 51
 IID IUnknown, 49
 specifying in code, 80
 type libraries, 26
granting permissions, roles, 361-363

groups, attribute, 23
GUIDs. *See* Globally Unique Identifiers

H

H files, generating, 26
handling
    exceptions, Visual Basic (VB), 39
    recovery, 274-275
hanging clients, troubleshooting, 343
hanging news feeders, 288-289
Happy and Done (HD) bits, 247
HashAlgorithm parameter, 419
Hauger, Doug, 311
HD (Happy and Done bits), 247
header files
    CALC.H, 44-45
    calcsdk.tlh and calcsdk.tli, 71-72
    comcalc.h, 28
HRESULT, 38, 73, 81

I

IAlarm interface, declarations, 116
ICalc class, creating instances, 70
ICalc interface, 42-43
    clients creating COMCalc instances, 51
    implementation of class supporting, 149-150
    inheriting from IDispatch interface, 146
    member functions, 151-152
    prototype, J++, 154
    releasing Calc objects, 43-48
    support, Calc objects, 49
ICalc object, Interface Definition Language (IDL) description, 22
ICalc vtables, relationship with COMCalc, 68-70

IClassFactory interface, 83-85
IClientSecurity interface, 384
IConnectionPointContainer interface, 334
IContextState interface, 251-252
IConvert method, Currency object implementation, 167-168
ICrmCompensator interface, 273-274
ICrmCompensatorVariants interface, 269, 273-274
ICrmLogControl interface, 260, 269, 275
ID. *See* identifiers
ID property, 173
id tag, 38
idempotence, 275
idempotent method calls, 307
identifiers (IDs)
    dispatch (DISPID), 132
    Globally Unique (GUID)
        apartments, 208
        components obtaining, 208, 212
        contexts, C++ components returning as strings, 210, 212
        IID IFinancial, 51
        IID IUnknown, 49
        specifying in code, 80
        type libraries, 26
Identify setting, 382
identities
    applications, 367-369
    callers, impersonating, 367-376
    changing, COM+ applications, 179-180
    setting, COM+ applications, 166
Identity property, 173
Identity tab, 368-369
IDispatch interface, 132-148, 372
    Asynchronous COM, 329
    ICalc interface inheriting from, 146
    inheriting from, 37-38

IDL. *See* Interface Definition Language
IEventSubscription interface, 352-355
IF, ELSE, 83
IFinancial interface
    clients creating COMCalc instances, 51-52
    implementation of class supporting, 149-150
IFinancial object, Interface Definition Language (IDL) description, 22
IFinancial vtables, relationship with COMCalc, 68-70
IFireControl interface, 347
IGetContextProperties interface, 222
IGetContextProperties method, 221-223
IID IFinancial GUID, 51
IID IUnknown GUID, 49
IIS. *See* Internet Information Server
IISIntrinsics property, 175
IISWAM.OutofProcessPool, 182
IISWAM.W3SVC, 182
Impersonate setting, 382
impersonating
    callers, 367-376, 385-394
    configuring, 381-383
    defined, 368
    Queued Components, 380
Impersonation drop-down box, 366
ImpersonationLevel property, 173
implementations
    COM classes, 66, 75-80
    functions, abstract base classes, 67
    methods, 81
    Release() function, 45
Implemented Categories entry, 57

implementing
    Asynchronous COM, 327-329
    coclasses, C++, 26-28
    COM objects, Visual C++, 21-28
    contexts, Component Object Model (COM), 207-217
    events, 332
    Microsoft Message Queue (MSMQ), 290-294
    publisher filters, 350-354
    Release() function, 43-45
    ServerCallBack class, 322
implements keyword, 12
importing components, 168-171
IMultiInterfacePublisherFilter interface, 346-351
[in] tags, 16
in-doubt state, 276
in-process applications, Internet Information Server (IIS), 181-182
in-process servers, library applications, 70
INFINITE value, 420
informational methods, 250-251
inheritance
    IDispatch interface, 37-38
    IUnknown interface, 49, 81
    multiple (MI), 81
    virtual, 68
INI files, 157-160
Initialize() method, 346-351
InprocServer32 entry, 57
INSET statement, 229
installing
    application proxies, 426-428
    COM+ applications, 164-166
    components, 168-171
    event classes, 337-338
instances
    COMCalc object, clients creating interfaces of, 51-52
    creating ICalc class, 70
    potential, 162

interfaces

instantiation
  debugging components, class factories, 84
  objects
    ASP pages, 221
    monikers, 298-300

instmsi.exe installing application proxies, 428

integrating Component Object Model (COM) and Microsoft Transaction Server (MTS), 197-199

IntelliSense, 19, 30

Interactive User radio button, 368

Interactive User setting, 166

interface blocks, 36

interface declarations, Interface Definition Language (IDL) events, 337

Interface Definition Language (IDL), 15-17, 21-22, 31-39
  Currency object, implementation for IConvert and ITransfer, 167-168
  event interface declarations, 337
  partial, TradeEntry component, 361
  declarations, 145
    adding QUEQUEABLE tags, 296
    interfaces with async uuid attribute, 327
  files, 143
    COMCalc object, 50
    dual interfaces, 152
    J++ coclass wrapper, 154

interfaces
  abstract base classes as, 64
  AsyncITester, 328-329
  attribute groups, 23
  Calc, generated in Visual Basic (VB), 36
  context, 218-223
  Currency, 169
  Currency object, 167-168
  custom, 143-154
  declarations, 23, 26, 327, 337
  defined, 8
  determining subscribers to, 352-354
  DLLRegisterServer, 336
  DLLUnregisterServer, 336
  dual, 145-154
  ICalc, 42-43
    clients creating COMCalc instances, 51
    implementation of class supporting, 149-150
    inheriting from IDispatch interface, 146
    member functions, 151-152
    prototype, J++, 154
    releasing Calc objects, 43-48
    support, Calc objects, 49
  IClassFactory, 83-85
  IClientSecurity, 384
  IConnectionPointContainer, 334
  IContextState, 251-252
  ICrmCompensator, 273-274
  ICrmCompensatorVariants, 269-274
  ICrmLogControl, 260, 269, 275
  IDispatch, 132-148, 372
    Asynchronous COM, 329
    ICalc interface inheriting from, 146
    inheriting from, 37-38
  IEventSubscription, 352-355
  IFinancial
    clients creating COMCalc instances, 51-52
    implementation of class supporting, 149-150
  IFireControl, 347
  IGetContextProperties, 222
  IMultiInterfacePublisherFilter, 346-351
  Interface Definition Language (IDL), 16-17, 145, 327
  IObjectContext, 194-197, 246-251
  IObjectControl, 408-409
  IOleItemContainer, 84
  IPersistStream, 292, 316
  IPlayBackControl, 324
  IPublisherFilter, 346-349

interfaces

IResponse, retrieving from contexts, 222
ISecurityCallContext, 366, 371
ISecurityCallersCall, 371
ISecurityCallersColl
  design of, 372
  determining call chains, 370
ISecurityIdentityColl, 370-372
ISynchronize, 328
IUnknown, 372
  inheritance, 81
  role of, 41-51
IWakeUp and IAlarm, declarations, 116
marking queueable, Admin objects, 295-296
marshaling, 111-117
methods, 367
Microsoft Transaction (MTS), IObjectContext interface, 194-197
object support, 75
Object. See IDispatch interface
passing between threads, multi-threaded clients, 115-116
pointers, passing between threads, 111-113
purpose of, 12-14
queued, restrictions on, 297
ValueProperty, 177

internal structures, virtual function tables (vtables), 68-70, 74

Internet Information Server (IIS)
  adding intrinsic objects to contexts, 222-223
  applications, in-process and out-of-process pooled, 181-182
  ASP pages, 221
  context extensibility, 221-222
  transactions, 252-253

interoperability, Microsoft Message Queue (MSMQ) and COM+ Queued Components, 311-315

invocation, method, 127-155

invoke arguments, marshaling, 134

Invoke() function, 134-147

IObjectContext interface, 194-197, 246-251
IObjectContextInfo method, 218
IObjectControl interface, methods, 408-409
IOleItemContainer interface, 84
IPersistStream interface, 292, 316
IPlayBackControl interface, 324
IPublisherFilter interface, 346-349
IResponse interface, retrieving from contexts, 222
IsCallerInRole method, 194, 250, 367
ISecurityCallContext interface, 366, 371
ISecurityCallContext method, 220
ISecurityCallersCall interface, properties, 371
ISecurityCallersColl interface
  determining call chains, 370
  interface, design of, 372
ISecurityIdentityColl interface
  design of, 372
  determining call chains, 370
IsEventClass property, 175
IsInTransaction method, 194, 250-251
isolation
  Compensating Resource Managers (CRMs), 284
  transactions, 228
IsSecurityEnabled method, 195, 251, 367
IsSystem property, 173
IsUserInRole method, 367
ISynchronize interface, 328
Item() method, 371
ITransfer method, Currency object implementation, 167-168

IUnknown interface, 372
  inheritance, 81
  role of, 41-51
IWakeUp interface,
  declarations, 116

J

J++ programming language
  custom interfaces, 152-154
  dual interfaces, 149-154
  ICalc interface prototype, 154
  IDispatch interface, 133, 139
  late binding, 140
  marshaling, 113
  Object data type, 136
Java Callable Wrappers (JCWs), 113
Java programming language, 10
JCW (Java Callable Wrappers), 113
JITA (Just In Time Activation),
  248, 405
Journal parameter, 420
Just-In-Time Activation (JITA),
  248, 405
JustInTimeActivation property, 175

K

keywords
  ByVal, 302
  implements, 12
  oleautomation, 131
  Set, 52
  virtual, 64, 67
  WithEvents, 333

L

Label parameter, 420
languages, programming. *See*
  programming languages
late binding, 37, 128-155

layers, administrative. *See* catalogs
Leave running when idle radio
  button, 162
legacy methods, 247
libraries
  Active Template (ATL), 21
  dblib, 236-239
  dynamic link (DLL), 53-61, 148
  type (TLB files), 8, 19-20, 44, 74-75
    coclasses, 26
    code for, 150-151
    declaration tags, 34
    late binding, 147
    listing, registered COM
      components, 29
    marshaling, 128-131
    registered, finding, 31-39
    registration, 55-59
    resources, 54-55
library applications, 106
  in-process servers, 70
  processes, 365-366
Lifetime methods, 195
lifetimes, objects, 47-48
Listen check box, 304
Listener object, 298-304
ListenerHelper class, 301, 304
listing type libraries, registered
  COM components, 29
listings. *See* source code listings
load balancing, 5
LoadBalancingSupported
  property, 175
locking, row level, 284
LockServer() function, 85
log entries, removing, 274
log files, 230-231, 260
LONG LIVED value, 420
loops, message, 98
lower level security, xi, 383-395

M

main function, 86

managers, proxy, 383

manual reading, messages, 312-315

marking applications and interfaces queueable, Admin objects, 295-296

marshalers, Free-Threaded (FTM), 119, 122-123, 215-217

marshaling
custom, 14
interfaces, 111-117
method invocation, 127
    late binding, 131-155
    type libraries, 128-131
standard, 411
type libraries (TLB files), 20, 411-412

MaxPoolSize property, 175

MaxTimeToReachQueue parameter, 415, 420-421

MaxTimeToReceive parameter, 421

member functions, ICalc interface, 151-152

menus, changing, 54

message loops, 98

message pumps, 98-100

message queues
protecting Single-Threaded Apartments (STAs) with, 109-110
serialization, 102
synchronization aides as, 97-101

message-only windows, 102-103

messages
defined, 289
error, similarly configured local queues, 326
failed queued component (QC), timeout periods and retry attempts, 309
passing objects through, 315, 319
playing, 308
reading manually, 312-315
received from queue by VB client, 293
receiving, 293, 304
retired, 307
sending, 292-293
sent to queue by VB client, 290
viewing method calls as, 305-307

method arguments
determining access, 367
variants as, 136

method calls
asynchronous, 288-289, 294-297
idempotent, 307
synchronous, 288
viewing as messages, 305-307

method invocation, marshaling, 127-155

methods
AbortRecordVariants(), 274
Activate, 408-409
Advise(), 334
BeginAbortVariance(), 274
BeginCommitVariants(), 272, 275
BeginPrepareVariants(), 271-272
CanBePooled, 408
CoCreateInstance, 247
CoGetClassObject(), 85-86
CoGetObjectContext(), 194
CoImpersonateClient(), 373, 377
CoInitializeSecurity(), 381-383
CoMarshalInterthreadInterfaceInStream(),215
CommitRecordsVariants(), 273
Context Flow, 195-196
ContextInformation(), 200-204
CoQueryProxyBlanket(), 384
CoSetProxyBlanket(), 383-384
CreateInstance, 247
CreateInstance(), 85, 195-196
CreateObject, 247
Deactivate, 408
declarations, 38-39
DisableCommit, 195

modifying **449**

Distributed Transaction Voting, 195
EnableCommit, 195
EndAbortVariants(), 274
EndCommitVariants(), 273
EndPrepareVariants(), 272
evaluating arguments, publisher filter properties, 356-357
FinalClientRetry, 324
FinalServerRetry, 324
GetDeactivateOnReturn, 251
GetMyTransactionVote, 252
GetObject(), 299-300
GetObjectContext(), 194
GetPublisherProperty(), 355
GetSubscriptions(), 351
IContextState interface, 251-252
IConvert, Currency object implementation, 167-168
IGetContextProperties, 221-223
implementations of, 81
Initialize(), 346-351
interfaces, 367
invoking, IDispatch interface, 140-141
IObjectContext interface, 246-251
IObjectContextInfo, 218
IObjectControl interface, 408-409
IsCallerInRole, 194, 250, 367
ISecurityCallContext, 220
IsInTransaction, 194, 250-251
IsSecurityEnabled, 195, 251, 367
IsUserInRole, 367
Item(), 371
ITransfer, Currency object implementation, 167-168
Lifetime, 195
New, 247
Open, 292
PrepareToFire(), 347-357
pure virtual, 67
QueryInterface(), aggregating FTM objects, 124
Receive, 293
RegisterCompensator(), 270
Send(), 293
SetAbort(), 195-196, 273, 309-310
SetComplete(), 195-196
SetDeactivateOnReturn, 251

SetMyTransactionVote, 251
See also functions
MI (multiple inheritance), 81
Microsoft Compiler (VC++), changing menus and dialog boxes, 54
Microsoft Installer files. *See* **MSI files, 165**
Microsoft Message Queue (MSMQ), 7, 257, 289-294, 311-315, 415-421
Microsoft Office as COM+ component, 142
Microsoft Press, 214
Microsoft Systems Journal, **214**
Microsoft Transaction Server (MTS), 7, 181, 194-199, 249
middleware, Microsoft Message Queue (MSMQ) as, 290
MIDL, generating files, 26, 44-45
migrating interfaces between processes, 116-117
MinAuthenticationLevel property, 371
MinPoolSize property, 175
Minutes until idle shutdown radio button, 162
models
    declarative, 5-11, 14
    Rental. *See* Thread Neutral Apartment, 125
    singleton, 8
    threading, 91
        apartments, 97-125
        marshaling interfaces, 111-117
        processes, 91-97
modes, Windows 2000 workgroup, 305
modifying
    cells in Excel spreadsheets, notifying Visual Basic (VB) clients, 332
    files
        callers, 374
        XML, account balances, 261-268

identities, COM+ applications, 179-180
menus and dialog boxes, 54
monikers
creating queued objects, 298-300
queue, parameters, 415-421
moving interfaces between processes, 116-117
MQMSG DEADLETTER value, 420-421
MQMSG DELIVERY EXPRESS value, 419
MQMSG DELIVERY RECOVERABLE value, 419
MQMSG JOURNAL NONE value, 420
MQMSG JOURNAL value, 420
MQMSG PRIV LEVEL BODY BASE value, 421
MQMSG PRIV LEVEL BODY ENHANCED value, 421
MQMSG PRIV LEVEL BODY value, 421
MQMSG PRIV LEVEL NONE value, 421
MQMSG SEND ROUTE TO REPORT QUEUE value, 422
MQMSG TRACE NONE value, 422
MSI files, 165
MSMQ. *See* **Microsoft Message Queue**
MTA (Multi-Threaded Apartments), 104-108
MTS. *See* **Microsoft Transaction Server**
Mts.Mtsgrp.1 component, 188
Multi-Threaded Apartment (MTA), 104-108
multi-threaded clients, passing interfaces between threads, 115-116
multi-threaded process, 92-97
multi-threaded programs, 94
MultiInterfacePublisherFilterCLSID property, 175
multiple inheritance (MI), 81
MustRunInClientContext property, 176

N

Name property, 173
named_guids argument, 72
names, non-MTS COM objects, 197
nested classes, 81
network protocols, 14
networks, propagating events across, 342-343
Neutral entry, 118
new class, 299-300
New method, 247
news feeders, hanging, 288-289
Newtonian universe, 225
non-transactional queues, 309-310
None setting, 381
nonextensible tag, 36
Not Supported option, 405
Not Supported property, 240
notifications, 321-325
cell changes in Excel spreadsheets, VB clients, 332
events, 4
no_namespace argument, 72
NT, Windows, 428-429
ADSI Scripting for System Administration, 311
installing application proxies, 428-429

NTFS files, permissions, 372
NumberClass class, 316
NumCallers property, 371

O

Object data type, 136
Object Definition Language (ODL) files, 142
Object interface. *See* **IDispatch interface**
Object Linking and Embedding (OLE) automation. *See* **late binding**
object pooling, 4, 407-408
object state, 248-249
object tag, 23
ObjectContext object, 194
ObjectPoolEnabled property, 176
objects
  ActiveX Data (ADO), 243, 399-401
  administration
    adding applications and components, 177-178
    components, 176-177
    marking applications and interfaces queueable, 295-296
    properties, 171-176
  apartment-threaded, 111
  Calc
    creating, Visual Basic (VB), 37
    method declarations, 38-39
    releasing, 43-48
    support, IUnknown interface, 49
  CalcSDK, Interface Definition Language (IDL), 22
  Calculator, creating, 21-28
  calculcation, support of C++ interfaces, 9
  COM
    implementing, Visual C++, 21-28
    location of, 53-59, 61
  COM+ administration, associating event classes with publisher filters, 348-349
  COMAdminCatalog, 176
  COMAdminCatalogCollection, 176-177
  COMAdminCatalogObject, 177
  COMCalc, 50-52
  context, 194
  ContextObject, 194
  Currency
    IDLs for interfaces of, 167
    Implementation for IConvert and ITransfer, 167-168
  deactivation, 245, 407
  FTM, 121, 124
  ICalc, Interface Definition Language (IDL), 22
  IFinancial, Interface Definition Language (IDL), 22
  instantiation, ASP pages, 221
  interface support, 75
  lifetimes, 47-48
  Listener, 298-304
  ObjectContext, 194
  Page, 252-253
  passing through messages, 315, 319
  Player, 298-304
  pooled
    determining current transactions upon activation, 218
    transaction enlistment, 237-239
  queued
    creating, monikers, 298-300
    writing, 302
  Receiver, parallel application configurations, 325
  Recorder, 298-304, 323
  releasing, 43-48
  Sender, parallel application configurations, 325
  STA, 121
  termination, 407
  threads and, 101-110
  TransactionContext, voting, 246
  VB, simple, 404
  VBCalc, type library, 33-34

OCX, 256
ODBC (Open Database Connectivity) vs. OLE-DB, 400-401
ODL (Object Definition Language files), 142
Office as COM+ component, 142
OLE automation. *See* late binding
OLE Transactions protocol, 257
OLE-DB, ActiveX Data Objects (ADOs), 399-401
oleautomation keyword, 131
oleautomation tag, late binding and marshaling, 147-155
OleMainThreadWndClass window, 104
OLEView.EXE, 31-34
Open Database Connectivity (ODBC) vs. OLE-DB, 400-401
Open method, 292
opening
　files, 388-394
　queues, 291-292
operators, AddressOf, 96
options, Concurrency tab, 405
Options tab, 342-343
OriginalCaller property, 371
[out,retval] tag, 39
out-of-process pooled applications, Internet Information Server (IIS), 181-182
out-of-process servers, 248
output, VB components, 375
output parameters, calling stored procedures, 402

P

Package files (PAK files), 165
Packet Integrity setting, 381
Packet Privacy setting, 381
Packet setting, 381
Page object, 252-253
pages, Active Server (ASP), 181-183
　contexts, 221
　transactions, 252-253
　type libraries, 129
PAK files (Package files), 165
parallel application configurations, Sender and Receiver objects, 325
parameters
　AppSpecific, 418
　AuthLevel, 418
　ComputerName, 417-418
　Delivery, 419
　EncryptAlgorithm, 419
　FormatName, 416-417
　HashAlgorithm, 419
　Journal, 420
　Label, 420
　MaxTimeToReachQueue, 415, 420-421
　MaxTimeToReceive, 421
　output, calling stored procedures, 402
　PathName, 417-418
　Priority, 421
　PrivLevel, 421
　queue monikers, 415-421
　QueueName, 417-418
　Trace, 422
　See also attributes
parsing process, 299
passing
　block data, SAFEARRAYs, 411-412
　interface pointers between threads, 111-113
　interfaces between threads, multi-threaded clients, 115-116
　objects through messages, 315, 319
Password property, 173

PathName parameter, 417-418
pbForget argument, 271
peer-to-peer connections, 333
Perform Access Checks radio buttons, 364-365
performance, COM+, 226
permissions
    granting, roles, 361-363
    NTFS files, 372
persistable component, 319-320
persistence, 315, 319
phases, Commit and Prepare, 233-234, 272-275
placing messages into queues manually, 315
Platt, David, 214
Player object, 298-304
Playing messages, 308
pointer default tag, 24
pointers
    interface, passing between threads, 111-113
    smart, 48
points, connection, 288, 332-336
polymorphism, 63-75, 81-85
pooled objects, 4, 407-408
    determining current transactions upon activation, 218
    transaction enlistment, 237-239
pools, thread, 107
potential instances, 162
PRC. *See* Remote Procedure Calls
pre-installed COM+ applications, 180-190
Prepare phase, 232-234, 270-275
PrepareToFire() method, 347-357
primary threads, 92
Priority parameter, 421
private queues, 310-311

PRIVATE specifier, 416
Private$ specifier, 417
PrivLevel parameter, 421
procedures
    stored, calling for ActiveX Data Objects (ADOs), 402
    window, 98-100
processes, 91
    COM+ library applications, 365-366
    moving interfaces between, 116-117
    multi-threaded, 92-97
processing transactions, 4
ProgID property, 176
program listings. *See* listings
Programmable entry, 57
programmatic security, xi, 363-369
programming languages
    C, generating files, 26
    C++
        clients, 70-73
        components, returning context GUIDs as strings, 210-212
        IDispatch interface, 138
        implementations, 26-28, 75-80
        interfaces, 9, 41-51
        raw functions, 39
        Variant data type, 136
        virtual function tables (vtables), abstract base classes, and polymorphism, 63-75, 81-85
        writing COM objects, 66-68
    Interface Definition (IDL), 15-17, 21-22, 31-39
        Currency object, implementation for IConvert and ITransfer, 167-168
        event interface declarations, 337
        partial, TradeEntry component, 361
        declarations, 145, 296, 327
        files, 50, 143, 152-154
    J++
        interfaces, 133, 139, 149-154
        late binding, 140
        marshaling, 113
        Object data type, 136

454 programming languages

Java, 10
Visual Basic (VB)
   arrays, passing block data, 411-412
   Calc interface, 36
   clients, 52, 290, 293, 332
   CoImpersonateClient() method, 373
   components, obtaining Globally Unique Identifiers (GUIDs), 212
   CreateInstance() method, 196
   creating Calc objects, 37
   creating COM components, 28
   exception handling, 39
   late binding, 137, 147
   objects, simple, 404
   persistable components, 319-320
   pseudo-clients, 12
   pseudo-servers, 11
   registering components in Registry, 55
   source code, subscribing components and tickers, 339
   TransactionContext object, 246
   Variant data type, 136
   writing queueable objects, 302
Visual C++ (VC++), 337
   changing menus and dialog boxes, 54
   implementing COM objects, 21-28
   IObjectContext() method, 196
   object components, retrieving IResponse interfaces from contexts, 222
   TransactionContext object, 246
Visual J++ (VJ++), implementation of class supporting ICalc and IFinancial interfaces, 149-150

programs. *See* **applications**

propagating events across networks, 342-343

properties
   3GigSupportEnabled, 174-177
   AccessChecksLevel, 171
   Activation, 172
   AllowInprocSubscribers, 174
   ApplicationAccessChecks-Enabled, 172
   ApplicationID, 174

ApplicationProxy, 172
ApplicationProxyServerName, 172
applications, 161-163
Authentication, 172
Callers, 371
Changeable, 172
CLSID, 174
COM+ administration objects, 171-176
CommandLine, 172
COMTIIntrinsics, 174
ConstructionEnabled, 174
CreatedBy, 172
CreationTimeout, 175
CRMEnabled, 172
CRMLogFile, 172
Deleteable, 173
Description, 173-175
DirectCaller, 371
Disabled, 240
EventsEnabled, 173
EventTrackingEnabled, 175
ExceptionClass, 175
FireInParallel, 175
ID, 173
Identity, 173
IISIntrinsics, 175
ImpersonationLevel, 173
ISecurityCallContext interface, 371
ISecurityCallersCall interface, 371
IsEventClass, 175
IsSystem, 173
JustInTimeActivation, 175
LoadBalancingSupported, 175
MaxPoolSize, 175
MinAuthenticationLevel, 371
MinPoolSize, 175
MultiInterfacePublisherFilterCLSID, 175
MustRunInClientContext, 176
Name, 173
Not Supported, 240
NumCallers, 371
ObjectPoolEnabled, 176
OriginalCaller, 371
Password, 173
ProgID, 176
publisher filters, 355

PublisherID, 176
QueueListenerEnabled, 173
QueuingEnabled, 173
Required, 241
Requires New, 241
RunForever, 174
ShutdownAfter, 174
Supported, 241
Synchronization, 176
ThreadingModel, 176
Transaction, 176
transaction, components, 240-241
VersionBuild, 176
VersionMajor, 176
VersionMinor, 176
VersionSubBuild, 176

protecting Single-Threaded Apartments (STAs) with message queues, 109-110

protocols
network, 14
OLE Transactions, 257
two-phase commit, 231-232, 256-257, 275-276
X/Open XA, 257

prototypes
AsyncITester interface, 328
ICalc interface inheriting from IDispatch interface, 146
ICalc interface, J++, 154
ICalc, MIDL generated files, 44-45
IDispatch interface, 132
Variant data type, 137

proxies, 14, 301, 423-428

proxy DLL, 129

proxy functions, 75

proxy managers, 383

proxy/stub dynamic link library (DLL), 148

pseudo-clients
Java, 10
Visual Basic (VB), 12

pseudo-servers, Visual Basic (VB), 11

public queues, 310-311
PUBLIC specifier, 416
publisher filters, 346-357
PublisherID property, 176
publishers, 335-344
pumps, message, 98-100
pure virtual methods, 67

Q

QC. *See* Queued Components
QC.DLQListener component, 180
QC.ListenerHelper.1 component, 181
QC.Recorder.1 component, 181
QUEQUEABLE tags, adding to IDL declarations, 296
QueryInterface() function, 47-51, 73-74, 82-83
QueryInterface() method, aggregating FTM objects, 124
queuable settings, 302-304
QUEUABLE tag, 24
queue class, 299-300
queue monikers, parameters, 415-421
queueable objects, writing, 302
Queued check box, 303-304
Queued Components (QCs), 287
Asynchronous COM, 327-330
COM+ Queued Components, 294-325
firing events, 343-344
hanging news feeders, 288-289
impersonation and delegation, 380
installing application proxies, 429
Microsoft Message Queue (MSMQ), 289-294
vs. COM events, 335
queued event classes vs. queued subscribers, 343

queued interfaces, restrictions on, 297
queued objects, creating, 298-300
queued subscribers vs. queued event classes, 343
QueueListenerEnabled property, 173
QueueName parameter, 417-418
queues
   closing, 293-294
   creating, 291-292
   dead, 303
   deleting, 294
   destination, parameters affecting, 416-418
   message
      protecting Single-Threaded Apartments (STAs) with, 109-110
      serialization, 102
      synchronization aides as, 97-101
   message received from by VB client, 293
   message sent to by VB client, 290
   Microsoft Message (MSMQ), 7, 257, 289-294
   non-transactional, 309-310
   opening, 291-292
   private, 310-311
   public, 310-311
   transactional, 309-310
queuing, 4
QueuingEnabled property, 173
quitting queues, 294

R

race conditions, 93-97
radio buttons
   Interactive User, 368
   Leave running when idle, 162
   Minutes until idle shutdown, 162
   Perform Access Checks at the Process and Component Level, 364-365
   Perform Access Checks Only at the Process Level, 364-365
   This User, 369
raw Distributed Transaction Coordinator (DTC), coordinating transactions across multiple databases, 234-236
Raw functions, 39
RD. *See* Resource Dispensers
RDBMS (relational database management systems), 225
reading messages manually, 312-315
Receive method, 293
Receiver object, parallel application configurations, 325
receivers, Microsoft Message Queue (MSMQ), implementing, 293-294
receiving
   messages, 293, 304
   SAFEARRAYs, 412
receiving events, 339, 341-342
Recorder objects, 298-304, 323
recordsets, retrieving, 401
recovery, handling, 274-275
reference counts, 47-48
references, 45, 95
REFIID, 73
RegisterCompensator() method, 270
registered COM components, listing, 29
registered type libraries, finding, 31-39
RegisterTypeLib() function, 58
registration
   type libraries, 55-59
   Visual Basic (VB), 29

Registry, 157-160
  entries, COM classes, 57
  non-MTS COM object listings in, 197
  registration, type libraries, 55-59
  ThreadingModel entry, 117-118
Regsvr32.exe, 56
relational database management systems (RDBMS), 225
Release() function, 43-48, 249
releasing objects, 43-48
remote control, Excel, 130-131
Remote Procedure Calls (RPCs), 7, 14, 19, 75, 288
RemoteHelper.RemoteHelper component, 181
removing
  log entries, 274
  queues, 294
Rental model, 125-126, 217
Required option, 405
Required property, 241
Requires New option, 405
Requires New property, 241
resolving authentication problems, Windows 2000 workgroup mode, 305
Resource Dispensers (RDs), 244-245, 401
resource editors, Watcom, 54
resource files, 54
Resource Managers (RMs), 256-258, 275-276
resources, type libraries, 54-55
restarting COM+ applications, 179-180
restrictions, queued interfaces, 297
resultsets, calling stored procedures, 402

retired messages, 307
retrieving
  caller chains, 370
  IResponse interfaces from contexts, VC++ object components, 222
  marshaled interfaces from streams, 112
  recordsets, ActiveX Data Objects (ADOs), 401
  SAFEARRAYs, 412
  subscribers, 354
retry attempts, failed queued component (QC) messages, 309
returning Booleans, CanBePooled method, 408
RM. *See* **Resource Managers**
role-based security, 4
roles, xi, 384-395
  defined, 359
  entering users, 360-361
  granting permissions, 361-363
ROLLBACK command, 227, 230-231, 244
row level locking, 284
RPC. *See* **Remote Procedure Calls**
RunForever property, 174

S

SAFEARRAYs, passing block data, 137, 411-412
schema, 310
SCM (Service Control Manager), 70
scope, global, 85
scripting-server-side, 221
searching
  message-only windows, 103
  registered type libraries, 31-39
security, xi, 359, 396
  boundaries, xi, 369-383
  declarative, xi, 359-366
  disabling, 304-305

458　security

    lower level, xi, 383-395
    programmatic, xi, 363-369
    role-based, 4
Security dialog box, 364-366
security information, objects, 207
Security tab, 383
Select Subscription Method(s) dialog box, 340
self-registration, type libraries, 55-59
Send() method, 293
Sender object, parallel application configurations, 325
senders, Microsoft Message Queue (MSMQ), implementing, 290-293
sending messages, 292-293
serialization
    message queues, 102
    Single-Threaded Apartments (STAs), 403-405
Server name text box, 342
server-side scripting, 221
Server.Execute command, 252
Server.Transfer command, 252
ServerCallBack class, implementing, 322
servers
    connection points, 334
    in-process, library applications, 70
    interface usage, 13
    Internet Information (IIS)
        adding intrinsic objects to contexts, 222-223
        applications, in-process and out-of-process pooled, 181-182
        ASP pages, 221
        context extensibility, 221-222
        transactions, 252-253
    Microsoft Transaction (MTS), 7, 181, 197-199, 249
    out-of-process, 248
    singleton, 109, 248-249
    Visual Basic (VB), 11

Service Control Manager (SCM), 70
Set keyword, 52
SetAbort() function, 243-252, 261
SetAbort() method, 195-196, 273, 309-310
SetComplete() function, 243-252
SetComplete() method, 195-196
SetDeactivateOnReturn method, 251
SetMyTransactionVote method, 251
setting
    identities, COM+ applications, 166
    publisher filters, event classes, 348
settings
    Anonymous, 382
    authentication, 381
    Call, 381
    Connect, 381
    declarative, COM+ transactions, 240-244
    Default Properties tab, 382
    Delegate, 382
    Identify, 382
    Impersonate, 382
    None, 381
    Packet, 381
    Packet Integrity, 381
    Packet Privacy, 381
    queuable, 302, 304
    Security tab, 383
    See also entries
shared property manager, 249
ShutdownAfter property, 174
shutting down COM+ applications, 179-180
Single-Threaded Apartments (STAs), 104-110
    pooled objects, 408
    serialization, 403-405
singleton model, 8
singleton servers, 109, 248-249

source code listings   459

sinks, event, 333-334
smart pointers, 48
software. *See* **applications**
software accounts, 369
source code
  Component A, 242
  Component B, 243
source code listings
  access, determining for
    programmatic security and method
    arguments, 367
  Active Server Page (ASP)
    example, 182
  ActiveX Data Objects (ADOs)
    calling stored procedures, 402
    retrieving recordsets, 401
  applications
    adding to catalogs, 177-178
    *COM+, shutting down, changing
      identities, and restarting, 179-180*
    *marking queueable, Admin objects,
      295-296*
  arguments
    *determining access for programmatic
      security and, 367*
    variants as, 136
  catalogs, adding applications,
    177-178
  Asynchronous COM, client-side
    code, 329
  C++
    *components returning context GUIDs
      as strings, 210-212*
    *implementation of CalcSDK
      coclass, 27*
    raw functions, 39
  caller chains, retrieving, 370
  casting to ICalc and IFinancial, 70
  classes
    CallBackObj, 323
    event, setting publisher filters, 348
    implementing, 149-150, 322
    ServerCallBack, 322

clients
  Asynchronous COM, 329
  *associating publisher filters with event
    classes, 349-350*
  creating COMCalc instances, 51-52
  comcalc.h file, 28
  Java pseudo-clients, 10
  *multi-threaded, passing between
    threads, 115-116*
coclasses
  Calc, 37
  CalcSDK, implementation of, 27
  Compensator, 276-283
  *Interface Definition Library
    (IDL), 25*
components
  *borrowing credentials of callers to
    modify files owned by, 374*
  *C++, returning context GUIDs as
    strings, 210-212*
  Component A, 242
  Component B, 243
  *object, retrieving IResponse interfaces
    from contexts, 222*
  obtaining GUIDs, 208, 212
  *persistable, written in Visual Basic
    (VB), 319-320*
  *worker, modifying account balances in
    XML files, 261-268*
  *TradeEntry, partial Interface
    Definition Language (IDL), 361*
declarations
  Add() and Subtract() functions, 38
  interfaces, 23, 116, 337
dispinterfaces, 143
DISPPARAMS structure, 139
early binding, remotely controlling
  Excel with, 130
exception handling, Visual Basic
  (VB), 39
events, determining subscribers to
  and firing, 352-354
files
  *binary, reading messages and dumping
    contents into, 314*
  Regsvr32.exe, 56
  *XML, worker component modifying
    account balances in, 261-268*

functions
    Add() and Subtract(), declarations, 38
    QueryInterface(), 7
    raw, C++, 39
    Release(), implementation of, 45
    virtual, trickle down effect of, 65
Global Interface Tables (GITs),
    obtaining interfaces to, 114
impersonations
    callers, 385-394
    COM classes, 66, 75-80
inheritance, ICalc interface from
    IDispatch interface, 146
Interface Definition Language (IDL)
    adding QUEQUEABLE tags, 296
    COMCalc object, 50
    Currency object, implementation for
        IConvert and ITransfer, 167-168
    describing ICalc, IFinancial, and
        CalcSDK objects, 22
    files, 16, 50, 154
    interface declarations, 145, 327, 337
    interfaces, 16-17
    partial, TradeEntry component, 361
Interface Definition Library (IDL)
    with coclasses, 25
interfaces
    attribute groups, 23
    Calc, generated in Visual Basic
        (VB), 36
    as native part of Java, 10
    declarations, 23, 116, 337
    determining subscribers to and firing
        events, 352, 354
    dual, 152
    ICalc, 44-45, 146, 154
    IDispatch, 138-139, 146
    Interface Definition Language (IDL),
        16-17
    IResponse, object components
        retrieving from contexts, 222
    marking queueable, Admin objects,
        295-296
    marshaled, retrieving from
        streams, 112
    marshaling, 112-113

    obtaining to Global Interface Tables
        (GITs), 114
    passing between threads, multi-
        threaded clients, 115-116
    SecurityCallContext interface,
        enumerating through, 220
J++ coclass wrapper, 154
Java pseudo-clients, 10
late binding
    J++, 140
    remotely controlling Excel with,
        130-131
    Visual Basic (VB), 147
message loop, 98
messages
    error, similarly configured local
        queues, 326
    manually placing into queues, 315
    reading and dumping contents into
        binary files, 314
method arguments
    determining access for programmatic
        security and, 367
    variants as, 136
methods, ContextInformation(),
    200-204
monikers, creating queued
    objects, 298
multi-threaded programs, 94
objects
    ActiveX Data (ADO), 401-402
    Admin, marking applications and
        interfaces queueable, 295-296
    Calc, creating in Visual Basic
        (VB), 37
    calculation, support with C++
        interfaces, 9
    Free-Threaded Marshaler (FTM),
        aggregating, 124
    pooled, 218, 239
    queued, creating, 298
    simple, Visual Basic (VB), 404
    VBCalc, 33-34
    Visual C++ (VC++) components
        retrieving IResponse interfaces from
        contexts, 222

prototypes
    ICalc interface, 44-45, 146, 154
    AsyncITester interface, 328
    IDispatch interface, 132
publisher filters, setting for event classes, 348
queues
    local, similarly configured, 326
    manually placing messages into, 315
tags
    declaration, type libraries, 34
    oleautomation, 148
threads
    creating, AddressOf operator, 96
    passing between, multi-threaded clients, 115-116
transactions
    aborting, 248
    creating, Distributed Transaction Coordinator (DTC), 235-236
    pooled objects, 218, 239
type libraries, 33-34, 44, 150-151
unions, C and discriminated, 135
Variant data type, 137
variants as method arguments, 136
Visual Basic (VB)
    component output, 375
    creating Calc objects, 37
    exception handling, 39
    persistable component written in, 319-320
    pseudo-clients, 12
    pseudo-servers, 11
    simple objects, 404
    subscribing components and tickers, 339
Visual Basic (VB) clients
    notifying of cell changes in Excel spreadsheets, 332
    receiving message from queue, 293
    sending message to queue, 290
Visual C++ (VC++) object components retrieving IResponse interfaces from contexts, 222
Visual J++ (VJ++), implementation of class supporting ICalc and IFinancial interfaces, 149-150

Win32 message pump and window procedure, 98-100
writing variant arrays to log files, 260
XML files, worker component modifying account balances, 261-268

specifiers, 416-417

specifying Globally Unique Identifiers (GUIDs) in code, 80

spreadsheets, changing cells, 332

Spy++, 102

SQLSetConnectOption() function, 236

STA objects, 121

STA. *See* **Single-Threaded Apartments**

standard marshaling, 411

state, object, 248-249

statements, 228-229

states, in-doubt, 276

static cloaking, 379

STDMETHOD, 81

STDMETHODIMP, 81

stored procedures, calling for ActiveX Data Objects (ADOs), 402

streams, 112

structures
    DISPPARAMS, 139
    internal, virtual function tables (vtables), 68-74

stubs, 14

subscribers, 335-344, 352-354

Subtract() function, declarations, 38

support
    calculation objects, C++ interfaces, 9
    dual and custom interfaces, J++, 152-154
    interfaces, 49, 75

Supported option, 405
Supported property, 241
surrogates, 60-61
SWITCH, CASE, 83
symmetry, client-side, 326
synchronization, 4, 206
   activities, 403-405
   thread, 93
synchronization aides, message queues as, 97-101
Synchronization property, 176
synchronous events, firing, 343
synchronous method calls, 288
systems, foreign exchange trading (FX systems), 7

T

tables
   Global Interface (GIT), 113-116, 215
   virtual function (vtables), 20, 63-75, 81-85
tabs
   Concurrency, options, 405
   Default Properties, settings, 382
   Identity, 368-369
   Options, 342-343
   Security, 383
tags
   declaration, type libraries, 34
   dual, 37
   id, 38
   [in], 16
   nonextensible, 36
   object, 23
   oleautomation, late binding and marshaling, 147-155
   [out,retval], 39
   pointer default, 24
   QUEQUEABLE, adding to IDL declarations, 296

QUEUABLE, 24
TRANSACTION_NOT_SUPPORTED, 24
TRANSACTION_REQUIRED, 24
TRANSACTION_REQUIRES_NEW, 24
TRANSACTION_SUPPORTED, 24
TCE (tightly coupled events), 333
termination, objects, 407
text boxes
   Filter Criteria, 345
   Server name, 342
This User radio button, 369
Thread Neutral Apartments (TNAs), 125-126, 217
thread pools, 107
thread synchronization, 93
threading models, 91
   apartments, 97-110, 117, 122-125
   marshaling interfaces, 111-117
   processes, 91-97
ThreadingModel entry, 117-118
ThreadingModel property, 176
threads, 8, 215
   creating, AddressOf operator, 96
   objects and, 101-106, 110
   primary, 92
threads, multi-threaded clients, passing interfaces between, 115-116
throughput, 226
tickers, subscribing, 339
tightly coupled events (TCEs), 333
timeout periods, failed queued component (QC) messages, 309
TLB files. *See* type libraries
TNA (Thread Neutral Apartment), 125-126, 217

tools. *See* applications

ToString function, 152

TPC-C (Transaction Processing Council), benchmark ranks COM+ top performer, 226

Trace parameter, 422

TrackerServer, 184

TradeEntry component, partial Interface Definition Language (IDL), 361

traditional COM events, 332-335

transaction information, objects, 207

transaction processing, 4

Transaction Processing Council (TPC-C), benchmark ranks COM+ top performer, 226

Transaction property, 176

transactional queues, 309-310

TransactionContext object, voting, 246

transactions, 225
 aborting, 273-274
 ACID, 227-228
 Active Server Pages (ASP) and Internet Information Server (IIS), 252-253
 activities, 405
 COM+, 239-252
 Distributed Transaction Coordinator (DTC), 231-239
 examples of, 228-231
 flow, 194-197
 ROLLBACK and COMMIT commands, 227
 success of, 275, 284

TRANSACTION_NOT_SUPPORTED tag, 24

TRANSACTION_REQUIRED tag, 24

TRANSACTION_REQUIRES_NEW tag, 24

TRANSACTION_SUPPORTED tag, 24

trickle down effect, virtual functions, 65

troubleshooting
 authentication, Windows 2000 workgroup mode, 305
 debugging components, class factories, 84
 hanging clients, 343

turning off security, 304-305, 364

turning on security, 363-366

two-phase commit protocol, 231-232, 256-257, 275-276

TxCTx.TransactionContext component, 181

TxCTx.TransactionContextEx component, 181

type libraries (TLB files), 8, 19-20, 44, 74-75
 coclasses, 26
 code for, 150-151
 declaration tags, 34
 late binding, 141-147
 listing, registered COM components, 29
 marshaling, 128-131, 411-412
 registered, finding, 31-39
 registration, 55-59
 resources, 54-55

Typelib entry, 57

464 UDA (Universal Data Access)

U

UDA (Universal Data Access), 400
unconfigured components, 158, 198
undoing log entries, 274
unions, 134-136
Universal Data Access (UDA), 400
universes, Newtonian, 225
unmarshaling interface pointers between threads, 113
UPDATE statement, 228
Use All Event Classes That Implement This Interface check box, 341
users, entering in roles, 360-361
utilities. *See* applications

V

ValueProperty interface, 177
values
    CALG RC2, 419
    CALG RC4, 419
    INFINITE, 420
    LONG LIVED, 420
    MQMSG DEADLETTER, 420-421
    MQMSG DELIVERY EXPRESS, 419
    MQMSG DELIVERY RECOVERABLE, 419
    MQMSG JOURNAL, 420
    MQMSG JOURNAL NONE, 420
    MQMSG PRIV LEVEL BODY, 421
    MQMSG PRIV LEVEL BODY BASE, 421
    MQMSG PRIV LEVEL BODY ENHANCED, 421
    MQMSG PRIV LEVEL NONE, 421
    MQMSG SEND ROUTE TO REPORT QUEUE, 422
    MQMSG TRACE NONE, 422
    ThreadingModel entry, 117-118
vargs array, 140
variant arrays, writing to log files, 260
Variant data type, 136-137
variants, 134-137
VB. *See* Visual Basic programming language
VBCalc object, type library, 33-34
VC++. *See* Visual C++ programming language
Version entry, 57
VersionBuild property, 176
VersionMajor property, 176
VersionMinor property, 176
VersionSubBuild property, 176
viewing
    method calls as messages, 305-307
    SAFEARRAYs, 412
Viper. *See* Microsoft Transaction Server
virtual function tables (vtables), 20, 63-75, 81-85
virtual functions, trickle down effect of, 65
virtual inheritance, 68
virtual keyword, 64, 67
Visual Basic (VB) programming language
    arrays, passing block data, 411-412
    Calc interface, 36
    clients
        creating COMCalc instances, 52
        message received from queue by, 293
        message sent to queue by, 290
        notifying of cell changes in Excel preadsheets, 332
    CoImpersonateClient() method, 373
    components, obtaining Globally Unique Identifiers (GUIDs), 212

CreateInstance() method, 196
creating Calc objects, 37
creating COM components, 28
exception handling, 39
late binding, 137-147
objects, simple, 404
persistable components, 319-320
pseudo-clients, 12
pseudo-servers, 11
registering components in Registry, 55
source code, subscribing components and tickers, 339
TransactionContext object, 246
Variant data type, 136
writing queueable objects, 302

Visual C++ programming language, 337
changing menus and dialog boxes, 54
implementing COM objects, 21-28
IObjectContext() method, 196
object components, retrieving IResponse interfaces from contexts, 222
TransactionContext object, 246

Visual J++ (VJ++) programming language, implementation of class supporting ICalc and IFinancial interfaces, 149-150

VJ++ (Visual J++ programming language), implementation of class supporting ICalc and IFinancial interfaces, 149-150

voting, COM+ transactions, 245-251

vtables. *See* **virtual function tables**

W

Wade, William C. III, 311

WAM (Web Applications Manager), 182-183

Watcom resource editor, changing menus and dialog boxes, 54

Web Applications Manager (WAM), 182-183

Win32 message pump and window procedure, 98-100

window procedure, 98-100

windows, 102-104

Windows 2000 Active Directory, 311

Windows 2000 workgroup mode, authentication problems, 305

Windows Installer (instmi.exe), installing application proxies, 428

Windows NT, installing application proxies, 428-429

Windows NT/2000 ADSI Scripting for System Administration, **311**

WithEvents keyword, 333

wizards
COM Application Install, 164-166
COM Component Install, 168-171

Word as COM+ component, 142

Worker coclass, 258-260, 269-275

worker components, modifying account balances in XML files, 261-268

workgroup mode, authentication problems, 305

wrappers
coclass, Interface Definnition Language (IDL) file, 154
Java Callable (JCW), 113

writing
Calculator objects, 21-28
COM objects in C++, 66-68

writing

   event classes, 336-338
   publisher filters, 350-352, 354
   queueable objects, 302
   variant arrays to log files, 260

X

X/Open XA protocol, 257

XML files, worker components modifying account balances in, 261-268

Windows 2000 Answers

Selected Windows 2000 Titles from New Riders Publishing

Building from the author-driven, no-nonsense approach of our *Landmark* books, New Riders proudly offers something unique for Windows 2000 administrators—an in-depth and discriminating book on Windows 2000 Server, written by someone in the trenches who can anticipate your situation and provide reliable answers.

INSIDE Windows 2000 Server

ISBN: 1-56205-929-7

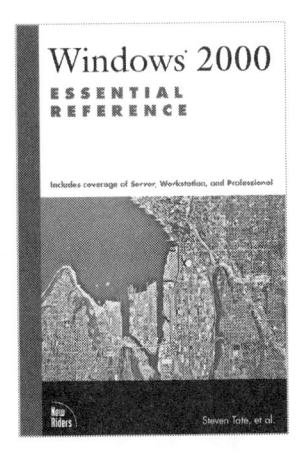

Architected to be the most navigable and useful reference available for Windows 2000, this book uses a creative "telescoping" design that you can adapt to your style of learning. It's a concise, focused, and quick reference for Windows 2000, providing the kind of practical advice, tips, procedures, and additional resources that every administrator will need.

Windows 2000 ESSENTIAL REFERENCE

ISBN: 0-7357-0869-X

Windows 2000 Active Directory is just one of several Windows 2000 titles from New Riders' acclaimed *Landmark* series. Ideal for network architects and administrators, this book describes the intricacies of Active Directory while keeping real-world systems and constraints in mind. It's a detailed, solution-oriented book that addresses the need for a single guide to planning, deploying, and managing Active Directory in an enterprise setting.

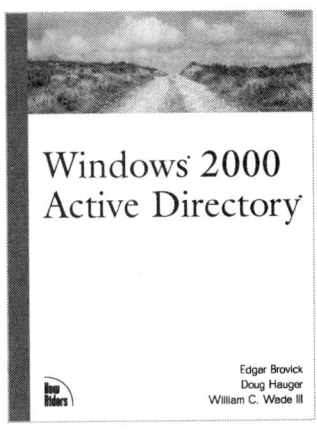

Windows 2000 Active Directory

Edgar Brovick
Doug Hauger
William C. Wade III

ISBN: 0-7357-0870-3

Advanced Information on Networking Technologies

New Riders Books Offer Advice and Experience

LANDMARK
Rethinking Computer Books

We know how important it is to have access to detailed, solution-oriented information on core technologies. *Landmark* books contain the essential information you need to solve technical problems. Written by experts and subjected to rigorous peer and technical reviews, *Landmark* books are hard-core resources that get to the heart of what you need to know.

ESSENTIAL REFERENCE
Smart, Like You

The *Essential Reference* series from New Riders provides answers when you know what you want to do but need to learn how to do it. Each title skips extraneous material and assumes a strong base of knowledge. These are indispensable books for the practitioner who wants to find specific features of a technology quickly and efficiently. Avoiding fluff and basic material, these books present solutions in an innovative, clean format.

MCSE CERTIFICATION
Engineered for Test Success

New Riders offers a complete line of test preparation materials to help you achieve your certification. With books like the *MCSE Training Guide*, and software like the acclaimed *MCSE Complete* and the revolutionary *ExamGear*, New Riders offers comprehensive products built by experienced professionals who have passed the exams and instructed hundreds of candidates.

New Riders: Books for Networking Professionals

Windows NT/2000 Titles

Windows 2000 Professional
By Jerry Honeycutt
1st Edition
350 pages, $34.99
ISBN: 0-7357-0950-5

Windows 2000 Professional explores the power available to the Windows workstation user on the corporate network and Internet. The book is aimed directly at the power user who values the security, stability and networking capabilities of NT alongside the ease and familiarity of the Windows 9X user interface. This book covers both user and administration topics, with a dose of networking content added for connectivity.

Windows 2000 Deployment & Desktop Management
By Jeffrey A. Ferris
1st Ediition
400 pages, $34.99
ISBN: 0-7357-0975-0

More than a simple overview of new features and tools, this solutions-driven book is a thorough reference to deploying Windows 2000 Professional to corporate workstations. The expert real-world advice and detailed exercises make this a one-stop, easy-to-use resource for any system administrator, integrator, engineer, or other IT professional planning rollout of Windows 2000 clients.

Windows 2000 DNS
By Herman Knief, Jeffrey Graham, Andrew Daniels, and Roger Abell
2nd Edition
450 pages, $39.99
ISBN: 0-7357-0973-4

Without proper design and administration of DNS, computers wouldn't be able to locate each other on the network, and applications like email and Web browsing wouldn't be feasible. Administrators need this information to make their networks work. *Windows 2000 DNS* provides a technical overview of DNS and WINS, and how to design and administer them for optimal performance in a Windows 2000 environment.

Planning for Windows 2000

By Eric K. Cone, Jon Boggs, and Sergio Perez
1st Edition
400 pages, $29.99
ISBN: 0-7357-0048-6

Planning for Windows 2000 lets you know what the upgrade hurdles will be, informs you how to clear them, guides you through effective Active Directory design, and presents you with detailed rollout procedures. Eric K. Cone, Jon Boggs, and Sergio Perez give you the benefit of their extensive experiences as Windows 2000 Rapid Deployment Program members by sharing problems and solutions they've encountered on the job.

Windows 2000 Security

By Roberta Bragg
1st Edition
500 pages, $39.99
ISBN: 0-7357-0991-2
October 2000

No single authoritative reference on security exists for serious network system administrators. The primary goal of this title is to assist the Windows networking professional in understanding and implementing Windows 2000 security in their organization. Included are best practices sections which make recommendations for settings and security practices.

Inside Windows 2000 Server

By William Boswell
1st Edition
1550 pages, $49.99
ISBN: 1-56205-929-7

Building on the author-driven, no-nonsense approach of our Landmark books, New Riders proudly offers something unique for Windows 2000 administrators—an in-depth, discriminating book on Windows 2000 Server written by someone who can anticipate your situation and give you workarounds that won't leave a system unstable or sluggish.

Windows 2000 Server Professional Reference

By Karanjit S. Siyan, Ph.D.
3rd Edition
1800 pages, $75.00
ISBN: 0-7357-0952-1

Windows 2000 Server Professional Reference is the benchmark of references available for Windows 2000. Although other titles take you through the setup and implementation phase of the product, no other book provides the user with detailed answers to day-to-day administration problems and tasks. Real-world implementations are key to help administrators discover the most viable solutions for their particular environments. Solid content shows administrators how to manage, troubleshoot, and fix problems that are specific to heterogeneous Windows networks, as well as Internet features and functionality.

Windows 2000 User Management
By Lori Sanders
1st Edition
300 pages, $34.99
ISBN: 1-56205-886-X

With the dawn of Windows 2000, it has become even more difficult to draw a clear line between managing the user and managing the user's environment and desktop. This book, written by a noted trainer and consultant, provides a comprehensive, practical guide to managing users and their desktop environments with Windows 2000.

Windows 2000 Active Directory Design & Deployment
By Gary Olsen
1st Edition
450 pages, $45.00
ISBN: 1-57870-242-9
September 2000

This book focuses on the design of a Windows 2000 Active Directory environment, and how to develop an effective design and migration plan. The reader is led through the process of developing a design plan by reviewing each pertinent issue, and then provided expert advice on how to evaluate each issue as it applies to the reader's particular environment. Practical examples illustrate all these issues.

Windows 2000 Quality of Service
By David Iseminger
1st Edition
300 pages, $45.00
ISBN: 1-57870-115-5

As the traffic on networks continues to increase, the strain on network infrastructure and available resources has also grown. *Windows 2000 Quality of Service* teaches network engineers and administrators to how to define traffic control patterns and utilize bandwidth in their networks.

Windows 2000 Server: Planning and Migration
By Sean Deuby
1st Edition
450 pages $40.00
ISBN: 1-57870-023-X

Windows 2000 Server: Planning and Migration can quickly save the NT professional thousands of dollars and hundreds of hours. This title includes authoritative information on key features of Windows 2000 and offers recommendations on how to best position your NT network for Windows 2000.

Windows 2000 and Mainframe Integration
By William Zack
1st Edition
400 pages, $40.00
ISBN: 1-57870-200-3

Windows 2000 and Mainframe Integration provides mainframe computing professionals with the practical know-how to build and integrate Windows 2000 technologies into their current environment.

Windows NT/2000 Thin Client Solutions
By Todd Mathers
2nd Edition
750 pages, $45.00
ISBN: 1-57870-239-9

A practical and comprehensive reference to MetaFrame 1.8 and Terminal Services, this book should be the first source for answers to the tough questions on the Terminal Server VCx2/MetaFrame platform. Building on the quality of the previous edition, additional coverage of installation of Terminal Services and MetaFrame on a Windows 2000 Serveris included, as well as chapters on Terminal Server management, remote access, and application integration.

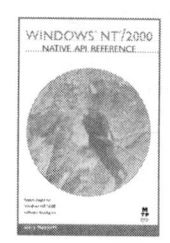

Windows NT/2000 Native API Reference
By Gary Nebbett
1st Edition
500 pages, $50.00
ISBN: 1-57870-199-6

This book is the first complete reference to the API functions native to Windows NT and covers the set of services that are offered by the Windows NT to both kernel- and user-mode programs. Coverage consists of documentation of the 210 routines included in the NT Native API, and the functions that have been be added in Windows 2000. Routines that are either not directly accessible via the Win32 API or offer substantial additional functionality are described in especially great detail. Services offered by the NT kernel, mainly the support for debugging user mode applications, are also included.

Windows NT/2000 ADSI Scripting for System Administration
By Thomas Eck
1st Edition
700 pages, $45.00
ISBN: 1-57870-219-4

Active Directory Scripting Interfaces (ADSI) allow administrators to automate administrative tasks across their Windows networks. This title fills a gap in the current ADSI documentation by including coverage of its interaction with LDAP and provides administrators with proven code samples that they can adopt to effectively configure and manage user accounts and other usually time-consuming tasks.

Windows 2000 Virtual Private Networking
By Thaddeus Fortenberry
1st Edition
400 pages, $45.00
ISBN 1-57870-246-1
December 2000

Because of the ongoing push for a distributed workforce, administrators must support laptop users, home LAN environments, complex branch offices, and more—all within a secure and effective network design. The way an administrator implements VPNs in Windows 2000 is different than that of any other operating system. In addition to discussions about Windows 2000 tunneling, new VPN features that can affect Active Directory replication and network address translation are also covered.

Windows NT Terminal Server and Citrix MetaFrame
By Ted Harwood
1st Edition
400 pages, $29.99
ISBN: 1-56205-944-0

It's no surprise that most administration headaches revolve around integration with other networks and clients. This book addresses these types of real-world issues on a case-by-case basis, giving tools and advice for solving each problem. The author also offers the real nuts and bolts of thin client administration on multiple systems, covering relevant issues such as installation, configuration, network connection, management, and application distribution.

Windows NT Power Toolkit
By Stu Sjouwerman and Ed Tittel
1st Edition
800 pages, $49.99
ISBN: 0-7357-0922-X

This book covers the analysis, tuning, optimization, automation, enhancement, maintenance, and troubleshooting of Windows NT Server 4.0 and Windows NT Workstation 4.0. In most cases, the two operating systems overlap completely. Where the two systems diverge, each platform is covered separately. This advanced title comprises a task-oriented treatment of the Windows NT 4 environment. By concentrating on the use of operating system tools and utilities, Resource Kit elements, and selected third-party tuning, analysis, optimization, and productivity tools, this book will show its readers how to carry out everyday and advanced tasks.

Windows NT Performance: Monitoring, Benchmarking, and Tuning
By Mark T. Edmead and Paul Hinsberg
1st Edition
288 pages, $29.99
ISBN: 1-56205-942-4

Performance monitoring is a little like preventive medicine for the administrator: No one enjoys a checkup, but it's a good thing to do on a regular basis. This book helps you focus on the critical aspects of improving the performance of your NT system by showing you how to monitor the system, implement benchmarking, and tune your network. The book is organized by resource components, which makes it easy to use as a reference tool.

Windows NT Device Driver Development
By Peter Viscarola and W. Anthony Mason
1st Edition
700 pages, $50.00
ISBN: 1-57870-058-2

This title begins with an introduction to the general Windows NT operating system concepts relevant to drivers, then progresses to more detailed information about the operating system, such as interrupt management, synchronization issues, the I/O Subsystem, standard kernel mode drivers, and more.

Windows NT Shell Scripting
By Tim Hill
1st Edition
350 pages, $32.00
ISBN: 1-57870-047-7

A complete reference for Windows NT scripting, this book guides you through a high-level introduction to the shell language itself and the shell commands that are useful for controlling or managing different components of a network.

Windows Script Host
By Tim Hill
1st Edition
400 pages, $35.00
ISBN: 1-57870-139-2

Windows Script Host is one of the first books published about this powerful tool. The text focuses on system scripting and the VBScript language, using objects, server scriptlets, and provides ready-to-use script solutions.

Internet Information Services Administration
By Kelli Adam
1st Edition
200 pages, $29.99
ISBN: 0-7357-0022-2

Are the new Internet technologies in Internet Information Services giving you headaches? Does providing security on the Web take up all of your time? Then this is the book for you. With hands-on configuration training, advanced study of the new protocols, coverage of the most recent version of IIS, and detailed instructions on authenticating users with the new Certificate Server and implementing and managing the new e-commerce features, *Internet Information Services Administration* gives you the real-life solutions you need. This definitive resource gives you detailed advice on working with Microsoft Management Console, which was first used by IIS.

Windows NT Win32 Perl Programming: The Standard Extensions
By Dave Roth
1st Edition
600 pages, $40.00
ISBN: 1-57870-067-1

See numerous proven examples and practical uses of Perl in solving everyday Win32 problems. This is the only book available with comprehensive coverage of Win32 extensions, where most of the Perl functionality resides in Windows settings.

SMS 2 Administration

By Michael Lubanski
and Darshan Doshi
1st Edition
350 pages, $39.99
ISBN: 0-7357-0082-6

Microsoft's new version of its Systems Management Server (SMS) is starting to turn heads. Although complex, it allows administrators to lower their total cost of ownership and more efficiently manage clients, applications, and support operations. So if your organization is using or implementing SMS, you'll need some expert advice. Michael Lubanski and Darshan Doshi can help you get the most bang for your buck with insight, expert tips, and real-world examples. Michael and Darshan are consultants specializing in SMS and have worked with Microsoft on one of the most complex SMS rollouts in the world, involving 32 countries, 15 languages, and thousands of clients.

SQL Server 7 Essential Reference

By Sharon Dooley
1st Edition
400 pages, $35.00 US
ISBN: 0-7357-0864-9

SQL Server 7 Essential Reference is a comprehensive reference of advanced how-tos and techniques for developing with SQL Server. In particular, the book addresses advanced development techniques used in large application efforts with multiple users, such as developing Web applications for intranets, extranets, or the Internet. Each section includes detail on how each component is developed and then integrated into a real-life application.

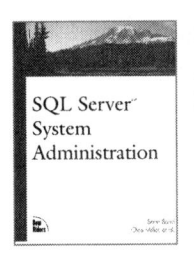

SQL Server System Administration

By Sean Baird,
Chris Miller, et al.
1st Edition
352 pages, $29.99
ISBN: 1-56205-955-6

How often does your SQL Server go down during the day when everyone wants to access the data? Do you spend most of your time being a "report monkey" for your coworkers and bosses? *SQL Server System Administration* helps you keep data consistently available to your users. This book omits introductory information. The authors don't spend time explaining queries and how they work. Instead, they focus on the information you can't get anywhere else, like how to choose the correct replication topology and achieve high availability of information.

Networking Titles

Network Intrusion Detection: An Analyst's Handbook

By Stephen Northcutt
and Judy Novak
2nd Edition
450 pages, $39.99
ISBN: 0-7357-1008-2
September 2000

Get answers and solutions from someone who has been in the trenches. Stephen Northcutt, original developer of the Shadow intrusion detection system and former director of the United States Navy's Information System Security Office at the Naval Security Warfare Center, gives his expertise to intrusion detection specialists, security analysts, and consultants responsible for setting up and maintaining an effective defense against network security attacks.

Understanding the Network: A Practical Guide to Internetworking
By Michael Martin
1st Edition
650 pages, $39.99
ISBN: 0-7357-0977-7

Understanding the Network addresses the audience in practical terminology, and describes the most essential information and tools required to build high-availability networks in a step-by-step implementation format. Each chapter could be read as a stand-alone, but the book builds progressively toward a summary of the essential concepts needed to put together a wide-area network.

Understanding Data Communications
By Gilbert Held
6th Edition
600 pages, $39.99
ISBN: 0-7357-0036-2

Updated from the highly successful fifth edition, this book explains how data communications systems and their various hardware and software components work. More than an entry-level book, it approaches the material in textbook format, addressing the complex issues involved in internetworking today. A great reference book for the experienced networking professional that is written by the noted networking authority, Gilbert Held.

Cisco Router Configuration & Troubleshooting
By Mark Tripod
2nd Edition
400 pages, $34.99
ISBN: 0-7357-0999-8

Want the real story on making your Cisco routers run like a dream? Pick up a copy of *Cisco Router Configuration & Troubleshooting* and see what Mark Tripod of Exodus Communications has to say. Exodus is responsible for making some of the largest sites on the Net scream, like Amazon.com, Hotmail, USAToday, Geocities, and Sony. In this book, the author provides advanced configuration issues, sprinkled with advice and preferred practices. By providing real-world insight and examples instead of rehashing Cisco's documentation, Mark gives network administrators information they can start using today.

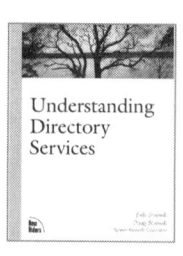

Understanding Directory Services
By Beth Sheresh and Doug Sheresh
1st Edition
400 pages, $39.99
ISBN: 0-7357-0910-6

Understanding Directory Services provides the reader with a thorough knowledge of the fundamentals of directory services: what DSs are, how they are designed, and what functionality they can provide to an IT infrastructure. This book provides a framework to the exploding market of directory services by placing the technology in context and helping people understand what directories can, and can't, do for their networks.

Local Area High Speed Networks
By Dr. Sidnie Feit
1st Edition
650 pages, $50.00
ISBN: 1-57870-113-9

A great deal of change is happening in the technology being used for local area networks. As Web intranets have driven bandwidth needs through the ceiling, inexpensive Ethernet NICs and switches have come into the market. As a result, many network professionals are interested in evaluating these new technologies for implementation. This book provides real-world implementation expertise for these technologies, including traces, so that users can realistically compare and decide how to use them.

Network Performance Baselining
By Daniel Nassar
1st Edition
700 pages, $50.00
ISBN: 1-57870-240-2

Network Performance Baselining focuses on the real-world implementation of network baselining principles and shows not only how to measure and rate a network's performance, but also how to improve the network's performance. This book includes chapters that give a real "how to" approach for standard baseline methodologies along with actual steps and processes to perform network baseline measurements. In addition, the proper way to document and build a baseline report is provided.

Directory Enabled Networks
By John Strassner
1st Edition
700 pages, $50.00
ISBN: 1-57870-140-6

Directory Enabled Networks is a comprehensive resource on the design and use of DEN. This book provides practical examples side-by-side with a detailed introduction to the theory of building a new class of network-enabled applications that will solve networking problems. It is a critical tool for network architects, administrators, and application developers.

Wide Area High Speed Networks
By Dr. Sidnie Feit
1st Edition
600 pages, $50.00
ISBN:1-57870-114-7

Networking is in a transitional phase between long-standing conventional wide area services and new technologies and services. This book presents current and emerging wide area technologies and services, makes them understandable, and puts them into perspective so that their merits and disadvantages are clear.

Quality of Service in IP Networks
By Grenville Armitage
1st Edition
300 pages, $50.00
ISBN: 1-57870-189-9

Quality of Service in IP Networks presents a clear understanding of the architectural issues surrounding delivering QoS in an IP network, and positions the emerging technologies within a framework of solutions. The motivation for QoS is explained with reference to emerging real-time applications such as Voice/Video over IP, VPN services, and supporting Service Level Agreements.

Intrusion Detection
By Rebecca Bace
1st Edition
300 pages, $50.00
ISBN: 1-57870-185-6

Intrusion detection is a critical new area of technology within network security. This comprehensive guide to the field of intrusion detection covers the foundations of intrusion detection and system audit. *Intrusion Detection* provides a wealth of information, ranging from design considerations to how to evaluate and choose the optimal commercial intrusion detection products for a particular networking environment.

The DHCP Handbook
By Ralph Droms and Ted Lemon
1st Edition
550 pages, $55.00
ISBN: 1-57870-137-6

The DHCP Handbook is an authoritative overview and expert guide to the setup and management of a DHCP server. This title discusses how DHCP was developed and its interaction with other protocols. Also, learn how DHCP operates, its use in different environments, and the interaction between DHCP servers and clients. Network hardware, inter-server communication, security, SNMP, and IP mobility are also discussed. Included in the book are several appendices that provide a rich resource for networking professionals working with DHCP.

Other Books By New Riders

Microsoft Technologies

ADMINISTRATION

Inside Windows 2000 Server
1-56205-929-7 • $49.99 US
Windows 2000 Essential Reference
0-7357-0869-X • $35.00 US
Windows 2000 Active Directory
0-7357-0870-3 • $29.99 US
Windows 2000 Routing and Remote Access Service
0-7357-0951-3 • $34.99 US
Windows 2000 Deployment & Desktop Management
0-7357-0975-0 • $34.99 US
Windows 2000 DNS
0-7357-0973-4 • $39.99 US
Windows 2000 User Management
1-56205-886-X • $34.99 US
Windows 2000 Professional
0-7357-0950-5 • $34.99 US
Planning for Windows 2000
0-7357-0048-6 • $29.99 US
Windows 2000 Server Professional Reference
0-7357-0952-1 • $75.00 US
Windows 2000 Security
0-7357-0991-2 • $39.99 US
Available October 2000
Windows 2000 Registry
0-7357-0944-0 • $34.99 US
Available December 2000
Windows 2000 Terminal Services and Citrix MetaFrame
0-7357-1005-8 • $39.99 US
Available December 2000
Windows NT/2000 Network Security
1-57870-253-4 • $45.00 US
Windows NT/2000 Thin Client Solutions
1-57870-239-9 • $45.00 US
Windows 2000 Virtual Private Networking
1-57870-246-1 • $45.00 US
Available December 2000
Windows 2000 Active Directory Design & Deployment
1-57870-242-9 • $45.00 US
Available September 2000
Windows 2000 and Mainframe Integration
1-57870-200-3 • $40.00 US
Windows 2000 Server: Planning and Migration
1-57870-023-X • $40.00 US
Windows 2000 Quality of Service
1-57870-115-5 • $45.00 US
Windows NT Power Toolkit
0-7357-0922-X • $49.99 US
Windows NT Terminal Server and Citrix MetaFrame
1-56205-944-0 • $29.99 US
Windows NT Performance: Monitoring, Benchmarking, and Tuning
1-56205-942-4 • $29.99 US
Windows NT Registry: A Settings Reference
1-56205-941-6 • $29.99 US
Windows NT?2000 Network Security
1-87870-253-4 $45.00 US

Windows NT Domain Architecture
1-57870-112-0 • $38.00 US

SYSTEMS PROGRAMMING

Windows NT/2000 Native API Reference
1-57870-199-6 • $50.00 US
Windows NT Device Driver Development
1-57870-058-2 • $50.00 US
DCE/RPC over SMB: Samba and Windows NT Domain Internals
1-57870-150-3 • $45.00 US

APPLICATION PROGRAMMING

Delphi COM Programming
1-57870-221-6 • $45.00 US
Windows NT Applications: Measuring and Optimizing Performance
1-57870-176-7 • $40.00 US

WEB PROGRAMMING

Exchange & Outlook: Constructing Collaborative Solutions
ISBN 1-57870-252-6 • $40.00 US

SCRIPTING

Windows Script Host
1-57870-139-2 • $35.00 US
Windows NT Shell Scripting
1-57870-047-7 • $32.00 US
Windows NT Win32 Perl Programming: The Standard Extensions
1-57870-067-1 • $40.00 US
Windows NT/2000 ADSI Scripting for System Administration
1-57870-219-4 • $45.00 US
Windows NT Automated Deployment and Customization
1-57870-045-0 • $32.00 US

BACK OFFICE

SMS 2 Administration
0-7357-0082-6 • $39.99 US
Internet Information Services Administration
0-7357-0022-2 • $29.99 US
SQL Server System Administration
1-56205-955-6 • $29.99 US
SQL Server 7 Essential Reference
0-7357-0864-9 • $35.00 US

Open Source

MySQL
0-7357-0921-1 • $49.99 US
Web Application Development with PHP
0-7357-0997-1 • $39.99 US
PHP Functions Essential Reference
0-7357-0970-X • $35.00 US
Available December 2000
Python Essential Reference
0-7357-0901-7 • $34.95 US
Autoconf, Automake, and Libtool
1-57870-190-2 • $35.00 US
Available October 2000

Linux/Unix

ADMINISTRATION

Linux System Administration
1-56205-934-3 • $29.99 US
Linux Firewalls
0-7357-0900-9 • $39.99 US
Linux Essential Reference
0-7357-0852-5 • $24.95 US
UnixWare 7 System Administration
1-57870-080-9 • $40.00 US

DEVELOPMENT

Developing Linux Applications with GTK+ and GDK
0-7357-0021-4 • $34.99 US
GTK+/Gnome Application Development
0-7357-0078-8 • $39.99 US
KDE Application Development
1-57870-201-1 • $39.99 US

GIMP

Grokking the GIMP
0-7357-0924-6 • $39.99 US
GIMP Essential Reference
0-7357-0911-4 • $24.95 US

SOLARIS

Solaris Advanced System Administrator's Guide, Second Edition
1-57870-039-6 • $39.99 US
Solaris System Administrator's Guide, Second Edition
1-57870-040-X • $34.99 US
Solaris Essential Reference
0-7357-0023-0 • $24.95 US

Networking

STANDARDS & PROTOCOLS

Cisco Router Configuration & Troubleshooting, Second Edition
0-7357-0999-8 • $39.99 US
Understanding Directory Services
0-7357-0910-6 • $39.99 US
Understanding the Network: A Practical Guide to Internetworking
0-7357-0977-7 • $39.99 US
Understanding Data Communications, Sixth Edition
0-7357-0036-2 • $39.99 US
LDAP: Programming Directory Enabled Applications
1-57870-000-0 • $44.99 US
Gigabit Ethernet Networking
1-57870-062-0 • $50.00 US
Supporting Service Level Agreements on IP Networks
1-57870-146-5 • $50.00 US
Directory Enabled Networks
1-57870-140-6 • $50.00 US
Differentiated Services for the Internet
1-57870-132-5 • $50.00 US
Quality of Service on IP Networks
1-57870-189-9 • $50.00 US

Designing Addressing Architectures for Routing and Switching
1-57870-059-0 • $45.00 US
Understanding & Deploying LDAP Directory Services
1-57870-070-1 • $50.00 US
Switched, Fast and Gigabit Ethernet, Third Edition
1-57870-073-6 • $50.00 US
Wireless LANs: Implementing Interoperable Networks
1-57870-081-7 • $40.00 US
Wide Area High Speed Networks
1-57870-114-7 • $50.00 US
The DHCP Handbook
1-57870-137-6 • $55.00 US
Designing Routing and Switching Architectures for Enterprise Networks
1-57870-060-4 • $55.00 US
Local Area High Speed Networks
1-57870-113-9 • $50.00 US
Network Performance Baselining
1-57870-240-2 • $50.00 US
The Economics of Electronic Commerce
1-57870-014-0 • $49.99 US

SECURITY

Intrusion Detection
1-57870-185-6 • $50.00 US
Understanding Public-Key Infrastructure
1-57870-166-X • $50.00 US
Network Intrusion Detection: An Analyst's Handbook, 2E
0-7357-1008-2 • $45.00 US
Linux Firewalls
0-7357-0900-9 • $39.99 US

LOTUS NOTES/DOMINO

Domino System Administration
1-56205-948-3 • $49.99 US
Lotus Notes & Domino Essential Reference
0-7357-0007-9 • $45.00 US

Software Architecture & Engineering

Designing for the User with OVID
1-57870-101-5 • $40.00 US
Designing Flexible Object-Oriented Systems with UML
1-57870-098-1 • $40.00 US
Constructing Superior Software
1-57870-147-3 • $40.00 US
A UML Pattern Language
1-57870-118-X • $45.00 US

Professional Certification

TRAINING GUIDES

MCSE Training Guide: Networking Essentials, 2nd Ed.
156205919X • $49.99 US

MCSE Training Guide: Windows NT Server 4, 2nd Ed.
1562059165 • $49.99 US
MCSE Training Guide: Windows NT Workstation 4, 2nd Ed.
1562059181 • $49.99 US
MCSE Training Guide: Windows NT Server 4 Enterprise, 2nd Ed.
1562059173 • $49.99 US
MCSE Training Guide: Core Exams Bundle, 2nd Ed.
1562059262 • $149.99 US
MCSE Training Guide: TCP/IP, 2nd Ed.
1562059203 • $49.99 US
MCSE Training Guide: IIS 4, 2nd Ed.
0735708657 • $49.99 US
MCSE Training Guide: SQL Server 7 Administration
0735700036 • $49.99 US
MCSE Training Guide: SQL Server 7 Database Design
0735700044 • $49.99 US
CLP Training Guide: Lotus Notes 4
0789715058 • $59.99 US
MCSD Training Guide: Visual Basic 6 Exams
0735700028 • $69.99 US
MCSD Training Guide: Solution Architectures
0735700265 • $49.99 US
MCSD Training Guide: 4-in-1 Bundle
0735709122 • $149.99 US
CCNA Training Guide
0735700516 • $49.99 US
A+ Certification Training Guide, 2nd Ed.
0735709076 • $49.99 US
Network+ Certification Guide
073570077X • $49.99 US
Solaris 2.6 Administrator Certification Training Guide, Part I
157870085X • $40.00 US
Solaris 2.6 Administrator Certification Training Guide, Part II
1578700868 • $40.00 US
MCSE Training Guide: Windows 2000 Professional
0735709653 • $49.99 US
MCSE Training Guide: Windows 2000 Server
0735709688 • $49.99 US
MCSE Training Guide: Windows 2000 Network Infrastructure
0735709661 • $49.99 US
MCSE Training Guide: Windows 2000 Network Security Design
073570984X • $49.99 US
MCSE Training Guide: Windows 2000 Network Infrastructure Design
0735709823 • $49.99 US
MCSE Training Guide: Windows 2000 Directory Svcs. Infrastructure
0735709769 • $49.99 US
MCSE Training Guide: Windows 2000 Directory Services Design
0735709831 • $49.99 US

MCSE Training Guide: Windows 2000 Accelerated Exam
0735709793 • $59.99 US
MCSE Training Guide: Windows 2000 Core Exams Bundle
0735709882 • $149.99 US

How to Contact Us

Visit Our Web Site

www.newriders.com

On our Web site you'll find information about our other books, authors, tables of contents, indexes, and book errata.

Email Us

Contact us at this address:

nrfeedback@newriders.com

- If you have comments or questions about this book
- To report errors that you have found in this book
- If you have a book proposal to submit or are interested in writing for New Riders
- If you would like to have an author kit sent to you
- If you are an expert in a computer topic or technology and are interested in being a technical editor who reviews manuscripts for technical accuracy

nrfeedback@newriders.com

- To find a distributor in your area, please contact our international department at this address.

nrmedia@newriders.com

- For instructors from educational institutions who want to preview New Riders books for classroom use. Email should include your name, title, school, department, address, phone number, office days/hours, text in use, and enrollment, along with your request for desk/examination copies and/or additional information.
- For members of the media who are interested in reviewing copies of New Riders books. Send your name, mailing address, and email address, along with the name of the publication or Web site you work for.

Write to Us

New Riders Publishing
201 W. 103rd St.
Indianapolis, IN 46290-1097

Call Us

Toll-free (800) 571-5840 + 9 + 7477

If outside U.S. (317) 581-3500. Ask for New Riders.

Fax Us

(317) 581-4663

New Riders: We Want to Know What You Think

To better serve you, we would like your opinion on the content and quality of this book. Please complete this card and mail it to us or fax it to 317-581-4663.

Name _____

Address _____

City_____ State_____ Zip _____

Phone _____

Email Address _____

Occupation _____

Operating System(s) that you use _____

What influenced your purchase of this book?
- ❏ Recommendation
- ❏ Cover Design
- ❏ Table of Contents
- ❏ Index
- ❏ Magazine Review
- ❏ Advertisement
- ❏ New Rider's Reputation
- ❏ Author Name

How would you rate the contents of this book?
- ❏ Excellent
- ❏ Very Good
- ❏ Good
- ❏ Fair
- ❏ Below Average
- ❏ Poor

How do you plan to use this book?
- ❏ Quick reference
- ❏ Self-training
- ❏ Classroom
- ❏ Other

What do you like most about this book? Check all that apply.
- ❏ Content
- ❏ Writing Style
- ❏ Accuracy
- ❏ Examples
- ❏ Listings
- ❏ Design
- ❏ Index
- ❏ Page Count
- ❏ Price
- ❏ Illustrations

What do you like least about this book? Check all that apply.
- ❏ Content
- ❏ Writing Style
- ❏ Accuracy
- ❏ Examples
- ❏ Listings
- ❏ Design
- ❏ Index
- ❏ Page Count
- ❏ Price
- ❏ Illustrations

What would be a useful follow-up book to this one for you? _____

Where did you purchase this book? _____

_____

Can you name a similar book that you like better than this one, or one that is as good? Why?

_____

How many New Riders books do you own? _____

What are your favorite computer books? _____

_____

What other titles would you like to see us develop? _____

_____

Any comments for us? _____

_____

_____

_____

Applying COM+, 0-7357-0978-5

www.newriders.com • Fax 317-581-4663

Fold here and tape to mail

Place
Stamp
Here

New Riders Publishing
201 W. 103rd St.
Indianapolis, IN 46290